WORLD PHILOSOPHY

WORLD PHILOSOPHY

A Contemporary Bibliography

Edited by
John R. Burr
Charlotte A. Burr, Research Editor

Bibliographies and Indexes in Philosophy, Number 3

GREENWOOD PRESS
Westport, Connecticut • London

Library of Congress Cataloging-in-Publication Data

World philosophy : a contemporary bibliography / edited by John R.
   Burr ; Charlotte A. Burr, research editor.
       p.   cm.—(Bibliographies and indexes in philosophy, ISSN
   0742-6887 ; no. 3)
     Includes bibliographical references and index.
     ISBN 0-313-24032-9 (alk. paper)
     1. Philosophy, Modern—20th century—Bibliography.   I. Burr, John
   Roy.   II. Series.
   Z7125.W87   1993
   [B801]
   016.1'09'047—dc20   93-18031

British Library Cataloguing in Publication Data is available.

Library of Congress Catalog Card Number: 93-18031
ISBN: 0-313-24032-9
ISSN: 0742-6887

First published in 1993

Greenwood Press, 88 Post Road West, Westport, CT 06881
An imprint of Greenwood Publishing Group, Inc.

Printed in the United States of America

The paper used in this book complies with the
Permanent Paper Standard issued by the National
Information Standards Organization (Z39.48-1984).

10 9 8 7 6 5 4 3 2 1

7637986

Contents

Acknowledgments

The preparation of a bibliography of this size, scope, and complexity would have been impossible without the assistance of many individuals. I particularly wish to express my appreciation to my research editor and librarian at Ripon College, Charlotte A. Burr, for her skilled and indefatigable help in obtaining and verifying publication data, as well as putting the content of this bibliography onto the computer database.

Professor Shokichi Uto, Philosophy, Nihon University School of Dentistry at Matsudo, Japan, provided valuable help in the selection of Japanese works and with translations into English. Expert advice on some translations from Chinese and Korean into English was given by University of Wisconsin-Oshkosh faculty colleagues Professors David W. Chang, Political Science; Tina Cheng Fu, Libraries; Hy Sang Lee, Economics; Kwang-ming Wu, Philosophy; and Patrick Hsu, formerly of Ripon College and now Director of Blumberg Memorial Library, Texas Lutheran College, Seguin, Texas. I am indebted also to Professor Lewis W. Tusken, Foreign Languages, and Professor Emeritus Arlow Anderson, History, both of the University of Wisconsin-Oshkosh, for their counsel on problems in translating, respectively, Russian and the Scandinavian languages.

Renee Duescher's knowledge of computer software and ability to surmount seemingly insurmountable obstacles were indispensable. Thanks for additional computer assistance are due to Tom Oyster, Coordinator of Academic Computing, Ripon College, and to Professor James Beatty, Chemistry, Ripon College.

I also want to express my appreciation to Nathalie M. Moore, secretary of the University of Wisconsin-Oshkosh Department of Philosophy, to the University of Wisconsin-Oshkosh Polk Library and Staff, and to the Ripon College Library and staff. Sally Feirer Wilke, Virgina Marcoe, and Christine Ann Clark assisted in the recording of materials for this work.

Without the encouragement, professional advice, and apparently endless patience of Dr. George F. Butler, Acquisitions Editor, and, in earlier stages, of Marilyn Brownstein and of Mary Sive of Greenwood Press, this bibliography would not be in your hands now.

Finally I would not have been able to endure, persevere, and complete this bibliography without the shrewd counsel and unflagging support of my wife, Marjorie Bakirakis Burr.

The brevity of these acknowledgments is in inverse proportion to my gratitude to all who helped make this work a reality. They have rescued me before publication from many errors and omissions large and small. Others, I fear, remain as yet undetected and for which I alone am responsible. I shall be grateful for any corrections and additions sent to me at the Department of Philosophy; University of Wisconsin-Oshkosh; Oshkosh, Wisconsin 54901; U.S.A.

Introduction

This bibliography is an updated supplement to the bibliographies in a <u>Handbook of World Philosophy: Contemporary Developments Since 1945</u>, which I edited and which was published in 1980 by Greenwood Press. Since the bibliographies in that earlier volume did not include, by and large, works published later than 1976, the time period covered by this companion bibliography begins with publications appearing in 1976 and extends to 1992. However, the majority of the works cited fall within the decade 1976-1986 because of the limits imposed by a single volume, by the great wealth of material, and by lacunae in the availability and completeness of the more recent records of publication on a world-wide scale. While it is true that computers certainly are multiplying the speed and volume of communication, translation still takes time; wars and social, religious, economic, and political changes interfere with the compiling of accurate and complete information on philosophic publications, particularly the more recent ones, throughout this still large, diverse, and often turbulent world of ours. The stunningly abrupt finis to the Cold War, which dominated the world scene from the end of World War II until the last few years, currently is the most striking and, in its only dimly foreseen and also unforeseen consequences, most immense of the changes taking place. It is as if the scenery of a play suddenly disappeared, leaving only an obscure and unfamiliar background behind what was once so clear and definite. From the point of view of this bibliography, that global alteration provides an appropriate time at which to close its listing of philosophical books and monographs. At present, what philosophic effect, if any, that seismic change will have remains to be seen. As the organization of this bibliography indicates, it belongs to the period of the worldwide dominance of the Cold War.

The governing aim of this supplementary bibliography is to give a representative sample of the books and monographs in philosophy that have been published throughout the world since 1976. The materials cited in this bibliography constitute entrances for exploration, the beginnings of various paths, like so many threads, that can be followed into an immense labyrinth of philosophic literature. In providing a representative sample of its subject matter, this current work is consistent with the fundamental orientation of my earlier <u>Handbook of World Philosophy: Contemporary Developments Since 1945</u>.

Restricting this single-volume bibliography to a representative sample of books and monographs seemed the most sensible ideal for a number of reasons. An exhaustive bibliography covering the world since 1976 would require many volumes were it even feasible, to put it mildly a somewhat dubious supposition. The articles and bibliographies of the earlier <u>Handbook of World Philosophy</u>, to which this present bibliography is a supplement, dealt not only with the time-honored fields of philosophy such as ethics, epistemology, logic, metaphysics, and political and social philosophy but added to them such newer ones such as aesthetics, philosophy of history, of science, of language, of mind, of feminism, and the other multiplying "philosophy of's." The steadily increasing diversity of philosophical subject matter, as well as the volume of philosophical publications, limits a one-volume bibliography of world philosophy only to specimens. Furthermore, since hardly a month seems to pass without the announcement of a new philosophy journal and because many books are collections of previously published journal articles or revised and enlarged versions of them, the citations of this bibliography are limited to books and monographs. Philosophical material obtainable only in the forms of audio recordings and tapes, motion pictures, video cassettes, and computer print-outs is omitted. On some tomorrow, the bulk of philosophical publication may be in some form other than what today we routinely think of as a book. Perhaps in that future more and more philosophical writ ing will be only on computer disks whose existence is known to but a few. The lure of the esoteric is as old as Pythagoras and may yet reduce bibliographers to despair. On the other hand, the desire to communicate the truth as widely as possible may prevail, and bibliographers will not lose their occupation. Denied the gift of prophecy, the editor makes no predictions. At any rate, that conjectural tomorrow has not yet become today.

While arbitrariness in the selection of representative works included in a world bibliography of this size could not be avoided entirely, the editor's choices have been guided by a number of considerations. It is true that some of the entries in this work could have been omitted in favor of others not listed on a "six of one, half a dozen of the other" basis. Nevertheless, this present bibliography is teleological; it supplements the bibliographies in my earlier Handbook of World Philosophy by extending them from 1976 to the present. Therefore, it is modeled on the organization and content of that previous volume. It is divided into regions and countries of the world, as was that handbook. What counts as "philosophy" is determined by the kinds of subject matter, the themes, problems, and issues and the methods of inquiry recognized as philosophical by the expert authors of the chapters in that 1980 handbook, as well as by what is called "philosophy" by philosophers in the various regions and countries treated. Similarly, identification as such by the experts in the earlier handbook and by practice in the various regions and countries determine who is a "philosopher." By and large these usages of the terms "philosophy" and "philosopher" coincide with common practice in Western Europe and the United States. This European-American classification constitutes the basis of the author and subject indices in this volume. This is not intended to imply that there is a global unanimity as to what is "philosophy" and who is a "philosopher." Not only are there disputable borderline cases as with any classificatory scheme, but the nature of philosophy itself is a salient contemporary issue about which philosophies and philosophers disagree. If err he must, the editor has tried to do so in favor of inclusiveness. A representative sample should reflect existing dis agreements as well as agreements.

Indeed, this bibliography, as was the case with its companion 1980 handbook, is first and foremost empirical in the sense that it attempts to state the facts whether or not they fit neatly into some classificatory scheme or organizational logic. Of course, some order is necessary if a mass of data is to be intelligible and usable. However, whenever the truth seemed to demand it, the editor has modified the organizational arrangement on an *ad hoc* basis or even ignored it here and there. This procedure has been applied not only to "What is philosophy?" and "Who is a philosopher?," but also to such other questions as "In what country or region should this work or philosopher be listed?" During the period of time encompassed by this bibliography, a number of philosophers moved from one country or region to another or others and published philosophical works in some or all of them. Yet national and regional distinctions cannot be dispensed with entirely because they still mark significant differences in philosophical training, traditions, methods, themes, problems, and standards. There is as yet no single comprehensive world philosophy and way of philosophizing. The most specific and efficient guide to the content of this bibliography is not the contents but the author and subject indices.

Though descriptive in its general design, this bibliography is not wholly devoid of evaluation. Certainly what is included in and what is excluded from this bibliography do not represent what its compiler deems philosophically sound and important as distinquished from what he believes is philosophically unsound and unimportant. However, a bibliographic representative sample would not be truly representative if it did not take into account the evaluations suggested by what and whom philosophers in the various countries and regions choose to write about and the evaluative judgments they explicitly pronounce on philosophies and philosophers in the neighborhood or on another continent. The marked penchant for skepticism or at least for critical assessment, particularly concerning the nature of proof and the nature, role, significance, and future of philosophy noted in the 1980 Handbook of World Philosophy, has continued apace. This bibliography illustrates these implicit and explicit evaluations without judging them. The editor does not champion any causes, whether seemingly successful or lost.

The category "World Philosophy" in the table of contents differs from those of the regions and countries that follow. The last paragraph of the introduction to the 1980 Handbook of World Philosophy said in part:

> it would seem that the most realistic ideal prospect would
> be the gradual growth of combined local-international
> philosophy, ineradicably indigenous yet carried on in the
> light of a full and up-to-date knowledge of and sympathetic,
> yet critical, understanding of relevant philosophical devel-
> opments everywhere in the world. Obviously, at present such
> a combined local-internationalized philosophizing remains
> more an ideal than a fact.

The category of "World Philosophy" in this bibliography calls attention, not to the world philosophy generally accepted, but to the growth since 1976 to a distinct class of philosophical publications emphasizing "relevant philosophical developments everywhere in the world," however modest their number may be in comparison with the world total of philosophical works. In the ensuing years, works have appeared that do not really fit into any regional or national classification or even into the familiar category of comparative philosophy, because they deliberately attempt to deal with philosophy as a world-wide enterprise rather than primarily as an individual, scholastic, national, or regional one. Whatever their shortcomings, these works attempt to cross all cultural, traditional, linguistic, national, and regional divisions in philosophy. However much these local-international philosophical publications individually may differ from one another, they evince an admittedly vague yet real sense that all philosophers are engaged in a common enterprise in spite of their disagreements about particular philosophical issues and even about the nature of philosophy itself. This emerging sense of world philosophy resembles the strengthening conviction that business and commerce are distinctly global phenomena, not primarily local, regional, national, or even international ones in the old meaning of involving more than one country or region. Although certainly without the agreed-upon results and methods of contemporary science, the sample of works in the World Philosophy category tend to view philosophers first and foremost as philosophers and only secondarily as citizens or natives of particular countries and regions and legatees of particular philosophical movements and traditions. Perhaps this slowly intensifying sense of philosophy as a distinct, common global activity in space and time, in spite of its diversity in detail, most closely resembles that of art. While there is no single, uniform, comprehensive world philosophy any more than there is a single, uniform, comprehensive art, there is an emerging conscience among more and more philosophers that they should take into account what other philosophers have thought or are thinking however much they may be separated in space, time, tradition, and outlook. Of course, this is not to say that after due consideration no philosopher should dismiss another philosopher as irrelevant to his or her own professional concerns. But it is to say that due consideration should be given, that philosophers distant in space and time and concepts, as well as the philosopher just down the street, should not be ignored *ab initio*, particularly for some transient doctrinal reason. In any event, the world philosophy category calls attention to a growing number of post-1976 works that seem to express this global sense of conscience about philosophy, that philosophy should be viewed from a distinct world perspective just as art and business are seen today.

Perforce a single volume bibliography of contemporary world philosophy must be an itinerary rather than a travelogue. Some bibliographic entries are annotated; many are not. Given the limitations of a single volume, the editor faced a dilemma: more annotations with fewer entries or fewer annotations with more entries. Careful consideration of the advantages and disadvantages of each choice compelled the conclusion that a surplus of books and monographs over annotations would in the long run provide the greater benefit to anyone consulting a bibliography sampling philosophy on a world-wide scale. The general empirical plan of this bibliography rules out the editor giving his own evaluations as annotations. In most cases, the titles and, where given, the subtitles of works indicate at least the general content--certainly to anyone sufficiently interested in and knowledgeable about philosophy to move them to consult this work. In addition, there are detailed author and subject indices to aid the inquirer. The fact that a particular work possesses an extensive bibliography is noted. Limitations of space, by and large, restrict works cited to the latest known revised editions and prevent an exhaustive listing of all translations. When this project was begun, computer software appropiate for all of the various languages in which philosophical works were published was not available. Consequently, the names of authors and the titles of books and monographs are romanized and diacritical marks omitted.

In conclusion, each book and monograph should be viewed as a port of entry into a larger terrain of which it is a part. This bibliography is a world route to such ports of entry.

WORLD
PHILOSOPHY

WORLD PHILOSOPHY

1. Bogdan, Radu J., ed. PROFILES: AN INTERNATIONAL SERIES ON CONTEM-
PORARY PHILOSOPHERS AND LOGICIANS. Vol. 1, PATRICK SUPPES (1979).
Vol. 2, KEITH LEHRER (1981). Vol. 3, HENRY E. KYBURG, JR. & ISAAC LEVI
(1982). Vol. 4, D. M. ARMSTRONG (1984). Vol. 5, ALVIN PLANTINGA, edited by
James R. Tomberlin and Peter Van Inwagen (1985). Vol. 6, HECTOR-NERI CASTANE-
DA, edited by James E. Tomberlin (1986). Vol. 7, RODERICK M. CHISHOLM
(1986). Vol. 8, JAAKKO HINTIKKA (1987). Dordrecht and Boston: Reidel, 1979-.

The design of this Profiles Series is to survey and analyze in depth the work and
achievements of "outstanding personalities" in contemporary philosophy and logic.
However, some volumes will not be devoted to individuals but to established or emerging schools of thought. This series will cover the international state of philosophy and
will present research being conducted and its results. Unique and concise autobiographical material is promised for each individual profile. The philosopher profiled also replies
to other philosophers discussing his work in the volume.

2. Bulygin, Eugenio, et al, eds. MAN, LAW, AND MODERN FORMS OF LIFE. Law
and Philosophy Library. Dordrecht and Boston: Reidel, 1985.

This volume contains the proceedings of the 11th IVR World Congress on Philosophy of
Law and Social Philosophy held on August 14-20, 1983 in Helsinki, Finland.

3. Burr, John R., ed. HANDBOOK OF WORLD PHILOSOPHY: CONTEMPORARY
DEVELOPMENTS SINCE 1945. Westport, CT: Greenwood Press, 1980.

This pioneer work consists of critical essays discussing important developments in philosophy after World War II in fifty-four countries. This work is organized by region or
country of the world. The author of each essay is an authority on the philosophy of the
country or region treated. The volume also includes detailed indexes of subjects and of
philosophers and directories of philosophical associations and congresses and their
schedules.

4. Bynagle, Hans Edward. PHILOSOPHY: A GUIDE TO THE REFERENCE LITERA-
TURE. Reference Sources in the Humanities Series. Littleton, CO: Libraries Unlimited,
1986.

This reference work designed for professional philosophers, students of philosophy and librarians describes and evaluates more than 200 works dealing with philosophy from throughout the world. Works in English are emphasized.

5. Cauchy, Venant, ed. PHILOSOPHIE ET CULTURE: ACTES DU XVIIE CONGRES MONDIAL DE PHILOSOPHIE=PHILOSOPHY AND CULTURE: PROCEEDINGS OF THE XVII WORLD CONGRESS OF PHILOSOPHY. 5 Vols. Montreal: Edition du Beffroi; Editions Montmorency, 1986-1988.

These volumes are in French, English, German, and Spanish.

6. Centre National de la Recherche Scientifique. BULLETIN SIGNALTIQUE. PART 519: PHILOSOPHIE. Paris: Centre National de la Recherche Scientifique, 1947-.

This bibliography provides world-wide coverage of books and periodicals. Each entry contains a brief abstract.

7. Cormier, Ramona and Richard H. Lineback, eds. INTERNATIONAL DIRECTORY OF PHILOSOPHY AND PHILOSOPHERS, 1990-1992. 7th ed. Bowling Green, OH: Philosophy Documentation Center, Bowling Green State Univ, 1990.

This comprehensive directory is published every three years and covers Europe, Central and South America, Asia, Africa, and Australia; however, it does not include the United States and Canada, which are treated in the DIRECTORY OF AMERICAN PHILOS-OPHERS, edited by Archie J. Bahm. Included are the addresses and telephone numbers of philosophy departments, department chairpersons, philosophy faculties, institutes and research centers, societies and associations, journals, and publishers.

8. Deutsch, Eliot, ed. CULTURE AND MODERNITY: EAST-WEST PHILOSOPHIC PERSPECTIVES. Honolulu: Univ. of Hawaii Press, 1991.

This volume consists of thirty-six selected papers from the Sixth East-West Philosophers' Conference held in August, 1989. The international roster of contributors includes Richard Rorty, Svetozar Stojanovich, Bimal K. Matilal, Jiang Tianji, A. C. Graham, Karl-Otto Apel, Margaret Chatterjee, Aziz Al-Azmeh, Kwame Gyerke, Maria Herrera, Megumi Sakabe, Li Zhilin, Ilkka Niiniluoto, R. R. Verma, and others.

9. Diemer, Alwin, ed. EROFFNUNGS UND SCHLUSSITZUNG; PLENARSITZUN GEN; ABENDVORTRAGE. 16 Weltkongress fur Philosophie 1978=SEANCE D'OUVERTURE ET DE CLOTURE; SESSIONS PLENIERES; CONFERENCES DU SOIR. 16eme Congresmondial de Philosophie 1978=OPENING AND CLOSING SESSION; PLENARY SESSIONS; EVENING LECTURES. 16th World Congress of Philosophy, 1978. Frankfurt am Main and New York: Peter Lang, 1983.

10. Dilworth, David A. PHILOSOPHY IN WORLD PERSPECTIVE: A COMPARA-TIVE HERMENEUTIC OF THE MAJOR THEORIES. New Haven and London: Yale Univ. Press, 1989.

11. Dorsey, Gray, ed. EQUALITY AND FREEDOM: INTERNATIONAL AND COMPARATIVE JURISPRUDENCE. 3 Vols. New York: Dobbs Ferry, 1977.

This volume contains the papers from the World Congress of Philosophy of Law and Social Philosophy held in St. Louis, August 24-29, 1975. This edition was authorized by the International Vereinigung fur Rechts- und Sozialphilosophie (IVR). The papers are written in English, French, German, or Spanish.

12. Eliade, Mircea, Editor in Chief. THE ENCYCLOPEDIA OF RELIGION. 16 Vols. New York: Macmillan, 1987.

13. Ericsson, Lars Olov, et al. JUSTICE, SOCIAL AND GLOBAL: PAPERS PRESENTED AT THE STOCKHOLM INTERNATIONAL SYMPOSIUM ON JUSTICE, HELD IN SEPTEMBER, 1978. Stockholm: Akademilitteratur, 1981.

14. Floistad, Guttorm, ed. CONTEMPORARY PHILOSOPHY: A NEW SURVEY. Vol. I, PHILOSOPHY OF LANGUAGE/PHILOSOPHICAL LOGIC. Vol. II, PHILOSO- PHY OF SCIENCE. Vol. III, PHILOSOPHY OF ACTION. Vol. IV, PHILOSOPHY OF MIND. Vol. V, AFRICAN PHILOSOPHY. Dordrecht: Nijhoff, 1981-1983.

This is a continuation of two earlier collections: PHILOSOPHY IN THE MID- CENTURY (Florence, 1958/59) and CONTEMPORARY PHILOSOPHY (Florence, 1968).

15. Geldsetzer, Lutz. BIBLIOGRAPHY OF THE INTERNATIONAL CONGRESSES OF PHILOSOPHY: PROCEEDINGS, 1900-1978=BIBLIOGRAPHIE DER INTERNATIONALEN PHILOSOPHIE KONGRESSE: BEITRAGE, 1900-1978. Munich and New York: Saur, 1981.

16. Guerry, Herbert, ed. A BIBLIOGRAPHY OF PHILOSOPHICAL BIBLIOGRA- PHIES. Westport, CT: Greenwood, 1977.

This work tries to list philosophical bibliographies published in all countries since about 1450 through 1974. The author has restricted his compilation to bibliographies pub- lished separately, as contributions to journals, and as appendices to monographs or as parts of larger bibliographies. The 2,353 entries are divided into two lists: (1) bibliogra- phies of the works by, and the literature about, individual philosophers; (2) bibliogra- phies on philosophical topics. The original languages of the bibliographies are identi- fied. The author has not translated titles in the major European languages. However, titles in other Roman alphabet languages are translated into English. Titles in non- Roman alphabets are transliterated into the Roman alphabet with English translations.

17. International Institute of Philosophy. BIBLIOGRAPHIE DE LA PHILOSOPHIE. BULLETIN TRIMESTRIEL (BIBLIOGRAPHY OF PHILOSOPHY. A QUARTERLY BULLETIN). Paris: Librairie Philosophique, J. Vrin, 1937-.

This bibliography covers books on philosophy and related subjects published throughout the world. Since 1954 it has been a quarterly bulletin and included substantial abstracts of books published for the first time. These abstracts are in the language of the original publication if it was written in English, French, German, Italian, or Spanish. Otherwise the abstracts are written in English or French. None of the works listed are evaluated. The summaries are preceded by the following data: author or editor, title and sub-titles, writer of preface, translator, place of publication, publisher, and date. Books are classified in eleven main sections: (1) Philosophy in General, Metaphysics, Ontology, Phenomenology, Philosophical Anthropology, Existential Philosophy; (2) Logic, Philos- ophy of Science, Methodology, Semantics, Philosophy of Language; (3) Philosophy of Mind; (4) Aesthetics; (5) Ethics, General Theory of Value; (6) Social Philosophy, Philosophy of Politics, Philosophy of Law; (7) Philosophy of History, Reflections on Culture, Philosophy of Education; (8) Philosophy of Religion; (9) History of Philosophy; (10) Dictionaries, Bibliographies, Miscellanea, Reference Works; and (11) Chinese books (translation of titles according to subject matter). The final issue of each year includes 3 indices: (1) authors, titles, subject matter; (2) proper names (editors, transla- tors, writers of prefaces, persons referred to; and (3) publishers.

18. Katz, Nathan, ed. BUDDHIST AND WESTERN PHILOSOPHY: A CRITICAL COMPARATIVE STUDY. Atlantic Highlands, NJ: Humanities Press; New Delhi: Sterling, 1981.

    Nineteen noted scholars from the United States, India, Japan, Sri Lanka and England have contributed twenty-eight essays. Each essay focuses on a particular topic, school or philosophy from within Buddhism and western traditions and analyzes them comparatively.

19. Lineback, Richard H., ed. THE PHILOSOPHER'S INDEX. Bowling Green, OH: Philosophy Documentation Center, Bowling Green University, 1967-.

    This index covers journals and books from over forty countries. While publications from North America and Western Europe are cited most often, the index also covers journals and books from Eastern Europe, Central and South America, Asia, Africa, and Australia. There are abstracts; subject, author, and book review indices; and cross references. The work is available as an online database or on CD-Rom.

20. MacGregor, Geddes. DICTIONARY OF RELIGION AND PHILOSOPHY. New York: Paragon House, 1989.

    In more than 3,000 entries, the author distills a lifetime of scholarship. The religious and philosophical concepts treated are not confined to Judeo-Christianity but range from those of Egyptian and Indian antiquity, Buddhism, Neoplatonism, the Vienna Circle, and Islam to bioethics and scientology. This work also contains entries on many individual philosophers. There are brief, selective bibliographies from African religions to Zoroastrianism.

21. McCormick, Peter J., ed. THE REASONS OF ART: ARTWORKS AND THE TRANSFORMATIONS OF PHILOSOPHY=L'ART A SES RAISONS: LES OEUVRES D'ART, D'EFIS A LA PHILOSOPHIE. Philosophia 30. Ottawa: Univ. of Ottawa Press, 1985.

    This collection contains almost 250 scholarly papers selected from those presented at the Xth International Congress in Aesthetics, Montreal, Canada, August 14-19, 1984, representing current work in the field in Europe, North and South America, Africa, the Far East, and Australia. These papers focus on the implications of works of art for the nature of philosophizing.

22. Mercier, Andre and Maja Svilar, eds. PHILOSOPHES CRITIQUES D'EUX MEMES/ PHILOSOPHERS ON THEIR OWN WORK/PHILOSOPHISCHE SELBSTBE-TRACHTUNGEN. Bern: Herbert Lang; Frankfurt am Main: Peter Lang, 1975-.

    Each volume in this series consists of critical articles by individual thinkers from around the world on their philosophies and philosophizing. There is a short biography of each philosopher and a list of his or her publications. By volume the philosophers included are : Vol. 1, Alfred Cyril Ewing, Marvin Farber, Kurt Hubner, Richard McKeon, John Passmore, Chaim Perelman, and Ioannis N. Theodoracopoulos. Vol. 2, Peter Caws, Hans-George Gadamer, Karel Kuypers, Franco Lombardi, Andre Mercier, Howard L. Parsons, and Adam Schaff. Vol. 3, Augustin Basave Fernandez Del Valle, Guido Calogero, George F. McLean, Maria Do Carmo Tavares De Miranda, Karl R. Popper, Clemence Ramnoux, and Fritz-Joachim von Rintelen. Vol. 4, Karl-Otto Apel, Joseph Bochenski, Leo Gabriel, Sava Zolov Ganovski, Henri Gouhier, Bonifatii Mikhailovich Kedrov, Raimundo Panikkar, Jean Pucell, and Alexandru Tanase. Vol. 5, Evandro Agazzi, Alwin Diemer, Ernesto Grassi, Mohamed Aziz Lahbabi, Teodor Ilich Oizerman, Jerzy Pelc, and Paul Weiss. Vol. 6, Milan Damnjanovic, Carlo Giacon, Olof Gigon, Florence M. Hetzler, Seyyed Hossein Nasr, Jeanne Parain-Vial, and John E. Smith. Vol. 7, Alberto Caturelli, Jeanne Hersch, Mihailo Markovic, Evanghelos Moutsopoulos,

Gerard Radnitsky, Stephan Strasser, Ernst Topitsch, and Alexandre Zinoviev. Vol. 8, Brand Blanshard, Augusto Guzzo, Charles Hartshorne, Helmut Kuhn, T.M.P. Mahadevan, Joseph Moreau, Miguel Reale, and Rene Schaerer. Vol. 9, Shlomo Avineri, Venant Cauchy, Richard T. De George, Justus Hartnack, Jaakko Hintikka, Francisco Larroyo, and Nicholas Rescher. Vol. 10, Margaret Chatterjee, Jose Luis Curiel Y Benfield, Alphonse De Waelhens, Ludwig Landgrebe, Emmanuel Levinas, Konrad Marc-Wogau, Arne Naess, and Wolfgang Stegmuller.

23. Oizerman, Teodor Ilich, et al. FILOSOFIIA MARKSIZMA I SOVREMENAIA NAUCHNO-TECHNICHESKAIA REVOLIUTSIIA: [MATERIALY] XV VESMIRNYI FILOS. KONGRESS. Moscow: Nauka, 1977.

This is a collection of articles analyzing and broadly summarizing the accomplishments of the 15th International Congress of Philosophy, Varna, Bulgaria, 1973.

24. Pelikan, Jaroslav Jan, et al. COMPARATIVE WORK ETHICS: JUDEO-CHRISTIAN, ISLAMIC, AND EASTERN. Washington, DC: Library of Congress, 1985.

25. Plott, John C., et al. GLOBAL HISTORY OF PHILOSOPHY. Vol. 1, THE AXIAL AGE. Vol. 2, THE HAN-HELLENISTIC-BACTRIAN PERIOD. Vol. 3, THE PATRISTIC-SUTRA PERIOD. Vols. 4-5, THE PERIOD OF SCHOLASTICISM. Ed. by Robert C. Richmond, et al. Delhi: Motilal Banarsidass, 1977-.

26. Rauh, Hans-Christoph, ed. DEUTSCHE ZEITSCHRIFT FUR PHILOSOPHIE. East Berlin: Deutscher Verlag der Wissenschaften, 1953-.

This annual is generally global in coverage but emphasizes works on dialectical materialism written in Eastern Europe.

27. Reese, William L., ed. THE BEST IN THE LITERATURE OF PHILOSOPHY AND WORLD RELIGIONS. New York and London: R. R. Bowker, 1988.

This is volume 4 of THE READER'S ADVISOR: A LAYMAN'S GUIDE TO LITERATURE, 13th ed. This single volume bibliography is designed for the non-specialist. Only books currently available in English from a publisher or distributor in the United States are listed; however some out-of-print titles are included"...because of their importance in the field". The volume is enhanced by name, title, and subject indices. 443 pages of this 714 page (minus indices) bibliography are devoted to philosophy, the remainder to world religions.

28. Reese, William L. DICTIONARY OF PHILOSOPHY AND RELIGIONS: EASTERN AND WESTERN THOUGHT. Atlantic Highlands, NJ: Humanities Press, 1980.

This comprehensive dictionary contains more than 3,500 entries ranging over ancient and modern philosophic and religious thought of the East and the West. Philosophical terms, intellectual figures and movements are carefully interrelated and extensively cross referenced.

29. Reich, Warren R., Editor in Chief. ENCYCLOPEDIA OF BIOETHICS. 4 Vols. New York: Free Press, 1978.

This reference work covers European and non-European thought and values, including Confucianism, Hinduism, Buddhism, and Taoism. The articles are by recognized scholars on their respective subjects.

30. Ruben, Douglas H., comp. PHILOSOPHY JOURNALS AND SERIALS: AN ANALYT-
ICAL GUIDE. Annotated Bibliographies of Serials: A Subject Approach, Vol. 2. Westport, CT: Greenwood Press, 1985.

This international bibliography consists of 335 annotated entries of twentieth century
periodicals with at least some articles in English covering thirty countries. "Periodical"
includes journals published less frequently than once a year, publications of professional
associations, magazines, selected newsletters, almanacs, and conference proceedings.
Countries covered are: Africa, Argentina, Australia, Austria, Belgium, Canada, China,
Denmark, Finland, France, Germany, Great Britain, Greece, Holland, Hungary, India,
Iceland, Israel, Italy, Malaysia, Mexico, Netherlands, Norway, Poland, Puerto Rico,
Romania, Scotland, Sweden, Switzerland and the United States. There are geographical
and subject indices.

31. Stein, Gordon, ed. THE ENCYCLOPEDIA OF UNBELIEF. 2 Vols. Buffalo:
Prometheus Books, 1985.

This encyclopedia focuses on expressions of religious skepticism, including atheism and
agnosticism, in countries and regions around the world from antiquity to the present. A
generous number of articles by philosophers are devoted to individual philosophers and
to philosophical movements.

32. Troisfontaines, Claude and Urbain Dhondt, eds. REPERTOIRE BIBLIOGRAPHIQUE
DE LA PHILOSOPHIE/INTERNATIONAL PHILOSOPHICAL BIBLIOGRAPHY/
BIBLIOGRAFISCH REPERTORIUM VAN DE WIJSBEGEERTE. Louvain- La-Neuve,
Belgium: Institut Superieur de Philosophie, 1949-.

The text is in the language of the authors. There are introductions in Dutch, English,
French, German, Italian, and Spanish. This bibliography covers books, articles, and
reviews of philosophical writings. There are no abstracts; however, the American work,
THE PHILOSOPHER'S INDEX (See entry 19), gives abstracts of many entries.

AFRICA

AFRICA

33. Apostel, Leo. AFRICAN PHILOSOPHY-MYTH OR REALITY? Ghent, Belgium: Storica-Scientia, 1981.

34. Diemer, Alwin, ed. PHILOSOPHY IN THE PRESENT SITUATION OF AFRICA. SYMPOSIUM, 16TH WORLD CONGRESS OF PHILOSOPHY, 1978. Wiesbaden: Steiner, 1981.

35. Etuk, Udo Akpan. ETHICAL POSTULATES FOR AFRICAN DEVELOPMENT. (Ph. D. Thesis). Bloomington: Indian University, 1982.

36. Hountondji, Paulin J. AFRICAN PHILOSOPHY: MYTH AND REALITY. Tr. of SUR LA PHILOSOPHIE AFRICAINE: CRITIQUE DE L`ETHNOPHILOSOPHIE. Paris: F. Maspero, 1977. Tr. by Henri Evans with the collaboration of Jonathan Ree. Bloomington, IN: Indiana Univ. Press, 1983.

37. Hountondji, Paulin J., ed. PHILOSOPHICAL RESEARCH IN AFRICA, A BIBLIOGRAPHIC SURVEY=BILAN DEL A RECHERCHE PHILOSOPHIQUE AFRICAINE REPERTOIRE ALPHABETIQUE. Cotonou, Benin: Inter-African Council for Philosophy, Conseil Interafricain de Philosophie, 1985-.

Part I, 1900-1985; Vol. 1, A-M has been published to date.

38. Hountondji, Paulin J. SUR LA PHILOSOPHIE AFRICAINE: CRITIQUE DE L'ETHNOPHILOSOPHIE. Paris: F. Maspero, 1977.

39. Karp, Ivan and Charles S. Bird, eds. EXPLORATIONS IN AFRICAN SYSTEMS OF THOUGHT. Bloomington: Indiana Univ. Press, 1980.

This is a collection of papers presented at a seminar organized for the African Studies Program at Indiana University.

40. Maurier, Henri. PHILOSOPHIE DE L'AFRIQUE NOIRE. St. Augustine bei Bonn: Verlag des Anthropos-Instituts, 1976.

There is an extensive bibliography on pages 253-271.

41. McKenzie-Rennie, Rhoda. NKRUMAH: GREATEST OF MODERN PHILOSOPHERS. New York: Vantage Press, 1977.

42. Ngubane, Jordan K. CONFLICT OF MINDS. New York: Books in Focus, 1979.

43. Ocholla-Ayayo, Andrev B. C. TRADITIONAL IDEOLOGY AND ETHICS AMONG THE SOUTHERN LUO. Uppsala: Scandinavian Institute of African Studies, 1976.

44. Okere, Theophilus. AFRICAN PHILOSOPHY: A HISTORICO-HERMENEUTICAL INVESTIGATION OF THE CONDITIONS OF ITS POSSIBILITY. Lanham, MD: Univ. Press of America, 1983.

45. Olela, Henry. FROM ANCIENT AFRICA TO ANCIENT GREECE: AN INTRODUC-TION TO THE HISTORY OF PHILOSOPHY. Ed. by Edward F. Collins and Alveda King Beal. Black Heritage Publication. Atlanta: Published for the Black Heritage Corp. by Select Publishing, 1981.

46. Oruka, Henry Odera. "FOUR TRENDS IN ANCIENT AFRICAN PHILOSOPHY" (xeroxed manuscript from author).

47. Outlaw, Lucius. INTERNATIONAL DIRECTORY OF PHILOSOPHERS OF AFRI-CAN DESCENT. Studies in African Philosophy. Haverford, PA: Dept. of Philoso phy, Haverford College, 1981.

48. Ruch, E. A. and K. Chukwulozie Anyanwu. AFRICAN PHILOSOPHY: AN INTRO-DUCTION TO THE MAIN PHILOSOPHICAL TRENDS IN CONTEMPORARY AFRICA. Rev ed. Rome: Catholic Book Agency, 1984.

The volume contains a bibliography on pages 385-412.

49. Serequeberhan, Tsenay, ed. AFRICAN PHILOSOPHY: THE ESSENTIAL READINGS. New York: Paragon House, 1991.

All of the eleven essays from the period 1967 to 1987 making up this collection deal with the question of what constitutes or would constitute African philosophy. Five answers emerge: ethnophilosophy; the second-level articulation of cultural beliefs; sagacity, or the tradition of tribal sages; nationalist-ideological thought; and professional philosophy from an African perspective.

50. Smet, Alphonse J. HISTOIRE DE LA PHILOSOPHIE AFRICAINE CONTEMPO-RAINE: COURANTS ET PROBLEMES. Kinshasa, Zaire: Department de Philosophie et Religions Africaines, Faculte de Theologie Catholique, 1980.

51. Thompson, Robert Farris. FLASH OF THE SPIRIT: AFRICAN AND AFRO-AMERI-CAN ART AND PHILOSOPHY. New York: Random House, 1983.

52. Wright, Richard A. AFRICAN PHILOSOPHY: AN INTRODUCTION. 3d ed. Lanham: Univ. Press of America, 1984.

This volume includes an extensive bibliography on pages 259-279.

ALGERIA

53. Onwuanibe, Richard C. A CRITIQUE OF REVOLUTIONARY HUMANISM: FRANTZ FANON. St. Louis: W. H. Green, 1983.

CAMEROON

54. Towa, Marcien. ESSAI SUR LA PROBLEMATIQUE PHILOSOPHIQUE DANS L'AFRICQUE ACTUELLE. 2d ed. Point de Vue, Vol. 8. Yaounde, Cameroon: Cle, 1979.

55. Towa, Marcien. IDEOLOGIES ET UTOPIES. [s.l.: s.n., 1977?].

   This volume consists of material from the Conference International de Philosophie, October 30-November 3, 1977 in Khartoum.

56. Towa, Marcien. L'IDEE D'UNE PHILOSOPHIE NEGRO-AFRICAINE. Point de Vue. Yaounde, Cameroon: Editions CLE, 1979.

EGYPT

57. Al-Ghazzali. LE LIVRE DU LICITE ET DE L'ILLICITE. Paris: J. Vrin, 1981.

   This is a translation of KITABAT ALHILAL WA-ALHARAM. The introduction, translation and notes are by Regis Morelon.

58. Anawati, Georges C. RECHERCHES D'ISLAMOLOGIE: RECEUIL D'ARTICLES AFFECTS A GEORGES C. ANAWATI ET LOUIS GARDET PAR LEURS COLLEQUES ET AMIS. Louvain: Peeters, 1977.

59. Anawati, Georges C., et al. LA PHILOSOPHIE DE LA NATURE DE SAINT THOMAS D'AQUIN: ACTES DU SYMPOSIUM SUR LE PENSEE DE SAINT THOMAS, TENU A ROLDUC LES 7 ET 8 NOV. 1981. Vatican City: Pontificia Academia de San Tommaso Libreria Editrice Vaticana, 1982.

60. Avicenna. LA METAPHYSIQUE DU SHIFA AVICENNE: TRADUCTION FRANCAISE DU TEXTE ARABE DE L'EDITION DU CAIRE. Vol. 1, LIVRES I a V. Vol. 2, LIVRES VI a X. Paris: J. Vrin, 1978-1985.

   This is a translation of AL-ILAHIYAT, which forms the fourth part of the author's AL-SHIFA. The introduction, notes and commentary are by Georges C. Anawati.

61. Wahba, Mourad, ed. PHILOSOPHY AND CIVILIZATION. Cairo: Faculty of Education, Ain Shams Univ., 1978.

   This book is the proceedings of the first Afro-Asian Philosophy Conference, March 13-16, 1978, Cairo, Egypt. Articles are written in English or French, with passages in Arabic.

62. Wahba, Mourad, ed. PHILOSOPHY AND MASS-MAN. Cairo, A. R. E.: Anglo-Egyptian Bookshop, 1985.

   This book is the Proceedings of the Fifth International Philosophy Conference, November 12-15, 1983

ETHIOPIA

63. Sumner, Claude. CLASSICAL ETHIOPIAN PHILOSOPHY. Addis Ababa: Commercial Print. Press, 1985.

   The forward to this volume is in English and French.

64. Sumner, Claude. ETHIOPIAN PHILOSOPHY. Addis Ababa: Central Print. Press, 1974-.

     The following volumes have been published: Vol. 1, THE BOOK OF THE WISE PHI-LOSOPHERS. Vol. 2-3, THE TREATISE OF ZARA YAEQUO AND OF WALDA HEYWAT. Vol. 4, THE LIFE AND MAXIMS OF SKENDES. Vol. 5, THE FISALG-WOS.

65. Sumner, Claude, ed. PROCEEDINGS OF THE SEMINAR ON AFRICAN PHILOSO-PHY, ADDIS ABABA, 1-3 DECEMBER, 1976/ACTES DU SEMINAIRE SUR LA PHILOSOPHIE AFRICAINE, ADDIS ABABA, 1-3 DECEMBRE, 1976. Addis Ababa: printed for Addis Ababa University by Chamber Print., 1980.

66. Sumner, Claude. THE SOURCE OF AFRICAN PHILOSOPHY: THE ETHIOPIAN PHILOSOPHY OF MAN. Stuttgart: F. Steiner Wiesbaden, 1986.

GHANA

67. Gyekye, Kwame. ARABIC LOGIC: IBN AL-TAYYIB'S COMMENTARY ON PORPHYRY'S EISAGOGE. Studies in Islamic Philosophy and Science, Vol. 68. Albany: State Univ. of New York Press, 1979.

     This work includes a translation of Ibn al-Tayyib's TALIQ ISAGHUJI ALA FUR FURIYUS.

68. Gyekye, Kwame. AN ESSAY ON AFRICAN PHILOSOPHICAL THOUGHT: THE AKAN CONCEPTUAL SCHEME. Cambridge and New York: Cambridge Univ. Press, 1987.

     There is a substantial bibliography included on pages 213-238.

69. Wiredu, Kwasi. PHILOSOPHY AND AN AFRICAN CULTURE. Cambridge and New York: Cambridge Univ. Press, 1980.

KENYA

70. Mbiti, John Samuel. AFRICAN RELIGIONS AND PHILOSOPHY. 2d., rev. and enl. ed. Oxford and Portsmouth, NH: Heinemann, 1990.

71. Mugambi, Jesse Ndwiga Kanyua. A COMPARATIVE STUDY OF RELIGIONS. Nairobi: Nairobi Univ. Press, 1990.

72. Oruka, Henry Odera. PUNISHMENT AND TERRORISM IN AFRICA: PROBLEMS IN THE PHILOSOPHY AND PRACTICE OF PUNISHMENT. Kampala: East African Literature Bureau, 1976.

73. Oruka, Henry Odera, ed. SAGE PHILOSOPHY: INDIGENOUS THINKERS AND MODERN DEBATE IN AFRICAN PHILOSOPHY. Leiden and New York: E. J. Brill, 1990.

74. Oruka, Henry Odera. TRENDS IN CONTEMPORARY AFRICAN PHILOSOPHY. Nairobi: Shirikon, 1990.

75. Oruka, Henry Odera, et al. THE RATIONAL PATH: A DIALOGUE ON PHILOSO-PHY, LAW AND RELIGION. Nairobi: Standard Textbooks Graphics and Publishing, 1989.

76. Oruka, Henry Odera and D. A. Masolo, eds. PHILOSOPHY AND CULTURES. Nairobi, Kenya: Bookwise, Ltd, 1983.

These are the Proceedings of the 2nd Afro-Asian Philosophy Conference, Nairobi, October and November, 1981. The text is in English and French.

NIGERIA

77. Agrawal, Murari Mohan. INDIVIDUALITY AND REINCARNATION. New Delhi: Sunrise International, 1978.

78. Agrawal, Murari Mohan. THE PHILOSOPHY OF NON-ATTACHMENT: THE WAY TO SPIRITUAL FREEDOM IN INDIAN THOUGHT. Delhi: Motilal Banarsidass, 1982.

79. Amadi, Elechi. ETHICS IN NIGERIAN CULTURE. Ibadan: Heinemann Educational Books, Nigeria, 1982.

80. Bodunrin, Peter Oluwambe, ed. PHILOSOPHY IN AFRICA: TRENDS AND PER-SPECTIVES. Ile-Ife, Nigeria: Univ. of Ife Press, 1985.

This volume consists of selected papers from an International Conference on African Philosophy held at the University of Ibadan, Ibada, February 15-19, 1985, with the assistance of UNESCO.

81. Hallen, Barry and J. O. Sodipo. KNOWLEDGE, BELIEF AND WITCHCRAFT: ANALYTIC EXPERIMENTS IN AFRICAN PHILOSOPHY. London: Ethnographica, 1986.

82. Makinde, Moses Akin. AFRICAN PHILOSOPHY, CULTURE, AND TRADITIONAL MEDICINE. Athens: Ohio Univ. Center for International Studies, 1988.

83. Mason, Thomas F. ETHICAL CONCEPTS AND THEIR ANALYSIS. Dublin: Good Counsel Press, 1979.

84. Momoh, Campbell Shittu. AN AFRICAN CONCEPTION OF BEING AND THE TRADITIONAL PROBLEM OF FREEDOM AND DETERMINISM (Ph. D. Thesis). Bloomington: Indiana Univ. Press, 1979.

85. Momoh, Campbell Shittu, ed. THE SUBSTANCE OF AFRICAN PHILOSOPHY. Auchi: African Philosophy Projects Publications, 1989.

86. Momoh, Campbell Shittu, et al, eds. NIGERIAN STUDIES IN RELIGIOUS TOLER-ANCE. Vol. 1, RELIGIONS AND THEIR DOCTRINES. Vol. 2, RELIGION AND MORALITY. Vol. 3, RELIGION AND NATION BUILDING. Vol. 4, PHILOSOPHY OF RELIGIOUS TOLERANCE. Lagos: Centre for Black and African Arts and Civilza-tion: National Association for Religious Tolerance, 1988.

87. Nwala, T. Uzodinma. IGBO PHILOSOPHY. Ikeja, Lagos: Lantern Books, 1985.

88. Onyewuenyi, Innocent Chilaka. AFRICAN ORIGIN OF GREEK PHILOSOPHY. Nsukka: Department of Philosophy, Univ. of Nigeria Nsukka, 1987.

SENEGAL

89. Ndaw, Alassane. LA PENSEE AFRICAINE: RECHERCHES SUR LA FONDEMENTS DE LA PENSEE NEGRO- AFRICAINE. Dakar: Nouvelles editions africaines, 1983.

SOUTH AFRICA

90. Schuurman, Egbert. TECHNOLOGY IN CHRISTIAN-PHILOSOPHICAL PERSPEC-
TIVE. Weetenskaplike bydraes of the Potchefstroom University for Christian Higher
Education: Series F, Institute for the Advancement of Calvinism. Potchefstroom: Potchef-
stroom Univ., 1980.

ZAIRE

91. Mudimbe, Vumbi Yoka. AFRICAN GNOSIS: PHILOSOPHY AND THE ORDER OF
KNOWLEDGE. Haverford, PA: V. Y. Mudimbe, 1984.

This work was commissioned by the ACLS/SSRC Joint Committee on African Studies
for presentation at the 27th annual meeting of the African Studies Association, October
25-28, 1984, Los Angeles, California. There is a 43 page bibliography.

92. Mudimbe, Vumbi Yoka. THE INVENTION OF AFRICA: GNOSIS, PHILOSOPHY,
AND THE ORDER OF KNOWLEDGE. Bloomington: Univ. of Indiana Press, 1988.

93. Mudimbe, Vumbi Yoka. VISAGE DE LA PHILOSOPHIE ET DE LA THEOLOGIE
CONTEMPORAINES AU ZAIRE. Brussels: CEDAF (Centre d'etude et de documentation africaines), 1981.

94. Tempels, Placide. LE CONCEPT FONDAMENTAL DE L'ONTOLOGIE BANTU.
Tr. of HET GRONDBEGRIP DER BANTU-ONTOLOGIE. Tr. from the Dutch by
Alphonse J. Smet. Kinshasa-Limite: Departement de Philosophie et Religions Africaines,
1977.

95. Tempels, Placide. PHILOSOPHIE BANTU. Kinshasa: Departement de Philosophie et
Religions Africaines Faculte de Theologie Catholique, 1979.

96. Tempels, Placide. PLAIDOYER POUR LA PHILOSOPHIE BANTU: ET QUELQUES
AUTRES TEXTES. Ed. by Alphonse J. Smet. Kinshasa-Limete: Departement de
Philosophie et Religions Africaines, Faculte de Theologie Catholique, 1982.

ZIMBABWE

97. Callinicos, Alex. MARXISM AND PHILOSOPHY. Oxford and New York: Oxford
Univ. Press, 1985, 1983.

MIDDLE
EAST

MIDDLE EAST

98. Al-Attas, Muhammed Naguib. ISLAM, SECULARISM, AND THE PHILOSOPHY OF THE FUTURE. London and New York: Mansell, 1985.

99. Averroes. AVERROES MIDDLE COMMENTARY ON ARISTOTLE'S POETICS. Tr. by Charles E. Butterworth. Tr. of TALKHIS KITAB AL-SHIR. Princeton: Princeton Univ. Press, 1986.

100. Averroes. IBN RUSHD'S METAPHYSICS: A TRANSLATION WITH INTRODUCTION OF IBN RUSHD'S COMMENTARY ON ARISTOTLE'S METAPHYSICS, BOOK L'AM. Tr. of TAFSIR MA BADA AL-TABIAH. Book 11. Tr. by Charles Genequand. Leiden: E. J. Brill, 1984.

101. Bosworth, Clifford Edmund, ed. THE ENCYCLOPEDIA OF ISLAM. Leiden: Brill, 1980-.

This is a new edition being prepared by a number of leading orientalists.

102. Hourani, Albert Habib. ISLAM IN EUROPEAN THOUGHT. Cambridge and New York: Cambridge Univ. Press, 1991.

103. Hourani, George F. REASON AND TRADITION IN ISLAMIC ETHICS. Cambridge and New York: Cambridge Univ. Press, 1985.

104. Kogan, Barry S. AVERROES AND THE METAPHYSICS OF CAUSATION. Albany: State Univ. of New York Press, 1985.

105. Leaman, Oliver. AN INTRODUCTION TO MEDIEVAL ISLAMIC PHILOSOPHY. London and New York: Cambridge Univ. Press, 1985.

106. Mahdi, Muhsin S. THE POLITICAL ORIENTATION OF ISLAMIC PHILOSOPHY. Washington, DC: Center for Contemporary Arab Studies, Georgetown Univ., 1982.

107. Marmura, Michael E., ed. ISLAMIC THEOLOGY AND PHILOSOPHY: STUDIES IN HONOR OF GEORGE F. HOURANI. Albany: State University of New York Press, 1984.

This work is in English and French.

108. Morewedge, Parviz, ed. ISLAMIC PHILOSOPHICAL THEOLOGY. Studies in Islamic Philosophy and Science. Albany: State Univ. of New York Press, 1979.

This work consists of eleven essays written by such internationally recognized authorities as L. Gardet, W. C. Smith, F. E. Peters, R. M. Frank, and G. F. Hourani.

109. Morewedge, Parviz, ed. ISLAMIC PHILOSOPHY AND MYSTICISM. Delmar, NY: Caravan Books, 1981.

110. Watt, William Montgomery. ISLAMIC PHILOSOPHY AND THEOLOGY. 2d ed. New York: Columbia Univ. Press; Edinburgh: Univ. Press, 1985.

This is a completely rewritten edition of a standard survey of Islamic thought. It traces its development from early religio-political sects through Aristotelian influences to the modern period.

IRAN

111. Hairi Yazdi, Mahdi. HIRAMI HASTI: TAHLILI AZ MABADI-I HASTI SHINASI-I TATBIQI. Tehran: Muassisah-i Mutali at va Tahqiqat-i Farhangi, 1983.

There is an added title page: THE PYRAMID OF EXISTENCE. The text is in Persian.

112. Hairi Yazdi, Mahdi. KAVUSH'HA-YI AQL-I AMALI: FALSAFAH-I AKHLAQ. Tehran: Muassisah-i Mutali at va Tahqiqat-i Farhangi, 1982.

There is an added title page: PRACTICAL REASON, METAETHICS. The text is in Persian.

113. Hairi Yazdi, Mahdi. THE PRINCIPLES OF EPISTEMOLOGY IN ISLAMIC PHILOSOPHY: KNOWLEDGE BY PRESENCE. Albany: State Univ. of New York Press, 1992.

There are bibliographical references on pages 191-222.

114. Hook, Sidney. QAHRAMAN DAR TARIKH. Persian translation of the HERO IN HISTORY. New York: John Day, 1943. Teheran, Iran: Intisharat-i-Ravaq, 1357, 1978.

115. Kirmani, Awhaduddin. HEART'S WITNESS. Tr. by Bernd Manuel Weischer and Peter Lamborn Wilson. Tehran: Imperial Iranian Academy, 1978.

116. Lawrence, Bruce B. NOTES FROM A DISTANT FLUTE. Tehran: Tehran Imperial Academy of Philosophy, 1978.

117. Nasr, Seyyed Hossein. ESSAIS SUR LA SOUFISME. Tr. of SUFI ESSAYS. New York: Schocken Books, 1972. Tr. by Jean Herbert. Paris: A. Michel, 1980.

118. Nasr, Seyyed Hossein. AN INTRODUCTION TO ISLAMIC COSMOLOGICAL DOCTRINES: CONCEPTIONS OF NATURE AND METHODS USED FOR ITS STUDY BY THE IKWAN AL-SAFA, AL BIRUNI, AND IBN SINA. Rev ed. London: Thames and Hudson; Boulder: Shambhala, 1978.

There is a bibliography on pages 287-308.

119. Nasr, Seyyed Hossein. ISLAMIC LIFE AND THOUGHT. London and Boston: G. Allen & Unwin; Albany: State Univ. of New York, 1981.

120. Nasr, Seyyed Hossein. KNOWLEDGE AND THE SACRED. The Gifford Lectures. Edinburgh: Univ. Press; New York: Crossroad Continuum, 1981.

These lectures by a specialist in Sufi doctrines explore the intellectual and spiritual chaos of modern times.

121. Nasr, Seyyed Hossein. L'HOMME, FACE A LA NATURE: LA CRISE SPIRI-TUELLE DE L'HOMME MODERNE. Tr. of MAN AND NATURE: THE SPIRITUAL CRISIS OF MODERN MAN. London: Unwin, 1976. Tr. from English by Gisele Kondracki and Jeanine Loreaux. Paris: Editions Buchet/Chastel, 1978.

The original volume was based on four lectures delivered at the University of Chicago during May, 1966.

122. Nasr, Seyyed Hossein, ed. MELANGES OFFERTS A HENRY CORBIN. Tehran: Institute of Islamic Studies, McGill Univ., Tehran Branch, 1977.

123. Nasr, Seyyed Hossein, ed. PHILOSOPHY, LITERATURE AND FINE ARTS. Dunton Green, Sevenoaks, Kent: Hodder and Stoughton; Jeddah: King Abdulaziz Univ., 1982.

124. Nasr, Seyyed Hossein. SADR AL-DIN SHIRAZI AND HIS TRANSCENDENT THEOSOPHY: BACKGROUND, LIFE AND WORKS. Imperial Iranian Academy of Philosophy Publication, Vol. 29. Tehran: Imperial Iranian Academy of Philosophy, 1978.

125. Sabzavari, Hadi ibn Mahdi. THE METAPHYSICS OF SABZAVARI. Tr. of SHARH AL-MAN ZUMAH FI AL-HIKMAH. Qum: Intirashati Allamah, 19--. Tr. from the Arabic by Mehdi Mohaghegh and Toshihiko Izutsu. Wisdom of Persia Series, Vol. 10. Delmar: Caravan Books, 1977.

126. Sadr al-Din Shirazi, Muhammad Ibn Ibrahim. AL-MABDA WA-AL-MAAD. Tehran: Anjuman-i Shahinshahii Falsafah-i Iran, 1976.

There is an added title page: AL-MABDA WA-AL-MA'AD (THE BEGINNING AND THE END) ed. with Prolegomena and notes by Jalal al-Din al Ashtiyani. The Persian and English introductions are by Seyyed Hossein Nasr. The text is in Arabic.

127. Zunuzi, Abdallah. LAMAAT-I ILAHIYAH. Tehran: Shahinshahi-yo Falsafah-i Iran, 1976.

There is an added title page and an introduction in English.

ISRAEL

128. Agassi, Joseph. SCIENCE AND SOCIETY: STUDIES IN THE SOCIOLOGY OF SCIENCE. Boston Studies in the Philosophy of Science, Vol. 65. Dordrecht and Boston: Reidel, 1981.

This work contains a bibliography of the works of Joseph Agassi on pages 502-511.

129. Agassi, Joseph. TECHNOLOGY, PHILOSOPHICAL AND SOCIAL ASPECTS. Dordrecht and Boston: Reidel, 1985.

130. Agassi, Joseph. TOWARDS A RATIONAL PHILOSOPHICAL ANTHROPOLOGY. The Hague: Nijhoff, 1977.

131. Agassi, Joseph and Ian Charles Jarvie, eds. RATIONALITY: THE CRITICAL VIEW. Nijhoff International Philosophy Series. Dordrecht and Boston: Reidel, 1986.

132. Amado Levy-Valensi, Eliane. LA NATURE DE LA PENSEE INCONSCIENTE: ENCYCLOPEDIE UNIVERSITAIRE. Paris: J-P. Delarge, 1978.

133. Amado Levy-Valensi, Eliane. LE MOISE DE FREUD, OU, LA REFERENCE OCCULTEE. Monaco: Editions du Rocher, 1984.

134. Avineri, Shlomo. THE MAKING OF MODERN ZIONISM: THE INTELLECTUAL ORIGINS OF THE JEWISH STATE. New York: Basic Books, 1981.

135. Avineri, Shlomo. MOSES HESS, PROPHET OF COMMUNISM AND ZIONISM. New York: New York Univ. Press, 1985.

136. Avineri, Shlomo, ed. THE VARIETIES OF MARXISM. Van Leer Foundation Series. Atlantic Highlands, NJ: Humanities Press, 1976c1975.

This volume is based on the 1974 International Symposium on Varieties of Marxism, Van Leer Jerusalem Foundation.

137. Batscha, Zevi. STUDIEN ZUR POLITISCHEN THEORIE DES DEUTSCHEN FRUHLIBERALISMUS. Frankfurt am Main: Suhrkamp, 1981.

138. Bergman, Samuel Hugo. TOLDOT HA-FILOSOFYAH HA-HADASHAH: MI-NIKOLUS KUZANUS AD TEKUFAT HA-HASKALAH. 3d ed. Jerusalem: Mosad Byalik, 1984.

139. Bertman, Martin A. BODY AND CAUSE IN HOBBES: NATURAL AND POLITICAL. Wakefield, NH: Longman Academic, 1991.

140. Bertman, Martin A. HOBBES, THE NATURAL AND THE ARTIFACTED GOOD. Bern and Las Vegas: P. Lang, 1981.

141. Bertman, Martin A., et al, eds. CENTRAL THEME: SPINOZA AND HOBBES. Studia Spinozana, Vol. 3. Hanover: Walther & Walther, 1986.

The text is in English, French and German.

142. Bertman, Martin A. and Michel Malherbe, eds. THOMAS HOBBES DE LA META-PHYSIQUE A LA POLITIQUE: ACTES DU COLLOQUE FRANCO-AMERICAIN DE NANTES. Paris: J. Vrin, 1989.

The text of this work is in French or English.

143. Brinker, Menahem, et al, eds. BARUKH SHPINOZA: KOVETS MAAMARIM AL MISHNATO. Tel Aviv: ifalim universitaim le-hotsaah le-or, 1979.

The title on the added title page is BARUCH DE SPINOZA, A COLLECTION OF PAPERS OF HIS THOUGHT. The volume contains summaries in English.

144. Cohen, Avener and Marcelo Dascal, eds. THE INSTITUTION OF PHILOSOPHY: BEYOND RORTY. Totowa, NJ: Rowman and Littlefield, 1986.

145. Dan, Joseph. JEWISH MYSTICISM AND JEWISH ETHICS. Seattle: Univ. of Washington Press, 1986.

146. Elkana, Yehuda. TRANSFORMATIONS IN REALIST PHILOSOPHY OF SCIENCE FROM VICTORIAN BACONIANISM TO THE PRESENT DAY. Cambridge: Cambridge Univ. Press, 1984.

147. Freund, Else-Rahel. FRANZ ROSENZWEIG'S PHILOSOPHY OF EXISTENCE: AN ANALYSIS OF THE STAR OF REDEMPTION. Ed. by Paul R. Mendes-Flohr. Tr. of rev. ed. of DIE EXISTENZPHILOSOPHIE FRANZ ROSENZWEIGS Hamburg: F. Meiner, 1959. Tr. by Stephen L. Weinstein and Robert Israel. The Hague and Boston: Nijhoff, 1979.

148. Fried, Yehuda and Joseph Agassi. PSYCHIATRY AS MEDICINE: CONTEMPORARY PSYCHOTHERAPIES. The Hague and Boston: Nijhoff, 1983.

149. Gabbay, Dov and Franz Guenthner, eds. HANDOOK OF PHILOSOPHICAL LOGIC. Vol. 1, ELEMENTS OF CLASSICAL LOGIC. Vol. 2, EXTENSIONS OF CLASSICAL LOGIC. Vol. 3, ALTERNATIVES TO CLASSICAL LOGIC. Vol. 4, TOPICS IN THE PHILOSOPHY OF LANGUAGE. Dordrecht and Boston: Reidel, 1984.

150. Heyd, David. SUPEREROGATION: ITS STATUS IN ETHICAL THEORY. Cambridge and New York: Cambridge Univ. Press, 1982.

151. Hoffmann, Yoel. IDEA OF SELF, EAST AND WEST: A COMPARISON BETWEEN BUDDHIST PHILOSOPHY AND THE PHILOSOPHY OF DAVID HUME. Calcutta: Firma KLM Private, 1980.

152. Horwitz, Rivka. BUBER'S WAY TO "I AND THOU": AN HISTORICAL ANALYSIS AND THE FIRST PUBLICATION OF MARTIN BUBER'S LECTURES "RELIGION ALS GEGENWART". Phronesis, Vol. 7. Heidelberg: Schneider, 1978.

This work contains material in English or in German.

153. Kasher, Asa, ed. LANGUAGE IN FOCUS: FOUNDATIONS, METHODS, AND SYSTEMS: ESSAYS IN MEMORY OF YEHOSHUA BAR-HILLEL. Boston Studies in the Philosophy of Science, Vol. 43. Dordrecht and Boston: Reidel, 1976.

154. Kasher, Asa and Mosheh Halamish. FILOSOFYAH YISRELIT. Tel-Aviv: Papirus, 1983.

155. Kasher, Asa and Sholom Lappin. ZERAMIM HADISHIM BE-FILOSOFYEH: MA'AMARIM BE-FILOSOFYAH UVE TOLDOTEHA. Tel-Aviv: Yahda, 1982-.

156. Kasher, Asa and Sholom Lappin. PHILOSOPHICAL LINGUISTICS: AN INTRODUCTION. Kronberg/Ts: Scriptor-Verlag, 1977.

157. Levy, Zeev. STRUKTURALIZM: BEN METOD U-TEMUNAT-OLAM (Structuralism: Method and Theory). Tel-Aviv: Sifriat Poalim, 1976.

158. Margalit, Avishai, ed. MEANING AND USE: PAPERS PRESENTED AT THE SECOND JERUSALEM PHILOSOPHICAL ENCOUNTER, APRIL, 1976. Dordrecht and Boston: Reidel, 1979.

159. Moonan, Willard. MARTIN BUBER: AN ANNOTATED BIBLIOGRAPHY OF WRITINGS IN ENGLISH THROUGH 1978. New York: Garland, 1981.

160. Pines, Shlomo. BEN MA HASHEVET YISRAEL LE-MAHASHEVET HA-AMIM MEHKARIM BE-TOLDOT HA-FILOSOFYAH HA-YEHUDIT. Jerusalem: Mosad Bialik, 1977.

161. Pines, Shlomo. COLLECTED WORKS OF SHLOMO PINES. Jerusalem: Magnes Press, The Hebrew Univ., 1979-.

162. Pines, Shlomo and Yirmiahu Yovel, eds. MAIMONIDES AND PHILOSOPHY: PAPERS PRESENTED AT THE SIXTH JERUSALEM PHILOSOPHY ENCOUNTER, MAY, 1985. Dordrecht and Boston: Nijhoff, 1986.

163. Raz, Joseph. AUTORIDAD DEL DERECHO: LA ENSAYOS SOBRE DERECHO Y MORAL. Tr. of THE AUTHORITY OF LAW: ESSAYS ON LAW AND MORALITY. Oxford: Clarendon Press; New York: Oxford Univ. Press, 1979 ed. Tr. by Rolando Tamayo y Salmoran. Mexico: Universidad Nacional Autonoma de Mexico Instituto de Investigaciones Juridicas, 1982.

164. Raz, Joseph, ed. PRACTICAL REASONING. Oxford and New York: Oxford Univ. Press, 1978.

165. Rosenzweig, Franz. BRIEFE UND TAGEBUCHER. 2 Vols. Ed. by Rachel Rosen-zweig-Scheinmann and Edith Rosenzweig. The Hague: Nijhoff, 1979.

166. Rotenstreich, Nathan. JEWS AND GERMAN PHILOSOPHY: THE POLEMICS OF EMANCIPATION. New York: Schocken Books, 1984.

167. Rotenstreich, Nathan. LEGISLATION AND EXPOSITION: CRITICAL ANALYSIS OF DIFFERENCES BETWEEN THE PHILOSOPHY OF KANT AND HEGEL. Bonn: Bouvier, 1984.

168. Rotenstreich, Nathan. MAN AND DIGNITY. Jerusalem: Magnus Press, 1983.

169. Rotenstreich, Nathan. PHILOSOPHY, HISTORY AND POLITICS: STUDIES IN CONTEMPORARY ENGLISH PHILOSOPHY OF HISTORY. Dordrecht and The Hague: Nijhoff, 1976.

170. Rotenstreich, Nathan. PRACTICE AND REALIZATION: STUDIES IN KANT'S MORAL PHILOSOPHY. Dordrecht and The Hague: Nijhoff, 1979.

171. Rotenstreich, Nathan. REFLECTION AND ACTION. Dordrecht and Boston: Nijhoff, 1985.

172. Rotenstreich, Nathan. WEGE ZUR ERKENNBARKEIT DER WELT. Freiburg: Alber, 1983.

173. Rotenstreich, Nathan and Norma Schneider, eds. SPINOZA: HIS THOUGHT AND WORK. Jerusalem: Israel Academy of Sciences and Humanities, 1983.

174. Scharfstein, Ben-Ami. THE PHILOSOPHERS: THEIR LIVES AND THE NATURE OF THEIR THOUGHT. Oxford: Blackwell; New York: Oxford Univ. Press, 1980.

175. Scharfstein, Ben-Ami, et al, eds. PHILOSOPHY EAST/PHILOSOPHY WEST: A CRITICAL COMPARISON OF INDIAN, CHINESE, ISLAMIC, AND EUROPEAN PHILOSOPHY. Oxford and New York: Oxford Univ. Press, 1978.

This work includes contributions by Shlomo Biderman, Dan Daor, Ilai Alon, Yoel Hoffmann, and Ben-Ami Scharfstein.

176. Schlanger, Jacques. L'ACTIVITE THEORETIQUE. Paris: Libraire philosophique J. Vrin, 1983.

177. Schlanger, Jacques. OBJETS IDEELS. Paris: J. Vrin, 1978.

178. Schlanger, Jacques. UNE THEORIE DU SAVOIR. Paris: Vrin, 1978.

179. Sirat, Colette. A HISTORY OF JEWISH PHILOSOPHY IN THE MIDDLE AGES. Cambridge and New York: Cambridge Univ. Press; Paris: Editions de la Maison des Sciences de L'Homme, 1984.

This volume is based on LA PHILOSOPHIE JUIVE AU MOYEN AGE. Paris: CNF, 1983 and contains a lengthy bibliography on pages 413-457.

180. Stemmer, Nathan. THE ROOTS OF KNOWLEDGE. New York: St. Martin's Press; Oxford: Basil Blackwell, 1983.

181. Twerskey, Isadore. INTRODUCTION TO THE CODE OF MAIMONIDES (Mishneh Torah). New Haven: Yale Univ. Press, 1980.

182. Twersky, Isadore, ed. STUDIES IN JEWISH LAW AND PHILOSOPHY. New York: Ktav Publishing House, 1982.

183. Ullmann-Margalit, Edna. THE EMERGENCE OF NORMS. Oxford: Clarendon Press, 1977.

184. Ullmann-Margalit, Edna, ed. THE ISRAEL COLLOQUIUM: STUDIES IN HISTORY, PHILOSOPHY, AND SOCIOLOGY OF SCIENCE. Vol. 1, THE KALEIDOSCOPE OF SCIENCE. Vol. 2, THE PRISM OF SCIENCE. Dordrecht and Boston: Reidel; Atlantic Highlands, NJ: Humanities Press, 1985.

185. Ullmann-Margalit, Edna, ed. SCIENCE IN REFLECTION. Dordrecht and Boston: Reidel, 1988.

186. Yovel, Yirmiahu. KANT AND THE PHILOSOPHY OF HISTORY. Princeton: Princeton Univ. Press, 1980.

187. Yovel, Yirmiahu, ed. NIETZSCHE AS AFFIRMATIVE THINKER. Dordrecht and Boston: Nijhoff, 1986.

This volume contains papers presented at the Fifth Jerusalem Philosophical Encounter, 1983.

188. Yovel, Yirmiahu, ed. PHILOSOPHY OF HISTORY AND ACTION. Dordrecht and Boston: Reidel, 1978.

This volume contains papers presented at the First Jerusalem Philosophical Encounter, December 1974.

189. Zemach, Eddy M. MAVO LE-ESTETIKAH. (Aesthetics). Tel Aviv: Univ. Publi cations, 1976.

LEBANON

190. Fakhry, Majid. AL-FIKR AL-AKHLAQI AL-ARABI. Vol. 1, AL-FUQAHA WA-AL--MUTAKALLIMUM. Vol. 2, AL-FALASIFAH AL-KHULQIYUN. Beirut: al-Ahliyah lil-Nashr wa-al-Tawzi, 1978-1979.

191. Fakhry, Majid. ARISTU: AL-MUALLIM AL-AWWAL. Beirut: al-Ahliyah lil-Nashr wa-al-Tawzi, 1977.

192. Fakhry, Majid. DIRASAT FI AL-FIKR AL-ARABI. 2d ed. Beirut: Dar al-Nahar lil-Nashr, 1977.

193. Fakhry, Majid. ETHICAL THEORIES IN ISLAM. Leiden and New York: E.J. Brill, 1991.

194. Fakhry, Majid. A HISTORY OF ISLAMIC PHILOSOPHY. 2d ed. Studies in Oriental Culture. New York: Columbia Univ. Press; London: Longman, 1983.

This work is a detailed survey of Islamic philosophy and theology from the seventeenth century to the present. It includes a bibliography on pages 368-375.

ASIA

ASIA

195. Fischer-Schreiber, Ingrid, et al. THE ENCYCLOPEDIA OF EASTERN PHILOSO-PHY AND RELIGION: BUDDHISM, HINDUISM, TAOISM, ZEN. Ed. by Stephan Schumacher and Gert Woerner. Tr. of LEXIKON DER OSTLICHEN WEISHEITS LEHREN: BUDDHISMUS, HINDUISMUS TAOISMUS, ZEN. Bern: O.W. Barth, 1986. Tr. by Michael H. Kohn, Karen Ready, and Werner Wunsche. Boston: Shambala, 1989.

196. Jaini, Padmanabh S. JAINA SAMPRADAYA MEM MOKSAHA AVATARA AURA PUNARJANMA: TNA VYAKHYANA. Ahamadabada: Setha Bholabhai Jesingabhai adhyayana-Samsodhana Vidyabhavana, 1982.

197. Riepe, Dale Maurice, ed. ASIAN PHILOSOPHY TODAY. New York, London and Paris: Gordon and Breach, 1981.

INDIA

198. Anacker, Stefan, ed. SEVEN WORKS OF VASUBANDHU, THE BUDDHIST PSYCHOLOGICAL DOCTOR. Tr. by Stefan Anacker. Delhi: Motilal Banarsidass, 1984.

This work includes translations of VADAVIDHI, PANCASKANDHAKA-PRAKARANA, KARMA-SIDDHI-PRAKARANA, VIMSATIKA-KARIKA-VRTTI, TRIMSIKA-KARI-KA, MADHYANTA-VIBHAGA-BHASYA, TRI-SVABHAVA-NIRDESA.

199. Anand, Kewal Krishna. INDIAN PHILOSOPHY (THE CONCEPT OF KARMA). Delhi and Benares: Bharatiya Vidya Prahashan, 1982.

In giving a review of the theory of karma, this doctoral dissertation covers all of the classical philosophical systems, as well as the epics.

200. Arapura, John Geeverghese. GNOSIS AND THE QUESTION OF THOUGHT IN VEDANTA: DIALOGUE WITH THE FOUNDATIONS. Dordrecht and Boston: Nijhoff, 1986.

The volume contains a bibliography on pages 201-211.

201. Balbir Singh. ATMAN AND MOKSHA: SELF AND SELF-REALIZATION. Studies in Indian Philosophy. Atlantic Highlands, NJ: Humanities Press; New Delhi: Arnold Heinemann, 1981.

202. Balbir Singh. THE CONCEPTUAL FRAMEWORK OF INDIAN PHILOSOPHY. Delhi: Macmillan, 1976.

203. Balbir Singh. DHARMA: MAN, RELIGION AND SOCIETY. New Delhi: Arnold-Heinemann, 1981.

204. Balbir Singh. ESSENCE OF BHAGAVADGITA: AN INTELLIGENT MAN'S GUIDE. Atlantic Highlands, NJ: Humanities Press, 1981.

205. Balbir Singh. KARMA YOGA: THE DISCIPLINE OF ACTION. Atlantic Highlands, NJ: Humanities Press, 1981.

   The author expounds the doctrine of Karma-Yoga and compares its ethical system with the moral philosophy of Immanuel Kant.

206. Balbir Singh. THE PHILOSOPHY OF TRUTH: THE QUEST FOR REALITY IN INDIAN THOUGHT. New Delhi: Arnold Heinemann, 1981.

207. Beardeau, Madeleine. ETUDES DE MYTHOLOGIE HINDOUE. Paris: Ecole Francaise d'Extreme Orient, 1981-.

208. Bedekar, V. M., ed. PHILOSOPHY IN THE FIFTEEN MODERN INDIAN LANGUAGES. Pune: Continental Prakashan, 1979.

209. Bharadwaja, Vijay K. NATURALISTIC ETHICAL THEORY. Delhi: Univ. of Delhi, 1978.

210. Bhatnagar, R. S. DIMENSIONS OF CLASSICAL SUFI THOUGHT. Delhi: Motilal Banarsidass, 1984.

211. Bhatt, Siddheswar Rameshwar, ed. REALITY, KNOWLEDGE AND VALUE: ESSAYS IN HONOUR OF PROFESSOR A. G. JAVADEKAR. Delhi: Bharatiya Vidya Prakashan, 1985.

212. Bhatta, Jayanta. JAYANTA BHATTA'S NYAYA-MANJARI (THE COMPENDIUM OF INDIAN SPECULATIVE LOGIC). Vol. 1. Tr. into English by Janaki Vallabha Bhattacharya. Delhi: Motilal Banarsidass, 1978.

213. Bhattacharya, Bishnupada. KABYA-MIMAMSA. Kalikata: Jijnasa: Paribesaka, Jijnasa Ejensija, 1982.

   The text of this work is written in Bengali with quotations in Sanskrit (Bengali script).

214. Bhattacharya, Harisatya. JAIN MORAL DOCTRINE. Bombay: Jain Sahitya Vikas Mandala, 1976.

215. Bhattacharya, Kalidas. GOPINATH KAVIRAJ'S THOUGHTS: TOWARDS A SYSTEMATIC STUDY. Calcutta: Univ. of Calcutta, 1982.

216. Bhattacharya, Kalidas. THE INDIAN CONCEPT OF MAN. Calcutta: Hirendranath Datta Foundation, Jandavpur Univ., 1982.

217. Bhattacharya, Kalidas. MANDUKYOPANISHADERA KATHA. Kalikata: Kalikata Bisvabidyalaya, 1982.

218. Bhattacharya, Kalidas. ON THE CONCEPTS OF RELATION AND NEGATION IN INDIAN PHILOSOPHY. Calcutta: Sanskrit College, 1977.

219. Bhattacharya, Kalidas, et al. PHILOSOPHY, THEORY AND ACTION. Poona: Continental Prakashan for Prof. S.S. Barlingay Felicitation Committee, 1980.

220. Bhattacharyya, Krishnachandra C. STUDIES IN PHILOSOPHY. Ed. by Gopinath Bhattacharyya. 2d. rev ed. Delhi: Motilal Banarsidass, 1983.

221. Biardeau, Madeleine. HINDUISM, THE ANTHROPOLOGY OF A CIVILIZATION. L'HINDOUISME: ANTHROPOLOGIE D'UNE CIVILISATION. Paris: Flammarion, 1981. Tr. by Richard Nice. Delhi and New York: Oxford Univ. Press, 1989.

The volume published in 1981 by Flammarion is a revised edition of CLEFS POUR LA PENSEE HINDOUE published in 1972 in Paris by Seghers. There is a bibliography on pages 195-203.

222. Bishop, Donald H., ed. THINKERS OF THE INDIAN RENAISSANCE. New Delhi: Wiley Eastern, 1982.

Contemporary Indian philosophers discuss different Indian philosophers of the past two centuries.

223. Broaue, Donald Allen. MAYA IN RADHAKRISHNAN'S THOUGHT: SIX MEAN-INGS OTHER THAN ILLUSION. Delhi: Motilal Banarsidass, 1984.

224. Brockington, Joseph L. THE SACRED THREAD: HINDUISM AND IT'S CONTINU-ITY AND DIVERSITY. Edinburgh: Univ. Press, 1981.

This introduction to Hinduism traces the concepts of the Hindu faith from its Vedic origins to its present development.

225. Candrakirti. LUCID EXPOSITION OF THE MIDDLE WAY: THE ESSENTIAL CHAPTERS FROM THE PRASANNAPADA OF CANDRAKIRTI. Tr. from Sanskrit by Mervyn Sprung in collaboration with T. R. V. Murti and U. S. Vyas. Boulder: Prajna Press; London: Routledge and Kegan Paul, 1979.

226. Cardona, George. PANINI: A SURVEY OF RESEARCH. Delhi: Motilal Banarsidass, 1980,1976.

227. Chakrabarti, Kisor Kumar. LOGIC OF GOTAMA. Monographs of the Society for Asian and Comparative Philosophy, Vol. 5. Honolulu: Univ. Press of Hawaii, 1978.

228. Chandra, Suresh. IDENTITY AND THOUGHT EXPERIMENT. Simla: Indian Institute of Advanced Study, 1977.

229. Chandra, Suresh. PHILOSOPHICAL DISCUSSIONS. Bareilly: Prakash Book Depot, 1979.

230. Chang, Chen-chi, ed. A TREASURY OF MAHAYANA SUTRAS. SELECTIONS FROM THE MAHARATNAKUTA SUTRA. Tr. of TRIPITAKA. SUTRAPITAKA. RATNAKUTA. (English Selections). Tr. by The Buddhist Association of the United States. London and University Park: Pennsylvania State Univ. Press, 1983.

This volume contains 22 of the 49 sutras of the MAHARATNAKUTA (or "Treasury") SUTRA, many translated into a Western language for the first time.

231. Chapple, Christopher. KARMA AND CREATIVITY. State University of New York Series in Religion. Albany: State Univ. of New York, 1986.

There is a bibliography on pages 127-136.

232. Chatterjee, Margaret. GANDHI'S RELIGIOUS THOUGHT. Notre Dame, IN: Univ. of Notre Dame Press; London: Macmillan, 1983.

233. Chatterjee, Margaret. THE LANGUAGE OF PHILOSOPHY. The Hague: Nijhoff, 1981.

This work deals with several aspects of the use of language in philosophy such as the role of metaphors in the formulating of metaphysical thought and the interrelatedness of philosophy and poetry. The author seeks to place philosophy among the Geisteswissenschaften and criticizes contemporary philosophers who assign philosophy the role of handmaiden to the natural sciences.

234. Chatterjee, Margaret. THE RELIGIOUS SPECTRUM: STUDIES IN AN INDIAN CONTEXT. New Delhi: Allied, 1984.

235. Chatterji, Probhat Chandra. SECULAR VALUES FOR SECULAR INDIA. New Delhi: Lola Chatterjo, 1984.

236. Chatterji, Probhat Chandra. TWO VOICES: ESSAYS IN COMMUNICATION AND PHILOSOPHY. New Delhi: Hem Publishers, 1979.

237. Chattopadhyay, Narayan Kumar. INDIAN PHILOSOPHY: ITS EXPOSITION IN THE LIGHT OF VIJNANABHIKSU'S BHASYA AND YOGAVARITTIKA: A MODERN APPROACH. Calcutta: Sanskrit Pustak Bhandar, 1979.

238. Chattopadhyaya, D. P. (Debi Prasad). ANTHROPOLOGY AND HISTORIOGRAPHY OF SCIENCE. Series in Continental Thought, Vol. 16. Athens: Ohio Univ. Press, 1990.

239. Chattopadhyaya, Debiprasad. KNOWLEDGE AND INTERVENTION: STUDIES IN SOCIETY AND CONSCIOUSNESS. Calcutta: Firma KLM, 1985.

240. Chattopadhyaya, Debiprasad. LENIN, THE PHILOSOPHER. New Delhi: Sterling, 1979.

241. Chattopadhyaya, Debiprasad. LOKAYATA: A STUDY IN ANCIENT INDIAN MATERIALISM. 8 Vols. 4th ed. New Delhi: People's Publishing House, 1978.

242. Chattopadhyaya, Debiprasad, ed. MARXISM AND INDOLOGY: THE TRANSACTION OF A SEMINAR ON MARXISM AND INDOLOGY JOINTLY SPONSORED BY THE ASIATIC SOCIETY, CALCUTTA, AND THE INDO GDR FRIENDSHIP SOCIETY, WEST BENGAL IN CELEBRATION OF THE 80TH BIRTHDAY OF PROFESSOR WALTER RUBEN. Calcutta: K.P. Bagchi, 1981.

243. Chattopadhyaya, Debiprasad, ed. STUDIES IN THE HISTORY OF INDIAN PHILOSOPHY: AN ANTHOLOGY OF ARTICLES BY SCHOLARS, EASTERN AND WESTERN. Vol. 1, THE PROTO-HISTORIC AND VEDIC PERIOD; Vol. 2, THE EARLY INDIAN SECTS AND SECULAR PHILOSOPHIES OF THE POST-VEDIC PERIOD; Vol. 3, JAINISM AND BUDDHISM. Calcutta: K. P. Bagchi, 1978-1979,1977.

244. Chattopadhyaya, Debiprasad. TWO TRENDS IN INDIAN PHILOSOPHY. Mysore: Prasaranga, Univ. of Mysore, 1977.

245. Chattopadhyaya, Debiprasad. WHAT IS LIVING AND WHAT IS DEAD IN INDIAN PHILOSOPHY. 8 Vols. 2d ed. New Delhi: People's Publishing House, 1977, 1976.

246. Chattopadhyaya, Latika. SELF IN SANKHYA PHILOSOPHY. Calcutta: Roy and Chowdhury, 1982.

247. Chemparathy, George. L'AUTORITE DE VEDA SELON LES NAYANA-VAISESI-KAS. Louvain-ta-Neuve: Centre d'histoire des religions, 1983.

248. Cheng, Hsueh-li. NAGARJUNA'S TWELVE GATE TREATISE. Tr. of DVADASA-NIKAYASASTRA. Dordrecht and Boston: Reidel, 1982.

This translation includes introductory essays, comments and notes.

249. Chennakesavan, Sarasvati. CONCEPT OF MIND IN INDIAN PHILOSOPHY. 2d. rev ed. Delhi: Motilal Banarsidass, 1980.

250. Chennakesavan, Sarasvati. A CRITICAL STUDY OF HINDUISM. 2d ed. Delhi-Varanasi-Parna: Motilal Banarsidass; Columbia, MO: South Asia Books, 1980.

251. Christanand, Maria Pavras. THE PHILOSOPHY OF INDIAN MONOTHEISM. Delhi: Macmillan, 1979.

252. Chubb, Jehangir Nasserwanji. FAITH POSSESSES UNDERSTANDING: A SUGGESTION FOR A NEW DIRECTION IN RATIONAL THEOLOGY. Atlantic Highlands, NJ: Humanities Press, 1982.

253. Collins, Steve. SELFLESS PERSONS: IMAGERY AND THOUGHT IN THERAVA-DA BUDDHISM. Cambridge: Cambridge Univ. Press, 1982.

254. Conze, Edward. BUDDHIST SCRIPTURES: A BIBLIOGRAPHY. Ed. by Lewis Lancaster. New York: Garland, 1982.

255. Conze, Edward. THE MEMOIRS OF A MODERN GNOSTIC. Sherborne, England: Samizdat, 1979-.

256. Conze, Edward. THE PRAJNAPARAMITA LITERATURE. 2d. rev and enl. ed. Tokyo: Ruyukai, 1978.

257. Coward, Harold G., ed. LANGUAGE IN INDIAN PHILOSOPHY AND RELIGION. Toronto: Canadian Corporation for Studies in Religion, 1978.

These papers were originally read at a seminar sponsored by the Canadian Society for the Study of Religion/Societe canadienne des sciences religieuses at Laval University, Quebec City, May 28th-30th, 1976.

258. Coward, Harold G. THE SPHOTA THEORY OF LANGUAGE: A PHILOSOPHICAL ANALYSIS. Delhi: Motilal Banarsidass, 1980.

This book is not only about Sphota but is also a detailed and knowledgeable general introduction to the whole field of Indian thought about language.

259. Coward, Harold G. and Krishna Sivaraman, eds. REVELATION IN INDIAN THOUGHT: A FESTSCHRIFT IN HONOUR OF T.R.V. MURTI. Emeryville, CA: Dharma Pub, 1977.

This volume contains essays by G. Staal, J. G. Arapua, K. Swaraman, H. G. Coward, K. Klostermeier, H. Nakamura, H. V. Guenther, A. K. Chatterjee, P. Jaini, M. Sprung, R.

K. Tripathi, and R. L. Slater, as well as a complete bibliography and an academic biography of Professor T. R. V. Murti.

260. Della Santina, Peter. MADHYAMIKA SHOOLS IN INDIA. Delhi: Motilal Banarsidass, 1986.

This volume contains a study of the Madhyamika philosophy and of the division of the system into the Prasangika and Svatantrika schools.

261. Feuerstein, Georg. YOGA-SUTRA OF PATANJALI: A NEW TRANSLATION AND COMMENTARY. Kent, England: Dawson and Sons Ltd., 1979.

262. Frauwallner, Erich. KLEINE SCHRIFTEN. Ed. by Gerhard Oberhammer and Ernst Steinkellner. Wiesbaden: F. Steiner, 1982.

This is a collection of Frauwallner's essays and articles published in various journals before 1962.

263. Frauwallner, Erich. NACHGELASSENE WERKE. Ed. by Ernst Steinkellner. Vienna: Verlag der Osterreichischen Akademie der Wissenschaften, 1984.

264. Gangesa. MANGALAVADAH. GANGESOPADHYAYARACITAH. Ed. by Gaurinath Bhattacharyya Shastri. Calcutta: Esiyatika Sosaiti, 1979.

265. Gangesa. SRIMADGANGESOPADHYAYAVIRACITATATTVACINTAMANIH UPAMANAKHANDATMAKAH: SRIPRAGALBHACARYAPRANITAYA PRAGALBHI TIKAYA SAMALANKRTAH. Ed. by Gaurinath Bhattacharyya Shastri. Benares: Sampurnanand Sanskrit Visvavidyalaya, 1983.

This basic work with the 15th century commentary of the Neo-Nyaya school in Indic philosophy includes the portion dealing with analogy (upamana).

266. Gangesa. TATTVACINTAMANAU PRAMANYAVADAH: PRAMANYAGRAHE MIMAMSAKAPAKSAPARYANTAH. Ed. by Gaurinath Bhattacharyya Shastri. Benares: Samurnananda Sanskrit Visvavidyalaya, 1983.

This portion of a basic work of the Neo-Nyaya school deals with the validity of knowledge. There is also prefatory matter in English.

267. Gangopadhyaya, Mrinalkanti. INDIAN ATOMISM: HISTORY AND SOURCES. Balchi Indological Series, No. 1. Calcutta: K.B. Balchi, 1980.

268. Granhoff, Phyllis Emily. PHILOSOPHY AND ARGUMENT IN LATE VEDANTA: SRI HARSA'S KHANDANAKHANDAKHADYA. Dordrecht and Boston: Reidel, 1978.

The preface of this work analyzes valid knowledge and perception and places Sri Harsa in the Vedantic tradition, while the second part is a translation of and commentary upon the introductory part of the KHANDANAKHANDAKHADYA.

269. Gudmunsen, Chris. WITTGENSTEIN AND BUDDHISM. New York: Barnes and Noble, 1977.

270. Guenther, Herbert V. PHILOSOPHY AND PSYCHOLOGY IN THE ABHIDHARMA. Berkeley: Shambhala, 1976.

271. Guha, Dinesh Chanira. NAVYA NYAYA SYSTEM OF LOGIC: BASIC THEORIES AND TECHNIQUES. 2d. rev ed. Delhi: Motilal Banarsidass, 1979.

272. Hacker, Paul. GRUNDLAGEN INDISCHER DICHTUNG UND INDISCHEN DENKENS. Vienna: Institut fur Indologie der Universitat Wien, Sammlung De Neobili; Leiden: Commission agents E. J. Brill, 1985.

273. Halder, Aruna. SOME PSYCHOLOGICAL ASPECTS OF EARLY BUDDHIST PHILOSOPHY BASED ON ABHIDHARMAKOSA OF VASUBANDHU. Asiatic Society Monograph Series, No. 25. Calcutta: Asiatic Society, 1981.

274. Herzberger, Radhika. BHARTRIHARI AND THE BUDDHISTS: AN ESSAY IN THE DEVELOPMENT OF FIFTH AND SIXTH CENTURY INDIAN THOUGHT. Dordrecht and Boston: Reidel, 1986.

275. Indich, William Martin. CONSCIOUSNESS IN ADVAITA VEDANTA. Delhi: Motilal Banarsidass, 1980.

276. Jaini, Padmanabh S., ed. ABHIDHARMADIPA WITH VIBHASAPRABHAVRT-TI. 2d ed. Patna: Kashi Prasad Jayaswal Research Institute, 1977.

This work is written in Sanskrit, but the introduction is in English. P. S. Jaini has supplied notes and annotations.

277. Jaini, Padmanabh S. THE JAINA PATH OF PUREFICATION. Delhi: Motilal Banarsidass; Berkeley: Univ. of California Press, 1979.

There is a bibliography on pages 317-334.

278. Jha, Durgadhara. PURVAMIMAMSA-PRAVESIKA. Patna: Maithili Akadami, 1982.

279. Jones, Richard H. SCIENCE AND MYSTICISM: A COMPARATIVE STUDY OF WESTERN NATURAL SCIENCE, THERAVADA BUDDHISM AND ADVAITA VEDANTA. Lewisburg, PA: Bucknell Univ. Press, 1986.

280. Junankar, N. S. GAUTAMA: THE NYAYA PHILOSOPHY. Delhi: Motilal Banarsidass, 1978.

281. Kalupahana, David J. FO CHIAO CHE HSUEH: I KO LO SHIH TI FEN HSI. Tr. of BUDDHIST PHILOSOPHY: A HISTORICAL ANALYSIS. Honolulu Univ. Press of Hawaii, 1976. Hsiang-kang: Fo chiao fa chu hsueh hui, 1984.

282. Kalupahana, David J. NAGARJUNA: THE PHILOSOPHY OF THE MIDDLE WAY. Albany: State Univ. of New York Press, 1986.

283. Kalupahana, David J. A PATH OF RIGHTEOUSNESS: DHAMMAPADA: AN INTRODUCTORY ESSAY, TOGETHER WITH THE PALI TEXT, ENGLISH TRANS-LATION AND COMMENTARY. Lanham, MD: Univ. Press of America, 1986.

284. Kalupahana, David J. WAY OF SIDDHARTHA: A LIFE OF BUDDHA. Boulder: Shambhala, 1982.

285. Kar, Sijayananda. INDIAN PHILOSOPHY: AN ANALYTICAL STUDY. Delhi: Ajanta Publications, 1985.

286. Kaviraj, Gopi Nath. THE HISTORY AND BIBLIOGRAPHY OF NYAYA-VAISESI-KA LITERATURE. Ed. by Gaurinath Bhattacharyya Shastri. Benares: Saravati Bhavana Library, Sampurnanand Sanskrit Vishvavidyalaya, 1982.

287. Kawamura, Leslie S. and Keith Scott, eds. BUDDHIST THOUGHT AND ASIAN CIVILIZATION: ESSAYS IN HONOR OF HERBERT V. GUENTHER ON HIS

SIXTIETH BIRTHDAY. Emeryville, CA: Dharma Pub., 1977.

This volume includes a bibliography of Herbert V. Guenther's works.

288. King, Winston Lee. THERAVADA MEDITATION: THE BUDDHIST TRANSFOR-MATION OF YOGA. University Park and London: Pennsylvania State Univ. Press, 1980.

289. Klostermaier, Klaus K. MYTHOLOGIES AND PHILOSOPHIES OF SALVATION IN THE THEISTIC TRADITIONS OF INDIA. Waterloo, Ontario, Canada: Wilfrid Laurier Univ. Press, 1984.

290. Krishna, Daya and B. V. Kishan, eds. WHAT IS LIVING AND WHAT IS DEAD IN INDIAN PHILOSOPHY? Waltair: Andhra Univ. Press, 1978.

291. Lal, Basant Kumar. CONTEMPORARY INDIAN PHILOSOPHY. 2d. rev ed. Delhi: Motilal Banarsidass, 1978.

292. Lancaster, Lewis, ed. PRAJNAPARAMITA AND RELATED SYSTEMS: STUDIES IN HONOR OF EDWARD CONZE. Berkeley: Regents of the Univ. of California Press, 1977.

293. Larson, Gerald James. CLASSICAL SAMKHYA: AN INTERPRETATION OF ITS HISTORY AND MEANING. 2d. rev ed. Delhi: Motilal Banarsidass, 1979.

This volume includes Isvarakrsna's SAYMKHYAKARIKA in English and Sanskrit (Roman script).

294. Lewis, Hywel David, ed. PHILOSOPHY, EAST AND WEST: ESSAYS IN HONOUR OF DR. T. M. P. MAHADEVAN. Bombay: Blackie & Son, 1976.

295. Ling, Trevor Oswald, ed. THE BUDDHA'S PHILOSOPHY OF MAN: EARLY INDIAN BUDDHIST DIALOGUES. London: Dent, 1981.

296. Lipner, Julius Joseph, et al, eds. A NET CAST WIDE: INVESTIGATIONS INTO INDIAN THOUGHT: IN MEMORY OF DAVID FRIEDMAN. Newcastle upon Tyne: Grevatt and Grevatt, 1986.

297. Lo, Shih-hsien. CHENG WEI SHIH LUN SHU CHI SHAN CHU. Hsiang-Kang: Fochia fa hsiang hsueh hui, 1977.

298. Lott, Eric. VEDANTIC: APPROACHES TO GOD. Totowa, NJ: Barnes and Noble, 1980.

299. Mahadevan, Telliyavaram Mahadevan Ponnambalam. A PHILOSOPHER LOOKS BACK. Bombay: Bharatiya Vidya Bhavan, 1982.

300. Mahadevan, Telliyavaram Mahadevan Ponnambalam. THE PHILOSOPHY OF ADVAITA WITH SPECIAL REFERENCE TO BHARATITIRTHA VIDYARANYA. 4th ed. New Delhi: Arnold-Heinemann Publishers, 1976.

This is a revision of the author's thesis for the degree of doctor of philosophy at the University of Madras, 1935.

301. Mahadevan, Telliyavaram Mahadevan Ponnambalam. SUPERIMPOSITION IN ADVAITA VEDANTA. New Delhi: Sterling Publishers Private, 1985.

302. Mahadevan, Telliyavaram Mahadevan Ponnambalam and Grace E. Cairns, eds. CONTEMPORARY INDIAN PHILOSOPHERS OF HISTORY. Calcutta: World Press, 1977.

303. Mahadevan, Telliyavaram Mahadevan Ponnambalam and G. V. Saroja. CONTEMPORARY INDIAN PHILOSOPHY. 2d ed. New Delhi: Sterling, 1983.

304. Mankha. SAHITYAMIMAMSA. MANKHAKAPRANITA. Ed. by Gaurinath Bhattacharyya Shastri. Benares: Sampurnanand Sanskrit Visvavrdyalaya, 1984.

305. Matilal, Bimal Krishna. THE CENTRAL PHILOSOPHY OF JAINISM: ANEKANTA- VADA. Ahmedabad: L. D. Institute of Indology, 1981.

The subtitle,"The Doctrine of the Non-onesidedness," refers to an elucidation of Buddha's Middle Way.

306. Matilal, Bimal Krishna. LOGIC AND ETHICAL ISSUES OF RELIGIOUS BELIEF. Calcutta: Univ. of Calcutta, 1982.

307. Matilal, Bimal Krishna. LOGIC, LANGUAGE AND REALITY: AN INTRODUCTION TO INDIAN PHILOSOPHICAL STUDIES. New Delhi: Motilal Banarsidass, 1985.

308. Matilal, Bimal Krishna. THE LOGICAL ILLUMINATION OF INDIAN MYSTICISM. Oxford and New York: Clarendon Press, 1977.

This is an inaugural lecture delivered before the University of Oxford on 5 May 1977.

309. Matilal, Bimal Krishna. PERCEPTION: AN ESSAY ON CLASSICAL INDIAN THEORIES OF KNOWLEDGE. Oxford: Clarendon Press; New York: Oxford Univ. Press, 1986.

310. Matilal, Bimal Krishna and Robert D. Evans. BUDDHIST LOGIC AND EPISTEMOLOGY: STUDIES IN THE BUDDHIST ANALYSIS OF INFERENCE AND LANGUAGE. Dordrecht and Boston: Reidel, 1986.

Most of these essays were part of a seminar at Oxford University, August, 1982, held under the auspices of the International Association of Buddhist Studies.

311. Matilal, Bimal Krishna and Jaysanker Lal Shaw, eds. ANALYTICAL PHILOSOPHY IN COMPARATIVE PERSPECTIVE: EXPLORATORY ESSAYS IN CURRENT THEORIES AND CLASSICAL INDIAN THEORIES OF MEANING AND REFERENCE. Dordrecht and Boston: Reidel, 1984.

312. Mayeda, Sengaku. A THOUSAND TEACHINGS: THE UPADESASAHASRI OF SANKARA. Tr. with introductory notes by Sengaku Mayeda. Tokyo: Univ. of Tokyo Press, 1979.

313. Mehta, Jarava Lal. J. L. MEHTA ON HEIDEGGER, HERMENEUTICS AND INDIAN TRADITION. Ed. by William J. Jackson. Leiden and New York: E. J. Brill, 1991.

314. Mishra, Sabhajit. THE ANQUISHED FREEDOM: A STUDY IN SARTRE'S PHILOSOPHY OF SUBJECTIVITY AND HUMAN FREEDOM. Delhi: GDK Publications, 1979.

315. Mittal, Kewal Krishan, ed. ETHICAL IDEAS OF MAHATMA GANDHI: SEMINAR PAPERS AND DISCUSSION. Delhi: Gandhi Bhavan, Univ. of Delhi, 1981.

This volume includes papers and discussions from the Seminar on Ethical Ideas of Gandhiji, Delhi, 1965, organized by the Gandhi Bhavan, University of Delhi.

316. Mittal, Kewal Krishan, ed. PERSPECTIVES OF THE PHILOSOPHY OF DEVATMA. Delhi: Motilal Banarsidass, 1983.

317. Mittal, Kewal Krishan, ed. QUEST FOR TRUTH: A FELICITATION VOLUME IN HONOUR OF PROF. S. P. KANAL=SATYANVESHANA. Delhi: Prof. S. P. Kanal Abhinandan Samiti, 1976.

This volume, which contains a bibliography of Prof. Kanal's writings on pages 717-731, is printed in English and Hindi.

318. Mittal, Kewal Krishan, ed. A TIBETAN EYE-VIEW OF INDIAN PHILOSOPHY: BEING TRANSLATION OF GRUB MTHASHEL GYI ME LONG OF THUU-BKWAN BLO-BZANG CHOS-KYI-NYI-MA. New Delhi: Munshiram Mancharlal, 1984.

319. Mohanty, Jitendranath N. and S. P. Banarjee, eds. SELF, KNOWLEDGE AND FREEDOM: ESSAYS FOR KALIDAS BHATTACHARYA. Calcutta: World Press, 1978.

320. Mukherjee, Soumyendra Nath, ed. INDIA, HISTORY AND THOUGHT: ESSAYS IN HONOR OF A. L. BASHAM. Calcutta: Subarnarekha, 1982.

This work includes a list of the publications of A. L. Basham compiled by S. N. Mukherjee.

321. Mukhopadhyay, Pradyot Kumar. INDIAN REALISM: A RIGOROUS DESCRIPTIVE METAPHYSICS. Calcutta: K. P. Bagchi, 1984.

322. Murti, Tirupattur Ramaseshayyer Venkatachala. STUDIES IN INDIAN THOUGHT: COLLECTED PAPERS OF PROF. T. R. V. MURTI. Ed. by Harold G. Coward. Delhi: Motilal Banarsidass, 1983.

This volume contains a complete bibliography of the writings of T. R. V. Murti.

323. Murty, Kotta Satchidananda. PHILOSOPHY IN INDIA: TRADITIONS, TEACHING AND RESEARCH. Delhi: Motilal Banarsidass; New Delhi: Indian Council of Philosophical Research, 1985.

324. Nakamura, Hajime. A HISTORY OF EARLY VEDANTA PHILOSOPHY. Tr. of SHOKI VEDANTA TETSUGAKUSHI. Tokyo: Iwanami Shoten, 1950. Tr. by Trevor Leggett et al. Delhi: Motilal Banarsidass, 1983-.

325. Nakamura, Hajime. THE IDEAL OF WORLD COMMUNITY: BUDDHIST ASPIRATION IN VIEW OF SRI AUROBINDO. Madras: Dr. S. Radhakrishnan Institute for Advanced Study in Philosophy, Univ. of Madras, 1981.

326. Nakamura, Hajime. INDIAN BUDDHISM: A SURVEY WITH BIBLIOGRAPHICAL NOTES. Hirakata: Kansai Univ. of Foreign Studies, 1980.

327. O'Flaherty, Wendy Doniger, ed. KARMA AND REBIRTH IN CLASSICAL INDIAN TRADITIONS. Berkeley and Los Angeles: Univ. of California Press, 1980.

This collection includes essays by Karl Potter, Wilhelm Halbfass, Gerald Larson and others focusing on the subjects of the title.

328. O'Flaherty, Wendy Doniger. THE ORIGINS OF EVIL IN HINDU MYTHOLOGY. Berkeley: Univ. of California Press, 1976.

329. O'Flaherty, Wendy Doniger and John Duncan M. Derrett, eds. THE CONCEPT OF DUTY IN SOUTH ASIA. New Delhi: Vikas Publishing House, 1977c1978.

330. O'Neil, L. Thomas. MAYA IN SANKARA. Delhi: Motitlal Banarsidass, 1979.

331. Oberhammer, Gerhard, ed. INKLUSIVISMUS: EINE INDISCHE DENKFORM. Vienna: Institute fur Indologie der Universitat, Wien, Sammlung De Nobili; Leiden: Brill, 1983.

This is a festschrift in honor of Paul Hacker's 70th Birthday.

332. Oberhammer, Gerhard. PARASARABHATTAS TATTVARATNAKARAH. Vienna: Verlag des Osterreichische Akademie der Wissenschaft, 1979.

This volume contains the extant fragmentary text of the TATTVARATNAKARA in transliterated Sanskrit with an extensive commentary in German.

333. Oberhammer, Gerhard. STRUCTUREN YOGISCHER MEDITATION: UNTER-SUCHUNGEN ZUR SPIRITUALITAT DES YOGA. Vienna: Verlag der Oester-reichischen Akademie der Wissenschaften (Veroffentlichungen der Kommmission fur Sprachen und Kulturen Sudasiens, Volume 13), 1977.

334. Oberhammer, Gerhard. WAHRHEIT UND TRANSZENDENZ: EIN BEITRAG ZUR SPIRITUALITAT DES NYAYA. Vienna: Verlag der Oesterreichischen Akademie der Wissenschaften, 1984.

335. Padma, Sudhi. AESTHETIC THEORIES OF INDIA. 1st ed. Poona: Bhandarkar Oriental Research Institute, 1983-.

336. Padmarajiah, Yelekyatharachalli Jinadathiah. THE JAINA THEORIES OF REALITY AND KNOWLEDGE: A COMPARATIVE STUDY. Delhi: Motilal Banarsidass, 1983.

337. Pandeya, Ram Chandra. INDIAN STUDIES IN PHILOSOPHY. Delhi: Motilal Banarsidass, 1977.

338. Pandeya, Ram Chandra and Siddeschwar Rameshwar, eds. KNOWLEDGE, CUL-TURE, AND VALUE. Delhi: Motilal Banarsidass, 1976.

This book consists of papers presented in Plenary Sessions, Panel Discussions, and Sectional Meetings of the World Philosophy Conference, Golden Jubilee of the Indian Philosophical Conference, December 28, 1975 to January 3, 1976.

339. Phillips, Stephen H. AUROBINDO'S PHILOSOPHY OF BRAHMAN. Leiden: Brill, 1986.

This book includes a preface by Robert Nozick.

340. Potter, Karl H., ed. THE ENCYCLOPEDIA OF INDIAN PHILOSOPHIES. Vol. 1, BIBLIOGRAPHY (1970). Vol. 2, INDIAN METAPHYSICS AND EPISTEMOLOGY: THE TRADITION OF NYAYA-VAISESIKA UP TO GANGESA (1977). Vol. 3, ADVAITA VEDANTA UP TO SAMKARA AND HIS PUPILS (1981). Vol. 4, SAMK-HYA: A DUALIST TRADITION IN INDIAN PHILOSOPHY (1987). Vol. 5, THE PHILOSOPHY OF THE GRAMMARIANS (1990). Vol. 6, INDIAN PHILOSOPHICAL ANALYSIS: NYAYA-VAISESIKA FROM GANGESA TO RAGHUNATHA SIROMANI (1991). Princeton: Princeton Univ. Press, 1970-.

A second revised edition of Volume I, BIBLIOGRAPHY, was published by Motilal Banarsidass and Princeton University Press in 1983.

341. Potter, Karl H. GUIDE TO INDIAN PHILOSOPHY. Ed. by Austin B. Creel and Edwin Gerow. Goston: G. K. Hall, 1988.

342. Puligandla, Ramakrishna. JNANA-YOGA, THE WAY OF KNOWLEDGE: AN ANALYTICAL INTERPRETATION. Lanham, MD: Univ. Press of America, 1985.

343. Raju, Poolla Tirupati. SPIRIT, BEING, AND SELF: STUDIES IN INDIAN AND WESTERN PHILOSOPHY. New Delhi: South Asian Publishers, 1982.

344. Ramachandran, T. P. THE INDIAN PHILOSOPHY OF BEAUTY. Vol. 1, PERSPECTIVE. Vol. 2, SPECIAL CONCEPTS. Madras: Univ. of Madras, 1979-1980.

345. Riepe, Dale Maurice. INDIAN PHILOSOPHY SINCE INDEPENDENCE. Calcutta: Research India Publications; Amsterdam: Gruner, 1979.

There is a bibliography on pages A1-A18.

346. Riepe, Dale Maurice. OBJECTIVITY AND SUBJECTIVISM IN THE PHILOSOPHY OF SCIENCE WITH SPECIAL REFERENCE TO INDIA. Calcutta: K. P. Bagchi, 1986.

347. Santideva. EINTRITT IN DAS LEBEN ZUR ERLEUCHTUNG (BODHICARYAVATARA): LEHRGEDICHT DER MAHAYANA. Tr. of BODHICARYAVATARA. Tr. from the Sanskrit by Ernst Steinkellner. Dusseldorf: Diederichs, 1981.

348. Sasadhara. SASADHARA'S NYAYASIDDHANTADIPA: WITH TIPPANA. Ed. by Bimal Krishna Matilal. Ahmedabad, India: L. D. Institute of Indology, 1976.

The text is in Sanskrit and the introduction is in English.

349. Saxena, Sushil Kumar. AESTHETICAL ESSAYS: STUDIES IN AESTHETIC THEORY, HINDUSTANI MUSIC AND KATHAK DANCE. Delhi: Chanakya Publications, 1981.

350. Sen Gupta, Anima. THE EVOLUTION OF THE SAMKHYA SCHOOL OF THOUGHT. 2d. rev ed. New Delhi: M. Manoharlal, 1986.

351. Sen, Debabrata. THE CONCEPT OF KNOWLEDGE: INDIAN THEORIES. Calcutta: K. B. Bagchi, 1984.

352. Sen, Pranab Kumar. LOGIC, INDUCTION AND ONTOLOGY: ESSAYS IN PHILOSOPHICAL ANALYSIS. Jadavpur Studies in Philosophy, Vol. 2. Delhi: Macmillan, 1980.

353. Sengupta, Swapna. LANGUAGE, STRUCTURE AND MEANING. Ed. by Pradip Kumar Sengupta. 1st ed. Santinikitan: Visva-Bharati, 1977.

This work was originally presented as the author's thesis under the title: SOME ASPECTS OF THE PHILOSOPHY OF LANGUAGE.

354. Sharma, Kanhayalal L., ed. PHILOSOPHY, SOCIETY, AND ACTION: ESSAYS IN HONOUR OF PROF. DAYA KRISHNA. In consultation with R. S. Bhatnagar. Jaipur: Aalekh, 1984.

355. Sharma, Kanhayalal L. SUBJECTIVITY AND ABSOLUTE: A STUDY OF K. C. BHATTACHARYYA'S PHILOSOPHY. Jaipur: Aalekh, 1986.

356. Shastri, Gaurinath Bhattacharyya. SRIGAUTINATHASASTRIPRANITO MUKTIVA-DAH. Naimasaranya, Sitapura: Pauranika tatha Vaidika Adhyayana evam Anusandhana-Samsthana, 1982.

This work is a treatise on salvation (mukti) in Hindu philosophy.

357. Shastri, Gaurinath Bhattacharyya. THE STUDY IN THE DIALECTICS OF SPHOTA. New rev ed. Delhi: Motilal Banarsidass, 1980.

358. Shastri, Pashupatinath. INTRODUCTION TO PURVA MIMAMSA. Ed. by Gaurinath Bhattacharyya Shastri. 2d ed. Benares: Chaukhambha, 1980.

359. Singh, Satya Prakash. UPANISADIC SYMBOLISM. New Delhi: Meharchand Lachhmandas, 1981.

360. Snellgrove, David L. INDO-TIBETAN BUDDHISM: INDIAN BUDDHISTS AND THEIR SUCCESSORS. 2 Vols. Boston: Shambhala; London: Serindia, 1987.

361. Srinivasan, Gummaraju. THE PHENOMENOLOGICAL APPROACH TO PHILOSO-PHY: INDIAN AND WESTERN. Delhi: Caravan, 1980.

362. Staal, Frits. THE SCIENCE OF RITUAL. Poona, India: Bhandarkar Oriental Research Institute, 1982.

363. Staal, Frits, et al. AGNI, THE VEDIC RITUAL OF THE FIRE ALTAR. 2 Vols. Berkeley: Asian Humanities Press, 1983.

364. Steinkellner, Ernst. VERSE-INDEX OF DHARMAKIRTI'S WORKS: (TIBETAN VERSION). Vienna: Arbeitskreis fur Tibetische und Buddistische Studien, 1977.

365. Subrahmanya Iyer, V. AN INQUIRY INTO TRUTH, OR, TATTVA VICARA: A COLLECTION OF SPEECHES AND WRITINGS. Ed. by Telliyavaram Mahadevan Ponnambalam Mahadevan. Salem: K. Subrahmanian, 1982.

366. Taber, John A. TRANSFORMATIVE PHILOSOPHY: A STUDY OF SANKARA, FICHTE, AND HEIDEGGER. Honolulu: Univ. of Hawaii Press, 1983.

367. Tachikawa, Musashi. STRUCTURE OF THE WORLD IN UDAYANA'S REALISM: A STUDY OF THE LAKA SANAVALI AND THE KIRANAVALI. Dordrecht and Boston: Reidel, 1981.

368. Tahtinen, Unto. AHIMSA: NON-VIOLENCE IN INDIAN TRADITION. London: Rider, 1976.

369. Tahtinen, Unto. THE CORE OF GHANDI'S PHILOSOPHY. New Delhi: Abhinao Publications, 1979.

370. Tahtinen, Unto. INDIAN TRADITIONAL VALUES. Atlantic Highlands, NJ: Humanities Press; New Delhi: Abhinav Publications, 1983.

371. Tarkunde, Vithal Mahadev, et al. RATIONALISM, HUMANISM AND DEMOCRA-CY: A COMMEMORATION VOLUME IN HONOR OF PROF. R. S. YADAVA. Ed. by Krishna Gopal. Meerut: Professor R. S. Yadava Commemoration Volume Committee, 1985.

372. Tuck, Donald R. THE CONCEPT OF MAYA IN SAMKARA AND RADHAKRISH-NAN. Columbia, MO: South Asia Books, 1986.

373. Udaycaryana. KIRANAVALI. UDAYANACARYAPRANITA: HINIBHASAVYAK-HYANASAMALANKRTA. Ed. by Gaurinath Bhattacharyya Shastri. Benares: Sampurnananda-Sanskrit Visvavidyalaya, 1980.

374. Valiuddin, Mir. THE QURANIC SUFISM. Delhi: Motilal Banarsidass, 1977.

375. Varma, Vishwanath Prasad. PHILOSOPHICAL HUMANISM AND CONTEMPORARY INDIA. 1st ed. Delhi: Motilal Banarsidass, 1979.

376. Vetter, Tilmann. STUDIEN ZUR LEHRE UND ENTWICKLUNG SANKARAS. Vienna and Leiden: Brill in Komm.; Vienna: Gerold in Komm. ; Delhi: Motilal Banarsidass in Komm., 1979.

377. Visweswari, Amma. UDAYANA AND HIS PHILOSOPHY. Delhi: Nag Publishers, 1985.

378. Vohra, Ashok. WITTGENSTEIN'S PHILOSOPHY OF MIND. La Salle, IL: Open Court; New York: St. Martins; London: Croom Helm, 1986.

379. Wayman, Alex. BUDDHIST INSIGHT: ESSAYS. Ed. by George Elder. Delhi: Motilal Banarsidass, 1984.

380. Werner, Karel. YOGA AND INDIAN PHILOSOPHY. Delhi: Motilal Banarsidass, 1977.

381. Willis, Janice Dean. ON KNOWING REALITY: THE TATTVARTHA CHAPTER OF ASANGA'S BODHISATTVABHUMI. Tr. of Asanga. TATTVARTHAPATAL, the 4th Chapter of Part I of BODHISATTVABHUMI, the 15th Section of YOGACARABHUMI. Tr. by Janice Dean Willis. New York: Columbia Univ. Press, 1979.

JAPAN

382. Abe, Masao. ZEN AND WESTERN THOUGHT. Ed. by William R. LaFleur. Honolulu: Univ. of Hawaii Press; London: Macmillan, 1984.

383. Adachi, Kazuhiro. NINGEN TO IMI NO KAITAI: GENSHOGAKUKOZOSHUGI-DERODA (The Dismemberment of Man and Meaning: Phenomenology-Structuralism-Derrida). Tokyo: Keiso Shobo, 1978.

384. Aso, Ken. KAISHAKUGAKU (Hermeneutics). Tokyo: Sekai Shoin, 1985.

385. Bernstein, Gail Lee. JAPANESE MARXIST: A PORTRAIT OF KAWAKAMI HAJIME, 1879-1946. Cambridge: Harvard Univ. Press, 1976.

386. Chao-chou, Shih. RADICAL ZEN: THE SAYINGS OF JOSHU. Trans. with commentary by Yoel Hoffmann. Preface by Hirano Sojo. Brookline, MA: Autumn Press, 1978.

387. Chih-yu, Shih. EVERY END EXPOSED: THE 100 KOANS OF MASTER KIDO: WITH THE ANSWERS OF HAKUIN-ZEN. Tr. with commentary by Yoel Hoffmann. Brookline, MA: Autumn Press, 1977.

This is a translation of part of the Japanese collection GENDAI SOJI ZEN HYORON, compiled by Hau Hoo. The original Chinese title is HSU-T'ANG HO SHANG YU LU.

388. Dogen. FLOWERS OF EMPTINESS: SELECTIONS FROM DOGEN'S SHOBO-GENZO. Tr. of SHOBOGENZO. Tr. by Hee-Jin Kim. Lewiston, NY: E. Mellen Press,

1985.

Hee-Jin Kim has written an introductory essay and notes for this volume.

389. Dogen. MOON IN A DEWDROP: WRITINGS OF ZEN MASTER DOGEN. Ed. by Kazuaki Tanahashi. Tr. by Robert Aitken, et al. San Francisco: North Point Press, 1985.

390. Dogen. RECORD OF THINGS HEARD, FROM THE TREASURY OF THE EYE OF THE TRUE TEACHING=THE SHOBOGENZO ZUIMONKI: TALKS OF ZEN MASTER DOGEN AS RECORDED BY ZEN MASTER EJO. Tr. of SHOBOGENZO ZUIMONKI. Tr. by Thomas Cleary. Boulder, CO: Prajna Press, 1980.

391. Dogen. SHOBOGENZO CHIKUGOKAI. Ed. by Mushika Kenichi. Tokyo: Seibundo, 1983-.

392. Dogen. SHOBOGENZO KAIDOKU. Ed. by Toshijiro Okada. Tokyo: Yayoi Shobo, 1978.

393. Dogen. SHOBOGENZO ZUIMONKI, EJOHEN, WATSUJI TETSURO KOTEI. Tokyo: Iwanami Shoten, 1983.

394. Dogen. SHOBOGENZO (Treasury of the Eye of True Teaching). Tr. by Thomas Cleary. Honolulu: Univ. of Hawaii Press, 1986.

395. Dogen. THE WAY OF EVERYDAY LIFE: ZEN MASTER DOGEN'S GENJOKOAN. Tr. of SHOBOGENZO. GENJOKOAN. Los Angeles: Zen Center of Los Angeles, 1978.

The volume contains a commentary by Hakuyu Taizan Maezumi, photos by John Daido Loori, calligraphy by Vo-Dingh and a foreward by W. S. Merwin.

396. Fujita, Kenji. TAIKEI TO TENBO (System and Perspective). Tokyo: Nigensha, 1981.

397. Furuta, Hikaru and Tadashi Suzuki, eds. KINDAI NIHON NO TETSUGAKU. Gendai Tetsugaku Sensho, Vol. 16. Tokyo: Hokuju Shuppan: Hatsubaimoto Gakubunsha Showa 58, 1983.

398. Hall, Edward Twitchell. BUNKA TO SHITE NO JIKAN (The Dance of Life: the Other Dimension of Time). Tokyo: TBS Buritanika, 1983.

There is a bibliography on pages 1-12.

399. Haruna, Sumito. TETSUGAKU TO SHINGAKU (PHILOSOPHY AND THEOLOGY). Kyoto: Horitsubunkasha, 1984.

400. Harunori, Izumi and Jiro Watanabe, eds. SEIYO NI OKERU SEI TO SHI NO SHISO: SEIYO SEISHINSHI NYUMON (The Concepts of Life and Death in the West: Introducing the History of Ideas in the West). Tokyo: Yuhikaku, 1983.

401. Heine, Steven. EXISTENTIAL AND ONTOLOGICAL DIMENSIONS OF TIME IN HEIDEGGER AND DOGEN. Albany: State Univ. of New York Press, 1985.

402. Hida, Shuichi. CHISEI NO TANKYU (Inquiries into Intellect). Kyoto: Horitsubunkasha, 1979.

403. Hiromatsu, Wataru. MONO-KOTO-KOTOBA (Things and Language). Tokyo: Keiso Shobo, 1979.

404. Hiromatsu, Wataru. SONZAI TO IMI: KOTOTEKI JITEKISEKAIKAN NO TEISO (Existence and Meaning: The Foundation of Abstract World-View). Tokyo: Iwanami Shoten, 1986.

405. Hozaka, Katsuyuki. TETSUGAKU NO GENRI NO HAKKEN: SHIN JITSUZAISHU-GI NO TETSUGAKU (Discoveries of the Principles of Philosophy: The Philosophy of True Realism). Niigata: Shunyokan Shoten, 1978.

406. Imamichi, Tomonobu. TOZAI NO TETSUGAKU (Eastern and Western Philosophy). Tokyo: TBS Britannica, 1981.

407. Inagaki, Fujimaro. NINSHIKI TO CHOHETSU (Cognition and Transcendence). Tokyo: Hokuju-Shuppan, 1981.

408. Iwasa, Shigeru. YUIBUTSURON TO KAGAKUTEKI SEISHIN: [YUIBUTSURON TO KEIKEN HIHANRON] NO SEKAI (Materialism and the Scientific Mind: The World of "Materialism and Empirio-Criticism"). Tokyo: Shiraishi Shoten, 1983.

409. Iwasaki, Takeo. SHINRIRON: TETSUGAKU TAIKEI DAI ICHUBU (The Theories of Truth: Philosophy I). Tokyo: Univ. of Tokyo Press, 1976.

410. Iwasaki, Takeo. SONZAIRON-JISSENRON: TETSUGAKU TAIKEI DAI 2-3BU (Ontology-Practical Philosophy: Philosophy II-III). Tokyo: Univ. of Tokyo Press, 1977.

411. Izutsu, Toshihiko and Toyo Izutsu. THE THEORY OF BEAUTY IN THE CLASSICAL AESTHETICS OF JAPAN. The Hague: Nijhoff, 1981.

412. Kamioka, Hiroshi. SONZAIRON NO HOHO (The Method of Ontology). Tokyo: Gakubunsha, 1984.

413. Kaneoka, Hidetomo, et al. NIHONBUKKYO TENSEKI DAIJITEN (The Large Dictionary of the Original Texts in Japanese Buddhism). Tokyo: Yuhzankaku, 1986.

This dictionary treats the original writings of the founders of Buddhist religious sects in Japan.

414. Kasulis, Thomas P. ZEN ACTION, ZEN PERSON. Honolulu: Univ. of Hawaii Press, 1981.

415. Kitagawa, Hidenori. INDO KOTEN RONRIGAKU NO KENKYU: CHINNA DIGNA-GA NO TAIKEI (Studies on Indian Classic Logic: The System of Dignaga). Kyoto: Rinsen Book Co., 1985.

There is a summary in English, with a caption title: A STUDY OF INDIAN CLASSICAL LOGIC, DIGNAGA'S SYSTEM.

416. Kodera, Takashi James. DOGEN'S FORMATIVE YEARS IN CHINA: AN HISTORICAL STUDY AND TRANSLATION OF THE "HOKYO-KI". Boulder, CO: Prajna Press, 1980.

417. Kono, Makoto. NINGEN TO JIYU (Man and Freedom). Tokyo: Ikubunsha, 1984.

418. Koyasu, Nobukuni and Hikaru Firusta, eds. NIHON SHISO SHI TOKUHON. Tokyo: Toyo Keizai Shimposha, 1979.

419. Kuno, Osamu. REKISHITEKI RISEIHIHAN JOSETSU (Introduction to the Criticism of Historical Reasons). Tokyo: Iwanami Shoten Publishers, 1977.

420. Kurahara, Korehito. REKISHI NO NAKA NO BENSHOHO (Dialectics in History). Tokyo: Shinnihonshuppansha Publishing Co, 1984.

421. Kuroda, Wataru. CHISHIKI TO KODO (Knowledge and Behavior). Tokyo: Univ. of Tokyo Press, 1983.

422. Kyushudaigaku Tetsugakukenkyushitsu, eds. KODO NO KOZO (The Structure of Behavior). Tokyo: Keiso Shobo, 1983.

423. LaFleur, William R., ed. DOGEN STUDIES. Honolulu: Univ. of Hawaii Press, 1985.

This collection of essays on the writings of the Zen monk Dogen was published in association with the Kuroda Institute.

424. Matsuda, Yoshio. ISO KOZORON: ISHIKI NO KAISOKOZONITSUITE (The Theory of Phase-Structure: On the Level-Structure of Consciousness). Tokyo: Marunouchi Shuppen, 1983.

425. Matsuo, Hosaku. THE LOGIC OF UNITY: THE DISCOVERY OF ZERO AND EMPTINESS IN PRAJNAPARAMITA THOUGHT. Tr. of ICHI NO RONRI. Tokyo: Hokuju Schuppan, 1981. Tr. by Kenneth K. Inada. Albany: State Univ. of New York Press, 1987.

426. Minamoto, Ryoen. KINSEI SHOKI JITSUGAKU SHISO NO KENKYO. Tokyo: Sobunsha, 1980.

427. Minamoto, Ryoen. NIHON NI OKERU SEI TO SHI NO SHISO: NIHONJIN NO SEISHINSHI NYUMON (The Concepts of Life and Death in Japan: Introducing the History of Ideas in Japan). Tokyo: Yuhikaku, 1977.

428. Mineshima, Akio. TETSUGAKU NO RONRI: TETSUGAKUTEKI RONRIGAKU JOSETSU (The Logic of Philosophy: Introduction to Philosophical Logic). Tokyo: Sekai Shoin, 1981.

429. Miwa, Masahi, ed. SEIMEI NO TETSUGAKU. Gendai Tetsugaku Sensho, Vol. 14. Tokyo: Hokuju Shuppan: Hatsubaimoto Gakubunsha, 1981.

430. Miyakawa, Toru, ed. GENDAI NIHON SHISO SHI. 5 Vols. (The History of Ideas in Contemporary Japan). Tokyo: Aoki Shoten, 1977.

This work is based on KINDAI NIHON SHISOSHI KENKYUKAI. KINDAI NIHON SHISO SHI. (The History of Ideas in Modern Japan: The Society of the Ideas in Modern Japan).

431. Miyamoto, Juzo. TETSUGAKU NYUMON: SHISO NO REKISHI TO RONRIGAKU (Introduction to Philosophy: History of Thought and Logic). Tokyo: Asakura Shoten, 1985.

432. Mizuno, Kogen. BUDDHIST SUTRAS: ORIGIN, DEVELOPMENT, TRANSMISSION. 1st. Eng. ed. Tr. of KYODEN: SONO SEIRITSU TO TENKAI, 1980. Tokyo: Kosei Publ, 1982.

433. Moriguchi, Mitsuo. "SEKAI" NO IMI O MOTOMETE (Inquiring into the Meaning of "World"). Tokyo: Koyo Shobo, 1979.

434. Nagai, Hiroshi. NINGEN TO SEKAI NO KEISHIJOGAKU: TETSUGAKUGENRI NO TANKYU (Metaphysics of Man and World: Inquiry into the Principles of Philosophy). Tokyo: Sobunsha, 1985.

435. Nagai, Nario. KISO RONRIGAKU (Fundamental Logic). Tokyo: Univ. of Waseda Press, 1977.

436. Nagai, Nario. SEKAIKAN NO RONRI (The Logic of World View). Tokyo: Univ. of Waseda Press, 1986.

437. Nagoya Tetsugaku Kenkyukai, eds. GENDAI NO TETSUGAKU KENKYU (Studies in Contemporary Philosophy). Tokyo: Godoshuppan, 1977.

438. Nakamura, Hajime. ANSATZE, MODERNEN DENKENS IN DEN RELIGIONEN JAPANS. Tr. of NIHON SHUKY NO KINDAISEI. Tokyo: Shunjusha, 1964. Tr. by Siegried Schultz with Anke Schomaker-Huett. Leiden: E. J. Brill, 1982.

439. Nakamura, Hajime. BUDDHA: DAIJO BUKKYO SHU. Tokyo: Tamagawa Daigaku Shippanbu, 1983.

440. Nakamura, Hajime, ed. BUKKYO KYOIKU HOTEN. Tokyo: Tamagawa Daigaku Shuppanbu, Showa 58, 1983.

441. Nakamura, Hajime, ed. BUTSUZO SANSAKU. Sculptures of Buddha. Tokyo: Shoseki, 1982.

442. Nakamura, Hajime. A COMPARATIVE HISTORY OF IDEAS. Rev ed. London and New York: KPI, 1986.

443. Nakamura, Hajime. GOTAMA BUDDHA. Tr. of GOTAMA BUDDHA: SHAKUSON NO SHOGAI. Tokyo: Shunjusha, 1969. Los Angeles: Buddhist Books International, 1977.

444. Nakamura, Hajime, et al. BUDDHA NO SEKAI=THE WORLD OF BUDDHA. Tokyo: Gakushu Kenkyusha, 1980.

445. Nakamura, Hajime, et al. KOFUKU NA SHINIKATA TO WA (How to Die Happy). Tokyo: Heibonsha, 1983.

This volume includes the proceedings of the 15th Nihon Bukkyo Kaigi held at Tokyo, Oct. 22, 1982, co-sponsored by Zen Nohon Bukkyokai and Kokusai Bukkyo Koryu Senta Shohan.

446. Nakamura, Hajime and Masutani Fumio. JIGOKU TO GOKURAKU (Hell and Paradise). Tokyo: Suzuki Shuppan, 1983.

447. Nakamura, Hajime and Masutani Fumio. SHAKUSON NO DESHITACHI. (Disciples of Buddha). 2 Vols. Tokyo: Suzuki Shuppan, 1982-1983.

448. Nakamura, Hajime and Minakami Tsutomu. ZOKUSE NO BUKKYO: BUKKYO SHI KOGI (Buddhism of the Common People: Lectures on the History of Buddhism). Tokyo: Asahi Shuppansha, 1980.

449. Nando, Hisashi. KIGORON HANDOBUKKU: ATARASHII CHI NO MIRYOKU (Handbook of Semiotics: Charm of New Understanding). Tokyo: Keiso Shobo, 1984.

450. Nishida, Kitaro. INTUITION AND REFLECTION IN SELF-CONSCIOUSNESS. Tr. of JIKAKU NI OKERU CHOKKAN TO HANSEI. Tokyo: Iwanami Shoten, 1917, 1941. Tr. by Valdo H. Viglielmo, with Takeuchi Yoshinori and Joseph S. O'Leary. Albany: State Univ. of New York Press, 1987.

451. Nishida, Kitaro. LAST WRITINGS: NOTHINGNESS AND THE RELIGIOUS WORLDVIEW. Tr. of BASHOTEKI RONRI TO SHUKYOTEKI SEKAIKAN and

WATAKUSHI NO RONRI NI TSUITE. Tr. with an introcution by David A. Dilworth. Honolulu: Univ. of Hawaii Press, 1987.

452. Nishitani, Keiji. NISHIDA KITARO. Tr. of NISHIDA KITARO. Tr. by Yamamoto Seisaku and James W. Heisig. Nanzan Studies in Religion and Culture, Vol. 15. Berkeley: Univ. of California Press, 1991.

This is an English translation of essays Keiji Nishitani wrote about his teacher, Kitaro Nishida, from 1936 to 1968 and published as a book in 1985. The book also has an introduction by D. S. Clarke.

453. Nishitani, Keiji. NISHITANI KEIJI CHOSAKUSHU. (Collected Works). 13 Vols. Tokyo: Sobunsha, 1986-1987.

454. Nishitani, Keiji. RELIGION AND NOTHINGNESS. Tr. by Jan Van Bragt. Berkeley: Univ. of California Press, 1982.

455. Nishitani, Keiji. THE SELF-OVERCOMING OF NIHILISM. Tr. NIHIRIZUMU. Tokyo: Sobunsha, 1986. Tr. by Graham Parkes with Setsuko Aihara. Albany: State Univ. of New York Press, 1990.

456. Nitta, Yoshihiro. GENSHOGAKU (Phenomenology). Tokyo: Inwanami Shoten, 1978.

457. Okada, Toshijiro. SHOBOGENZO KAIDOKU. Tokyo: Yayoi Shobo, 1978.

458. Okazaki, Kimiyoshi. "ARU" NO KENKYO: SONZAIRON NO TETSUGAKU (Studies on "Being Existent": The Philosophy of Ontology). Tokyo: Shinjyusha, 1978.

459. Okuda, Heihachiro. FUKACHI NO KUMO (The Cloud of the Unknowable). Tokyo: Gendai Shichosha, 1977.

460. Omori, Shozo. MONO TO KOKORO (Thing and Mind). Tokyo: Tokyo Daigaku Shuppan-kai, 1976.

461. Ota, Kanji. RONRIGAKU GAIRON (Introduction to Logic). Kyoto: Showado Ltd, 1981.

462. Sagara, Toru. EDO NO SHISOKATACHO. 2 Vols. Tokyo: Kenkyusha, 1979.

463. Sagara, Toru, ed. TOYO RINRI SHISO SHI (The History of Ethical Thought in Asia). Gendai Tetsugaku Sensho, Vol. 7. Tokyo: Gakubunsha, 1977.

464. Sawada, Nobushige, ed. KAGAKU TO SONZAIRON (Science and Ontology). Tokyo: K-I-C Shisakusha, 1986.

465. Shaner, David Edward. THE BODYMIND EXPERIENCE IN JAPANESE BUDDHISM: A PHENOMENOLOGICAL STUDY OF KUKAI AND DOGEN. Albany: State Univ. of New York Press, 1985.

466. Shibata, Shingo. JISSENTEKI YUIBUTSURON NO KONPON MONDAI (Fundamental Problems of Practical Materialism). Tokyo: Aoki Shoten Publishers, 1987.

467. Shimizu, Masumi. DAS "SELBST" IM MAHAYANA-BUDDHISMUS IN JAPANISCHER SICHT UND DIE "PERSON" IM CHRISTENTUM IM LICHT DES NEUEN TESTAMENTS. Leiden: E. J. Brill, 1981.

This work includes a summary in English and a bibliography on pages 206-223.

468. Shimizu, Yoshio. KIGO RONRIGAKU (Symbolic Logic). Tokyo: Univ. of Tokyo Press, 1984.

469. Shimomura, Torataro. BURKUJARUTO NO SEKAI: BIJUTSU SHIKAN, BUNKA SHIKAN, REKISHI TETSUGAKUSHA. Tokyo: Iwanami Shoten, 1983.

470. Shimomura, Torataro. ENKACHO. Tokyo: Nansosha, 1982.

471. Shozo, Omori and Ito Shuntaro. KAGAKU TO TETSUGAKU NO KAIMEI. (Inquiry into Science and Philosophy). Tokyo: Asahi Shuppansha, 1981.

472. Sibatani, Atsuhiro. ENVIRONMENT, MAN, SCIENCE AND TECHNOLOGY IN JAPAN. Melbourne: Japanese Center, 1984.

473. Sueki, Takehiro. UITTOGENSHUTAIN RONRI-TETSUGAKU RONKO NO KENKYO (Researches in Wittgentstein's Tractatus Logico-Philosophicus). 2 Vols. Tokyo: Koron-sha, 1976-1977.

474. Sueki, Takehiro. NISHIDA KITARO: SONO TETSUGAKU TAIKEI. 4 Vols. Tokyo: Shunjyusha, 1983-1988.

475. Sueki, Takehiro. UITTOGENSHUTAIN RONRI TETSUGAKU RONKO NO KENKYU [2. CHUHSHAKU HEN] (Studies on Wittgenstein's `Tractatus' [2. Explanatory Notes]. Tokyo: Koron Sha, 1977.

476. Suzuki, Shigeru. CHISHIKI TOWA NANI KA (What is Knowledge?). Tokyo: Aoki Shoten Publishers, 1984.

477. Takahashi, Shoji. TETSUGAKU NO SHOMONDAI (Problmes of Philosophy). Tokyo: Koyo Shobo, 1984.

478. Takeichi, Akihiro. BUNSEKI TETSUGAKU NO KONPON MONDAI: GENDAI TETSUGAKU NO KONPON MONDAI (Fundamental Problems of Analytical Philosophy: Fundamental Problems of Contemporary Philosophy). Kyoto: Koyo Shobo, 1985.

479. Takeuchi, Yoshinori. HEART OF BUDDHISM: IN SEARCH OF THE TIMELESS SPIRIT OF PRIMITIVE BUDDHISM. Ed. by James W. Heisig. New York: Crossroad, 1983.

480. Takeuchi, Yoshinori. TETSUGAKU NO SEKAI (The World of Philosophy). Tokyo: Sobunsha, 1985.

481. Takeuchi, Yoshio. MARUKUSUSHUGI NO UNMEI (The Trend of Marxism). Tokyo: Daisan Bunmei Sha, 1980.

482. Tamura, Yoshiro. JAPANESE BUDDHISM. Tokyo: Centre for East Asian Cultural Studies, 1980.

Titles cited in the bibliography are in Japanese, romanized Japanese and English.

483. Tanaka, Michitaro. NINGEN DE ARU KOTO (To Be A Human Being). Tokyo: Bungei Shunju, 1984.

This volume contains essays, addresses, and lectures.

484. Tanaka, Michitaro. SHIMIN TO KOKKA: TANAKA MICHITARO SEJI RONSHU. Tokyo: Sankei Shuppan, 1983.

485. Tanaka, Michitaro. TETSUGAKU SONOMONO (Philosophy for Itself). Kyoto: Jinbun Shoin, 1977.

486. Tanikawa, Tetsuzo. NIHONJIN NI TOTTENO TOYO TO SEIYO [Taidan] (The East and the West for the Japanese [Conversation]). Tokyo: Univ. of Hosei Press, 1981.

487. Tetsugakukai (Editors). CHISHIKI TO SHINNEN (Knowledge and Belief). Tokyo: Yuhikaku Publishing Co, 1983.

488. Tsurumi, Shunsuke. TSURUMI SHUNSUKE CHOSAKI-SHU (Collected Papers of Tsurumi Shunsuke). 5 Vols. Tokyo: Chikuma Shobo, 1975-1976.

489. Uchiyama, Kosho. SHOBOGENZO: MAKA HANNYA PAPMITSU, IKKA MEISHU, SOKUSHIN JOBUTSU O AJIWAU. Tokyo: Hakujush, 1982.

490. Ueda, Yoshifumi, ed. LETTERS OF SHINRAN: A TRANSLATION OF MAT-TOSHO. Shin Buddhism Translation Series, Vol. I. Kyoto: Honganji International Center, 1978.

The Shin Buddhism Translation Series is a collaborative effort of scholars from Japan, the United States, and Great Britain.

491. Ueda, Yoshifumi, et al. SHINRAN KARA NO SHATEI: SHUKYO HEIWA KOKKA. (From the Shinran Point of View: Religious Concept of a Peaceful Nation). Kyoto: Nagata Bunshodo, 1983.

492. Ueno, Chizuko. KOZOSHUGI NO BOKEN (The Adventure of Stucturalism). Tokyo: Keiso Shobo, 1985.

493. Umehara, Takeshi, ed. KAISHAKUGAKU NO KIDAI TO TENKAI: KAISHAKUGA-KU NO RIRONTEKI HATTEN TO GUTAITEKI TE KIYO (Tasks and Development of Hermeneutics: Theoretical Development and Concrete Application of Hermeneutics). Kyoto: Koyo Shobo, 1981.

494. Umehara, Takeshi. TETSUGAKU NO FUKKO (Happiness of Philosophy). Tokyo: Shueisha, 1983.

This collection consists of addresses, essays and lectures on philosophy and civilization.

495. Unami, Akira. HIHYOSURU KIKAI. Tokyo: Natsumesha, 1980.

496. Usuki, Hideo, ed. HIKAKUSHISOH TO HIKAKUBUNKA (Comparative Thought and Comparative Culture). Tokyo: Gakubunsha, 1980.

497. Watanabe, Yasuo. SEIKATSUSHA NO TETSUGAKU: TETSUGAKU-SHAKAI-SHIZEN (Philosophy of Living Persons: Philosophy-Society-Nature). Tokyo: Risohsha, 1981.

498. Yamada, Munemutsu. GENDAI TETSUGAKU NO SEKKEI (A Plan of Contemporary Philosophy). Tokyo: San Ichi Shobo, 1978.

499. Yamaguchi, Ichiro. PASSIVE SYNTHESIS UND INTERSUBJECTIVITAT BEI EDMUND HUSSERL. The Hague and Boston: Nijhoff, 1982.

500. Yamaguchi, Yusuke. RONRI NO TETSUGAKU (Philosophy of Logic). Tokyo: Daizo Shuppan, 1979.

501. Yamakawa, Hideya. NINGEN TO IDEA (Man and Idea). Kyoto: Horitsubunkasha, 1977.

502. Yamamoto, Haruyoshi. MARUKUSUSHUGI TO YUIBUTSURON TETSUGAKU (Marxism and Philosophy of Materialism). Tokyo: San Ichi Shobo, 1980.

503. Yamamoto, Shin. KEISHIJOGAKU NO KANOSEI (The Possibility of Ontology). Tokyo: Univ. of Tokyo Press, n.d.

504. Yokochi, Fusahiko. GENDAI SHISO NO HANSEI (Reflections on Contemporary Thought). Tokyo: Gakubunsha, 1983.

This book contains addresses, essays and lecures on nineteenth and twentieth century philosophy.

505. Yonemori, Yuji. PASU NO KIGOGAKU (Semiotics of Charles Sanders Peirce). Tokyo: Keiso Shobo, 1981.

506. Yuasa, Shinichi. CHIKAKU TO SHINTAI NO GENSHOGAKU (Phenomenology of Perception and Body). Tokyo: Taiyoshuppan, 1978.

507. Yuasa, Yasuo. THE BODY: TOWARD AN EASTERN MIND-BODY THEORY. Ed. by Thomas P. Kasulis. Tr. of SHINTAI: TOYOTEKI SHINSHINRON NO KOKO-ROMI. Tokyo: Sobunsha, Showa 52, 1977. Tr. by Nagatomo Shigenori and Thomas P. Kasulis. Albany: State Univ. of New York Press, 1967.

The volume contains a bibliography on pages 241-251.

KOREA

508. Bary, William Theodore de and JaHyun Kim Haboush, eds. THE RISE OF NEO-CONFUCIANISM IN KOREA. New York: Columbia Univ. Press, 1985.

509. Buswell, Robert E. THE KOREAN APPROACH TO ZEN: THE COLLECTED WORKS OF CHINUL. Honolulu: Univ. of Hawaii Press, 1983.

510. Choe, Min-Hong. COMPARATIVE PHILOSOPHY: WESTERN AND KOREAN PHILOSOPHIES COMPARED. Seoul: Seong Moon Sa, 1980.

511. Choe, Min-Hong. A MODERN HISTORY OF KOREAN PHILOSOPHY. 3d ed. Seoul: Seong Moon Sa, 1983.

512. Hwang, Philip Ho. A CRITICAL STUDY OF MENCIUS' PHILOSOPHY OF HUMAN NATURE WITH SPECIAL REFERENCE TO KANT AND CONFUCIUS. Norman, OK: [s.n.], 1978.

This is the author's Ph.D Thesis at the University of Oklahoma, 1978.

513. Kim, Hyo-Myung. CONSTANT AND NECESSITY: A STUDY IN HUME'S THEORY OF CAUSATION. Bloomington, IN: [s.n.], 1982.

This is the author's Ph.D. Thesis at Indiana University, 1982.

514. Kim, Tyong-Ho. SOOE SIDAE UI CH'ORHAK. Seoul: Munumsa, 1981.

515. Nam, Kyung-Hee. LOGOS, KNOWLEDGE, AND FORMS IN PLATO'S THEAETE-TUS AND SOPHIST. Austin, TX: [s.n.], 1982.

This is the author's Ph.D Thesis at the University of Texas at Austin, 1982.

516. Pak, Chong-hong. HANGUK SASANGSA NONBAK: YUHAK PYON. (History of Korean Thought). Seoul: Somundanng, 1977.

517. Pak, Chong-hong. HANGUK SASANGSA NONGO: YUHAK PYON. (History of Korean Thought). Seoul: Somundang, 1977.

518. Pak, Chong-hong. HANGUKUI SASANGCHOK PANGHYANG: KU MYOT KAJIUI KOCHA (Direction of Korean Thought). Seoul Tukpyolsi: Pagyongsa, 1982.

519. Pak, Chong-hong. WORKS OF PAK CHONG-HONG. Vol.1; CHOGI NONGO. Vol. 2; NOLLIHAK NONJO. Vol. 3; CHORHAK KAESOL. Vols. 4-5; HANGUK SASANGSA. Vol. 6; CHORHAKCHOK SUSANG. Vol. 7; ILGI, SUPIL, SOHAN. Seoul: Hyongsol Chulpansa, 1980.

The volumes are written in English, Japanese and Korean and each volume contains a bibliography of the author's published works.

520. Park, Soon-Young. DIE REZEPTION DER DEUTSCHEN PHILOSOPHIE IN JAPAN AND KOREA: DARGESTELLT ALS PROBLEM DER UBERSETZUNG PHILOSO-PHISCHE TEXTE. Bochum, Germany: [s.n.], 1976.

This is the author's Ph.D. Thesis at Ruhr-Universitat at Bochum, 1976.

521. Shin, Gui Hyun. DIE STRUKTUR DES INNEREN ZEITBEWUSSTSEINS: EINE STUDIE UBER DEN BEGRIFF DER PROTENTION IN DEN VEROFFENTLICHEN DER SCHRIFTEN EDMUND HUSSERLS. Bern and Las Vegas: P. Lang, 1978.

522. So, Hung-yol. CAUSAL EXPLANATION OF HUMAN ACTION. Sepol: T'ap Ch'ulp' ansa: ch'ongp'an Kwangmunsa, 1976.

523. Song, Sok-ku. HANGUKUI YUBUL SASANG (Confucianism/Korean Buddhism). Seoul: Sasayon, 1985.

524. Tu, Wei-Ming. CENTRALITY AND COMMONALITY: AN ESSAY ON CONFU-CIAN RELIGIOUSNESS. Albany: State Univ. of New York Press, 1989.

This is a revised and enlarged edition of CENTRALITY AND COMMONALITY: AN ESSAY ON CHUNG-YUNG published in Honolulu by the University Press of Hawaii in 1976.

525. Tu, Wei-Ming. CONFUCIAN THOUGHT: SELFHOOD AS CREATIVE TRANS-FORMATION. Albany: State Univ. of New York Press, 1985.

There is a bibliography of Tu Wei-ming's writings on pages 189-196.

526. Tu, Wei-ming. HUMANITY AND SELF-CULTIVATION: ESSAYS IN CONFUCIAN THOUGHT. Berkeley: Asian Humanities Press, 1978.

527. Yi, Hwang. WORKS. Seoul: Toegyehak Yonguwon, 1988.

Each page of this reprint, first published in 1869, represents 2 leaves of the original. A new introduction has been written in Korean, Chinese and English.

PEOPLE'S REPUBLIC OF CHINA

528. Adelmann, Frederick J., ed. CONTEMPORARY CHINESE PHILOSOPHY. Boston College Studies in Philosophy, Vol. 4. The Hague, Boston and London: Nijhoff, 1982.

This is a compilation of scholarly articles dealing with various aspects of contemporary Chinese philosophy.

529. Allinson, Robert E., ed. UNDERSTANDING THE CHINESE MIND: THE PHILO-SOPHICAL ROOTS. New York and Hong Kong: Oxford Univ. Press, 1989.

This work contains essays on various aspects of traditional Chinese philosophy and Western philosophy by John E. Smith, Robert C. Neville, Chad Hansen, Christoph Harbsmeier, Chung-ying Chen, Antonia S. Cua, Kuang-ming Wu, and Lao Sze-kwang (Lao Yung-wei). There is also a comprehensive bibliography of Chinese and Western language sources.

530. Ames, Roger T. THE ART OF RULERSHIP: A STUDY IN ANCIENT CHINESE POLITICAL THOUGHT. Honolulu: Univ. Of Hawaii Press, 1983.

This volume includes an English translation of HUAI-NAN TZU. 9. CHU SHU HSUN.

531. Bary, William Theodore de. THE LIBERAL TRADITION IN CHINA. New York: Columbia Univ. Press; Hong Kong: Chinese Univ. Press, 1983.

These essays examine the history and contemporary significance of the Neo-Confucian school of thinking, emphasizing its liberal approaches to issues of education, individualism, moral cultivation, and criticism of political despotism.

532. Bary, William Theodore de. NEO-CONFUCIAN ORTHODOXY AND THE LEARN-ING OF MIND-AND-HEART. New York: Columbia Univ. Press, 1981.

This first study of the formative stages of Neo-Confucianism in 13th and 14th century China is a major addition to the understanding of the development of Neo-Confucianism.

533. Bary, William Theodore de and Irene Bloom, eds. PRINCIPLE AND PRACTICALI-TY: ESSAYS IN NEO-CONFUCIANISM AND PRACTICAL LEARNING. New York: Columbia Univ. Press, 1979.

534. Ch'en, Ch'i-yun. HSUN YUEH AND THE MIND OF LATE HAN CHINA. Princeton Library of Asian Translations. Princeton: Princeton Univ. Press, 1980.

This volume contains a translation of Hsun's HAN-CHI and an annotated translation of his major philosophical work, the SHEN-CHIEN, as well as chapters on Hsun and his thought. There also is an introduction by Ch'i-yun Ch'en in addition to a bibliography, an index, and a glossary.

535. Chan, Hok-Lam, et al. YUAN THOUGHT: CHINESE THOUGHT AND RELIGION UNDER THE MONGOLS. New York: Columbia Univ. Press, 1982.

This volume contains ten papers dealing with the areas of thought and religion that reaffirm the classical heritage from the Tang and Sung periods in response to alien rule and that provide the basis for further intellectual growth in the Ming and Ch'ang periods.

536. Chan, Wing-tsit, ed. CHU HSI AND NEO-CONFUCIANISM. Honolulu: Univ.of Hawaii Press, 1986.

This collection consists of essays on Chu Hsi's achievement by scholars from around the world, including Taiwan and the People's Republic of China.

537. Chih, Andrew. CHINESE HUMANISM: A RELIGION BEYOND RELIGION. Hsin- chuang, Taiwan: Fu Jen Catholic Univ. Press, 1981.

538. Chin, Yueh-lin, ed. CHIN-SHIH LUN. Pei-ching: Shang wu yin shu kuan, 1983.

539. Chin, Yueh-lin, ed. LUN TAO. Pei-ching: Shang wu yin shu kuan, 1985.

540. Ching, Julia. TO ACQUIRE WISDOM: THE WAY OF WANG YANG-MING. New York: Columbia Univ. Press, 1976.

This work includes selected essays and poems by Wang Yang-ming in English. There is a bibliography on pages 331-367.

541. Chuang Tzu. CHUANG-TZU: THE SEVEN INNER CHAPTERS AND OTHER WRITINGS FROM THE BOOK CHUANG-TZU. Tr. of selections from NANHUA-CHING. Tr. by Angus Charles Graham. London and Boston: Allen & Unwin, 1981.

542. Cleary, Thomas. ENTRY INTO THE INCONCEIVABLE: AN INTRODUCTION TO HUA-YEN BUDDHISM. Honolulu: Univ. of Hawaii Press, 1983.

543. Coleman, Earle Jerome. PHILOSOPHY OF PAINTING BY SHIH T'AO: A TRANS-LATION AND EXPOSITION OF HIS HUA-P'U. (Treatise on the Philosophy of Painting). The Hague: Mouton, 1978.

This edition includes an uninterrupted English translation of HUA-P'U.

544. Cua, Antonio S. ETHICAL ARGUMENTATION: A STUDY IN HSIIN TZU'S MORAL EPISTEMOLOGY. Honolulu: Univ. of Hawaii Press, 1985.

545. Cua, Antonio S. THE UNITY OF KNOWLEDGE AND ACTION: A STUDY IN WANG YANG-MING'S MORAL PSYCHOLOGY. Honolulu: Univ. of Hawaii Press, 1982.

546. Delza, Sophia. TAI-CHI CHUAN (WU STYLE): BODY AND MIND IN HARMONY: THE INTEGRATION OF MEANING AND METHOD. Rev ed. Albany: State Univ. of New York Press, 1985.

547. Elman, Benjamin A. FROM PHILOSOPHY TO PHILOLOGY: INTELLECTUAL AND SOCIAL ASPECTS CHANGE IN LATE IMPERIAL CHINA. Cambridge: Harvard Univ. Press, 1984.

548. Fu, Charles Wei-Hsun and Wing-tsit Chan. GUIDE TO CHINESE PHILOSOPHY. Boston: G. K. Hall, 1978.

The general purpose of this bibliographical guide is to serve as a teaching and research aid to college students and teachers. Fu and Chan express the "...hope that sinological scholars and students might find our GUIDE useful." This bibliography is limited mainly to writings in English; however, it does include some material in French and German. This bibliography is organized under the headings: History of Chinese Philosophy; Human Nature; Ethics; Philosophy of Religion; Philosophical Psychology; Epistemology; Metaphysics and Ontology; Philosophy of Language; Logic; Social and Political Philosophy; Philosophy of History and Philosophy of Science; Aesthetics; Philosophy of Education; Presuppositions and Methods; Comparisons; and Authoritative Texts and their Philosophical Significance. There is an author/title index.

549. Fu, Charles Wei-hsun and Gerhard E. Spiegler, eds. MOVEMENTS AND ISSUES IN WORLD RELIGIONS: A SOURCEBOOK AND ANALYSIS OF DEVELOPMENTS SINCE 1945: RELIGION, IDEOLOGY, AND POLITICS. Westport, CT: Greenwood Press, 1987-.

550. Fudan Xuebao Shehuikexueban Bianjibu. ZHONGGUO GUDAI MEIXUESHI YANJIU (Study of Ancient Chinese Aesthetics). Shanghai: Fudan Daxue Chubanshe, 1983.

551. Girardot, Norman J. MYTH AND MEANING IN EARLY TAOISM: THE THEME OF CHAOS (HUN-TUN). Berkeley: Univ. of California Press, 1983.

552. Graham, Angus Charles. LATER MOHIST LOGIC, ETHICS AND SCIENCE. London: School of Oriental and African Studies, Univ. of London; Hong Kong: Chinese Univ. Press, 1978.

This is a study of six chapters from the MO-TZU: TA CH'U, Canon I, Canon II, Explanation I, Explanation II, and HSIAO CH'U. It includes an annotated Chinese text and an English translation of MO-TZU.

553. Graham, Angus Charles. STUDIES IN CHINESE PHILOSOPHY AND PHILOSOPH-ICAL LITERATURE. Studies in Chinese Philosophy and Philosophical Literature. Boston: Cheng and Tsui; Singapore: The Institute of East Asian Philosophies, National Univ. of Singapore, 1986.

This is a one volume collection of some of the Sinologist A.C. Graham's works previously published in journals. Original Chinese texts are included.

554. Guenther, Herbert V. TIBETAN BUDDHISM IN WESTERN PERSPECTIVE: COLLECTED ARTICLES OF HERBERT V. GUENTHER. Emeryville, CA: Dharma Publishing Co., 1977.

555. Gurley, John G. CHALLENGES TO CAPITALISM: MARX, LENIN, AND MAO. 3d. ed. Reading, MA: Addison Wellesley, 1988.

556. Gurley, John G. CHINA'S ECONOMY AND THE MAOIST STRATEGY. New York: Monthly Review Press, 1976.

557. Hall, David L. and Roger T. Ames. THINKING THROUGH CONFUCIUS. Albany: State Univ. of New York PRess, 1987.

558. Hansen, Chad. LANGUAGE AND LOGIC IN ANCIENT CHINA. Ann Arbor: Univ. of Michigan Press, 1983.

559. Jiang Kongyang. ZHONGGUO GUDAI MEIXUE YISHU LUNWENJI (Essays on Aesthetics and the Arts in Ancient China). Shanghai: Guji Chubanshe, 1981.

560. Jiang, Paul Yun-Ming. THE SEARCH FOR MIND: CH'EN PAI-SHA, PHILOSO-PHER POET. Singapore: Singapore Univ. Press, 1980.

561. Kasoff, Ira E. THOUGHT OF CHANG TSAI (1020-1077). Cambridge, London and New York: Cambridge Univ. Press, 1984.

562. Knight, Nick, ed. THE PHILOSOPHICAL THOUGHT OF MAO ZEDONG: STUD-IES FROM CHINA, 1981-1989. Special Journal Issue of CHINESE STUDIES IN PHILOSOPHY: A TRANSLATION JOURNAL. Armonk, NY: M. E. Sharpe, 1992.

This is a collection of English translations of papers by Chinese Mao scholars in the 1980's. Topics discussed include Mao's epistemology, his treatment of the laws of dialectics, bibliographic research on his philosophy, and comparisons with Stalin's philosophy. The editor provides an introduction analyzing the field of Chinese Mao studies.

563. Larson, Gerald James and Eliot Deutsch. INTERPRETING ACROSS BOUNDARIES: NEW ESSAYS IN COMPARATIVE PHILOSOPHY. Princeton: Princeton Univ. Press, 1988.

These are papers from a conference sponsored by the Society for Asian and Comparative Philosophy in 1984.

564. Loewe, Michael. WAYS TO PARADISE: THE CHINESE QUEST FOR IMMORTAL- ITY. London: Allen and Unwin, 1979.

565. Mair, Victor H., ed. EXPERIMENTAL ESSAYS ON CHUANG-TZU. Honolulu: Univ. of Hawaii Press, 1983.

566. McRae, John R. THE NORTHERN SCHOOL AND THE FORMATION OF EARLY CH'AN BUDDHISM. Studies in East Asian Buddhism, Vol. 3. Honolulu: Univ. of Hawaii Press, 1986.

The texts are in English and Chinese, specifically the Chinese texts of the HSIU-HSIN YAO LUN and YUAN-MING LUN on pages 1-44 (3rd group). There is a bibliography on pages 349-360.

567. Munro, Donald J. THE CONCEPT OF MAN IN CONTEMPORARY CHINA. Ann Arbor: Univ. of Michigan Press, 1977.

568. Munro, Donald J., ed. INDIVIDUALISM AND HOLISM: STUDIES IN CONFU- CIAN AND TAOIST VALUES. Michigan Monographs in Chinese Studies. Ann Arbor: Center for Chinese Studies Publications, the Univ. of Michigan, 1985.

Contributors to this monograph on Chinese philosophy and literature from Confucius to the present include Arthur Danto, Ying-shih Yu, Tu Wei-ming and others.

569. Neville, Robert C. THE TAO AND THE DAIMON: SEGMENTS OF A RELIGIOUS INQUIRY. Albany: State Univ. of New York Press, 1982.

570. Norman Bethune Institute. A BASIC UNDERSTANDING OF THE COMMUNIST PARTY OF CHINA (Shanghai, 1974). Toronto: Norman Bethune Institute, 1976.

This is a translation by the Norman Bethune Institute of the French edition published in 1976, which was a translation from the original Chinese.

571. Paul, Diana Y. PHILOSOPHY OF MIND IN SIXTH-CENTURY CHINA: PARA- MARTHA'S "EVOLUTION OF CONSCIOUSNESS." Stanford, CA: Stanford Univ. Press, 1984.

This book includes a translation of Paramartha's CHUAN SHI LUN (Treatise on the Evolution of Consciousness), the first Chinese translation of Vasubandhu's TRIMSEKA- KARIKA with Paramartha's own exegesis.

572. Rosemont, Henry and Benjamin Isadore Schwartz, eds. JOURNAL OF THE AMERI- CAN ACADEMY OF RELIGION THEMATIC ISSUE: "STUDIES IN CLASSICAL CHINESE THOUGHT." Chico, CA: American Academy of Religion, 1979.

This special issue of the JOURNAL OF THE AMERICAN ACADEMY OF RELIGION contains selected workshops on classical Chinese thought held at Harvard University in 1976. The authors of the papers and their commentators include

H. Fingarette, H. S. Creel, A. C. Graham, Robin D. S. Yates and others.

573. Schwartz, Benjamin Isadore. THE WORLD OF THOUGHT IN ANCIENT CHINA. Cambridge: Harvard Univ. Press, 1985.

574. Soo, Francis Y. K. MAO TSE-TUNG'S THEORY OF DIALECTIC. Dordrecht and Boston: Reidel, 1981.

575. Tang, Chun-i. TANG, CHUN-I CHUAN CHI. Taipai: Tai-wan hsueh sheng shu chu, 1988.

576. Tson-kha-pa blo-bzan-grags-pa. CALMING THE MIND AND DISCERNING THE REAL: BUDDHIST MEDITATION AND THE MIDDLE VIEW, FROM THE LAM RIN CHEN MO TSON-KHA=PA. Tr. by Alex Wayman. New York: Columbia Univ. Press; Delhi: Motilal Banarsidass, 1978.

577. Tu, Wei-Ming. CONFUCIAN ETHICS TODAY: THE SINGAPORE CHALLENGE. Singapore: Curriculum Development Institute of Singapore: Federal Publications, 1984.

578. Wang, Pi. COMMENTARY ON THE LAO TZU. Tr. by Ariadne Rump in collaboration with Wing-tsit Chan. Monograph of the Society for Asian and Comparative Philosophy, Vol. 6. Honolulu: Univ. Press of Hawaii, 1979.

579. Wu, Kuang-ming. THE BUTTERFLY AS COMPANION: MEDITATIONS ON THE FIRST THREE CHAPTERS OF THE CHUANG TZU. Albany: State Univ. of New York Press, 1990.

Chuang Tzu's first three chapters are translated almost verbatim into free verse. The translator has supplied extensive critical glosses taking into account over fifty Chinese, Japanese, and Western commentators. Wu then meditates on the exegetical, philosophical and contemporary implications of the first three chapters of the Chuang Tzu text.

580. Wu, Kuang-ming. CHUANG TZU: WORLD PHILOSOPHER AT PLAY. New York: Crossroad Pub. Co.; Chico, CA: Scholars Press, 1982.

581. Wu, Laurence C. FUNDAMENTALS OF CHINESE PHILOSOPHY. Ed. by Robert Ginsberg. Lanham, MD and London: Univ. Press of America, 1986.

This work is intended to be a guide to the main schools of thought in Chinese philosophy.

582. Zedong, Mao. MAO'S ROAD TO POWER: REVOLUTIONARY WRITINGS, 1912-1949. Vol. 1, THE PRE-MARXIST PERIOD, 1912-1920. Ed. by Stuart R. Sharamm. Armonk, NY: M. E. Sharpe, 1992.

This new edition of Mao Zedong's writings seeks to provide annotated English translations of every text by Mao obtainable.

583. Zedong, Mao. THE WRITINGS OF MAO ZEDONG, 1949-1976. Vol. 1, SEPTEMBER 1949-DECEMBER 1955. Ed. by Michael Y. M. Kau and John K. Leung. Armonk, NY: M. E. Sharpe, 1986-.

The other volumes in this projected critical edition of Mao's writings will be published over the next four years. These authoritative translations will include full source and editorial annotations as well as comprehensive bibliographies.

584. Zhu Guangquan. ZHU GUANGQIAN MEIXUE WENJI (Collected Works on Aesthetics by Zhu Guangqian). Shanghai: Wenyi Chubanshe, 1982.

TAIWAN

585. Fang, Thome H. CHINESE PHILOSOPHY: ITS SPIRIT AND ITS DEVELOPMENT. Taipei, Taiwan, Republic of China: Linking Pub. Co., 1981.

This is an English translation of CHUNG-KUO CHE HSUEH CHIH CHING SHEN CHI CHI FA CHAN. There is also a bibliography of the author's principle works.

586. Fu, Charles Wei-hsun. HSI YANG CHE HSUEH SHIH (History of Western Philosophy). Taipei: San min Book Publishing Co, 1984.

587. Fu, Charles Wei-hsun. PI PAN TI CHI CHENG YU CHUANG TSAO TO FA CHAN. Taipei: Tung ta Book Co, 1986.

588. Hsiao Kung-Ch'uan. A HISTORY OF CHINESE POLITICAL THOUGHT. Vol. 1, FROM BEGINNINGS TO THE SIXTH CENTURY, A. D. Tr. of CHUNG-KUO CHENG CHIH SU HSIANG SHIH. 2 Vols. Taipei: Hua kang, Min kuo 66 [1977]. Tr. by Frederick Mote. Princeton: Princeton Univ. Press, 1979.

589. Li Disheng. XUNZI ZHISHI (Xunzi: Collected Commentaries). Taipei: Xuesheng, 1979.

590. Liang Qixiong. XUNZI JIANSHI (Xunzi: Selected Interpretations). Taipei: Shangwu Yinshuju, 1978.

591. Wu, Joseph S. CLARIFICATION AND ENLIGHTENMENT: ESSAYS IN COMPARATIVE PHILOSOPHY. Washington, D. C.: Univ. Press of America, 1978.

592. Wu, Joseph S. PI CHIAO CHIEH HSUEH YU WEN HUA (Comparative Philosophy and Culture). Taipei: Tung Ta, 1978.

593. Wu, Yi. CHIEH HSUEH LUN CHI (Collected Essays in Philosophy). Taipei: Hua Kang, 1976.

This work is a collection of fifty essays written by contemporary Chinese thinkers representing all trends in Chinese philosophy today with the exception of Maoism.

594. Wu, Yi. CHINESE PHILOSOPHICAL TERMS. San Francisco: California Institute of Integral Studies; Lanham, MD: Univ. Press of America, 1986.

In addition to an analysis of fifty key words, this work includes a series of brief essays explaining the central concepts of China's greatest thinkers and their schools.

595. Zhongguo Wenshiciliao Bianji Weiyuanhui. ZHONGGUO MEIXUESHI CILIAO XUANBIAN (Anthology of Materials on Chinese Aesthetics). Taipei: Guangmei shuju, 1984.

TIBET

596. Tson-kha-pa blo-bzan-grags-pa. TSONG KHAPA'S SPEECH OF GOLD IN THE ESSENCE OF TRUE ELOQUENCE: REASON AND ENLIGHTENMENT IN THE CENTRAL PHILOSOPHY OF TIBET. Tr. of LEGS BSAD SNIN PO. Tr. with an introduction by Robert A. F. Thurman. Princeton: Princeton Univ. Press, 1984.

A substantial introduction provides a study of Tibetan philosophy, its roots in India, and its relevance to 20th century Western thought. The second part of the book is a translation of Tsong Khapa's text.

VIETNAM

597. Tran, Duc Thao. INVESTIGATIONS INTO THE ORIGIN OF LANGUAGE AND CONSCIOUSNESS. Tr. of RECHERCHES SUR L'ORIGINE DU LANGAGE ET DE LA CONSCIENCE. Paris: Editions Sociales, 1973. Tr. by Daniel J. Herman and Robert L. Armstrong. Dordrecht and Boston: Reidel, 1984.

There is a bibliography on pages 199-212.

598. Tran, Duc Thao. PHENOMENOLOGY AND DIALECTICAL MATERIALISM. Ed. by Robert Sonne Cohen. Tr. of PHENOMENOLOGIE ET MATERIALISME DIALECTIQUE. Paris: Editions Minh-Tan, 1951. Tr. by Daniel J. Herman and Donald V. Morano. Dordrecht and Boston: Reidel, 1985.

EASTERN
EUROPE

EASTERN EUROPE

BULGARIA

599. Piryov, Gencho. ABSTRACTS OF BULGARIAN SCIENTIFIC LITERATURE. PHILOSOPHY, SOCIOLOGY, SCIENCE OF SCIENCES, PSYCHOLOGY AND PEDAGOGICS. Sofia, Bulgaria: Bulgarian Academy Sciences, Center for Scientific Information and Documentation, 1958-.

Editions in English and Russian are published. There is an author index.

CZECHOSLOVAKIA

600. Beranek, Jan and Josef Muzik. CITANKA Z MARXISTICKA FILOZOFIE NA VYS. SKOLACH CSR. Prague: SPN, 1976.

601. Biemel, Walter and Husserl-Archiv zu Lowen, eds. DIE WELT DES MENSCHEN, DIE WELT DER PHILOSOPHIE: FESTSCHRIFT FUR JAN PATOCKA. The Hague: Nijhoff, 1976.

602. Godel, Kurt. COLLECTED WORKS. Ed. by Solomon Feferman, et al. Oxford: Clarendon Press; New York: Oxford University Press, 1986-.

This complete edition features the German texts with parallel English translations. There is a complete bibliography of Godel's works. Two volumes have been published so far: Vol. 1, PUBLICATIONS, 1929-1936. Vol. 2, PUBLICATIONS, 1938-1974.

603. Kohak, Erazim V. JAN POTOCKA: BIBLIOGRAPHY. Flushing, NY: Czechoslovak Society for Arts and Sciences, 1987.

604. Kohak, Erazim V. THE EMBERS AND THE STARS: A PHILOSOPHICAL INQUIRY INTO THE MORAL SENSE OF NATURE. Chicago: Univ. of Chicago Press,1984.

605. Kohak, Erazim V. IDEA AND EXPERIENCE: EDMUND HUSSERL'S PROJECT OF PHENOMENOLOGY IN IDEAS I. Chicago: Univ. of Chicago Press, 1978.

606. Kohak, Erazim V., ed. JAN POTOCKA: PHILOSOPHY AND SELECTED WRIT-
INGS. Chicago: Univ. of Chicago Press, 1990.

607. Kohak, Erazim V. NAROD V NAS: CESKA OTAZKA AIDEAL HUMANITNE V
UDOBI NORMALIZACE. Toronto, Ont: Sixty-Eight Publishers, 1978.

608. Kosik, Karel. DIALECTICS OF THE CONCRETE: A STUDY ON PROBLEMS
OF MAN AND WORLD. Tr. of DIALEKTIKA KONKRETNIHO: STUDIE PROB-
LEMATICE CLOVEKA A SVETA. Prague: Nakl. Ceskoslovenske Akademie ved, 1963.
Tr. by Karle Kovavda with James Schmidt. Dordrecht and Boston: Reidel, 1976.

The table of contents and a summary are written in German. This work was published in
French as LA DIALECTIQUE DU CONCRET. Paris: Maspero, 1970; in German as DIE
DIALEKTIK DES KONKRETEN. EINE STUDIE ZUR PROBLEMATIK DES
MENSCHEN UND DER WELT. Frankfurt am Main: Suhrkamp, 1967; and in Spanish as
DIALECTICA DE LO CONCRETO: ESTUDIO SOBRE LOS PROBLEMAS DEL
HOMBRE Y EL MUNDO. Mexico: Editorial Grijalbo, 1967.

609. Machovec, Milan, et al. MASARYKUV SBORNIK VIII. Microform. Prague: s.n.,
1980.

This samizdat work was published in Czechoslovakia in 1980 by a group of Czech and
Slovak intellectuals who continue the tradition of the prewar Masaryk's SBORNIK published in six volumes between 1925 and 1932.

610. Mukarovsky, Jan. STRUCTURE, SIGN AND FUNCTION. Ed. by John Burbank
and Peter Steiner. New Haven, CT. and London: Yale Univ. Press, 1978.

There is a bibliography on pages 251-266.

611. Muzik, Josef. K FILOZOFICKYM A METODOLOGICKYM OTAZKAM SPOLE-
CENSKYCH VED. Prague: Ustav pro vyzkum kultury, 1979.

612. Patocka, Jan. CHARTA 77: DOCUMENTS. s. l.: s. n., 1977.

This xerox copy of type-written documents includes, Packet 1, Mylnar Zdenek. POLIC-
TICKA SITUACE KOLEM CHARTY 77. Packet 2, Patocka, Jan et al. CHARTER 77;
DOCUMENTS. Packet 3, MISCELLANEOUS LETTERS, FEUILLETONS, ETC. Packet
4, CZECHOSLOVAK DISSIDENT POLITICAL DOCUMENTS. Packet 5, CZECHO-
SLOVAK DISSIDENT POLITICAL DOCUMENTS.

613. Patocka, Jan. DVE STUDIE O MASARYKOVI 1977. Toronto: Sixty-Eight Publishers
Corporation, 1980.

614. Patocka, Jan. ESSAIS HERETIQUES SUR LA PHILOSOPHIE DE L'HISTOIRE.
Preface by Paul Ricoeur. Afterward by Roman Jakobson. Tr. of KACIRSKE ESJE O
FILOZOFIE DEJIN. Munich: K. Jadrny', 1980. Tr. by Erika Abrams. Paris: Verdier,
1981.

The title on the verso of the original title page reads: HERETICAL ESSAYS ON THE
PHILOSOPHY OF HISTORY.

615. Patocka, Jan. KJETTERSKE STUDIER I HISTORIENS FILOSOFI: MED ET TIL-
LEGG: JAN PATOCKA OG CHARTA 77. Oslo: Norli, 1979.

616. Patocka, Jan. LE MONDE NATUREL COMME PROBLEME PHILOSOPHIQUE.
Tr. of PRIROZENY SVET JAKO FILOSOFICKY PROBLEM. Tr. by Jaromir Danek
and Henri Decleve. The Hague: Nijhoff, 1976.

617. Patocka, Jan. LOS INTELLECTUALES ANTE LA NUEVA SOCIEDAD. Tr. by Fernando Valenzuela. Madrid: Ahal, 1976.

618. Patocka, Jan. OSOBNOST A DILO. Cologne: Index, 1980.

There is a bibliography on pages 133-150.

619. Patocka, Jan. PLATON ET L'EUROPE: SEMINAIRE PRIVE DU SEMESTRE D'ETE 1973. Tr. by Erika Abrams. Paris: Verdier, 1981.

620. Patocka, Jan, et al. LA SCIENZA ASSEDIATO: LIBERTA DELLA RICERCA SCIENTIFICA NELL'EUROPA DELL'EST. Venice: La Bienale de Venezia and Marsilio, 1977.

621. Ruml, Vladimir. MARXISTICO-LENINSKA FILOSOFIE, FILOSOFIE KOMUNISMU. Prague: Horizon, 1978.

622. Ruml, Vladimir, et al. POZITIVISMUS A VEDECKE POZNANI. Prague: Horizon, 1976.

623. Svitak, Ivan. BARON D'HOLBACH, PHILOSOPHER OF COMMON SENSE. FILOSOF ZDRZVEHO ROZUMU, HOLBACH. Tr. by Jarmila Viltrusky. Chico: California State Univ., 1976.

624. Svitak, Ivan. THE DIALECTIC OF COMMON SENSE: THE MASTER THINKERS. Tr. by Jarmila Veltrusky. Washington, DC: Univ. Press of America, 1979.

625. Svitak, Ivan. DIOGENES. Chico: California State Univ, 1976.

626. Zeleny, Jindrich. POJEDNANI O DIALEKTICE. Prague: Akademia, 1982.

This work contains a summary in English and Russian.

EAST GERMANY

627. Beyer, Wilhelm Raimund. DER "ALTE POLITIKUS" HEGEL. Frankfurt am Main: Verlag Marxistische Blatter, 1980.

628. Beyer, Wilhelm Raimund. FREIBEUTER IN HEGELISCHEN GEFILDEN. Frankfurt am Main: Sendler, 1983.

629. Beyer, Wilhelm Raimund. HEGEL, DER TRIUMPH DES NEUEN RECHTS. Hamburg: VSA-Verlag, 1981.

630. Beyer, Wilhelm Raimund, ed. DIE LOGIK DES WISSENS UND DAS PROBLEM DER ERZIEHUNG. Hamburg: Meiner, 1982.

631. Buhr, Manfred, ed. DENKEN UND BEDENKEN: HEGEL AUFSATZE: ZUM 75 GEBURTSTAG VON WILHELM RAIMUND BEYER. Berlin: Akademie-Verlag, 1977.

632. Buhr, Manfred. DER MUT DER WAHRHEIT: 150 JAHRE NACH HEGEL. Berlin: Akademie-Verlag, 1982.

633. Buhr, Manfred. UBER DIE HISTORISCHE NOTWENDIGKEIT DES IDEOLOGISCHEN KLASSENKAMPFES. Frankfurt am Main: Verlag Marxistische Blatter, 1976.

634. Buhr, Manfred. VERNUNFT, MENSCH, GESCHICHTE: STUDIEN ZUR EN-TWICKLUNGSGESCHICHTE DER KLASISCHEN BURGERLICHEN PHILOSOPHIE. Berlin: Akademie-Verlag, 1977.

635. Buhr, Manfred. VERNUNFTIGE GESCHICHTE: ZUM DENKEN UBER GESCHICHTE IN DER KLASSISCHEN DEUTSCHEN PHILOSOPHIE. Berlin: Akademie-Verlag, 1986.

636. Buhr, Manfred. WILHELM RAIMUND BEYER: EINE BIBLIOGRAPHIE. Rev. ed. Vienna: Europaverlag, 1982.

This volume includes an appendix by Wilhelm Raimund Beyer entitled "Auf der Suche nach Hegels Weltbegriff".

637. Buhr, Manfred and Gerd Irrlitz. DER ANSPRUCH DER VERNUNFT: DIE KLAS-SISCHE BURGERLICHE DEUTSCHE PHILOSOPHIE ALS THEORETISCHE QUELLE DES MARXISMUS, KANT, FICHTE, SCHELLING, LESSING, GOETHE, SCHILLER. Cologne: Pahl-Rugenstein, 1976-.

638. Buhr, Manfred and Alfred Kosing. KLEINES WORTERBUCH DER MARXISTISCH-LENINISTISCHEN PHILOSOPHIE. 7th. rev ed. Berlin: Dietz Verlag, 1984.

639. Buhr, Manfred and Gunter Krober, eds. MENSCH, WISSENSCHAFT, TECHNIK: VERSUCH EINER MARXISTISCHEN ANALYSE DER WISSENSCHAFTLICH-TECHNISCHEN REVOLUTION. Berlin: Akademie-Verlag, 1977.

This is a translation by Harro Lucht of CHELOVEK-NAUKA-TEKHNIKA: OPYT MARKSISTSKOGO ANALIZA NAUCHO-TEKHNICHESKO I REVOLIUTSII, which appeared in 1973 under the auspices of Akademiia Nauk SSSR, Institut Filosofii, Institut Istorii Estestvozaniia i Tekhniki, Ceskoslovenska Akademie ved, Ustav pro filosofii a sociologii.

640. Buhr, Manfred and Teodor Ilich Oizerman, eds. REVOLUTION DER DENKART ODER DENKART DER REVOLUTION: BEITRAGE ZUR PHILOSOPHIE IMMA-NUEL KANTS. Berlin: Akademie-Verlag, 1976.

This volume contains papers from a meeting sponsored by the Institut filosofii of the Akademi nauk SSSR and the Zentralinstitut fur Philosophie of the Akademie der Wissen-schaften der DDR, March 28-29, 1974 in Berlin.

641. Buhr, Manfred and Teodor Ilich Oizerman, eds. VOM MUTE DES ERKENNENS: BEITRAGE ZUR PHILOSOPHIE G. W. F. HEGELS. Frankfurt am Main: Verlag Marxistische Blatter, 1981.

At the head of the title is Akademie der Wissenschaften der USSR, Institute fur Phi-losophie, Akademie der Wissenschaften der DDR, Zentral institut fur Philosophie.

642. Buhr, Manfred and Jorg Schreiter. ERKENNTNISTHEORIE, KRITISCHER RA-TIONALISMUS, REFORMISMUS: ZUR JUNGSTEN METAMORPHOSE D. POSI-TIVISMUS. Berlin: Akademie-Verlag, 1979.

643. Buhr, Manfred and Robert Steigerwald. VERZICHT, AUF FORTSCHRIFT, GESCHICHTE, ERKENNTNIS UND WAHRHEIT: ZU DEN GRUNDTENDENZEN DER GEGENWARTIGEN BURGERLICHEN PHILOSOPHIE. Frankfurt am Main: Verlag Marxistische Blatter, 1981.

644. Eichhorn, Wolfgang. DIALEKTISCHER UND HISTORISCHER MATERIALISMUS, EIN BESTANDTEIL DES MARXISMUS-LENINISMUS. Berlin: Dietz, 1976.

645. Eichhorn, Wolfgang, et al, eds. ERKENNTNIS UND WAHRHEIT. Wissenschaftlichen Rates fur Marxistich-Leninistische Philosophie der D D R. Berlin: Dietz, 1983.

646. Eichhorn, Wolfgang, et al. GRUNDLAGEN DES HISTORISCHEN MATERIALIS-MUS. Ed. by Institute fur Gesellschaftswissenschaften. 2d ed. Berlin: Dietz, 1977.

This volume contains contributions by O. Asheim, J. Hellesnes, K.O. Apel, D. Bohler, T. Nordenstam, A. Maseide, A. Haga, G. Skirbekk, K. S. Johannessen, R. Slagstad, E. A. Wyller, and H. Hoibraaten.

647. Eichhorn, Wolfgang, et al. MARXISTISCH-LENINISTISCHE PHILOSOPHIE. 2d ed. Berlin: Dietz, 1982.

648. Engelberg, Ernst and Wolfgang Kuttler, eds. FORMATIONSTHEORIE UND GESCHICHTE: STUDIEN ZUR HISTORISCHE UNTERSUCHUNG VON GE-SELLSCHAFTSFORMATIONEN IM WERK VON MARX, ENGELS UND LENIN. Berlin: Akademie Verlag, 1978.

649. Engelberg, Ernst and Wolfgang Kuttler, eds. PROBLEME DER GESCHICHTS-WISSENSCHAFTLICHEN ERKENNTNIS. Berlin: Akademie-Verlag, 1977.

650. Erpenbeck, John. MOTIVATION: IHRE PSYCHOLOGIE UND PHILOSOPHIE. Berlin: Akademie-Verlag, 1984.

651. Erpenbeck, John. PSYCHOLOGIE ERKENNTNISTHEORIE: ZU PHILOSO-PHISCHEN PROBLEMEN PSYCHISCHER ERKENNTNIS-PROGRESSE. Berlin: Akademie-Verlag, 1980.

652. Erpenbeck, John and Herbert Horz. PHILOSOPHIE CONTRA NATURWIS-SENSCHAFT? Berlin: Deutscher Verlag der Wissenschaften, 1977.

653. Finger, Otto. JOSEPH DIETZGEN: BEIT. ZU D. PHILOSOPHI. LEISTUNGEN D. DT. ARBEITERPHILOSOPHEN. Berlin: Dietz Verlag, 1977.

654. Finger, Otto. DER MATERIALISMUS DER KRITISCHEN THEORIE. Frankfurt am Main: Verlag Marxistische Blatter, 1976.

655. Finger, Otto. UBER HISTORISCHEN MATERIALISMUS UND ZEITGENOS-SISCHE TENDENZEN SEINER VERFALSCHUNG. Berlin: Akademie-Verlag, 1977.

656. Frolov, Ivan Timofeevich. WISSENSCHAFTLICHER FORTSCHRITT UND ZUKUNFT DES MENSCHEN: KRITIK DES SZIENTISMUS, BIOLOGISMUS UND ETHISCHEN NIHILISMUS. Tr. of PROGRESS NAUKI I BUDUSHCHEE CHELO-VEKA: OPYT POSTANOVKI PROBLEMY, DISKUSSII OBOBSHCHENIIA Moscow: Politizdat, 1975. Tr. by Niels Jensen. Frankfurt am Main: Verlag Marxistische Blatter, 1978.

There is a preface by Manfred Buhr.

657. Hahn, Erich, et al. IDEOLOGIE UND KUNST. Berlin: Akademie-Verlag, 1984.

658. Hollitscher, Walter. NATUR UND MENSCH IM WELTBILD DER WIS-SENSCHAFT. Vol. 1, DIE MENSCHLICHE PSYCHE. Vol. 2, MATERIE,BEWE-GUNG, KOMISCHE ENTWICKLUNG UND ENTWICKLUNG DES LEBENS. Vol. 3, URSPRUNG UND ENTWICKLUNG DES LEBENS. Vol. 4, not listed. Vol. 5, MENSCHE UND GESELLSCHAFT. Vol. 6, NATURBILD UND WEL-TANSCHAUUNG. Ed. by Hubert Horstmann. Vienna: Globus; Cologne: Pahl-Rugenstein, 1983-.

659. Horstmann, Hubert, ed. DENKWEISE UND WELTANSCHAUUNG: STUDIEN ZUR WELTANSCHAULICHEN UND METHODOLOGISCHEN FUNKTION DER MATERIALISTISCHEN DIALEKTIK. Berlin: Akademie-Verlag, 1981.

660. Horstmann, Hubert. STUDIEN ZUR METHAPHYSISCHEN UND DIALEKTISCHE-MATERIALISTISCHEN DENKWEISE. Berlin: Akademie-Verlag, 1977.

661. Horz, Herbert. MARXISTISCHE PHILOSOPHIE UND NATURWISSENSCHAFTEN. 2d. rev ed. Berlin: Akademie-Verlag, 1976,1974.

662. Horz, Herbert. MATERIALISTISCHE DIALEKTIK UND WISSENSCHAFTSENT-WICKLUNG. Berlin: Akademie-Verlag, 1981.

663. Horz, Herbert. MENSCH CONTRA MATERIE?: STANDPUNKTE D. DIALEKT. MATERIALISMUS ZUR BEDEUTUNMG NATURWISS. ERKENNTNISSE FUR D. MENSCHEN. Berlin: Deutscher Verlag d. Wiss., VEB, 1976.

664. Horz, Herbert. MODELLE IN DER WISSENSCHAFTLICHEN ERKENNTNIS: PHILOSOPHISCHERKENNTNISTHEORETISCHE PROBLEME. Berlin: Akademie-Verlag, 1978.

665. Horz, Herbert, et al. PHILOSOPHICAL PROBLEMS IN PHYSICAL SCIENCE. Ed. by Erwin Marquit. Rev. English language ed. Revised translation of PHILOSOPHISCHE PROBLEME DER PHYSIK. Berlin: VEB Deutscher Verlag der Wissenschaften, 1978. Tr. by Salomea Genin. Studies in Marxism, Vol. 7. Minneapolis: Marxist Educational Press, 1980.

666. Horz, Herbert, et al. PHILOSOPHIE UND NATURWISSENSCHAFTEN: WORTER-BUCH ZU DEN PHILOSOPHISCHEN FRAGEN DER NATURWISSEN SCHAFTEN. 2d. rev ed. Berlin: Dietz, 1983.

667. Horz, Herbert and Czeslaw Nowinski, eds. GESETZ, ENTWICKLUNG, INFORMA-TION: ZUM VERHALTNISS VON PHIL. UND BIOLOG. ENTWICKLUNGSTHEOR-IE. Berlin: Akademie-Verlag, 1979.

668. Horz, Herbert and Ulrich Roseberg. MATERIALISTISCHE DIALEKTIK IN DER PHYSIKALISCHEN UND BIOLOGISCHEN ERKENNTNIS. Frankfurt am Main: Verlag Marxistische Blatter, 1981.

669. Horz, Herbert and Karl-Friedrich Wessel. PHILOSOPHISCHE ENTWICKLUNG-STHEORIE: ERKENNTNISTHEORETISCHE UND METHODOLOGISCHE PROB-LEME DER NATURWISSENSCHAFTEN. Berlin: Deutscher Verlag der Wissenschaften, 1983.

There are summaries in German, Russian, English, French and Spanish.

670. Klaus, Georg. BEITRAGE ZU PHILOSOPHISCHEN PROBLEMEN DER EINZEL-WISSENSCHAFTEN. Ed. by Heinz von Liebscher. Berlin: Akademie-Verlag, 1978.

This work includes a bibliography of George Klaus' works.

671. Klaus, Georg. PHILOSOPHIEHISTORISCHE ABHANDLUNGEN: KOPERNIKUS, D'ALEMBERT, CONDILLAC, KANT. Ed. by Manfred Buhr. Berlin: Akademie-Ver-lag, 1977.

672. Klenner, Hermann. JOHN LOCKE UND DER FORMIERUNGSPROZESS DER POLITISCHE-JURISTISCHEN STANDARDTHEORIE DES BURGERTUMS. Berlin: Akademie Verlag, 1979.

673. Klenner, Hermann. MARXISMUS MENSCHENRECHTE: STUDIEN ZUR RE-CHTSPHILOSOPHIE: ANHANG, MENSCHENRECHTSKATALOGE AUS ORGAN-GENHEIT UND GEGENWART. Berlin: Akademie-Verlag, 1982.

674. Klenner, Hermann. RECHTSPHILOSOPHIE IN DER KRISE. Berlin: Akademie-Verlag, 1976.

675. Korch, Helmut. MATERIEAUFFASSUNG DER MARXISTISCHE-LENINIS-TISCHEN PHILOSOPHIE. Ed. by Wolfgang Eichhorn, et al. Berlin: Dietz, 1980.

676. Kosing, Alfred. NATION IN GESCHICHTE UND GEGENWART: STUDIE ZUR HISTOR. -MATERIALIST. THEORIE DER NATION. Berlin: Dietz, 1976.

677. Kosing, Alfred, et al. DIALEKTIK DER SOZIALISMUS. Ed. by Der Akademie fur Gesellschaftswissenschaften beim ZK der SED. Berlin: Dietz, 1981.

678. Ley, Hermann. ATHEISMUS, MATERIALISMUS, POLITIK. Berlin: Deutscher Verlag der Wissenschaften, 1978.

679. Lother, Rolf, et al. PHILOSOPHISCHE SCHRIFTEN VON MARX, ENGELS UND LENIN UND IHRE BEDEUTUNG FUR DIE MEDIZIN HEUTE. Jena: Gustav Fischer Verlag, 1979.

680. Lother, Rolf and Klaus Fuchs-Kittkowski. DAS REDUKTIONISMUSPROBLEM IN DER BIOLOGIE. Berlin: Akademie-Verlag, 1979.

681. Schlenstedt, Dieter, et al, eds. LITERARISCHE WIDERSPIEGELUNG: GESCHICH-TLICHE UND THEORETISCHE DIMENSIONEN EINES PROBLEMS. Akademie der Wissenschaften der DDR Zentral institut fuer Literaturgeschichte. Berlin: Aufbau, 1981.

682. Schreiter, Jorg. WAHRHEIT, WISSENSCHAFTLICHKEIT, GESELLSCHAFTSWIS-SENSCHAFTEN. Berlin: Akademie-Verlag, 1979.

683. Schreiter, Jorg. ZUR KRITIK DER PHILOSOPHISCHEN GRUNDPOSITIONEN DES WIENER KREISES. Frankfurt am Main: Verlag Marxistische Blatter, 1977.

684. Seidel, Helmut. MARXISMUS UND SPINOZISMUS: MATERIALIEN EINER WISSENSCHAFTLICHEN KONFERENZ. Leipzig: Karl-Marx-Universitat, 1981.

685. Treder, Hans-Jurgen, ed. FRIEDRICH ENGELS UND DIE WEGEWEISENDE BEDEUTUNG DER PHILOSOPHIE FUR DIE NATURWISSENSCHAFT. Berlin: Akademie Verlag, 1982.

686. Wahsner, Renate. AKTIVE UND DAS PASSIVE: ZUR ERKENNTNISTHEORE-TISCHEN BEGRUNDUNG DER PHYSIK DURCH DEN ATOMISMUS, DARGES-TELLT AN NEWTON UND KANT. Berlin: Akademie-Verlag, 1981.

687. Wahsner, Renate. MENSCH UND KOSMOS, DIE COPERNICANISCHE WENDE. Berlin: Akademie-Verlag, 1978.

688. Wessel, Karl-Friedrich, ed. STRUKTUR UND PROZESS. Berlin: Deutscher Verlag der Wissenschaften, 1977.

HUNGARY

689. Almasi, Miklos. THE PHILOSOPHY OF APPEARANCES. Tr. of A LATSZAT VALOSAGA. Budapest: Magveto Konyvkiado, 1971. Tr. by Andreas Vitanyi.

Translation revised by N. Horton Smith. Dordrecht and Boston: Kluwer, 1989.

Agnes Vertes tranlated this work into German and it was published in Budapest in 1977 by Akademiai Kiado as PHANOMENOLOGIE DES SCHEINS: DIE SEINSWEISE DER GESELLSCHAFTLICHEN SCHEINFORMEN.

690. Fodor, Judit. DIE ENTWICKLUNG DER DETERMINISMUS-KONZEPTION UND IHRE BEZIEHUNGEN ZUR QUANTENMECHANIK. Tr. of DETERMINIZ-MUS-KONCEPCIO FELODESEES KAPCSOLATAI A KVANTUMMECHANIKAV-AL. Tr. by Gaspar Soltesz. Budapest: Akademiai Kiado, 1980.

691. Gluck, Mary. GEORG LUKACS AND HIS GENERATION, 1900-1918. Cambridge: Harvard Univ. Press, 1985.

692. Heller, Agnes, ed. LUKACS REAPPRAISED. New York: Columbia Univ. Press, 1983.

693. Heller, Agnes, et al. DIE SEELE UND DAS LEBEN: STUDIEN ZUM FRUHEN LUKACS. Frankfurt am Main: Suhrkamp, 1977.

694. Hermann, Istvan. AZ ERTELEMIG ES TOVABB!: A FILOSZOFIA NAGY PROB-LEMAI. Budapest: Kozmiz Konyvek, 1982.

695. Hermann, Istvan. DIE GEDANKENWELT VON GEORG LUKACS. Tr. of LUKACS GYORGY (GONDOLTVILAGA): TANULMANY A XX. SZAZADEMBEERI LEHTO-SEGEIROL. Budapest: Magveto Kiado, 1974. Tr. by Endre Kiss. Budapest: Akademiai Kiado, 1978.

696. Hermann, Istvan. A GONDOLAT HATALMA: TANULMANYOK. Budapest: Szepir-od. Kaido, 1978.

697. Hermann, Istvan. IDEOLOGIA ES KULTURA A HELVENES EVEKBEN. Budapest: Kossuth Konyvkiado, 1982.

698. Hermann, Istvan. LUKACS GYORGY elete. Budapest: Corvina, 1985.

699. Hermann, Istvan. PROBLEME DER SOZIALISTISCHEN KULTUR. Tr. of SZO-CIALISTA KULTURA PROBLEMAI. Budapest: Kossuth Konyvkiado, 1970. Tr. from Hungarian by Endre Kiss and Javos Kristof Nyiri. Budapest: Corvina, 1978.

700. Hermann, Istvan. TELEOLOGIA ES TORTENETISEG. Budapest: Gondolat, 1979.

701. Kirtian, Garbis. METACRITIQUE: THE PHILOSOPHICAL ARGUMENT OF JURGEN HABERMAS. Tr. by John Raffin. Paris: Edition de Minuet, 1979.

702. LaPointe, Francois H. GEORG LUKACS AND HIS CRITICS: AN INTERNATION-AL BIBLIOGRAPHY WITH ANNOTATIONS (1910-1982). Westport, CT: Green-wood Press, 1983.

703. Lukacs, Gyorgy. THE DESTRUCTION OF REASON. Tr. of AZ ESZ TRONFOSZ-TASA: AZ IRRACIONALISTA FILOSZOFIA KRITIKAJA. Budapest: Akademia, 1954. London: Merlin, 1980.

This work develops a reconsideration of the history of German irrationalism using the investigative tools of historical materialism.

704. Lukacs, Gyorgy. GEORG LUKACS: SELECTED CORRESPONDENCE, 1902-1920: DIALOGUES WITH WEBER, SIMMEL, BUBER, MANNHEIM AND OTHERS.

Ed. by Marcus Tar and Zoltan Tar. New York: Columbia Univ. Press, 1986.

705. Lukacs, Gyorgy. WIE IST DEUTSCHLAND ZUM ZENTRUM DER REAKTION-AREN IDEOLOGIE GEWORDEN? Ed. by Laszlo Sziklai. Budapest: Akademiai Kiado, 1982.

706. Lukacs, Gyorgy. WIE IST DIE FASCHISTISCHE PHILOSOPHIE IN DEUTSCH-LAND ENSTANDEN? Ed. by Laszlo Sziklai. Budapest: Akademiai Kiado, 1982.

707. Lukacs, Jozsef and Ferenc Todei, eds. PHILOSOPHY AND CULTURE: STUDIES FROM HUNGARY PUBLISHED ON THE OCCASION OF THE 17TH WORLD CONGRESS OF PHILOSOPHY. Budapest: Akademiai Kiado, 1983.

708. Matrai, Laszlo. A KULTURA TORTENETISEGE: VALOGATOTT TANULMAN-YOK ES CIKKEK. Budapest: Gondolat, 1977.

709. Matrai, Laszlo. MUHELYEIM TORTENETE. Budapest: Szepirodalmi Konyvkiado, 1982.

710. Tamas, Gyorgy. THE LOGIC OF CATEGORIES. Ed. by Robert Sonne Cohen. Tr. of KATEGORIAK LOGIKAJA. Budapest: Akademiai Kiado, 1975. Tr. by Ildiko Berkes. Dordrecht and Boston: Reidel; Budapest: Akademiai Kiado, 1986.

POLAND

711. Ajdukiewicz, Kazimierz. THE SCIENTIFIC WORLD-PERSPECTIVE AND OTHER ESSAYS, 1931-1963. Ed. by Jerzy Giedymin. Dordrecht and Boston: Reidel, 1978.

This volume contains a translation of essays selected from the author's JEZYK I POZNANIE, with two articles added and a bibliography of Ajdukiewicz's works on pages 363-369.

712. Amsterdamski, Stefan. MIEDZY HISTORIA A METODA: SPORY O RACJONAL-NOSC NAUKI. Warsaw: Panstwowy Institut Wydowniczy, 1983.

713. Augustynek, Zdzislaw. TIME PAST, PRESENT AND FUTURE. Tr. of PRZES-ZLOSC TERAZNIEJSZOSC, PRZYSZLOSC STUDIUM FILOZOFICZNE. Warsaw: Panstwowe Wydawn, Naukowe, 1979. Dordrecht and Boston: Kluwer Academic Publishers, 1989.

714. Bialostocki, Jan. REFLEKSJE I SYNTEZY ZE SWIATA SZTUKI:CYKL DRUGI. Warsaw: Panstwowe Wydawnictwo Naukowe, 1974-.

715. Bochenski, Joseph M. LOGICA Y ONTOLOGIA. Valencia: Revista Teorema, 1977.

716. Borzym, Stanislaw, et al. ZARYS DZIEJOW FILOZOFII POLSKIEJ, 1815-1918. Warsaw: Panstwowe Wydawnictwo Naukowe, 1983.

717. Dambska, Izydora. WPROWADZENIE DO STARO ZYTNEJ SEMIOTYKI GRECK-IEJ: STUDIA I TEKSTY. Warsaw: Zaklad Narodowyy im. Ossolinskich, 1984.

718. Dziemidok, Bohdan. TEORIA PRZEZYC I WARTOSCI ESTETYCZNYNYCH W POLSKIEJ ESTETYCE DWUDZIESTOLECIA MIEDZYWOJENNEGO (Theories of Aesthetic Experience and Value in Polish Aesthetics During the Period Between the Wars). Warsaw: PWN, 1980.

The table of contents is printed in English and Polish.

719. Gasparski, Wojciech and Tadeusz Pszczolowski, eds. PRAXIOLOGICAL STUDIES: POLISH CONTRIBUTIONS TO THE SCIENCE OF EFFICIENT ACTION. Warsaw: Polish Scientific Publications; Dordrecht and Boston: Reidel, 1983.

720. Hoffman, Piotr. ANATOMY OF IDEALISM: PASSIVITY AND ACTIVITY IN KANT, HEGEL, AND MARX. The Hague and Boston: Nijhoff, 1982.

721. Hoffman, Piotr. DOUBT, TIME, VIOLENCE. Chicago: Univ. of Chicago Press, 1986.

722. Hoffman, Piotr. THE HUMAN SELF AND THE LIFE AND DEATH STRUGGLE. Gainesville: University of Florida Presses, 1983.

723. Hoffman, Piotr. VIOLENCE IN MODERN PHILOSOPHY. Chicago: Univ. of Chicago Press, 1989.

724. Ingarden, Roman. GEGENSTAND UND AUFGABEN DER LITERATURWIS-SENSCHAFT: AUFSATZE UND DISKUSSIONSBEITRAGEN (1937-1964). Ed. by Rolf Fieguth. Tubingen: Niemeyer, 1976.

725. Ingarden, Roman. MAN AND VALUE. Tr. from Polish and German by Arthur Szylewicz. Washington, DC: Catholic Univ. of America Press; Munich: Philosophia, 1983.

726. Ingarden, Roman. ONTOLOGY OF THE WORK OF ART: THE MUSICAL WORK, THE PICTURE, THE ARCHITECTURAL WORK, THE FILM. Tr. of UNTER-SUCHUNGEN ZUR ONTOLOGIE DER KUNST: MUSIKWERK, BILD, ARCHITEK-TUR, FILM. Tubingen: M. Niemeyer, 1962. Tr. by Raymond Meyer and John T. Gold-thwait. Series in Continental Thought, Vol. 12. Athens: Ohio Univ. Press, 1989.

727. Ingarden, Roman. SELECTED PAPERS IN AESTHETICS. Ed. by Peter J. McCormick. Washington, DC: Catholic Univ. of America Press; Munich: Philosophia, 1984.

728. Ingarden, Roman. THE WORKD OF MUSIC AND THE PROBLEM OF ITS IDEN-TITY. Tr. of UTWOR MUZYCYNY I SPRAWA JEGO TO ZSAMO SCI. Cracow: Polskie Wydawn. Muzyczzne, 1973. Tr. from the original Polish by Adam Czer niawski. Berkeley: Univ. of California Press; London: Macmillan, 1986.

This volume contains a list of works by Roman Ingarden in English translation.

729. Ingarden, Roman. WYKLADY I DYSKUSJE Z ESTETIYKI. Ed. by Wladyslaw Strozewski. Tr. of DZIE A FILOZOFICZNE. Warsaw: Panstwowe Wydawnictwo Naukowe, 1981.

730. Kolakowski, Leszek. MAIN CURRENTS OF MARXISM: ITS RISE, GROWTH, AND DISSOLUTION. 3 Vols. Tr. of GLOWNE NURTY MARKSIZMU: POWSTANIE, ROZWOJ ROZKLAD 3.Vols. Paryz: Instytut Literacki, 1976-1978. Tr. by P. S. Falla. Oxford: Clarendon Press, 1978.

731. Kolakowski, Leszek. RELIGION, IF THERE IS NO GOD: ON GOD, THE DEVIL, SIN AND OTHER WORRIES OF THE SO-CALLED PHILOSOPHY OF RELIGION. New York and Oxford: Oxford Univ. Press, 1982.

732. Kotarbinski, Tadeusz. DROGI DOCIEKA N WASNYCH: FRAGMENTY FILOZO-FICZNE. Warsaw: Panstwowe Wydawnictwo Naukowe, 1986.

733. Kotarbinski, Tadeusz. MYSLI I LUDZIACH I LUDZKICH SPRAWACH. Ed. by Janina Kotarbinska. Warsaw: Zaklad Narodowy, 1986.

734. Kotarbinski, Tadeusz. PISMA ETYCZNE. Ed. by Pawe Smoczynski. Warsaw: Zaklad Narodowy im. Ossolinskich Wydawnictwo, 1987.

735. Kotarbinski, Tadeusz. SZKICE Z HISTOIRII FILOZOFII I LOGIKI. Ed. by Klemens Szaniawski. Warsaw: Panstwowe Wydawnictwo Naukowe, 1979.

736. Krajewski, Wladyslaw. CORRESPONDENCE PRINCIPLE AND GROWTH OF SCIENCE. Dordrecht and Boston: Reidel, 1977.

737. Krajewski, Wladyslaw. KONIECZNOSC, PRZYPADEK, PRAWO STATYSTYCNE. Warsaw: Panstwowe Wydawnictwo Naukowe, 1977.

738. Krajewski, Wladyslaw, ed. POLISH ESSAYS IN THE PHILOSOPHY OF THE NATURAL SCIENCES. Tr. from the Polish. Dordrecht and Boston: Reidel, 1982.

739. Krajewski, Wladyslaw, et al. RALACJE MIEDZY TEORIAMI A ROZWAJ NAUKI. Warsaw: Zaklad Narodowy im Ossolinskich, 1978.

740. Kurczewska, Joanna. NAROD W SOCJOLOGII I IDEOLOGII POLSKIEJ: ANALZA POROWNAWCZA WYBRANZCH KONCEPCJI Z PRZELOMU XIX I XX WIEKU. Warsaw: Panstowowe Wydawnictwo Naukowe, 1979.

This work contains a summary in English.

741. Kurczewska, Joanna and Jerzy Szacki, eds. TRADYCJA I NOWOCZESNOSC. Warsaw: Czytelnik, 1984.

This volume contains a selection of articles translated from American, English, French, German, Japanese, and Russian.

742. Malinowski, Grzegorz. TOPICS IN THE THEORY OF STRENGTHENINGS OF SENTENTIAL CALCULI. Warsaw: Institute of Philosophy and Sociology of the Polish Academy of Sciences, 1979.

743. Marciszewski, Withold, ed. DICTIONARY OF LOGIC AS APPLIED IN THE STUDY OF LANGUAGE: CONCEPTS-METHODS-THEORIES. The Hague and Boston: Nijhoff, 1981.

744. Marek, Wiktor and Janusz Onyszkiewicz. ELEMENTS OF LOGIC. Tr. of ELEMENTY LOGIKI I TEORII MNOGOSCI W ZADIOCH. Warsaw: Panstwowe Wydawn Naukowe, 1975. Tr. by Ezbieta Tarantowicz-Marek. Dordrecht and Boston: Reidel; Warsaw: PWN Scientific Publishers, 1982.

745. Nowak, Lenzek. PROPERTY AND POWER: TOWARDS A NON-MARXIAN HISTORICAL MATERIALISM. Dordrecht and Boston: Reidel, 1983.

746. Nowak, Stefan. UNDERSTANDING AND PREDICTION: ESSAYS IN THE METHODOLOGY OF SOCIAL AND BEHAVIORAL THEORIES. Dordrecht and Boston: Reidel, 1976.

747. O'Rourke, James J., et al. CONTEMPORARY MARXISM: ESSAYS IN HONOR OF J. M. BOCHENSKI. Dordrecht and Boston: Reidel, 1984.

This volume includes a bibliography of works by J. M. Bochenski on pages 257-261.

748. Ossowska, Maria. MORAL NORMS: A TENTATIVE SYSTEMATIZATION. Ed. by Peter Thomas Geach. Tr. of NORMY MORALNE: PROBA SYSTEMATYZACJI.

Warsaw: Pannstwowe Wydawn. Naukowe, 1971. Tr. by Irena Gulowska. Amsterdam and New York: North-Holland; Warsaw: PWN-Polish Scientific Publishers, 1980.

This work contains a summary in English.

749. Ossowski, Stanislaw. THE FOUNDATIONS OF AESTHETICS. Tr. of U PODSTAW ESTETYKI. Warsaw: Czytelnik, 1949. Tr. by Janina and Witold Rodzinski. Dordrecht and Boston: Reidel, 1978.

750. Pawlowski, Tadeusz. BEGRIFFSBILDUNG UND DEFINITION. Tr. from Polish by George Grzyb. Berlin and New York: DeGruyter, 1980.

751. Pelc, Jerzy, comp. SEMIOTICS IN POLAND, 1894-1969. Tr. of SEMIOTYKA POLSKA, 1894-1969 Warsaw: Pastwowe Wydawnictwo Naukowe, 1971. Dordrecht and Boston: Reidel, 1979.

752. Pelc, Jerzy. WSTEP DO SEMIOTYKI. Warsaw: Wiedza Powszechna, 1982.

753. Pelc, Jerzy, et al, eds. SIGN, SYSTEM, AND FUNCTION: PAPERS OF THE FIRST AND SECOND POLISH-AMERICAN SEMIOTICS COLLOQUIUM. Berlin and New York: Mouton, 1984.

This volume consists of papers from a Semiotic Symposium held at Radziejowice, Poland, May 22-28, 1978 and the U. S. Polish Bilateral Conference "Semiotic Systems and Their Functions" held at Indiana University, Bloomington, October 1-3, 1979.

754. Polish Academy of Sciences, Branch in Lodzi. STUDIES IN THE THEORY AND PHILOSOPHY OF LAW. Wroclaw: Zaklad Narodowy im. Ossolinskich, 1986.

This publication is issued every year in Poland.

755. Prokopczyk, Czeslaw. TRUTH AND REALITY IN MARX AND HEGEL: A REAS-SESSMENT. Amherst: Univ. of Massachusetts Press, 1980.

756. Przelecki, Marian, et al, Eds. FORMAL METHODS IN THE METHODOLOGY OF EMPIRICAL SCIENCES. Dordrecht and Boston: Reidel, 1976.

These are the Proceedings of the Conference for Formal Methods in Methodology of Empirical Sciences, Warsaw, June 17-21, 1974.

757. Przelecki, Marian and Ryszard Wojcicki, eds. TWENTY-FIVE YEARS OF LOGICAL METHODOLOGY IN POLAND. Tr. from the Polish by Edmund Ronowicz and Stanis law Wojnicki. Dordrecht and Boston: Reidel, 1977.

758. Schaff, Adam. ENTFREMDUNG ALS SOZIALES PHANOMEN. Vienna: Europa-verlag, 1977.

759. Schaff, Adam. STRUCTURALISM AND MARXISM. Tr. of STRUKTURALIZM I MARKSIZM. Oxford and New York: Pergamon Press, 1978.

760. Strozewski, Wladyslaw. DIALEKTYJA TWORCZOSCI. Cracow: Polskie Wydaw-nictwo Muzyczne, 1983.

761. Strozewski, Wladyslaw, ed. STUDIA Z TEORII POZANANIA I FILOZOFII WARTOSCI. Warsaw: Zaklad Narodowy im. Ossolinskich, 1978.

There is a bibliography of the works of Izydora Dambska published from 1926-1974 on pages 207-220.

762. Swiezawski, Stefan. DZIEJE FILOZOFI EUROPEJESKIEJ W XV WIEKU. Warsaw: Akademia Teologii Katolickiej, 1974-.

Six volumes have been published to date: Vol. 1, POZNANIE. Vol. 2, WIEDZA, Vol. 3, BYT. Vol. 4, BOG. Vol. 5, WSZECH SWIAT. Vol. 6, CZOWIEK.

763. Szacki, Jerzy. HISTORIA MYSLI SOCJOLOGICZNEJ. 2 Vols. 2d ed. Tr. of 1st. ed. HISTORY OF SOCIOLOGICAL THOUGHT. Westport, CT Greenwood Press, 1979. Warsaw: Panstwowe Wydawnictwo Naukowe, 1983.

764. Szacki, Jerzy, ed. IDEA SPOLECZENSTWA KOMUNISTYCZNEGO W PRACACH KLASYKOW MARKSIZM: OPRACOWANIE ZBIORWE. Warsaw: Panstwowe Wydawnictwo Naukowe, 1977.

765. Szacki, Jerzy. SPOTKANIA Z UTOPIA. Warsaw: Iskry, 1980.

766. Tatarkiewicz, Wladyslaw. ANALYSIS OF HAPPINESS. Tr. of O SZCZE'SCIU. Warsaw: Panstwowe Wydawnictwo Naukowe, 1965. Tr. from Polish by Edward Rothert and Danuta Zielinska. Warsaw: PWN. Polish Scientific Publishers, 1976.

767. Tatarkiewicz, Wladyslaw. A HISTORY OF SIX IDEAS: AN ESSAY IN AESTHETICS. Tr. of DZIEJE SZESCIU POJEC-SZTUKA, PIEKNO, FORMA, TWORCZOSC, ODTWORCZOSC, PRZEZYCIE ESTETYCZNE. Warsaw: Panstwowe Wydawnictwo Naukowe, 1975. Tr. by Christopher Kasparek. The Hague and Boston: Nijhoff, 1980.

768. Tatarkiewicz, Wladyslaw. PARERGA. Warsaw: Panstwowe Wydawnictwo Naukowe, 1978.

769. Tatarkiewicz, Wladyslaw and Teresa Tatarkiewiczowa. WSPOMNIENIA. Warsaw: Panstwowe Instytut Wydawniczy, 1979.

770. Tymieniecka, Anna-Teresa, ed. ANALECTA HUSSERLIANA: THE YEARBOOK OF PHENOMENOLOGICAL RESEARCH. Dordrecht and Boston: Reidel, 1971-.

Vol. 4, INGARDIANA: A SPECTRUM OF SPECIALISED STUDIES ESTABLISHING THE FIELD OF RESEARCH (1976); Vol. 5, THE CRISIS OF CULTURE: STEPS TO REOPEN THE PHENOMENOLOGICAL INVESTIGATION OF MAN: THE MODALITIES OF HUMAN LIFE, THE IRREDUCIBLE IN VALUES AND THEIR FLUCTUATING FRAMEWORK OF REFERENCE, FROM REASON TO ACTION, ALIENATION, AND BELONGING (1976); Vol. 6, THE SELF AND THE OTHER: THE IRREDUCIBLE ELEMENT IN MAN: THE CRISIS OF MAN (1977); Vol. 7, THE HUMAN BEING IN ACTION: THE IRREDUCIBLE ELEMENT IN MAN, PART II: INVESTIGATIONS AT THE INTERSECTION OF PHILOSOPHY AND PSYCHIATRY (1978); Vol. 8, JAPANESE PHENOMENOLOGY: PHENOMENOLOGY AS THE TRANSCULTURAL PHILOSOPHICAL APPROACH (1978); Vol. 9, THE TELEOLOGIES IN HUSSERLIAN PHENOMENOLOGY (1979); Vol. 10, THE ACTING PERSON by John Paul II (Karol Wojtyla) (1979); Vol. 11, THE GREAT CHAIN OF BEING AND ITALIAN PHENOMENOLOGY (1981); Vol. 12, THE PHILOSOPHICAL REFLECTION OF MAN IN LITERATURE (1982); Vol. 13, THE UNHAPPY CONSCIOUSNESS: THE POETIC PLIGHT OF SAMUEL BECKETT: AN INQUIRY AT THE INTERSECTION OF PHENOMENOLOGY AND LITERATURE (1981); Vol. 14, THE PHENOMENOLOGY OF MAN AND THE HUMAN CONDITION: INDIVIDUALISATION OF NATURE AND THE HUMAN BEING (1983); Vol. 15, FOUNDATIONS OF MORALITY, HUMAN RIGHTS, AND THE HUMAN SCIENCES: PHENOMENOLOGY IN A FOUNDATIONAL DIALOGUE WITH THE HUMAN SCIENCES (1983); Vol. 16, SOUL AND BODY IN HUSSERLIAN PHENOMENOLOGY: MAN AND NATURE (1983); Vol. 17, PHENOMENOLOGY OF LIFE IN A DIALOGUE BETWEEN CHINESE AND OCCIDENTAL PHILOSOPHY (1984); Vol. 18, THE EXISTENTIAL

COORDINATES OF THE HUMAN CONDITION, POETIC--EPIC--TRAGIC: THE LITERARY GENRE (1984); Vol. 19, POETICS OF THE ELEMENTS IN THE HUMAN CONDITION: THE SEA: FROM ELEMENTAL STIRRINGS TO SYMBOLIC INSPIRATION, LANGUAGE, AND LIFE-SIGNIFICANCE IN LITERARY INTERPRETATION AND THEORY (1985); Vol. 20, THE MORAL SENSE IN THE COMMUNAL SIGNIFICANCE OF LIFE: INVESTIGATIONS IN PHENOMENOLOGICAL PRAXEOLOGY: PSYCHIATRIC THERAPEUTICS, MEDICAL ETHICS, AND SOCIAL PRAXIS WITHIN THE LIFE AND COMMUNAL WORLD; Vol.21, THE PHENOMENOLOGY OF MAN AND OF THE HUMAN CONDITION (1986).

771. Tymieniecka, Anna-Teresa. POETICA NOVA: THE CREATIVE CRUCIBLES OF HUMAN EXISTENCE AND OR ART. Dordrecht and Boston: Reidel, 1982.

772. Walentynowicz, Bohdan, ed. POLISH CONTRIBUTIONS TO THE SCIENCE OF SCIENCE. Dordrecht and Boston: Reidel, 1983.

773. Walicki, Andrzej. A HISTORY OF RUSSIAN THOUGHT FROM THE ENLIGHTENMENT TO MARXISM. Tr. of ROSYJSKA FILOZOFIA I MYSL SPOLECZNA OD OSWIECENIA DO MARKSIZMU. Warsaw: Wiedza Powszechna, 1973. Tr. by Hilda Andrews-Rusiecka. Stanford: Stanford Univ. Press, 1979.

774. Walicki, Andrzej. LEGAL PHILOSOPHIES OF RUSSIAN LIBERALISM. Oxford: Clarendon Press; New York: Oxford Univ. Press, 1986.

775. Wiatr, Jerzy, ed. POLISH ESSAYS IN THE METHODOLOGY OF THE SOCIAL SCIENCES. Dordrecht and Boston: Reidel, 1979.

776. Wojcicki, Ryszard. LECTURES ON PROPOSITIONAL CALCULI. Ossolineum, Poland: Publishing House of the Polish Academy of Sciences, 1984.

777. Wojcicki, Ryszard, ed. SELECTED PAPERS ON LUKASIEWICZ SENTENTIAL CALCULI. Wroclaw: Zaklad Narodowy im Ossolinskich, 1977.

This volume contains a bibliography of Lukasiewicz's logics on pages 189-199.

778. Wojcicki, Ryszard. TOPICS IN THE FORMAL METHODOLOGY OF EMPIRICAL SCIENCES. Tr. of METODOLOGIA FORMALNA NAUK EMPIRYCZ NYCH. Tr. by Ewa Jansen. Dordrecht and Boston: Reidel, 1979.

779. Wroblewski, Jerzy. MEANING AND TRUTH IN JUDICIAL DECISION. Ed. by Aulis Aarnio. 2d ed. Helsinki: A-TIETO Oy, 1983.

ROMANIA

780. Allen, Douglas and Dennis Doeing. MIRCEA ELIADE: AN ANNOTATED BIBLIOGRAPHY. New York: Garland, 1980.

781. Berar, Petru. RELIGIA IN LUMEA CONTEMPORANA (Religion in the World Today). Bucharest: Editura Politica, 1976.

782. Berar, Petru. UMANISM SI ATEISM: STUDII. Bucharest: Editura Stiintifica si Enciclopedica, 1980.

783. Blaga, Lucian. ASPECTE ANTROPOLOGICE (Anthropological Aspects). Timisoara and Bucharest: Facla, 1976.

784. Bogdan, Radu J., ed. LOCAL INDUCTION. Dordrecht and Boston: Reidel, 1976.

This volume consists of essays by the editor, I. Levi, W.K. Goosens, K. Lehrer, I. Niini luoto, R. Tuomela, and other logicians. It also contains a selected bibliography on local induction by Radu J. Bogdan on pages 329-336.

785. Dumitriu, Anton. A HISTORY OF LOGIC. 4 Vols. Tunbridge Wells: Abacus Press, 1977.

This is a revised, updated and enlarged translation of the 2d. ed. of ISTORIA LOGICII, published in Budapest by Editura Didactica si Pedagaoica in 1975.

786. Eliade, Mircea. HISTORY OF RELIGIOUS IDEAS. Vol. 1, FROM THE STONE AGE TO THE ELEUSINIAN MYSTERIES. Vol. 2, FROM GAUTAMA BUDDHA TO THE TRIUMPH OF CHRISTIANITY. Vol. 3, FROM MUHAMMAD TO THE AGE OF REFORMS. Tr. of HISTOIRES DES CROYANCES ET DES IDEES RELIGIEUSES. Vol. 1, DE L'AGE DE LA PIERRE AUX MYSTERES D'ELUSIS. Vol. 2, DE GAUTA-MA BOUDDHA AU TRIOMPHE DU CHRISTIANISME. Vol. 3, DE MAHOMET A L'AGE DES REFORMES. Paris: Payot, 1976-. Tr. by William R. Trask. Volume 3 translated by Alf Hiltenbeitel and Diane Apostolow-Cappadona. Chicago: Univ. of Chicaago, 1978-1985.

787. Joja, Athanase. STUDII DE LOGICA. 4 Vols. Bucharest: Editura Academiei Republicii Socialiste Romania, 1968-1976.

788. Miros, Liubomira. ECHITE, SI DREPTATE. Bucharest: Editura Stiintifica Enciclopedica, 1977.

789. Miros, Liubomira. RAPORTUL DINTRE INDIVID SI SOCIETATE, REALIZAREA, LIBERTATII IN CONDITULLE SOCIALISMULUI. Bucharest: Editura Politica, 1980.

790. Pascadi, Ion. ARTA SI CIVILIZATIE: ESEURI. Bucharest: Meridiane, 1976.

This book includes a summary in French and a table of contents in Romanian and English.

791. Rautu, Leonte, ed. PROGRESUL ISTORIC SI CONTEMPORANEITATEA: CULEGERE DE STUDII. Bucharest: Editura Politica, 1976.

This book includes a table of contents in Romanian, English, French, German and Russian.

792. Smeu, Grigore. RELATIA SOCIAL-AUTONOM IN ARTA: STUDIU. Bucharest: Editura Academiei Republicii Socialiste Romania, 1976.

This book includes a summary in French and a table of contents in Romanian and English.

793. Smeu, Grigore and Dimitu Matei, coor. ESTETICUL IN SFERA CULTURII: STUDII DE ESTETICA SI TEORIA ARTEI. Bucharest: Meridiane, 1976.

794. Tamas, Sergiu. CERCETAREA VIITORULUI. Bucharest: Editura Political, 1976.

This volume includes a table of contents in Romanian, English, French, and Russian.

795. Tanase, Alexandru, ed. CIVILZATIA SOCIALISTA DIMENSIUNI SI CONFRON-TARI CONTEMPORANE. Bucharest: Editura Academia de Stinte Sociale si Politici. Institutul de Filozofie, 1979.

The table of contents is in Romanian, English and Russian.

796. Tanase, Alexandru. CULTURA SI CIVILIZATIE: STUDII. Bucharest: Editura Politica, 1977.

This work includes a table of contents in Romanian, English, French and Russian.

797. Tanase, Alexandru. DIALOGURI DESPRE UMANISM. Bucharest: Albatros, 1976.

798. Tanase, Alexandru. ESEURI DE FILOSOFIE A LITERATURII SI ARTEI. Bucharest: Editura Eminescu, 1980.

799. Tanase, Alexandru. LUCIEN BLAGA: FILOSOFUL POET, POETUL FILOSOF. Bucharest: Cartea Romaneasca, 1977.

800. Tanase, Alexandru, et al. DIMENSIUNI SI FUNCTII ALE CULTURII IN SOCIAL-ISM. Bucharest: Editura Academiei Republicii Socialiste Romania, 1984-.

The table of contents is in English, Romanian and Russian.

801. Tanase, Alexandru and Victor Isac. REALITATE SI CUONSTERE IN ISTORIE. Bucharest: Editura Politica, 1980.

This work includes a table of contents in Romanian and French.

802. Tanase, Alexandru and C. Gh Marinescu, eds. CONFRUNTARI IDEOLOGICE CONTEMPORANE: STUDII. Iasi: Junimea, 1981.

803. Tanase, Alexandru and Liubomira Miros, eds. COORDONATE VALORICE ALE CIVILZATIIEI SOCIALISTE: CULEGERE DE STUDII (Value Landmarks of Socialist Civilization). Bucharest: Editura Academiei Socialiste Romania, 1976.

The volume contains summaries in English.

804. Tanase, Alexandru and Ion Rebedeu, eds. ARTA SI IDEOLOGIE. Iasi: Junimea, 1979.

805. Tanase, Alexandru and Georgeta Todea. OMUL, CREATOR DE CULTURA, CIVI-LIZATIE. Bucharest: Editura Stiintifica si Enciclopedica, 1979.

806. Vieru, Sorin. NORME, VALORI, ACTIUNE: ANALIZA LOGICA A DISCURSULUI PRACTIC, CU APLICATII IN ETICA SI IN DREPT. Bucharest: Editura Politica, 1979.

This work is a collection of articles in Romanian translated from various English, French and Russian books and periodicals.

807. Wald, Henri. IDEEA VINE VORBIND. Bucharest: Cartea Romaneasca, 1983.

808. Wald, Henri, ed. ORIENTARI CONTEMPORANE IN TEORIA CUONASTERRII (Contemporary Orientations in the Theory of Cognition). Bucharest: Editura Academiei Republicii Socialiste Romania, 1976.

The Table of Contents of the volume is printed in Romanian and English.

809. Wald, Henri. TEORIE SI METODA IN STIINTELE SOCIALE (Theory and Method in the Social Sciences). Bucharest: Editura Politica, 1965-.

SOVIET UNION

810. Adelmann, Frederick J. SOVIET PHILOSOPHY REVISITED. Boston College Studies in Philosophy, Vol. 5. The Hague and Boston: Nijhoff; Chestnut Hill: Boston College, 1977.

811. Afanasev, Viktor Grigorevich. MARXIST PHILOSOPHY. Ed. by J. Riordan. 4th rev. ed. Tr.of OSNOVY FILOSOFSKIKH ZNANII. Moscow: Izd-vo Mysl', 1976. Tr.by David Fidlon. Moscow: Progress Publishers, 1980.

812. Alekseev, Igor Serafimovich. KONTSEPTSIIA DOPOLNITEL'NOSTI. Moscow: Nauka, 1978.

813. Alekseev, Peter Vasilevich. PREDMET, STRUKTURA I FUNKTSII DIALEK-TICHESKOGO MATERIALIZMA. Moscow: Izd-vo Moskovskogo Universiteta, 1978.

814. Andropov, Iurii Vladmirovich. SPEECH AT THE CPSU CENTRAL COMMITTEE PLENARY MEETING, JUNE 15, 1983. Moscow: Novesti Press Agency, 1983.

815. Andropov, Iurii Vladmirovich. UCHENIE KARLA MARKSA I NEKOTORYE VOPROSY SOSTSIALISTICHESKOGO STROITEL'STVA V SSSR. Moscow: Izd-vo Politicheskoi Literatury, 1983.

816. Anismov, Sergei Fedorovich. MORAL' I POVEDENIE. Moscow: Mysl', 1979.

817. Anufriev, Evgenii Aleksandrovich, et al. NAUCHNYI KOMMUNIZM. OPYT RAZRABOTKI I CHTENIIA LEKSTII. Moscow: Izd-vo Moskovskogo Universiteta, 1982.

818. Arkhangel'skii, Leonid Mikhailovich, ed. METODOLOGIIA ETICHESKIKH ISSLEDOVANII. Moscow: Nauka, 1982.

819. Bakhtomin, N. K. PRAKTIKA-MYSHLENIE-ZNANIE: PROBLEME TVORCHES-KOGO MYSHLENIIA. Moscow: Nauka, 1978.

820. Bakshtanovskii, Vladimir Iosifovich, ed. PRAKTIKUM PO ETIKE. 2d ed. Tiumen': Tiumenskii Industrial'nyi Institut, 1979.

821. Bakshtanovskii, Vladimir Iosifovich, et al. NAUCHNOE UPRAVLENIE NRAV-STVENNYMI PROTSESSAMI I ETIKO-PRIKLADNYE ISSLEDOVANIIA. Novosi-birsk: Nauka, Sibirskoe Otdelenie, 1980.

822. Barabash, Iurii IAkovlevych. AESTHETICS AND POETICS. Tr. of VOPROSY ESTHETIKI I POETIKI. 3d. ed. Moscow: Sovetskaia Rossiia, 1978. Moscow: Progress Publishers, 1977.

823. Blauberg, Igor Viktorovich, et al. SYSTEMS THEORY: PHILOSOPHICAL AND METHODOLOGICAL PROBLEMS. Tr. from the Russian by Sergei Syrovathkin and Olga Germodenoval. Moscow: Progress Publishers, 1977.

824. Bogomolov, Aleksei Sergeevich and Teodor Ilich Oizerman. OSNOVY TEORII ISTORIKO-FILOSOFSKOGO PROTSESSA. Moscow: Izd-vo Nauka, 1983.

825. Bykhovskii, Bernard Emmanuilovich. SCHOPENHAUER AND THE GROUND OF EXISTENCE. Tr. with an introductory essay by Philip Moran. Amsterdam: B. R. Grun-er, 1984.

826. Chudinov, Engel's Matveevich, ed. EINSHTEIN: FILOSOFSKIE PROBLEMY FIZIKI XX VEKA. Moscow: Nauka, 1979.

827. Copleston, Frederick Charles. PHILOSOPHY IN RUSSIA: HERZEN TO LENIN. Indiana: Notre Dame Press, 1986.

This comprehensive work traces the development of philosophical thought in Russia from Peter the Great through the years after Stalin's death.

828. Copleston, Frederick Charles. RUSSIAN RELIGIOUS PHILOSOPHY: SELECTED ASPECTS. Notre Dame, IN: Univ. of Notre Dame Press; Tunbridge Wells, Kent, Eng.: Search, 1988.

The author discusses the views of Soloviev, Florensky, Frank, Bulgakov, Shestov, and others on the divine wisdom, God, manhood, history and freedom.

829. Davydov, Iu. ETIKA LIUBVI I METAFIZIKA SVOEVOLIIA: PROBLEMY NRAVSTVENNO FILOSOFII. Moscow: Molodaia Gvardiia, 1982.

830. Drobnitskii, Oleg Grigorevich. PROBLEMY NRAVSTVENNOSTI. Moscow: Nauka, 1977.

831. Dubrovin, Artemii Grigorevich. KOMMUNISTICHESKOE MIROVOZZRENIE I ISKUSSTVO SOTSIALISTICHESKOGO REALIZMA (SBORNIK). Moscow: Znanie, 1977.

832. Eiermacher, Karl and Serge Shishkoff. SUBJECT BIBLIOGRAPHY OF SOVIET SEMIOTICS: THE MOSCOW-TARTU SCHOOL. Ann Arbor: Dept. of Slavic Languages and Literatures, Univ. of Michigan, 1977.

833. Fedoseev, Petr Nikolaevich, ed. FILOSOFIIA I MIROVOZZRENCHESKIE PROBLEMY SOVREMENNO I NAUKI:XVI VSEMIRNY I FILOSOFSKI I KONGRESS, AUGUST 27-SEPTEMBER 2, 1972, IN DUSSELDORF. Moscow: Izd-vo Nauka, 1981.

834. Fedoseev, Petr Nikolaevich. PHILOSOPHY AND SCIENTIFIC COGNITION. Tr. of FILOSOFIIA I NAUCHOE POZNANIE. Moscow: Izd-vo Nauka, 1983. Tr, from the Russian by Stannislav Pshennikov. Moscow: General Editorial Board for Foreign Publications, Nauka Publishers, 1985.

835. Fedoseev, Petr Nikolaevich, et al. PHILOSOPHY IN THE USSR: PROBLEMS OF DIALECTICAL MATERIALISM. Moscow: Progress Publishers, 1977.

836. Frolov, Ivan Timofeevich, ed. DICTIONARY OF PHILOSOPHY. Ed. by Murad Saifulin and Richard R. Dixon. 2d. rev ed. Tr. of FILOSOFSKII SLOVAR. 4th ed. Moscow: Izd-vo polit. lit-ry, 1980. Moscow: Progress Publishers, 1984.

This dictionary, translated from the fourth Russian edition (1980), contains about 1,300 cross-referenced entries and a glossary of mainly Greek and Latin philosophical terms.

837. Gavin, William J. and Thomas J. Blakeley. RUSSIA AND AMERICA: A PHILOSOPHICAL COMPARISON: DEVELOPMENT AND CHANGE OF OUTLOOK FROM THE NINETEENTH TO THE TWENTIETH CENTURY. Dordrecht and Boston: Reidel, 1976.

838. Ginzburg, Vitali Lazarevich. KEY PROBLEMS OF PHYSICS AND ASTROPHYSICS. Tr. of O FIZIKI I ASTROFIZIKE. Tr. by Oleg Glebov. Moscow: Mir Publishers, 1976.

839. Goldentrikht, Semen Semenovich. O PRIRODE ESTETICHESKOGO TVORCHES-TVA. 2d rev ed. Moscow: Izd-vo Moskovskogo Universiteta, 1977.

840. Gorskii, Dimitrii Pavlovich. DEFINITION: LOGICO-METHODOLOGICAL PROB-LEMS. Tr. of OPREDELENIE: LOGIKO-METODOLOGICHESKIE PROBLEMY. Moscow: Mysl', 1974. English translation by Sergei Syrovatin from the Russian text of 1974. Moscow: Progress Publishers, 1981.

This work discusses logical rules of definition in formalized theories and systems, in physical theories, and in the social sciences, as well as applicability of truth valuations to definitions.

841. Gott, Vladimir Spiridonovich. THIS AMAZING, AMAZING, AMAZING BUT KNOWABLE UNIVERSE. Tr. of UDIVITELNYI NEISCHERPAEMYI POZNAVEMYI MIR. Tr. by John Bushnell and Kristine Bushnell. Moscow: Progress Publishers, 1977.

842. Grier, Philip T. MARXIST ETHICAL THEORY IN THE SOVIET UNION. Dordrecht and Boston: Reidel, 1978.

843. Il'enkov, Evald Vasilevich. DIALECTICAL LOGIC: ESSAYS ON ITS HISTORY AND THEORY. Tr. by H. Campbell Creighton. Moscow: Progress Publishers, 1977.

844. Il'ichev, Leonid Fedorovich. FILOSOFIIA I NAUCHNYI PROGRESS: NEKOTORYE METODOL. PROBLEMY ESTESTVOZENANIIA I OBSHCHEST VOZNANIIA. Moscow: Nauka, 1977.

845. Il'ichev, Leonid Fedorovich, ed. MATERIALISTICHESKAIA DIALEKTIKA KAK OBSHCHAIA TEORIIA RAZVITIIA. 3 Vols. to date. Moscow: Nauka, 1982-.

846. Il'ichev, Leonid Fedorovich, et al, eds. FILOSOFSKII ENTSIKLOPEDICHESKII SLOVAR'. Moscow: Sovietskaia Entsiklopediia, 1983.

847. Karmin, Anatolii Solomonovich. POZANIE BESKONECHNOGO. Moscow: Mysl', 1981.

848. Kedrov, Bonifatii Mikhailovich. DIALEKTICHESKOE PROTIVORECHIE. Moscow: Politizdat, 1979.

849. Kedrov, Bonifatii Mikhailovich. ENGEL'S O RAZVITII KHIMII. 2d ed. Moscow: Nauka, 1979.

850. Kedrov, Bonifatii Mikhailovich. FILOSOFSKIE OSNOVANIIA NAUKI: MATERI-ALY K VIII VSESOIUZNOI KONFERENTSII "LOGIKA I METODOLOGIIA" NAUKI 26-28 SENTIABRIA 1982. Vilnius: In-t filosofii, sosiologii i prava an Litovskoi, 1982.

851. Kedrov, Bonifatii Mikhailovich. FRIEDRICH ENGELS UBER DIE DIALEKTIK DER NATURWISSENSCHAFT: TEXTE. Tr. of Fridrikh Engel's O DILEKTIKE ESTESTVOZNANIIA. Berlin: Dietz, 1979.

852. Kedrov, Bonifatii Mikhailovich. MARKSISTSKAIA KONTSEPTSIIA ISTORII ESTESTVOZNANIIA: XIX V. Moscow: Nauka, 1978.

853. Kharin, IUrii Andreevich. FUNDAMENTALS OF DIALECTICS. Tr. by Konstantin Kostrov. Moscow: Progress Publishers, 1981.

This work presents dialectical materialism as a philosophy of physical science and a guide to social action in opposition to idealistic and positivistic theories of knowledge and logic.

854. Kirchoff, Rolf and Teodor Ilich Oizerman, eds. 100 JAHRE "ANTI-DUHRING": MARXISMUS, WELTANSCHAUNG WISSENSCHAFT. Berlin: Akademie-Verlag, 1978.

855. Kolesnikov, Aleksandr Stepanovich, ed. NAUCHNO-TEKHNICHESKAIA REVO-LIUTSIIA I FILOSOFSKAIA NAUKA (Scientific-technological Revolution and Philosophical Science). Leningrad: Izd-vo Leningrad unta, 1977.

The Russian text is in Cyrillic script.

856. Kommunisticheskaia partiia Sovetskogo Soiuza skaia partiia. DOCUMENTS AND RESOLUTIONS. THE TWENTY-SIXTH CONGRESS OF THE COMMUNIST PARTY OF THE SOVIET UNION, FEBRUARY, 23-MARCH 3, 1981. Moscow: Novosti Press Agency, 1981.

857. Konkin, Mikhail Ivanovich. PROBLEMA FORMIROVANIIA I RAZVITIIA FILOSO-FISKIKH KATEGORII. Moscow: Vysshaia Shkola, 1980.

858. Konstantinov, Fedor Vasilevich, ed. FUNDAMENTALS OF MARXIST-LENINIST PHILOSOPHY. Tr. of OSNOVY MARKSISTKO-LENINSKOI FILOSOFII. 4th rev. ed. Moscow: Izd-vo Politicheskoi Literatury, 1978. Tr. by Robert Daglish. Moscow: Progress Publishers, 1982.

859. Konstantinov, Fedor Vasilevich and Vladimir Grigorevich Marakov, eds. MATERI-ALISTICHESKAIA DIALEKTIKA. Vol. 1, OBEKTIVNAIA DIALEKTIKA. Vol. 2, SUBEKTIVNAIA DIALEKTIKA. Vol. 3, DIALEKTIKA PRIRODY I ESTESTVOZ NANIIA. Vol. 4, DIALEKTIKA OBSHCHESTVENNENOGO RAZVITIIA. Vol. 5, KRITIKA IDEALISTICHESKIKH KONTSEPTSII DIALEKTIKI. Moscow: Mysl', 1981-1985.

860. Korshunov, Anatoli Mikhailovich. OTRAZHENIE, DEIATEL`NOST', POZNANIE. Moscow: Politizdat, 1979.

861. Kosolapov, Richard Ivanovich. SOTSIALIZM: K VOPROSAM TEORII. 2d ed. Moscow: Mysl', 1979.

862. Kozhanov, Nikolai Mikhailovich. NRAVSTVENNYE PRINTSIPY KOMMUNISTA. Moscow: Izd-vo Politicheskoi Literatury, 1979.

863. Kulikova, Irina Sergeevna and Avner IAkovlevich Zis', eds. MARXIST-LENINIST AESTHETICS AND THE ARTS. Tr. of MARKSISTSKO-LENINSKAIA ESTETIKA I KHUDOZHESTVENNO TVORCHESTVO. Moscow: Progress Publishers, 1979. Moscow: Progress Publishers, 1980.

864. Kumpf, Fritz and Zaid M. Orudzhev. DIALEKTICHESKAIA LOGIKA: OSNOVNYE PRINTSIPY I PROBLEMY. Moscow: Izd-vo Politcheskoi Literatury, 1979.

865. Kuzmin, Vsevolod Petrovich. PRINTSIP SISTEMNOSTI V TEORII I METODOLOGII K. MARKSA. 3d ed. Moscow: Izd-vo Politicheskoi Lit-ry, 1986.

866. Laptenok, Sergei Danilovich. AKTUAL'NYE VOPROSY METODIKI PREPODAVA-NIIA MARKSISTSKI-LENINSKOI ETIKI. Minsk: Izd-vo BGU im. V.I. Lenina, 1980.

867. Lebedev, Valerii Petrovich. BESKONECHNA LI VSELENNAIA? Minsk: Nauka i Tekhnika, 1978.

868. Letorski, Vladislav Aleksandrovich. SUB'EKT, OB'EKT, POZNANIE. Moscow: Nauka, 1980.

869. Loone, Eero Nikolaevich. SOUVREMENNAIA FILOSOFIIA ISTORII. Tallin: Eesti Raamat, 1980.

There is a summary in English as well as a bibliography on pages 279- 293.

870. Lorentson, V. and Boris Grigorevich Iudin. MARXIST DIALECTICS TODAY. 2d ed. Moscow: Social Sciences Today Editorial Board,, USSR Academy of Sciences, 1979.

871. Lorentson, V. and A. Shatalov, eds. PHILOSOPHY AND THE WORLD-VIEWS OF MODERN SCIENCES. Tr. of FILOSOFIIA I MIROVOSSRENCHESKIE PROBLEMY SOVREMENNYKH NAUK. Moscow: Social Sciences Today Editorial Board, USSR Academy of Sciences, 1978.

This volume is in English, French, German, and Spanish.

872. Lucid, Daniel Peri, ed. SOVIET SEMIOTICS: AN ANTHOLOGY. Baltimore: Johns Hopkins Univ. Press, 1977.

873. Marakhov, Vladimir Grigoroevich and Viktor D. Komararova, eds. FILOSOFIIA V PROTSESSES NAUCHNO-TECHNICHESKOI REVOLIUTSII (Philosophy in the Scientific-Technological Revolution). Leningrad: Izd-vo Leningradskogo Universiteta, 1976.

874. Mitin, Mark Borisovich, et al, eds. MARKSISTSKO-LENINSKAIA DIALEKTIKA V VOS'MI KNIGAKH. Vol. 1, MATERIALISTICHESKAIA DIALEKTIKA KAK NAUCHNAIA SISTEMA, Vol. 3, DIALEKTIKA PROTSESSA POZNANIIA, and Vol. 5, DIALEKTIKA ZHIVOI PRIRODY have been published to date. Moscow: Izd-vo Moskovskogo Universiteta, 1983-.

875. Nersesiants, Vladik Sumbatovich. POLITICAL THOUGHT OF ANCIENT GREECE. Tr. of POLITICHESKIE UCHENIIA DREVNE I GRETSII. Moscow: Nauka, 1979. Tr. by Vladimir Stankeevich. Moscow: Progress Publishers, 1986.

876. Novikov, Vasilii Vasilevich. ARTISTIC TRUTH AND DIALECTICS OF CREATIVE WORK. Tr. of: KHUDOZHESLVENNAIA PRAVDA I DIALEKTIKA TVORCHESTVA. Tr. by Evgeni Filippov. Moscow: Progress Publishers, 1981.

877. Oizerman, Teodor Ilich. DIALECTICAL MATERIALISM AND THE HISTORY OF PHILOSOPHY: ESSAYS ON THE HISTORY OF PHILOSOPHY. Tr. of DIALEKTICHESKII MATERIALIZM I ISTORIIA FILOSOFII. Moscow: Mysl', 1979. Tr. by Dmitri Beliavsky. Moscow: Progress Publishers, 1982.

878. Oizerman, Teodor Ilich. ISTORIKO-FILOSOFSKOE UCHENIE GEGELIA. Moscow: Izd-vo Znanie, 1982.

879. Oizerman, Teodor Ilich. DER `JUNGE' MARX IM IDEOLOGISCHEN KAMPF DER GEGENWART. Berlin: Akademie Verlag, 1976.

880. Oizerman, Teodor Ilich. KRITIKA BURZHUAZNOI KONTSEPTSII SMERTI FILOSOFII. Novoe v Zhizni, Nauke, Tekhnike: Seriia Filosfiia, Vol. 4. Moscow: Znanie, 1980.

881. Oizerman, Teodor Ilich. THE MAKING OF THE MARXIST PHILOSOPHY. Tr. of FORMIROVANIE FILOSOFII MARKSIZMA. Moscow: Izd-vo sotsial'no ekon lit-ry, 1962. Tr. into English by Yuri Sdobnikov. Moscow: Progress Publishers, 1981.

This work is organized into Part I: From Idealism and Revolutionary Democracy to Dialectical Materialism and Scientific Communism; and Part II: The Foundations of Dialectical and Historical Materialism.

882. Oizerman, Teodor Ilich. DIE PHILOSOPHISCHEN GRUNDRICHTUNGEN. Tr. of GLAVNNYE FILOSOFSKIE NAPRAVLENIIA: TEORETICHESKII ANALIZ ISTORIKO- FILOSOFSKOGO PROTSESSA. Moscow: Mysl', 1971. Tr. by Helmut Wolle. Berlin: Dietz, 1976.

883. Oizerman, Teodor Ilich. PROBLEMY ISTORIKO-FILOSOFSKOI NAUKI. 2d ed. Moscow: Mysl', 1982.

884. Oizerman, Teodor Ilich, et al. ISTORIAIA DIALEKTIKI: NEMETSKAIA KLAS-SICHESKAIA FILOSOFIIA. Moscow: Mysl', 1978.

885. Oizerman, Teodor Ilich, et al. KRATKII OCHERK ISTORII FILOSOFII. Moscow: Mysl', 1981.

886. Oizerman, Teodor Ilich and Aleksei Sergeevich Bogomolov. PRINCIPLES OF THE THEORY OF THE HISTORICAL PROCESS IN PHILOSOPHY. Tr. of OSNOVY TEORII ISTORIKO-FILOSOFSKOGO PROTSESSA. Moscow: Izd-vo Nauka, 1983. Tr. by H. Campbell Greighton. Moscow: Progress Publishers, 1986.

887. Omelianovskyi, Mykhailo Erazmovych. DIALECTICS IN MODERN PHYSICS. Tr. of DIALEKTIKA V SOVREMENNOI FIZIKI. Moscow: Nauka, 1973. Tr. by H. C. Creighton. Moscow: Progress Publishers, 1979.

888. Omelianovskyi, Mykhailo Erazmovych, ed. LENIN AND MODERN NATURAL SCIENCE. Tr. by Sergei Syrovatkin. Moscow: Progress Publishers, 1978.

889. Platonov, Georgii Vasilevich, et al. MARKSISTKO-LENINSKAIA FILOSOFIIA KAK SISTEMA: PREDMET, STRUKTURA I FUNDKTSII. Moscow: Izd-vo Moskovs-kogo Universiteta, 1981.

890. Scanlan, James Patrick. MARXISM IN THE USSR: A CRITICAL SURVEY OF CURRENT SOVIET THOUGHT. Ithaca and London: Cornell Univ. Press, 1985.

There is a bibliography on pages 336-354.

891. Shakhnazarov, Georgi Khosroevich. FUTUROLOGY FIASCO: A CRITICAL STUDY OF NON-MARXIST CONCEPTS OF HOW SOCIETY DEVELOPS. Tr. of FIASKO FUTUROLOGII: KRITISCHESKII OCHUK NEMARKSISTSKIKH TEORII OB-SHCHESLVENNOGO RAZVILIIA. Moscow: Politizsat, 1979. Tr. by Vic Schneierson. Moscow: Progress Publishers, 1982.

892. Sheptulin, Aleksandr Petrovich. MARXIST-LENINIST PHILOSOPHY. Tr. by S. Ponomarenko and A. Timofeyev. Moscow: Progress Publishers, 1978.

893. Sheptulin, Aleksandr Petrovich, ed. MATERIALISTICHESKAIA DIALEKTIKA KAK NAUCHNAIA SISTEMA. Vol. 1: MARKSISTSKO-LENINSKAIA DIALEKTIKA V VOS'MI TOMAKH. Ed. by Mark Borisovich Mitin, et al. Moscow: Izd-vo Mosko-voskogo, 1983.

894. Shinkaruk, Vladimir Illarionovich, et al, eds. DIALEKTICHESKII I ISTORICHESKII MATERIALISM: FILOSOFSKAIA ISNOVA KOMMUNISTICHESKOGO MIROVOZ ZRENIIA. Kiev: Naukova Dumka, 1977.

895. Shukman, Ann. LITERATURE AND SEMIOTICS: A STUDY OF THE WRITINGS OF YU. M. LOTMAN. Amsterdam and New York: North Holland Publishing, 1977.

896. Solopov, Evgennii Frolovich. VEDENIE V DIALEKTICHESKUIU LOGIKU. Leningrad: Nauka, 1979.

897. Soviet Communist Party. DOCUMENTS AND RESOLUTIONS: THE 26TH CONGRESS OF THE COMMUNIST PARTY OF THE SOVIET UNION, MOSCOW, FEBRUARY 23-MARCH 3, 1981. Moscow: Novosti Press Agency Pub. House, 1981.

898. Suvorow, Lev Nikolaevich. MARXIST PHILOSOPHY AT THE LENINIST STAGE. Moscow: Progress Publishers, 1982.

899. Swiderski, Edward M. THE PHILOSOPHICAL FOUNDATIONS OF SOVIET AESTHETICS: THEORIES AND CONTROVERSIES IN THE POST-WAR YEARS. Dordrecht and Boston: Reidel, 1979.

900. Syrovatkin, Sergei, tr. PHILOSOPHY IN THE USSR: PROBLEMS OF HISTORICAL MATERIALISM. Moscow: Progress Publishers, 1981.

901. Titarenko, Aleksandr Ivanovich, ed. MARKSISTSKAIA ETIKA. Moscow: Izd-vo Poli ticheskoi Literatury, 1976.

902. Tselishchev, Vitali Valentinovich, et al, eds. LOGIKA I ONTOLOGIIA. Moscow: Nauka, 1978.

903. Tucker, Robert C., ed. THE MARX-ENGELS READER. 2d ed. New York: W. W. Norton, 1978.

904. USSR Academy of Science. Members of the Institute of Linguistics. ESSAYS ON LINGUISTICS: LANGUAGE SYSTEMS AND STRUCTURES. Tr. from the Russian by Christopher English. Moscow: Progress Publishers, 1980.

905. Vartanov, Rober Gareginovich. SOTSIALIZM: STUPENI RAZVITIIA. Erevan: Izd-vo Aiastan, 1982.

906. Viakkerev, Fedor Fedorovich, et al, eds. EDINSTVO DIALELKTICHESKOGO I ISTORICHESKOGO MATERIALIZMA. Leningrad: Izd-vo Leningradskogo Universiteta, 1978.

907. Voishvillo, Evgenii Kazimirovich, et al. DIALEKTIKA NAUCHNOGO POZNANIIA: OCHERK DIALEKTICHESKOI LOGIKI. Moscow: Nauka, 1978.

908. Voloshinov, Valentin Nikolaevic. MARXISM AND THE PHILOSOPHY OF LANGUAGE. Tr. of MARKSIZM I FILOSOFIIA IAZYKA: OSNOVNYE PROBLEMY SOTSIOLOGICHESKOGO METODA V NAUKAOI AZYKE. The Hague: Mouton, 1972. Tr. by Ladislav Matejka and I. R. Titunik. Cambridge: Harvard Univ. Press, 1986.

909. Zinoviev, Aleksandr. LOGICAL PHYSICS. Ed. by Robert Sonne Cohen. Tr. of LOGOCHESKAIA FIZIKA. Moscow: Nauka, 1972. Tr. by O. A. Germogenova. Boston Studies in the Philosophy of Science, Vol. 74. Dordrecht and Boston: Reidel, 1983.

910. Zis', Avner IAkovlevich. FOUNDATIONS OF MARXIST AESTHETICS. Tr. by Katharine Judelson. Moscow: Progress Publishers, 1977.

YUGOSLAVIA

911. Damnjanovic, Milan, et al. SVIJET UMJETNOSTI: MARKSISTICKE INTERPRE-TACIJE. Zagreb: Skolska Kvjiga, 1976.

912. Kosik, Karel. DIJALEKTIKA KRIZE. Belgrade: NIP Mladost, 1983.

913. Markovic, Mihailo. DIALECTICAL THEORY OF MEANING. Tr. by David Rouge and Joan Coddington from the Serbo-Croatian. Boston Studies in the Philosophy of Science, Vol. 81. Dordrecht and Boston: Reidel, 1984.

This is a new edition based on the work originally published in 1971 by Nolit in Belgrade under the title: DIJALEKTICKA TEORIJA ZNACENJA.

914. Markovic, Mihailo. FILOZOFSKI OSNOVI NAUKI. Belgrade: Srpska Akademija Nauka i Umetnosti, 1981.

This work includes a summary in English.

915. Markovic, Mihailo. MARX CONTEMPORENEO. Tr. of CONTEMPORARY MARX: ESSAYS ON HUMANIST COMMUNISM. Nottingham: Spokesman Books, 1974. Mexico: Fondo de Cultura Economica, 1978.

916. Markovic, Mihailo and Gajo Petrovic, eds. PRAXIS: YUGOSLAV ESSAYS IN THE PHILOSOPHY AND METHODOLOGY OF THE SOCIAL SCIENCES. Tr. by Joan Coddington. Dordrecht and Boston: Reidel, 1979.

917. Stojanovic, Svetozar. IN SEARCH OF DEMOCRACY IN SOCIALISM: HISTORY AND PARTY CONSCIOUSNESS. Tr. of GESCHICHTE UND PARTEIBEWUSST-SEIN: AUF DER SUCHE NACH DEMOKRATIE IM SOZIALISMUS. Munich: Hanser, 1978. Tr. by Gerson S. Sher. Buffalo: Prometheus Books, 1981.

The original edition, ISTORIJA I PARTIJSKA SVEST, was translated from Serbo-Croation by Elizabeth Prager.

WESTERN EUROPE, AUSTRALIA and NEW ZEALAND

WESTERN EUROPE, AUSTRALIA and NEW ZEALAND

AUSTRALIA

918. Anderson, Janet, et al. ART AND REALITY: JOHN ANDERSON ON LITERA-
TURE AND AESTHETICS. Sydney: Hale and Iremonger, 1982.

919. Armstrong, David Malet. A COMBINATORIAL THEORY OF POSSIBILITY.
Cambridge and New York: Cambridge Univ. Press, 1989.

920. Armstrong, David Malet. THE NATURE OF MIND: AND OTHER ESSAYS. St.
Lucia Queensland, Australia: Univ. of Queensland Press; Ithaca: Cornell
Univ. Press, 1980.

921. Armstrong, David Malet. UNIVERSALS AND SCIENTIFIC REALISM. Vol. 1,
NOMINALISM AND REALISM. Vol. 2, A THEORY OF UNIVERSALS. Cambridge
and New York: Cambridge Univ. Press, 1978.

922. Armstrong, David Malet. WHAT IS A LAW OF NATURE? Cambridge and New
York: Cambridge Univ. Press, 1984,1985.

923. Armstrong, David Malet and Norman Malcolm. CONCIOUSNESS AND CAUSAL-
ITY: A DEBATE ON THE NATURE OF MIND. New York: Blackwell, 1984.

924. Attridge, Derek, et al. POST-STRUCTURALISM AND THE QUESTION OF HIS-
TORY. Cambridge and New York: Cambridge Univ. Press, 1987.

925. Baier, Kurt, et al. JUST BUSINESS: NEW INTRODUCTORY ESSAYS IN BUSI-
NESS ETHICS. Ed. by Tom Regan. Philadelphia: Temple Univ. Press, 1983.

926. Baker, Allan James. ANDERSON'S SOCIAL PHILOSOPHY. London: Angus and
Robertson, 1979.

927. Baker, Allan James. AUSTRALIAN REALISM: THE SYSTEMATIC PHILOSO-
PHY OF JOHN ANDERSON. Cambridge: Cambridge Univ. Press, 1986.

928. Benn, Stanley I. POLITICAL PARTICIPATION: A DISCUSSION OF POLITICAL RATIONALITY. Canberra, Australia and Norwalk, CT: Australian National Univ. Press, 1978.

This book contains essays by Richard Wollheim and others on a discussion initiated by S.I. Benn.

929. Benn, Stanley I. A THEORY OF FREEDOM. Cambridge and New York: Cambridge Univ. Press, 1988.

This work presents a theory of rational action that analyzes the ways which value conflicts can be rationally resolved, the objectivity of value, the concept of moral personality, the ideal of autonomy, and the rights to freedom, welfare, and privacy.

930. Benn, Stanley I. and Gerald F. Gaus. PUBLIC AND PRIVATE IN SOCIAL LIFE. London: Croom Helm; New York: St. Martin's Press, 1983.

931. Benn, Stanley I. and G. W. Mortimore. RATIONALITY AND THE SOCIAL SCIENCES: CONTRIBUTIONS TO THE PHILOSOPHY AND METHODOLOGY OF THE SOCIAL SCIENCES. London: Routledge and Kegan Paul, 1976.

932. Boucher, David. TEXTS IN CONTEXT: REVISIONIST METHODS FOR STUDYING THE HISTORY OF IDEAS. Dordrecht and Boston: Nijhoff, 1985.

933. Campbell, Richard. FROM BELIEF TO UNDERSTANDING: A STUDY OF ANSELM'S PROSLOGION ARGUMENT ON THE EXISTENCE OF GOD. Canberra: Faculty of Arts, Australian National Univ. 1976.

934. Chalmers, Alan Francis. WHAT IS THIS THING CALLED SCIENCE?: AN ASSESSMENT OF THE NATURE AND STATUS OF SCIENCE AND ITS METHODS. 2d ed. St. Lucia, Queensland: Queensland Univ. Press, 1982,1976.

935. Colman, John. JOHN LOCKE'S MORAL PHILOSOPHY. Edinburgh: Edinburgh Univ. Press, 1983.

936. Cristaudo, Wayne. THE METAPHYSICS OF SCIENCE AND FREEDOM: FROM DESCARTES TO KANT TO HEGEL. Aldershot, Hants, England: Avebury; Brookfield, VT: Gower, 1991.

937. Crocker, Lawrence. POSITIVE LIBERTY: AN ESSAY IN NORMATIVE POLITICAL PHILOSOPHY. The Hague and Boston: Nijhoff, 1980.

938. Delahunty, R. J. SPINOZA. The Arguments of the Philosophers. London and Boston: Routledge and Kegan Paul, 1985.

939. Detmold, Michael J. THE UNITY OF LAW AND MORALITY: A REFUTATION OF LEGAL POSITIVISM. International Library of Philosophy. London and Boston: Routledge and Kegan Paul, 1984.

940. Devitt, Michael. DESIGNATION. New York: Columbia Univ. Press, 1981.

941. Devitt, Michael. REALISM AND TRUTH. Princeton: Princeton Univ. Press, 1984.

An extensive bibliography is included.

942. Eddy, William Henry Charles. UNDERSTANDING MARXISM: AN APPROACH THROUGH DIALOGUE. Oxford: Blackwell; Totowa, NJ: Rowman and Littlefield, 1979.

943. Elliot, Robert and Arran Gare. ENVIRONMENTAL PHILOSOPHY: A COLLECTION OF READINGS. St. Lucia, Queensland and New York: Univ. of Queensland Press; Milton Keynes: Open Univ. Press, 1983.

An international group of contributors examines traditional ideas, Western and non-Western. The book is divided into three parts. Part I, Environmental Policy and Human Welfare; Part II, Toward a New Environmental Ethic; and Part III, Attitudes to the Natural Environment. The work contains contributions by Robert Goodin, Gregory S. Kavka, Virginia Warren, C. A. Hooker, Janna L. Thompson, Mary Anne Warren, Holmes Rolston III, Mary Midgley, Stephen R. L. Clark, Robin Attfield, J. Baird, and Richard Routley.

944. Ewin, Robert E. LIBERTY, COMMUNITY AND JUSTICE. Totowa, NJ: Rowman and Littlefield, 1987.

945. Fang, Wan-Chuan. A STUDY OF DAVIDSONIAN EVENTS. Nanking: Institute of American Culture, 1985.

946. Goddard, Leonard and Brenda Judge. THE METAPHYSICS OF WITTGENSTEIN'S TRACTATUS. Melbourne: The Australasian Association of Philosophy, 1982.

947. Goldman, Alvin I. EPISTEMOLOGY AND COGNITION. Cambridge: Harvard Univ. Press, 1986.

948. Goldman, Alvin I. and Jaegwon Kim. VALUES AND MORALS: ESSAYS IN HONOR OF WILLIAM FRANKENA, CHARLES STEVENSON, AND RICHARD BRANDT. Dordrecht and Boston: Reidel, 1978.

The volume includes bibliographies of Frankena, pages 317-321, of Stevenson, pages 323-324, and of Brandt, pages 325-327.

949. Grave, Selwyn A. CONSCIENCE IN NEWMAN'S THOUGHT. Oxford and New York: Clarendon Press, 1982.

950. Grave, Selwyn A. HISTORY OF AUSTRALIAN PHILOSOPHY. St. Lucia, Queensland: Univ. of Queensland Press, 1984.

951. Grave, Selwyn A. PHILOSOPHY IN AUSTRALIA SINCE 1958. Sydney: Sydney Univ. Press for the Australian Academy of the Humanities, 1976.

952. Harries, Owen. LIBERTY AND POLITICS: STUDIES IN SOCIAL THEORY. Rushcutters Bay, NSW: Pergaman Press, 1976.

This book is in memory of William Henry Charles Eddy and contains essays by David Armstrong, John Passmore, F. Knopfelmacher and others.

953. Harris, Kevin. EDUCATION AND KNOWLEDGE: THE STRUCTURED MISREPRESENTATION OF REALITY. London and Boston: Routledge and Kegan Paul, 1979.

954. Harris, Kevin. TEACHERS AND CLASSES: A MARXIST ANALYSIS. London and Boston: Routledge and Kegan Paul, 1982.

955. Hooker, Clifford Alan. A REALISTIC THEORY OF SCIENCE. Albany: State Univ. of New York Press, 1987.

956. Hooker, Clifford Alan, et al. FOUNDATIONS AND APPLICATION OF DECISION THEORY. Vol. 1, THEORETICAL FOUNDATIONS. Vol. 2, EPISTEMIC AND SOCIAL APPLICATIONS. Ed. by James Leach and Edward Francis McClennen. Dordrecht and Boston: Reidel, 1978.

These are papers resulting from a workshop held at the University of Western Ontario, Canada in the spring of 1975.

957. Hughes, George Edward and Max J. Cresswell. EINFUHRUNG IN DIE MODALLO-GIK. Ed. by Florian Coulmas, et al. Berlin and New York: De Gruyter, 1978.

958. Hume, L. J. BENTHAM AND BUREAUCRACY. Cambridge and New York: Cambridge Univ. Press, 1981.

959. Jackson, Frank. PERCEPTION: A REPRESENTATIVE THEORY. Cambridge and New York: Cambridge Univ. Press, 1977. .

960. Kamenka, Eugene and Martin Krugier. BUREAUCRACY: THE CAREER OF A CONCEPT. New York: St. Martin's Press, 1979.

961. Kamenka, Eugene and Francis Barrymore Smith. THE INTELLECTUALS AND REVOLUTIONS: SOCIALISM AND THE EXPERIENCE OF 1848. London: E. Arnold, 1979.

962. Kleinig, John. PATERNALISM. Philosophy and Society Series. Manchester: Manchester Univ. Press, 1983.

There is a bibliography on pages 218-235.

963. Kuhse, Helga and Peter Singer. SHOULD THE BABY LIVE?: THE PROBLEMS OF HANDICAPPED INFANTS. Oxford and New York: Oxford Univ. Press, 1985.

964. Langford, Peter E. MODERN PHILOSOPHIES OF HUMAN NATURE: THEIR EMERGENCE FROM CHRISTIAN THOUGHT. Dordrecht and Boston: Nijhoff, 1986.

965. Lloyd, Genevieve. THE MAN OF REASON: "MALE" AND "FEMALE" IN WESTERN PHILOSOPHY. Minneapolis: Univ. of Minnesota Press, 1984.

966. Mackie, John Leslie. HUME'S MORAL THEORY. London and Boston: Routledge & Kegan Paul, 1980.

967. Mackie, John Leslie. THE MIRACLE OF THEISM: ARGUMENT FOR AND AGAINST THE EXISTENCE OF GOD. Oxford: Clarendon Press; New York: Oxford Univ. Press, 1982.

968. Mackie, John Leslie. PROBLEMS FROM LOCKE. Oxford: Clarendon Press, 1976.

969. Mackie, John Leslie. SELECTED PAPERS. Vol. 1, LOGIC AND KNOWLEDGE. Vol. 2, PERSONS AND VALUES. Ed. by Joan Mackie and Penelope Mackie. Oxford: Clarendon Press; New York: Oxford Univ. Press, 1985-.

970. Mannison, Don S., et al. ENVIRONMENTAL PHILOSOPHY. Australian National Monograph Series. Canberra: RSSS (Research School of Social Sciences), Australian National Univ., 1980.

971. McCloskey, Henry John. ECOLOGICAL ETHICS AND POLITICS. Totowa, NJ: Rowman and Littlefield, 1983.

972. Nerlich, Graham. THE SHAPE OF SPACE. Cambridge and New York: Cambridge Univ. Press, 1976.

The author argues for an absolutist conception of space and illustrates the thesis that "the senses do not bind the intellect."

973. Oakley, Allen. THE MAKING OF MARXIST CRITICAL THEORY: A BIBLIO-GRAPHIC ANALYSIS. London and Boston: Routledge and Kegan Paul, 1983.

This is an analytical guide to Marx's writings on critical theory.

974. Oldroyd, David Roger. DARWINIAN IMPACTS: AN INTRODUCTION TO THE DARWINIAN REVOLUTION. Totowa, NJ: Humanities Press, 1980.

The volume contains a bibliography on pages 369-379.

975. Papineau, David. THEORY AND MEANING. Oxford: Clarendon Press; New York: Oxford Univ. Press, 1979.

This volume is based on the author's thesis and its discussion of theory-choice in science.

976. Passmore, John Arthur. LOCKE AND THE ETHICS OF BELIEF. London: Oxford Univ. Press, 1980.

The text is from the Proceedings of the British Academy, London, Vol. LXIV, 1978.

977. Passmore, John Arthur. THE PHILOSOPHY OF TEACHING. London: Duckworth, 1980.

978. Passmore, John Arthur. RECENT PHILOSOPHERS: A SUPPLEMENT TO A HUNDRED YEARS OF PHILOSOPHY. LaSalle, IL: Open Court, 1985c1984.

979. Passmore, John Arthur. SERIOUS ART. Peru, IL: Open Court, 1991.

980. Pateman, Carole. THE PROBLEM OF POLITICAL OBLIGATION: A CRITICAL ANALYSIS OF LIBERAL THEORY. Chichester and New York: Wiley, 1979.

This work was reprinted by the University of California Press in 1986.

981. Pateman, Carole and Elizabeth Gross. FEMINIST CHALLENGES: SOCIAL AND POLITICAL THEORY. Boston: Northeastern Univ. Press, 1986.

982. Petit, Philip. JUDGING JUSTICE: AN INTRODUCTION TO CONTEMPORARY POLITICAL PHILOSOPHY. London and Boston: Routledge and Kegan Paul, 1982.

This is a discussion of the role and method of political philosophy, including material on utilitarianism and the philosophies of Robert Nozick and John Rawls.

983. Phillips, Dewi Zephaniah. EDUCATION AND INQUIRY/JOHN ANDERSON. Totowa, NJ: Barnes and Noble, 1980.

This book contains Anderson's articles and lecture notes on education, as well as essays by Eugene Kamenka, J. L. Mackie and P. H. Partridge.

984. Redner, Harry. THE ENDS OF PHILOSOPHY: AN ESSAY IN THE SOCIOLOGY OF PHILOSOPHY AND RATIONALITY. Totowa, NJ: Rowman and Allenheld, 1986.

985. Rose, Margaret A. MARX'S LOST AESTHETIC: KARL MARX AND THE VISUAL ARTS. Cambridge and New York: Cambridge Univ. Press, 1984.

This study looks at Marx's views from a history of art perspective and locates those views in the context of Marx's own time.

986. Routley, Richard. WAR AND PEACE: ON THE ETHICS OF LARGE-SCALE NUCLEAR WAR AND NUCLEAR DETERRENCE AND THE POLITICAL FALL-OUT. Canberra: Australian National University, 1984.

987. Routley, Richard, et al. RELEVANT LOGICS AND THEIR RIVALS. Part 1: THE BASIC PHILOSOPHICAL AND SEMANTICAL THEORY. Atascadero, CA: Ridgeview, 1982-.

Volume one contains a lengthy bibliography on pages 435-451.

988. Singer, Peter. A COMPANION TO ETHICS. Oxford and Cambridge, MA: Blackwell Reference, 1991.

In nearly fifty essays, contemporary philosophers survey the entire field of ethics. This reference work is extensively indexed.

989. Singer, Peter. IN DEFENSE OF ANIMALS. New York: Blackwell, 1985.

990. Singer, Peter. PRACTICAL ETHICS. Cambridge and New York: Cambridge Univ. Press, 1980,1979.

991. Singer, Peter and Deane Wells. MAKING BABIES: THE NEW SCIENCE AND ETHICS OF CONCEPTION. New York: Charles Scribner's Sons, 1985.

This is a revised edition of THE REPRODUCTION REVOLUTION. 1st ed. Oxford and New York: Oxford Univ. Press, 1984.

992. Smart, John Jamieson Carswell. ESSAYS METAPHYSICAL AND MORAL: SELECTED PHILOSOPHICAL PAPERS. Oxford and New York: B. Blackwell, 1987.

993. Smart, John Jamieson Carswell. OUR PLACE IN THE UNIVERSE: A METAPHYSICAL DISCUSSION. Oxford and New York: Blackwell, 1989.

994. Snare, Francis. MORALS, MOTIVATION, AND CONVENTION: HUME'S INFLUENTIAL DOCTRINES. Cambridge and New York: Cambridge Univ. press, 1991.

995. Stove, David Charles. THE PLATO CULT AND OTHER PHILOSOPHICAL FOLLIES. Oxford and Cambridge: B. Blackwell, 1991.

996. Stove, David Charles. THE RATIONALITY OF INDUCTION. Oxford and New York: Oxford Univ. Press, 1986.

997. Suchting, Wallis Arthur. MARX AND PHILOSOPHY: THREE STUDIES. New York: New York Univ. Press; London: Macmillan, 1986.

998. Ten, Chin Liew. CRIME, GUILT, AND PUNISHMENT: A PHILOSOPHICAL INTRODUCTION. Oxford: Clarendon Press; New York: Oxford Univ. Press, 1987.

999. Ten, Chin Liew. MILL ON LIBERTY. New York: Oxford Univ. Press; Oxford: Clarendon Press, 1980.

This study argues for the consistency and coherence of Mill's defense of individual liberty. But the author maintains that there are substantial non-utilitarian elements in his arguments.

1000. Thom, Paul. THE SYLLOGISM. ANALYTICA: INVESTIGATIONS IN LOGIC, ONTOLOGY, AND THE PHILOSOPHY OF LANGUAGE. Munich: Philosophia, 1981.

1001. Tucker, David F. B. LAW, LIBERALISM AND FREE SPEECH. Totowa, NJ: Rowman and Allenheld, 1985.

1002. Tucker, David F. B. MARXISM AND INDIVIDUALISM. New York: St. Martin's Press; Oxford: Blackwell, 1986.

1003. Walters, William A. W. and Peter Singer. TEST-TUBE BABIES: A GUIDE TO MORAL QUESTIONS, PRESENT TECHNIQUES AND FUTURE POSSIBILITIES. Melbourne and New York: Oxford Univ. Press, 1984.

1004. Young, Robert. PERSONAL AUTONOMY: BEYOND NEGATIVE AND POSITIVE LIBERTY. London: Croom Helm; New York: St. Martin`s Press, 1986.

AUSTRIA

1005. Coreth, Emerich, et al. CHRISTLICHE PHILOSOPHIE IM KATHOLISCHEN DENKEN DES 19. UND 20. JAHRHUNDERTS. Graz: Styria, 1987-.

1006. Ehrenfels, Christian von. PHILOSOPHICAL SCHRIFTEN IN VIER BANDEN. Vol. 1, WERTTHEORIE; Vol. 2, ASTHETIK; Vol. 3, PSYCHOLOGIE, ETHIK, ERKENNTNISTHEORIE; Vol. 4, METAPHYSIK. Munich: Philosophie Verlag, 1982-.

1007. Feigl, Herbert. INQUIRIES AND PROVOCATIONS: SELECTED WRITINGS, 1929-1974. Ed. by Robert Sonne Cohen. Vienna Circle Collection, Vol. 14. Dordrecht and Boston: Reidel, 1980.

1008. Gabriel, Leo. DIE WAHRHEIT DES GANZEN. Ed. by Helmut Karl Kohlenberger. Vienna, Freiburg and Basel: Herder, 1976.

The volume includes a tribute to Leo Gabriel in French and a bibliography of his works on pages 233-237.

1009. Gabriel, Leo. WAHRHEIT UND WIRKLICHKEIT: FESTGABE FUR LEO GABRIEL ZUM 80 GEBURTSTAG. Ed. by Peter Kampits, et al. Berlin: Duncker and Humblot, 1983.

1010. Gadol, Eugene T. RATIONALITY AND SCIENCE: A MEMORIAL VOLUME FOR MORITZ SCHLICK IN CELEBRATION OF THE CENTENNIAL OF HIS BIRTH. Vienna and New York: Springer Verlag, 1982.

1011. Gombocz, Wolfgang L., et al. INTERNATIONAL BIBLIOGRAPHY OF AUSTRIAN PHILOSOPHY=INTERNATIONALE BIBLIOGRAPHIE ZUR OSTERREICHISCHEN PHILOSOPHIE. Amsterdam: Rodopi, 1986-.

While this bibliography is mainly in German, some information is also in English.

1012. Hahn, Hans. EMPIRICISM, LOGIC, AND MATHEMATICS: PHILOSOPHICAL PAPERS. Ed. by Brian McGuinness. Vienna Circle Collection, Vol. 13. Dordrecht and Boston: Reidel, 1980.

This volume includes an introduction by Karl Menger.

1013. Haller, Rudolf. SCIENCE AND ETHICS. Grazer Philosophische Studien. Amsterdam: Rodopi, 1981.

This volume continues the Dubrovnic studies in science and ethics published in RATIONALITY IN SCIENCE: STUDIES IN THE FOUNDATIONS OF SCIENCE AND

ETHICS, Reidel, 1980. Contributing philosophers include Mikhailo Markovic, Ernan McMullin, Patrick Suppes, Rudolf Haller, Ryszard Wojcicki, Gerald Dworkin, Harald Ofstad, Ivan Supek, Michael Dummett, and others.

1014. Haller, Rudolf. SPRACHE UND ERKENNTNIS ALS SOZIALE TATSACHE: BEITRAGE DES WITTGENSTEIN-SYMPOSIUMS VON ROM 1979. Vienna: Holder-Pichler-Temsky, 1981.

1015. Haller, Rudolf. STUDIEN ZUR OSTERREICHISCHEN PHILOSOPHIE: VARIA-TIONEN UBER EIN THEMA. Amsterdam: Rodopi, 1979.

1016. Hayek, Friedrich August von. NEW STUDIES IN PHILOSOPHY, POLITICS, ECONOMICS, AND THE HISTORY OF IDEAS. Chicago: Univ. of Chicago Press, 1978.

1017. Heintel, Erich. GRUNDRISS DER DIALEKTIK: EIN BEITRAG ZU IHRER FUNDAMENTALPHILSOPHISCHEN BEDEUTUNG. Vol. 1, ZWISCHEN WIS-SENSCHAFTSTHEORIE UND THEOLOGIE; Vol.2, ZUM LOGOS DER DIALEKTIK UND ZU SEINER LOGIK. Darmstadt: Wissenschaftliche Buchgesellschaft, 1984.

1018. Heintel, Erich and Susanne Heine. GOTT OHNE EIGENSCHAFTEN? Vienna: Evangelischer Pressverband, 1983.

1019. Henrich, Dieter. IDENTITAT UND OBJEKTIVITAT: E. UNTERS. UBER KANTS TRANZENDENTALE DEDUKTION. Heidelberg: C. Winter, 1976.

1020. Henrich, Dieter. SELBSTVERHALTNISSE: GEDANKEN UND AUSLEGUN-GEN ZU DEN GRUNDLAGEN DER KLASSICHEN DEUTSCHEN PHILOSOPHIE. Stuttgart: Reclam, 1982.

1021. Henrich, Dieter. STUTTGARTER HEGEL-KONGRESS 1975: IST SYSTEMA-TISCHE PHILOSOPHIE MOGLICH? Bonn: Bouvier, 1977.

This congress was put on by the Internationnalen Hegel-Vereinigung in cooperation with the Heidelberger Akademie der Wissenschaften der Schelling-Kommision der Bayeris-chen Akademie der Wissenschaftern and the city of Stuttgart.

1022. Henrich, Dieter and Wolfgang Iser. THEORIEN DER KUNST. Frankfurt am Main: Suhrkamp, 1982.

1023. Herms, Eilert and Joachim Ringleben. VERGESSENE THEOLOGEN DES 19. UND FRUHEN 20. JAHRHUNDERTS: STUDIEN ZUR THEOLOGIEGESCHICHTE. Gottingen: Vandenhoeck & Ruprecht, 1984.

This work includes essays by Johann Christoph Wedeke, Gunter Meckenstock, Manfred Marquardt, Michael Bromse, Bernd Jaeger, Ulrich Kopf, and the editors.

1024. International Wittgenstein Symposium. PROCEEDINGS. 2nd, WITTGENSTEIN AND HIS IMPACT ON CONTEMPORARY THOUGHT edited by Elisabeth Leinfellner et al, 1978. 3rd, WITTGENSTEIN, THE VIENNA CIRCLE AND CRITICAL RATION-ALISM edited by Hal Berghel et al, 1979. 4th, LANGUAGE, LOGIC AND PHILOSO-PHY edited by Rudolf Haller and Wolfgang Grassl, 1980. 5th, ETHICS: FOUNDA-TIONS, PROBLEMS, AND APPLICATIONS. 7th, EPISTEMOLOGY AND THE PHILOSOPHY OF SCIENCE edited by Paul Weingartner and Johannes Cermak, 1983. 8th, Pt. 1, AESTHETICS edited by Rudolf Haller, and Pt. 2, PHILOSOPHY OF RELI-GION edited by Wolfgang L. Gombocz, 1984. 9th, PHILOSOPHY OF MIND, PHILOS-OPHY OF PSYCHOLOGY edited by Roderick M. Chisholm et al., 1985. 10th, THE TASKS OF CONTEMPORARY PHILOSOPHY edited by Werner Leinfellner and Franz

M. Wuketits, 1987. 11th, LOGIC, PHILOSOPHY OF SCIENCE AND EPISTEMOLO-GY. 12th, LAW, POLITICS, SOCIETY edited by Ota Weinberger, Peter Koller and Alfred Schramm, 1988. Vienna: Holder-Pichler-Tempsky, 1977-.

The texts are written in German and English.

1025. Janik, Allan. ESSAYS ON WITTGENSTEIN AND WEININGER. Amsterdam: Rodopi, 1985.

1026. Levinson, Paul. IN PURSUIT OF TRUTH: ESSAYS IN HONOUR OF KARL POPPER`S 80TH BIRTHDAY. Atlantic Highlands, NJ: Humanities Press, 1982.

Isaac Asimov, Helmut Schmidt, Sir E. H. Gombrich and Sir John Eccles have written essays exploring and explaining Popper's approaches to science and social science. His "three worlds" philosophy is examined, extending its application to education, literary criticism and technology. The final section discusses Popper himself and the prospects of his approach. There is a bibliography on pages 297-316.

1027. Luckardt, C. Grant. WITTGENSTEIN, SOURCES AND PERSPECTIVES. Ithaca: Cornell Univ. Press; Hassocks: Harvester Press, 1979.

1028. Musil, Robert. GESAMMELTE WERKE. Vol. 1, DER MANN OHNE EI-GENSCHAFTEN. Vol. 2, PROSA UND STUCKE. KLEINE PROSA. APHORISMEN. AUTOBIOGRAPHISCHES. ESSAYS UND REDEN. KRITIK. Ed. by Adolf Frise. Reinbek bei Hamburg: Rowohlt, 1978.

1029. Nyiri, Janos Kristof. AUSTRIAN PHILOSOPHY: STUDIES AND TEXTS. Munich: Philosophia Verlag, 1981.

This volume includes studies by Lee Congdon, Allan Janik, William M. Johnston, Rudolf Haller, Ferruccio Rossi-Landi, Josef Eotvos and Robert Musil.

1030. Nyiri, Janos Kristof. GEFUHL UND GEFUGE: STUDIEN ZUM ENTSTEHEN DER PHILOSOPHIE WITTGENSTEINS. Amsterdam: Rodopi, 1986.

1031. Popper, Karl Raimund. BEIDEN GRUNDPROBLEME DER ERKENNTNISTHEOR-IE: AUFGRUND VON MS. AUS D. JAHREN 1930-1933. Tubingen: Mohr, 1979.

1032. Popper, Karl Raimund. POST SCRIPTUM A LA LOGICA DE LA INVESTIGA-CION CIENTIFICA. Vol. 1, REALISMO Y EL OBJETIVO DE LA CIENCIA. Vol. 2, EL UNIVERSO ABIERTO: UN ARGUMENTO EN FAVOR DEL INDETERMINIS-MO. Vol. 3, TEORIA CUANTICA Y EL CISMA EN FISICA. Tr. of POSTSCRIPT TO THE LOGIC OF SCIENTIFIC DISCOVERY. Vol. 1, REALISM AND THE AIM OF SCIENCE. Vol. 2, THE OPEN UNIVERSE: AN ARGUMENT FOR INDETERMIN-ISM. Vol. 3, QUANTUM THEORY AND THE SCHISM IN PHYSICS. Edited by W. W. Routley. Totowa, NJ: Rowman and Littlefield, 1981. Tr. by Marta Sansigre Vidal. Madrid: Editorial Tecnos, 1985.

1033. Popper, Karl Raimund. UNENDED QUEST: AN INTELLECTUAL BIOGRAPHY. Rev. ed. La Salle, IL: Open Court, 1982.

1034. Popper, Karl Raimund and John Carew Eccles. THE SELF AND ITS BRAIN: AN ARGUMENT FOR INTERACTIONISM. New York: Springer International, c1977.

1035. Rhees, Rush. LUDWIG WITTGENSTEIN, PERSONAL RECOLLECTIONS. Oxford: Blackwell; Totowa, NJ: Rowman and Littlefield, 1981.

This volume includes contributions by his sister, Hermine Wittgenstein, and Famia

Pascal, F.R. Leavis and two of his students, John King and M.O.C. Drury.

1036. Ringleben, Joachim. ANEIGNUNG: DIE SPEKULATIVE THEOLOGIE SOREN KIERKEGAARDS. Berlin and New York: De Gruyter, 1983.

1037. Ringleben, Joachim. HEGELS THEORIE DER SUNDE: DIE SUBJEKTIVITATSLO-GISCHE KONTRUKTION EINES THEOLOGISCHEN BEGRIFFS. Berlin and New York: De Gruyter, 1976.

1038. Rod, Wolfgang. DESCARTES: DIE GENESE DES CARTESIANISCHE RATIONA-LISMUS. 2d. rev and exp. ed. Munich: Beck, 1982.

1039. Runggaldier, Edmund. CARNAP'S EARLY CONVENTIONALISM: AN INQUIRY INTO THE HISTORICAL BACKGROUND OF THE VIENNA CIRCLE. Amsterdam: Rodopi, 1984.

1040. Sauer, Werner. OSTERREICHISCHE PHILOSOPHIE ZWISCHEN AUFKLARUNG UND RESTAURATION. Amsterdam: Rodopi, 1982.

1041. Schlick, Moritz. MORITZ SCHLICK: PHILOSOPHICAL PAPERS. Vol. 1, 1909-1922. Vol. 2, 1925-1936. Ed. by Henk L. Mulder and Barbara F. B. van de Velde Schlick. Tr. by Peter Heath. Vienna Circle Collection, Vol. 11. Dordrecht and Boston: Reidel, 1979-.

1042. Smith, Barry. STRUCTURE AND GESTALT: PHILOSOPHY AND LITERATURE IN AUSTRIA-HUNGARY AND HER SUCCESSOR STATES. Amsterdam: John Benjamins B. V., 1981.

This book consists of eleven essays read at a seminar on Austro-German philosophy (Bolzano, Brentano, Freud, and Wittgenstein).

1043. Stock, Mechtild and Wolfgang G. Stock. PSYCHOLOGIE UND PHILOSOPHIE DER GRAZER SCHULE: EINE DOKUMENTATION ZU WERK UND WIRKUNGS-GESCHICHTE, ALEXIUS MEINONG...ET AL. Amsterdam and Atlanta: Rodopi, 1990.

1044. Topitsch, Ernst and Gerhard Streminger. HUME. Darmstadt: Wissenschaftliche Buchgesellschaft, 1981.

1045. Waismann, Friedrich. LECTURES ON THE PHILOSOPHY OF MATHEMATICS. Ed. by Wolfgang Grassl. Amsterdam: Rodopi, 1982.

The work is in English and German.

1046. Waismann, Friedrich. WITTGENSTEIN AND THE VIENNA CIRCLE: CONVER-SATIONS. Ed. by Brian McGuinness. Tr. of WITTGENSTEIN UND DER WIENER KREIS. Frankfurt am Main: Suhrkamp, Oxford: B. Blackwell, 1967. Tr. by Joachim Schulte and Brian McGuinness. Totowa, NJ: Rowman and Allanheld; New York: Barnes and Noble Books, 1979.

This volume consists of conversations among Wittgenstein, Waismann, and Schlick between 1929 and 1932. Wittgenstein expounds views similar to theses in PHILOSO-PHISCHE BEMERKUNGEN and to some of the themes of the TRACTATUS and responds to questions and criticisms from his interlocuters.

1047. Werle, Josef M. FRANZ BRENTANO UND DIE ZUKUNFT DER PHILOSOPHIE: STUDIEN ZUR WISSENSCHAFTSGESCHICHTE UND WISSENSCHAFTSSYSTE-MATIK IM 19 JAHRHUNDERT. Amsterdam and Atlanta: Rodopi, 1989.

1048. Wittgenstein, Ludwig. BRIEFWECHSEL MIT B. RUSSELL, G. E. MOORE, J. M. KEYNES, F. P. RAMSEY, W. ECCLES, P. ENGELMANN UND L. VON FICKER. Ed. by Brian McGuinness and Georg Henrik von Wright. Frankfurt am Main: Suhrkamp, 1980.

1049. Wittgenstein, Ludwig. CULTURE AND VALUE. Ed. by Georg Henrik von Wright. Amended 2d ed. Tr. of VERMISCHTE BERMERKUNGEN. Frankfurt am Main: Suhrkamp, Oxford: B. Blackwell, 1977. Tr. by Peter Winch. Oxford: B. Blackwell, 1980.

This edition contains the German text with a parallel English translation.

1050. Wittgenstein, Ludwig. NOTEBOOKS, 1914-1916. (TAGEBUCHER, 1914-1916). Ed. by Georg Henrik von Wright and Gertrude Elizabeth Margaret Anscombe. 2d ed. Tr. by G. E. M. Anscombe. Oxford: B. Blackwell, 1979.

1051. Wittgenstein, Ludwig. REMARKS ON COLOUR. Ed. by Gertrude Elizabeth Margaret Anscombe. Tr. of BEMERKUNGEN UBER DIE FARBEN. Tr. by Linda L. McAlister and Margarete Schattle. Oxford: Blackwell, 1977.

1052. Wittgenstein, Ludwig. REMARKS ON FRAZER'S GOLDEN BOUGH. Ed. by Rush Rhees. Tr. by A. C. Miles. Atlantic Highlands, NJ: Humanities Press, 1979.

1053. Wittgenstein, Ludwig. REMARKS ON THE FOUNDATIONS OF MATHEMATICS. Ed. by Georg Henrik von Wright, et al. 3d. rev ed. Tr. of BEMERKUNGEN UBER DIE GRUNDLAGEN DER MATHEMATIK. Frankfurt am Main: Suhrkamp, 1956. Tr. by G. E. M. Anscombe. Oxford: B. Blackwell; Cambridge: MIT Press, 1978.

1054. Wittgenstein, Ludwig. REMARKS ON THE PHILOSOPHY OF PSYCHOLOGY. 2 Vols. Ed. by Gertrude Elizabeth Margaret Anscombe and Georg Henrik von Wright. Tr.of BEMERKUNGEN UBER DIE PHILOSOPHIE DER PSYCHOLOGIE. Oxford: B.Blackwell; Chicago: Univ. of Chicago Press, 1980.

1055. Wittgenstein, Ludwig. WITTGENSTEIN'S LECTURES, CAMBRIDGE, 1930-1932: FROM THE NOTES OF JOHN KING AND DESMOND LEE. Ed. by Desmond Lee. Totowa, NJ: Rowman and Littlefield; Oxford: Blackwell, 1980.

1056. Wittgenstein, Ludwig. WITTGENSTEIN'S LECTURES, CAMBRIDGE, 1932-1935: FROM THE NOTES OF ALICE AMBROSE AND MARGARET MACDONALD. Ed. by Alice Ambrose. Totawa, NJ: Rowman and Littlefield; Oxford: Blackwell, 1979.

These are lecture notes taken down by two of Wittgenstein's students as he began to rethink the logical atomism of the TRACTATUS.

1057. Zilian, Hans-Georg. KLARHEIT UND METHODE: FELIX KAUFMANNS WISSENSCHAFTSTHEORIE. Amsterdam and Atlanta: Rodopi, 1990.

BELGIUM

1058. Abensor, Miguel, et al. PHENOMENOLOGIE ET POLITIQUE: MELANGES OFFERTS A JACQUES TAMINIAUX. Brussels: Ousia, 1989.

1059. Boehm, Rudolf. VOM GESICHTSPUNKT DER PHANOMENOLOGIE. 2 Vols. The Hague: Nijhoff, 1981.

1060. Burggraeve, Roger. EMMANUEL LEVINAS: THE ETHICAL BASIS FOR A HUMANE SOCIETY: BIBLIOGRAPHY 1929-1977, 1977-1981. Louvain: Center for

Metaphysics and Philosophy of God, Institute of Philosophy, 1981.

This work contains a bibliography of Levinas's works and secondary literature to 1981.

1061. Burggraeve, Roger. EMMANUEL LEVINAS: UNE BIBLIOGRAPHIE PRIMAIRE ET SECONDAIRE, 1929-1985. Leuven: Hoger Instituut voor Wijsbegeerte, Centrum voor Metafysica en Wijsgerige Godsleer, Peeters, 1986.

1062. Couloubaritsis, Lambros. L'AVENEMENT DE LA SCIENCE PHYSIQUE: ESSAI SUR LA PHYSIQUE D'ARISTOTE. Brussels: Ousia, 1980.

1063. Griffin-Collart, Evelyne. LA PHILOSOPHIE ECOSSAISE DU SENS COMMUN: THOMAS REID ET DUGALD STEWART. Brussels: Academie Royale de Belgique, 1980.

1064. Hegel, George Wilhelm Friedrich. LES ECRITS DE HAMANN. Ed. by Jacques Colette. Paris: Aubier-Montagne, 1981.

The introduction, notes and index to this volume, as well as the translation were written by Jacques Colette.

1065. Leonardy, Heinz. LIEBE UND PERSON: MAX SCHELERS VERSUCH EINES "PHANOMENOLOGISCHEN" PERSONALISMUS. The Hague: Nijhoff, 1976.

1066. Lories, Danielle. PHILOSOPHIE ANALYTIQUE ET ESTHETIQUE. Preface by Jacques Taminiaux. Paris: Meridiens Klincksieck, 1988.

1067. Lories, Danielle. RAISON ET FINITUDE. Louvain-la-Neuve: Institut superieur de philosophie: Cabay, 1983.

1068. McCarthy, Marie, et al. HANNAH ARENDT. Paris: Deuxtemps Tierce, 1991.

1069. Melle, Ulrich. WAHRNEHMUNGSPROBLEM UND SEINE VERWANDLUNG IN PHANOMENOLOGISCHER EINSTELLUNG: UNTERSUCHUNGEN ZU DEN PHANOMENOLOGISCHEN WAHRNEHMUNGSTHEORIEN VON HUSSERL, GURWITSCH, UND MERLEAU-PONTY. The Hague and Boston: Nijhoff, 1983.

1070. Parret, Herman. CONTEXTS OF UNDERSTANDING. Amsterdam: Benjamins, 1980.

1071. Parret, Herman. FILOSOFIE EN TAALWETENSCHAP. Assen: Van Gorcum, 1979.

1072. Parret, Herman. HISTORY OF LINGUISTIC THOUGHT AND CONTEMPO-RARY LINGUISTICS. Berlin and New York: De Gruyter, 1976.

1073. Parret, Herman. ON BELIEVING: EPISTEMOLOGICAL AND SEMIOTIC APPROACHES=DE LA CROYANCE: APPROCHES EPISTEMOLOGIQUES ET SEMIOTIQUES. Berlin and New York: De Gruyter, 1983.

1074. Parret, Herman. SEMIOTICS AND PRAGMATICS: AN EVALUATIVE COMPAR-ISON OF CONCEPTUAL FRAMEWORKS. Amsterdam and Philadelphia: Benjamins, 1985.

1075. Parret, Herman, et al. LE LANGAGE EN CONTEXTE: ETUDES PHILOSO-PHIQUES ET LINGUISTIQUES DE PRAGMATIQUE. Amsterdam: Benjamins, 1980.

1076. Parret, Herman, et al. POSSIBILITIES AND LIMITATION OF PRAGMATICS. Amsterdam: Benjamins, 1981.

These are the Proceedings of the Conference on Pragmatics held in Urbino, July 8-14, 1979.

1077. Parret, Herman and Jacques Bouveresse. MEANING AND UNDERSTANDING. Berlin and New York: De Gruyter, 1981.

1078. Parret, Herman and Hans-George Ruprecht. EXIGENCES ET PERSPECTIVES DE LA SEMIOTIQUE: RECUEIL D`HOMMAGES POUR ALGIRDAS JULIEN GREIMAS=AIMS AND PROSPECTS OF SEMIOTICS: FESTSCHRIFT FOR ALGIRDAS JULIEN GREIMAS. Vol. 1, LE PARADIGME THEORIQUE=THE THEORETICAL PARADIGM; Vol. 2, LES DOMAINES D'APPLICATION=DOMAINS OF APPLICATION. Amsterdam and Philadelphia: Benjamins, 1985.

1079. Pinxten, Rik. UNIVERSALISM VERSUS RELATIVISM IN LANGUAGE AND THOUGHT. The Hague and Paris: Mouton, 1976.

These are the Proceedings of a Colloquium on the Sapir-Whorf Hypotheses.

1080. Taminiaux, Jacques. DIALECTIC AND DIFFERENCE: FINITUDE IN MODERN THOUGHT. Ed. by James Decker and Robert Crease. Atlantic Highlands, NJ: Humanities Press: Macmillan, 1985.

1081. Taminiaux, Jacques. HEIDEGGER AND THE PROJECT OF FUNDAMENTAL ONTOLOGY. Tr. of LECTURE DE L'ONTOLOGIE FONDAMENTALE: ESSAIS SUR HEIDEGGER. Grenoble: J. Millon, 1989. Ed. and tr. by Michael Gendre. Albany: State Univ. of New York Press, 1991.

1082. Taminiaux, Jacques, et al. FIGURES DE LA FINITUDE: ETUDES D'ANTHROPOLOGIE PHILOSOPHIQUE. Ed. by Ghislaine Florival. Louvain-la-Neuve: Editions de l'Institute superieur de philosophie, 1988.

1083. Waelhens, Alphonse de. ETUDES D'ANTHROPOLOGIE PHILOSOPHIQUE. Louvain la Neuve: Editions de l'institut superieur de philosophie; Paris: J. Vrin; Leuven: Peeters, 1980.

1084. Waelhens, Alphonse de. QU'EST-CE QUE L'HOMME?: PHILOSOPHIE/PSYCHOLANALYSE: HOMMAGE A ALPHONSE DE WAELHENS, (1911-1981). Brussels: Facultes universitaires Saint Louis, 1982.

There is a bibliography of the works of Alphonse de Waelhens on pages 9-21.

1085. Waelhens, Alphonse de. SCHIZOPHRENIA: A PHILOSOPHICAL REFLECTION ON LACAN'S STRUCTURALIST INTERPRETATION. Tr. of LA PSYCHOSE: ESSAI D'INTERPRETATION ANALYTIC ET EXISTENTIALE. Louvain: Editions Nauwelaerts, Paris: Beatrice-Nauwelaerts, 1972. Pittsburgh: Duquesne Univ. Press, 1978.

DENMARK

1086. Collin, Finn. THEORY AND UNDERSTANDING: A CRITIQUE OF INTERPRETIVE SOCIAL SCIENCE. Oxford and New York: B. Blackwell, 1985.

1087. Engberg-Pedersen, Troels. ARISTOTLE'S THEORY OF MORAL INSIGHT. New York and Oxford: Clarendon Press, 1983.

1088. Favrholdt, David. LENIN, HANS FILOSOFI OF VERDENSANSKUELSE. Copenhagen: Gad, 1978.

1089. Favrholdt, David, et al. MENNESKEOPFATTELSEN: ARTIKLER OF REPLIK-KER. Haarby: Forlageet i Haarby, 1980.

1090. Hartnack, Justus. FRA KANT TIL HEGEL: EN NYTOLKNING. Copenhagen: Berlingske, 1979.

1091. Hartnack, Justus. LA TEORIA DEL CONOCIMIENTO DE KANT. 2d ed. Tr. by Carmen Garcia and J. A. Llorente. Madrid: Ediciones Catedra, 1979.

1092. Hartnack, Justus. MENNESKERETTIGHEDER: GRUNDLAGGENDE POLITISKE BEGREBER OG FORHOLD I NY BELYSING. Haarby: Forlaget i Haarby, 1980.

1093. Hartnack, Justus. WITTGENSTEIN AND MODERN PHILOSOPHY. 2d ed. Notre Dame, IN: Notre Dame Press, 1985.

An afterword brings up to date this study first published in English in 1965.

1094. Hartnack, Justus. IDEOLOGI, SPLITTELSE, FALLESSLAB: DEBATINDLAG. Skodsborg: Rolighed, 1981.

In addition to an essay by Hartnack, this volume contains essays by Anders Munk, Poul Bjerre, Stig Moller, and Paul Schluter.

1095. Jensen, Uffe Juul and Rom Harre. THE PHILOSOPHY OF EVOLUTION. New York: St. Martin's Press; Sussex: Harvester Press, 1981.

These are papers based on a symposium held at the Institute of Philosophy, University of Aarhus, Denmark. They include a critical survey of concepts of evolution and an analysis of their varied contexts of application by ten experts in the history and philosophy of biology and sociology.

1096. Kierkegaard, Soren. KIERKEGAARD'S WRITINGS. Ed. by Howard Vincent Hong and Edna Hatlestad Hong. Tr. by the Editors. Princeton: Princeton Univ. Press, 1978-.

1097. Kierkegaard, Soren. SOREN KIERKEGAARD'S JOURNALS AND PAPERS. 7 Vols. Ed. by Howard Vincent Hong and Edna Hatlestad Hong. Tr. by the Editors. Bloomington, IN: Indiana Univ. Press, [1967-1978].

The editors were assisted by Gregor Malantschuk.

1098. Kloeden, W. von, et al. KIERKEGAARD'S VIEW OF CHRISTIANITY. Copenhagen: Reitzel, 1978.

This volume contains a bibliography of works by Kierkegaard on pages 192-194.

1099. Koch, Carl Henrik. FRANCIS BACON OG DET 17. ARHUNDREDES VIDENS-KABELIGE REVOLUTION. Copenhagen: Museum Tusculanum, 1979.

1100. Ostenfeld, Erik Nis. FORMS, MATTER AND MIND: THREE STRANDS IN PLATO'S METAPHYSICS. The Hague and Boston: Nijhoff, 1982.

This work seeks to demonstrate how Plato's conception of man is an integral part of his metaphysics. This book also seeks to show that Plato's view of man differs fundamentally from Cartesianism.

1101. Thulstrup, Niels. COMMENTARY ON KIERKEGAARD'S CONCLUDING UNSCIENTIFIC POSTSCRIPT: WITH A NEW INTRODUCTION. Tr. of SOREN KIERKEGAARD, AFSLUTTENDE UVIDENSKABELIG EFTERSKRIFT. Tr. by Robert J.

Widenmann. Princeton: Princeton Univ. Press, 1984.

1102. Thulstrup, Niels. KIERKEGAARD'S RELATION TO HEGEL. Tr. of Kierkegaard's FORHOLD TIL HEGEL OG TIL DEN SPEKULATIVE IDEALISME INDTIL 1846. Copenhagen: Gyldendal, 1967. Tr. by George L. Stengren. Princeton: Princeton Univ. Press, 1980.

FINLAND

1103. Aarnio, Aulis. DENKWEISEN DER RECHTSWISSENSCHAFT: EINFUHRUNG IN DIE THEORIE DER RECHTSWISSENSCHAFTLICHEN FOR SCHUNG. Vienna and New York: Springer, 1979.

1104. Aarnio, Aulis. LEGAL POINT OF VIEW: SIX ESSAYS ON LEGAL PHILOSO-PHY. 2 Vols. Ed. by Urpo Kangas. Tr. by Jyrki Uusitalo. Helsinki: Helsingin Yliopisto, 1978.

1105. Aarnio, Aulis. MITA LAINOPPI ON. Helsinki: Tammi, 1978.

1106. Aarnio, Aulis. ON LEGAL REASONING. Turku: Turun Yliopisto, 1977.

1107. Aarnio, Aulis. PHILOSOPHICAL PERSPECTIVES ON JURISPRUDENCE. Acta Philosophica Fennica, Vol. 36. Helsinki: Philosophical Society of Finland, 1983.

This volume offers a selection of Aarnio's essays on the philosophy of law and legal theory originally produced in the period 1975-1982.

1108. Aarnio, Aulis and Mark van Hoecke. ON THE UTILITY OF LEGAL THEORY. Tampere: A-Tieto Oy, 1985.

This volume is based on the Proceedings of the Benelux-Scandinavian Symposium, Antwerp, 1983.

1109. Aarnio, Aulis and Ilkka Niiniluoto. METHODOLOGIE ERKENNTNISTHEORIE DER JURISTISCHEN ARGUMENTATION: BEITRAGE DES INTERNATIONA-LEN SYMPOSIONS "ARGUMENTATION IN LEGAL SCIENCE" VOM 10 BIS 12 DEZEMBER 1979 IN HELSINKI. Berlin: Duncker and Humblot, 1981.

The contributions in this volume are in English and in German.

1110. Airaksinen, Timo. ETHICS OF COERCION AND AUTHORITY: A PHILO-SOPHICAL STUDY OF SOCIAL LIFE. Pittsburgh: Univ. of Pittsburgh Press, 1988.

1111. Airaksinen, Timo. OF GLAMOUR, SEX, AND DE SADE. Wakefield, NH: Long-wood Academic, 1991.

1112. Airaksinen, Timo. OGOLNA TEORIA WARTOSCI I JEJ ZASTOSOWANIE W NAUCE I TECHNNICE. Warsaw: Zaklad Narodowy im. Ossolinskich, 1986.

1113. Airaksinen, Timo, et al. TIEDEPOLITIIKAN OIKEUDENMUKAISUUS JA TUTKIJAN VASTUU. Helsinki: Gaudeamus, 1987.

1114. Airaksinen, Timo and Martin A. Bertman. HOBBES: WAR AMONG NATIONS. Aldershot, Hants, Eng. and Brookfield, VT: Avebury, 1989.

These are the Proceedings of the Hobbes Conference held at the University of Helsinki in May, 1987, sponsored by the Philosophical Society of Finland.

1115. Alanen, Lilli. STUDIES IN CARTESIAN EPISTEMOLOGY AND PHILOSOPHY OF MIND. Acta Philosophica Fennica, Vol. 33. Helsinki: Societas Philosophica Fennica, 1982.

1116. Apel, Karl-Otto, et al. NEUE VERSUCHE UBER ERKLAREN UND VERSTEHEN. Frankfurt am Main: Suhrkamp, 1978.

This work includes essays by M. Riedel, L. Hertzberg, J. Kim, F. Stoutland, R. Martin, I. Niiniluoto, G. Meggle, and G. H. von Wright.

1117. Asztalos, Monkika, et al. KNOWLEDGE AND THE SCIENCES IN MEDIEVAL PHILOSOPHY. Acta Philosophica Fennica, Vol. 48. Helsinki: Yliopistopaino, 1990.

This is Vol. 1 of the Proceedings of the the Eighth International Congress of Medieval Philosophy held in Helsinki, August 24-29, 1987. Vol. 2 was published as B 19 of the Publications of the Luther-Agricola-Society and Vol. 3 as Number 55 of the Missiologian Ja Ekumeniikan Seuran Julkaisuja.

1118. Bogdan, Radu J. BELIEF: FORM, CONTENT, AND FUNCTION. Oxford: Clarendon Press; New York: Oxford Univ. Press, 1986.

1119. Carlson, Lauri. DIALOGUE GAMES: AN APPROACH TO DISCOURSE ANALYSIS. Dordrecht and Boston: Reidel, 1983.

1120. Conte, Amadeo G., et al. DEONTISCHE LOGIK UND SEMANTIK. Wiesbaden: Athenaion, 1977.

This book consists of revised papers originally presented at a meeting held March 17-22, 1975 at the Zentrum fur Interdisziplinare Forschung, Bielefeld University.

1121. Day, John Patrick. HOPE: A PHILOSOPHICAL INQUIRY. Acta Philosophica Fennica, Vol. 51. Helsinki: Philosophical Society of Finland, 1991.

1122. ESSAYS ON WITTGENSTEIN IN HONOUR OF G. H. VON WRIGHT. Acta Philosophica Fennica, Vol. 28. Amsterdam: North-Holland, 1976.

1123. Haapala, Arto. WHAT IS A WORK OF LITERATURE? Acta Philosophica Fennica, Vol. 46. Helsinki: Philosophical Society of Finland, 1989.

1124. Haaparanta, Leila. FREGE'S DOCTRINE OF BEING. Acta Philosophica Fennica, Vol. 39. Helsinki: Societas Philosophica Fennica, 1985.

1125. Haaparanta, Leila and Jaakko Hintikka. FREGE SYNTHESIZED: ESSAYS ON THE PHILOSOPHICAL AND FOUNDATIONAL WORK OF GOTTLOB FREGE. Dordrecht and Boston: Reidel, 1986.

1126. Haaparata, Leila, et al. LANGUAGE, KNOWLEDGE, AND INTENTIONALITY: PERSPECTIVES ON THE PHILOSOPHY OF JAAKKO HINTIKKA. Acta Philosophica Fennica, Vol. 49. Helsinki: Philosophical Society of Finland, 1990.

This work consists of papers from a symposium held in 1989 to celebrate the sixtieth birthday of Prof. Hintikka.

1127. Hautamaki, Antti. POINTS OF VIEW AND THEIR LOGICAL ANALYSIS. Acta Philosophica Fennica, Vol. 41. Helsinki: Philosophical Society of Finland, 1986.

1128. Heiskanen, Heikki and Timo Airaksinen. FROM SUBJECTIVE WELFARE TO SOCIAL VALUE: AXIOLOGY IN METHODOLOGICAL AND PHILOSOPHICAL

PERSPECTIVE. Helsinki: Suomalainen Tiedeakatamia, 1979.

1129. Hilpinen, Risto. NEW STUDIES IN DEONTIC LOGIC: NORMS, ACTIONS, AND THE FOUNDATIONS OF ETHICS. Dordrecht and Boston: Reidel, 1981.

This collection includes essays by Georg Henrik von Wright, Hector-Neri Castaneda, Richmond H. Thomason, Lennart Aqvist, and others.

1130. Hilpinen, Risto. RATIONALITY IN SCIENCE: STUDIES IN THE FOUNDATIONS OF SCIENCE AND ETHICS. Dordrecht and Boston: Reidel, 1980.

1131. Hilpinen, Risto, et al. LOGIC AND LINGUISTICS: PART I. Dordrecht and Boston: Reidel, 1978.

1132. Hintikka, Jaakko. THE GAME OF LANGUAGE: STUDIES IN GAME-THEORETICAL SEMANTICS AND ITS APPLICATION. Ed. by Jack Kulas. Dordrecht and Boston: Reidel, 1983.

1133. Hintikka, Jaakko. THE SEMANTICS OF QUESTIONS AND THE QUESTIONS OF SEMANTICS: CASE STUDIES IN THE INTERRELATION OF LOGIC, SEMANTICS AND SYNTAX. Acta Philosophica Fennica, Vol. 28. Amsterdam: North-Holland, 1976.

1134. Hintikka, Jaakko, et al. ARISTOTLE ON MODALITY AND DETERMINISM. Acta Philosophica Fennica, Vol. 29. Helsinki: Societas Philosophica Fennica, 1977.

1135. Hintikka, Jaakko, et al. ESSAYS ON MATHEMATICAL AND PHILOSOPHICAL LOGIC. Dordrecht and Boston: Reidel, 1979.

These are the Proceedings of the Fourth Scandinavian Logic Symposium of the First Soviet-Finnish Logic Conference, Jyvaskyla, Finland, June 29- July 6, 1976.

1136. Hintikka, Jaakko, et al. PROCEEDINGS OF THE 1978 PISA CONFERENCE ON THE HISTORY AND PHILOSOPHY OF SCIENCE. Vol. 1, THEORY CHANGE, ANCIENT AXIOMATICS, AND GALILEO'S METHODOLOGY. Vol. 2, PROBABILISTIC THINKING, THERMODYNAMICS, AND THE INTERACTION OF THE HISTORY AND PHILOSOPHY OF SCIENCE. Dordrecht and Boston: Reidel, 1981.

1137. Hintikka, Jaakko and Jack Kulas. ANAPHORA AND DEFINITE DESCRIPTIONS: TWO APPLICATIONS OF GAME-THEORETICAL SEMANTICS. Dordrecht and Boston: Reidel, 1985.

1138. Hintikka, Merrill Bristow and Jaakko Hintikka. INVESTIGATING WITTGENSTEIN. Oxford: Blackwell, 1986.

1139. Holmstrom-Hintikka, Ghita and Andrew J. I. Jones. ACTION, LOGIC, AND SOCIAL THEORY: DEDICATED TO INGMAR PORN ON THE OCCASION OF HIS 50TH BIRTHDAY. Acta Philosophica Fennica, Vol. 38. Helsinki: Philosophical Society of Finland, 1985.

There is a list of publications by Ingmar Porn on pages 348-349.

1140. Holmstrom-Hintikka, Ghita. ACTION, PURPOSE, AND WILL: A FORMAL THEORY. Acta Philosophica Fennica, Vol. 50. Helsinki: Philosophical Society of Finland, 1991.

1141. Kaila, Eino. REALITY AND EXPERIENCE: FOUR PHILOSOPHICAL ESSAYS. Ed. by Robert Sonne Cohen. Tr. from German by Peter Kirschenmann and Ann

Kirschenmann. Vienna Circle Collection, Vol. 12. Dordrecht and Boston: Reidel, 1978.

This work includes an introduction by G. H. von Wright.

1142. Kannisto, Heikki. THOUGHTS AND THEIR SUBJECT: A STUDY OF WITTGEN-STEIN'S TRACTATUS. Acta Philosophica Fennica, Vol. 40. Helsinki: Philosophical Society of Finland, 1986.

1143. Knuuttila, Simo Jussi Irsakki. REFORGING THE GREAT CHAIN OF BEING: STUDIES OF THE HISTORY OF MODAL THEORIES. Dordrecht and Boston: Reidel; Helsinki: Univ. of Helsinki, 1981.

1144. Knuuttila, Simo Jussi Irsakki, et al. AATE JA MAAILMANKUVA: SUOMEN FILOSOFISTA PERINT OA KESKIAJALTA VUOSISADALLEMME: PROFESSORI JUSSE TENKUN 60 VUOTISPAIVAKSI TOIMITTANEET. Porvoo: Soderstrom, 1979.

This volume contains contributions by A. I. Lehtinen, J. Lounela, I. Patoluoto, V. Oitti nen, J. Manninen, G. H. von Wright, O. Ketonen, N.Luukanen, I. Niiniluoto, J. V. Snellman, E. Westermarck, and E. Kaila.

1145. Knuuttila, Simo Jussi Irsakki and Jaakko Hintikka. THE LOGIC OF BEING: HISTORICAL STUDIES. Dordrecht and Boston: Reidel, 1986.

This volume includes essays by the editors and by Charles H. Kahn, Benson Mates, Russell M. Dancy, Klaus Jacobi, Hermann Weidemann, Lilli Alanen, and Leila Haaparanta.

1146. Krawietz, Werner and Robert Alexy. METATHEORIE JURISTISCHER ARGU-MENTATION IN VERBINDUNG. Berlin: Duncker and Humblot, 1983.

1147. Lagerspetz, Eerik. A CONVENTIONAL THEORY OF INSTITUTIONS. Acta Philosophica Fennica, Vol. 44. Helsinki: Philosophical Society of Finland, 1989.

1148. Lemmon, Edward John. THE "LEMMON NOTES": AN INTRODUCTION TO MODAL LOGIC. By E. J. Lemmon in collaboration with Dana Scott. Ed. by Krister Segerberg. Bristol: Blackwell for the American Philosophical Quarterly, 1977.

1149. Lenzen, Wolfgang. RECENT WORK IN EPISTEMIC LOGIC. Acta Philosophica Fennica, Vol. 30. Helsinki: Societas Philosophica Fennica; Amsterdam: North-Holland, 1978.

The volume includes a bibliography on pages 181-219.

1150. Liehu, Heidi. SOREN KIERKEGAARD'S THEORY OF STAGES AND ITS RELATION TO HEGEL. Acta Philosophica Fennica, Vol. 47. Helsinki: Philosophical Society of Finland, 1990.

1151. Lounela, Jaako. DIE LOGIK IM XVII JAHRHUNDERT IN FINLAND. Helsinki: Suomalainen Tiedeakatemia; Akateeminen Kirjakauppa, 1978.

1152. Manninen, Juha. AJATUS 36. AISTHESES: ESSAYS ON THE PHILOSOPHY OF PERCEPTION. YEARBOOK OF THE PHILOSOPHICAL SOCIETY OF FINLAND. Helsinki: The Philosophical Society of Finland, 1976.

1153. Manninen, Juha. AUFKLARUNG UND FRANZOSISCHE REVOLUTION: EIN SYMPOSION ZUR IDEEN- UND WISSENSCHAFTSGESCHICHTE IN OULU, NOV. 29, 1985. Oulu: Oulun Yliopisto, 1989.

This volume contains contributions by Anto Leikola, Jouni Alavuotunki, Martin Kusch, Manfred Buhr, Jorg Schreiter, Vesa Ottinen, and the editor.

1154. Manninen, Juha. DIALEKTIIKAN YDIN. Oulu: Pohjoinen, 1987.

1155. Manninen, Juha. MAAILMANKUVA KULTTUURIN KOKONAISUUDESSA: AATE- JA OPPIHISTORIAN, KIRJALLISUUSTIETEEN JA KULTTUURIANTRO-POLOGIAN NAK OKULMIA. Oulu: Pohjoinen, 1989.

1156. Manninen, Juha. MITEN TULKITA J.V. SNELLMANIA?: KIRJOITUKSIA J.V. SNELLMANIN AJATTELUN KEHITTYMISEST A JA TAUSTOISTA? Kuipio: Kustan-nuskiila, 1987.

The volume contains a bibliography on pages 181-209.

1157. Manninen, Juha and Hans-Jorg Sandkuhler. REALISMUS UND DIALEKTIK, ODER, WAS KONNEN WIR WISSEN? Cologne: Pahl-Rugenstein, 1984.

1158. Manninen, Juha and Raimo Tuomela. ESSAYS ON EXPLANATION AND UNDER-STANDING: STUDIES IN THE FOUNDATIONS OF HUMANITIES AND SOCIAL SCIENCES. Dordrecht and Boston: Reidel, 1976.

This international anthology contains essays on the general subject of its title by Rudiger Bubner, Jaegwon Kim, G. H. von Wright and other philosophers from various countries.

1159. Mattila, Jorma K. and Arto Siitonen. ANALYSIS, HARMONY AND SYNTHESIS IN ANCIENT THOUGHT. Acta Universitatis Ouluensis: Series B, Humaniora, No. 6; Historica, no.3. Oulu: Univ. of Oulu, 1977.

1160. Maury, Andre. CONCEPTS OF "SINN" AND "GEGENSTAND" IN WITTGEN-STEIN'S "TRACTATUS". Acta Philosophica Fennica, Vol. 29. Helsinki: Societas Philo-sophica Fennica; Amsterdam: North-Holland, 1977.

1161. Niiniluoto, Ilkka. TIEDE, FILOSOFIA GA MAAILMANKATSOMUS: FILOSOFI-SIA EPSEITA TIEDOSTA JA SEN ARVOSTA. Helsinki: Otava, 1984.

1162. Niiniluoto, Ilkka and Esa Saarinen. INTENSIONAL LOGIC: THEORY AND APPLICATIONS. Acta Philosophica Fennica, Vol. 35. Helsinki: Philosophical Society of Finland, 1982.

1163. Niiniluoto, Ilkka and Raimo Tuomela. THE LOGIC AND EPISTEMOLOGY OF SCIENTIFIC CHANGE. Acta Philosophica Fennica, Vol. 30. Helsinki: Societas Philo-sophica Fennica, 1979.

1164. Nyberg, Tauno. AJATUS JA ANALYYSI. Porvoo: Soderstrom, 1977.

1165. Peczenik, Aleksander and Jyrki Uusitalo. REASONING ON LEGAL REASONING. Helsinki: Society of Finnish Lawyers, 1979.

1166. Pitkanen, Risto. ON THE ANALYSIS OF PICTORIAL REPRESENTATION. Acta Philosophica Fennica, Vol. 31. Amsterdam: North-Holland, 1981.

1167. Porn, Ingmar. ACTION THEORY AND SOCIAL SCIENCE: SOME FORMAL MODELS. Dordrecht and Boston: Reidel, 1977.

1168. Porn, Ingmar. ESSAYS IN PHILOSOPHICAL ANALYSIS: DEDICATED TO ERIK STENIUS ON THE OCCASION OF HIS 70TH BIRTHDAY. Acta Philosophica Fennica, Vol. 32. Helsinki: Societas Philosophica Fennica, 1981.

1169. Rantala, Veikko. ASPECTS OF DEFINABILITY. Acta Philosophica Fennica, Vol. 29. Helsinki: Societas Philosophica Fennica; Amsterdam: North-Holland, 1977.

1170. Rantala, Veikko, et al. ESSAYS ON THE PHILOSOPHY OF MUSIC. Acta Philo sophica Fennica, Vol. 43. Helsinki: Philosophical Society of Finland, 1988.

1171. Saarinen, Esa. GAME-THEORETICAL SEMANTICS: ESSAYS ON SEMANTICS. Dordrecht and Boston: Reidel, 1979.

1172. Saarinen, Esa, et al. ESSAYS IN HONOUR OF JAAKKO HINTIKKA ON THE OCCASION OF HIS FIFTIETH BIRTHDAY ON JANUARY 12, 1979. Dordrecht and Boston: Reidel, 1979.

1173. Saarinen, Esa, et al. RAKKAUDEN FILOSOFIA. Porvoo: Soderstrom, 1984.

1174. Sandbacka, Carola. UNDERSTANDING OTHER CULTURES: STUDIES IN THE PHILOSOPHICAL PROBLEMS OF CROSS-CULTURAL INTERPRETATION. Acta Philosophica Fennica, Vol. 42. Helsinki: Philosophical Society of Finland, 1987.

1175. Schilpp, Paul Arthur and Lewis Edwin Hahn. THE PHILOSOPHY OF GEORG HENRIK VON WRIGHT. Library of Living Philosophers, Vol. XIX. LaSalle, IL: Open Court, 1989.

In addition to Von Wright's intellectual autobiography and a complete bibliography of his writings up to the date of publication, this volume contains critical articles on Von Wright's philosophy by other philosophers and Wright's replies to each of them.

1176. Segerberg, Krister. CLASSICAL PROPOSITIONAL OPERATORS: AN EXERCISE IN THE FOUNDATIONS OF LOGIC. Oxford Logic Guides, Vol. 2. Oxford: Clarendon Press; New York: Oxford Univ. Press, 1982.

1177. Segerberg, Krister. WRIGHT AND WRONG: MINI ESSAYS IN HONOUR OF GEORG HENRIK VON WRIGHT ON HIS SIXTIETH BIRTHDAY, JUNE 14, 1976. Real: Group in Logic and Methodology of Real Finland, 1976.

1178. Sintonen, Arto and Timo Airaksinen. VALUE, CONSCIOUSNESS, AND ACTION. Turku: Turun Yliopisto, 1976.

The selections in this volume are in English or German.

1179. Sintonen, Matti. THE PRAGMATICS OF SCIENTIFIC EXPLANATION. Acta Philosophica Fennica, Vol. 37. Helsinki: Philosophical Society of Finland, 1984.

There is a bibliography on pages 237-254.

1180. Stroup, Timothy. EDWARD WESTERMARCK: ESSAYS ON HIS LIFE AND WORKS. Acta Philosophica Fennica, Vol. 34. Helsinki: Societas Philosophica Fennica, 1982.

The volume includes a lengthy bibliography on pages 274-292.

1181. Stroup, Timothy. WESTERMARCK'S ETHICS. Publications of the Research Institute of the Abo Akademi Foundation, Vol. 76. Abo: Abo Akademi, 1982.

1182. Tahtinen, Unto. NON-VIOLENT THEORIES OF PUNISHMENT, INDIAN AND WESTERN. Helsinki: Suomalainen Tiedeakatemia, 1982.

1183. Tammelo, Ilmar and Aulis Aarnio. FORTSCHRITT VON THEORIE UND TECHNIK IN RECHT UND ETHIK=ON THE ADVANCEMENT OF THEORY AND TECHNIQUE IN LAW AND ETHICS. Berlin: Duncker and Humblot, 1981.

1184. Tuomela, Raimo. HUMAN ACTION AND ITS EXPLANATION: A STUDY ON THE PHILOSOPHICAL FOUNDATION OF PSYCHOLOGY. Dordrecht and Boston: Reidel, 1977.

1185. Tuomela, Raimo. A THEORY OF SOCIAL ACTION. Dordrecht and Boston: Reidel, 1984.

1186. Vaina, Lucia and Jaakko Hintikka. COGNITIVE CONSTRAINTS ON COMMUNICATION: PROCESSES AND REPRESENTATIONS. Synthese Language Library, Vol. 18. Dordrecht and Boston: Reidel, 1984.

1187. Wilenius, Reijo. IHMINEN, LUONTO JA TEKNIIKKA. Jyvaskyla: Gummerus, 1978.

1188. Wilenius, Reijo. IHMISKESKEISSEN KULTUURIIN: RUDOLF STEINER JA ANTROPOSOFINEN HENGENTIEDE. Oulu: Pohjoinen, 1976.

1189. Wilenius, Reijo. SNELLMANIN LINJA: HENKISEN KASVUN FILOSOFIA. Jyvaskyla: Gummerus, 1978.

1190. Wilson, George M. THE INTENTIONALITY OF HUMAN ACTION. Acta Philosophica Fennica, Vol. 31. Helsinki: Societas Philosophica Fennica; Amsterdam: North-Holland, 1980.

1191. Wright, Georg Henrik von. FREEDOM AND DETERMINATION. Acta Philosophica Fennica, Vol. 31. Amsterdam: North-Holland, 1980.

1192. Wright, Georg Henrik von. HANDLUNG, NORM UND INTENTION: UNTERSUCHUNG ZUR DEONTISCHEN LOGIK. Ed. by Hans Poser. Berlin and New York: De Gruyter, 1977c1976.

1193. Wright, Georg Henrik von. HUMANISM AND THE HUMANITIES. Ithaca: Society for the Humanities, Cornell University, 1976.

This sound recording was made on October 25, 1976 at Cornell University.

1194. Wright, Georg Henrik von. HUMANISMENN SOM LIVSH ALLNING OCH ANDRE ESSAYER. Helsingfors: Soderstrom, 1978.

1195. Wright, Georg Henrik von. LOGIC AND PHILOSOPHY. The Hague: Nijhoff, 1980.

This volume grew out of the International Institute of Philosophy Symposium in Dusseldorf August 27-September 1, 1978.

1196. Wright, Georg Henrik von. PHILOSOPHICAL PAPERS. Vol. 1, PRACTICAL REASON. Vol. 2, PHILOSOPHICAL LOGIC. Vol. 3, TRUTH, POSSIBILITY AND CERTAINTY. Oxford: Blackwell; Ithaca: Cornell Univ. Press, 1983-.

1197. Wright, Georg Henrik von. WHAT IS HUMANISM. A Lindley Lecture. Lawrence: University of Kansas, 1977.

1198. Wright, Georg Henrik von. WITTGENSTEIN. Minneapolis: Univ. of Minnesota Press; Oxford: Blackwell, 1982.

FRANCE

1199. Adloff, Jean Gabriel. SARTRE: INDEX DU CORPUS PHILOSOPHIQUE. Paris: Klincksieck, 1981-.

1200. Althusser, Louis. CE QUI NE PEUT PLUS DURER DANS LE PARTI COMMU-NISTE. Paris: F. Maspero, 1978.

The volume contains articles originally published in Le Monde, April 24-27, 1978.

1201. Althusser, Louis. ESSAYS ON IDEOLOGY. London: Verso, 1984.

1202. Althusser, Louis. FREUD UND LACAN. Berlin: Merve, 1976.

1203. Althusser, Louis. POSITIONS, 1964-1975. Paris: Editions Sociales, 1976.

1204. Amsterdamski, Stefan, et al. LA QUERELLE DU DETERMINISME: PHILOSOPHIE DE LA SCIENCE D'AUJOURD'HUI. Paris: Gallimard, 1990.

1205. Armogathe, Jean Robert. THEOLOGIA CARTESIANA: L'EXPLICATION PHY-SIQUE DE L'EUCHARISTIE CHEZ DESCARTES ET DOM DESGABETS. The Hague: Nijhoff, 1977.

1206. Aron, Raymond. POLITICS AND HISTORY: SELECTED ESSAYS. Ed. by Miriam Bernheim Conant. New York: Free Press, 1978.

1207. Auroux, Sylvain. LA SEMIOTIQUE DES ENCYCLOPEDISTES: ESSAI D'EPIS-TEMOLOGIE HISTORIQUE DES SCIENCE DU LANGAGE. Paris: Payot, 1980.

1208. Bachelard, Gaston. THE NEW SCIENTIFIC SPIRIT. Tr. of LE NOUVELLE ESPRIT SCIENTIFIQUE. Vol. 2 of the NOUVELLE ENCYCLOPEDIE PHILOSO-HIQUE. Paris: Librarie Felix Alcan, 1934. Tr. by Arthur Goldhammer. Boston: Beacon Press, 1984.

The author argues that scientific breakthroughs result from intuitive insights later tested empirically. In defending this thesis, he draws on the meaning of post-Newtonian physics.

1209. Barthes, Roland. RUSTLE OF LANGUAGE. Tr. of BRUISSEMENT DE LA LANGUE. Paris: Seuil, 1984. Tr. by Richard Howard. New York: Hill and Wang; Oxford: B. Blackwell, 1986.

1210. Biard, Joel, et al. INTRODUCTION A LA LECTURE DE LA SCIENCE DE LA LOGIQUE DE HEGEL. Paris: Aubier-Montaigne, 1981-.

1211. Birault, Henri. HEIDEGGER ET L'EXPERIENCE DE LA PENSEE. Paris: Galli-mard, 1978.

1212. Blondel, Maurice. ACTION: ESSAYS ON A CRITIQUE OF LIFE AND SCIENCE OF PRACTICE. Tr. of Blondel's L'ACTION: ESSAI D'UNE CRITIQUE DE LA VIE ET D'UNE SCIENCE DE LA PRATIQUE, originally published in 1893. Vol. 1, LE PROBLEME DES CAUSES SECONDES ET LE PUR AGER. Vol. 2, L'ACTION HUMAINE ET LES CONDTIONS DE SON ABOUTISSEMENT. Tr. by Olivia Blanchette. Notre Dame: Univ. of Notre Dame, 1984.

1213. Bourdieu, Pierre. DISTINCTION: A SOCIAL CRITIQUE OF THE JUDGMENT OF TASTE. Tr. of LA DISTINCTION, CRITIQUE SOCIALE DU JUGEMENT. Paris, Les Editions de Minuet, 1979. Tr. by Richard Nice. Cambridge: Harvard Univ. Press, 1984.

1214. Bourdieu, Pierre. LE SENS PRATIQUE. Paris: Editions de Minuit, 1980.

1215. Bourdieu, Pierre. OUTLINE OF A THEORY OF PRACTICE. Tr. with revisions of ESQUISSE D'UNE THEORIE DE LA PRATIQUE: PRECEDE DE TROIS ETUDES D'ETHNOLOGIE KABYLE. Geneva and Paris: Droz, 1972. Tr. by Richard Nice. Cambridge and New York: Cambridge Univ. Press, 1977.

1216. Bourdieu, Pierre, et al. RECHERCHES SUR LA PHILOSOPHIE ET LE LANGAGE: CONFERENCES. Grenoble: Universite des sciences de Grenoble, 1981.

1217. Bourdieu, Pierre and Jean-Claude Passeron. REPRODUCTION IN EDUCATION, SOCIETY AND CULTURE. Tr. of LA REPRODUCTION: ELEMENTS POUR UNE THEORIE DU SYSTEME D'ENSEIGNEMENT. Paris: Editions de Minuit, 1970. Tr. by Richard Nice with a foreward by Tom Bottomore. London and Beverly Hills: Sage Publications, 1977.

1218. Bouveresse, Jacques. LE MYTHE DE L'INTERIORITE: EXPERIENCE, SIGNIFICATION, ET LANGAGE PRIVE CHEZ WITTGENSTEIN. Paris: Editions de Minuit, 1976.

An extensive biography is included on pages 677-693.

1219. Bouveresse, Jacques. LE PHILOSOPHE CHEZ LES AUTOPHAGES. Paris: Editions de Minuit, 1984.

1220. Bouveresse, Jacques. RATIONALITE ET CYNISME. Paris: Editions de Minuit, 1984.

1221. Brague, Remi. DU TEMPS CHEZ PLATON ET ARISTOTE: QUATRE ETUDES. Paris: Presses Universitaires de France, 1982.

1222. Canguilhem, Georges. ETUDES D'HISTOIRE ET DE PHILOSOPHIE DES SCIENCES. 5th enl ed. Paris: J. Vrin, 1983.

1223. Canguilhem, Georges. IDEOLOGY AND RATIONALITY IN THE HISTORY OF THE LIFE SCIENCES. 2d. rev ed. Tr. of IDEOLOGIE ET RATIONALITE DANS L'HISTOIRE DES SCIENCES DE LA VIE: NOUVELLES ETUDES D'HISTOIRE ET DE PHILOSOPHIE DES SCIENCES. Paris: J. Vrin, 1981. Tr. by Arthur Goldhammer. Cambridge: MIT Press, 1988.

1224. Canguilhem, Georges. ON THE NORMAL AND THE PATHOLOGICAL. Tr. of NORMAL ET LE PATHOLOGIQUE. Paris: Presses Universitaires de France, 1966. Tr. by Carolyn R. Fawcett. Dordrecht and Boston: Reidel, 1978.

This work includes an introduction by Michel Foucault.

1225. Canguilhem, Georges, et al. ANATOMIE D'UN EPISTEMOLOGUE: FRANCOIS DAGOGNET. Paris: Libraries Philosophique J. Vrin, 1984.

This work contains an epilogue of objections with responses by Francois Dagognet.

1226. Castelli, Enrico, et al. HERMENEUTIQUE DE LA SECULARISATION: ACTES. Tr. of ERMENEUTICA DELLA SECOLAIZZAZIONE. Padua: CEDAM, 1976. Paris: Aubier Montaigne, 1976.

This work derives from a colloquium organized by la Centre International d'etudes humanistes and by the l'Institut d'etudes de philosophiques de Rome in Rome, January 3-8, 1976.

1227. Centre national de la recherche scientifique (France). PHILOSOPHES IBERIQUES ET IBERO-AMERICAINS EN EXIL. Toulouse: Association des publications de l'Universite de Toulousse-Le Mirail, 1977.

1228. Centre national de la recherche scientifique (France). PHILOSOPHIE DU LANGAGE ET GRAMMAIRE DANS L'ANTIQUITE. Brussels: Editions Ousia; Grenoble: Universite des science sociales de Grenoble, 1986.

This volume contains the Proceedings of the Colloque sur philosophies du langage et theories linguistiques dans l'antiquite, Grenoble, September 3-6, 1985.

1229. Chedin, Olivier. SUR L'ESTHETIQUE DE KANT: ET LA THEORIE CRITIQUE DE LA REPRESENTATION. Paris: J. Vrin, 1982.

1230. Clark, Michael. MICHEL FOUCAULT, AN ANNOTATED BIBLIOGRAPHY: TOOL KIT FOR A NEW AGE. New York: Garland, 1982.

1231. Cohen-Solal, Annie. SARTRE: A LIFE. Tr. of SARTRE. Paris: Gallimard, 1985. Tr. by Anna Cancogni. New York: Pantheon, 1987.

1232. Comte, Auguste. CORRESPONDENCE GENERALE ET CONFESSIONS. Ed. by Paulo E. de Berredo Carneiro and Pierre Arnaud. Paris: Mouton, 1973-.

1233. Conche, Marcel. TEMPS ET DESTIN. Villers-sur-Mer: Editions de Megare, 1980.

1234. Culler, Jonathan D. FERDINAND DE SAUSSURE. New York: Penguin Books, 1977c1976.

1235. Dagognet, Francois. FACES, SURFACES, INTERFACES. Paris: J. Vrin, 1982.

1236. Dagognet, Francois. MEMOIRE POUR L'AVENIR: VERS UNE METHODOLOGIE DE L'INFORMATIQUE. Paris: J. Vrin, 1979.

1237. Dagognet, Francois. REMATERIALISER: MATIERES ET MATERIALISMES. Paris: J. Vrin, 1985.

1238. Dagognet, Francois. UNE EPISTEMOLOGIE DE L'ESPACE CONCRET: NEO-GEOGRAPHIE. Paris: J. Vrin, 1977.

1239. Deleuze, Gilles. CINEMA. Vol. 1, THE MOVEMENT-IMAGE. Vol.2, THE TIME IMAGE. Tr. of CINEMA. Vol. 1, L'IMAGE MOUVEMENT. Vol. 2, L'IMAGE-TEMPS. Paris: Minuit, 1983-1985. Tr. by Hugh Tomlinson and Barbara Habberjam. Minneapolis: Univ. of Minnesota Press, 1986-1989.

1240. Deleuze, Gilles. EMPIRICISM AND SUBJECTIVITY: AN ESSAY ON HUME'S THEORY OF HUMAN NATURE. Tr. of EMPIRISME ET SUBJECTIVITE: ESSAI SUR LA NATURE SELON HUME. Paris: Presses Universitaires de France, 1980. Tr. with an introduction by Constantin V. Boundas. New York: Columbia Univ. Press, 1991.

1241. Deleuze, Gilles. FOUCAULT. Ed. by Sean Hand. Tr. of FOUCAULT. Paris: Minuit, 1986. Tr. by Sean Hand. Minneapolis: Univ. of Minnesota Press, 1988.

1242. Deleuze, Gilles. KANT'S CRITICAL PHILOSOPHY: THE DOCTRINE OF THE FACULTIES. Tr. of the 5th ed. of LA PHILOSOPHIE CRITIQUE DE KANT: DOCTRINE DES FACULTIES. Paris: Presses Universitaires de France, 1983. Tr. by Hugh Tomlinson and Barbara Habberjam. Minneapolis: Univ. of Minnesota Press; London: Athlone, 1984.

1243. Deleuze, Gilles. NIETZSCHE AND PHILOSOPHY. Tr. of NIETZSCHE ET LA PHILOSOPHIE. 6th ed. Paris: Presses Universitaires de France, 1962. Tr. by Hugh Tomlinson. London: Athlone Press; New York: Columbia University Press, 1983.

1244. Deleuze, Gilles. SPINOZA, PRACTICAL PHILOSOPHY. Tr. of SPINOZA, PHILOSOPHIE PRATIQUE. Paris: Editions de Minuit, 1981,1970. Tr. by Robert Hur ley. San Francisco: City Lights Books, 1988.

This work was translated into Spanish by Antonio Escochotado and published as SPINO-ZA: FILOSOFIA PRACTICA, in Barcelona by Tusquets in 1984.

1245. Deleuze, Gilles and Felix Guattari. MILLE PLATEAUX. Paris: Editions de Minuit, 1980.

1246. Deleuze, Gilles and Felix Guattari. ANTI-OEDIPUS: CAPITALISM AND SCHIZO-PHRENIA. Tr. of L'ANTI-EDIPE. Paris: Editions de Minuit, 1972. Tr. from the French by Robert Hurley, Mark Seeme, and Helen R. Lane. New York: Viking Press, 1977.

This work also has been translated into Spanish by Francisco Mongel as EL ANTI-EDIPO: CAPITALISMO Y ESQUIZOFRENIA. Barcelona: Paidos, 1985.

1247. Deprun, Jean. LA PHILOSOPHIE DE L'INQUIETUDE EN FRANCE AU XVIIIe SIECLE. Paris: J. Vrin, 1979.

1248. Derrida, Jacques. THE ARCHAEOLOGY OF THE FRIVOLOUS: READING CONDILLAC. 1st ed. Tr. of L'ARCHEOLOGIE DU FRIVOLE: LIRE CONDILLAC. Paris: Denoel/Gonthier, 1976 c1973. Tr. by John P. Leavey. Atlantic Highlands, NJ: Humanities Press; Pittsburgh: Duquesne Univ. Press, 1980.

1249. Derrida, Jacques. DISSEMINATION. Tr. of LA DISSEMINATION. Paris: Editions du Seuil, 1972. Tr. by Barbara Johnson. Chicago: Univ. of Chicago Press; London: Athlone Press, 1981.

This translation includes an introduction and additional notes by Barbara Johnson.

1250. Derrida, Jacques. EDMUND HUSSERL'S "ORIGIN OF GEOMETRY": AN INTRODUCTION. Tr. of INTRODUCTION A "L'ORIGINE DE LA GEOMETRIE" DE HUSSERL. Paris: Presses universitaires de France, 1962. Tr. by J. P. Leavey. Stony Brook, NY: Hays; Hassocks: Harvester, 1978.

This work includes a French and English bibliography of Jacques Derrida; the Appendix, pages 155-180, contains THE ORIGIN OF GEOMETRY by Edmund Husserl, first published in 1939 under the title: DIE FRAGE NACH DEM URSPRUNG DER GEO-METRIE ALS INTENTIONAL-HISTORISCHES PROBLEM.

1251. Derrida, Jacques. EPERONS: LES STYLES DE NIETZSCHE: SPURS: NIETZSCHE'S STYLES=SPOREN DIE STILE NIETZSCHES=SPRONI: GLI STILI DI NIETZSCHE. Venice: Corbo e fiore, 1976.

This French work also has English, German, and Italian translations. An edition with English and French on facing pages was published by the University of Chicago Press in 1978.

1252. Derrida, Jacques. MARGINS OF PHILOSOPHY. Tr. of MARGES DE LA PHI-LOSOPHIE. Paris: Editions Minuit, 1972. Tr. by Alan Bass. Chicago: Univ. of Chicago Press; Sussex: Harvester, 1982.

1253. Derrida, Jacques. MEMOIRES FOR PAUL DE MAN. Tr. by Cecile Lindsay,

Jonathan Culler and Eduardo Cadova.´ New York: Columbia Univ. Press, 1986.

These are the Wellek Library Lectures given at the University of California, Irvine.

1254. Derrida, Jacques. OF GRAMMATOLOGY. 1st American ed. Tr. of DE LA GRAMMATOLOGIE. Paris: Editions de Minuit, 1967. Tr. by G. C. Spivak. Baltimore: Johns Hopkins, 1976.

1255. Derrida, Jacques. OF SPIRIT: HEIDEGGER AND THE QUESTION. Tr. of DE L'ESPRIT: HEIDEGGER ET LA QUESTION. Paris: Editions Galilee, 1987. Tr. by Geoffrey Bennington and Rachel Bowlby. Chicago: Univ. of Chicago Press, 1989.

This conference was held on March 14, 1987, at the time of a colloquium on Heidegger organized by the International College of Philosophy at Paris. This work contains a bibliography on pages 115-139.

1256. Derrida, Jacques. POSITIONS. Tr. of POSITIONS: ENTRETIENS AVEC HENRI RONSE, JULIA KRISTEVA, JEAN-LOUIS HOUDEBINE, GUY SCARPETTA. Paris: Editions de Minuit, 1972. Tr. and annotated by Alan Bass. Chicago: Univ. of Chicago Press; London: Athlone, 1981.

1257. Derrida, Jacques. THE POST CARD: FROM SOCRATES TO FREUD AND BEYOND. LA CARTE POSTALE DE SOCRATE A FREUD ET AU-DELA. Paris: Flammarion, 1980. Tr. by Alan Bass. Chicago: Univ. of Chicago Press, 1987.

The translation includes an introduction and additional notes by Alan Bass.

1258. Derrida, Jacques. THE TRUTH IN PAINTING. Tr. of VERITE EN PEINTURE. Paris: Flammarion, 1978. Tr. by Geoff Bennington and Ian McLeod. Chicago: Univ. of Chicago Press, 1987.

1259. Derrida, Jacques. WRITING AND DIFFERENCE. Tr. of L'ECRITURE ET LA DIFFERENCE. Paris: Edition de Seuil, 1967. Tr., with an introduction and additional notes by Alan Bass. Chicago: Univ. of Chicago Press, 1978.

A complete bibliography of Derrida's works through 1978, together with critical commentary, is provided in RESEARCH IN PHENOMENOLOGY 8 (1978).

1260. Desanti, Jean Toussaint. LES PHILOSOPHIE ET LES POUVOIRS: ENTRETIENS AVEC PASCAL LAINE ET BLANDINE BARRET-KRIEGEL. Paris. Calman-Levy: 1976.

1261. Desanti, Jean Toussaint. UN DESTIN PHILOSOPHIQUE. Paris: B. Grosset, 1982.

1262. Descombes, Vincent. L'INCONSCIENT MALGRE LUI. Paris: Editions de Minuit, 1977.

1263. Descombes, Vincent. MODERN FRENCH PHILOSOPHY. Tr. of LE MEME ET L'AUTRE: QUARANNTE-CINQ ANS DE PHILOSOPHIE FRANCAISE (1933-1978). Paris: Editions de Minuit, 1979. Tr. by Lorna Scott-Fox and Jeremy M. Harding. Cambridge and New York: Cambridge Univ. Press, 1980.

1264. Descombes, Vincent. OBJECTS OF ALL SORTS: A PHILOSOPHICAL GRAMMAR. Tr. of GRAMMAIRE D'OBJECTS EN TOUS GENRES. Paris: Editions de minuit, 1983. Tr. by Lorna Scott-Fox and Jeremy Harding. Baltimore: Johns Hopkins Univ. Press, 1986.

1265. Descombes, Vincent. PHILOSOPHIE PAR GROS TEMPS. Paris: Minuit, 1989.

1266. Dillon, Martin C. MERLEAU-PONTY VIVANT. Albany: New York State Univ. Press, 1991.

This work contains essays by Edward. S. Casey, Duane H. Davis, David Michael Levin, Alphonso Lingis, G. B. Madison, Joseph Margolis, Hugh J. Silverman, and Jacques Tamineaux.

1267. Dillon, Martin C. MERLEAU-PONTY'S ONTOLOGY. Bloomington: Indiana Univ. Press, 1988.

1268. Dreyfus, Hubert L. and Paul Rabinow. MICHEL FOUCAULT, BEYOND STRUCTURALISM AND HERMENEUTICS. 2d ed. Chicago: Univ. of Chicago Press, 1983.

1269. Duby, George and Guy Lardreau. DIALOGUES. Paris: Flammarion, 1980.

1270. Ducrot, Oswald. STRATEGIES DISCURSIVES: ACTES DU COLLOQUE DU CENTRE DE RECHERCHES LINGUISTIQUES ET SEMIOLOGIQUES DE LYON, 20-22 MAY 1977. Lyons: Presses Universitaires de Lyons, 1978.

1271. Dufour-Kowalska, Gabrielle. MICHEL HENRY, UN PHILOSOPHE DE LA VIE ET DE LA PRAXIS. Paris: Librairie Philosophique J. Vrin, 1980.

1272. Dufrenne, Mikel. IN THE PRESENCE OF THE SENSUOUS: ESSAYS IN AESTHETICS. Ed. by Mark S. Roberts and Dennis Gallagher. Tr. by the editors. Atlantic Highlands, NJ: Humanities Press International, 1986.

The work includes a bibliography of Mikel Dufrenne on pages 199-207.

1273. Dufrenne, Mikel. L`INVENTAIRE DES A PRIORI: RECHERCHE DE L`ORIGINAIRE. Paris: C. Bourgois, 1981.

1274. Dufrenne, Mikel. MAIN TRENDS IN AESTHETICS AND THE SCIENCES OF ART. New York and London: Holmes and Meier, 1979c1978.

This work was originally published as Chapters 4 and 5 of MAIN TRENDS OF RESEARCH IN THE SOCIAL AND HUMAN SCIENCES, UNESCO, 1978. There is a bibliography on pages 353-418.

1275. Dufrenne, Mikel. SUBVERSION-PERVERSION. Paris: Presses Universitaires de France, 1977.

1276. Dufrenne, Mikel, et al. SARTRE/BARTHES. Toulouse: Privat, 1982.

1277. Dumont, Louis. ESSAYS ON INDIVIDUALISM: MODERN IDEOLOGY IN ANTHROPOLOGICAL PERSPECTIVE. Tr. of ESSAIS SUR L'INDIVIDUALISME: UNE PERSPECTIVE ANTHROPOLOGIQUE SUR L'IDEOLOGIE MODERNE. Paris: Editions du Seuil, 1983. Tr. by Louis Dumont. Chicago: Univ. of Chicago, 1986.

There is a bibliography on pages 269-278.

1278. Eribon, Didier. MICHEL FOUCAULT. Tr. of MICHEL FOUCAULT: 1926-1984. Paris: Flammarion, 1989. Tr. by Betsy Wing. Cambridge: Harvard Univ. Press, 1991.

1279. Ey, Henri. CONSCIOUSNESS: A PHENOMENOLOGICAL STUDY OF BEING CONSCIOUS AND BECOMING CONSCIOUS. Tr. of LA CONSCIENCE. Paris: Presses de Universitaires de France, 1963. Tr. from the French by John H. Flodstrom. Bloomington: Indiana Univ. Press, 1978.

This work was tranlated into German in 1967 as DAS BEWUSSTSEIN. It was published in Berlin by de Gruyter.

1280. Farias, Victor. HEIDEGGER AND NAZISM. Ed. by Joseph Zalman Margolis and Tom Rockmore. Tr. of HEIDEGGER ET LE NAZISME. Paris: Verdier, 1987. French materials were translated by Paul Burrell with the advice of Dominic Di Bernardi and German materials were translated by Gabriel R. Ricci. There is an extensive bibliography on pages 303-338. Philadelphia: Temple Univ. Press, 1989.

1281. Fauconnier, Gilles. ESPACES MENTAUX: ASPECTS DE LA CONSTRUCTION DU SENS DANS LES LANGUES NATURELLES. Paris: Editions de Minuit, 1984.

1282. Ferry, Luc. POLITICAL PHILOSOPHY. Vol. 1, RIGHTS: THE NEW QUARREL BETWEEN THE ANCIENTS AND THE MODERNS. 2d. corr ed. Tr. of PHILOSOPHIE POLITIQUE. Vol. 1, LE DROIT: LA NOUVELLE QUERELLE DES ANCIENS ET DES MODERNES. Vol. 2, LE SYSTEME DES PHILOSOPHIES DE L'HISTOIRE. Vol. 3, DES DROITS DE L'HOMME A L'IDEE REPUBLICAINE. Paris: P. Tr. by Franklin Philip. Chicago: Univ. of Chicago Press, 1990-.

1283. Ferry, Luc and Alain Renaut. HEIDEGGER AND MODERNITY. Tr. of HEIDEGGER ET LES MODERNES. Paris: B. Grasset, 1988. Tr. by Franklin Philip. Chicago: Univ. of Chicago Press, 1990.

1284. Ferry, Luc and Alain Renaut. LA PENSEE 68: ESSAI SUR L'ANTI-HUMANISME CONTEMPORAINE. Paris: Gallimard, 1985.

1285. Ferry, Luc and Alain Renaut. SYSTEME ET CRITIQUE: ESSAIS SUR LA CRITIQUE DE LA RAISON DANS LA PHILOSOPHIE CONTEMPORAINE. Brussels, Ousia, 1984.

1286. Forget, Philippe. TEXT UND INTERPRETATION: DEUTSCH-FRANZOSISCHE DEBATTE. Munich: W. Fink, 1984.

This German-French debate includes contributions by Hans-Georg Gadamer, Manfred Frank, Jacques Derrida, Philippe Forget, Jean Greisch, and Francois Laruelle.

1287. Foucault, Michel. DISCIPLINE AND PUNISH: THE BIRTH OF THE PRISON. Tr. of SURVEILLER ET PUNIR: NAISSANCE DE LA PRISON. Paris: Gallimard, 1975. Tr. by Alan Sheridan. New York: Pantheon, 1977.

In 1976 the German translation, UBERWACHEN UND STRAFEN: GEBURT. D. GEFANGNISSES, was published by Suhrkamp in Frankfurt am Main. The translator was Walter Seitter.

1288. Foucault, Michel. THE HISTORY OF SEXUALITY. Vol. 1, AN INTRODUCTION. Vol. 2, THE USE OF PLEASURE. Vol. 3, THE CARE OF THE SELF. Tr. of HISTOIRE DE LA SEXUALITE. Vol. 1, LA VOLONTE DE SAVOIR. Vol. 2, L'USAGE DES PLAISIRS. Vol. 3, LE SOUCI DE SOI. Paris: Gallimard, 1976-. Tr. by Robert Hurley. New York: Pantheon, 1978-1987.

The Spanish translation, HISTORIA DE LA SEXUALIDAD, Vol. 1, VOLUNTAD DE SABER. Vol. 2, EL USO DE LOS PIACERES. Vol. 3, LA INQUIETUD DE SI, was published in Mexico by Siglio Veintiuno Editores in 1977. Ulises Guinaz was the translator.

1289. Foucault, Michel. LANGUAGE, COUNTER-MEMORY, PRACTICE: SELECTED ESSAYS AND INTERVIEWS. Ed. by Donald F. Bouchard. Tr. by Donald F. Bouchard and Sherry Simon. Ithaca: Cornell Univ. Press; Oxford: B. Blackwell, 1977.

1290. Foucault, Michel. POWER/KNOWLEDGE: SELECTED INTERVIEWS AND OTHER WRITINGS, 1972-1977. Ed. by Colin Gordon. Tr. by Colin Gordon et al. New York: Pantheon Books; Sussex: Harvester Press, 1980.

The bibliography includes the Writings of Michel Foucault on pages 261-270.

1291. Foucault, Michel. THIS IS NOT A PIPE. Ed. by James Harkness. Tr. of CECI N'EST PAS UNE PIPE. Montpelier: Fata Morgana 1973. Berkeley: Univ. of California Press, 1983.

The volume contains illustrations and letters by Rene Magritte.

1292. Gasche, Rodolphe. THE TAIN OF THE MIRROR: DERRIDA AND THE PHILOSOPHY OF REFLECTION. Cambridge: Harvard Univ. Press, 1986.

1293. Gerard, Gilbert. CRITIQUE ET DIALECTIQUE: L'ITINERAIRE DE HEGEL A IENA (1801-1805). Brussels: Facultes Universitaires Saint-Louis, 1982.

1294. Gerassi, John. JOHN-PAUL SARTRE: HATED CONSCIENCE OF HIS CENTURY. Vol. 1, PROTESTANT OR PROTESTER? Chicago: Univ. of Chicago Press, 1989.

1295. Gilson, Etienne. FROM ARISTOTLE TO DARWIN AND BACK AGAIN: A JOURNEY IN FINAL CAUSALITY, SPECIES AND EVOLUTION. Tr. of D'ARISTOTE A DARWIN ET RETOUR: ESSAI SUR QUELQUES CONSTANTES DE LA BIOPHILOSOPHIE. Paris: J. Vrin, 1971. Tr. by John Lyon. Notre Dame, IN: Univ. of Notre Dame Press, 1984.

1296. Glucksmann, Andre. CYNISME ET PASSION. Paris: B. Grasset, 1981.

1297. Glucksmann, Andre. THE MASTER THINKERS. Tr. of LES MAITRES PENSEURS. Paris: B. Grasset, 1977. Tr. by Brian Pearce. New York: Harper and Row; Sussex: Harvester, 1980.

1298. Goederts, Georges. NIETZSCHE, CRITIQUE DES VALEURS CHRETIENNES: SOUFFRANCE ET COMPASSION. Paris: Edition Beauchesne, 1977.

1299. Goldmann, Lucien. LUKACS AND HEIDEGGER: TOWARDS A NEW PHILOSOPHY. Tr. of LUKACS ET HEIDEGGER: FRAGMENTS POSTHUMES ETABLIS ET PRESENT ES PAR YOUSSEF ISHAGHPOUR. Paris: Denoel/Gonthier, 1973. Tr. by William Q. Boelhower. London and Boston: Routledge & Kegan Paul, 1977.

1300. Granier, Jean. NIETZSCHE. QUE SAIS-JE? Paris: Presses Universitaires de France, 1982.

1301. Granier, Jean. PENSER LA PRAXIS. 1st rev ed. Paris: Presses Universitaires de France, 1980.

1302. Greimas, Algirdas Julien. DESCRIPTION ET NARRATIVITE: SUIVI DE A PROPOS DU JEU. Paris: Groupe de recherches semio-linguistiques, Ecole des hautes etudes en sciences sociales, Centre Nacional de la recherche scientifique, 1980.

DESCRIPTION ET NARRATIVITE DAN "LA FICELLE" DE GUY DE MAUPASSANT is the title of the first essay which includes the full text of LA FICELLE.

1303. Greimas, Algirdas Julien. DU SENS II: ESSAIS SEMIOTIQUES. Paris: Seuil, 1983.

1304. Greimas, Algirdas Julien. MAUPASSANT: THE SEMIOTICS OF TEXT: PRACTICAL EXERCISES. Tr. of MAUPASSANT: LA SEMIOTIQUE DU TEXTE: EXERCI-

CES PRACTIQUES. Paris: Editions du Seuil, 1976. Tr. by Paul Perron. Amsterdam and Philadelphia: J. Benjamins, 1988.

1305. Greimas, Algirdas Julien. ON MEANING: SELECTED WRITINGS IN SEMIOTIC THEORY. Tr. by Paul J. Pereron and Frank H. Collins. Minneapolis: Univ. of Minnesota Press, 1987.

1306. Greimas, Algirdas Julien, et al. INTRODUCTION A L'ANALYSE DU DISCOURS EN SCIENCES SOCIALES. Paris: Hachette, 1979.

1307. Greisch, Jean. HERMENEUTIQUE ET GRAMMATOLOGIE. Paris: Editions du Centre national de la recherche scientifique, 1977.

1308. Gueroult, Martial. DESCARTES' PHILOSOPHY INTERPRETED ACCORDING TO THE ORDER OF REASON. Vol. 1, THE SOUL AND GOD. Vol. 2, THE SOUL AND THE BODY. Tr. of DESCARTES SELON L'ORDRE DES RAISONS. Paris: Aubier, 1953. Vol 1, L'AME ET DIEU. Vol. 2, L'AME ET LE CORP. Tr. by Roger Ariew. Minneapolis: Univ. of Minnesota Press, 1984-1985.

1309. Gunter, Pete Addison. HENRI BERGSON: A BIBLIOGRAPHY. Rev. 2d ed. Bibliographies of Famous Philosophers. Bowling Green, OH: Philosophy Documentation Center, 1986.

This volume contains over 2,000 new entries and over 1,000 new annotations.

1310. Haar, Michel. MARTIN HEIDEGGER. L'Herne. Paris: L'Herne, 1983.

In addition to the bibliography on pages 477-513, this volume includes texts by Heidegger translated into French.

1311. Habachi, Rene. LE MOMENT DE L'HOMME. Paris: Desclee de Brouwer, 1984.

1312. Habachi, Rene. TROIS ITINERAIRES UN CARREFOUR: GABRIEL MARCEL, MAURICE ZUNDEL ET PIERRE TEILHARD DE CHARDIN. Quebec: les Presses de l'Universite Laval, 1983.

1313. Helvetius, Claude Adrien. CORRESPONDANCE GENERALE D'HELVETIUS. Vol. 1, 1737-1756, LETTRES 1-249. Vol. 2, 1757-1760, LETTRES 250-464. Vol. 3, LETTRES 465-719 (1761-1774). Ed. by David Smith, et al. Toronto: University of Toronto Press; Oxford: The Voltaire Foundation, 1981-.

1314. Henry, Michel. MARX: A PHILOSOPHY OF HUMAN REALITY. Tr. of MARX. Vol. 1, UNE PHILOSOPHIE DE LE REALITE. Vol. 2, UNE PHILOSOPHIE DE L'ECONOMIE. Paris: Gallimard, 1976. Tr. by Kathleen McLaughlin. Bloomington: Indiana Univ. Press, 1983.

This is an abridged translation of a two volume work in which the usual depiction of Marxist thought as an economically oriented analysis of social reality is contrasted with the author's contention that in Marx's theory philosophy is primary. Central to this author's reading of Marx is the theory of praxis.

1315. Hill, Claire Ortiz. WORD AND OBJECT IN HUSSERL, FREGE, AND RUSSELL: THE ROOTS OF TWENTIETH-CENTURY PHILOSOPHY. Series in Continental Thought, Vol. 17. Athens: Ohio Univ. Press, 1991.

1316. Irigaray, Luce. AMANTE MARINE: DE FRIEDRICH NIETZSCHE. Paris: Editions de Minuit, 1980.

1317. Irigaray, Luce. L'OUBLI DE L'AIR CHEZ MARTIN HEIDEGGER. Paris: Editions de Minuit, 1983.

1318. Jambet, Christian. APOLOGIE DE PLATON: ESSAIS DE METAPHYSIQUE. Paris: B. Grasset, 1976.

1319. Jambet, Christian. HENRY CORBIN. Paris: Herne, 1981.

There is a bibliography on pages 345-360.

1320. Jambet, Christian. LA LOGIQUE DES ORIENTAUX: HENRY CORBIN ET LA SCIENCE DES FORMES. Paris: Editions du Seuil, 1983.

1321. Jambet, Christian and Guy Lardreau. ONTOLOGIE DE LA REVOLUTION. Vol. 1, L'ANGE: POUR UNE CYNEGETTIQUE DE SEMBLANT. Vol. 2, LE MONDE: RESPONSE A LA QUESTION, QU'EST-CE QUE LES DROITS DE L'HOMME? Paris: B. Grasset, 1976-1978.

1322. Jeanson, Francis. SARTRE AND THE PROBLEM OF MORALITY. Tr. of LA PROBLEME MORAL ET LA PENSEE DE SARTRE. Paris: Editions du Seuil, 1947. Tr. by Robert V. Stone. Bloomington: Indiana Univ. Press, 1980.

This study has been said to be the only detailed interpretation of his work Sartre every fully recommended.

1323. Koyre, Alexandre. GALILEO STUDIES. Tr. of: ETUDES GALILEENNES. Vol. 1, A. L'AUBE DE LA SCIENCE CLASSIQUE. Vol. 2, LA LOI DE LA CHUTE DES CORPS. DESCARTES ET GALILEE. Vol. 3, GALILEE ET LA LOI D'ENERTIE. Paris: Hermann, 1939. Atlantic Highlands, NJ: Humanities Press; Sussex: Harvester, 1978.

1324. Kremer-Marietti, Angele. LA MORALE. Paris: Presses Universitaires de France, 1982.

1325. Kruks, Sonia. THE POLITICAL PHILOSOPHY OF MERLEAU-PONTY. Atlantic Highlands NJ: Humanities Press; Brighton, Sussex: Harvester Press, 1981.

1326. Kurzweil, Edith. THE AGE OF STRUCTURALISM: LEVI-STRAUS TO FOUCAULT. New York: Columbia Univ. Press, 1980.

1327. Labica, Georges. MARXISM AND THE STATUS OF PHILOSOPHY. Tr. of LE STATUT MARXISTE DE LA PHILOSOPHIE. Brussels: Editions Complexe, 1976. Tr. from the French by Kate Soper and Martin Ryle. Atlantic Highlands, NJ: Humanities Press; Sussex: Harvester Press, 1980.

1328. Lacan, Jacques. ECRITS: A SELECTION. Tr. by Alan Sheridan. New York: Norton, 1977.

1329. Lacoue-Labarthe, Philippe. L'IMITATION DES MODERNES. Paris: Galilee, 1986.

The book brings together the author's papers and talks from 1978-1985.

1330. Lacoue-Labarthe, Philippe. LA POESIE COMME EXPERIENCE. Paris: C. Bourgois, 1986.

1331. Lacoue-Labarthe, Philippe. LE SUJET DE LA PHILOSOPHIE (TYPOGRAPHIES I). Paris: Aubier Flammarion, 1979.

1332. Lacoue-Labarthe, Philippe and Jean-Luc Nancy. LES FINS DE L`HOMME: A PARTIRE DU TRAVAIL DE JACQUES DERRIDA: COLLOQUE DE CERISY, 23 JUILLET-2 AUOT 1980. Paris: Éditions Galilee, 1981.

1333. LaPointe, Francois H. JEAN-PAUL SARTRE AND HIS CRITICS: AN INTERNATIONAL BIBLIOGRAPHY, 1938-1980. Annotated and revised 2d ed. Bibliographies of Famous Philosophers. Bowling Green, OH: Philosophy Documentation Center, 1981.

1334. LaPointe, Francois H. and Claire C. LaPointe. CLAUDE LEVI-STRAUSS AND HIS CRITICS: AN INTERNATIONAL BIBLIOGRAPHY OF CRITICISM (1950-1976). New York: Garland, 1977.

1335. LaPointe, Francois H. and Claire C. LaPointe. GABRIEL MARCEL AND HIS CRITICS: AN INTERNATIONAL BIBLIOGRAPHY (1928-1976). New York: Garland, 1977.

1336. LaPointe, Francois H. and Claire C. LaPointe. MAURICE MERLEAU-PONTY AND HIS CRITICS: AN INTERNATIONAL BIBLIOGRAPHY (1942-1976). New York: Garland, 1976.

1337. Lardreau, Guy. DISCOURS PHILOSOPHIQUE ET DISCOURS SPIRITUEL: AUTOUR DE LA PHILOSOPHIE SPIRITUELLE DE PHILOXENE DE MABBOUG. Paris: Editions du Seuil, 1985.

The volume contains a bibliography on pages 153-185.

1338. Lardreau, Guy. LA MORT DE JOSEPH STALINE: BOUFFONNERIE PHILOSOPHIQUE. Paris: B. Grasset, 1978.

1339. Largeault, Jean. PRINCIPES DE PHILOSOPHIE REALISTE. Paris: Klincksieck, 1985.

1340. Largeault, Jean. SYSTEMES DE LA NATURE. Paris: J. Vrin, 1985.

1341. Laruelle, Francois. LE PRINCIPE DE MINORITE. Paris: Aubier-Montaigne, 1981.

In this work, the author claims that minority groups are essential parts of the state's unity.

1342. Laruelle, Francois. PHILOSOPHIE ET NON-PHILOSOPHIE. Liege and Brussels: P. Mardaga, 1989.

1343. Le Doeuff, Michele. HIPPARCHIA'S CHOICE: AN ESSAY CONCERNING WOMEN, PHILOSOPHY, ETC. Tr. of L'ETUDE ET LE ROUET. Vol. 1, FEMMES DE LA PHILOSOPHIE, ETC. Paris: Seuil, 1989-. Tr. by Trista Selous. Oxford and Cambridge: Blackwell, 1991.

There is a bibliography on pages 317-356.

1344. Lecercle, Jean-Jacque. PHILOSOPHY THROUGH THE LOOKING-GLASS: LANGUAGE, NONSENSE, DESIRE. La Salle, IL: Open Court, 1985.

1345. Lefebvre, Henri. THE PRODUCTION OF SPACE. Tr. of LA PRODUTION DE L'SPACE. Paris: Editions Anthropos, 1974. Tr. of Donald Nicholson-Smith. Oxford and Cambridge: Blackwell, 1991.

1346. Lefebvre, Jean-Pierre and Pierre Macherey. HEGEL ET LA SOCIETE. 2d. ed. Paris: Presses Universitaires de France, 1987.

1347. Levi-Strauss, Claude. MYTH AND MEANING. New York: Schocken Books, 1979.

1348. Levi-Strauss, Claude and Didier Eribon. CONVERSATIONS WITH CLAUDE LEVI-STRAUSS. Tr. of DE PRES ET DE LOIN. Paris: Victor Magan, 1937. Tr. by Paula Wissing. Chicago: Univ. of Chicago Press, 1991.

1349. Levinas, Emmanuel. COLLECTED PHILOSOPHICAL PAPERS OF EMMANUAL LEVINAS. Ed. by Alphonso Lingis. Tr. by Alphonso Lingis. Dordrecht: Nijhoff, 1986.

1350. Levinas, Emmanuel. DE DIEU QUI VIENT A L'IDEE. 2d. rev. and aug ed. Paris: J. Vrin, 1986.

1351. Levinas, Emmanuel. EMMANUEL LEVINAS. Ed. by Joseph Rolland. LaGrasse: Verdier, 1984.

1352. Levinas, Emmanuel. EN D'ECOUVRANT L'EXISTENCE AVEC HUSSERL ET HEIDEGGER: REIMPRESSION CONFROME A LA PREMIERE EDITION SUIVIE D'ESSAIS NOUVEAUX. Paris: Librarie Philosophique, 1982.

1353. Levinas, Emmanuel. ETHICS AND INFINITY: CONVERSATIONS WITH PHILLIPPE NEMO. Tr. of ETHIQUE ET INFINI: DIALOGUES AVEC PHILLIPPE NEMO Paris: Fayard: France Culture, 1982. Tr. by Richard A. Cohen. Pittsburgh: Duquesne Univ. Press, 1985.

1354. Levinas, Emmanuel. EXISTENCE AND EXISTENTS. Tr. of DE L'EXISTENCE A L'EXISTANT. Paris: Fontaine, 1947. Tr. by Alphonso Lingis. The Hague: Nijhoff, 1978.

1355. Levinas, Emmanuel. GOTT NENNEN: PHANOMENOLOGISCHE ZUGANGE. Ed. by Berkhard Casper. Freiburg and Munich: Alber, 1981.

1356. Levinas, Emmanuel. NOMS PROPRES: AGNON, BUBER, CELAN, DEHOMME, DERRIDA, JABES, KIERKEGAARD, LACROIX, LAPORTE, PICARD, PROUST, VAN BREDA, WAHL. Montpellier: Fata Morgana, 1976.

This is a collection of the author's previously published articles.

1357. Levinas, Emmanuel. OTHERWISE THAN BEING: OR BEYOND ESSENCE. Tr. of AUTREMENT QU'ETRE OU, AU-DELA DE L'ESSENCE. 2d. ed. The Hague: Nijhoff, 1978. Tr. by Alphonso Lingis. The Hague and Boston: Nijhoff, 1981.

1358. Levinas, Emmanuel. TIME AND THE OTHER AND ADDITIONAL ESSAYS. Tr. of LE TEMPS ET L'AUTRE, DIACHRONIE ET REPRESENTATION, AND L'ANCIEN ET LE NOUVEAU. Montpellier: Fata Morgana, 1979. Tr. by Richard A. Cohen. Pittsburgh: Duquesne Univ. Press, 1987.

1359. Levinas, Emmanuel. TOTALITE ET INFINI: ESSAI SUR L'EXTERIORITE. 4th ed. TOTALITY AND INFINITY: AN ESSAY ON EXTERIORITY. Tr. of 3d. ed. The Hague and Boston: Nijhoff, 1979. Tr. by Alphonso Lingis. Phenomenologica, Vol. 8. The Hague and Boston: Nijhoff, 1984.

1360. Levinas, Emmanuel. TRANSCENDANCE ET INTELLIGIBILITE: SUIVI D'UN ENTRETIEN. Geneva: Labor et Fides: Centre Protestant d'Etudes, 1984.

1361. Levinas, Emmanuel, et al. JEAN WAHL AND GABRIEL MARCEL. Paris: Beauchesne, 1976.

1362. Levy, Bernard Henri. BARBARISM WITH A HUMAN FACE. Tr. of BARBARIE A VISAGE HUMAIN. Paris: B. Grasset, 1977. Tr. by George Holoch. New York: Harper and Row, 1979.

1363. Levy, Bernard Henri. QUESTIONS DE PRINCIPE. Paris: Dennoel/Gonthier, 1983.

1364. Llewelyn, John. DERRIDA ON THE THRESHOLD OF SENSE. New York: St. Martin's Press; Basingstoke: Macmillan, 1986.

1365. Lyotard, Jean-Francois. LE DIFFEREND: PHRASES IN DISPUTE. Tr. of LE DIFFEREND. Paris: Editions de Minuit, 1983 1986. Tr. by Georges Van Den Abbeele. Minneapolis: Univ. of Minnesota Press; Manchester: Manchester Univ. Press, 1988.

1366. Lyotard, Jean-Francois. LE POSTMODERN EXPLIQUE AUX ENFANTS: CORRE-SPONDANCE 1982-1985. Paris: Editions Galilee, 1986.

1367. Lyotard, Jean-Francois. LES TRANSFORMATEURS DUCHAMP. Paris: Editions Galilee, 1977.

1368. Lyotard, Jean-Francois. THE POSTMODERN CONDITION: A REPORT ON KNOWLEDGE. Tr. of LA CONDITION POSTMODERNE: RAPPORT SUR LA SAVOIR. Paris: Editions de Minuit, 1979. Tr. by Geoff Bennington and Brian Massumi. Minneapolis: Univ. of Minnesota Press, 1984.

1369. Lyotard, Jean-Francois. RUDIMENTS PAIENS. Paris: U.S.E., 1977.

1370. Lyotard, Jean-Francois. TOMBEAU DE L'INTELLECTUEL: ET AUTRES PAPI-ERS. Paris: Editions Galilee, 1984.

1371. Lyotard, Jean-Francois and Annie Cazenave. L'ART DES CONFINS: MELANGES OFFERTS A MAURICE DE GANDILLAC. Paris: Presses Universitaires de France, 1985.

1372. Lyotard, Jean-Francois and Jean-Loup Theobaud. JUST GAMING. Tr. of AU JUSTE: CONVERSATIONS. Paris: Bourgeois, 1979. Tr. by Wlad Godzick. Theory and History of Literature, Vol. 20. Minneapolis: Univ. of Minnesota Press, 1985.

1373. Macherey, Pierre. COMTE, LA PHILOSOPHIE ET LES SCIENCES. Paris: Press Universitaires de France, 1989.

1374. Macherey, Pierre. HEGEL OU SPINOZA. Paris: F. Maspero, 1979.

1375. Macherey, Pierre. A QUOI PENSE LA LITTERATURE?: EXERCICES DE PHIL-OSOPHIE LITTERAIRE. Paris: Press Universitaires de France, 1990.

This work includes bibliographic references on pages 204-253.

1376. Macherey, Pierre. A THEORY OF LITERARY PRODUCTION. Tr. of POUR UNE THEORIE DE LA PRODUCTION LITTERAIRE. Paris: F. Maspero, 1966. Tr. from the French by Geoffrey Wall. London and Boston: Routledge & Kegan Paul, 1978.

1377. Major, Rene. AFFRANCHISSEMENT DU TRANSFERT ET DE LA LETTRE: COLLOQUE AUTOUR DE LA CARTE POSTALE DE JACQUE DERRIDA, 4 ET 5 AVRIL 1981. Paris: Confrontation, 1982.

1378. Marin, Louis. UTOPICS: SPATIAL PLAY. Tr. of UTOPIQUES: JEUX DESPAC-ES. Paris: Editions de Minuit, 1973. Tr. by Robert A. Vollrath. Atlantic Highlands, NJ: Humanities Press; London: Macmillan, 1984.

1379. Marion, Jean-Luc. SUR LA THEOLOGIE BLANCHE DE DESCARTES: ANALO-GIE, CREATION, DES VERITES ETERNELLES ET FONDEMENT. Paris: Presses Universitaires de France, 1981.

1380. Marty, Francois. LA NAISSANCE DE LA METAPHYSIQUE CHEZ KANT: UNE ETUDE SUR LA NOTION KANTIENNE D'ANALOGIE. Paris: Beauchesne, 1980.

1381. McCarthy, Joseph M. PIERRE TEILHARD DE CHARDIN: A COMPREHENSIVE BIBLIOGRAPHY. New York: Garland, 1981.

1382. Menage, Gilles. THE HISTORY OF WOMEN PHILOSOPHERS. Tr. of HISTORIA MULIERUM PHILOSOPHARUM: SCRIPTORE GIDIO MENAGIO: ACCEDIT EJUSDEM COMMENTARIUS ITALICUS IN VII. SONETTUM FRANCIS CI PE-TRARCHA, A. RE NON ALIENUS. Lugduni: Apud Anissonios, Joan. Posuel, & Claudium . Tr. from the Latin with an introduction by Beatrice Hope Zedler. Lanham, MD: Univ. Press of America, 1984.

1383. Mongis, Henri. HEIDEGGER ET LA CRITIQUE DE LA NOTION DE VALEUR: LA DESTRUCTION DE LA FONDATION METAPHYSIQUE. The Hague: Nijhoff, 1976.

This work contains a preface in the form of a letter from Heidegger.

1384. Montefiore, Alan. PHILOSOPHY IN FRANCE TODAY. Cambridge and New York: Cambridge Univ. Press, 1983.

1385. Moraux, Paul. LE COMMENTAIRE D'ALEXANDRE D'APHRODISE AUX `SECONDS ANALTIQUES' D'ARISTOTE. Berlin and New York: De Gruyter, 1979.

1386. Moreau, Joseph. DE LA CONNAISSANCE SELON THOMAS D'AQUIN. Paris: Beauchesne, 1976.

1387. Moreau, Joseph. STOICISM, EPICURISME, TRADITION HELLINIQUE. Paris: Vrin, 1979.

1388. Nancy, Jean-Luc. L'IMPERATIF CATEGORIQUE. Paris: Flammarion, 1983.

1389. Nancy, Jean-Luc. LE PARTAGE DES VOIX. Paris: Galilee, 1982.

1390. Parain-Vial, Jeanne. LES PHILOSOPHIES DE L'EXISTENCE ET LES LIMITES DE L'HOMME. Paris: J.Vrin, 1981.

1391. Parain-Vial, Jeanne. L`ESTHETIQUE MUSICALE DE GABRIEL MARCEL. Paris: Aubier, 1980.

1392. Parain-Vial, Jeanne. PHILOSOPHIE DES SCIENCES DE LA NATURE: TEN-DANCES NOUVELLES. 2d ed. Paris: Klincksieck, 1983.

1393. Parain-Vial, Jeanne. TENDANCES NOUVELLES DE LA PHILOSOPHIE. Paris: Centurion, 1978.

1394. Piattelli-Palmarini, Massimo. LANGUAGE AND LEARNING: THE DEBATE BETWEEN JEAN PIAGET AND NOAM CHOMSKY. Tr. of THEORIES DU LAN-GAGE, THEORIES DE L'APPRENTISSAGE: LE DEBAT ENTRE JEAN PIAGET ET NOAM CHOMSKY. Paris: Editions du Seuil, 1979. Cambridge: Harvard Univ. Press; London: Routledge & Kegan Paul, 1980.

The volume is based on the transcription of the debate held October, 1975 at Abbaye de

Royaumont near Paris, and it also includes 2 papers written for the participants and distributed before the colloquium. The work has been translated into Spanish: TEORIAS DEL LANGUAJE, TEORIAS DEL APRENTIZAJE: EL DEBATE ENTRE JEAN PIAGET Y NOAM CHOMSKY. Barcelona: Editorial Critica, 1983. Silvia Furio translated the text.

1395. Polin, Raymond. HOBBES, DIEU ET LES HOMMES. Paris: Presses Universitaires de France, 1981.

1396. Ramnoux, Clemence. PARMENIDE ET SES SUCCESSEURS IMMEDIATS. Monte Carlo: Editions du Rocher, 1979.

1397. Recanti, Francois. LA SIGNALISATION DU DISCOURSE. Paris: Larousse, 1982.

1398. Recanti, Francois. LA TRANSPARENCE ET L'ENONCIATION: POUR INTRODUIRE A LA PRAGMATIQUE. Paris: Editions du Seuil, 1979.

1399. Recanti, Francois. MEANING AND FORCE: THE PRAGMATICS OF PERFORMATIVE UTTERANCES. Tr. of LES ECONCES PERFORMATIFS: CONTRIBUTION A LA PRAGMATIQUE. Paris: Editions de Minuit, 1981. Cambridge and New York: Cambridge Univ. Press, 1987.

1400. Recanti, Francois and Anne Marie Diller. LA PRAGMATIQUE. Paris: Larousse, 1979.

1401. Ricoeur, Paul. HERMENEUTICS AND THE HUMAN SCIENCES: ESSAYS ON LANGUAGE, ACTION, AND INTERPRETATION. Ed. by John Brookshire Thompson. Cambridge and New York: Cambridge Univ. Press; Paris: Edition de la Maison des science de l'homme, 1981.

1402. Ricoeur, Paul. INTERPRETATION THEORY: DISCOURSE AND THE SURPLUS OF MEANING. Fort Worth: Texas Christian Univ. Press, 1976.

1403. Ricoeur, Paul. PHILOSOPHICAL HERMENEUTICS AND THEOLOGICAL HERMENEUTICS: IDEOLOGY, UTOPIA, AND FAITH: PROTOCOL OF THE SEVENTEENTH COLLOQUY, 4 NOVEMBER, 1974. Berkeley: Center for Hermeneutical Studies in Hellenistic and Modern Culture, 1976.

1404. Ricoeur, Paul. PHILOSOPHY OF THE WILL. Rev ed. Tr. of PHILOSOPHIE DE LA VOLONTE. 2 Vols. in 3. Vol. 1, LE VOLONTAIRE ET L'INVOLONTAIRE. Vol. 2, FINITUDE ET CULPABILITE: Pt. 1, L'HOMME FAILLIBLE. Pt. 2, LA SYMBOLIQUE DU MAL. Paris: Aubier-Editions Montaigne,. A revised translation by Charles A. Kelbley with an introduction by Walter J. Lowe. New York: Fordham Univ. Press, 1986.

The following have been published to date: Vol. 1, THE VOLUNTARY AND THE INVOLUNTARY. Vol. 2, FINITUDE AND GUILT: Pt. 1, FALLIBLE MAN. Pt. 2, SYMBOLISM AND EVIL.

1405. Ricoeur, Paul. THE RULE OF METAPHOR: MULTIDISCIPLINARY STUDIES OF THE CREATION OF MEANING IN LANGUAGE. Tr. of METAPHORE VIVE. Paris: Seuil, 1975. Tr. by Robert Czerny with Kathleen McLaughlin and John Costello. Toronto: Univ. of Toronto Press, 1977.

LA METAFORA VIVA: DALLA RETORICA ALLA POETICA, PER UN LINGUAGGIO DI RIVELAZIONE is the Italian translation published in Milan in 1976 by Jaca Book. Giuseppe Grampa was the translator. This work has been translated into Spanish at least twice. Graziella Baravelle translated the edition published in 1977 in Buenos

Aires by Ediciones Megapolis. The other Spanish translation, LA METAPHORE VIVA, was published in Madrid by Ediciones Europa in 1980.

1406. Ricoeur, Paul. TIME AND NARRATIVE. Tr. of TEMPS ET RECIT. Vol. 1, without special title], Vol. 2, LA CONFIGURATION DANS LE RECIT DE FICTION, Vol. 3, LE TEMPS RACONTE. Paris: Seuil, 1983-1985. Tr. by Kathleen McLaughlin and David Pallauer. Chicago: Univ. of Chicago Press, 1984-1988.

This first volume of a three-volume study pairs Ricoeur's earlier RULE OF META-PHOR with an analysis of how the plot narrative temporalizes and discloses meaning in history.

1407. Ricoeur, Paul, et al. RECHERCHES SUR LA PHILOSOPHIE ET LE LANGAGE. Grenoble: Vrin, 1982.

1408. Robinet, Andre. ACTES DU COLLOQUE POUR LE CINQUENTENAIRE DE L'ASSOCIATION DES PHILOSOPHIE DE LANGUE FRANCAISE, PARIS, 6-8 JUILLET 1987. Paris: J. Vrin, 1988.

1409. Rosset, Clement. L'ANTI-NATURE: ELEMENTS POUR UNE PHILOSOPHIE TRAGIQUE. 2d ed. Paris: Presses Universitaires de France, 1986.

1410. Rosset, Clement. L'OBJET SINGULIER. New and enl. ed. Paris: Editions de Minuit, 1985c1979.

1411. Rosset, Clement. LA FORCE MAJEURE. Paris: Editions de Minuit, 1983.

1412. Rosset, Clement. LE PHILOSOPHE ET LES SORTILEGES. Paris: Editions de Minuit, 1985.

1413. Rosset, Clement. LE REEL ET SON DOUBLE: ESSAI SUR L'ILLUSION. Rev. and enl. ed. Paris: Gallimard, 1985.

1414. Rosset, Clement. LE REEL: TRAITE DE L'IDIOTIE. Paris: Editions de Minuit, 1977.

1415. Roustang, Francois. DIRE MASTERY: DISCIPLESHIP FROM FREUD TO LACAN. Tr. of DESTIN SI FUNESTE. Paris: Editions de Minuit, 1976. Tr. by Ned Lukacher. Baltimore: Johns Hopkins Univ. Press, 1982.

1416. Roustang, Francois. LACAN DE L'EQUIVOQUE A L'IMPASSE. Paris: Editions de Minuit, 1986.

1417. Roustang, Francois. PSYCHOANALYSIS NEVER LETS GO. Tr. of--ELLE NE LE LACHE PLUS. Paris: Editions de minuit, 1980. Tr. by Ned Lukacher. Baltimore: Johns Hopkins Univ. Press, 1983.

1418. Sartre, Jean-Paul. CRITIQUE OF DIALECTICAL REASON. Vol. 1, THEORY OF PRACTICAL ENSEMBLES. Ed. by Jonathan Ree. Tr. by Alan Sheridan-Smith. London: NLB; Atlantic Highlands, N J: Humanities Press, 1976.

Vol. 2, THE INTELLIGIBILITY OF HISTORY (unfinished) edited by Arlette Elkaim-Sartre and translated by Quintin Hoare was published in 1991 in London and New York by Verso Press.

1419. Sartre, Jean-Paul. THE FAMILY IDIOT: GUSTAVE FLAUBERT, 1821-1857. 4 Vols. Tr. of: IDIOT DE LA FAMILLE. Paris: Gallimard, 1971. Tr. by Carol Cosman. Chicago: Univ. of Chicago Press, 1981-1991.

1420. Sartre, Jean-Paul. THE FREUD SCENARIO. Ed. by J. B. Ponntalis. Tr. of LE SCENARIO FREUD. Paris: Gallimard, 1984. Tr. by Quintin Hoare. Chicago: Univ. of Chicago Press, 1985.

FREUD, ALEM DE ALMA: ROTEIRO PARA UM FILME is the title of Jorge Laelette's Portuguese translation. It was published in Rio de Janeiro by Editora Nova Fronteira in 1986.

1421. Sartre, Jean-Paul. SARTRE BY HIMSELF. Tr. by Richard Seaver. New York: Urizen Books, 1978.

The text of this book has been taken from the film directed by Alexandre Astruc and Michel Contat.

1422. Schilpp, Paul Arthur. THE PHILOSOPHY OF JEAN-PAUL SARTRE. Library of Living Philosophers, Vol. XVI. LaSalle, IL: Open Court, 1981.

The transcript of a long taped interview with Sartre replaces the usual intellectual biography and reply to critics, which Sartre's failing eyesight prevented him from writing. Thirty philosophers contribute descriptive and critical essays.

1423. Schilpp, Paul Arthur and Lewis Edwin Hahn. THE PHILOSOPHY OF GABRIEL MARCEL. 1st ed. Library of Living Philosophers, Vol. XVII. LaSalle, IL: Open Court, 1984.

This volume contains an autobiographical essay and descriptive and critical essays on Gabriel Marcel's philosophy with his replies and a bibliography of the writings of Gabriel Marcel compiled by Francois H. LaPointe.

1424. Schneiderman, Stuart. RETURNING TO FREUD: CLINICAL PSYCHOANALYSIS IN THE SCHOOL OF LACAN. New Haven: Yale Univ. Press, 1980.

1425. Schurmann, Reiner. HEIDEGGER ON BEING AND ACTING: FROM PRINCIPLES TO ANARCHY. Tr of LE PRINCIPE D'ANARCHIE: HEIDEGGER ET LA QUESTION DE L'AGIR. Paris: Seuil, 1982. Tr. by Christine Marie Gros in collaboration with the author. Bloomington: Univ. of Indiana Press, 1986.

1426. Searle, John R. SENS ET EXPRESSION: ETUDES DE THEORIE DES ACTES DE LANGAGE. Tr. of EXPRESSION AND MEANING: STUDIES IN THE THEORIES OF SPEECH ACTS Cambridge and New York: Cambridge Univ. Press, 1979. Tr. by Joelle Proust. Paris: Les Editions de Minuit, 1982.

1427. Serres, Michel. CARPACCIO: AESTHETISCHE ZUGANGE. Tr. of ESTHETIQUES SUR CARPACCIO. Paris: Hermann, 1975. Tr. by Ulrich Raulff. Reinbek bei Hamburg: Rowohlt, 1981.

1428. Serres, Michel. DETACHMENT. Tr. of DETACHEMENT: APOLOQUE. Paris: Flammarion, 1983. Tr. by Genevieve James and Raymond Federman. Athens, OH: Ohio Univ. Press, 1989.

1429. Serres, Michel. GENESE: RECITS METAPHYSIQUES. Paris: B. Grasset, 1982.

1430. Serres, Michel. HERMES. Paris: Editions de Minuit, 1968-.

These collected essays now number 5 volumes: Vol. 1, LA COMMUNICATION (1968). Vol. 2, L'INTERFERENCE (1972). Vol. 3, LA TRADUTION (1974). Vol. 4, LA DISTRIBUTION (1977). Vol. 5, LE PASSAGE DU NORD-OUEST (1980).

1431. Serres, Michel. HERMES: LITERATURE, SCIENCE, PHILOSOPHY. Baltimore: Johns Hopkins Univ. Press, 1982.

1432. Serres, Michel. LA NAISSANCE DE LA PHYSIQUE DANS LE TEXTE DE LUCRECE; FLEUVES ET TURBULENCES. Paris: Éditions de Minuit, 1977.

1433. Serres, Michel. MICHEL SERRES, INTERFERENCES ET TURBULENCES: HOMMAGE. Paris: Edition de Minuit, 1979.

This work contains a bibliography of the works of Michel Serres and contributions by S. Felman, R. Girard, R. Debray, I. Prigogne, I. Steingers, C. Fremont, P. Pachet, C. Rabant, M. A. Sinaceur, M. Pierssens and C. Mouchard.

1434. Serres, Michel. THE PARASITE. Tr. of LE PARASITE. Paris: B. Grasset, 1980. Tr. with notes, by Lawrence R. Schehr. Baltimore: Johns Hopkins Univ. Press, 1982.

1435. Sturrock, John. STRUCTURALISM AND SINCE: FROM LEVI-STRAUSS TO DERRIDA. Oxford and New York: Oxford Univ. Press, 1979.

1436. Thierry, Yves. SENS ET LANGUAGE. Brussells: Ousia, 1983.

1437. Turlot, Fernand. IDEALISME, DIALECTIQUE, ET PERSONALISME: ESSAI SUR LA PHILOSOPHIE D'HAMELIN. Paris: J. Vrin, 1976.

1438. Veto, Miklos. LE FONDEMENT SELON SCHELLING. Paris: Beauchesne, 1977.

1439. Vieillard-Baron, Jean-Louis. PLATON ET L'IDEALISME ALLEMAND (1770-1830). Paris: Beauchesne, 1979.

1440. Wade, Ira Owen. THE STRUCTURE AND FORM OF THE FRENCH ENLIGHTENMENT. Vol. 1, ESPRIT PHILOSOPHIQUE. Vol. 2, ESPRIT REVOLUTIONNAIRE. Princeton: Princeton Univ. Press, 1977.

Vol. 1 contains a bibliography on pages 652-670 and Vol. 2 on pages 417-435.

1441. Whitford, Margaret. THE IRIGARAY READER. Tr. from the French. Oxford and Cambridge: Basil Blackwell, 1991.

This comprehensive collection of Irigary's work includes a number of writings appearing for the first time in English. There are also bibliographies of works by and about Irigary.

GREAT BRITAIN

1442. Abraham, William James and Steven W. Holtzer. THE RATIONALITY OF RELIGIOUS BELIEF. Oxford: Clarendon Press; New York: Oxford Univ. Press, 1987.

This tribute includes contributions by Richard Swinburne, Rom Harre, Michael Dummett, and others. B.G. Mitchell's principle writings are listed on pages 263-264.

1443. Ackrill, John Lloyd. ARISTOTLE THE PHILOSOPHER. Oxford and New York: Oxford Univ. Press, 1981.

1444. Alexander, Peter. IDEAS, QUESTIONS, AND CORPUSCLES: LOCKE AND BOYLE ON THE EXTERNAL WORLD. Cambridge and New York: Cambridge Univ. Press, 1985.

1445. Annas, Julia. AN INTRODUCTION TO PLATO'S REPUBLIC. Oxford: Clarendon

Press; New York: Oxford Univ. Press, 1981.

There is a 1982 edition printed with corrections.

1446. Annas, Julia. OXFORD STUDIES IN ANCIENT PHILOSOPHY: VOLUME I, 1983. New York: Oxford Univ. Press, 1984.

1447. Annas, Julia and Jonathan Barnes. THE MODES OF SKEPTICISM: ANCIENT TEXTS AND MODERN INTERPRETATIONS. Cambridge and New York: Cambridge Univ. Press, 1985.

This is a non-technical translation.

1448. Anscombe, Gertrude Elizabeth Margaret. THE COLLECTED PHILOSOPHICAL PAPERS OF G.E.M. ANSCOMBE. Vol. 1, FROM PARMENIDES TO WITTGEN-STEIN. Vol. 2, METAPHYSICS AND THE PHILOSOPHY OF MIND. Vol. 3, ETHICS, RELIGION, AND POLITICS. Minneapolis: Univ. Of Minnesota Press, 1981.

1449. Appiah, Anthony. ASSERTION AND CONDITIONALS. Cambridge and New York: Cambridge Univ. Press, 1985.

1450. Appiah, Anthony. FOR TRUTH IN SEMANTICS. Oxford and New York: B. Blackwell, 1986.

1451. Archard, David. CONSCIOUSNESS AND THE UNCONSCIOUS. LaSalle, IL: Open Court; London: Hutchinson, 1984.

1452. Aristotle. ARISTOTLE: THE REVISED OXFORD TRANSLATION. 2 Vols. Ed. by Jonathan Barnes. Princeton and Guildford, Eng: Princeton Univ. Press, 1984.

1453. Atiyah, Patrick S. PROMISES, MORALS, AND LAW. Oxford: Clarendon Press; New York: Oxford Univ. Press, 1981.

1454. Atkinson, Ronald F. KNOWLEDGE AND EXPLANATION IN HISTORY: AN INTRODUCTION TO THE PHILOSOPHY OF HISTORY. Ithaca: Cornell Univ. Press, 1978.

1455. Austin, John Langshaw. PHILOSOPHICAL PAPERS. Ed. by James Opie Urmson and Geoffrey James Warnock. 3d ed. Oxford: Clarendon; New York: Oxford Univ. Press, 1979.

This volume includes a new essay entitled "The Line and the Cave in Plato's Republic" which has not appeared anywhere before the publication of this edition.

1456. Ayer, Alfred Jules. CONTEMPORARY PHILOSOPHY. Guilford: Univ. of Surrey, 1983.

1457. Ayer, Alfred Jules. FREEDOM AND MORALITY AND OTHER ESSAYS. Oxford: Clarendon Press; New York: Oxford Univ. Press, 1984.

1458. Ayer, Alfred Jules. THE MEANING OF LIFE. New York: Scribner's, 1990.

1459. Ayer, Alfred Jules. MORE OF MY LIFE. Oxford and New York: Oxford Univ. Press, 1985,1984.

1460. Ayer, Alfred Jules. PART OF MY LIFE: THE MEMOIRS OF A PHILOSOPHER. London: Collins; New York: Harcourt, Brace, Jovanovich, 1977.

1461. Ayer, Alfred Jules. PHILOSOPHY IN THE TWENTIETH CENTURY. London: Weidenfeld and Nicolson; New York: Random House, 1982.

1462. Ayer, Alfred Jules. VOLTAIRE. New York: Random House, 1986.

1463. Ayer, Alfred Jules. WITTGENSTEIN. London: Weidenfeld and Nicolson; New York: Random House, 1985.

1464. Ayres, Michael. LOCKE'S LOGICAL ATOMISM. London: British Academy, 1983.

The text was taken from the Proceedings of the British Academy, London, Vol. LXII 1981.

1465. Baker, Gordon P. and Peter Michael Stephan Hacker. AN ANALYTICAL COMMENTARY ON THE PHILOSOPHICAL INVESTIGATIONS. Vol. 1, WITTGENSTEIN: UNDERSTANDING AND MEANING. Vol. 2, WITTGENSTEIN, RULES, GRAMMAR, AND NECESSITY. Vol. 3, WITTGENSTEIN: MEANING AND MIND. Chicago: Univ. of Chicago Press, 1980-.

1466. Baker, Gordon P. and Peter Michael Stephan Hacker. FREGE, LOGICAL EXCAVATIONS. New York: Oxford Univ. Press; Oxford: Blackwell, 1984.

1467. Baker, Gordon P. and Peter Michael Stephan Hacker. LANGUAGE, SENSE AND NONSENSE: A CRITICAL INVESTIGATION INTO MODERN THEORIES OF LANGUAGE. Oxford: B. Blackwell, 1984.

1468. Baker, Gordon P. and Peter Michael Stephan Hacker. SCEPTICISM, RULES AND LANGUAGE. Oxford and New York: B. Blackwell, 1984.

1469. Baker, Gordon P. and Peter Michael Stephan Hacker. WITTGENSTEIN, RULES, GRAMMAR AND NECESSITY. Oxford and New York: Blackwell, 1985.

This volume includes an analytical commentary on the PHILOSOPHICAL INVESTIGATIONS.

1470. Bambrough, Renford. MORAL SKEPTICISM AND MORAL KNOWLEDGE. London: Routledge and Kegan Paul; Atlantic Highlands, NJ: Humanities Press, 1979.

1471. Barnes, Jonathan. THE PRESOCRATIC PHILOSOPHERS. Vol. 1, THALES TO ZENO. Vol. 2, EMPEDOCLES TO DEMOCRITUS. Rev ed. The Arguments of the Philosophers. London and Boston: Routledge & Kegan Paul, 1982.

1472. Barnes, Jonathan. TERMS AND SENTENCES: THEOPHRASTUS ON HYPOTHETICAL SYLLOGISMS. Oxford: Oxford Univ. Press, 1983c1984.

The text is taken from the Proceedings of the British Academy, London, Vol. LXIX, 1983.

1473. Barnes, Jonathan, et al. ARTICLES ON ARISTOTLE, Vol. 1-4. London: Duckworth, 1975-1979.

1474. Barrow, John D. and Frank J. Tipler. THE ANTHROPIC COSMOLOGICAL PRINCIPLE. Oxford: Oxford Univ. Press, 1986.

1475. Bentham, Jeremy. COLLECTED WORKS. Ed. by James Henderson Burns. London: Athlone Press; Oxford: Clarendon Press; New York: Oxford Univ. Press, 1968-.

1476. Berlin, Isaiah. SELECTED WRITINGS. Ed. by Henry Hardy. London: Hogarth Press; New York: Viking Press, 1978-.

The volumes published are : Vol. 1, RUSSIAN THINKERS. Vol. 2, CONCEPTS AND CATEGORIES: PHILOSOPHICAL ESSAYS. Vol. 3, AGAINST THE CURRENT: ESSAYS IN THE HISTORY OF IDEAS. Vol. 4, PERSONAL IMPRESSIONS. Vol. 5, THE CROOKED TIMBER OF HUMANITY: CHAPTERS IN THE HISTORY OF IDEAS. (Vol. 5 was published by Knopf in New York City and it contains five essays which have never been published before in a book).

1477. Berlin, Isaiah. VICO AND HERDER: TWO STUDIES IN THE HISTORY OF IDEAS. London: Hogarth, 1976.

1478. Bhaskar, Roy. HARRE AND HIS CRITICS: ESSAYS IN HONOUR OF ROM HARRE WITH HIS COMMENTARYON THEM. Oxford, and Cambridge, MA: B. Blackwell, 1990.

1479. Bhaskar, Roy. THE POSSIBILITY OF NATURALISM: A PHILOSOPHICAL CRITIQUE OF THE CONTEMPORARY HUMAN SCIENCES. Atlantic Highlands, NJ: Humanities Press, 1979.

1480. Bhaskar, Roy. A REALISTIC THEORY OF SCIENCE. Atlantic Highlands, NJ: Humanities Press; Sussex: Harvester Press, 1978.

1481. Blackburn, Simon. KNOWLEDGE, TRUTH, AND RELIABILITY. London: Oxford Univ. Press, 1986.

The text is taken from the Proceedings of the British Academy, London, Vol. LXX 1984.

1482. Blackburn, Simon. SPREADING THE WORD. Oxford: Clarendon Press, 1984.

1483. Bloch, Maurice. MARXISM AND ANTHROPOLOGY: THE HISTORY OF A RELATIONSHIP. Oxford: Clarendon Press; New York: Oxford Univ. Press, 1983.

1484. Blumenthal, Henry J. and Robert Austin Markus. ON NEOPLATONISM AND EARLY CHRISTIAN THOUGHT: ESSAYS IN HONOUR OF A. H. ARMSTRONG. London: Variorum Publications, 1981.

This volume contains fourteen essays by J. Whittaker, J. M. Rist, D. O'Brien, P. Hadot, J. Igal, M. T. Clark, R. Russell, G. J. P. O'Daly, and other scholars.

1485. Boden, Margaret A. ARTIFICIAL INTELLIGENCE AND NATURAL MAN. New York: Basic Books; Sussex: Harvester, 1977.

A substantial bibliography is included on pages 475-494.

1486. Bottomore, Tom. A DICTIONARY OF MARXIST THOUGHT. Cambridge: Harvard Univ. Press, 1983.

1487. Bottomore, Tom and Patrick Goode. AUSTRO-MARXISM. Tr. by Tom Bottomore and Patrick Goode. Oxford: Clarendon Press, 1978.

1488. Brown, Harvey R. and Rom Harre. PHILOSOPHICAL FOUNDATIONS OF QUANTUM FIELD THEORY. Oxford: Clarendon Press; New York: Oxford Univ. Press, 1988.

1489. Brown, Stuart C. LEIBNIZ. Philosophers in Context. Minneapolis: Univ. of Minnesota Press; Sussex: Harvester, 1984.

1490. Brown, Stuart C. OBJECTIVITY AND CULTURAL DIVERGENCE. Royal Institute of Philosophy, Lecture Series, Vol. 17. Cambridge and New York: Cambridge Univ.

Press, 1984.

This is a supplement to the journal PHILOSOPHY, 1984.

1491. Brown, Stuart C. PHILOSOPHERS OF THE ENLIGHTENMENT. Atlantic Highlands, NJ: Humanities Press; Sussex: Harvester Press, 1979.

1492. Brown, Stuart C. PHILOSOPHICAL DISPUTES IN THE SOCIAL SCIENCES. Sussex: Harvester Press; Atlantic Highlands, NJ: Humanities Press, 1979.

1493. Burns, James Henderson. THE CAMBRIDGE HISTORY OF MEDIEVAL POLITICAL THOUGHT c.350-c1450. Cambridge and New York: Cambridge Univ. Press, 1991.

There is an extensive bibliography on pages 691-777.

1494. Burns, James Henderson and Mark Goldie. THE CAMBRIDGE HISTORY OF POLITICAL THOUGHT, 1450-1700. Cambridge and New York: Cambridge Univ. Press, 1991.

This work include contributions by Anthony Grafton, Nicolai Rubenstein, Donald R. Kelley, Brendan Bradshaw, Robert M. Kingdon, J.H.M. Salmon, Howell A. Lloyd, Julian H. Franklin, J.C. Davis, J.P. Sommerville, Corinne C. Weston, David Wootton, Blair Worden, Peter Burke, Richard Tuck, Noel Marcum, Alfred Dufour, James Tully, and the editors.

1495. Burnyeat, Myles. CONFLICTING APPEARANCES. London: British Academy, 1981.

The text is taken from the Proceedings of the British Academy, London, Vol. LXV, 1979.

1496. Carrithers, Michael, et al. CATEGORY OF THE PERSON: ANTHROPOLOGY, PHILOSOPHY, HISTORY. Cambridge and New York: Cambridge Univ. Press, 1985.

1497. Carver, Terrell. FRIEDRICH ENGELS: HIS LIFE AND THOUGHT. New York: St. Martin's Press, 1989.

1498. Carver, Terrell. A MARX DICTIONARY. Cambridge: Polity; Totowa, NJ: Barnes & Noble Books, 1986.

1499. Carver, Terrell. MARX'S SOCIAL THEORY. Oxford and New York: Oxford Univ. Press, 1982.

1500. Chadwick, Henry. BOETHIUS: THE CONSOLATIONS OF MUSIC, LOGIC, THEOLOGY, AND PHILOSOPHY. Oxford and New York: Clarendon Press, 1981.

1501. Clarke, Desmond M. DESCARTES' PHILOSOPHY OF SCIENCE. Univ. Park: Pennsylvania Univ. Press; Manchester: Manchester Univ. Press, 1982.

This major new study of Descartes explores several issues, including his use of experience and reason in science, the metaphysical foundations of Cartesian science, the Cartesian concept of explanation and proof, and an empiricist interpretation of the REGULAE and the DISCOURSE.

1502. Clarke, Simon. THE FOUNDATIONS OF STRUCTURALISM: A CRITIQUE OF LEVI STRAUSS AND THE STRUCTURALIST MOVEMENT. Studies in Philosophy, Vol. 17. Totowa, NJ: Barnes and Noble Books; Sussex: Harvester, 1981.

This book is based on the author's doctoral thesis, University of Essex, 1975, under the title: THE STRUCTURALISM OF CLAUDE LEVI-STRAUSS. The published works of Claude Levi-Strauss are listed on pages 239-253. There also is a bibliography, pages 255-264.

1503. Coburn, Kathleen. THE COLLECTED WORKS OF SAMUEL TAYLOR COLERIDGE. Vol.13, LOGIC. Ed. by J. R. de Jackson. Princeton NJ: Princeton Univ. Press; Boston, London and Henley: Routledge & Kegan Paul, 1981.

1504. Cohen, Gerald Allan. KARL MARX'S THEORY OF HISTORY: A DEFENCE. Oxford: Clarendon Press; New York: Oxford Univ. Press, 1978.

1505. Cohen, Laurence Jonathan. THE DIALOGUE OF REASON: AN ANALYSIS OF ANALYTICAL PHILOSOPHY. Oxford: Clarendon Press; New York: Oxford Univ. Press, 1986.

1506. Cohen, Laurence Jonathan. THE PROBABLE AND THE PROVABLE. Oxford: Clarendon Press, 1977.

1507. Cohen, Laurence Jonathan, et al. METHODOLOGY, AND PHILOSOPHY OF SCIENCE VI. Amsterdam and New York: North-Holland; Warsaw: PWN-Polish Scientific Publishers, 1982.

The contents of this book come from the Sixth International Congress of Logic, Methodology, and Philosophy of Science, Hanover, 1979.

1508. Cohen, Laurence Jonathan and Mary B. Hess. APPLICATIONS OF INDUCTIVE LOGIC. Oxford: Clarendon Press; New York: Oxford Univ. Press, 1980.

This book is the proceedings of a conference at Queen's College, Oxford August 21-24, 1978.

1509. Cooper, David E. METAPHOR. Oxford and New York: B. Blackwell, 1986.

1510. Cooper, Neil. THE DIVERSITY OF MORAL THINKING. Clarendon Library of Logic and Philosophy. Oxford: Clarendon Press; New York: Oxford Univ. Press, 1981.

The author discusses three theses: the diversities of moral judgment, their normativeness, and their possible rationality.

1511. Copleston, Frederick Charles. ON THE HISTORY OF PHILOSOPHY. New York: Barnes and Noble Books; London: Search Press, 1979.

1512. Copleston, Frederick Charles. PHILOSOPHIES AND CULTURES. Oxford and New York: Oxford Univ. Press, 1980.

1513. Copleston, Frederick Charles. RELIGION AND THE ONE: PHILOSOPHIES EAST AND WEST. Gifford Lectures. Crossroad, 1982.

1514. Cornforth, Maurice Campbell. COMMUNISM AND PHILOSOPHY: CONTEMPORARY DOGMAS AND REVISIONS OF MARXISM. Atlantic Highlands, NJ: Humanities Press; London: Lawrence and Wishart, 1980.

1515. Cottingham, John, et al. PHILOSOPHICAL WRITINGS OF DESCARTES. 3 Vols. Cambridge: Cambridge Univ. Press, 1984-1991.

The third volume is devoted to Descartes' correspondence and contains 207 of his letters, over half of which have not been translated previously into English. It includes in its entirety Anthony Kenny's translation of selected philosophical letters.

1516. Craib, Ian. EXISTENTIALISM AND SOCIOLOGY: A STUDY OF JEAN-PAUL SARTRE. Cambridge and New York: Cambridge Univ. Press, 1976.

1517. Cranach, Mario von and Rom Harre. THE ANALYSIS OF ACTION: RECENT THEORETICAL AND EMPIRICAL ADVANCES. Cambridge and New York: Cambridge Univ. Press; Paris: Editions de la Maison des Sciences de l'Homme, 1982.

1518. Cranston, Maurice William. JEAN-JACQUES ROUSSEAU. Vol. 1, THE EARLY LIFE AND WORK OF JEAN-JACQUES ROUSSEAU, 1712-1754. New York: Norton, 1983. Vol. 2, THE NOBLE SAVAGE: JEAN-JACQUES ROUSSEAU, 1754-1762. Chicago: Univ. of Chicago Press, 1991.

1519. Cranston, Maurice William. PHILOSOPHERS AND PAMPHLETEERS: POLITICAL THEORISTS OF THE ENLIGHTENMENT. Oxford and New York: Oxford Univ. Press, 1986.

This work is based on the Carlyle Lectures which were delivered at the University of Oxford in Trinity Term, 1984.

1520. Cranston, Maurice William, et al. HUMAN RIGHTS. Cambridge: American Academy of Arts and Sciences, 1983.

This work first appeared as the Fall 1983 issue of DAEDALUS, Journal of the American Academy of Arts and Sciences, and also as Vol. 112, no. 4 of the Proceedings of the Ameri
can Academy of Arts and Sciences.

1521. Cranston, Maurice William and Peter Mair. LANGAGE ET POLITIQUE=LANGUAGE AND POLITICS. Brussels: Bruylant, 1982.

This volume is a publication of the European University Institute.

1522. Crowe, Michael Bertram. THE CHANGING PROFILE OF NATURAL LAW. The Hague: Nijhoff, 1977.

1523. Dancy, Jonathan, et al. HUMAN AGENCY: PHILOSOPHICAL ESSAYS IN HONOR OF J. O. URMSON. Stanford: Stanford Univ. Press, 1988.

1524. Davie, George Elder. THE CRISIS OF THE DEMOCRATIC INTELLECT: THE PROBLEM OF GENERALISM AND SPECIALISATION IN TWENTIETH-CENTURY SCOTLAND. Edinburgh: Polygon, 1986.

1525. Dawson, Raymond Stanley. CONFUCIUS. Oxford: Oxford Univ. Press, 1981.

1526. Dent, Nicholas John Henry. THE MORAL PSYCHOLOGY OF THE VIRTUES. Cambridge and New York: Cambridge Univ. Press, 1984.

1527. Dummett, Michael A. E. ELEMENTS OF INTUITIONISM. Oxford: Oxford Univ. Press, 1977.

1528. Dummett, Michael A. E. FREGE AND OTHER PHILOSOPHERS. Oxford: Clarendon Press; New York: Oxford Univ. Press, 1991.

This book includes all of Dummett's published and previously unpublished essays on Frege except those in the author's TRUTH AND OTHER ENIGMAS.

1529. Dummett, Michael A. E. FREGE: PHILOSOPHY OF LANGUAGE. 2d ed. Cambridge: Harvard Univ. Press, 1981.

This study includes chapters on the evolution of Frege's thought and his place in the history of philosophy.

1530. Dummett, Michael A. E. THE INTERPRETATION OF FREGE'S PHILOSOPHY. Cambridge: Harvard Univ. Press; London: Duckworth, 1981.

1531. Dummett, Michael A. E. TRUTH AND OTHER ENIGMAS. Cambridge: Harvard Univ. Press; London: Duckworth, 1978.

1532. Dummett, Michael A. E. THE LOGICAL BASIS OF METAPHYSICS. Cambridge: Harvard Univ. Press; London: Duckworth, 1991.

1533. Dworkin, Ronald M. THE PHILOSOPHY OF LAW. Oxford: Oxford Univ. Press, 1977.

1534. Easton, Susan M. HUMANIST MARXISM AND WITTGENSTEINIAN SOCIAL PHILOSOPHY. Manchester, UK and Dover, NH: Manchester Univ. Press, 1983.

1535. Eccles, John Carew. THE HUMAN MYSTERY. Berlin and New York: Springer-Verlag, 1979.

These are the Gifford Lectures, 1977-1978.

1536. Ehrenfeld, David W. THE ARROGANCE OF HUMANISM. New York: Oxford Univ. Press, 1978.

1537. Elder, Crawford. APPROPRIATING HEGEL. Scots Philosophical Monographs. Aberdeen: Aberdeen Univ. Press, 1980.

1538. Emmet, Dorothy. THE EFFECTIVENESS OF CAUSES. Albany: State Univ. of New York Press, 1985.

1539. Evans, Gareth. COLLECTED PAPERS. New York: Oxford Univ. Press; Oxford: Clarendon Press, 1985.

1540. Evans, Gareth. THE VARIETIES OF REFERENCE. Ed. by John McDowell. Oxford: Clarendon Press; New York: Oxford Univ. Press, 1982.

1541. Evans, Gareth and John McDowell. TRUTH AND MEANING: ESSAYS IN SEMANTICS. Oxford: Clarendon Press, 1976.

1542. Evans, John David Gemmill. ARISTOTLE'S CONCEPT OF DIALECTIC. Cambridge and New York: Cambridge Univ. Press, 1977.

1543. Falk, W. David. OUGHT, REASONS, AND MORALITY: THE COLLECTED PAPERS OF W. D. FALK. Ithaca: Cornell Univ. Press, 1986.

1544. Feaver, George and Frederick Rosen. LIVES, LIBERTIES, AND THE PUBLIC GOOD: NEW ESSAYS IN POLITICAL THEORY FOR MAURICE CRANSTON. New York: St. Martins' Press, 1987.

This work contains a bibliography of Maurice Cranston compiled by Calliope Farsides on pages 259-266 and essays contributed by Raymond Polin, Harvey C. Mansfield, Jr., Robert Orr, Robert Wokler, Sanford Lakhoff, Sergio Cotta, William Letwin, Kenneth Minogue, Shirley Robin Letwin, Maurice Cranston and the editors.

1545. Findlay, John Niemeyer. WITTGENSTEIN: A CRITIQUE. Boston: Routledge and Kegan Paul, 1984.

1546. Fine, Kit. REASONING WITH ARBITRARY OBJECTS. Aristotelian Society Series, Vol. 3. Oxford and New York: Blackwell, 1985.

1547. Finnis, John. NATURAL LAW AND NATURAL RIGHTS. Oxford: Clarendon Press; New York: Oxford Univ. Press, 1980.

1548. Flew, Antony G. N. DARWINIAN EVOLUTION. London: Paladin, 1984.

1549. Flew, Antony G. N. DAVID HUME: PHILOSOPHER OF MORAL SCIENCE. Oxford and New York: B. Blackwell, 1986.

1550. Flew, Antony G. N. A DICTIONARY OF PHILOSOPHY. Rev. 2d ed. New York: St. Martin's Press, 1984c1979.

1551. Flew, Antony G. N. GOD: A CRITICAL ENQUIRY. 2d ed. LaSalle, IL: Open Court Press, 1984.

This is a revised edition of Flew's GOD AND PHILOSOPHY. London: Hutchinson; New York: Harcourt, Brace and World, 1966.

1552. Flew, Antony G. N. THE LOGIC OF MORTALITY. Oxford and New York: Blackwell, 1987.

This volume is based on Flew's Gifford Lectures of 1986-1987.

1553. Flew, Antony G. N. THE POLITICS OF PROCRUSTES: CONTRADICTIONS OF ENFORCED EQUALITY. Buffalo: Prometheus, 1981.

1554. Flew, Antony G. N. A RATIONAL ANIMAL AND OTHER PHILOSOPHICAL ESSAYS ON THE NATURE OF MAN. Oxford: Clarendon Press, 1978.

1555. Flew, Antony G. N. SOCIOLOGY, EQUALITY AND EDUCATION: PHILO-SOPHICAL ESSAYS IN DEFENCE OF A VARIETY OF DIFFERENCES. London: Macmillan; New York: Barnes and Noble, 1976.

1556. Flew, Antony G. N. THINKING ABOUT SOCIAL THINKING: THE PHILOSOPHY OF THE SOCIAL SCIENCES. Oxford and New York: Blackwell, 1985.

1557. Foot, Philippa. MORAL RELATIVISM. Lawrence: Univ. of Kansas, 1979.

1558. Foot, Philippa. VIRTUES AND VICES AND OTHER ESSAYS IN MORAL PHI-LOSOPHY. Berkeley: Univ. of California Press; Oxford: B. Blackwell, 1978.

1559. Foster, John. AYER. The Arguments of the Philosophers. London and Boston: Routledge & Kegan Paul, 1985.

1560. Foster, John and Howard Robinson. ESSAYS ON BERKELEY: A TERCENTENNI-AL CELEBRATION. Oxfrod: Clarendon Press, 1985.

1561. Frey, Raymond Gillespie. UTILITY AND RIGHTS. Minneapolis: Univ. of Minnesota Press, 1984.

1562. Gallie, Walter Bryce. PHILOSOPHERS OF PEACE AND WAR: KANT, CLAUSE-WITZ, MARX, ENGELS, AND TOLSTOY. Cambridge and New York: Cambridge Univ. Press, 1978.

1563. Gaskin, John Charles Addison. HUME'S PHILOSOPHY OF RELIGION. 2d ed. Atlantic Highlands, NJ: Humanities Press International, 1988.

1564. Gaskin, John Charles Addison. THE QUEST FOR ETERNITY. Harmondsworth: Penguin Books, 1984.

1565. Gauld, Alan and John Shotter. HUMAN ACTION AND ITS PSYCHOLOGICAL INVESTIGATION. London and Boston: Routledge and Paul, 1977.

1566. Gavison, Ruth. ISSUES IN CONTEMPORARY LEGAL PHILOSOPHY: THE INFLUENCE OF H.L.A. HART. Oxford: Clarendon Press; New York: Oxford Univ. Press, 1987.

This volume contains papers from a conference held in Jerusalem in March, 1984. There is a bibliography of H.L.A. Hart on pages 351-354.

1567. Geach, Peter Thomas. REASON AND ARGUMENT. Berkeley: Univ. of California Press; Oxford: B.Blackwell, 1976.

1568. Geach, Peter Thomas. REFERENCE AND GENERALITY: AN EXAMINATION OF SOME MEDIEVAL AND MODERN THEORIES. 3d ed. Ithaca: Cornell Univ. Press, 1980.

1569. Geach, Peter Thomas. TRUTH, LOVE, AND IMMORTALITY: AN INTRO- DUCTION TO MCTAGGERT'S PHILOSOPHY. London: Hutchinson; Berkeley: Univ. of California Press, 1979.

1570. Gellner, Ernest. LEGITIMATION OF BELIEF. Cambridge and New York: Cambridge Univ. Press, 1979.

1571. Gellner, Ernest. REASON AND CULTURE: A SOCIOLOGICAL AND PHILO- SOPHICAL STUDY OF THE ROLE OF RATIONALITY AND RATIONALISM. Oxford and Cambridge: Basil Blackwell, 1992.

1572. Gellner, Ernest. RELATIVISM AND THE SOCIAL SCIENCES. Cambridge and New York: Cambridge Univ. Press, 1985.

1573. Gellner, Ernest. WORDS AND THINGS: AN EXAMINATION OF, AND AN ATTACK ON, LINGUISTIC PHILOSOPHY. Rev ed. London and Boston: Routledge & Kegan Paul, 1979.

Bertrand Russell wrote the forward to this work.

1574. Gellner, Ernst. SPECTACLES AND PREDICAMENTS: ESSAYS IN SOCIAL THEORY. Cambridge and New York: Cambridge Univ. Press, 1979.

1575. Gillies, Douglas Angus. FREGE, DEDEKIND AND PEANO ON THE FOUNDA- TION OF ARITHMETIC. Assen,Netherlands: Van Gorcum, 1982.

1576. Glover, Jonathan. CAUSING DEATH AND SAVING LIVES. Harmondsworth and New York: Penguin, 1977.

1577. Glover, Jonathan. I, THE PHILOSOPHY AND PSYCHOLOGY OF PERSONAL IDENTITY. London: Allen Lane; New York: Viking Penguin, 1988.

1578. Glover, Jonathan. THE PHILOSOPHY OF MIND. Oxford: Oxford Univ. Press, 1976.

1579. Glover, Jonathan. SELF-CREATION. London: British Academy; Oxford: Oxford Univ. Press, 1984.

The text is taken from the Proceedings of the British Academy, London, Vol. LXIX 1983.

1580. Gombrich, Ernst Hans. THE IMAGE AND THE EYE: FURTHER STUDIES IN THE PSYCHOLOGY OF PICTORIAL REPRESENTATION. Oxford: Phaidon, 1982.

1581. Gordon, Peter and John White. PHILOSOPHERS AS EDUCATIONAL REFORMERS: THE INFLUENCE OF IDEALISM ON BRITISH EDUCATIONAL THOUGHT AND PRACTICE. London and Boston: Routledge & Paul, 1979.

1582. Gosling, Justin Cyril Bertrand and Christopher Charles Whiston Taylor. THE GREEKS ON PLEASURE. Oxford: Clarendon Press, 1982.

1583. Graham, Keith. J. L. AUSTIN: A CRITIQUE OF ORDINARY LANGUAGE PHILOSOPHY. Atlantic Highlands, NJ: Humanities Press; Sussex: Harvester, 1977.

1584. Grattan-Guinness, Ivor. DEAR RUSSELL-DEAR JOURDAIN: A COMMENTARY ON RUSSELL'S LOGIC BASED ON HIS CORRESPONDENCE WITH PHILIP JOURDAIN. New York: Columbia Univ. Press, 1977.

1585. Gray, John. HAYEK ON LIBERTY. 2d ed. Oxford and New York: B. Blackwell, 1986.

The volume contains a bibliography on pages 148-249.

1586. Gray, John. MILL ON LIBERTY: A DEFENSE. International Library of Philosophy. London and Boston: Routledge and Kegan Paul, 1983.

1587. Grayling, Anthony C. BERKELEY, THE CENTRAL ARGUMENTS. London: Duckworth, 1985.

1588. Grayling, Anthony C. AN INTRODUCTION TO PHILOSOPHICAL LOGIC. Totowa, NJ: Barnes and Noble; Sussex: Harvester Press, 1982.

1589. Grayling, Anthony C. THE REFUTATION OF SCEPTICISM. LaSalle, IL: Open Court, 1985.

1590. Gregory, Richard L. THE OXFORD COMPANION TO THE MIND. Ed. by Oliver Louis Zangwill. Oxford: Oxford Univ. Press, 1987.

This work contains over nine hundred entries, ranging from brief definitions to essays. It is not confined to psychology and psychologists but also includes expert treatments of philosophers and philosophical theories and issues. Contributors include such philosophers as D.M. Armstrong, A. J. Ayer, D. C. Dennett, J. Hick, D. Pears, W. V. O. Quine, P. Strawson, and others.

1591. Grice, H. Paul. STUDIES IN THE WAY OF WORDS. Cambridge: Harvard Univ. Press, 1989.

This volume includes Grice's revision of his 1967 James lectures.

1592. Griffiths, A. Phillips. OF LIBERTY. Cambridge and New York: Cambridge Univ. Press, 1983.

1593. Grossman, Reinhardt. PHENOMENOLOGY AND EXISTENTIALISM: AN INTRODUCTION. London and Boston: Routledge and Kegan Paul, 1984.

1594. Guthrie, William Keith Chambers. A HISTORY OF GREEK PHILOSOPHY. Vol. 1, EARLIER PRESOCRATICS AND THE PYTHAGOREANS. Vol. 2, THE PRESO-CRATIC TRADITION FROM PARMENIDES TO DEMOCRITUS. Vol. 3, THE FIFTH CENTURY ENLIGHTENMENT: Part 1, THE SOPHISTS. Part 2, SOCRATES. Vol.4, PLATO: THE MAN AND HIS DIALOGUES: EARLIER PERIOD. Vol. 5, THE LATER PLATO AND THE ACADEMY. Vol. 6, ARISTOTLE, AN ENCOUNTER. London and New York: Cambridge Univ. Press, 1962-1981.

The set contains bibliographies in Vol. 1, pp. 493-503; Vol. 2, pp. 508--522; Vol. 3, pp. 508-523; and Vol. 4, pp. 562-581.

1595. Haack, Susan. PHILOSOPHY OF LOGICS. Cambridge and New York: Cambridge Univ. Press, 1978.

1596. Hacker, Peter Michael Stephan and Joseph Raz. LAW, MORALITY, AND SOCIE-TY: ESSAYS IN HONOUR OF H. L. A. HART. Oxford: Clarendon Press, 1977.

There is a bibliography of the works of H. L. A. Hart on pages 309-312.

1597. Hahn, Frank Horace and Martin Hollis. PHILOSOPHY AND ECONOMIC THEO-RY. Oxford and New York: Oxford Univ. Press, 1979.

1598. Hahn, Lewis Edwin. THE PHILOSOPHY OF A. J. AYER. The Library of Living Philosophers, Vol. XXI. Peru, IL: Open Court, 1992.

In addition to Ayer's intellectual autobiography and a complete bibliography of his writings up to the date of publication, this volume contains 24 descriptive and critical essays on Ayer's philosophy by other philosophers. Before his death, Ayer completed 20 detailed replies to his critics.

1599. Haight, Mary Rowland. A STUDY OF SELF-DECEPTION. Atlantic Highlands, NJ: Humanities Press; Sussex: Harvester Press, 1980.

1600. Hall, Roland and Roger S. Woolhouse. 80 YEARS OF LOCKE SCHOLARSHIP: A BIBLIOGRAPHICAL GUIDE. Edinburgh: Univ. Press, 1983.

1601. Hamlyn, David Walter. METAPHYSICS. Cambridge and New York: Cambridge Univ. Press, 1984.

1602. Hamlyn, David Walter. PERCEPTION, LEARNING AND THE SELF: ESSAYS IN THE PHILOSOPHY OF PSYCHOLOGY. London and Boston: Routledge and Kegan Paul, 1983.

This work argues that the information-processing model is insufficient to stand on its own. Any framework used to view cognition must be an essentially social one.

1603. Hamlyn, David Walter. SCHOPENHAUER. The Arguments of the Philosophers. London and Boston: Routledge and Kegan Paul, 1980.

1604. Hampsher-Monk, Iain. THE POLITICAL PHILOSOPHY OF EDMUND BURKE. London and New York: Longman, 1987.

1605. Hampshire, Stuart. INNOCENCE AND EXPERIENCE. Cambridge: Harvard Univ. Press, 1989.

1606. Hampshire, Stuart. MORALITY AND CONFLICT. Cambridge: Harvard Univ. Press, 1983.

1607. Hampshire, Stuart, ed. PUBLIC AND PRIVATE MORALITY. Cambridge and New York: Cambridge Univ. Press, 1978.

This book contains essays by the editor, Bernard A.O. Williams, Thomas Nagel, Thomas M. Scanlon, and Richard Dworkin.

1608. Hampshire, Stuart. TWO THEORIES OF MORALITY. Oxford: Oxford Univ. Press, 1977.

1609. Hanfling, Oswald, ed. ESSENTIAL READINGS IN LOGICAL POSITIVISM. Oxford: B. Blackwell, 1981.

1610. Hanfling, Oswald. LOGICAL POSITIVISM. New York: Columbia University Press; Oxford: B. Blackwell, 1981.

1611. Hare, Richard Mervyn. ESSAYS ON POLITICAL MORALITY. Oxford: Clarendon Press; New York: Oxford Univ. Press, 1989.

Three of the essays in this volume have not been published previously.

1612. Hare, Richard Mervyn. MORAL THINKING: ITS LEVELS, METHOD, AND POINT. Oxford: Clarendon Press; New York: Oxford Univ. Press, 1982.

1613. Harman, Peter Michael. METAPHYSICS AND NATURAL PHILOSOPHY. Totowa, NJ: Barnes and Noble, 1982.

1614. Harre, Rom. INTRODUCTION TO THE LOGIC OF THE SCIENCES. 2d ed. New York: St. Martin's Press; London: Macmillan, 1983.

1615. Harre, Rom. THE PHILOSOPHIES OF SCIENCE. 2d ed. Oxford and New York: Oxford Univ. Press, 1984.

1616. Harrison, Jonathan. HUME'S THEORY OF JUSTICE. Oxford: Clarendon Press; New York: Oxford Univ. Press, 1981.

1617. Harrison, Ross. BENTHAM. The Arguments of the Philosophers. London and Boston: Routledge and Kegan Paul, 1983.

A critical examination of Bentham's theory about the nature of language and its relation to the world. The author has drawn on previously unpublished work by Bentham to conduct an in-depth study of his utilitarianism.

1618. Hart, Herbert Lionel Adolphus. ESSAYS IN JURISPRUDENCE AND PHILOSOPHY. Oxford: Clarendon Press; New York: Oxford Univ. Press, 1983.

1619. Hart, Herbert Lionel Adolphus. ESSAYS ON BENTHAM: STUDIES IN JURISPRUDENCE AND POLITICAL THEORY. Oxford: Clarendon Press; New York: Oxford Univ. Press, 1982.

1620. Hart, Herbert Lionel Adolphus and Tony Honore. CAUSATION IN THE LAW. Oxford: Clarendon Press; New York: Oxford Univ. Press, 1985.

1621. Himsworth, Harold. SCIENTIFIC KNOWLEDGE AND PHILOSOPHIC THOUGHT. Baltimore and London: Johns Hopkins Univ. Press, 1986.

This book contains an extensive bibliography.

HERBERT HART ZUM 70 GEBURTSTAG. Munich: Deutscher Taschenbuch-Verlag, 1977.

1623. Hollis, Martin. MODELS OF MAN: PHILOSOPHICAL THOUGHT ON SOCIAL ACTION. Cambridge and New York: Cambridge Univ. Press, 1977.

1624. Hollis, Martin and Steven Lukes. RATIONALITY AND RELATIVISM. Cambridge: MIT Press; Oxford: Blackwell, 1982.

1625. Honderich, Ted. A THEORY OF DETERMINISM: THE MIND, NEUROSCIENCE, AND LIFE-HOPES. Oxford: Clarendon Press; New York: Oxford Univ. Press, 1988.

1626. Honderich, Ted. THREE ESSAYS ON POLITICAL VIOLENCE. Oxford: B. Blackwell, 1976.

1627. Hookway, Christopher. MINDS, MACHINES AND EVOLUTION. Cambridge: Cambridge Univ. Press, 1985.

This work includes contributions by the editor, David Hull, Elliott Sober, John Maynard Smith, Neil Tennant, Yorick Wilks, Daniel Dennett, and Margaret Boden.

1628. Hookway, Christopher. PEIRCE. The Arguments of the Philosophers. London: Routledge & Kegan Paul, 1985.

1629. Hornsby, Jennifer. ACTIONS. International Library of Philosophy. London and Boston: Routledge & Kegan Paul, 1980.

1630. Hudson, William Donald. A CENTURY OF MORAL PHILOSOPHY. New York: St. Martin's Press, 1980.

1631. Hudson, William Donald. MODERN MORAL PHILOSOPHY. New York: St. Martin's Press; Guilford, Eng.: Lutterworth Press, 1983.

1632. Hughes, Gerard J. THE PHILOSOPHICAL ASSESSMENT OF THEOLOGY: ESSAYS IN HONOUR OF FREDERICK C. COPLESTON. Kent: Search Press; Washington, D.C.: Georgetown Univ. Press, 1987.

1633. Hunnings, Gordon. THE WORLD AND LANGUAGE IN WITTGENSTEIN'S PHILOSOPHY. Contributions in Philosophy of Language. London: Macmillan, 1987.

1634. Inwood, Michael J. HEGEL. The Arguments of the Philosophers. London and Boston: Routledge and Kegan Paul, 1983.

1635. Ishiguro, Hide. LEIBNIZ'S PHILOSOPHY OF LOGIC AND LANGUAGE. 2d ed. Cambridge and New York: Cambridge Univ. Press, 1990.

1636. Ishiguro, Hide. PRE-ESTABLISHED HARMONY VERSUS CONSTANT CON-JUNCTION: A RECONSIDERATION OF THE DISTINCTION BETWEEN RATION-ALISM AND EMPIRICISM. Oxford: Oxford Univ. Press, 1978.

The text is taken from the Proceedings of the British Academy, London, Vol. LXIII, 1977.

1637. Jay, Martin. ADORNO. Cambridge: Harvard Univ. Press, 1984.

1638. Jay, Martin. MARXISM AND TOTALITY; THE ADVENTURES OF A CONCEPT FROM LUKACS TO HABERMAS. Berkeley: Univ. of California Press, 1984.

1639. Kearney, Richard. DIALOGUES WITH CONTEMPORARY CONTINENTAL THINKERS: THE PHENOMENOLOGICAL HERITAGE: PAUL RICOEUR, EMMANUEL LEVINAS, HERBERT MARCUSE, STANISLAS BRETON, JACQUES DERRIDA. Manchester, UK and Dover, NH: Manchester Univ. Press, 1984.

1640. Kenny, Anthony John Patrick. AQUINAS. Oxford: Oxford Univ. Press, 1980.

1641. Kenny, Anthony John Patrick. ARISTOTLE'S THEORY OF THE WILL. New Haven: Yale Univ. Press, 1979.

1642. Kenny, Anthony John Patrick. FREEWILL AND RESPONSIBILITY. London and Boston: Routledge and Kegan Paul, 1978.

1643. Kenny, Anthony John Patrick. THE IVORY TOWER: ESSAYS IN PHILOSOPHY AND PUBLIC POLICY. Oxford and New York: Blackwell, 1985.

1644. Kenny, Anthony John Patrick. THE LEGACY OF WITTGENSTEIN. Oxford and New York: B. Blackwell, 1984.

1645. Kenny, Anthony John Patrick. THE METAPHYSICS OF THE MIND. Oxford: Clarendon Press; New York: Oxford Univ. Press, 1989.

1646. Kenny, Anthony John Patrick, et al. WITTGENSTEIN AND HIS TIMES. Ed. by Brian McGuinness. Oxford: Blackwell; Chicago: Univ. of Chicago Press, 1982.

This is a collection of essays on Wittgenstein and his philosophizing by Anthony Kenny, Brian McGuinness, J. C. Nyeri, Rush Rhees, and Georg Henrik von Wright.

1647. Kerferd, George Briscoe. THE SOPHISTIC MOVEMENT. Cambridge and New York: Cambrige Univ. Press, 1981.

1648. Kerferd, George Briscoe. THE SOPHISTS AND THEIR LEGACY. Wiesbaden: Steiner, 1981.

These are the Proceedings of the Fourth International Colloquium on Ancient Philosophy held in cooperation with Projektgruppe Altertumswissenschaften der Thyssen Stiftung at Bad Homburg, August 29-September 1, 1979.

1649. Kirk, Geoffrey Stephen, et al. THE PRESOCRATIC PHILOSOPHERS: A CRITICAL HISTORY WITH A SELECTION OF TEXTS. 2d ed. Cambridge and New York: Cambridge Univ. Press, 1983.

1650. Kissin, S. F. FAREWELL TO REVOLUTION: MARXIST PHILOSOPHY AND THE MODERN WORLD. New York: St. Martin's Press; London: Weidenfield and Nicolson, 1978.

1651. Korner, Stephan. EXPERIENCE AND CONDUCT: A PHILOSOPHICAL ENQUIRY INTO PRACTICAL THINKING. Cambridge and New York: Cambridge Univ. Press, 1976.

1652. Korner, Stephan. METAPHYSICS, ITS STRUCTURE AND FUNCTION. Cambridge and New York: Cambridge Univ. Press, 1984.

1653. Korner, Stephan. PHILOSOPHY OF LOGIC: PAPERS AND DISCUSSIONS. Berkeley and Los Angeles: Univ. of California Press; Oxford: B. Blackwell, 1976.

This book is the Proceedings of the Third Bristol Conference on Critical Philosophy.

1654. Krell, David Farrell. INTIMATIONS OF MORTALITY: TIME, TRUTH AND FINITUDE IN HEIDEGGER'S THINKING OF BEING. University Park and London: Pennsylvania State Univ. Press, 1986.

1655. Kretzmann, Norman, et al. THE CAMBRIDGE HISTORY OF LATER MEDIEVAL PHILOSOPHY: FROM THE REDISCOVERY OF ARISTOTLE TO THE DISINTE-GRATION OF SCHOLASTICISM, 1100-1600. Cambridge and New York: Cambridge Univ. Press, 1982.

This work contains forty-six chapters by forty-one historians of philosophy, religion and science from Great Britain, Canada, Australia, Finland, France, Germany, Denmark, Holland and Poland. There is a bibliography on pages 893-977.

1656. Kuntz, Paul Grimley. BERTRAND RUSSELL. Twayne English Author Series. Boston: Twayne, 1986.

1657. Lamb, David. HEGEL: FROM FOUNDATION TO SYSTEM. The Hague: Nijhoff, 1980.

1658. Laslett, Peter and James Fishkin. PHILOSOPHY, POLITICS AND SOCIETY; FIFTH SERIES: A COLLECTION. New Haven: Yale Univ. Press; Oxford: B. Blackwell, 1979.

1659. Lawson, Hilary. REFLEXIVITY: THE POST-MODERN PREDICAMENT. London: Hutchinson; LaSalle, IL: Open Court, 1986.

1660. Lawson, Hilary and Lisa Appignanesi. DISMANTLING TRUTH: REALITY IN THE POST MODERN WORLD. London: Weidenfeld and Nicolson; New York: St. Martin's Press, 1989.

This collection consists of 13 essays by such philosophers and scientists as Richard Rorty, Bruno Latour, and Richard Gregory questioning the validity of any context independent conception of truth. The volume is based on a series of papers presented at a conference at the Institute of Contemporary Arts in London.

1661. Lee, Keekok. A NEW BASIS FOR MORAL PHILOSOPHY. London: Routledge and Kegan Paul, 1985.

1662. Lewis, Hywel David. CONTEMPORARY BRITISH PHILOSOPHY: PERSONAL STATEMENTS. London: Allen & Unwin; Atlantic Highlands, NJ: Humanities Press, 1976.

1663. Lewis, Hywel David. THE ELUSIVE SELF: BASED ON THE GIFFORD LEC-TURES DELIVERED IN THE UNIVERSITY OF EDINBURGH, 1966-1968. London: Macmillan; Philadelphia: Westminster Press, 1982.

1664. Lewis, Hywel David. FREEDOM AND ALIENATION: THE THIRD VOLUME BASED ON THE GIFFORD LECTURES DELIVERED IN THE UNIVERSITY OF EDINBURGH, 1966- 1968. Edinburgh: Scottish Academic Press, 1985.

1665. Lewis, Hywel David. PERSONS AND LIFE AFTER DEATH: ESSAYS BY HYWEL D. LEWIS AND SOME OF HIS CRITICS. New York: Barnes and Noble, 1978.

1666. Lewis, Hywel David, et al. LOGIC, ONTOLOGY AND ACTION. Delhi: Macmillan; Atlantic Highlands, NJ: Humanities Press, 1982,1979.

1667. Llewelyn, John. BEYOND METAPHYSICS?: THE HERMENEUTIC CIRCLE IN

CONTEMPORARY CONTINENTAL PHILOSOPHY. Atlantic Highlands, NJ: Humanities Press International; London: Macmillan, 1985.

1668. Lloyd, Christopher. SOCIAL THEORY AND POLITICAL PRACTICE. Oxford: Clarendon Press; New York: Oxford Univ. Press, 1983.

This 1981 volume of Wolfson College Lectures includes contributions by Ralf Dahrendorf, Tom Bottomore, Charles Taylor, Amartya Sen, David Marquand, and Wlodzimierz Brus.

1669. Lloyd, Geoffrey Ernest Richard and Gwilym Ellis Lane Owen. ARISTOTLE ON MIND AND THE SENSES. Cambridge and New York: Cambridge Univ. Press, 1978.

These are the Proceedings of the Seventh Symposium Aristotelicum.

1670. Locke, John. THE CORRESPONDENCE OF JOHN LOCKE. Vol. 1, INTRODUCTION; LETTERS NOS. 1-461. Vol. 2, LETTERS NOS. 462-848. Vol. 3, LETTERS NOS. 849-1241. Vol 4, LETTERS NOS. 1242-1701. Vol 5, LETTERS NOS. 1702-2198. Vol. 6, LETTERS NOS. 2199-2665. Vol. 7, LETTERS NOS. 2665-3286. Vol. 8, LETTERS 3287-3848. Ed. by Esmond Samuel de Beer. Oxford: Clarendon Press, 1976-1989.

1671. Lovibond, Sabina. REALISM AND IMAGINATION IN ETHICS. Oxford: B. Blackwell; Minneapolis: Univ. of Minnesota Press, 1983.

This volume examines non-cognitivist theories of ethics in opposition to new theories of moral realism. The author discusses the empiricist tradition in moral philosophy and the attractions of a radical alternative inspired by Hegel and Wittgenstein.

1672. Lucas, John Randolph. ON JUSTICE=PERI DIKAIOU. Oxford: Clarendon Press; New York: Oxford Univ. Press, 1980.

1673. Lukes, Steven. MARXISM AND MORALITY. Oxford: Clarendon Press; New York: Oxford Univ. Press, 1985.

1674. Lyons, William. EMOTION. Cambridge and New York: Cambridge Univ. Press, 1980.

1675. Lyons, William. GILBERT RYLE: AN INTRODUCTION TO HIS PHILOSOPHY. Atlantic Highlands, NJ: Humanities Press; Sussex: Harvester Press, 1980.

1676. MacCormick, Neil. LEGAL REASONING AND LEGAL THEORY. Oxford: Clarendon Press; New York: Oxford Univ. Press, 1978.

1677. MacCormick, Neil. LEGAL RIGHT AND SOCIAL DEMOCRACY. Oxford: Clarendon Press; New York: Oxford Univ. Press, 1982.

1678. MacDonald, Graham F. PERCEPTION AND IDENTITY: ESSAYS PRESENTED TO A. J. AYER, WITH HIS REPLIES. London: Macmillan; Ithaca: Cornell Univ. Press, 1979.

A. J. Ayer replies to essays by Michael Dummett, P. F. Strawson, David M. Armstrong and other philosophers. A bibliography of the works of A. J. Ayer is on pages 334-341.

1679. Madell, Geoffrey. THE IDENTITY OF THE SELF. Edinburgh: Univ. Press, 1981.

1680. Magee, Bryan. MEN OF IDEAS: SOME CREATORS OF CONTEMPORARY PHILOSOPHY: DIALOGUES BETWEEN BRYAN MAGEE AND ISAIAH BERLIN

AND OTHERS. London: British Broadcasting Corp., 1978.
Bryan Magee, the interlocuter, discusses contemporary individual philosophers, philosophical movements and fields of philosophy viewed as important by Anglo-American philosophy with Isaiah Berlin, Charles Taylor, Herbert Marcuse, William Barrett, Anthony Quinton, Alfred Jules Ayer, Bernard Williams, Richard Mervyn Hare, William Van Orman Quine, John Searle, Noam Chomsky, Hilary Putnam, Ronald Dworkin, Iris Murdoch, and Ernest Gellner. This book derives from a series of television programs screened by the BBC in January-April, 1978.

1681. Magee, Bryan. PHILOSOPHY AND THE REAL WORLD: AN INTRODUCTION TO POPPER. LaSalle, IL: Open Court, 1985.

This is a revised edition of POPPER. Collins, 1973.

1682. Magee, Bryan. THE PHILOSOPHY OF SCHOPENHAUER. New York: Oxford Univ. Press; Oxford: Clarendon Press, 1983.

1683. Manser, Anthony. BRADLEY'S LOGIC. Totowa, NJ: Barnes and Noble, 1983.

1684. Marenbon, John. EARLY MEDIEVAL PHILOSOPHY (480-1150). 2d ed. London and Boston: Routledge and Kegan Paul, 1988.

This work includes studies not only of such well-known thinkers as Boethius and Eriugena but also of lesser known figures.

1685. Marenbon, John. FROM THE CIRCLE OF ALCUIN TO THE SCHOOL OF AUXERRE: LOGIC, THEOLOGY, AND PHILOSOPHY IN THE EARLY MIDDLE AGES. Cambridge Studies in Medieval Life and Thought. Third Series, Vol. 15. New York: Cambridge Univ, Press, 1981.

1686. Martin, Werner. BERTRAND RUSSELL: A BIBLIOGRAPHY OF HIS WRITINGS=EINE BIBLIOGRAPHIE SEINER SCHRIFTEN, 1895-1976. Munich: K. G. Sauer; Hamden, CT: Linnet Books, 1981.

This bibliography is published in English and German.

1687. Mays, Wolfe. WHITEHEAD'S PHILOSOPHY OF SCIENCE AND METAPHYSICS: AN INTRODUCTION TO HIS THOUGHT. The Hague and Boston: Nijhoff, 1977.

1688. McDowell, John. CRITERIA, DEFEASIBILITY, AND KNOWLEDGE. London: British Academy, 1982.

1689. McEvoy, James. THE PHILOSOPHY OF ROBERT GROSSETESTE. Oxford: Clarendon Press; New York: Oxford Univ. Press, 1982.

Grosseteste favored mathematical science and ancient classical languages and the development of the scholastic method in logic and metaphysics.

1690. McGinn, Colin. WITTGENSTEIN ON MEANING: AN INTERPRETATION AND EVALUATION. Aristotelian Society Series, Vol. 1. Oxford and New York: Blackwell, 1984.

1691. McGuinness, Brian. MORITZ SCHLICK. Dordrecht and Boston: Reidel, 1985.

1692. McGuinness, Brian. WITTGENSTEIN AND HIS TIMES. Oxford: B. Blackwell, 1981.

This collection of essays takes Wittgenstein's major achievements for granted and raises issues about how to think of those achievements.

1693. McGuinness, Brian. WITTGENSTEIN, A LIFE: YOUNG LUDWIG, 1889-1921. London: Duckworth; Berkeley: Univ. of California Press, 1988.

1694. McGuinness, Brian and Aldo Giorgio Gargani. WITTGENSTEIN AND CONTEMPORARY PHILOSOPHY. Pisa: ETS, 1985.

The volume is printed in English and German and includes bibliographies.

1695. McMilllan, Carol. WOMEN, REASON, AND NATURE: SOME PHILOSOPHICAL PROBLEMS WITH FEMINISM. Princeton, NJ: Princeton Univ. Press; Oxford: B. Blackwell, 1982.

1696. Meikle, Scott. ESSENTIALISM IN THE THOUGHT OF KARL MARX. LaSalle, IL: Open Court, 1984.

1697. Mellor, David Hugh. THE POSSIBILITY OF PREDICTION. London: British Academy, 1981.

The text is taken from the Proceedings of the British Academy, London, Vol. LXV 1979.

1698. Mellor, David Hugh. REAL TIME. Cambridge and New York: Cambridge Univ. Press, 1981.

1699. Mellor, David Hugh. SCIENCE, BELIEF AND BEHAVIOR: ESSAYS IN HONOUR OF R. B. BRAITHWAITE. New York and Cambridge: Cambridge Univ. Press, 1980.

This volume includes contributions by G. Buchdahl, N. Jardine, S. Korner, and others. There is a bibliography of the philosophical writing of R. B. Braithwaite on pages 219-227.

1700. Mepham, John and David- Hillel Ruben. ISSUES IN MARXIST PHILOSOPHY. Vol. 1, DIALECTICS AND METHOD. Vol. 2, MATERIALISM. Vol. 3, EPISTEMOLOGY, SCIENCE, IDEOLOGY. Vol. 4, SOCIAL AND POLITICAL PHILOSOPHY. Atlantic Highlands, NJ: Humanities Press; Sussex: Harvester Press, 1979-.

The aim of this series is to bring together articles written by contemporary Marxist philosophers in the English speaking world.

1701. Meszaros, Istvan. THE WORK OF SARTRE. Atlantic Highlands, NJ: Humanities Press, 1979-.

1702. Midgley, E. Brian F. THE IDEOLOGY OF MAX WEBER: A THOMIST CRITIQUE. Totowa, NJ: Barnes and Noble; Aldershot, Hants: Gower, 1983.

1703. Midgley, Mary. ANIMALS AND WHY THEY MATTER: A JOURNEY AROUND THE SPECIES BARRIER. Marmondsworth, Middlesex and New York: Penguin Books, 1983.

1704. Midgley, Mary. BEAST AND MAN: THE ROOTS OF HUMAN NATURE. Ithaca: Cornell Univ. Press, 1978.

1705. Midgley, Mary. EVOLUTION AS A RELIGION: STRANGE HOPES AND STRANGER FEARS. London and New York: Metheun, 1985.

1706. Midgley, Mary. WICKEDNESS: A PHILOSOPHICAL ESSAY. London and Boston: Routledge and Kegan Paul, 1984.

1707. Midgley, Mary and Judith Hughes. WOMEN'S CHOICES: PHILOSOPHICAL PROBLEMS FACING FEMINISM. London: Weidenfeld and Nicolson; New York: St. Martin's Press, 1983.

1708. Miller, David Leslie. ANARCHISM. London: J. M. Dent, 1984.

1709. Miller, David Leslie. THE BLACKWELL ENCYCLOPEDIA OF POLITICAL THOUGHT. Oxford and New York: B. Blackwell, 1987.

1710. Miller, David Leslie. SOCIAL JUSTICE. Oxford: Clarendon Press, 1976.

1711. Miller, David Leslie and Larry Siedentop. THE NATURE OF POLITICAL THEORY. Oxford and New York: Clarendon Press, 1983.

This work includes contributions by the editors and A. MacIntyre, John Gray, S. Lukes, B. Barry, P. Jones, G. Marshall, A. Ryan, and R. Wokler. Also included is a bibliography of the published works of John Plamenatz.

1712. Milligan, David. REASONING AND THE EXPLANATION OF ACTIONS. Atlantic Highlands, NJ: Humanities Press, 1980.

1713. Mitchell, Basil. MORALITY: RELIGIOUS AND SECULAR: THE DILEMMA OF THE TRADITIONAL CONSCIENCE. Oxford: Clarendon Press; New York: Oxford Univ. Press, 1980.

1714. Mitchell, Sollace and Michael Rosen. THE NEED FOR INTERPRETATION: CONTEMPORARY CONCEPTIONS OF THE PHILOSOPHER'S TASK. London: Athlone Press; Atlantic Highlands, NJ: Humanities Press, 1983.

This work includes contributions by David Kirsh, Christopher M. Leich, Theodore R. Schatzki, Charles Taylor and the editors.

1715. Monk, Ray. LUDWIG WITTGENSTEIN: THE DUTY OF GENIUS. New York: Free Press: Maxwell Macmillan International, 1990.

1716. Moore, George Edward. G. E. MOORE: THE EARLY ESSAYS. Ed. by Tom Regan. Philadelphia: Temple Univ. Press, 1986.

1717. Mure, Geoffrey R. G. IDEALIST EPILOGUE. Oxford: Clarendon Press, 1978.

1718. Newton-Smith, William Herbert. THE RATIONALITY OF SCIENCE. Boston: Routledge and Kegan Paul, 1981.

1719. Newton-Smith, William Herbert. THE STRUCTURE OF TIME. Boston and London: Routledge and Kegan Paul, 1980.

1720. Noonan, Harold W. OBJECTS AND IDENTITY: AN EXAMINATION OF THE RELATIVE IDENTITY THESIS AND IT'S CONSEQUENCES. The Hague and Boston: Nijhoff, 1980.

1721. Norman, Richard J. and Sean Sayers. HEGEL, MARX, AND DIALECTIC: A DEBATE. Atlantic Highlands, NJ: Humanities Press; Sussex: Harvester, 1980.

1722. O'Hear, Anthony. KARL POPPER. The Arguments of the Philosophers. Boston and London: Routledge and Kegan Paul, 1980.

1723. Osborne, Harold. ABSTRACTION AND ARTIFICE IN TWENTIETH-CENTURY ART. Oxford: Clarendon Press; New York: Oxford Univ. Press, 1979.

1724. Osler, Margaret J. and Paul Lawrence Farber. RELIGION, SCIENCE, AND WORLDVIEW: ESSAYS IN HONOR OF RICHARD S. WESTFALL. Cambridge and New York: Cambridge Univ. Press, 1985.

This volume contains a bibliography of Richard S. Westfall's writings on the history of science on pages 341-344.

1725. Parfit, Derek. PRUDENCE, MORALITY, AND THE PRISONER'S DILEMMA. Oxford: Oxford Univ. Press, 1981.

The text is taken from the Proceedings of the British Academy, Vol. 65.

1726. Parfit, Derek. REASONS AND PERSONS. Oxford: Clarendon Press, 1984.

1727. Parkinson, George Henry Radcliffe. GEORG LUKACS. London and Boston: Routledge & Paul, 1977.

1728. Parkinson, George Henry Radcliffe. THE HANDBOOK OF WESTERN PHILOSO-PHY. New York: Macmillan, 1988.

The British edition is published under the title: AN ENCYCLOPEDIA OF PHILOSO-PHY. This volume includes the 1976-1986 period covered by this supplementary bibliography. Most of its 37 original articles were written by contemporary British and Australian philosophers, although several are by contemporary American philosophers and one by a contemporary Greek philosopher. This single volume also includes indices of names and subjects, a glossary of philosophical terms, and a 1600-1960 chronological survey of philosophy and the arts and sciences.

1729. PAST MASTERS SERIES. Oxford: Oxford Univ. Press, 1980-.

Each volume in this series is devoted to a particular individual. Included among the musicians, poets, religious leaders, and others are the following volumes on philosophers by contemporary philosophers: Aristotle (J. Barnes), Vico (P. Burke), Augustine (H. Chadwick), Bentham (J. Dinwiddy), Locke (J. Dunn), Diderot (P. France), Kierkegaard (P. Gardiner), Wittgenstein (A.C. Grayling), Plato (R. M. Hare), Bergson (L. Kolakowski), Leibniz (G. McDonald Ross), Bacon (A. Quinton), Kant (R. Scruton), Spinoza (R. Scruton), Montesquieu (J. N. Sklar), Hegel (P. Singer), Machiavelli (Q. Skinner), Descartes (T. Sorell), Mill (W. Thomas), Hobbes (R. Tuck), Berkeley (J. O. Urmson), Aquinas (A. Kenny), The Buddha (M. Carrithers), Confucius (R. Dawson), Engels (T. Carver), Jesus (H. Carpenter), Marx (P. Singer), Muhammed (M. Cook), More (A. Kenny), Newman (O. Chadwick), Paine (M. Philp), Wycliff (A. Kenny), Hume (A. J. Ayer).

1730. Peacocke, Christopher. HOLISTIC EXPLANATION: ACTION, SPACE, INTER-PRETATION. Oxford: Clarendon Press; New York: Oxford Univ. Press, 1979.

1731. Peacocke, Christopher. SENSE AND CONTENT: EXPERIENCE, THOUGHT, AND THEIR RELATIONS. Oxford: Clarendon Press; New York: Oxford Univ. Press, 1983.

1732. Peacocke, Christopher. THOUGHTS: AN ESSAY ON CONTENT. Aristotelian Society Series, Vol. 4. New York: Blackwell, 1985.

1733. Pears, David Francis. THE FALSE PRISON: A STUDY OF THE DEVELOPMENT OF WITTGENSTEIN'S PHILOSOPHY. 2 Vols. Oxford: Clarendon Press; New York: Oxford Univ. Press, 1987-1988.

1734. Pears, David Francis. MOTIVATED IRRATIONALITY. Oxford: Clarendon, 1984.

1735. Pears, David Francis. THE NATURALISM OF BOOK I OF HUME'S TREATISE ON HUMAN NATURE. London: Oxford Univ. Press [for the British Academy], 1976.

This is the Dawes Hicks lecture on philosophy and is reprinted from the Proceedings of the British Academy, vol. 62, 1976.

1736. Pelczynski, Zbigniew A. THE STATE AND CIVIL SOCIETY: STUDIES IN HEGEL'S POLITICAL PHILOSOPHY. Cambridge and New York: Cambiridge Univ. Press, 1984.

1737. Pelczynski, Zbigniew A. and John Gray. CONCEPTIONS OF LIBERTY IN POLITICAL PHILOSOPHY. New York and London: St. Martin's Press, 1985.

This work consists of 17 essays on important political philosophers including Hobbes by D.D. Raphael, Rousseau by Patrick Gardiner, Kant by Charles Taylor, Hegel by Zbigniew A. Pelczynski, Marx, by Andrzej Walicki, and Habermas, by Jay Bernstein.

1738. Penelhum, Terence. BUTLER. The Arguments of the Philosophers. London and Boston: Routledge and Kegan Paul, 1985.

1739. Peters, Richard S. JOHN DEWEY RECONSIDERED. London and Boston: Routledge and Paul, 1977.

1740. Phillips, Dewi Zephaniah. RELIGION WITHOUT EXPLANATION. Oxford: Blackwell, 1976.

This book consists of addresses, essays, and lectures.

1741. Phillips, Dewi Zephaniah. THROUGH A DARKENING GLASS: PHILOSOPHY, LITERATURE AND CULTURAL CHANGE. Notre Dame, IN: Univ. of Notre Dame Press, 1982.

This book consists of addresses, essays and lectures.

1742. Piatigorsky, Alexander. THE BUDDHIST PHILOSOPHY OF THOUGHT: ESSAYS IN INTERPRETATION. London: Curzon Press; Totowa, NJ: Barnes and Noble, 1984.

1743. Pitcher, George. BERKELEY. The Arguments of the Philosophers. London and Boston: Routledge & Kegan Paul, 1977.

1744. Platts, Mark de Bretton. REFERENCE, TRUTH, REALITY: ESSAYS ON THE PHILOSOPHY OF LANGUAGE. London and Boston: Routledge & Kegan Paul, 1980.

1745. Plotinus. PLOTINUS. Vol. 1, PORPHYRY ON THE LIFE OF PLOTINUS AND THE ORDER OF HIS BOOKS. ENNEADS I. Vol. 2, ENNEADS II. Vol. 3, ENNEADS III. Vol. 4, ENNEADS IV. Vol. 5. ENNEADS V. Vol. 6, ENNEADS VI, 1-5. ENNEADS VI, 6-9. Tr. of ENNEADS (English and Greek). English translation by Arthur Hilary Armstrong. Cambridge: Harvard Univ. Press; London: Heinemann, 1966-1988.

The Greek text is essentially that of Paul Henry and Hans-Rudolf Schwyzer.

1746. Pole, David. AESTHETICS, FORM AND EMOTION. Ed. by George Roberts. New York: St. Martin's Press; London: Duckworth, 1983.

1747. Pompa, Leon and William H. Dray. SUBSTANCE AND FORM IN HISTORY: A COLLECTION OF ESSAYS IN PHILOSOPHY OF HISTORY. FESTSCHRIFT IN HONOR OF W. H. WALSH. New York: Columbia Univ. Press; Edinburgh: Univ. Press, 1981.

This Festschrift contains essays written by thirteen philosophers in appreciation of Walsh's contributions to the philosophy of history.

1748. Punter, David Godfrey. BLAKE, HEGEL, AND DIALECTIC. Elementa, Vol. 25. Amsterdam: Rodopi, 1982.

1749. Quinn, Arthur. THE CONFIDENCE OF BRITISH PHILOSOPHERS: AN ESSAY IN HISTORICAL NARRATIVE. Leiden: E.J. Brill, 1977.

1750. Radford, Colin and Sally Minogue. THE NATURE OF CRITICISM. Sussex: Harvester Press; Atlantic Highlands, NJ: Humanities Press, 1981.

The complex problematic aspects of criticism are discussed by a philosopher and a literary critic.

1751. Rankin, Herbert David. SOPHISTS, SOCRATICS AND CYNICS. Totowa, NJ: Barnes and Noble; London: Croom Helm, 1983.

1752. Ree, Jonathan, et al. PHILOSOPHY AND ITS PAST. Sussex: Harvester Press, 1978.

1753. Richards, Janet Radcliffe. THE SCEPTICAL FEMINIST: A PHILOSOPHICAL ENQUIRY. Boston and London: Routledge and Kegan Paul, 1982,1980.

1754. Rickman, Hans Peter. THE ADVENTURE OF REASON: THE USES OF PHILOSOPHY IN SOCIOLOGY. Westport, CT: Greenwood Press, 1983.

1755. Rickman, Hans Peter. WILHELM DILTHEY: PIONEER OF THE HUMAN STUDIES. London: Elek; Berkeley: Univ. of California Press, 1979.

1756. Robbins, Peter. THE BRITISH HEGELIANS, 1875-1925. Ed. by Peter Stansky and Leslie Hume. New York: Garland, 1982.

1757. Rose, Gillian. THE MELANCHOLY SCIENCE: AN INTRODUCTION TO THE THOUGHT OF T. W. ADORNO. London: Macmillan; New York: Columbia Univ. Press, 1978.

A bibliography is included on pages 193-205.

1758. Rosen, Frederick. JEREMY BENTHAM AND REPRESENTATIVE DEMOCRACY: A STUDY OF THE CONSTITUTIONAL CODE. Oxford and New York: Clarendon Press, 1983.

1759. Rundle, Bede. GRAMMAR IN PHILOSOPHY. New York: Oxford Univ. Press; Oxford: Clarendon, 1979.

The author presents a thorough and wide ranging study of the philosophy of language. He concentrates on the constituents of noun and verb phrases and the questions of meaning and reference which these involve.

1760. Russell, Bertrand. THE COLLECTED PAPERS OF BERTRAND RUSSELL. The McMaster University Edition in twenty-eight volumes. Ed. by John Arthur Passmore. London and Boston: Allen & Unwin, 1983-.

1761. Ryan, Alan. THE IDEA OF FREEDOM: ESSAYS IN HONOUR OF ISAIAH BERLIN. Oxford and New York: Oxford Univ. Press, 1979.

There is a bibliography of Isaiah Berlin on pages 271-288.

1762. Ryder, Richard and David Patterson. ANIMAL RIGHTS-A SYMPOSIUM. Fontwell, Sussex: Centaur Press, 1979.

This is a record of the proceedings of a symposium held under the auspices of the Royal Society for the Prevention of Cruelty to Animals at Trinity College, Cambridge, August 18-19, 1977, on the ethical aspects of man's relationships with animals.

1763. Ryle, Gilbert. CONTEMPORARY ASPECTS OF PHILOSOPHY. Oxford International Symposium (Christ Church College, 1975). Stocksfield, Eng. and Boston: Oriel Press, 1977.

1764. Ryle, Gilbert. ON THINKING. Totowa, NJ: Rowman and Littlefield, 1979.

An anthology that consists of the later writings of one of the major figures in twentieth-century British philosophy.

1765. Sainsbury, Richard Mark. RUSSELL. The Arguments of the Philosophers. Boston: Routledge and Kegan Paul, 1979.

1766. Savile, Anthony. THE TEST OF TIME: AN ESSAY IN PHILOSOPHICAL AESTHETICS. Oxford and New York: Clarendon Press, 1982.

1767. Sayers, Sean. REALITY AND REASON: DIALECTIC AND THE THEORY OF KNOWLEDGE. Oxford and New York: B. Blackwell, 1985.

1768. Schilcher, Florian von and Neil Tennant. PHILOSOPHY, EVOLUTION AND HUMAN NATURE. London and Boston: Routledge and Kegan Paul, 1984.

There is a bibliography on pages 251-269.

1769. Schmitt, Charles B. THE CAMBRIDGE HISTORY OF RENAISSANCE PHILOSOPHY. Ed. by Quentin Skinner, et al. Cambridge and New York: Cambridge Univ. Press, 1988.

1770. Scholfield, Malcolm. AN ESSAY ON ANAXAGORAS. Cambridge and New York: Cambridge Univ. Press, 1980.

1771. Scholfield, Malcolm, et al. DOUBT AND DOGMATICISM: STUDIES IN HELLENISTIC EPISTEMOLOGY. Oxford: Clarendon Press; New York: Oxford Univ. Press, 1980.

1772. Scholfield, Malcolm and Martha Craven Nussbaum. LANGUAGE AND LOGOS: STUDIES IN ANCIENT PHILOSOPHY PRESENTED TO G. E. L. OWEN. Cambridge and New York: Cambridge Univ. Press, 1982.

1773. Scruton, Roger. THE AESTHETIC UNDERSTANDING: ESSAYS IN THE PHILOSOPHY OF ART AND CULTURE. London and New York: Metheun, 1983.

1774. Scruton, Roger. THE AESTHETICS OF ARCHITECTURE. Princeton Essays on the Arts. Princeton: Princeton Univ. Press, 1979.

1775. Scruton, Roger. FROM DESCARTES TO WITTGENSTEIN: A SHORT HISTORY OF MODERN PHILOSOPHY. London and Boston: Routledge & Kegan Paul, 1981.

1776. Scruton, Roger. KANT. Oxford and New York: Oxford Univ. Press, 1982.

1777. Seavor, Douglas and Nicholas Fotion. HARE AND CRITICS: ESSAYS ON MORAL THINKING. Oxford: Clarendon Press; New York: Oxford Univ. Press, 1988.

In thirteen original essays such philosophers as Thomas Nagel, Peter Singer, J.O. Urmson, R.B. Brandt, T.M. Scanlon and others discuss Hare's philosophy as expounded in his MORAL THINKING. Hare replies to his critics in a detailed, critical essay.

1778. Sen, Amartya and Bernard Arthur Owen Williams. UTILITARIANISM AND BEYOND. Cambridge and New York: Cambridge Univ. Press, 1982.

1779. Sharpe, Robert A. CONTEMPORARY AESTHETICS: A PHILOSOPHICAL ANALYSIS. New York: St. Martin's Press; Sussex: Harvester Press, 1983.

1780. Sheehan, Helena. MARXISM AND THE PHILOSOPHY OF SCIENCE: A CRITI- CAL HISTORY Vol. 1, THE FIRST HUNDRED YEARS. Atlantic Highlands, NJ: Humanities Press, 1985-.

The first volume covers the period from the 1940's to the end of the Second World War. A promised second volume will bring the account to the present.

1781. Smart, Barry. FOUCAULT, MARXISM, AND CRITIQUE. London and Boston: Routledge and Kegan Paul, 1983.

This work is concerned with the relevance of Foucault's work for developing an under- standing of those issues that lie beyond the limits of Marxist theory.

1782. Smiley, Timothy John. THE THEORY OF DESCRIPTIONS. London: Oxford Univ. Press, 1983.

The text is from the Proceedings of the British Academy, London, Vol. LXVII 1981.

1783. Smith, Barry. PARTS AND MOMENTS: STUDIES IN LOGIC AND FORMAL ONTOLOGY. Amsterdam and Philadelphia: John Benjamins; Munich: Philosophia Ver- lag, 1982.

1784. Soper, Kate. HUMANISM AND ANTI-HUMANISM. London: Hutchinson; LaSalle, IL: Open Court, 1986.

1785. Soper, Kate. ON HUMAN NEEDS: OPEN AND CLOSED THEORIES IN A MARXIST PERSPECTIVE. Sussex: Harvester Press; Atlantic Highlands, NJ: Humanities Press, 1981.

1786. Sorabiji, Richard R. K. IS TIME REAL?: RESPONSES TO AN UNAGEING PARADOX. London: British Academy, 1983.

The text is from the Proceedings of the British Academy, London, Vol. LXVIII, 1982.

1787. Sorell, Tom. HOBBES. The Arguments of the Philosophers. London and New York: Routledge and Kegan Paul, 1986.

1788. Sprigge, Timothy L. THE VINDICATION OF ABSOLUTE IDEALISM. Edinburgh: Univ. Press, 1983.

1789. Srednicki, Jan T. J. STEPHAN KORNER--PHILOSOPHICAL ANALYSIS AND RECONSTRUCTION: CONTRIBUTIONS TO PHILOSOPHY. Dordrecht and Boston: M. Nijhoff, 1987.

There is a bibliography of Stephan Korner's works on pages 161-167.

1790. Steiner, George. MARTIN HEIDEGGER. Glasgow: Fontana/Collins; Sussex:

Harvester, 1978.

1791. Stern, Joseph Peter. A STUDY OF NIETZSCHE. Cambridge and New York: Cambridge Univ. Press, 1979.

1792. Stewart, Michael Alexander. SELECTED PHILOSOPHICAL PAPERS OF ROBERT BOYLE. Manchester: Univ. Press, Totowa, NJ: Barnes and Noble, 1979.

1793. Stockman, Norman. ANTIPOSITIVIST THEORIES OF THE SCIENCES: CRITICAL RATIONALISM, CRITICAL THEORY, AND SCIENTIFIC REALISM. Dordrecht and Boston: Reidel, 1983.

1794. Straaten, Zak van. PHILOSOPHICAL SUBJECTS: ESSAYS PRESENTED TO P. F. STRAWSON. Oxford: Clarendon Press; New York: Oxford Univ. Press, 1980.

The twelve contributors are A. J. Ayer, Jonathan Bennett, J. L. Mackie, Hide Ishiguro, Gareth Evans, John McDowell, L. Jonathan Cohen, W. V. Quine, Peter Thomas Geach, David Wiggins, David Pears, and John R. Searle.

1795. Strawson, Peter Frederick. SKEPTICISM AND NATURALISM: SOME VARIETIES. The Woodbriddge Lectures 1983. New York: Columbia Univ. Press; London: Metheun, 1985.

1796. Stroud, Barry. HUME. The Arguments of the Philosophers. London: Routledge & Kegan Paul, 1977.

1797. Swinburne, Richard. THE COHERENCE OF THEISM. Oxford: Clarendon Press, 1977.

The COHERENCE OF THEISM is the first volume in the author's trilogy on philosophical theology. The second and third and their dates of publication by Clarendon Press are, respectively: THE EXISTENCE OF GOD (1979) and FAITH AND REASON (1981).

1798. Swinburne, Richard. THE EVOLUTION OF THE SOUL. New York: Oxford Univ. Press; Oxford: Clarendon Press, 1986.

1799. Swinburne, Richard. SPACE AND TIME. 2d ed. New York: St. Martin's Press, 1981.

1800. Swinburne, Richard. SPACE, TIME AND CAUSALITY. Dordrecht and Boston: Reidel, 1983.

1801. Taylor, Barry M. MICHAEL DUMMETT: CONTRIBUTIONS TO PHILOSOPHY. Dordrecht and Boston: Nijhoff, 1985.

This work includes original essays on this contemporary British philosopher.

1802. Taylor, C. M. THEORIES OF MEANING. London: Oxford Univ. Press, 1982.

The text is from the Proceedings of the British Academy, London, Vol. LXVI, 1980.

1803. Taylor, Charles. HEGEL AND MODERN SOCIETY. Cambridge and New York: Cambridge Univ. Press, 1979.

1804. Taylor, Michael. ANARCHY AND COOPERATION. London and New York: Wiley, 1976.

1805. Teichman, Jenny. PACIFICISM AND THE JUST WAR: A STUDY IN APPLIED PHILOSOPHY. Oxford and New York: B. Blackwell, 1986.

1806. Thompson, John Brookshire. CRITICAL HERMENEUTICS: A STUDY IN THE THOUGHT OF PAUL RICOEUR AND JURGEN HABERMAS. Cambridge and New York: Cambridge Univ. Press, 1981.

1807. Thompson, John Brookshire. STUDIES IN THE THEORY OF IDEOLOGY. Berkeley: Univ. of California Press; Cambridge: Polity Press, 1984.

There is a bibliography on pages 303-342.

1808. Thompson, John Brookshire and David Held. HABERMAS, CRITICAL DEBATES. Cambridge: MIT Press; London and Basingstoke: Macmillan, 1982.

This volume collects critical essays on Habermas's philosophizing by Rudiger Bubner, Henning Ottmann, Mary Hess, Andrew Arato, and others. In the final essay Habermas replies to his critics.

1809. Thompson, Kenneth A. and Margaret Thompson. SARTRE: LIFE AND WORKS. New York and Bicester, England: Facts on File, 1984.

This work contains a chronology of Sartre's life and a bibliography of his works.

1810. Thomson, Garrett. NEEDS. London and New York: Routledge and Kegan Paul, 1987.

1811. Tiles, James Edward. THINGS THAT HAPPEN. Scots Philosophical Monographs, Vol. 1. Aberdeen: Aberdeen Univ. Press, 1981.

1812. Trigg, Roger. THE SHAPING OF MAN: PHILOSOPHICAL ASPECTS OF SOCIO-BIOLOGY. Oxford: B. Blackwell, 1982.

1813. Uchida, Hiroshi. MARX'S GRUNDRISSE AND HEGEL'S LOGIC. Ed. by Terrell Carver. London: Croom Helm, 1988.

1814. Urmson, James Opie and Jonathan Ree. THE CONCISE ENCYCLOPEDIA OF WESTERN PHILOSOPHY AND PHILOSOPHERS. Completely rev. 3d ed. London and Boston: Unwin Hyman, 1989.

The original articles of the first edition (1960) have been revised and updated and 80 articles by 31 new authors have been added. New contributors include Ian Hacking, Jean-Jacques Lecercle, A. J. Ayer, R. M. Hare, Ernest Nagel, Gilbert Ryle, the editors and others.

1815. Vesey, Godfrey. COLLINS DICTIONARY OF PHILOSOPHY. London: Collins, 1990.

1816. Vesey, Godfrey. HUMAN VALUES. Royal Institute of Philosophy Lectures. Hassocks, Sussex: Harvester Press; Atlantic Highlands, NJ: Humanities Press, 1978.

1817. Vesey, Godfrey. IDEALISM: PAST AND PRESENT. Hassocks: Harvester; Cambridge and New York: Cambridge Univ. Press, 1982.

1818. Walker, Ralph Charles Sutherland. KANT. The Arguments of the Philosophers. London and Boston: Routledge & Kegan Paul, 1978.

1819. Walker, Ralph Charles Sutherland. KANT ON PURE REASON. Oxford and New York: Oxford Univ. Press, 1982.

This book is a collection of recent essays, mainly by Anglo-American philosophers, on various aspects of Kant's epistemology and metaphysics.

1820. Warnock, Geoffrey James. MORALITY AND LANGUAGE. Totowa, NJ: Barnes and Noble Books; Oxford: B. Blackwell, 1983.

1821. Warnock, Mary. IMAGINATION. Berkeley: Univ. of California Press, 1976.

1822. Waterhouse, Roger. A HEIDEGGER CRITIQUE: A CRITICAL EXAMINATION OF THE EXISTENTIAL PHENOMENOLOGY OF MARTIN HEIDEGGER. Atlantic Highlands, NJ: Humanitites Press; Sussex: Harvester Press, 1981.

A bibliography of Heidegger's works is included on pages 222-230.

1823. White, Alan. ABSOLUTE KNOWLEDGE: HEGEL AND THE PROBLEM OF METAPHYSICS. Series in Continental Thought, Vol. 4. Athens: Ohio Univ. Press, 1983.

1824. Wiggins, David. SAMENESS AND SUBSTANCE. Cambridge: Harvard Univ. Press; Oxford: B. Blackwell, 1980.

1825. Williams, Bernard Arthur Owen. DESCARTES: THE PROJECT OF PURE ENQUIRY. Atlantic Highlands, NJ: Humanities Press; Sussex: Harvester, 1978.

1826. Williams, Bernard Arthur Owen. ETHICS AND THE LIMITS OF PHILOSOPHY. Cambridge: Harvard Univ. Press, 1985.

1827. Williams, Bernard Arthur Owen. MORAL LUCK: PHILOSOPHICAL PAPERS, 1973-1980. Cambridge and New York: Cambridge Univ. Press, 1981.

1828. Williams, Howard Lloyd. KANT'S POLITICAL PHILOSOPHY. Oxford: B. Blackwell; New York: St. Martin's Press, 1983.

1829. Wilson, Edgar. THE MENTAL AS PHYSICAL: MIND-BRAIN IDENTITY THEORY, ETHICS AND JURISPRUDENCE. London and Boston: Routledge and Kegan Paul, 1979.

1830. Wilson, Margaret Dauler. DESCARTES. The Arguments of the Philosophers. London and Boston: Routledge and Kegan Paul, 1978.

1831. Winch, Peter. CEASING TO EXIST. London: British Academy, 1983.

This text was taken from the Proceedings of the British Academy, London, Vol. LXVIII 1982.

1832. Wohlheim, Richard. THE THREAD OF LIFE. Cambridge: Harvard Univ. Press, 1984.

1833. Wollheim, Richard. ART AND ITS OBJECTS: WITH SIX SUPPLEMENTARY ESSAYS. 2d ed. Cambridge and New York: Cambrdige Univ. Press, 1980.

1834. Wollheim, Richard and James Hopkins. PHILOSOPHICAL ESSAYS ON FREUD. Cambridge and New York: Cambridge Univ. Press, 1982.

1835. Woodfield, Andrew. TELEOLOGY. Cambridge: Cambridge Univ. Press, 1976.

1836. Woods, Michael. A FESTSCHRIFT FOR J. L. ACKRILL. Oxford: Clarendon Press, 1986.

This work contains a bibliography of the publications of J. L. Ackrill.

1837. Woolhouse, Roger S. LOCKE. Philosophers in Context. Minneapolis: Univ. of Minnesota Press; Sussex: Harvester Press, 1983.

The author examines Locke's ideas in the light of the philosopher's overall aim of tracing the origin, certainty and extent of knowledge. Locke's thought is placed in an intellectual context that includes Bacon, Boyle, Glanville, Lee, Leibniz, Lowde, More, Norris, Sargeant, Sprat, and Webster.

1838. Wright, Crispin. WITTGENSTEIN ON THE FOUNDATION OF MATHEMATICS. Cambridge: Harvard Univ. Press; London: Duckworth, 1980.

GREECE

1839. Boudouves, Constantine. PHILOSOPHY OF EDUCATION. Athens: n. p., 1976.

1840. Boudouves, Constantine. THE THEORY OF KNOWLEDGE. Athens: n. p., 1977.

1841. Despotopolos, Constantin. ARISTOTE SUR LA FAMILLE ET LA JUSTICE. Brussels: Ousia, 1983.

1842. Kanellopoulos, Panagiotes, et al. MELETEMATA GIA TON E. P. PAPANOUTSOS: HEORTASMOS STA OGDONTACHRONA TOU. Athens: Euthynes, 1981.

1843. Kyriazopoulos, Spyridon. LOGOS AND ETHOS. Ioannina: Philosophike Schole Panepistemiou Ionninon, 1976.

1844. Kyriazopoulos, Spyridon. SOCIALISTIC REALISM. Athens: Tropes, 1977.

1845. Moukanos, Demetrios D. ONTOLOGIE DER METAPHYSIK DES ARISTOTELES. Athener Abhandlungen zu Antiken Philosophie. Athens: D. Moukanos, 1981.

1846. Moutsopoulos, Evangelos. KAIROS: LA MISE ET L'ENJEU. Paris: Librarie philosophique J. Vrin, 1991.

1847. Moutsopoulos, Evanghelos. CONFORMISME ET DEFORMATION: MYTHES CONFORMISTES ET STRUCTURES DEFORMANTES. Paris: J. Vrin, 1978.

1848. Moutsopoulos, Evanghelos. DU VRAI, DU BEAU, DU BIEN: ETUDES PHILOSO-PHIQUES PRESENTEES AU PROFESSEUR EVANGHELOS A. MOUTSOPOULOS. Paris: Librairie philosophique J. Vrin, 1990.

1849. Moutsopoulos, Evanghelos. HISTORIA TES PHILOSOPHIAS. Athens: Ekdoseis Gregore, 1979-.

1850. Moutsopoulos, Evanghelos. LA CRITIQUE DU PLATONISME CHEZ BERGSON. Athens: Editions Grigoris, 1980.

1851. Moutsopoulos, Evanghelos. LE PROBLEME DE L'IMAGINAIRE CHEZ PLOTIN. Athens: Editions Grigoris, 1980.

1852. Moutsopoulos, Evanghelos. LES STRUCTURES DE L'IMAGINAIRE DANS LA PHILOSOPHIE DE PROCLUS. Paris: Belles Lettres, 1985.

1853. Moutsopoulos, Evanghelos. P. BRAILAS ARMENIS PHILOSOPHICAL WORKS. 5 Vols. Athens: n.p., 1969-1977.

1854. Moutsopoulos, Evanghelos. PLEASURES, A PHENOMENOLOGICAL STUDY (in Greek). Athens: n.p., 1977.

1855. Moutsopoulos, Evanghelos. THE PROCEDURE OF SPIRIT (in Greek). 3 Vols. Athens: n.p., 1974-1977.

1856. Moutsopoulos, Evanghelos, et al. ENERGEIA: ETUDES ARISTOTELICIENNES OFFERTES A MGR. ANTONIO JANNONE. Paris: J. Vrin, 1986.

1857. Moutsopoulos, Evanghelos and Antonio T. de Nicholas. GOD, EXPERIENCE OR ORIGIN? New York: Paragon, 1985.

1858. Papanoutsos, Evangelos P. APOMNEMONEUMATA. Athens: Ekdoseis Philoppote, 1982.

1859. Papanoutsos, Evangelos P. ART AND EMOTION: THE AESTHETICS OF E. P. PAPANOUTSOS. Tr. and introduction by N. Georgopoulos. New York: Peter Lang, 1989.

1860. Papanoutsos, Evangelos P. EPHEMERA EPIKAIRA ANEPITKAIRA. Athens: Ikaros, 1980.

1861. Papanoutsos, Evangelos P. HOI DROMOI TES ZOES. Athens: Philippotes, 1979.

1862. Papanoutsos, Evangelos P. PHILOSOPHIA KAI PAIDEIA. Athens: Ikaros, 1977.

1863. Papanoutsos, Evangelos P. PHILOSOPHIKA PROVLEMATA. 2d ed. Athens: Ikaros, 1978.

1864. Papanoutsos, Evangelos P. POLITEIA KAI DIKAIOSYNE: KAI ALLOI DIALOGOI. 2d ed. Athens: Ekdoseis Philippote, 1984.

1865. Papanoutsos, Evangelos P. TA METRA TES EPOCHES MAS. Athens: Ekdoseis Philippote, 1981.

1866. Tatakes, B. BYZANTINE PHILOSOPHY. Athens: Moraites School, 1977.

1867. Voros, Phanoures K., et al. APHIEROMASTON EUANGELO PAPNOUTSO: ME TEN EPIMELEIA EPITROPES. 2 Vols. Athens: Ekdidetai apotrimel e Epitrope, 1980-1983.

The contributions to this work are in Greek, English, French, and German.

ITALY

1868. Agazzi, Evandro. IL CONCETTO DI PROGRESSO NELLA SCIENZA. Milan: Feltrinelli, 1976.

1869. Agazzi, Evandro. IL PENSIERO CRISTIANO NELLA FILOSOFIA ITALIANA DEL NOVACENTO. Lecci: Milella, 1980.

1870. Agazzi, Evandro. MODERN LOGIC: A SURVEY: HISTORICAL, PHILOSOPH-ICAL, AND MATHEMATICAL ASPECTS OF MODERN LOGIC AND ITS APPLI-CATIONS. Proceedings of the 1978 Pisa Conference on the History and Philosophy of Science. Dordrecht and Boston: Reidel, 1981.

1871. Agazzi, Evandro. NORMALITA E DEVIANZA: ANALISI EPISTEMOLOGICHE

E FONDAZIONALI IN PSICOPATOLOGIA. Ed. by Orazio Siciliano, et al. Milan: F. Angeli, 1981.

1872. Agazzi, Evandro. STUDI SUL PROBLEMA DEL SIGNIFICATO. Florence: F. Le Monnier, 1979.

1873. Agazzi, Evandro, et al. LE SENS DE LA MORT=VOM SINN DES TODES. Freiburg, Switzerland: Editions Universitaires, 1980.

1874. Agazzi, Evandro, et al. SCIENZA E CULTURA CONTEMPORANEA. Ed. by Lido Valdre. Bologna: Univ. of Bologna, 1982.

1875. Agazzi, Evandro, et al. TEORIE METODO DELLE SCIENZE. Ed. by Carlo Huber. Rome: Universita Gregoriana, 1981.

1876. Agazzi, Evandro and Carlo Cellucci. LOGICHE MODERNE: ASPETTI, STORICI, FILOSOFICI E MATEMATICI. 2 Vols. Proceedings of the 1978 Pisa Conference on the History and Philosophy of Science. Rome: Istituto della Enciclopedia Italiana, 1981.

1877. Agazzi, Evandro and Dario Palladino. GEOMETRIE NON EUCLIDEE E I FONDAMENTI DELLA GEOMETRIA. Milan: A. Mondadori, 1978.

1878. Albertoni, Ettore A. STUDIES ON THE POLITICAL THOUGHT OF GAETANO MOSCA 1858-1931: THE THEORY OF THE RULING CLASS AND ITS DEVELOP-MENT ABROAD. Milan: A.Giuffre Academic Press, 1982.

1879. Alici, Luigi, et al. I LINGUAGGI DELLA COMUNICAZIONE. Ed. by Giovanni Santinello. Padua: Libreria Gregoriana, 1987.

This volume consists of papers presented at the 30th conference of the Ricercatori di Filosofia held in Padua, September 9-11, 1985.

1880. ARCHIVIO DI FILOSOFIA. Padua: CEDAM, 1976-.

The individual works in this series are in English, French, German, or Italian. Each volume is the proceedings of a conference devoted to a particular philosophical subject or philosopher. There are bibliographical references.

1881. Armogathe, Jean Robert and Jean-Luc Marion. INDEX DES REGULAE AD DIRECTIONEM INGENII DE RENE DESCARTES: AVEC DES LISTES DE LECONS ET CONJECTURES ETABLIE PAR G. CRAPULLE. Rome: Edizioni dell' Ateneo, 1976.

1882. Auciello, Nicola. RAGIONE POLITICA: SAGGIO SULL'INTELLETTO EURO-PEO. Bari: De Donato, 1981.

1883. Auciello, Nicola. SENSO E COMMUNITA: STUDIO SU DILTHEY. Naples: Edizioni Scientifice Italiane, 1982.

This work offers a rethinking of Dilthey's EINLEITUNG IN DIE GEISTESWISSEN-SCHAFT (1833) and its influence on Heidegger, Gadamer and Habermas.

1884. Badaloni, Nicola, et al. LA STORIA DELLA FILOSOFIA COME SAPERE CRITI-CO: STUDI OFFERTI A MARIO DAL PRA. Milan: F. Angeli, 1984.

1885. Ballarini, Adriano. ESSERE COLLETTIVO DOMINATO: NIETZSCHE E IL PROBLEMA DELLA GIUSTIZIA. Milan: A. Giuffre, 1982.

1886. Bellezza, Vito A. LA PROBLEMATICA GENTILIANA DELLA STORIA. Rome: Bulzoni, 1983.

1887. Bello, Angela Ales. THE GREAT CHAIN OF BEING AND ITALIAN PHENOME-NOLOGY. Analecta Husserliana: Yearbook of Phenomenological Research, Vol. XI. Dordrecht and Boston: Reidel, 1981.

1888. Beltrametti, Enrico G. and Bastiaan C. Van Fraassen. CURRENT ISSUES IN QUANTUM LOGIC. New York and London: Plenum, 1981.

This is the Proceedings of the Workshop on Quantum Logic, held December 2-9, 1979 at the Ettore Majorana Center for Scientific Culture, Erice, Sicily.

1889. Bertola, Francesco and Umberto Curi. THE ANTHROPIC PRINCIPLE: PROCEED-INGS OF THE SECOND VENICE CONFERENCE ON COSMOLOGY AND PHILOS-OPHY , NOVEMBER 18-19, 1988. Cambridge: Cambridge Univ. Press, 1989.

1890. Biasutti, Franco. ASSOLUTEZZA E SOGGETTIVITA: L'IDEA DI RELIGIONE IN HEGEL. Trent: Verifiche, 1979.

1891. Biasutti, Franco. LA DOTTRINA DELLA SCIENZA IN SPINOZA. Bologna: Patron, 1979.

1892. Boccara, Nadia. VITTORIANI E RADICALI: DA MILL A RUSSELL: ETICA E POLITICA NELLA CULTURA INGLESE TRA `800 E `900. Rome: Edizione dell'Ateneo, 1981.

This work discusses Victorian ethical and political ideas and the "Bloomsbury group" (Bertrand Russell, Lytton Strachey, Leonard and Virginia Woolf and John Maynard Keynes).

1893. Bodei, Remo, et al. HEGEL INTERPRETE DI KANT. Ed. by Valerio Verra. Naples: Prismi, 1981.

1894. Bonomi, Andrea. EVENTI MENTALI. Milan: Saggiatore, 1983.

1895. Bonomi, Andrea. UNIVERSI DI DISCORSO. Milan: Feltrinelli; Milan: Bocca, 1979.

1896. Bonomi, Andrea, et al. MERLEAU-PONTY ESISTENZA, FILOSOFIA, POLITICA. Naples: Guida, 1982.

1897. Booth, Edward. ARISTOTELIAN APORETIC ONTOLOGY IN ISLAMIC AND CHRISTIAN THINKERS. Cambridge Studies in Medieval Life and Thought, 3rd series, Vol. 20. Cambridge and New York: Cambridge Univ. Press, 1983.

This work contains an extensive bibliography on pages 276-304.

1898. Borradori, Giavanna. RECODING METAPHYSICS: THE NEW ITALIAN PHILOS-OPHY. Translated from the Italian. Evanston, IL: Northwestern Univ. Press, 1988.

There is a bibliography on pages 201-222.

1899. Bottin, Francesco. LA SCIENZA DEGLI OCCAMISTI: LA SCIENZA TARDOME-DIEVALE DALLE ORIGINI DEL PARADIGMA NOMINALISTA ALLA RIVO-LUZIONE SCIENTIFICA. Rimini: Maggioli, 1982.

1900. Bottin, Francesco. LE ANTINOMIE SEMANTICHE NELLA LOGICA ME-DIEVALE. Padua: Antenore, 1976.

1901. Bottin, Francesco. PROBLEMI DI EPISTEMOLOGIA NEL PENSIERO ANTICO E MEDIOEVALE. Padua: Cleup, 1977.

1902. Buzzetti, Dino and Maurizio Ferriani. LA GRAMMATICA DEL PENSIERO: LOGICAL, LINGUAGGIO E CONOSCENZA NELL'ETA DELL'ILLUMINISMO. Bologna: Mulino, 1982.

The editors and Sylvain Auroux, Barries E. Bartlett, Hans Werner-Arndt, Mirella Capozzi, Luigi Rosiello, and Massimo Mugnai discuss the ideas of Wolff, Leibniz, Locke, Condillac, Bernoulli, and Boole.

1903. Cacciari, Massimo. CRUCIALITA DEL TEMPO: SAGGI SULLA CONCEZIONE NIETZCHIANA DEL TEMPO. Naples: Liguori, 1980.

1904. Cacciari, Massimo. DIALETTICA E CRITICA DEL POLITICO: SAGGIO SU HEGEL. Milan: Feltrinelli, 1978.

1905. Cacciari, Massimo. ICONE DELLA LEGGE. Milan: Adelphi, 1985.

The volume contains a bibliography on pages 301-336.

1906. Cacciari, Massimo. KRISIS: SAGGIO SULLA CRISI DEL PENSIERO NEGATIVO DA NIETZSCHE A WITTGENSTEIN. Milan: Feltrinelli, 1976.

1907. Cacciari, Massimo. PENSIERO NEGATIVO E RAZIONALIZZAZIONE. Venice: Marsilio, 1977.

1908. Cacciari, Massimo, et al. IL DISPOSITIVO FOUCAULT. Venice: Cluva, 1981.

1909. Cambiano, Giuseppe. LA FILOSOFIA IN GRECIA E A ROMA. Roma and Bari: Laterza, 1983.

1910. Cappellini, Susanna. IL "RAZIONALISMO" MORALE DI WILLIAM WHEWELL. Lucca: M. Pacini Fazzi, 1983.

1911. Casini, Paolo. FILOSOFIA E FISICA DA NEWTON A KANT. Turin: Loescher, 1978.

1912. Casini, Paolo. INTRODUZIONE ALL'ILLUMINISMO DA NEWTON A ROUS-SEAU. Vol. 1, SCIENZA MISCREDENZA E POLITICA. Vol. 2, L'ENCICLOPEDIA E LE RIFORME. Rome: Laterza, 1980.

1913. Casini, Paolo. LA POLITICA DELLA RAGIONE: STUDI SULL'ILLUMINISMO: FRANCESE. Bologna: Mulino, 1978.

1914. Casini, Paolo. PER CONOSCERE ROUSSEAU. Milan: A. Mondadori, 1976.

1915. Cavallaro, Anna. PITTURA VISIONARIA E METAFISICA. Milan: Fratelli Fabbri, 1978.

This work contains contributions by Franco Rella and others.

1916. Centro di Studi Filosofici di Gallarate. DIZIONARIO DEI FILOSOFI. Florence: G. C. Sansoni, 1976.

1917. Chiereghin, Franco. DIALETTICA DELL'ASSOLUTO E ONTOLOGIA DELLA SOGGETTIVITA IN HEGEL: DALL'IDEALE GIOVANILE ALLA FENOMENOLO-GIA DELLO SPIRITO. Trent: Verifiche, 1980.

1918. Chiereghin, Franco. G. W. F. HEGEL: LOGICA ET METAFISICA DI JENA (1804-1805). Tr. by F. Biasutti et al. Trent: Verifiche, 1982.

This is an Italian translation of Hegel's logical and metaphysical writings during his Jena stay (1804-1805).

1919. Chiereghin, Franco. IMPLICAZIONE ETICHE DELLA STORIOGRAFIA FILOSO-FICA DI PLATONE. Padua: Liviana, 1976.

1920. Cirillo, Antonio. TH. ADORNO-M. HORKHEIMER: LEZIONI DI SOCIOLOGIA. L'Aquila: L.U. Japare Editore, 1980.

1921. Coffa, J. Alberto. THE SEMANTIC TRADITION FROM KANT TO CARNAP: TO THE VIENNA STATION. Ed. by Linda Wessels. Cambridge and New York: Cambridge Univ. Press, 1991.

1922. Colli, Giorgio. LA RAGIONE ERRABONDA: QUADERNI POSTUMI. Ed. by Enrico Colli. Milan: Adelphi, 1982.

1923. Coppola, Francesco. ARTE E CIVILITA IN ALFRED NORTH WHITEHEAD. Salerno: Palladio, 1983.

1924. Coppola, Francesco. ESPERIENZA E VALORE NEL PENSIERO DI JOHN DEWEY. Naples: Morano, 1978.

1925. Cotta, Sergio. GIUSTIFICAZIONE E OBBLIGATORIETA DELLE NORME. Milan: A. Giuffre Editore, 1981.

1926. Craven, William G. GIOVANNI PICO DELLA MIRANDOLA, SYMBOL OF HIS AGE: MODERN INTERPRETATIONS OF A RENAISSANCE PHILOSOPHER. Geneva: Droz, 1981.

1927. Crease, Robert. VICO IN ENGLISH: A BIBLIOGRAPHY OF WRITINGS BY AND ABOUT GIAMBATTISTA VICO (1668-1744). Atlantic Highlands, NJ: Humanities Press, 1978.

1928. Cremaschi, Sergio. L'AUTOMA SPIRITUALE: LA TEORIA DELLA MENTE E DELLA POSSIONI IN SPINOZA. Milan: Vita e Pensiero, 1979.

1929. Crispini, Franco. MENTALISMO A STORIA NATURALE NELL'ETA DI CONDILLAC: STUDI E RICERCHE. Naples: Morano, 1982.

Some of the articles in this volume are revisions of articles published in various journals.

1930. Crispini, Franco. NEOKANTISMO STRUTTURALISMO, SCIENZE UMANE: GURVITCH E GOLDMANN. Cosenza: Lerici, 1979.

1931. Dal Pra, Mario. STORIA DELLA FILOSOFIA. Vol. 1, FILOSOFIA INDIANA by Giuseppina Scalabrino Borsani. Vol. 2, LA FILOSOFIA CINESE E DELL'ASIA ORIENTALE. Vol. 3, LA FILOSOFIA GRECA DAL VI AL IV SECOLO. Vol. 4, LA FILOSOFIA ELLENISTICA E LA PATRISTICA CRISTIANA DAL III SECOLO A. C. A V SECOLO D. C. Vol. 5, LA FILOSOFIA MEDIEVALE DAL SECOLO VI AL SECOLO XII. Vol. 6, LA FILOSOFIA MEDIEVALE by Tullio Gregory. Vol. 7, LA FILOSOFIA MODERN, DAL QUATTROCENTO A SEICENTO. Vol. 8, LA FILOSO-FIA MODERNA, IL SETTECENTO by Paolo Casini. Vol. 9, LA FILOSOFIA CON-TEMPORANEA, L'OTTOCENTO. Vol. 10, LA FILOSOFIA CONTEMPORANEA, IL NOVECENTO. Milan: Vallardi, 1975-1978.

1932. Dal Pra, Mario, et al. LA STORIOGRAFIA FILOSOFICA E LA SU STORIA. Padua: Antenore, 1982.

This work is in French, German and Italian.

1933. DeLacy, Philip Howard and Estelle Allen DeLacy. PHILODEMUS ON METHODS OF INFERENCE. Rev. ed. Naples: Bibliopolis, 1978.

This volume was prepared with the collaboration of Marcello Gigante, Buricchio L. Francesca, and Guerra T. Adele.

1934. Della Volpe, Galvano. CRITIQUE OF TASTE. Tr. of CRITICA DEL GUSTO. Milan: Feltrinelli, 1960. Tr. by Michael Caesar. London and New York: Verso, 1991.

1935. Della Volpe, Galvano. ROUSSEAU AND MARX AND OTHER WRITINGS. Tr. of ROUSSEAU E MARX E ALTRI SAGGI DI CRITICA MATERIALISTICA. Rome: Editorial Riuniti, 1957. Tr. by John Fraser. Atlantic Highlands, NJ: Humanities Press; London: Lawrence and Weishart, 1978.

This work was translated into Spanish in 1963, French in 1974 and German in 1975.

1936. Deregibus, Arturo. BRUNO E SPINOZA: LA REALITA DELL'INFINITO E IL PROBLEMA DELLA SUA UNITA. 2 Vols. Turin: Giappichelli, 1981.

1937. Doria, Paolo Mattia. MANOSCRITTO NAPOLETAI DI PAOLO MATTIA DORIA. Galatina: Congedo, 1979-.

1938. Dufrenne, Mikel and Dino Formaggio. TRATTATO DI ESTETICA. 2 Vols. Milan: A. Mondadori, 1981.

1939. Eco, Umberto. ART AND BEAUTY IN THE MIDDLE AGES. Tr. by Hugh Biedin. New Haven and London: Yale Univ. Press, 1986.

1940. Eco, Umberto. IL SEGNO. 2d. ed. Enciclopedia Filosofica Oscar Studie, Vol. 6. Milan: A. Mondadori, 1980,1985.

1941. Eco, Umberto. LA DEFINIZIONI DELL'ARTE. Milan: Garzanti, 1978,1983.

1942. Eco, Umberto. LA STUTTURA ASSENTE. Milan: Tascabili Bompiani, 1980.

1943. Eco, Umberto. OPERA APERTA. 4th ed. Milan: Tascabili Bompiani, 1985.

1944. Eco, Umberto. SEMIOTICS AND THE PHILOSOPHY OF LANGUAGE. Tr. of SEMIOTICS E FILOSOFIA DEL LINGUAGGIO. Turin: Einaudi, 1984. Bloomington: Indiana University Press; London: Macmillan, 1984.

The author delves into the nature of signs, the concept of dictionary versus encyclopedia, metaphor, symbol, abduction, coding, isotopy, and mirrors.

1945. Eco, Umberto. A THEORY OF SEMIOTICS. Bloomington: Indiana Univ. Press, 1976.

An extensive bibliography is included on pages 319-346.

1946. Eco, Umberto. TRAVELS IN HYPER REALITY: ESSAYS. Tr. from the Italian by William Weaver. San Diego: Harcourt Brace Jovanovich, 1986.

1947. Eco, Umberto and Thomas A. Sebeok. IL SEGNO DEI TRE: HOLMES, DUPIN,

PEIRCE. THE SIGN OF THE THREE: DUPIN, HOLMES, PEIRCE. Bloomington: Indiana Univ. Press, 1983. Milan: Tascabili Bompiani, 1983.

1948. Evain, Francois. ETRE ET PERSONNE CHEZ ANTONIO ROSMINI. Paris: Beauchesne; Rome: Universita Gregoriana, 1981.

1949. Facco, Maria Luisa. METAFISICA E DIARISTICA IN GABRIEL MARCEL. Genoa: Univ. di Genova, 1982.

1950. Fasso, Guido. SCRITTI DI FILOSOFIA DEL DIRITTO. 3 Vols. Ed. by Enrico Pattaro, et al. Milan: A. Giuffre, 1982.

1951. Femia, Joseph V. GRAMSCI'S POLITICAL THOUGHT: HEGEMONY, CON-SCIOUSNESS, AND THE REVOLUTIONARY PROCESS. Oxford: Clarendon Press, 1981.

1952. Ficino, Marsilio. LETTERS OF MARSILIO FICINO. Tr. of EPISTOLAE. 2 Vols. Venice: Appresso Gabriel Giolito de Ferrari, 1546-1548. Tr. from Latin by members of the Language Department of the School of Economic Science, London. The preface is by Paul Oskar Kristeller. London: Shepheard-Walwyn, 1975-.

1953. Focher, Ferrucio. I QUATTRO AUTORI DI POPPER. Milan: F. Angeli, 1982.

1954. Focher, Ferrucio. VICO ET HOBBES. Naples: Giannini, 1977.

1955. Franchini, Raffaello. IL DIRITTO ALLA FILOSOFIA: SISTEMATICA, ESEGETI-CA, STORIOGRAFIA, FILOSOFICA, STORIA DELLA CULTURA. Naples: Societa Editrice Napoletana, 1982.

1956. Frongia, Guido and Brian McGuinness. WITTGENSTEIN: A BIBLIOGRAPHI-CAL GUIDE. Tr. of GUIDA ALLA LETTERATURA SU WITTGENSTEIN: STORIA E ANALISI DELLA CRITICA. Urbino: Argalia Editore, 1981. Oxford and Cambridge, MA: Basil Blackwell, 1990.

This completely revised and updated translation of Frongia's original Italian work examines two thousand titles in chronological order. This work is designed as a guide to anyone studying Wittgenstein for the first time.

1957. Galeazzi, Giancarlo. SCIENZA E FILOSOFIA OGGI: ATTI DEL CONVEGNO DI STUDIO SU "IL RUOLO DELL'EPISTEMOLOGIA NELLA CULTURA CON-TEMPORANEA", SVOLTOSI AD ANCONA NEL 1979. Milan: Massimo, 1980.

1958. Gallupi, Pasquale. OPUSCOLI POLITICO-FILOSOFICI SULLA LIBERTA. Naples: Morano, 1976.

1959. Garfagnini, Gian Carlo. MARSILIO FICINO E IL RITORNO DI PLATONE: STUDI E DOCUMENTI. 2 Vols. Florence: L.S. Olschki, 1986.

This work is in Italian, English, French, German, Greek, and Latin.

1960. Gargani, Aldo Giorgio. CRISIS DE LA RAZON; NUEVOS MODELOS E LA RELACION ENTRE SABER Y ACTIVADADES HUMANAS. Tr. of CRISI DELLA RAGIONE. Torino: G. Einaudi, 1979. Mexico, D.F.: Siglio Veintiuno Editores, 1983.

1961. Gargani, Aldo Giorgio. FREUD, WITTGENSTEIN, MUSIL. Brescia: Shakespeare & Company, 1982.

1962. Gargani, Aldo Giorgio. IL CIRCULO DI VIENNA: TRA LA SCOPERTA DEL

SENSO E LA SCOPERTA DELLA VERITA: ATTI DEL CONVEGNO DI STUDI BIBLIOTECA CLASSENSE DI RAVENNA 19-20 APRILE 1983. Ravenna: Longo, 1984.

1963. Gargani, Aldo Giorgio. L'ETONNEMENT ET LE HASARD. Tr. of LO STU-PORE E IL CASO. Bari: Laterza, 1985. Tr. by Jean-Pierre Cometti and Jutta Hansen. Marseilles: Chemin de ronde; Sommieres: Editions de l'Eclat, 1988.

1964. Gargani, Aldo Giorgio. STILI DI ANALISI. Ed. by Rosaria Egidi. Milan: Feltrinelli, 1980.

1965. Gargani, Aldo Giorgio. WITTGENSTEIN TRA AUSTRI E INGHILTERRA. Turin: Stampatori, 1979.

1966. Gargani, Aldo Giorgio, et al. WITTGENSTIN: MOMENTI DI UNA CRITICA DEL SAPERE. Ed. by Rosaria Egidi. Naples: Guida, 1983.

1967. Garin, Eugenio. UMANISTI, ARTISTI, SCIENZIATI: STUDI SUL RINASCIMEN-TO ITALIANO. Rome: Riuniti, 1989.

1968. Garin, Eugenio. VITO E OPERE DI CARTESIO. New ed. Rome: Laterza, 1984.

This work was originally published as INTRODUZIONE A CARTESIO IN OPERE. RENE DESCARTES. The new edition contains an extensive bibliography on pages 205-233.

1969. Garroni, Emilio. ESTETICA E LINGUISTICA. Bologna: Mulino, 1985.

1970. Gentile, Giovanni. LETTERE A BENEDETTO CROCE: SIMONA GIANNANTONI. Florence: G. G. Sansoni, 1982.

1971. Ghisalberti, Alesandro. LE QUESTIONES DE ANIMA ATTRIBUITE A MATTEO DA GUBBIO. Milan: Vita e Pensiero, 1981.

1972. Giacon, Carlo. ASPETTI DELLA CRISI FILOSOFICA: E SAGGI STORICI. Padua: Antenore, 1978.

1973. Giacon, Carlo. ERMENEUTICA LOGICA E ATRI SAGGI. Padua: Antenore, 1977.

1974. Giacon, Carlo. ITINERARIO TOMISTICO. Rome: La Goliardica, Editrice Universitata di Roma, 1983.

1975. Giacon, Carlo. VETERA NOVIS AUGERE: STUDI IN ONORE DI CARLO GIACON PER IL 25 CONVEGNO DEGLI ASSISTENTI UNIVERSITARI DEL MOVIMENTO DI GALLARATE. Rome: La Goliardica, 1982.

1976. Gianformaggio Bastida, Letizia. DIRITTO E FELICITA: LA TEORIA DEL DIRIT-TO IN HELVETIUS. Milan: Edizioni di Comunita, 1979.

1977. Giannantoni, Gabriele. SOCRATICORUM RELIQUIAE. 4 Vols. Naples: Edizioni dell'Ateneo, 1983-1985.

The text is written in Greek, Italian, and Latin.

1978. Gily Reda, Clementina. GUIDO DE RUG GIERO: UN RITRATTO FILOSOFICO. Naples: Societa Editrice Napoletana 1981.

1979. Gramsci, Antonio. SELECTIONS FROM CULTURAL WRITINGS. Ed. by David Forgads and Geoffrey Nowell-Smith. Tr. by William Boelhower. Cambridge: Harvard

Univ. Press, 1985.

1980. Grassi, Ernesto. DIE MACHT DER PHANTASIE: ZUR GESCHICHTE ABEN-DLANDISCHE DENKENS. Konigstein/Ts: Athenaum, 1979.

1981. Greppi Olivetti, Alessandra. DUE SAGGI SU R. G. COLLINGWOOD. Padua: Liviana, 1977.

This work includes an appendix of unpublished letters from Collingwood to G. Ruggiero.

1982. Guzzo, Augusto. STORIA DELLA FILOSOFIA E DELLA CIVILITA. Padua: La Garangola, 1973-1977.

1983. Hobsbawm, Eric J., et al. THE HISTORY OF MARXISM. Vol. 1, MARXISM IN MARX'S DAY. Tr. of STORIA DEL MARXISMO. Turin: Einaudi, 1978-1982. Bloomington: Indiana Univ. Press; Sussex: Harvester, 1982-.

The Spanish translation, HISTORIA DEL MARXISMO, is being published in Barcelona by Bruguera. Vol. 2, EL MARXISMO EN LA EPOCA DE LA SEGUNDA INTERNACIONAL, which was published in 1980, was translated by Maximo Loizu.

1984. Huber, Carlo. TEORIA E METODO DECLE SCIENZA. Rome: Universita Gregoriana, 1981.

1985. Ingegno, Alfonso. SAGGIO SULLA FILOSOFIA DI CARDANO. Florence: La Nuova Italia Editrice, 1980.

1986. Kramer, Hans Joachim. PLATONE E I FONDAMENTI DELLA METAFISICA: SAGGIO SULLA DEI PRINCIPI E SULLADOTTRINE NON SCRITTE DE PLATONE CON UNA RACCOLTA DEI DOCUMENTI FONDAMENTALI IN EDIZIONE BILINGUE E BIBLIOGRAFIA PLATO. Milan: Vita e Pensiero, 1982.

The volume is printed in German and Italian and contains a bibliography on pages 418-432.

1987. Landucci, Sergio. LA TEODICEA NELL'ETA CARTESIANA. Naples: Bibliopolis, 1986.

1988. Leo, Gian Filippo. CRITICA E SCIENZA NEL GIOVANE KANT (1747-1769). Padua: Tipografia Editrice, 1977.

1989. Leszel, Walter. I PRESOCRATICI. Bologna: Mulino, 1982.

1990. Linguiti, Gennar Luigi. IMRE LAKATOS E LA FILOSOFIA SCOPERTA. Lucca: M. Pacini Fazzi, 1981.

1991. Lombardiu, Franco. UNA SVOLTA DI CIVITA: ARTE, FILOSOFIA, ECONOMIA E POLITICA: l'EUROPA, IERI E DOMANI. Turin: ERI, 1981.

1992. Lucchetta, Guilio A. UNA FISICA SENZA MATEMATICA: DEMOCRITO, ARISTOTELE, FILOPONO. Trent: Verifiche, 1978.

1993. Lupi, Walter, et al. SCRITTO IN ONORE DI EUGENIO GARIN. Pisa: Scuola Normale Superiore, 1987.

1994. Mamiani, Maurizio. TEORIE DELLO SPAZIO DA DESCARTES A NEWTON. Milan: F. Angeli, [1980].

1995. Marcucci, Silvestro. BENTHAM E LINNEO: UNA INTERPRETAZIONE SINGO-
LARE. Lucca: M. Pacini Fazzi, 1979.

1996. Mathieu, Vittorio, et al. FILOSOFIA E RELIGIONE DI FRONTE ALLA MORTE.
Archivo di Filosofia. Padua: CEDAM, 1981.

These are the Proceedings of the International Colloquium sponsored by the Instituto di
Studi Filosofici "Enrico Castelli" by the Centro Internazionale di Studi Umanistici at
Rome, January 3-7, 1980. The text is printed in English, French, German and Italian.

1997. Meattini, Valerio. ANNAMNESI E CONOSCENZA IN PLATONE. Pisa: ETS,
1981.

1998. Meotti, Alverto. L'INDUZIONE E PORDINE DELL'UNIVERSO. Milan: Edizione
di Comunita, 1978.

1999. Montuori, Mario. DE SOCRATE IUSTE DAMNATO: THE RISE OF THE SO-
CRATIC PROBLEM IN THE 18TH CENTURY. Amsterdam: J. C. Gieben, 1981.

The texts in French and Latin were originally published between 1736 and 1799. There
is an introduction in English and there is a bibliography of 18th century writings on Socrates on pages 147-153.

2000. Montuori, Mario. SOCRATES: PHYSIOLOGY OF A MYTH. Tr. of SOCRATE:
FISIOLOGIE DI UN MITRO. Florence: G. C. Sansoni, 1974. Tr. by J. M. P. and
M. Langdale. Amsterdam: J. C. Gieben, 1981.

2001. Moravia, Sergio. FILOSOFIA E SCIENZE UMANE NELL'ETA DEI LUMI.
Florence: G. C. Sansoni, 1982.

These essays were originally published in the period 1972-1982.

2002. Moravia, Sergio. IL PUNGOLO DELL'UMANO: CONVERSAZIONE SU UN
IMPEGNO FILOSOFICO, 1964-1984. Ed. by Giovanni Invitto. Milan: F. Angeli, 1984.

2003. Moravia, Sergio. L'ENIGMA DELA MENTE: IL MIND-BODY PROBLEM NEL
PENSIERO CONTEMPORANEO. Rome: Laterza, 1986.

2004. Mouffe, Chantal. GRAMSCI AND MARXIST THEORY. London and Boston:
Routledge & Kegan Paul, 1979.

2005. Mugnai, Paolo F. STEGNO E LINGUAGGIO IN GEORGE BERKELEY. Rome:
Edizioni dell'Ateneo & Bizzarri, 1979.

2006. Nebuloni, Roberto. DIALETTICA E STORIA IN TH. W. ADORNO. Milan: Vita
e Pensiero, Universitta Cattolica del Sacro Cuore, 1978.

2007. Nemeth, Thomas. GRAMSCI'S PHILOSOPHY: A CRITICAL STUDY. Atlantic
Highlands, NJ: Humanities Press; Sussex: Harvester, 1980.

2008. Olivetti, Marco M. NUOVI STUDI DE FILOSOFIA DELLA RELIGIONE. Padua:
CEDAM, 1982.

2009. Olivetti, Marco M., et al. ETICA E PRAGMATICA. Padua: CEDAM, 1989.

This work is in English, French, German, and Italian.

2010. Olivetti, Marco M., et al. INTERSOGGETTIVITA, SOCIALITA, RELIGIONE.

Padua: CEDAM, 1986.

These are the Proceedings of the International Colloquium on Intersubjectivity, Society and Religion sponsored jointly by L'Institut d'Etudes Philosophiques "Enrico Castelli" and by la chaire de Philosophie de la religion de la Facultee de Lettres et Philosophie de l'Universite de Roma I, "La Sapienza'... January 4-7, 1986 in Rome.

2011. Olivetti, Marco M., et al. SCHLEIERMACHER. Padua: CEDAM, 1984.

These critical and interpretive essays in English, French, German, and Italian are presented in honor of the 150th aniversary of Schleiermacher's death.

2012. Pacchi, Arrigo. FILOSOFIA E TEOLOGIA IN HOBBES: DISPENSE DEL CORSO DI STORIA DELLA FILOSOFIA PER L'A.A. 1984-1985. Milan: UNICOPLI, 1985.

2013. Pacchiani, Claudio. FILOSOFIE PRATICA E SCIENZA POLITICA. Abano Terme: Francisci, 1980.

2014. Paganini, Gianni. ANALISI DELLA FEDE E CRITICA DELLA RAGIONE NELLA FILOSOFIA DI PIERRE BAYLE. Florence: La Nueva Italia, 1980.

2015. Palazzolo, Vincenzo. LA FILOSOFIA DEL DIRITTO DI GUSTAV RADBRUCH E DI JULIUS BINDER. Milan: A. Giuffre, 1983.

2016. Pallodini, Fiammetta. DISCUSSIONI SEICENTESCHE SU SAMUEL PUFENDORF: SCRITTI LATINI: 1663-1700. Bologna: Mulino, 1978.

2017. Pareyson, Luigi. ETICA ED ESTETICA IN SCHILLER. Milan: Mursia, 1983.

2018. Pareyson, Luigi. FICHTE: IL SISTEMA DELLA LIBERTA. 2d enl ed. Milan: Mursia, 1976.

2019. Pareyson, Luigi. L'ESTETICA DI KANT: LETTURA DELLA "CRITICA DEL GUIDIZIO". New enl ed. Milan: Mursia, 1984.

2020. Pareyson, Luigi. LA NUOVA EDIZIONE CRITICA DI SCHELLING. Turin: Filosofia, [1977?].

This volume contains a survey of editions of Schelling and of works about Schelling.

2021. Pareyson, Luigi. ROMANTICISMO, EXISTENZIALISMO, ONTOLOGIA DELLA LIBERTA. Milan: Mursia, 1979.

This Festschrift commemorates the sixtieth birthday of Luigi Pareyson.

2022. Pareyson, Luigi. SCHELLINGIANA RARIORA: GESAMMELT UND EINGELEI-TET VON LUIGI PARYEYSON. Turin: Bottea d'Erasomo, 1977.

2023. Penco, Carlo. MATEMATICA E GIOCO LINGUISTICO: WITTGENSTEIN E LA FILOSOFIA DELLA MATEMATICA DEL ˋ900. Florence: Felice le Monnier, 1981.

2024. Pera, Marcello. APOLOGIA DEL METODO. Rome: Laterza, 1982.

2025. Pera, Marcello. HUME, KANT E L'INDUZIONE. Bologna: Mulino, 1982.

2026. Pera, Marcello. POPPER E LA SCIENZA SU PALAFITTE. Rome: Laterza, 1981.

2027. Pera, Marcello and Joseph Pitt. RATIONAL CHANGES IN SCIENCE: ESSAYS

ON SCIENTIFIC REASONING. Tr. of I MODI DEL PROGRESSO: TEORIE E EPISODI DELLA RAZIONALITA SCIENTIFICA. Milan: Saggiatore, 1985. Dordrecht and Boston: Reidel, 1987.

This work contains contributions by Karl Popper, John Watkins, Raimo Tuomela, Thomas Nickles, Joseph Pitt, William Shea, Marcello Pera, and Rachel Laudan.

2028. Perniola, Mario. DOPO HEIDEGGER: FILOSOFIA E ORGANIZZAZIONE DELLA CULTURA. Milan: Feltrinelli, 1982.

2029. Perniola, Mario. L'ALIENATION ARTISTIQUE. Tr. of L'ALIENAZIONE ARTIS-TICA. Tr. by A. Harstein. Milan: U. Mursia, 1971.

2030. Perniola, Mario. L'INSTANT ETERNEL: BATAILLE ET LA PENSEE DE LA MARGINALITE. Tr. of GEORGES BATAILLE E IL NEGATIVO. Milan: Feltrinelli, 1977. Tr. by Francois Pelletier. Paris: Meridiens/Anthropos, 1982.

2031. Perniola, Mario. LA SOCIETA DEI SIMULACRI. Bologna: Cappelli, 1980.

2032. Perniola, Mario. PRESA DIRETTA: ESTETICA E POLITICA. Venice: Cluva, 1986.

2033. Perniola, Mario. TRANSITI: COME SI VA DALLO STESSO ALLO STESSO. Bologna: L. Cappelli, 1985.

2034. Perniola, Mario, et al. OGGI L'ARTE E UN CARCERE? Ed. by Luigi Russo. Bologna: Mulino, 1982.

2035. Piattelli-Palmarini, Massimo. LIVELLI DI REALTA. 2d ed. Milan: Feltrinelli, 1987.

The volume contains a bibliography on pages 527-542.

2036. Piccone, Paul. ITALIAN MARXISM. Berkeley: Univ. of California Press, 1983.

2037. Postigliola, Alberto. MONTESQUIEU: LE LEGGI DELLA POLITICA. Rome: Editori Riuniti, 1979.

2038. Pozzi, Lorenzo. DA RAMUS A KANT: IL DIBATTITO SULLA SILLOGISTICA. Milan: F. Angeli, 1981.

This volume contains chapters on Ramus, Wallis, Hobbes, Gassendi, LA LOGICA DI PORT ROYAL (1662), Leibniz, Lambert, and Kant. An appendix on Lewis Carroll refers to his unpublished SYMBOLIC LOGIC discovered and edited by W. W. Bartley, in 1977.

2039. Predaval Magrini, Maria Vittoria. FILOSOFIA ANALITICA E CONOSCENZA STORICA. Florence: La Nuova Italia, 1979.

2040. Radice, Roberto and David T. Runia. PHILO OF ALEXANDRIA: AN ANNOTAT-ED BIBLIOGRAPHY, 1937-1986. Leiden and New York: E. J. Brill, 1988.

2041. Reale, Giovanni. THE CONCEPT OF FIRST PHILOSOPHY AND THE UNITY OF METAPHYSICS OF ARISTOTLE. Ed. by John R. Catan. Tr. of IL CONCETTO DI FILOSOFIA PRIMA E L'UNITA DELLA METAFISICA DI ARISTOTELE. Milan: Vita e Pensiero, 1967. Albany: State Univ. of New York Press, 1980.

This is an authorized translation of the third edition, which contains a bibliography on pages 462-532.

2042. Reale, Giovanni. A HISTORY OF ANCIENT PHILOSOPHY. Ed. by John R. Catan. Tr. of STORIA DELLA FILOSOFIA ANTICA. Vol. 1, DALLE ORIGINE A SOCRATE, Vol. 2, PLATONE E. ARISTOTELE, Vol. 3, I. SISTEMI DELL'ETA ELLENISTICA, Vol. 4, LE SCUOLE DELL'ETA IMPERIALE, Vol. 5, LESSICO INDICI E BIBLIOGRAFIA. 2d.ed. Milan: Vita e Pensiero, 1976-1980. Tr. by John R. Catan. Albany: State Univ. of New York Press, 1985-.

The first four volumes of the original Italian edition cover the historical development of western philosophy from its Pre-Socratic origins through the schools of the imperial age of Rome. The fifth volume contains lexicon, index, and bibliography. To date, the following volumes have been translated: Vol. 1, FROM THE ORIGINS THROUGH SOCRATES (1987); Vol. 2, PLATO AND ARISTOTLE (1990); Vol. 3 THE SYSTEMS OF THE HELLENISTIC AGE (1985); Vol. 4, THE SCHOOLS OF THE IMPERIAL AGE (1990).

2043. Reale, Mario. LE RAGIONI DELLA POLITICA: J. J. ROUSSEAU DAL "DICORSI SULL'INEGUAGELIANZA' AL CONTRATTO". Rome: Edizioni dell'Ateneo, 1983.

2044. Rella, Franco. CRITICA E STORIA: MATERIALI SU BENJAMIN. Venice: Cluva, 1980.

2045. Rella, Franco. IL MITO DELL'ALTRO: LACAN, DELEUZE, FOUCAULT. Milan: Feltrinelli, 1978.

2046. Rella, Franco. IL SILENZIO E LE PAROLE: IL PENSIERO NEL TEMPI DELLA CRISI. Milan: Feltrinelli, 1981.

2047. Rella, Franco. LA BATTAGLIA DELLA VERITA. Milan: Feltrinelli, 1986.

2048. Rella, Franco. LIMINA: IL PENSIERO E LE COSE. Milan: Feltrinelli, 1987.

2049. Rovatti, Pier Aldo. BISOGNI E TEORIA MARXISTA. Milan: Mazzotta, 1976.

Roberta Tomassini and Amedeo Vigorelli are listed as joint authors of this work.

2050. Rovatti, Pier Aldo. INTORNO A LEVINAS. Milan: Unicopli, 1987.

This volume contains contributions by Graziella Berto and others.

2051. Santinello, Giovanni. GIAMBATTISTA VICO: POESIA, LOGICA, RELIGIONE. Brescia: Morcelliana, 1986.

This volume contains contributions to the XL Convegno del Centro di studi filosofici di Gallarate aprile 1985.

2052. Santinello, Giovanni. IMMAGINI E IDEA DELL'UOMO: INTRODUZIONE ANTROPOLOGICA ALLA FILOSOFIA. Rimini: Maggioli, 1984.

2053. Santinello, Giovanni. LA FILOSOFIA ITALIANA ATTRAVERSO LE RIVISTE (1900-1925): ATTI DEL CONVEGNO DELLA S..F.I. (LECCE, 10-12 DICEMBRE 1981). Ed. by Antonio Verri. Lecce: Milella, 1983.

2054. Santinello, Giovanni. STORIA DELLE STORIE GENERALI DELLA FILOSO-FIA, Vol. 1-2. Brescia: LaScuola, 1981-.

Vol. 1, DALLE ORIGINI RINASCIMENTALI ALLA "HISTORIA PHILOSOPHICA," by Francesco Bottin et al, and Vol. 2, DALL'ERA CARTESIANA A BRUCKER, by Francesco Bottan, Mario Longo, and Gregorio Piaia, have been published to date.

2055. Sarti, Sergio. PANORAMA DELLA FILOSOFIA ISPANOAMERICANA CON-
TEMPORANEA. Milan: Editoriale Cisalpina-Goliardica, 1976.

2056. Savonarola, Girolamo. SCRITTI FILOSOFICI. Vol. 1, COMPENDIUM LOGICAE.
APOLOGETICUS DE RATIONE POETICAE ARTIS. TRATTATO CONTRA LI
ASTROLOGI. Vol. 2, COMPENDIUM PHILOSOPHIAE NATURALIS, COMPENDI-
UM PHILOSOPHIAE MORALIS. Ed. by Gian Carlo Garfangnini and Eugenio Garin.
Rome: A Belardetti, 1982.

2057. Scribano, Maria Emanuela. NATURA UMANA SOCIETA COMPETITIVA:
STUDIO SU MANDEVILLE. Milan: Feltrinelli, 1980.

2058. Severino, Emanuele. DESTINO DELLA NECESSITA: KATA TO CHREON.
Milan: Adelphi, 1980.

2059. Severino, Emanuele. ESSENZA DEL NICHILISMO. New and enl ed. Milan:
Adelphi, 1982.

2060. Severino, Emanuele. GLI ABITATORI DEL TEMPO: CRISTIANESIMO, MARX-
ISMO, TECHNICA. Rome: A. Armando, 1978.

2061. Severino, Emanuele. LA FILOSOFIA ANTICA. Milan: Rizzoli, 1984.

2062. Severino, Emanuele. LA FILOSOFIA CONTEMPORANEA. 2d ed. Milan:
Rizzoli, 1986.

2063. Severino, Emanuele. LA FILOSOFIA MODERNA. Milan: Rizzoli, 1984.

2064. Severino, Emanuele. LEGGE E CASO. Vol. 1, LEGGE E CASO. Vol. 2, NOTE
SUL PROBLEMA DELL'INTERSOGGETTIVITA NELLA COSTRUZIONE LOGICA
DEL MONDO DI R. CARNAP. Milan: Adelphi, 1979.

2065. Silvestrini, Daniela. INDIVIDUI E MONDI POSSIBILI: PROBLEMI DI SEMANTI-
CA MODALE. Milan: Feltrinelli, 1979.

2066. Sorgi, Giuseppe. PER UNO STUDIO DELLA PARTECIPAZIONE POLITICA:
HOBBES, LOCKE, TOCQUEVILLE. Lecce: Milella, 1981.

2067. Tagliacozzo, Giorgio. VICO AND MARX: AFFINITIES AND CONTRASTS.
Atlantic Highlands, NJ: Humanities Press; London: Macmillan, 1983.

2068. Tagliacozzo, Giorgio. VICO: PAST AND PRESENT. 2 Vols. in 1. Atlantic
Highlands, NJ: Humanities Press, 1981.

This book originated as papers invited for presentation at the 1978 Vico/Venezia
Conference.

2069. Tagliacozzo, Giorgio, et al. A BIBLIOGRAPHY OF VICO IN ENGLISH (1884-
1984). Bibliographies of Famous Philosophers. Bowling Green, OH: Philosophy Documentation Center, Bowling Green Univ., 1986.

2070. Tagliacozzo, Giorgio, et al. VICO AND CONTEMPORARY THOUGHT. Atlantic
Highlands, NJ: Humanities Press, 1979c1976.

This volume consists of papers originally presented at a conference held in New York
City, Jan. 27-31, 1976, sponsored by the Institute for Vico Studies in association with the
Casa Italiana of Columbia University and the Graduate School of the New School for
Social Research. This is the first publication of an English translation of Vico's essay "On

the Heroic Mind."

2071. Taranto, Domenico. ABILITA DEL POLITICO E MECCANISMO ECONOMICO: SAGGIO SULLA `FAVOLA DELLE API'. Naples: Edizioni Scientifiche Italiane, 1982.

2072. Tarello, Giovanni. MATERIALI PER UNA STORIA DELLA CULTURA GIURIDI-CA: MOMINTI E FIGURE DELL "TEORIA GENERALE DEL DIRITTO". Bologna: Il Mulino, 1978.

2073. Turco, Luigi. LO SCETTICISMO MORALE DE DAVID HUME. Bologna: CLUEB (Cooperativea Libreria Universidad Bologna), 1984.

2074. Ugazio, Ugo Maria. IL PROBLEMA DELLA MORTE NELLA FILOSOFIA DI HEIDEGGER. Milan: Mursia, 1976.

2075. Urbinati, Nadia, et al. STUDI SULLA CULTRA FILOSOFICA ITALIANA FRA OTTOCENTO E NOVOCENTO. Ed. by Walter Tega. 2d ed. Bologna: Cooperative Libraria Universitaria, 1982.

2076. Valenziani, Enrichetta. INDICI DEGLI ATTI DEI CONVEGNI ROMANI SULLA DEMITIZZAZIONE E L'ERMENEUTICA (1961-1977). Padua: CEDAM, 1979.

2077. Valla, Lorenzo. REPASTINATIO DIALECTICE ET PHILOSOPHIE. 2 Vols. Ed. by Gianni Zippel. Padua: Atenore, 1982.

The text is in Latin with introduction and commentary in Italian.

2078. Vattimo, Gianni. ESTETICA MODERNA. Bologna: Mulino, 1977.

2079. Vattimo, Gianni. IL SOGGETTO E LA MASCHERA: NIETZSCHE E IL PROB-LEMA DELLA LIBERAZIONE. 2d ed. Milan: Tascabili Bompiani, 1983.

2080. Vattimo, Gianni. INTRODUZIONE A HEIDEGGER. 2d ed. Rome and Bari: Later-za, 1980.

This work contains a bibliography on pages 165-201.

2081. Vattimo, Gianni. INTRODUZIONE A NIETZSCHE. Rome: Laterza, 1985.

This volume contains a bibliography on pages 157-190.

2082. Vattimo, Gianni. JENSEITS VOM SUBJEKT: NIETZSCHE, HEIDEGGER UND DIE HERMENEUTIK. Tr. of AL DI LA DEL SOGGETTO: NIETZSCHE, HEIDEG-GER E. L'ERMENEUTICA. Milan: Feltrinelli, 1981. Tr. by Sonja Puntscher Riekmann. Graz: H. Bohlau, 1986.

2083. Vattimo, Gianni. LA FINE DELLA MODERNITA. Milan: Garzanti, 1985.

2084. Vattimo, Gianni. LAS AVENNTURAS DE LA DIFERENCIA: PENSAR DESPUES DE NIETZSCHE Y HEIDEGGER. Tr. of LE AVVENTURE DELLA DIFFERENZA. Milan: Garzanti, 1980. Tr. by Juan Carlos Gentile. Barcelona: Ediciones Peninsula, 1986.

LES AVENTURES DE LA DIFFERENCE, translated from the Italian by Pascal Gabellone, Riccardo Pineri and Jacques Rolland, was published in Paris by Les Editions de Minuit in 1985.

2085. Vattimo, Gianni. POESIA E ONTOLOGIA. New aug. ed. Milan: Mursia, 1985.

2086. Vattimo, Gianni and Pier Aldo Rovatti. IL PENSIERO DEBOLE. Milan: Feltrinelli, 1983.

This volume includes writings by Umberto Eco, G. Carchia, A. Dal Lago, M. Ferraris, Leonard Amoroso, D. Marconi, G. Comolli, F. Costa, F. Crespi and the editors.

2087. Velocci, Giovanni. LA DONNA IN KIERKEGAARD. L'Aquila: L. U. Japadres, 1980.

2088. Ventimiglia, Carmine. SOCIETA POLITICA, DIRITTO: IL CRISTIANO E IL MONDO IN PASCAL E DOMAT. Parma: Edizione Zara, 1983.

2089. Ventura, Pierfranco. NORMALITA E NORMATIVITA. PROSPETTIVE FILOSO-FICOGIURIDICHE PER UNA FENOMENOLOGIA DELLA ANORMALITA. Milan: A. Giuffre, 1982.

2090. Verra, Valerio. LA FILOSOFIA DAL '45 AD OGGI. Turin: Fri, 1976.

2091. Vico, Giambattista. THE NEW SCIENCE OF GIAMBATTISTA VICO. Tr. of PRINCIPI DI UNA SCIENZA NUOVA. Tr. by Thomas Goddard Bergin and Max Harold Fisch. Ithaca and London: Cornell Univ. Press, 1984.

This is an unabridged translation of the 3d ed. (1744) with the addition of "Practice of the New Science."

2092. Vico, Giambattista. PRINCIPJ DI UNA SCIENZA NUOVA INTORNO ALLA NATURA DELLE NAZIONI: RISTAMPA ANASTATICA DELL'EDIZIONE NAPOLI 1725, SEGUITA DA CONCORDANZE E INDICI DE FREQUENZA GIAMBATTISTA VICO. Ed. by Tullio Gregory. Rome: Edizioni dall Ateneo and Bizzari, 1979-.

2093. Vico, Giambattista. SELECTED WRITINGS. Ed. by Leon Pompa. Cambridge and New York: Cambridge Univ. Press, 1982.

2094. Viola, Francesco. CONCEZIONI DELL' AUTORITA E TEORIE DEL DIRITTO. L'Aquila: Japadre Editore, 1982.

This work discusses concepts of authority in philosophical theories of law in Aquinas, Hobbes, Hans Kelsen, and Alf Ross.

2095. Viti, Cavaliere Renata. HEIDEGGER E LA STORIA DELLA FILOSOFIA. Naples: Giannini Editore, 1979.

2096. Vitiello, Vincenzo. DIALETTICA ED ERMENEUTICA: HEGEL E HEIDEG-GER. Naples: Guida, 1979.

2097. Vitiello, Vincenzo. HEIDEGGER: IL NULLA E LA FONDAZIONE DELLA STORICITA: DALLA UBERWINDUNG DER METAPHYSIC ALLA DASEINANA-LYSE. Urbino: Argalia, 1976.

NETHERLANDS

2098. Ankersmit, Franklin R. NARRATIVE LOGIC: A SEMANTIC ANALYSIS OF THE HISTORIAN'S LANGUAGE. The Hague and Boston: Nijhoff, 1983.

2099. Baal, Jan van. MAN'S QUEST FOR PARTNERSHIP: ANTHROPOLOGICAL FOUNDATION OF ETHICS AND RELIGION. Assen: Van Gorcum, 1981.

2100. Bakker, Reinout. WIJSGERIGE ANTROPOLOGIE VAN DE TWINSTIGSTE EEUW. Assen: Van Gorcum, 1981.

2101. Bakker, Reinout, et al. INLEIDING TOT DE WIJSBEGEERTE IN CHRISTELIJK PERSPECTIEF. Kampen: Kok, 1981.

2102. Bakker, Reinout and Hubertus Gezinus. DE FILOSOFIE VAN BERNARD DELF-GAAUW. Bussum: Werevenster, 1982.

2103. Bakker, Reinout and Jan de Graaf. WIJSGERIGE ETHIEK VAN DE TWINTIGSTE EEUW: HOOFDLIHNEN IN HET HUIDIGE DENKEN OVER MENS EN MORAAL. Utrecht: Bijleveld, 1979.

2104. Beerling, Reinier Franciscus. HET CULTURPROTEST VAN J. J. ROUSSEAU. Devanter: Van Loghum Slaterus, 1977.

2105. Beerling, Reinier Franciscus. NIET TE GELOVEN: WIJSGERIG SCHAATSEN OP GODGELEERD IJS. Deventer: Van Loghum Slaterus, 1979.

This work includes critical commentary by H. J. Adriaanse, H. Berkof, and H. J. Heering.

2106. Beerling, Reinier Franciscus. VAN NIETZSCHE TOT HEIDEGGER: DRIE STUDIES. Deventer: Van Loghum Slaterus, 1977.

2107. Bend, J. G. van der. THOMAS HOBBES: HIS VIEW OF MAN: PROCEEDINGS OF THE HOBBES SYMPOSIUM AT THE INTERNATIONAL SCHOOL OF PHILOSOPHY IN THE NETHERLANDS (LEUSDEN, SEPTEMBER 1979). Elementa. Amsterdam: Rodopi, 1982.

2108. Benthem, Johan F. A. K. van. ESSAYS IN LOGICAL SEMANTICS. Studies in Linguistics and Philosophy, Vol. 29. Dordrecht and Boston: Reidel, 1986.

2109. Benthem, Johan F. A. K. van. THE LOGIC OF TIME: A MODEL THEORETIC INVESTIGATION INTO THE VARIETIES OF TEMPORAL DISCOURSE. Dordrecht and Boston: Reidel, 1983.

2110. Beth, Eevert Willelm. IMPLICACION SEMANTICA Y DERIVABILIDAD FORMAL. Tr. of KONINKLIJKE NEDERLANDSE AKADEMIE VAN WETENSCHAPPEN. Tr. by Wonfilio Trejo. Mexico: Universidad Nacional Autonoma de Mexico Facultad de Filosofia y Letras, 1978.

2111. Boer, Theodorus de. THE DEVELOPMENT OF HUSSERL'S THOUGHT. Tr. of ONTWIKKELINGSGANG IN HET DENKEN VAN HUSSERL: Assen: Van Gorcum, 1966. Tr. by Theodore Plantinga. The Hague and Boston: Nijhoff, 1978.

2112. Boer, Theodorus de. FOUNDATION OF A CRITICAL PSYCHOLOGY. Tr. of GRONDSLAGEN VAN EEN KRITSCHE PSYCHOLOGIE. Baarn: Ambo, 1980. Tr. by Theodore Plantinga. Pittsburgh: Duquesne Univ. Press, 1983.

2113. Boer, Theodorus de. TUSSEN FILOSOFIE EN PROFETIE: DE WIJSBEGEERTE VAN EMMANUEL LEVINAS. Baarn: Ambo, 1976.

There is a bibliography by Kees Meerhoff of works by and about Emmanuel Levinas on pages 160-173.

2114. Boer, Theodorus de, et al. EEN STROOIEN SOORTJE: NADENDEN OVER DE MENS. Baarn: Bosch and Keuning, 1981.

2115. Boer, Theodorus de, et al. FENOMENOLOGIE EN KRITIEK. Assen: Van Gorcum, 1981.

2116. Bos, A. P. PROVIDENTIA DIVINA: THE THEME OF DIVINE PRONOIA IN PLATO AND ARISTOTLE. Assen: Van Gorcum, 1976.

2117. Bos, A. P. WETENSCHAP EN ZIN-ERVARING. Amsterdam: VU Uitgeverij, 1985.

2118. Bos, Egbert P. TREATISES ON THE PROPERTIES OF TERMS: MARSILIUS OF INGHEN: A FIRST CRITICAL EDITION OF THE SUPPOSITIONES, AMPLIA-TIONES, APPELATIONES, RESTRICTIONES AND ALIENATIONES. Dordrecht, Boston and Lancaster: Reidel, 1983.

This edition contains annotations as well as translations from the Latin.

2119. Braakhuis, H. A. G., et al. ENGLISH LOGIC AND SEMANTICS FROM THE END OF THE TWELFTH CENTURY TO THE TIME OF OCKHAM AND BURLEIGH: ACTS OF THE 4TH EUROPEAN SYMPOSIUM ON MEDIEVAL LOGIC AND SEMANTICS, LEIDEN- NIJMEGEN, 23-27 APRIL, 1979. Nijmegen: Ingenium, 1981.

2120. Broekman, Jan Maurits. EL STRUCTURALISMO. 2d ed. Tr. of STRUKTURALIS-MUS: MOSCOW, PRAGUE, PARIS. Munich: Alber, 1981.

2121. Broekman, Jan Maurits. MENS ENB MENSBEELD VAN ONS RECHT. Leuven: Acco, 1986-.

2122. Broekman, Jan Maurits. RECHT UND ANTHROPOLOGIE. Freiburg and Munich: Alber, 1979.

2123. Broekman, Jan Maurits, et al. DE LIJDENDE MENS. Vol. 1, ALGEMENE BENADERING by J. M. Broekman et al. Vol. 2, INDIVIDUELE LIJDENSVORMEN by J. van der Veken et al. Leuven: Acco, 1976-.

2124. Bulhof, Ilse Nina. WILHELM DILTHEY: A HERMENEUTIC APPROACH TO THE STUDY OF HISTORY AND CULTURE. The Hague and Boston: Nijhoff, 1980.

2125. Delfgaaw, Bernardus Maria Ignatious. WAT IS EXISTENTIALISME?: KIERKE-GAARD, MARCEL, JASPERS, HEIDEGGER, SARTRE. 9th ed. Baarn: Wereldven-ster, 1977.

2126. Deugd, Cornelis de. SPINOZA'S POLITICAL AND THEOLOGICAL THOUGHT. Amsterdam and New York: North Holland, 1984.

These are the proceedings of an international symposium held under the auspices of the Royal Netherlands Academy of Arts and Sciences and commemorating the 350th anninver-sary of the birth of Spinoza, Amsterdam, November 24-27, 1982.

2127. Doeser, Marinus C. and John N. Kraay. FACTS AND VALUES: PHILOSOPHICAL REFLECTIONS FROM WESTERN AND NON-WESTERN PERSPECTIVES. Dor-drecht and Boston: Nijhoff, 1986.

This work includes contributions by M .C. Doeser, J. R. Lucas, G. H. von Wright, W. H. Walsh, J. Degenaar, H. Lubbe, A. Begiaschwili, E. Levinas, P. Ricoeur, W. Biemel, T. Imamichi, B. H. Son, H. Hanafi, A. Ndaw, M. Chatterjee and S. T. Alisjahbana.

2128. Draaisma, Douwe and Rob de Vries. LICHAAM EN GEET IN PSYCHOLOGIE EN GENEESKUNDE: WAARNEMING, GEHEUGEN, MOTIVATUEM PLACEBO'S ANOREXIA. Amsterdam: Swets & Zeitlinger, 1989.

2129. Duintjer, Otto D. RONDON REGELS: WIJSGERIGE GEDACHTEN OMTRENT REGELGELEID GETRAG. Meppel: Boom, 1977.

2130. Dussen, W. J. van der. HISTORY AS A SCIENCE: THE PHILOSOPHY OF R. G. COLLINGWOOD. The Hague and Boston: Nijhoff, 1981.

2131. Elders, Leo J. DE METAPHISICA VAN ST. THOMAS VAN AQUINO IN HISTOR-ISCH PERSPECTIEF. Brugge: Tabor; Vught: J. Richt, 1982.

2132. Elders, Leo J. QUINQUE SUNT VIAE. Ed. by Bernhard Lakebrink, et al. Vatican City: Pontificia Accademia di S Tommaso: Libreria Editrice Vaticana, 1980.

These are the Proceedings of the Symposiume sur les Cinq Voies de la Somme Theologique, Rolduc 1979. This work includes essays by Bernhard Lakebrink, Gerard Verbeke, N. Luyten, J. Walgrave, M. Corvez, F. Van Steenberghen, J. Malik, and the editor.

2133. Elders, Leo J. and Klaus Hedwig. ETHICS OF ST. THOMAS AQUINAS. Vatican City: Lireria Editrice Vaticana, 1984.

These are the Proceedings of the Third Symposium on St. Thomas Aquinas' Philosophy, Rolduc, November 5 and 6, 1983. The contributions are in English, French and German.

2134. Griffioen, Sander. DE ROOS EN HET KRUIS: DE WAARDERING VAN DE EINDIGHEID IN HET LATERE DENKEN VAN HEGEL. Assen and Amsterdam: Van Gorcum, 1976.

2135. Groot, Adrianus Dingeman de. REDE ALS RICHTSNOER: BIJDRAGEN OVER METHODEN VAN DENKEN EN WERKEN IN DE GEDRAGSWETENSCHAPPEN AANGEBODEN AAN. Prof. DR. A. D. de GROOT BIJ ZIJN AFSCHEID VAN DE UNIVERSITEIT VAN AMSTERDAM. 's-Gravenhage: Mouton, 1979.

The volume contains a bibliography of A. D. de Groot on pages 359-368.

2136. Heering, Herman Johan. GOED EN KWAAD: FEESTBUNDEL'TER ERE VAN DE VIJFENZESTIGSTE VER JAARDAG BAN PROF. H.J. HEERING. S'Gravenhage: Boekeneentrum, 1977.

2137. Hesling, Willem and L. Van Poecke. COMMUNICATIE VAN TEKEN TOT MEDIUM: LIBER AMICORUM PROFESSOR J. M. PETERS. Leuven: Universitaire Pers Leuven, 1985.

2138. Hoeven, Johan van der. KARL MARX: THE ROOTS OF HIS THOUGHT. Assen and Amsterdam: Van Gorcum; Toronto: Wedge Publishing Foundation, 1976.

This volume is based on lectures delivered in 1971 at Calvin College in Grand Rapids, Michigan.

2139. Hubbeling, Hubertus Gezinus. BRIEFWISSELING: VERTAALD UIT HET LATIJN EN UITG, NAAR DE BRONNEN ALSMEDE VAN EEN INLEIDING EN VERKLAR-ENDE TEKSTKRITISCHE AANTEKENIGEN VOORZIEN DOOR. Amsterdam: Wer-eldbibliotheek, 1977.

2140. Hubbeling, Hubertus Gezinus. DENKIND GELOVEN: INLEIDING TOT DE WIJSBEGEERTE VAN DE GODSDIENST. Assen: Van Gorcum, 1976.

2141. Hubbeling, Hubertus Gezinus. EINFUHRUNG IN DIE RELIGIONSPHILOSOPHIE. Gottingen: Vandenhoeck and Ruprecht, 1981.

2142. Hubbeling, Hubertus Gezinus. SPINOZA. 2d. ed. Baarn: Wereldvenster, 1978.

2143. Hubbeling, Hubertus Gezinus, et al. LOGIC AND RELIGION. Ghent, Belgium: Communication and Cognition, 1982.

2144. IJsseling, Samuel. HUSSERLIANA DOKUMENTE: VEROFFENTLICHT VOM HUSSERL- ARCHIV. The Hague: Nijhoff, 1977-.

This is a companion to the edition of Husserl's works published under the title HUSSERLIANA, 1950.

2145. IJsseling, Samuel. JACQUES DERRIDA: EEN INLEIDING IN ZIJN DENKEN. Baarn: Ambo, 1986.

This volume includes essays by Paul Moyaert, Rudolf Bernet, Jacques Deryckere, Egide Berns, Arnold Burns and the editor.

2146. IJsseling, Samuel. RHETORIC AND PHILOSOPHY IN CONFLICT: AN HISTORICAL SURVEY. Tr. of RETORIEK EN FILOSOFIE. Bilthoven: Ambo, 1975. The Hague: Nijhoff, 1976.

2147. Jong, Willem Remmelt de. THE SEMANTICS OF JOHN STUART MILL. Tr. of SEMANTIEK VAN JOHN STUART MILL. Amsterdam: Academische Press, 1979. Tr. from the Dutch by Herbert Donald Morton. Dordrecht and Boston: Reidel, 1982.

2148. Kimmerle, Heinz. MODELLE DER MATERIALISTISCHEN DIALEKTIK: BEITRAGE DER BOCHUMER DIALEKTIK-ARBEITSGEMEINSCHAFT. The Hague: Nijhoff, 1978.

2149. Kimmerle, Heinz. PHILOSOPHIE DER GEISTESWISSENSCHAFTEN ALS KRITIK IHRER METHODEN. The Hague: Nijhoff, 1978.

2150. Klapwijk, Jacob. DIALEKTIEK DER VERLICHTING: EEN VERKENNING IN HET NEOMARXISME VAN DE FRANKFURTER SCHULE. Assen: Van Gorcum, 1976.

2151. Kroes, Peter. TIME: ITS STRUCTURE AND ROLE IN PHYSICAL THEORIES. Dordrecht and Boston: Reidel, 1985.

2152. Kwant, Remigius C. STRUCTURALISTEN EN STRUCTURALISME. Alphen aan den Rijn: Samsom, 1978.

2153. Kwant, Remigius C. and Samuel IJsseling. FILOSOFEREN: GANGBARE VORMEN VAN WIJSGERIG DENKEN. Alphen aan den Rijn: Samsom, 1977.

2154. Leeuwen, Theodoor Marius van. THE SURPLUS OF MEANING: ONTOLOGY AND ESCHATOLOGY IN THE PHILOSOPHY OF PAUL RICOEUR. Amsterdam: Rodopi, 1981.

2155. Lemaire, Ton. HET VERTOOG OVER DE ONGELIJKHEID VAN JEAN-JACQUES ROUSSEAU, DE AMBIVALENTIE VAN DE VOORUITGANG. Baarn: Ambo, 1980.

There is a bibliography on pages 282-295.

2156. Lemaire, Ton. OVER DE WAARDE VAN KULTUREN: EEN INLEIDING IN DE KULTUURFILOSOFIE TUSSEN EUROPACENTRISME EN RELATIVISME. Baarn: Ambo, 1976.

This work contains a bibliography on pages 473-396.

2157. Luijpen, Wilhelmus A. MYTH AND METAPHYSICS. Tr. of THEOLOGIE IS ANTROPOLOGIE. Meppel: Boom, 1974. Tr. by Henry J. Koren. The Hague: Nijhoff, 1976.

2158. Maris, C. W. CRITIQUE OF THE EMPIRICIST EXPLANATION OF MORALITY: IS THERE A NATURAL EQUIVALENT OF CATEGORICAL MORALITY? Tr. of EEN NATUURLIJK EQUIVALENT VAN DE PLICHT. Tr. by Jane Fenoulhet. Boston: Kluwer-Deventer, 1981.

2159. Melsen, Andreas Gerardus Maria van. NATUURWETENSCHAP EN NATUUR: EEN INLEIDING IN DE NAUTUURFILOSOFIE. Nijmegan: Katholiek Studiecentrum; Baarn: Ambo, 1983.

2160. Melsen, Andreas Gerardus Maria van. WETENSCHAP IN DISCUSSIE. Amsterdam and New York: North Holland, 1982.

2161. Melsen, Andreas Gerardus Maria van, et al. WIE BEN IK, WIE ZIJN JULLIE/ EEN WAARDENVASTE OPVOEDING IM EEN WAARDENLOZE WERELD? Baarn: Ambo, 1980.

2162. Nota, Johannes Hille. MAX SCHELER, THE MAN AND HIS WORK. Tr. of MAX SCHELER, DE MAN EN ZIJN WERK. Baarn: Wereldvenster, 1979. Tr. by Theodore Plantinga and John H. Nota. Chicago: Franciscan Herald Press, 1983.

2163. Nuchelmans, Gabriel. JUDGMENT AND PROPOSITION: FROM DESCARTES TO KANT. Amsterdam and New York: North-Holland, 1983.

2164. Nuchelmans, Gabriel. LATE SCHOLASTIC AND HUMANIST THEORIES OF THE PROPOSITION. Amsterdam and New York: North-Holland, 1980.

2165. Nuchelmans, Gabriel. TAALFILOSOFIE: EEN INLEIDING. Muiderberg: D. Coutiinho, 1978.

2166. Nuchelmans, Gabriel. WIJSBEGEERTE EN TAAL: TWAALF STUDIES. Meppel: Boom, 1976.

2167. Pater, Wilhelmus Antonius de. FILOSOFISCHE TAALANALYSE IN ENGLAND NA 1900: EEN OVERZICHT. 2d. rev ed. Louvain: Acco, 1979.

2168. Pater, Wilhelmus Antonius de. IMMORTALITY, ITS HISTORY IN THE WEST. Louvain: Acco, 1984.

2169. Pater, Wilhelmus Antonius de and Willem Remmelt de Jong. VAN REDENERING TOT FORMELE STRUKTUUR: ENIGE HOOFDSTUKKEN UIT DE LOGIKA. Assen: Van Gorcum, 1981.

2170. Peperzak, Adriaan Theodoore. PHILOSOPHY AND POLITICS: A COMMENTARY ON THE PREFACE TO HEGEL'S PHILOSOPHY OF RIGHT. Tr. of FILOSOFIE EN POLITIEK: EEN KOMMENTAAR OPHET VOORWOORD VAN HEGELS RE-CHTSFILO SOFIE. Baarn: Ambo, 1981. Dordrecht and Boston: Nijhoff, 1987.

2171. Peperzak, Adriaan Theodoore. SYSTEM AND HISTORY IN PHILOSOPHY: ON THE UNITY OF THOUGHT AND TIME, TEXT AND EXPLANATION, SOLITUDE AND DIALOGUE, RHETORIC AND TRUTH IN THE PRACTICE OF PHILOSO-PHY. Tr. of SYSTEMATIEK EN GESCHIEDENIS: EEN INLEIDING IN DIE FILOS-OFIE VAN DE FILOSOFIEGESCHIEDENIS: OVER TEKST EN UITLEG, DENKEN

EN TIJD, EENZAAMHEID EN DIALOOG, WAARHEID EN RETORIEK, IN DIE
BEOEFENING VAN DE WIJSBEGEERTE. Alphen aan den Rijn Samson, 1981. Albany:
State Univ. of New York Press, 1986.

2172. Peters, Jan Marie Lambert. PICTORIAL SIGNS AND THE LANGUAGE OF FILM.
Amsterdam: Rodopi, 1981.

2173. Peursen, Cornelius Anthonie van. DE OPBOUW VAN DE WETENSCHAP: EEN
INLEIDING IN DE WETENSCHAPSTEER. Meppel: Boom, 1980.

2174. Peursen, Cornelius Anthonie van. EINDIGHEID BIJ SPINOZA. Leiden: Brill, 1977.

2175. Peursen, Cornelius Anthonie van. FILOSOFISHE IN DIE WIJSGERIGE PROBLEM-
ATIEK. Kampen: Kok, 1977.

2176. Peursen, Cornelius Anthonie van. LE CORPS-L'AME-L'ESPRIT: INTRODUCTION
A UNE ANTHROPOLOGIE PHENOMENOLOGIQUE. Tr. of LICHAAM--ZIEL--
GEEST: INLEIDING TOT EEN WIJSGERIGE ANTROPOLOGIE. Utrecht: Bijleveld,
1978. Tr. by Marie Claes. The Hague and Boston: Nijhoff, 1979.

2177. Peursen, Cornelius Anthonie van, et al. DE PLAATS VAN DE WETENSCHAP IN
DE HUIDIGE EN TOEKOMSTIGE SAMENLEVING. Haarlem: Hollandische
Matschappij der Wetenschappen, 1977.

2178. Peursen, Cornelius Anthonie van, et al. INLEIDING TOT DE WIJSBEGEERTE IN
CHRISTELIJK PERSPETIEF. Kampen: Kok, 1981.

2179. Peursen, Cornelius Anthonie van and Errit J. Petersma. METAPHYSICA: DE
GESCHIEDENIS VAN EEN BEGRIP. Meppel: Boom, 1981.

In addition to van Peursen's contribution, this volume includes essays on metaphysics by
J. Mansfeld, K.J. Brons, J. Bor, P.G.E. Wesly, and M. van Asperen.

2180. Poortman, Johannes Jacobus. RAAKVLAKKEN TUSSEN OOSTERSE EN WEST-
ERSE FILOSOFIE: EEN BUNDEL WIJSGERIGE OPSTELLEN. Assen: Van Gorcum,
1976.

2181. Poortman, Johannes Jacobus. VEHICLES OF CONSCIOUSNESS: THE CONCEPT
OF HYLIC PLURALISM (OCHEMA). 4 Vols. Tr. of OCHEMA: GESCHIEDENIS EN
ZIN VAN HET HYLISCH PLURALISME, HET Z. G. DUALISTISCH MATERIALIS-
ME. Assen: Van Gorcum, 1954-. Tr. by N. D. Smith. Utrecht and Wheaton, IL: The
Theosophical Society of West Netherlands, 1978.

2182. Rijk, Lambertus Marie de. ANONYMI AUCTORIS FRANCISCANI LOGICA
"AD RUDIUM". Nijmegen: Ingenium Publishers, 1981.

This has been edited from the MS. Vat. lat. 946 with a short introduction, notes and
indices.

2183. Rijk, Lambertus Marie de. LA PHILOSOPHIE AU MOYEN AGE. Tr. of MIDDE-
LEEUWSE WIJSBEGEERTE: TRADITIE EN VERNIEUWING. 2d. rev. ed. Assen: Van
Gorcum, 1981. Tr. by P. Swiggers. Leiden: E.J. Brill, 1985.

2184. Rijk, Lambertus Marie de. DIE MITTELATERLICHEN TRAKTATE: DE MODO
OPPONENDI ET RESPONDENDE. Munster: Aschendorff, 1980.

2185. Rijk, Lambertus Marie de. PIERRE ABELARD (1079-1142): SCHERPZINNIGHEID
ALS HARTSTACHT. Amsterdam and New York: North Holland, 1981.

2186. Rijk, Martien C., et al. ONTWIKKELINGEN IN HET SOCIALE DENKEN: OPGEDRAGEN AAN PROFESSOR DR. M. G. PLATTEL. Baarn: Ambo, 1978.

This volume contains a bibiography of works by Martin G. Plattel and essays by M. C. Rijk, H. M. Lange, N. A. Luyten, H. H. Berger, R. C. Kwant and others.

2187. Runia, David T. EXEGESIS AND PHILOSOPHY: STUDIES ON PHILO OF ALEXANDRIA. Aldershot, Hampshire, Great Britain: Variorum; Brookfield, VT: Gower, 1991.

2188. Runia, David T. PHILO OF ALEXANDRIA AND THE TIMAEUS OF PLATO. Leiden: E.J. Brill, 1986.

2189. Runia, David T. PLOTINUS AMID GNOSTICS AND CHRISTIANS. Amsterdam: VU Uitgeverij/Free Univ. Press, 1984.

These are papers presented at the Plotinus Symposium held at the Free University, Amsterdam, on January 25, 1984. This volume contains contributions by A. P. Bos, A. M. Armstrong, R. Ferwerda, and Th. G. Sinnige.

2190. Soeteman, Arend. LOGIC IN LAW: REMARKS ON LOGIC AND RATIONALITY IN NORMATIVE REASONING, ESPECIALLY IN LAW. Dordrecht and Boston: Kluwer, 1989.

2191. Soeteman, Arend and Popke Wieger Brouwer. LOGICA EN RECHT. Zwolle: Tjeennk Willink, 1982.

This work includes contributions by A. H. de Wild, P. W. Brouwer, A. Soeteman, Ch. Perelman, and J. F. A. K. van Benthem.

2192. Swart, Henricus Cornelius Maria de and Hubertus Gezinus Hubbeling. INLEIDING TOT DE SYMBOLISCHE LOGICA. Assen: Van Gorcum, 1976.

2193. Travis, Charles. MEANING AND INTERPRETATION. Oxford and New York: B. Blackwell, 1986.

Eleven eminent scholars from a broad variety of philosophical and linguistic backgrounds examine the relationship between the meaning and use of words.

2194. Van Fraassen, Bastiaan C. IMAGES OF SCIENCE: ESSAYS ON REALISM AND EMPIRICISM, WITH A REPLY FROM BAS C. VAN FRAASSEN. Ed. by Paul Montgomery Churchland and Clifford Alan Hooker. Chicago: Univ. of Chicago Press, 1985.

This work includes contributions by Richard N. Boyd, Paul M. Churchland, Brian Ellis, Ronald N. Giere, Clark Glymour, Gary Gutting, Ian Hacking, Clifford A. Hooker, Alan Musgrave, and Mark Wilson, together with replies by Van Fraassen.

2195. Van Fraassen, Bastiaan C., et al. STUDIES IN ONTOLOGY: ESSAYS. Oxford: B. Blackwell, 1978.

These essays were part of the International Philosophy Conference held in New York in 1976.

2196. Ver Eecke, Wilfried. NEGATIVITY AND SUBJECTIVITY: A STUDY ABOUT THE FUNCTION OF NEGATION IN FREUD, LINGUISTICS, CHILD PSYCHOLOGY, AND HEGEL. Brussels: Paleis der Academien, 1977.

The text is summarized in Dutch.

2197. Vogel, Cornelia J. de. RETHINKING PLATO AND PLATONISM. Leiden: E. J. Brill, 1986.

2198. Vroon, Pieter Adrianus and Douwe Draaisma. DE MENS ALS METAFOOR: OVER VERGELIJKINGEN VAN MENS EN MACHINE IN FILOSOFIE EN PSYCHOLOGIE. Baarn: Ambo, 1985.

2199. Waldenfels, Bernard Jan M., et al. PHENOMENOLOGY AND MARXISM. Tr. of PHANOMENOLOGIE UND MARXISMUS. Frankfurt am Main: Suhrkamp, 1977. Tr. by J. Claude Evans. London and Boston: Routledge and Kegan Paul, 1984.

These are papers originally presented at an annual workshop held in 1975-1978 at the Inter-University Centre in Dubrovnik, Yugoslavia.

2200. Wetlesen, Jon. THE SAGE AND THE WAY. Assen: Van Gorcum, 1979.

2201. Wijsenbeek-Wijler, H. ARISTOTLE'S CONCEPT OF SOUL, SLEEP, AND DREAMS. Amsterdam: Hakkert, 1978.

NEW ZEALAND

2202. Bishop, John. NATURAL AGENCY: AN ESSAY ON THE CAUSAL THEORY OF ACTION. Cambridge and New York: Cambridge Univ. Press, 1989.

2203. Cresswell, Max J. STRUCTURED MEANINGS: THE SEMANTICS OF PROPOSITIONAL ATTITUDES. Cambridge: MIT Press, 1985.

2204. Currie, Gregory. FREGE: AN INTRODUCTION TO HIS PHILOSOPHY. Totowa, NJ: Barnes and Noble Books, 1982.

2205. Goldblatt, Robert. AXIOMATISING THE LOGIC OF COMPUTER PROGRAMMING. Berlin and New York: Springer-Verlag, 1982.

2206. Goldblatt, Robert. TOPOI: THE CATEGORIAL ANALYSIS OF LOGIC. Rev. ed. Amsterdam and Oxford: North-Holland, 1984.

2207. Maxwell, William. THINKING, THE EXPANDING FRONTIER. Philadelphia: Franklin Institute Press, 1983.

These are the Proceedings of the International Interdisciplinary Conference on Thinking held at the University of the South Pacific, January, 1982. There is a preface by Jerome Bruner. Selections were made and edited by John Bishop, and others.

2208. Novitz, David. PICTURES AND THEIR USE IN COMMUNICATION: A PHILOSOPHICAL ESSAY. The Hague: Nijhoff, 1977.

2209. Oddie, Graham. LIKENESS TO TRUTH. Dordrecht and Boston: Reidel, 1986.

2210. Ziman, John Michael. AN INTRODUCTION TO SCIENCE STUDIES: THE PHILOSOPHICAL AND SOCIAL ASPECTS OF SCIENCE AND TECHNOLOGY. Cambridge and New York: Cambridge Univ. Press, 1984.

NORWAY

2211. Berg, Kare and Knut Erik Tranoy. RESEARCH ETHICS. New York: Liss, 1983.

This volume contains the proceedings of a symposium organized by the Norwegian Academy of Science and Letters and others.

2212. Bohler, Dietrich, et al. DIE PRAGMATISCHE WENDE: SPRACHSPIEL PRAG-MATIK ODER TRANSZEDENTALPRAGMATIK? Frankfurt am Main: Suhrkamp, 1986.

2213. Elster, Jon. LOGIC AND SOCIETY: CONTRADICTIONS AND POSSIBLE WORLDS. Chichester and New York: Wiley, 1978.

2214 Elster, Jon. MAKING SENSE OF MARX. Studies in Marxism and Social Theory. Cambridge: Cambridge Univ. Press, 1985.

There is a bibliography on pages 533-548.

2215. Elster, Jon. SOLOMONIC JUDGEMENTS: STUDIES IN THE LIMITATIONS OF RATIONALITY. Cambridge and New York: Cambridge Univ. Press; Paris: Editions de la Maison des sciences de l'homme, 1989.

This volume of essays is a sequal to the two earlier collections by Elster: SOUR GRAPES: STUDIES IN THE SUBVERSION OF RATIONALITY (1983) and ULYSSES AND THE SIRENS: STUDIES IN RATIONALITY AND IRRATIONALITY (1984).

2216. Eriksen, Trond Berg. BIOS THEORETIKOS: NOTES ON ARISTOTLE'S ETHICA NICOMACHEA X, 6-8. Oslo: Universitetsforlaget, 1976.

2217. Gullvag, Ingemund and Jon Wetlesen. IN SCEPTICAL WONDER: INQUIRIES INTO THE PHILOSOPHY OF ARNE NAESS ON THE OCCASION OF HIS 70TH BIRTHDAY. Oslo: Universitetsforlaget, 1982.

2218. Haga, Anund, et al. REFLEKSJON OG HANDLING: FESTSKRIFT TIL HANS SKJERVHEIM PA 50-ORSDAGEN 9. OKTOBER, 1976 (Reflection and Action: Festschrift for Hans Skjervheim on his 50th Birthday October 9, 1976). Oslo: Gyldendal, 1976.

There is a bibliography of Skjervhelm's works (1948-1975) on pages 256- 262.

2219. Hannay, Alastair. KIERKEGAARD. The Arguments of the Philosophers. London and Boston: Routledge and Kegan Paul, 1982.

2220. Hoibraaten, Helge and Ingemund Gullvag. ESSAYS IN PRAGMATIC PHILOSO-PHY. 2d ed. Oslo: Norwegian Univ. Press, 1990.

2221. Johannessen, Kjell S. KUNST OG KUNSTFORST AELSE: EN ANALYSE AV SENTRALE BEGREPER I ESTETISK TEORI. Bergen: Univeritetsforlaget, 1978.

2222. Johannessen, Kjell S. and Tore Nordenstam. HISTORIE, VITENSKAP OG SAM-FUNN, DEL II: STUDIEKRETS--VITENSKAPSHISTORIE. Bergen: Nordiska Sommar-universitet, 1976.

This collection contains contributions by Lennart Nilsson, Jan Barmark, Ingemar Nilsson, Risto Ersaari, Keijo Rahdonen, Pasi Falk, Lars-Henrik Schmidt, H. P. Clausen, Poul Enemark, and Otto Larsen.

2223. Johannessen, Kjell S. and Tore Nordenstam. WITTGENSTEIN, ASTHETIK UND TRANSZENDENTAL PHILOSOPHIE: AKTEN EINES SYMPOSIUMS IN BERGEN (NORWEGEN) 1980. Vienna: Holder-Pichler-Tempsky; Dordrecht and Boston: Reidel, 1981.

An added title page, in English, states: WITTGENSTEIN, AESTHETICS AND TRANSCENDENTAL PHILOSOPHY. The volume is printed in English and in German.

2224. Jones, Andrew J. I. COMMUNICATION AND MEANING: AN ESSAY IN APPLIED MODAL LOGIC. Dordrecht and Boston: Reidel, 1983.

2225. Naess, Arne. ANKLAGENE MOT VITENSKAPEN. (The Case Against Science). Oslo: Universitetsforlaget, 1980.

2226. Naess, Arne. COMMUNICATION AND ARGUMENT: ELEMENTS OF APPLIED SEMANTICS. Tr. from the Norwegian by Alastair Hannay. Oslo: Universitetsforlaget, 1981.

2227. Naess, Arne. ECOLOGY, COMMUNITY AND LIFESTYLE: OUTLINE OF AN ECOSOPHY. Ed. and tr. by David Rothenberg. Cambridge and New York: Cambridge Univ. Press, 1989.

2228. Naess, Arne. FILOSOFIENS HISTORIE: EN INNFORING I FILOSOFISKE PROBLEMER. Vol. 1, FRA OLDTID TIL RENESSANSE. Vol. 2, FRA RENESSANCE TIL V'AR TID. 6th rev. ed. Oslo: Universitetsforlaget, 1978.

2229. Naess, Arne. HVILKEN VERDEN ER DEN VIRKELIGE?: GIR FILOSOFI OG KULTUR SVAR? Oslo: Universitetsforlaget, 1982.

2230. Naess, Arne. JEG VELGER SANNHETEN: EN DIALOG MELLOM PETER WESSEL ZAPFFE OG HERMAN TONNESSEN. Oslo: Universitetsforlaget, 1983.

There also are commentaries by Arne Naess and Herman Tonnessen and an epilogue by Peter Wessel Zapffe.

2231. Naess, Arne. OKOLOGI SAMFUNN OG LIVSSTIL: ULKAST TIL EN OKOSOFI. Oslo: Universitetsforlaget, 1976.

2232. Naess, Arne. A SCEPTICAL DIALOGUE ON INDUCTION. Assen: Van Gorcum, 1984.

2233. Naess, Arne. TEKNIKK, PEDAGOGIK OG EN NY LIVSSTIL: EN DEL ARTIKLER OG FOREDRAG GJENNOM 25 AR. Oslo: Universitetsforlaget, 1978.

This work contains articles published from 1954-1977.

2234. Naess, Arne and Danilo Dolci. HOLISM AND ECOLOGY. Tokyo: United Nations Univ., 1981.

This work was originally presented as a paper to the EDA (Environment, Debate, Action) Conference on the Environment, Beatenberg, Switzerland, September 28 to October 1, 1978.

2235. Ofstad, Harald. ANSVAR OG HANDLING: DISKUSJONER AV MORAL-SOCIAL- OG RETTSFILOSOFISKE SPORSMAL. Oslo: Universitetsforlaget, 1980.

2236. Ofsti, Audun. DAS "ICH DENKE" UND KANTS TRANSZENDENTALE DEDUKTION IM LICHTE DER SPRACHPHILOSOPHISCHEN (PRAGMATISCHEN) WENDE. Trondheim: Tapir, 1988.

2237. Ofsti, Audun. VITENSKAPSTEORI OG TRANSCENDENTALFILOSOFI: EN KRITISK KOMMENTAR TIL FOLLESDAL OG WALLOE, "ARGUMENTASJONSTEORI OG VITENSKAPSFILOSOFI". Trondheim: Tapir, 1980.

2238. Skagestad, Peter. THE ROAD OF INQUIRY, CHARLES PEIRCE'S PRAGMAT-IC REALISM. New York: Columbia Univ. Press, 1981.

This work defends Peirce's evolutionary experimental theory of knowledge.

2239. Skirbekk, Gunnar. ORD ESSAY I UTVAL. Oslo: Norske samlaget, 1984.

2240. Skirbekk, Gunnar. WAHRHEITSTHEORIEN: E. AUSW. AUS D. DISKUSSIONEN UBER WAHRHEIT IM 20. JH. Frankfurt am Main: Suhrkamp, 1977.

2241. Skirbekk, Gunnar, et al. PRAXEOLOGY: AN ANTHOLOGY. Bergen: Universitets-forlaget, 1983.

SPAIN

2242. Abellan, Jose Luis. PANORAMA DE LA FILOSOFIA ESPANOLA ACTUAL: UNA SITUACION ESCANDALOSA. Proloque by Vicente Llorens. Madrid: Espasa-Culpe, 1978.

2243. Ariel del Val, Fernando. FILOSOFI IDEOLOGIA LIBERAL, FASCISMO. Valencia: F. Torres, 1976.

2244. Asin Palacios, Miquel. THE MYSTICAL PHILOSOPHY OF IBN MASARRA AND HIS FOLLOWERS. Tr. of ABENMASARRA Y SU ESCUELA: ORIGENES DE LA FILOSOFIA HISPANOMUSULMANA. Madrid: Imprenta Iberica, 1914. Tr. by Elmer H. Douglas and Howard W. Yoder. Leiden: J. Brill, 1978.

2245. Cabada Castro, Manuel. FEUERBACH Y KANT: DOS ACTITUDES ANTROPO-LOGICAS. Madrid: La Universidad Pontificia Comillas, 1980.

2246. Caffarena, Jose Gomez, et al. EN FAVOR DE BLOCH. Madrid: Taurus, 1979.

2247. Caturelli, Alberto. LA FILOSOFIA. 2d rev. and enl. ed. Madrid: Editorial Gredos, 1977.

2248. Cortina Orts, Adela. DIOS EN LA FILOSOFIA DE KANT. Salamanca: Universidad Pontifica, 1982.

2249. Diaz Diaz, Gonzalo. HOMBRES Y DOCUMENTOS DE LA FILOSOFIA ESPANO-LA. Madrid: Consejo Superior de Investigaciones Cientificas, Instituto de Filosofia "Luis Vives," Departamento de Filosofia Espanola, 1980-.

Vol. 1, A-B; Vol. 2, C-D; Vol. 3, E-G have been published so far.

2250. Diaz Diaz, Gonzalo and Ceferino Santos Escudero. BIBLIOGRAPHIA FILOSOFICA HISPANICA (1901-1970). Madrid: Consejo Superior de Investigaciones Cientificas, Insti-tuto de Filosofia "Luis Vives," Departamento de Filosofia Espanola, 1982.

2251. Diaz, Elias. LA FILOSOFIA SOCIAL DEL KRAUSISMO ESPANOL. Valencia: F. Torres, 1983.

There is s bibliography on pages 225-237.

2252. Donoso, Anton and Harold Rale. JOSE ORTEGA Y GASSET: A BIBLIOGRAPHY OF SECONDARY SOURCES. Bibliographies of Famous Philosophers. Bowling Green, OH: Philosophy Documentation Center, Bowling Green State University, 1986.

The introduction to this comprehensive secondary bibliography of over 4,000 works is in Spanish and English.

2253. Fernandez de la Mora, Gonzalo. FILOSOFOS ESPANOLES DEL SIGLO XX. Barcelona: Planeta, 1987.

2254. Ferrater Mora, Jose. CUATRO VISIONE DE LA HISTORIA UNIVERSAL: SAN AUGUSTIN, VICO, VOLTAIRE, HEGEL. Madrid: Alianza, 1982.

2255. Ferrater Mora, Jose. DE LA MATERIA A LA RAZON. Madrid: Alianza, 1979.

2256. Ferrater Mora, Jose. DICCIONARIO DE FILOSOPHIA DE BOLSILLO. 2 Vols. Madrid: Alianza, 1983.

2257. Ferrater Mora, Jose. DICCIONARIO DE FILOSOPHIA. 4 Vols. 6th ed. Madrid: Alianza, 1982.

2258. Ferrater Mora, Jose. EL SER Y MUERTE: BOSQUEJO DE FILOSOFIA INTEGRACIONISTA. New, rev. and aug ed. Barcelona: Planeta, 1979.

2259. Ferrater Mora, Jose. ETICA APLICADA: DEL ABORTO A LA VIOLENCIA. Madrid: Alianza, 1981.

2260. Ferrater Mora, Jose. MODOS DE HACER FILOSOFIA. Barcelona: Critica, 1985.

2261. Ferrater Mora, Jose. TRANSPARENCIES: PHILOSOPHICAL ESSAYS IN HONOR OF J. FERRATER MORA. Ed. by Priscilla Cohn. Atlantic Highlands, NJ: Humanities Press, 1981.

These essays discuss Ferrater Mora's idea of the continuum of nature and the concomitant notion that being has meaning and meaning has being. The thinking of the contributors is diverse, existential, phenomenological, analytical and religious. The volume includes a bibliography of J. Ferrater Mora's published writings compiled by Leopoldo Montoya on pages 201-232.

2262. Forment Giralt, Eualdo. PERSONA Y MODO SUBSTANCIAL. Barcelona: Promociones Publicaciones Universitatias, 1983.

2263. Garcia Cue, Juan Ramon. APROXIMACION AL ESTUDIO DEL KRAUSISMO ANDALUZ. Madrid and Technos: Fudacion Cultural E. Luno Pena, 1985.

2264. Greimas, Algirdas Julien. ENSAYOS DE SEMIOTICA POETICA. Tr. of ESSAIS DE SEMIOTIQUE POETIQUE. AVEC DES ETUDES SUR APPOLLINAIRE, BATAILLE, BAUDELAIRE, HUGO, JARRY, MALLARME, MICHAUX, NERVAL, RIMBAUD, ROUBAUD. Paris: Larousse, 1971. Tr. by Carmenn de Fezy Asuncion Rallo. Barcelona: Planeta, 1976.

2265. Greimas, Algirdas Julien and Joseph Courtes. SEMIOTICS AND LANGUAGE: AN ANALYTICAL DICTIONARY. Tr. of SEMIOTIQUE: DICTIONNAIRE RAISONNE DE LA THEORIE DU LANGAGE. Paris: Hachette, 1979. Tr. by Larry Crist et al. Bloomington: Indiana univ. Press, 1982.

This work also was translated into Portuguese by Alceu Dias Lima and others in 1979. It was published by Cultrix of Sao Paulo under the title, DICIONARIO DE SEMIOTICA. The Spanish edition, SEMIOTICA: DICCIONARIO RAZONADO DE LA TEORIA DEL LENGUAJE, translated by Enrique Ball and Aquirre Hermis Campodonnico Carrion, was published in 1979 in Madrid by Editorial Grados.

2266. Guy, Alain. HISTOIRE DE LA PHILOSOPHIE ESPAGNOLE. Toulouse: Association des publications de l'Universite de Toulouse-le Mirail, 1983.

2267. Heredia Soriano, Antonio. ACTAS DEL SEMINARIO DE HISTORIA DE LA FILOSOFIA ESPAÑOLA: SALAMANCA. I (1978); II (1980); III (1982); IV (1984); V (1986). Salamanca: Ediciones Universidad de Salamanca, Departamento de Historia de la Filosofia y la Ciencia, 1978-.

The texts are in French and Spanish.

2268. Krings, Hermann, et al. CONCEPTOS FUNDAMENTALES DE FILOSOFIA. 3 Vols. Barcelona: Editorial Herder, 1977-1979.

2269. Lacasta Zabalza, Jose Ignacio. HEGEL EN ESPANA: UN ESTUDIO SOBRE LA MENTALIDAD SOCIAL DEL HEGELISMO HISPANICO. Madrid: Centro de Estudios Constitucionales, 1984.

This volume contains a bibliography on pages 336-350.

2270. Marias, Julian. A BIOGRAPHY OF PHILOSOPHY. Tr. by Harold C. Raley. University: Univ. of Alabama Press, 1984.

2271. Muguerza, Javier. LA CONCEPCION ANALITICA DE LA FILOSOFIA. 2d ed. Madrid: Alianza, 1981.

2272. Nebreda, Jesus J. FENOMENOLOGIA DEL LENGUAGE DE MAURICE MERLEAU-PONTY: PROLEGOMENOS PARA UNA ONTOLOGIA DIACRITICA. Madrid: Publicaciones de la Universidad Pontificia Comillas, 1981.

2273. Passmore, John Arthur. 100 [CEIN] ANOS DE FILOSOFIA. Tr. by Pilar Castrillo. Madrid: Alianza, 1981.

2274. Penalver Gomez, Patricio. MARGENES DE PLATON: LA ESTRUCTURA DIALECTICA DEL DIALOGO Y LA IDEA EXTERIORIDAD. Murcia: Secretariada de Publicaciones e Intercambio Cientifico Universidad de Murcia, 1986.

2275. Pintor Ramos, Antonio. EL DEISMO RELIGIOSO DE ROUSSEAU: ESTUDIOS SOBRE SU PENSAMIENTO. Salamanca: Universidad Pontificia, 1982.

2276. Ramos Mattei, Carlos. ETHICAL SELF-DETERMINATION IN DON JOSE ORTEGA Y GASSET. New York: Peter Lang, 1987.

2277. Ripalda, Jose Maria. THE DIVIDED NATION: THE ROOTS OF A BOURGEOIS THINKER, G. W. F. HEGEL. Tr. from the Spanish manuscript by Fay Franklin and Maruja Tillman. Assen: Van Gorcum, 1977.

The volume contains a bibliography on pages 203-216.

2278. Scanone, Juan Carlos. TEOLOGIA DE LA LIBERACION Y PRAXIS POPULAR: APORTES CRITICOS PARA UNA TEOLOGIA DE LA LIBERACION. Salamanca: Ediciones Sigueme, 1976.

2279. Searle, John R. ACTOS DE HABLA: ENSAYO DE FILOSOFIA DEL LENGUAJE. Tr. of SPEECH ACTS: AN ESSAY IN THE PHILOSOPHY OF LANGUAGE. London: Cambridge Univ. Press, 1977. Madrid: Ediciones Catedra, 1980.

2280. Tyedor Campomanes, Cesar. UNA ANTROPOLOGIA DEL CONOCIMIENTO: ESTUDIO SOBRE SPINOZA. Madrid: Publicaciones de la Universidad Pontificia

Comillas de Madrid, 1981.

SWEDEN

2281. Aagaard-Mogensen, Lars. ASTETISK KULTUR. Copenhagen: Berlingske, 1979.

2282. Aagaard-Mogensen, Lars. CULTURE AND ART. Nyborg: F. Lokke; Atlantic Highlands, NJ: Humanities Press, 1976.

This anthology of essays includes contributions by contemporary aestheticians and philosophers of art such as Arthur Danto, Monroe C. Beardsley, Leonard B. Meyer, and Ted Brunius.

2283. Aagaard-Mogensen, Lars. HVAD ER OPLYSINING? Nyborg: Lokke, 1976.

This is a collection of essays by J. Hartnack, K.E. Legstrup, D. Favrholdt, J. Slok, and F. Palle Hansen.

2284. Aagaard-Mogensen, Lars. THE IDEA OF THE MUSEUM: PHILOSOPHICAL, ARTISTIC, AND POLITICAL QUESTIONS. Lewiston/Queenston, NY: E. Mellen Press, 1987.

2285. Aagaard-Mogensen, Lars. THE JOURNAL OF AESTHETICS AND ART CRITICISM CUMULATIVE INDEX, VOLUMES I-XXXV, 1941-1977. Philadelphia: American Society for Aesthetics, 1979.

2286. Aagaard-Mogensen, Lars and Goran Hermeren. CONTEMPORARY AESTHETICS IN SCANDINAVIA. Lund: Doxa, 1980.

2287. Aagaard-Mogensen, Lars and Luk de Vos. TEXT, LITERATURE, AND AESTHETICS: IN HONOR OF MONROE C. BEARDSLEY. Elementa. Wurzburg: Konigshausen and Neumann; Amsterdam: Rodopi; Atlantic Highlands, NJ: Humanities Press, 1986.

2288. Anderberg, Thomas, et al. AESTHETIC DISTINCTION: ESSAYS PRESENTED TO GORAN HERMEREN ON HIS 50TH BIRTHDAY. Lund: Lund Univ. Press; Bromley: Chartwell-Bratt, 1988.

2289. Aqvist, Lennart. A CONJECTURED AXIOMATIZATION OF TWO-DIMENSIONAL REICHENBACHIAN TENSE LOGIC. Uppsala: Filosofiska Foreningen och Filosofiska Institutionen, Uppsala Universitet, 1977.

2290. Aqvist, Lennart and Franz Guenthner. TENSE LOGIC. Publication du Centre National Belge de Recherches de Logique. Louvain: Nauweelaerts Print. S. A., 1977.

2291. Brakenhielon, Carl Reinhold. PROBLEMS OF RELIGIOUS EXPERIENCE. Uppsala: Uppsala Univ, 1985.

2292. Carlstedt, Ulla, et al. FILOSOFISKA SMULOR: TILLAGNADE KONRAD MARCWOGAU, 75 AR 4 APRIL 1977. Uppsala: Filosofiska Foreningen och Filosofiska Institutionen, Vid Uppsala Universitet, 1977.

This book contains essays by L. Aqvist, S. Kanger, J. S. Andersson, I. Tonisson, and others and a bibliography of works by K. Marc-Wogau.

2293. Dahl, Eva-Lena. OVERIDEOLOGI OCH POLITISKT HANDLINGSPROGRAM: EN STUDIE LOCKES OCH ROUSSEAUS TANKANDE=IDEOLOGY AND POLITICAL PROGRAM OF ACTION: A STUDY IN THE POLITICAL THOUGHT OF LOCKE

AND ROUSSEAU. Gothenburg: Acta Universitatis Gothoburgensis, 1980.

2294. Dilworth, Craig. SCIENTIFIC PROGRESS: A STUDY CONCERNING THE NATURE OF THE RELATION BETWEEN SUCCESSIVE SCIENTIFIC THEORIES. Dordrecht and Boston: Reidel, 1981.

2295. Ericsson, Lars Olov. JUSTICE IN THE DISTRIBUTION OF ECONOMIC RESOURCES: A CRITICAL AND NORMATIVE STUDY. Stockholm: Almqvist & Wiksell International, 1976.

2296. Eyerman, Ron. FALSE CONSCIOUSNESS AND IDEOLOGY IN MARXIST THEORY. Stockholm: Almqvist & Wiksell; Atlantic Highlands: Humanities Press, 1981.

2297. Frandberg, Ake and Mark Van Hoecke. THE STRUCTURE OF LAW. Uppsala: Iustus, 1987.

This volume contains the papers presented at the Second Benelux-Scandinavian Symposium on Legal Theory held in Uppsala, Dec. 11-13, 1986.

2298. Furberg, Mats. VERSTEHEN OCH FORSTA: FUNDERINGAR KRING ETT TEMA HOS DILTHEY, HEIDEGGER OCH GADAMER. Lund: Doxa, 1981.

2299. Furberg, Mats, et al. LOGIC AND ABSTRACTION: ESSAYS DEDICATED TO PER LINDSTROM ON HIS FIFTIETH BIRTHDAY. Gothenburg: Acta Universitatis Gothoburgensis, 1986.

2300. Gardenfors, Peter, et al. EVIDENTIARY VALUE: PHILOSOPHICAL, JUDICIAL AND PSYCHOLOGICAL ASPECTS OF A THEORY: ESSAYS DEDICATED TO SOREN HALLDEN ON HIS SIXTIETH BIRTHDAY. Lund: GWK Gleerups, 1983.

2301. Gardenfors, Peter and Nils-Eric Sahlin. DECISION, PROBABILITY AND UTILITY: SELECTED READINGS. Cambridge and New York: Cambridge Univ. Press, 1988.

2302. Hanson, Bo. APPLICATION OF RULES IN NEW SITUATIONS: HERMENEUTICAL STUDY. Lund: Liber Laromedel/Gleerup, 1977.

2303. Hanson, Bo, et al. RELIGIONSFILOSOFISKA PERSPEKTIV: FRYA PROVFORELASNINGAR TILL PROFESSUREN I RELIGIONSFILOSOFI 1982. Lund: Telogiska Institutionen i Lund, 1983.

2304. Hanson, Bo, et al. VARDAG OCH EVIGHET: FESTSKRIFT TILL HAMPUS LYTTKENS PA HANS 65 ARSDAG DEN 19 FEBRUARI 1981. Lund: Doxa, 1981.

There is a bibliogaphy of the works of Hampus Lyttkens on pages 253-259.

2305. Hansson, Bengt. METOD ELLER ANARKI: [MODERNA TEORIER OM VETENSKAPENS VASENT OCH METODER]. Lund: Doxa, 1980.

2306. Hermeren, Goran. ASPECTS OF AESTHETICS. Lund: CWK Gleerup, 1983.

2307. Israel, Joachim. THE LANGUAGE OF DIALECTICS AND THE DIALECTICS OF LANGUAGE. Copenhagen: Munksgaard; Atlantic Highlands, NJ: Humanities Press, 1979.

2308. Kanger, Stig and Sven Ohman. PHILOSOPHY AND GRAMMAR: PAPERS ON THE OCCASION OF THE QUINCENTENNIAL OF UPPSALA UNIVERSITY. Dordrecht and Boston: Reidel, 1981.

This volume includes contributions by D. Follesdal, J. Hintikka, W. V. Quine, G. H. Von Wright and others. The papers are written in both English and German.

2309. Krause-Jensen, Esbern. FILOSOFI, POLITIK OG PSYKOANALYSE: JACQUES DERRIDA. Kongerslev: GMT, 1980.

2310. Malmgren, Helge. IMMEDIATE KNOWLEDGE: A STUDY IN G. E. MOORE'S EPISTEMOLOGY. Bodafors, Sweden: Doxa, 1983.

2311. Marc-Wogau, Konrad, et al. LEHRSTUCKE DER PRAKTISCHEN PHILOSO- PHIE UND DER AESTHETIK. Ed. by Karl Barthlein and Gerd Wolandt. Basel and Stuttgart: Schwabe, 1977.

2312. Nordenfelt, Lennart. CAUSATION: AN ESSAY. Stockholm: Akademilitt, 1981.

2313. Nordenfelt, Lennart. CAUSES OF DEATH: A PHILOSOPHICAL ESSAY. Stock- holm: Forskningsradsnamnden, Delegationen for l'angsiklmotiverod Forsking, 1983.

2314. Nordenfelt, Lennart. EVENTS, ACTIONS, AND ORDINARY LANGUAGE. Lund: Doxa, 1977.

2315. Nordenfelt, Lennart. KUNSKAP, VARDERING, FORSTAELSE: INTRODUKTION TILL HUMANVETENSKAPERNAS TEORI OCH METOD. Stockholm: Liber Forlag, 1979.

The volume contains a bibliography on pages 124-154.

2316. Nordenfelt, Lennart. OMORSAKER OCH EFFEKTER I SPRAKET: NAGRA REFLEKTIONER MED UTGANGSPUNKT IN BENNY BRODDAS KASUSGRAMMA- TIK FOR SVENSKAN. Stockholm: Akademilitt, 1977.

2317. Nordenfelt, Lennart. ON THE NATURE OF HEALTH: AN ACTION-THEORETIC APPROACH. Dordrecht and Boston: Reidel, 1987.

2318. Nordenfelt, Lennart. TILL SJUKDOMSBEGREPPETS SEMANTIK: EN BEGREP- PSANALYTISK STUDIE. Stockholm: Akademilitt, 1979.

2319. Nordenfelt, Lennart and Borje Ingemar Bertil Lindahl. HEALTH, DISEASE, AND CAUSAL EXPLANATIONS IN MEDICINE. Dordrecht and Boston: Reidel, 1984.

2320. Ohlsson, Ragnar. THE MORAL IMPORT OF EVIL: ON COUNTERBALANCING DEATH, SUFFERING, AND DEGRADATION. Stockholm: Akdemilitt, 1979.

2321. Pauli, Tom. PHILOSOPHICAL ESSAYS DEDICATED TO LENNART AQVIST ON HIS FIFTIETH BIRTHDAY. Uppsala: Philosophical Society and Dept. of Philoso- phy, Univ. of Uppsala, 1982.

The text is written in English, German and Swedish.

2322. Ryding, Erik. STATEMENTS AND EXHORTATIONS. Lund: Doxa, 1980.

2323. Sahlin, Nils-Eric. THE PHILOSOPHY OF F. P. RAMSEY. Cambridge and New York: Cambridge Univ. Press, 1990.

2324. Sellberg, Erland. FILOSOFIN OCH NYTTAN=PHILOSOPHY AND USE: I. PETRUS RAMUS AND RAMISM. Gothenburg: Acta Universitatis Gothoburgensis, 1979-.

2325. Sjoberg, Lennart, et al. HUMAN DECISION MAKING. Bodafors: Doxa, 1983.

The authors represent such disciplines as psychology, philosophy, and economics, and come from all over the world. This book provides an overview of recent international developments in decision making.

2326. Teodorsson, Sven-Tage. ANAXAGORAS' THEORY OF MATTER. Studia Graeca and Latina Gothoburgensia. Gothenburg: Acta Universitatis Gothoburgensis, 1982.

2327. Tigerstedt, Eugene Napoleon. INTERPRETING PLATO. Stockholm Studies in History of Literature, Vol. 17. Stockholm: Almquist and Wiksell International, 1977.

2328. Wedberg, Anders. EN FILOSOFIBOK: TILLAGNAD ANDERS WEDBERG. Stockholm: Bonnier, 1978.

The volume contains essays by M. Furberg, D. Prawitz, H. Ofstad, E. Stenius, G. H. von Wright and others and a bibliography of the works of Anders Wedberg.

2329. Wedberg, Anders. A HISTORY OF PHILOSOPHY. Vol. 1, ANTIQUITY AND THE MIDDLE AGES. Vol. 2, THE MODERN AGE TO ROMANTICISM. Vol. 3, FROM BOLZANO TO WITTGENSTEIN. Tr. of FILOSOFINS HISTORIA. Vol. 1, ANTIKEN OCH MEDELTIDEN. Vol. 2, NYARE TIDEN TILL ROMANTIKEN. Vol. 3, FRAN BOLZANO TILL WITTGENSTEIN. Stockholm: Bonnier, 1958-. Oxford: Clarendon Press, 1982-1984.

Although this is a history of Western philosophy from Ancient Greece to the present, its focus is on philosophical problems, themes and theories at the center of comtemporary philosophic interest.

2330. Westin, Charles. SELF STEREOTYPES: CONSCIOUSNESS AND TIME. Atlantic Highlands, NJ: Humanities Press, 1984.

2331. Wetterstrom, Thomas. INTENTION AND COMMUNICATION: AN ESSAY IN THE PHENOMENOLOGY OF LANGUAGE. Lund: Doxa, 1977.

This work is a revision of the author's thesis at Gothenburg.

2332. Wetterstrom, Thomas. TOWARDS A THEORY OF BASIC ETHICS. Oxford: Doxa, 1986.

SWITZERLAND

2333. Corti, Walter Robert. THE PHILOSOPHY OF WILLIAM JAMES. Hamburg: Felix Meiner, 1976.

A bibliography of writings by and about William James compiled by C. H. Siegfried will be found on pages 385-393.

2334. Feyerabend, Paul K. AUSGEWAHLTE SCHRIFTEN. 2 Vols. Braunschweig: Vieweg, 1978-1981.

2335. Feyerabend, Paul K. PHILOSOPHICAL PAPERS. Vol. 1, REALISM, RATIONALISM, AND SCIENTIFIC METHOD; Vol. 2, PROBLEMS OF EMPIRICISM. Cambridge and New York: Cambridge Univ. Press, 1981.

2336. Feyerabend, Paul K. SCIENCE IN A FREE SOCIETY. London: NLB, 1978.

2337. Feyerabend, Paul K. THREE DIALOGUES ON KNOWLEDGE. Oxford and Cambridge: Blackwell, 1991.

2338. Hasler, Ludwig. SCHELLING, SEINE BEDEUTUNG FUR EINE PHILOSO-PHIE DER NATUR UND GESCHICHTE: REFERATE UND KOLLOQUIEN DER INTERNATIONALEN SCHELLING-TAGUNG ZURICH 1979. Stuttgart-Bad Connstatt: Frommann-Holzboog, 1981.

The thirty two papers from the colloquium discuss: 1. Schelling's relation to natural science and medicine; 2. perspectives on Schelling's philosophy of history; 3. Schelling's and Hegel's early political philosophies.

2339. Hersch, Jeanne. KARL JASPERS. Lausanne: L`Age d'Homme, 1978.

2340. Kohler, Georg. GESCHMACKSURTEIL UND ASTHETISCHE ERFAHRUNG: BEITRAGE ZUR AUSLEGUNG VON KANTS "KRITIK DE ASTHETISCHEN UR-TEILSKRAFT". Ed. by Gerhard Funke and Joachim Kopper. Berlin and New York: De Gruyter, 1980.

2341. Lauener, Henri. ZEITGENOSSISCHE PHILOSOPHIE IN DER SCHWEIZ. Bern: P. Haupt, 1984.

2342. Mercier, Andre. AGGRESSION UND TOLERANZ: WESEN UND UNWESEN MENSCHLICHEN VERHALTENS. Bern: Herbert Lang, 1977.

2343. Mercier, Andre. METAPHYSIK, EINE WISSENSCHAFT SUI GENERIS: THEORIE UND ERFAHRUNG AUF DEM GEBIET DES INKOMMENSURABLEN. Berlin: Dunker and Humblot, 1980.

2344. Mercier, Andre, et al. ON GENERAL RELATIVITY: AN ANALYSIS OF THE FUNDAMENTALS OF THE THEORY OF GENERAL RELATIVIY AND GRAVITA-TION. Berlin: Akademie Verlag, 1979.

2345. Mercier, Andre and Maja Svilar. SPACE: ENTRETIENS IN BERNE, 12-16 SEPTEMBER, 1976. Bern: Peter Lang, 1978.

2346. Ruef, Hans. AUGUSTIN UBER SEMIOTIK UND SPRACHE: SPRACHTHEORE-TISCHE ANALYSEN ZU AUGUSTINS SCHRIFT "DE DIALECTICA", MIT EINER DEUTSCHEN UBERSETZUNG. Bern: K. J. Wyss, 1981.

2347. Schaerer, Rene. PHILOSOPHIE ET FICTION: LES ITINERAIRES DE LA PENSEE. Lausanne: L'Age d'Homme, acheve d'impr., 1979.

2348. Schulthess, Peter. RELATION AND FUNKTION: EINE SYSTEMATISCHE UND ENTWICKLUNGSGESCHICHTLICHE UNTERSUCHUNG ZUR THEORE-TISCHEN PHILOSOPHIE KANTS. Berlin and New York: De Gruyter, 1981.

2349. Schuon, Frithjof. FROM THE DIVINE TO THE HUMAN: SURVEY OF META-PHYSICS AND EPISTEMOLOGY. Tr. of DU DIVIN A L'HUMAIN: TOUR D'HORI-ZON DE METAPHYSIQUE ET D'EPISTEMOLOGIE. Paris: Le Courier du Livre, 1981. Tr. by Gustavo Polit and Deborah Lambert. Bloomington, IN: World Wisdom Books, 1982.

2350. Schuon, Frithjof. SURVEY OF METAPHYSICS AND ESOTERISM. Tr. of RESUME DE METAPHYSIQUE INTEGRALE, AND SUR LES TRACES DE LA RELIGION PERENNE. Tr. by Gustavo Polit. Bloomington, IN: World Wisdom Books, 1986.

WEST GERMANY

2351. Abel, Gunter. STOIZISMUS UND FRUHE NEUZEIT: ZUR ENTSTEHUNGS-GESCHICHTE MODERNEN DENKENS IM FELDE VON ETHIK UND POLITIK. Berlin and New York: De Gruyter, 1977.

2352. Acham, Karl. PHILOSOPHIE DER SOCIALWISSENSCHAFTEN. Freiburg: K. Alber, 1983.

2353. Adorno, Theodor Wiesengrund. AESTHETIC THEORY. Boston: Routledge and Kegan Paul, 1984.

2354. Adorno, Theodor Wiesengrund. AGAINST EPISTEMOLOGY: A METACRITIQUE. STUDIES IN HUSSERL AND THE PHENOMENOLOGICAL ANTINOMIES. Tr. of ZUR METAKRITIK DER ERKENNTNISTHEORIE. Stuttgart: Kolhammer, 1956. Tr. by Willis Domingo. Studies in Contemporary German Social Thought. Oxford: B. Blackwell, 1982.

This is Bd. 5 of Adorno's GESAMMELTE SCHRIFTEN.

2355. Adorno, Theodor Wiesengrund, et al. THE POSTIVIST DISPUTE IN GERMAN SOCIOLOGY. Tr. of DER POSITIVISMUSSTREIT IN DER DEUTSCHEN SOZIOLO-GIE. Neuwied and Berlin: Luchterhand, 1969. Tr. by Glyn Adey and David Frisbey. London: Heinemann; New York: Harper & Row, 1976.

2356. Albert, Hans. AUFKLARUNG UND STEUERUNG: AUFSATZE ZUR SO-ZIALPHILOSOPHIE UND ZUR WISSENSCHAFTSLEHRE D. SOZIALWISS. Hamburg: Hoffmann und Campe, 1976.

These essays were originally published in various periodicals and anthologies during the period 1963-1975.

2357. Albert, Hans. DAS ELEND DER THEOLOGIE, KRIT. AUSEINANDERSET-ZUNG MIT HANS KUNG. Hamburg: Hoffmann und Campe, 1979.

2358. Albert, Hans. ETICA Y METAETICA: EL DILEMA DE LA FILOSOFIA MORAL ANALITICA. Tr. of ETHIK UND METAETHIK which originally appeared in Archiv fur Philosophy, Band 11 (1961), Hefte 1-2, SS. 28-63e. Tr. from the German by Manuel Jimenez Redonda. Valencia: Revista Teorema, 1978.

2359. Albert, Hans. FREIHEIT UND ORDNUNG: ZWEI ABHANDLUNGEN ZUM PROBLEM EINER OFFENEN GESELLSCHAFT. Tubingen: Mohr, 1986.

2360. Albert, Hans. KRITISCHE VERNUNFT UND MENSCHLICHE PRAXIS. Stuttgart: Reclam, 1977.

This book contains a collection of previously published material and a bibliography of the author's works on pages 212-213.

2361. Albert, Hans. TRAKTAT UBER RATIONALE PRAXIS. Tubingen: Mohr, 1978.

2362. Albert, Hans. TREATISE ON CRITICAL REASON. Tr. of TRAKTAT UBER KRITISCHE VERNUNFT. Tubingen: Mohr (Siebich), 1968. Tr. by Mary Varney Rorty. Princeton: Princeton Univ. Press, 1985.

There is a Spanish translation TRATADO DA RAZAO CRITICA, published in Rio de Janeiro by Tempo Brasileiro in 1976.

2363. Albert, Hans. DIE WISSENSCHAFT UND DIE FEHLBARKEIT DER VERNUNFT. Tubingen: Mohr, 1982.

2364. Albert, Hans and Kurt H. Stapf. THEORIE UND ERFAHRUNG: BEITRAGE ZUR GRUNDLAGENPROBLEMATIK DER SOZIALWISSENSCHAFTEN. Stuttgart: Klett-Cotta, 1979.

This volume contains papers from an interdisciplinary symposium held in Tubingen November 23-25, 1977. Chapters 1, 2, and 10 have been translated from English by Margarete Albert.

2365. Albert, Hans and Ernst Topitsch. WERTURTEILSSTREIT. Darmstadt: Wissenschaftliche Buchgesellschaft, 1979.

2366. Alther, Eduard. DAS ABSOLUTE ALS ZEIT-RAUM-VERHALTNIS UND VORGANG: BEZIEHUNGSWEISE, DAS WESEN UND GESETZ DER DEN ERSCHEINUNGEN IM GESAMTEN ZU GRUNDE LIEGENDEN URSACHE ODER KRAFT: DARGELEGET FUR DENKENDE, WISSENSCHAFTLER UND FORSCHER. Zurich: Kreis-Verlag, 1979.

2367. Andersson, Gunnar. RATIONALITY IN SCIENCE AND POLITICS. Dordrecht and Boston: Reidel, 1984.

2368. Andersson, Gunnar and Gerard Radnitzky. PROGRESO Y RACIONALIDAD EN LA CIENCIA. Tr. of FORTSCHRITT UND RATIONALITAT DER WISSENSCHAFT. Tubingen: Mohr, 1980. Madrid: Alianza Editorial, 1982.

FORTSCHRITT UND RATIONALITAT DER WISSENSCHAFT is a revised and expanded German translation of PROGRESS AND RATIONALITY IN SCIENCE published by Reidel in Boston and Dordrecht in 1978, the first of two volumes presenting the results of a workshop held July 6-18, 1975, near Frankfurt. The second volume based on this workshop was published by Reidel in 1979 under the title THE STRUCTURE AND DEVELOPMENT OF SCIENCE, also edited by Andersson and Radnitsky.

2369. Angehern, Emil. FREIHEIT UND SYSTEM BEI HEGEL. Berlin and New York: De Gruyter, 1977.

2370. Apel, Karl-Otto. CHARLES S. PEIRCE: FROM PRAGMATISM TO PRAGMATICISM. Tr. of DER DENKWEG VON CHARLES S. PEIRCE: EINE EINFUHRUNG IN DEN AMERIKANISCHEN PRAGMATISMUS. Frankfurt am Main: Suhrkamp, 1975, c1970. Tr. by John Michael Krois. Amherst: Univ. of Massachusetts Press, 1981.

2371. Apel, Karl-Otto. SPRACHPRAGMATIK UND PHILOSOPHIE. Frankfurt am Main: Suhrkamp, 1976,1984.

This book consists of essays on language and pragmatics by the editor and others.

2372. Apel, Karl-Otto. TOWARDS A TRANSFORMATION OF PHILOSOPHY. Tr. of TRANSFORMATION DER PHILOSOPHIE. Frankfurt am Main: Suhrkamp, 1973. Eng. tr. by Glyn Adey and David Frisby. London: Routledge and Kegan Paul, 1980.

2373. Apel, Karl-Otto. UNDERSTANDING AND EXPLANATION: A TRANSCENDENTAL- PRAGMATIC PERSPECTIVE. Tr. of DIE ERKLAREN-VERSTEHEN-KONTROVERSE IN TRANSZENDENTALPRAGMATISCHER SICHT. Frankfurt am Main: Suhrkamp, 1979. Tr. by Georgia Warnke. Cambridge: MIT Press, 1984.

2374. Apel, Max and Peter Ludz. PHILOSOPHISCHES WORTERBUCH. 6th ed. Berlin and New York: De Gruyter, 1976.

2375. Arato, Andrew and Eike Gebhardt. THE ESSENTIAL FRANKFURT SCHOOL READER. Oxford: Blackwell; New York: Urizen Books, 1978.

This work contains a bibliography on pages 530-541.

2376. Baldinger, Kurt. VERS UNE SEMANTIQUE MODERNE. Tr. of TEORIA SEMANTICA: HACIA UNA SEMANTICA MODERNA. 2d. ed. corr. and aug. Madrid: Ediciones Alcala, 1977. Paris: Klincksieck, 1984.

The English translation, SEMANTIC THEORY: TOWARD A MODERN SEMANTICS, was published in Oxford by B. Blackwell and in New York by St. Martin's Press in 1980. The work was translated by William C. Brown and edited by Roger Wright.

2377. Balmer, Hans Peter. PHILOSOPHIE DER MENSCHLICHEN DINGE: DIE EUROPAISCHE MORALISTIK. Bern and Munich: Francke, 1981.

2378. Bartels, Martin. SELBSTBEWUSSTSEIN UND UNBEWUSSTES: STUDIEN ZU FREUD UND HEIDEGGER. Berlin and New York: De Gruyter, 1976.

2379. Barth, Karl. THE THEOLOGY OF SCHLEIERMACHER: LECTURES AT GOT-TINGEN, WINTER SEMESTER OF 1923-1924. Tr. of DIE THEOLOGIE SCHLEIER-MACHERS VORLESUNG GOTTINGEN WINTERSEMESTER 1923/24. Ed. by Dietrich Ritschl. Zurich: Theologischer Verlag, 1978. Tr. by Geoffrey W. Bromley. Edinburgh: T. & T. Clark; Grand Rapids: Eerdmans, 1982.

2380. Baumgartner, Hans Michael. KANTS "KRITIK DER REINEN VERKNUNFT": ANLEITUNG ZUR LEKTURE. Freiburg and Munich: Alber, 1985.

2381. Baumgartner, Hans Michael. PRINZIP FREIHEIT: AUSEINANDERSETZUNG UM CHANCEN U. GRENZEN TRANSZENDENTALPHILOS. DENKENS: ZUM 65. GEBURTSTAG VON HERMANN KRINGS. Freiburg and Munich: K. Alber, 1979.

The volume contains a bibliography of Hermann Kring's works.

2382. Baumgartner, Hans Michael and Albin Eser. SCHULD UND VERANTWOR-TUNG: PHILOSOPHISCHE UND JURISTISCHE BEITRAGE ZUR ZURECKEN-BARKEIT MENSCHLICHEN HANDELNS. Tubingen: Mohr (Paul Siebeck), 1983.

2383. Baumgartner, Hans Michael and Bernhard Irrgang. AM ENDE DER NEUZEIT?: DIE FORDERUNG EINES FUNDAMENTALEN WERTWANDELS UND IHRE PROBLEME. Wurzburg: Konigshausen and Neumann, 1985.

This work includes contributions by Arnold Kopke-Dutter, Gunter Seubold, Peter Fonk, Karl-Heinz Hillmann, Walther C. Zimmerli, and the editors at the Colloquium "Technologie und Wertwandel" in Wolfenbuttel on October 13-15, 1983.

2384. Baumgartner, Hans Michael and Jorn Rusen. SEMINAR GESCHICHTE UND THEORIE: UMRISS E HISTORIK. Frankfurt am Main: Suhrkamp, 1976.

2385. Baumgartner, Hans Michael and Hans-Martin Sass. PHILOSOPHIE IN DEUTSCH-LAND 1945-1975: STANDPUNKT, ENTWICKLUNGEN, LITERATUR. Meisenheim: Hain, 1978.

2386. Beck, Heinrich. KULTURPHILOSOPHIE DER TECHNIK: PERSPEKTIVEN ZU TECHNIK, MENSCHHEIT, ZUKUNFT. Trier: Spee-Verlag, 1979.

2387. Beckermann, Ansgar. DESCARTES' METAPHYSISCHER BEWEIS FUR DEN DUALISMUS: ANALYSE UND KRITIK. Freiburg: K. Alber, 1986.

2388. Beckermann, Ansgar. GRUNDE UND URSACHEN: ZUM VERMEINTL. GRUND-SATZL. UNTERSCHIED ZWISCHEN MENTALEN HANDLUNGSERKLARUNGEN U. WISSENSCHAFTL. - KAUSALEN ERKLARUNGEN. Kronberg/Ts.: Scriptor-Verlag, 1977.

2389. Beckmann, Jan P., et al. SPRACHE UND ERKENNTNIS IM MITTELALTER. 2 Vols. Berlin: De Gruyter, 1981.

These are the Proceedings of the VI International Congress of Medieval Philosophy of the Societe Internationale pour l'Etude de la Philosophie Medievale. August 29-September 3, 1977 in Bonn. The text is in English, French, Italian, Latin or Spanish.

2390. Benjamin, Walter. GESAMMELTE SCHRIFTEN: UNTER MITWIRKUNG VON THEODORE W. ADORNO UND GERSHOM SCHOLEM. 12 Vols. Ed. by Rolf von Tiedemann and Hermann Schweppenhauser. Frankfurt am Main: Suhrkamp, 1980.

2391. Berding, Helmut. BIBLIOGRAPHIE ZUR GESCHICHTSTHEORIE. Gottingen: Vandenhoeck und Ruprecht, 1977.

2392. Biemel, Walter. MARTIN HEIDEGGER: AN ILLUSTRATED STUDY. Tr. of MARTIN HEIDEGGER IN SELBZEUGNISSEN UND BILDDOKUMENTEN. Reinbeck (bei Hamburg): Rowohlt, 1973. Tr. by J. L. Mehta. New York: Harcourt Brace Jovanovich, 1976.

This volume contains a bibliography on pages 187-206.

2393. Bieri, Peter, et al. TRANSCENDENTAL ARGUMENTS AND SCIENCE: ESSAYS IN EPISTEMOLOGY. Dordrecht and Boston: Reidel, 1979.

This book contains papers originally presented at a symposium held in July, 1977, and sponsored by the Center for Interdisciplinary Research of the University of Bielefeld.

2394. Bieri, Rolf. ANALYTISCHE PHILOSOPHIE DES GEISTES. Konigsten/TS: Hain, 1981.

A bibliography is included on pages 327-350.

2395. Bittner, Rudiger. MORALISCHE GEBOT ODER AUTONOMIE. Freiburg: Alber, 1983.

This is the author's doctoral thesis, Free University of Berlin, 1983.

2396. Bittner, Rudiger and Peter Pfaff. ASTHETISCHE URTEIL: BEITRAGE ZUR SPRACHANALYTISCHEN AESTHETIK. Cologne: Klepenheuer and Witsch, 1977.

2397. Bloch, Ernst. ESSAYS ON THE PHILOSOPHY OF MUSIC. Tr. of ZUR PHILOS-OPHIE DER MUSIK. Frankfurt am Main: Suhrkamp, 1974. Tr. by Peter Palmer. Cambridge and New York: Cambridge Univ. Press, 1985.

2398. Bloch, Ernst. GESAMTAUSGABE. Frankfurt am Main: Suhrkamp, 1985-.

2399. Bloch, Ernst. NATURAL LAW AND HUMAN DIGNITY. Tr. of NATURRECHT UND MENSCHLICHE WURDE. Frankfurt am Main: Suhrkamp, 1961. Tr. by Dennis J. Schmidt. Cambridge: MIT Press, 1985.

2400. Bloch, Ernst. THE PRINCIPLE OF HOPE. 3 Vols. Tr. of DAS PRINZIP HOFF-NUNG. Frankfurt am Main: Suhrkamp, 1959. Tr. by Neville Plaice, Stephen Plaice, and Paul Knight. Cambridge: MIT Press; Oxford: Basil Blackwell, 1986.

2401. Bloch, Ernst. REVOLUTION DER UTOPIE: TEXTE VON U. UBER ERNST BLOCH. Ed. by Helmut Reinicke. Frankfurt am Main and New York: Campus Verlag, 1979.

2402. Bloch, Ernst. TAGTRAUME VOM AUFRECHTEN GANG: SECHS INTERVIEWS MIT ERNST BLOCH. Ed. by Arno Munster. Frankfurt am Main: Suhrkamp, 1977.

2403. Bloch, Ernst, et al. AESTHETICS AND POLITICS. Ed. by Ronald Taylor. London: NLB, 1977.

2404. Blumenberg, Hans. THE LEGITIMACY OF THE MODERN AGE. Tr. of DIE LEGITIMITAT DER NEUZEIT. Vol. 1, SAKULARISIERUNG UND SELBSTBE-HAUPTUNG. Vol. 2, DER PROZESS DER THEORETISCHEN NEUGIERDE. Vol. 3, ASPEKTE DER EPOCHENSCHWELLE: CUSANER UND NOLANER. Frankfurt am Main: Suhrkamp, 1966. Tr. by Robert M. Wallace. Cambridge: MIT Press, 1983.

2405. Blumenberg, Hans. DIE LESBARKEIT DER WELT. Frankfurt am Main: Suhrkamp, 1981.

2406. Blumenberg, Hans. SCHIFFBRUCH MIT ZUSCHAUER: PARADIGMA E. DA SEINS METAPHER. Frankfurt am Main: Suhrkamp, 1979.

2407. Blumenberg, Hans. WIRKLICHKEITEN IN DENEN WIR LEBEN: AUFSATZE UND EINE REDE. Stuttgart: Reclam, 1981.

2408. Blumenberg, Hans. WORK ON MYTH. ARBEIT AM MYTHOS. Frankfurt am Main: Suhrkamp. 1979. Tr. by Robert M. Wallace. Cambridge: MIT Press, 1985.

2409. Bohme, Gernot, et al. EXPERIMENTELLE PHILOSOPHIE: URSPRUNGE AUTONOMER WISSENSCHAFTSENTWICKLUNG. Frankfurt am Main: Suhrkamp, 1977.

2410. Bolz, Norbert W. and Wolfgang Hubner. SPIEGEL AND GLEICHNIS: FES-TSCHRIFT FUR JACOB TAUBES. Wurzburg: Konigshausen and Neumann, 1983.

This volume contains contributions in English and French and a bibliography of Jacob Taubes's works.

2411. Brand, Gerd. WELT, GESCHICHTE, MYTHOS UND POLITIK. Berlin and New York: De Gruyter, 1977.

2412. Brandt, Reinhard. JOHN LOCKE; SYMPOSIUM, WOLFENBUTTEL, 1979. Berlin and New York: De Gruyter, 1981c1980.

The Symposium was held at the Herzog August Bibliotek on July 10-12, 1979.

2413. Brandt, Reinhard. RECHTSPHILOSOPHIE DIE AUFKLARUNG. Berlin and New York: De Gruyter, 1982.

This work was included in the Wolfenbuttel Symposium held at the Herzog August Bibliothek July 10-12, 1981.

2414. Brendel, Otto J. SYMBOLISM OF THE SPHERE: A CONTRIBUTION TO THE HISTORY OF EARLIER GREEK PHILOSOPHY. Tr. by Maria W. Brendel. Leiden: Brill, 1977.

2415. Brentano, Franz Clemens. ARISTOTLE AND HIS WORLD VIEW. Ed. by Rolf George and Roderick M. Chisholm. Tr. of ARISTOTELE UND SEINE WEL-

TANSCHAUUNG. Hamburg: Felix Meiner, 1977. Tr. by George Rolf and Roderick M. Chisholm. Berkeley: Univ. of California Press, 1978.

2416. Brentano, Franz Clemens. SENSORY AND NOETIC CONSCIOUSNESS: PSY-CHOLOGY FROM AN EMPIRICAL STANDPOINT III. English edition edited by Linda L. McAlister. Tr. of PSYCHOLOGIE VOM EMPIRISCHEN STANDPUNKT. Vol. 3, VOM SINNLICHEN UND NOETISCHEN BEWUSSTSEIN. Edited by Oscar Kraus. Leipzig: Dunker and Humblot, 1974. Tr. by Margaret Schattle and Linda L. McAlister. London: Routledge and Kegan Paul; New York: Humanities, 1981.

This volume covers Brentano's revisions of his earlier views on direct and oblique modes of perception, objects of mental acts, and perception of space and time.

2417. Brentano, Franz Clemens. THE THEORY OF CATEGORIES. Tr. of KATEGORI-ENLEHRE. Leipzig: F. Meiner, 1933. Tr. by Roderick Chisholm and Norbert Guterman. The Hague and Boston: Nijhoff, 1980.

2418. Brinkmann, Klaus. ARISTOTELES' ALLGEMEINE UND SPEZIELLE METAPHY-SIK. Berlin and New York: De Gruyter, 1979.

2419. Bubner, Rudiger. GESCHICHTSPROZESSE UND HANDLUNGSNORMEN: UNTERSUCHUNGEN ZUR PRAKTISCHEN PHILOSOPHIE. Frankfurt am Main: Suhrkamp, 1984.

2420. Bubner, Rudiger. HANDLUNG, SPRACHE UND VERNUNFT: GRUNDBE-GRIFFE PRAKTISCHER PHILOSOPHIE. Frankfurt am Main: Suhrkamp, 1976.

2421. Bubner, Rudiger. HEGEL UND GOETHE. Heidelberg: Winter, 1978.

2422. Bubner, Rudiger. MODERN GERMAN PHILOSOPHY. Tr. by Eric Matthews. Cambridge and New York: Cambridge Univ. Press, 1981.

This is a translation of the author's unpublished German manuscript.

2423. Bubner, Rudiger. ZUR SACHE DER DIALEKTIK. Stuttgart: P. Reclam, 1980.

2424. Bubner, Rudiger, et al. NEUE HEFTE FUR PHILOSOPHIE. Gottingen: Vanden-hoeck and Ruprecht, 1971-.

Vol. 10, MODERNE SOPHISTIK (1976); Vol. 11, PHILOSOPHISCHE PSYCHOLO-GIE? (1977); Vol. 12, SPINOZA: 1677-1977 (1977); Vol. 13, MARX' METHODOLOGIE (1978); Vol. 14, ZUR ZUKUNFT DER TRANSZENDENTALPHILOSOPHIE (1978); Vol. 15/16, AKTUALITAT DER ANTIKE (1979); Vol. 17, RECHT UND MORAL (1979); Vol. 18/19, ANSCHAUUNG ALS ASTHETISCHE KATEGORIE (1980); Vol. 20, TELEOLOGIE (1981); Vol. 21, POLITIKBEGRIFFE (1982); Vol. 22, KANTS ETHIK HEUTE (1983); Vol. 23, WIRKUNGEN HEIDEGGERS (1984); Vol. 24/25, KONTINGENZ (1985); Vol. 26, ARGUMENTATION IN DER PHILOSOPHIE (1986); Vol. 27/28, SUBJEKT UND PERSON (1988).

2425. Burkhardt, Hans. LOGIK UND SEMIOTIK IN DER PHILOSOPHIE VON LEIBNIZ. Munich: Philosophia, 1980.

2426. Burkhardt, Hans and Barry Smith. HANDBOOK OF METAPHYSICS AND ONTOLOGY. 2 Vols. Munich and Philadelphia: Philosophia Verlag, 1991.

This is a reference work concentrating on the metaphysical themes currently being debated in analytic philosophy. It contains more than 450 shorter articles on specific themes and methods in metaphysics and ontology as well as biographical essays summarizing the thought of those philosophers judged to be the most important in connection with those themes and methods. In addition, there are some twenty longer articles surveying historically and systematically the main area of metaphysics and ontology. Each article has an up-to-date bibligraphy. There is a detailed index of cross-references. Limiting itself to metaphysics and ontology in Western philosophy from the point of view of analytic philosophy, this handbook ranges from classical Greece to the present.

2427. Busch, Werner. ENTSTEHUNG DER KRITISCHEN RECHTSPHILOSOPHIE KANTS 1762-1780. Berlin and New York: De Gruyter, 1979.

2428. Cattepoel, Jan. ANARCHISMUS: GESTALTEN, GESCHICHTE, PROBLEME. Munich: Beck, 1979.

2429. Chisholm, Roderick M. and Rudolf Haller. DIE PHILOSOPHIE FRANZ BRENTANOS: BEITRAGE ZUR BRENTANO-KONFERENCZ GRAZ, 4-8 SEPTEMBER 1977. Amsterdam: Rodopi, 1978.

The volume contains contributions in English, French, and German.

2430. Christensen, Darrel E., et al. CONTEMPORARY GERMAN PHILOSOPHY. University Park: Pennsylvania State Univ. Press, 1982-.

This annual makes available essays in English by leading twentieth century German philosophers. This annual series also contains book reviews.

2431. Cramer, Konrad, et al. SPINOZA ETHIK UND IHRE FRUHE WIRKUNG. Wolfenbuttel: Herzog August Bibliothek, 1981.

This work is taken from the 8th Wolfenbuttel Symposium held at the Herzog August Bibliotek December 6-8, 1979.

2432. Cranach, Mario von. METHODS OF INFERENCE FROM ANIMAL TO HUMAN BEHAVIOR. Chicago: Aldine, 1976.

This book contains the Proceedings of the Conference on the Logic of Inference from Animal to Human Behavior, 1973, sponsored by the Maison des sciences de l'homme, Paris, with the aid of the Fonds national suisse de la recherche scientifique.

2433. David, Marian and Leopold Stubenberg. PHILOSOPHISCHE AUFSATZE ZU EHREN VON RODERICK M. CHISHOLM. Amsterdam: Rodopi, 1986.

2434. Deppert, Wolfgang, et al. EXACT SCIENCES AND THEIR PHILOSOPHICAL FOUNDATIONS=EXAKTE WISSENSCHAFTEN UND IHRE PHILOSOPHISCHE GRUNDLEGUNG: VORTRAGE DES INTERNATIONALEN HERMANN-WEYL-KONGRESSES, KIEL 1985. Frankfurt am Main and New York: Peter Lang, 1988.

The text is in both English and German.

2435. Detel, Wolfgang. SCIENTIA RERUM NATURA OCCULTARUM: METHODOLOGISCHE STUDIEN ZUR PHYSIK PIERRE GASSENDIS. Ed. by Gunther Patzig, et al. Berlin and New York: De Gruyter, 1978.

2436. Diaz, M. Richard. TOPICS IN THE LOGIC OF RELEVANCE. Munich: Philosophia, 1981.

2437. Diemer, Alwin. DIALEKTIK. Dusseldorf: Econ, 1976.

2438. Diemer, Alwin. HERMENEUTIK. Dusseldorf: Econ, 1977.

2439. Diemer, Alwin. PHILOSOPHISCHE ANTHROPOLOGIE. Dusseldorf: Econ, 1978.

2440. Dilthey, Wilhelm. DESCRIPTIVE PSYCHOLOGY AND HISTORICAL UNDER-
STANDING. Tr. of IDEEN UBER EINE BESCHREIBENDE UND ZERLIEDERNDE
PSYCHOLOGIE and DAS VERSTEHEN ANDERER PERSONEN UND IHRER
LEBENAUSSERUNGEN, originally published in the authors' GESAMMELTE SCHRIF-
TEN, 1924-1927. Tr. by R. M. Zaner and K. L. Heiges. The Hague: Nijhoff, 1977.

2441. Dilthey, Wilhelm. GESAMMELTE SCHRIFTEN. SELECTIONS. 1983. TEXTE
ZUR KRITIK DER HISTORISCHEN VERNUNFT. Ed. by Hans-Ulrich Lessing.
Gottingen: Vandenhoek and Ruprecht, 1983.

2442. Dilthey, Wilhelm. SELECTED WORKS. Ed. by Rudolf A. Makkreel and Frithjof
Rodi. Princeton: Princeton Univ. Press, 1985-.

Volume 5, POETRY AND EXPERIENCE, is the first published volume in this project
ed six volume English translation of the main works of Wilhelm Dilthey.

2443. Dilthey, Wilhelm. SELECTED WRITINGS. Ed. by Hans Peter Rickman. Cambridge
and New York: Cambridge Univ. Press, 1976.

2444. Drue, Hermann. PSYCHOLOGIE AUS DEM BEGRIFF: HEGELS PERSONLICH-
KEITSTHEORIE. Berlin and New York: De Gruyter, 1976.

2445. Durbin, Paul T. and Friedrich Rapp. PHILOSOPHY AND TECHNOLOGY. Dordrecht and Boston: Reidel, 1983.

This is a revised and enlarged English version of the Proceedings of the joint German-
North American Conference on the Philosophy of Technology, held at the Werner-
Reimers Stiftung, Bad Homburg, West Germany, April 7-11, 1981. The proceedings were
published in German in an abridged version as TECHNIKPHILOSOPHIE IN DER
DISKUSSION. F. Vieweg, 1982.

2446. Dutz, Klaus. ZEICHENTHEORIE UND SPRACHWISSENSCHAFT BEI G.W.
LEIBNIZ=EINE KRITISCH ANNOTIERTE BIBLIOGRAPHIE DER SEKUNDARLIT-
ERATUR. MIT EINEM ANHANG, SEKUNDAKITERATUR ZUR SPRACH-
FORSCHUNG IM 17 JAHRHUNDERT VOM ULRIKE KLINKHAMMER. Munster:
Institut fur Allegemeine Sprachwissenschaft der Westfalischen Wilhelms-Universitat, 1983.

2447. Engfer, Hans-Jurgen. PHILOSOPHIE ALS ANALYSIS: STUDIEN ZUR EN-
TWICKLUNG PHILOSOPHICHER ANALYSISKONZEPTIONEN UNTER DEM
EINFLUSS MATHEMATISCHER METHODENMODELLE IM 17. UND FRUHEN 18.
JAHRHUNDERT. Stuttgart-Bad Cannstatt: Frommann-Holzboog, 1982.

This volume includes a summary in English as well as a bibliography on pages 264-275.

2448. Engfer, Hans-Jurgen. PHILOSOPHISCHE ASPEKTE SCHULISCHER FACHER
UND PADAGOGISCHER PRAXIS. Munich, Vienna and Baltimore: Urban und
Schwarzenberg, 1978.

The volume contains a bibliography on pages 206-213.

2449. Enskat, Rainer. KANTS THEORIE DES GEOMETRISCHEN GEGENSTANDES:
UNTERSUCHUNGEN UBER DIE VORAUSSETZUNGEN DER ENTDECKBARKEIT
GEOMETRISCHER GEGENSTANDE BEI KANT. Berlin and New York: De Gruyter,
1978.

2450. Eschbach, Achim and Viktoria Eschbach-Szabo. BIBLIOGRAPHY OF SEMIOTICS.

2 Vols. Amsterdam and Philadelphia: John Benjamin, 1986.

Covering the years 1975-1985, this bibliography has been compiled at the Institute for Semiotic and Communication Research in Essen. This work contains 10,000 entries ordered alphabetically and with many cross-references, a very detailed subject and name index, and an index of reviews. Supplements will be available.

2451. Fellmann, Ferdinand. GELEBTE PHILOSOPHIE IN DEUTSCHLAND: DENK-FORMEN DER LEBENSWELT PHANOMENOLOGIE UND DER KRITISCHEN THEORIE. Freiburg: Alber, 1983.

2452. Fellmann, Ferdinand. PHANOMENOLOGIE UND EXPRESSIONISMUS. Freiburg: K. Alber, 1982.

2453. Fellmann, Ferdinand. DAS VICO-AXIOM, DER MENSCH MACHT DIE GESCHICHTE. Freiburg im Breisgau and Munich: K. Alber, 1976.

2454. Ferber, Rafael. PLATOS IDEE DES GUTEN. Sankt Augustin: H. Recharz, 1984.

There is a bibliography on pages 233-243.

2455. Ferber, Rafael. ZENONS PARADOXIEN DER BEWEGUNG UND DIE STRUK-TUR VON RAUM UND ZEIT. Munich: C. H. Beck, 1981.

2456. Fleischer, Margot. HERMENEUTISCHE ANTHROPOLOGIE. Berlin and New York: De Gruyter, 1976.

2457. Frank, Manfred. DAS INDIVIDUELLE ALLGEMEINE: TEXTSTRUKTURIE-RUNG UND INTERPRETATION NACH SCHLEIERMACHER. Frankfurt am Main: Suhrkamp, 1977.

2458. Frank, Manfred. DAS SAGBARE UND DAS UNSAGBARE: STUDIEN ZUR NEUESTEN FRANZOSISCHEN HERMENEUTIK UND TEXTTHEORIE. Frankfurt am Main: Suhrkamp, 1980.

2459. Franzen, Winfried. MARTIN HEIDEGGER. Stuttgart: J. B. Metzler, 1976.

This short introduction contains important bibliographies.

2460. Frege, Gottlob. COLLECTED PAPERS ON MATHEMATICS, LOGIC AND PHILOSOPHY. Ed. by Brian McGuinness. Tr. of KLEINE SCHRIFTEN. Ed. by Ignacio Angelli. Hildesheim: G. Olms, 1967. Tr. by Max Black, et al. Oxford and New York: B. Blackwell, 1984.

This is a translation of most of the papers which appeared in KLEINE SCHRIFTEN.

2461. Frege, Gottlob. LOGICAL INVESTIGATIONS. Ed. by Peter Thomas Geach. Tr. of LOGISCHE UNTERSUCHUNGEN. Vandenhoech and Ruprecht, 1966. Tr. by Peter Thomas Geach and R. H. Stoothoff. Oxford: Blackwell; New Haven: Yale Univ. Press, 1977.

2462. Frege, Gottlob. PHILOSOPHICAL AND MATHEMATICAL CORRESPONDENCE. Abridged from the German ed. by Brian McGuinness. Ed. by Gottfried Gabriel, et al. Tr. of selections from Vol. 2 of NACHGELASSENESCHRIFTEN UND WISSENSCHAF-TLICHER BRIEFWECHSEL. Hamburg: Meiner, 1969- 1976. Tr. by Hans Kaal. Chicago: Univ. of Chicago Press; Oxford: B. Blackwell, 1980.

2463. Frege, Gottlob. TRANSLATIONS FROM THE PHILOSOPHICAL WRITINGS

OF GOTTLOB FREGE. Ed. by Peter Thomas Geach and Max Black. 3d ed. Totowa, NJ: Rowan and Littlefield, 1980.

2464. Freising, Wolfgang. KRITISCHE PHILOSOPHIE UND GLUCKSELIGKEIT: KANTS AUSEINANDERSETZUNG MIT EUDAMONISMUS SEINER ZEIT. Luneburg: J. Schmidt-Neubauer, 1983.

2465. Freudenthal, Gideon. ATOM AND INDIVIDUAL IN THE AGE OF NEWTON: ON THE GENESIS OF THE MECHANISTIC WORLD VIEW. Tr. of ATOM UND INDIVIDUUM IM ZEITALTER NEWTONS: ZUR GENESEDER MECHANISTIS-CHEN NATUR- UND SOZIALPHILOSOPHIE. Frankfurt am Main: Suhrkamp, 1982. Tr. by Peter McLaughlin. Dordrecht and Boston: Reidel, 1986.

2466. Fries, Jakob Friedrich. DIALOGUES ON MORALITY AND RELIGION. Ed. by Dewi Zephaniah Phillips. Tr. by David Walford. Totowa, NJ: Barnes & Noble; Oxford: Blackwell, 1982.

2467. Funke, Gerhard. PHENOMENOLOGY, METAPHYSICS OR METHOD? Tr. of PHANOMENOLOGIE, METAPHYSIK ODER METHODE?. Bonn: H. Bouvier, 1966. Tr. by David J. Parent. Series in Continental Thought, Vol. 13. Athens: Ohio Univ. Press, 1987.

This volume contains an extensive bibliography on pages 179-223.

2468. Gadamer, Hans-Georg. DIALOGUE AND DIALECTIC: EIGHT HERMENEU-TICAL STUDIES ON PLATO. Tr. by P. Christopher Smith. New Haven: Yale Univ. Press, 1980.

2469. Gadamer, Hans-Georg. HEGEL'S DIALECTIC: FIVE HERMENEUTICAL STUD-IES. Tr. of HEGELS DIALEKTIK: FUNF HERMENEUTISCHE STUDIEN. Tubingen: Mohr, 1971. Tr. by P. Christopher Smith. New Haven: Yale Univ. Press, 1976.

2470. Gadamer, Hans-Georg. THE IDEA OF THE GOOD IN PLATONIC-ARISTOTE-LIAN PHILOSOPHY. Tr. of DIE IDEE DES GUTEN ZWISCHEN PLATO UND ARISTOTELES. Heidelberg: Winter, 1978. Translated with an introduction and annotations by P. Christopher Smith. New Haven and London: Yale Univ. Press, 1986.

2471. Gadamer, Hans-Georg. KLEINE SCHRIFTEN. Vol. 1, PHILOSOPHIE: HERME-NEUTIK; Vol. 2, INTERPRETATIONEN; Vol. 3, IDEE UND SPRACHE: PLATON, HUSSERL, HEIDEGGER; and Vol. 4, VARIATIONEN. Tubingen: Mohr, 1967-1977.

2472. Gadamer, Hans-Georg. PHILOSOPHICAL APPRENTICESHIPS. Tr. of PHILOSO-PHISCHE LEHRJAHRE: EINE RUCKSCHAU. Frankfurt am Main: Klostermann, 1977. Tr. by Robert R. Sullivan. Cambridge: MIT Press, 1985.

2473. Gadamer, Hans-Georg. PHILOSOPHICAL HERMENEUTICS. Ed. by David E. Linge. Berkeley: Univ. of California Press, 1976.

This is a translation of essays selected from Hans-Georg Gadamer's KLEINE SCHRIF-TEN published in three volumes by Mohr Verlag, Tubingen, 1967-1972.

2474. Gadamer, Hans-Georg. REASON IN THE AGE OF SCIENCE. Tr. by Frederick G. Lawrence. Cambridge: MIT Press, 1981.

Included in this volume are selected essays from the author's VERNUNFT IM ZEIT-ALTER DER WISSENSCHAFT. Frankfurt am Main, 1976, and two others not in that work.

2475. Gadamer, Hans-Georg. TRUTH AND METHOD. 2d ed. Tr. of WAHRHEIT UND DIE METHOD: GRUNDZUGE EINER PHILOSOPHISCHEN HERMENEU-TIK. Tubingen: Mohr, 1960. Tr. revised by Joel Weinsheimer and Donald C. Marshall. New York: Crossroad, 1989.

2476. Gadamer, Hans-Georg, et al. WAS IST LITERATUR? Ed. by Ernst Wolfgang Orth. Phanomenologische Forschungen. Freiburg im Breisgau: K. Alber, 1981.

2477. Gadamer, Hans-Georg and Gottfried Boehm. SEMINAR, DIE HERMENEUTIK UND DIE WISSENSCHAFTEN. Frankfurt am Main: Suhrkamp, 1978.

2478. Gadamer, Hans-Georg and Gottfried Boehm. SEMINAR, PHILOSOPHISCHE HERMENEUTIK. Frankfurt am Main: Suhrkamp, 1976.

2479. Gadamer, Hans-Georg and Carl Friedrich von Weizsacker. HEIDEGGER: THE UNIVERSITY OF FREIBURG MEMORIAL LECTURES. Ed. by Werner Marx. Tr. of HEIDEGGER, FREIBURGER UNIVERSITATVORTRAGE ZU SEINEM GEDENKEN. Freiburg and Munich: Alber, 1977. Tr. by Steven W. Davis. Pittsburgh: Duquesne Univ. Press, 1982.

2480. Gauvin, Joseph. WORTINDEX ZU HEGELS PHANOMENOLOGIE DES GEISTES UNTER MITARBEIT VON CHARLES BAILLY. Bonn: Bouvier, 1977,1984.

The introduction is in English, French, and German. This index in based on the Johannes Hoffmeister edition of Hegel's work, sixth printing, Hamburg, 1952.

2481. Gehlen, Arnold. GESAMTAUSGABE. Vol. 1, PHILOSOPHISCHE SCHRIFTEN, I (1925-1933); Vol. 2, PHILOSOPHISCHE SCHRIFTEN II (1933-1938); Vol. 4, PHILOSOPHISCHE ANTHROPOLOGIE UND HANDLUNGSLEHRE. Ed. by Lothar Samson. Frankfurt am Main: Klostermann, 1978-.

Volume 4 was edited by Karl-Siegbert Rehberg with the collaboration of Heinrich Wahlen and Albert Bilo.

2482. Gehlen, Arnold. ZEIT-BILDER: ZUR SOZIOLOGIE UND ASTHETIK DER MODERNEN MALEREI. Ed. by Karl-Siegbert Rehberg. Frankfurt am Main: Klostermann, 1986.

2483. Gethmann-Seifert, Annemarie and Otto Poggeler. HEIDEGGER UND DIE PRAK-TISCHE PHILOSOPHIE. Frankfurt: Suhrkamp, 1988.

2484. Gloy, Karen. EINHEIT UND MANNIGFALTIGKEIT: EINE STRUKTURANA-LYSE DES "UND": SYSTEMATISCHE UNTERSUCHUNGEN ZUM EINHEITS- UND MANNIGFALTIGSKEITBEGRIFF BEI PLATON, FICHTE, HEGEL SOWIE IN DER MODERNE. Berlin and New York: De Gruyter, 1981.

2485. Gloy, Karen. DIE KANTISCHE THEORIE DER NATURWISSENSCHAFT: EINE STRUKTURANALYSE IHRER MOGLICHKEIT, IHRES UMFANGS UND IHRER GRENZEN. Berlin and New York: De Gruyter, 1976.

2486. Gorland, Ingtraud. TRANSZENDENZ UND SELBST: EINE PHASE IN HEIDEG-GERS DENKEN. Frankfurt am Main: Klostermann, 1981.

2487. Grassi, Ernesto. HEIDEGGER AND THE QUESTION OF RENAISSANCE HUMANISM: FOUR STUDIES. Binghamton, NY: Center for Medieval and Early Renaissance Studies, 1983.

2488. Grassi, Ernesto and Hugo Schamale. DAS GRESPRACH ALS EREIGNIS: EIN

SEMIOTISCHEN PROBLEM. Munich: Fink, 1982.

2489. Grimm, Rudiger Hermann. NIETZSCHE'S THEORY OF KNOWLEDGE. Berlin and New York: De Gruyter, 1977.

2490. Gruber, Joachim. KOMMENTAR ZU BOETHIUS DE CONSOLATIONE PHILO-SOPHIAE. Berlin and New York: De Gruyter, 1978.

2491. Habermas, Jurgen. COMMUNICATION AND THE EVOLUTION OF SOCIETY. Tr. of four essays from ZUR REKONSTRUKTION DES HISTORISCHEN MATERIAL-ISMUS. Frankfurt am Main: Suhrkamp, 1976, and one essay from SPRACHPRAGMATIK UND PHILOSOPHIE. Frankfurt am Main: Suhrkamp, 1976. Tr. by Thomas McCarthy. London: Heinemann; Boston: Beacon Press, 1979.

2492. Habermas, Jurgen. PHILOSOPHICAL-POLITICAL PROFILES. Tr. of the revised edition of PHILOSOPHISCH-POLITISCHE PROFILE. Frankfurt am Main: Suhrkamp, 1981. Tr. by Frederick G. Lawrence. London: Heinemann; Cambridge: MIT Press, 1983.

These essays originally appeared in German as parts of Habermas's books PHILOSO-PHISCH-POLITISCHE PROFILE published by Suhrkamp Verlag in 1971 and KULTUR UND KRITIK. VERSTREUTE AUFSATZE, also published by Suhrkamp in 1973. These essays range over such German-trained thinkers as M. Heidegger, K. Jaspers, K. Lowith, E. Bloch, T. Adorno, W. Benjamin, H. Marcuse, H. Arendt, H.-G. Gadamer, G. Scholem, and others.

2493. Habermas, Jurgen. THE THEORY OF COMMUNICATIVE ACTION. Vol. 1, REASON AND THE RATIONALIZATION OF SOCIETY. Vol. 2, LIFEWORLD AND SYSTEM: A CRITIQUE OF FUNCTIONALIST REASON. Tr. of THEORIE DES KOMMUNIKATIVEN HANDELNS. 1st. ed. Frankfurt am Main: Suhrkamp, 1981. Tr. by Thomas McCarthy. Boston: Beacon Press, 1984-1987.

2494. Hagler, Rudolf-Peter. PLATONS "PARMENIDES": PROBLEME DER INTERPRE-TATION. Berlin and New York: De Gruyter, 1983.

2495. Hartmann, Klaus. DIE ONTOLOGISCHE OPTION: STUDIEN ZU HEGELS PROPADEUTIK, SCHELLINGS HEGEL-KRITIK UND HEGELS PHANOME-NOLOGIE DES GEISTES. Berlin and New York: De Gruyter, 1976.

2496. Harvey, Irene E. DERRIDA AND THE ECONOMY OF DIFFERANCE. Blooming-ton: Univ. of Indiana Press, 1985.

2497. Heckmann, Reinhard, et al. NATUR UND SUBJEKTIVITAT: ZUR AUSEINAN-DERSETZUNG MIT DER NATURPHILOSOPHIE DES JUNGEN SCHELLING: REFERATE, VOTEN UND PROTOKOLLE DER II INTERNATIONALEN SCHELL-ING-TAGUNG ZURICH 1983. Stuttgart- Bad Cannstatt: Frommann-Holzboog, 1985.

2498. Heidegger, Martin. THE BASIC PROBLEMS OF PHENOMENOLOGY. Tr. of: DIE GRUNDPROBLEME DER PHENOMENOLOGIE. Frankfurt am Main: Kloster-mann, 1975. Translation, Introduction and Lexicon by Albert Hofstadter. Bloomington: Indian Univ. Press, 1982.

Heidegger explains what he calls the ontological difference. This volume, which is Bd. 24 of the GESAMTAUSGABE, places the ontological orientation of BEING AND TIME in its philosophical context.

2499. Heidegger, Martin. GESAMTAUSGABE. Ed. by Friedrich Wilhelm von Hermann. Frankfurt am Main: Klostermann, 1976-.

2500. Heidegger, Martin. HISTORY OF THE CONCEPT OF TIME: PROLEGOMENA. Tr. of PROLEGOMENA ZUR GESCHICHTE DES ZEITBEGRIFFS. Frankfurt am Main: Klostermann, 1979. Tr. by Theodore Kisiel. Bloomington: Indiana Univ. Press, 1985.

This is Bd. 20 of the GESAMTAUSGABE.

2501. Heidegger, Martin. THE METAPHYSICAL FOUNDATIONS OF LOGIC. Tr. of METAPHYSICHE ANFANGSGRUNDE DER LOGIK IM AUSGANG VON LEIBNIZ. Frankfurt am Main: Klostermann, 1978. Tr. by Michael Heim. Bloomington: Indiana Univ. Press, 1984.

This volume is central for understanding the transition in Heidegger's thought from the existential analysis of BEING AND TIME to the overcoming of metaphysics in his later philosophy.

2502. Heidegger, Martin. NIETZSCHE. Vol.1, THE WILL TO POWER AS ART. Vol.2, THE ETERNAL RECURRANCE OF THE SAME. Vol. 3, THE WILL TO POWER AS KNOWLEDGE AND AS METAPHYSICS. Vol. 4, NIHILISM. Tr. of NIETZSCHE. 2 Vols. Pfullingin: Neske, 1961. Translated from the German with notes and an analysis by David Farrell Krell. Volume 3 was translated by Joan Stambaugh, David Farrell Krell, and Frank A. Capuzzi. Volume 4 was translated by Frank A. Capuzzi. San Francisco: Harper and Row, 1979-1987.

2503. Heidegger, Martin. THE QUESTION CONCERNING TECHNOLOGY AND OTHER ESSAYS. 1st ed. Tr. by W. Lovitt. New York: Harper and Row, 1977.

This work includes essays which originally appeared in DIE TECHNIK UND DIE KEHRE, HOLZWEGE. Pfullingen: Neske, 1962 and VORTRAGE UND AUFSATZE. Pfullingen: Neske, 1954. Titles of the essays are: The Turning, The Word of Nietzsche: "God is Dead", The Age Of The World Picture, and Science and Reflection.

2504. Heidegger, Martin. SCHELLING'S TREATISE ON THE ESSENCE OF HUMAN FREEDOM. Tr. of SCHELLINGS ABHANDLUNG UBER DAS WESEN DER MENSCHLICHEN FREIHEIT. Ed. by Hildegard Fieck. Tubingen: M. Niemeyer, 1971. Tr. by Joan Stambaugh. Series in Continental Thought, Vol. 8. Athens: Ohio Univ. Press, 1985.

2505. Held, Klaus. HERAKLIT, PARMENIDES UND DER ANFANG VON PHILOSO-PHIE UND WISSENSCHAFT: EINE PHANOMENOLOGISCHE BESINNUNG. Berlin and New York: De Gruyter, 1980.

Part two is a revision of the author's Habilitationsschrift, Cologne, 1969, presented under the title: HERAKLIT.

2506. Hempel, Carl Gustav. ASPEKTE WISSENSCHAFTLICHER ERKLARUNG. Berlin and New York: De Gruyter, 1977.

2507. Hempel, Carl Gustav, et al. METHODOLOGY, EPISTEMOLOGY AND PHILOSO-PHY OF SCIENCE: ESSAYS IN HONOUR OF WOLFGANG STEGMULLER ON THE OCCASION OF HIS 60TH BIRTHDAY, JUNE 3, 1983. Dordrecht and Boston: Reidel, 1983.

The text, in English and German, is reprinted from ERKENNTNIS, Vol. 19, nos. 1, 2, and 3.

2508. Hoffe, Otfried. UBER JOHN RAWLS' THEORIE DER GERECHTIGKEIT. Freiburg and Frankfurt am Main: Suhrkamp, 1977.

2509. Holenstein, Elmar. LINGUISTIK, SEMIOTIK, HERMENEUTIK: PLADOYERS FUR EINE STRUKTURALE PHANOMENOLOGIE. Frankfurt am Main: Suhrkamp, 1976.

2510. Holz, Harald and Ernest Wolf-Gazo. WHITEHEAD AND DER PROZESSBEGRIFF: BEITRAGE ZUR PHILOSOPHIE ALFRED NORTH WHITEHEADS AUF DEM ERSTEN INTERNATIONALEN WHITEHEAD-SYMPOSION 1981=WHITEHEAD AND THE IDEA OF PROCESS: PROCEEDINGS OF THE FIRST INTERNATIONAL WHITEHEAD-SYMPOSIUM 1981. Freiburg: K. Alber, 1984.

These essays on Whitehead's philosophy are in English and German.

2511. Holzhey, Helmut and Walther Christoph Zimmerli. ESOTERIK UND EXOTERIK DER PHILOSOPHIE: BEITRAGE ZU GESCHICHTE UND SINN PHILOSOPHISCHER SELBSTBESTIMMUNG: RUDOLF W. MEYER ZUM 60. GEBURTSTAG. Basel and Stuttgart: Schwabe, 1977.

2512. Hornung, Klaus. DER FASZINIERENDE IRRTUM-KARL MARX UND DIE FOLGEN. Freiburg im Breisgau: Herder, 1978.

2513. Horstmann, Rolf-Peter. SEMINAR, DIALEKTIK IN DER PHILOSOPHIE HEGELS. Frankfurt am Main: Suhrkamp, 1978.

2514. Hossenfelder, Malte. KANTS KONSTITUTIONSTHEORIE UND DIE TRANZENDENTALE DEDUKTION. Berlin and New York: De Gruyter, 1978.

2515. Hubig, Christoph and Wolfert von Rahden. KONSEQUENZEN KRITISCHER WISSENSCHAFTSTHEORIE. Berlin and New York: De Gruyter, 1978.

There is a bibliography on pages 353-389.

2516. Hubner, Kurt. CRITIQUE OF SCIENTIFIC REASON. Tr. of KRITIK DER WISSENSCHAFTLICHEN VERNUNFT. Freiburg and Munich: K. Alber, 1978. Tr. by Paul R. Dixon, Jr. and Hollis M. Dixon. Chicago: Univ. of Chicago Press, 1983.

2517. Hubner, Kurt and Werner Becker. OBJEKTIVITAT IN DEN NATUR UND GEISTESWISSENSCHAFTEN. Hamburg: Hoffmann and Campe, 1976.

2518. Hubner, Kurt and Jule Vuillemin. WISSENSCHAFTLICHE UND NICHTWISSENSCHAFTLICHE RATIONALITAT: EIN DEUTSCH- FRANZOSISCHES KOLLOQUIUM. Stuttgart-Bad Canstatt: Frommann-Holzboog, 1983.

2519. Hubscher, Arthur. SCHOPENHAUER-BIBLIOGRAPHIE. Stuttgart-Bad Cannstatt: Frommann-Holzboog, 1981.

2520. Hufnagel, Erwin. EINFUHRUNG IN DIE HERMENEUTIK. Stuttgart, Berlin, Cologne, and Mainz: Kohlhammer, 1976.

2521. Huppertz, Norbert. DIE WERTKRISE DES MENSCHEN: PHILOS. ETHIK IN D. HEUTIGEN WELT. Meisenheim am Glan: Hain, 1979.

2522. Husserl, Edmund. COLLECTED WORKS. Tr. of HUSSERLIANA: GESAMMELTE WERKE. The Hague: Nijhoff, 1950. The Hague and Boston: Nijhoff, 1980-.

The translations are prepared under the auspices of the Husserl Archives at Louvain.

2523. Husserl, Edmund. PHENOMENOLOGICAL PSYCHOLOGY: LECTURES, SUMMER SEMESTER, 1925. Tr. of PHANOMENOLOGISCHE PSYCHOLOGIE from

HUSSERLIANA published in the Hague in 1962. Tr. by John Scanlon. The Hague: Nijhoff, 1977.

2524. Jakobson, Roman, et al. DAS ERBE HEGELS II. Frankfurt am Main: Suhrkamp, 1984.

This book consists of speeches given on the occasion of the fifth Hegel award to Roman Jakobson on June 22, 1982.

2525. Janke, Wolfgang. HISTORISCHE DIALEKTIK: DESTRUKTION DIALEKTISCHER GRUNDFORM VON KANT BIS MARX. Berlin and New York: De Gruyter, 1977.

2526. Jaspers, Karl. KARL JASPERS: BASIC PHILOSOPHICAL WRITINGS: SELEC-TIONS. Edited, translated, with introductions by Edith Ehrlich, Leonard H. Ehrlich, and George B. Pepper. Series in Continental Thought, Vol. 10. Athens: Ohio Univ. Press, 1986.

2527. Jaspers, Karl. NOTIZEN ZU MARTIN HEIDEGGER. Ed. by Hans Saner. Munich and Zurich: Piper, 1978.

2528. Jauss, Hans Robert. AESTHETIC EXPERIENCE AND HERMENEUTICS. Tr. of ASTHETISCHE ERFAHRUNG UND LITERARISCHE HERMENEUTIC. Munich: Fink, 1977. Tr. from the German by Michael Shaw. Minneapolis: Univ. of Minnesota Press, 1982.

2529. Joas, Hans. G. H. MEAD: A CONTEMPORARY RE-EXAMINATION OF HIS THOUGHT. Tr. of PRAKTISCHE INTERSUBJEKTIVAT: D. ENTWICKLUNG D. WERKES VON GEORGE HERBERT MEAD. Frankfurt am Main: Suhrkamp, 1980. Tr. by Raymond Meyer. Cambridge: MIT press, 1985.

There is a bibliography on pages 240-262.

2530. Kanitscheider, Bernulf. MODERNE NATURPHILOSOPHIE. Wurzburg: Konighau-sen and Neumann, 1984c1983.

2531. Kanitscheider, Bernulf. PHILOSOPHIE UND MODERNE PHYSIK: SYSTEME, STRUKTUREN, SYNTHESEN. Darmstadt: Wissenschaftliche Buchgesellschaft, 1979.

2532. Kanitscheider, Bernulf. SPRACHE UND ERKENNTNIS. FESTSCHRIFT FUR GERHARD FREY ZUM 60. GEBURTSTAG. Innsbruck: Institut fur Sprachwissenschaft der Universitat Innsbruck, 1976.

The volume contains a bibliography of Frey's works on pages 335-346.

2533. Kanitscheider, Bernulf. VOM ABSOLUTEN RAUM ZU DYNAMISCHEN GEO-METRIE. Mannheim, Vienna and Zurich: Bibliographiches Institut, B.-I. Wissenschafts-verlag, 1976.

2534. Kanitscheider, Bernulf. WISSENSCHAFTSTHEORIE DER NATURWIS-SENSCHAFT. Berlin and New York: De Gruyter, 1981.

2535. Kaufmann, Felix. INFINITE IN MATHEMATICS: LOGICO-MATHEMATICAL WRITINGS. Ed. by Brian McGuinness. Tr. of DAS UNENDLICHE IN DER MATHE-MATIK UND SEINE AUSSCHALTUNG: EINE UNTERSUCHUNG UBER DIE GRUNDLAGEN DER MATHEMATIK. Leipzig and Vienna: F. Deuticke, 1930. Tr. by Paul Foulkes. Vienna Circle Collection, Vol. 9. Dordrecht and Boston: Reidel, 1978.

The volume contains an introduction by Ernest Nagel, the American philosopher of science, and a bibliography of the published works of Felix Kaufmann on pages 225-228.

2536. Kaulbach, Friedrich. DAS PRINZIP HANDLUNG IN DER PHILOSOPHIE KANT. Berlin and New York: De Gruyter, 1978.

2537. Kohlenberger, Helmut Karl. REASON, ACTION, AND EXPERIENCE: ESSAYS IN HONOR OF RAYMOND KLIBANSKY. Hamburg: Meiner, 1979.

The essays are in English, German and French. There is a bibliography on pages 243-250.

2538. Kohnke, Klaus Christian. THE RISE OF NEO-KANTIANISM: GERMAN ACADE-MIC PHILOSOPHY BETWEEN IDEALISM AND POSITIVISM. Tr. of ENSTEHUNG UND AUFSTIEG DES NEUKANTIANISMUS: DIE DEUTSCHE UNIVERSITATSPHI-LOSOPHIE ZWISCHEN IDEALISMUS UND POSITIVISMUS. Frankfurt am Main: Suhrkamp, 1986. Tr. by R.J. Hollingdale. Cambridge and New York: Cambridge Univ. Press, 1991.

2539. Kopper, Joachim. REFLEXION UND DETERMINATION. Berlin and New York: De Gruyter, 1976.

2540. Korsch, Karl. GESAMTAUSGABE. Bd. 1, RECHT, GEIST UND KULTUR, SCHRIFTEN 1908-1918. Bd. 2, RATEBEWEGUNG UND KLASSENKAMPF, SCHRIFTEN ZUR PRAXIS DER ARBEITERBEWEGUNG 1919-1923. Ed. by Michael Buckmiller. Frankfurt am Main: Europaische Verlagsanstalt, 1980-.

2541. Kraft, Viktor. FOUNDATIONS FOR A SCIENTIFIC ANALYSIS OF VALUE. Ed. by Henk L. Mulder. Tr. of DIE GRUNDLAGEN EINER WISSENSCHAFTLICHEN WERTLEHRE. 2d. ed., Vienna: Springer, 1951. Tr. by Elizabeth Hughes Schneewind. Vienna Circle Collection, Vol. 15. Dordrecht and Boston: Reidel, 1981.

2542. Krebs, Inge. PAUL NATORPS ASTHETIK: EINE SYSTEMTHEORETISCHE UNTERSUCHUNG. Berlin and New York: De Gruyter, 1976.

2543. Kreimendahl, Lother. HUMES VERBORGENER RATIONALISMUS. New York and Berlin: De Gruyter, 1982.

The author elucidates and examines what he claims to be the hidden rationalism in Hume's analysis of causality, his theory of possibility, and his axiom of the difference between the distinguishable and the separable and between truths of fact and relations of ideas.

2544. Krings, Hermann. DIE ENTFREMDUNG ZWISCHEN SCHELLING UND HEGEL (1801- 1807): VORGETRAGEN AM 7 MAI 1976. Munich: Verlag der Bayrischen Akademie der Wissenschaften; in Kommission bei C. H. Beck, 1977.

2545. Krings, Hermann. ORDO: PHILOSOPHISCH-HISTORISCHE GRUNDLEGUNG EINER ABERLANDISCHEN IDEE. 2d. rev ed. Hamburg: F. Meiner, 1982.

2546. Krings, Hermann. SYSTEM AND FREIHEIT: GESAMMELTE AUFSATZE. Freiburg: K. Alber, 1980.

2547. Kummer, Irene Elisabeth. BLAISE PASCAL, DAS HEIL IM WIDERSPRUCH: STUDIEN ZU DEN PENSEE IM ASPEKT PHILOSOPHISCH-THEOLOGISCHER ANSCHAUUNGEN, SPRACHLICHER GESTALTUNG UND REFLEXION. Berlin and New York: De Gruyter, 1978.

2548. Landgrebe, Ludwig. FAKTIZITAT UND INDIVIDUATION: STUDIEN ZU DEN GRUNDFRAGEN DER PHANOMENOLOGIE. Hamburg: F. Meiner, 1981.

2549. Landgrebe, Ludwig. PHANOMENOLOGIE UND PRAXIS. Freiburg and Munich: K. Alber, 1976.

This volume consists of contributions by Ludwig Landgrebe and others.

2550. Landgrebe, Ludwig. PHENOMENOLOGY OF EDMUND HUSSERL: SIX ESSAYS. Ed. by Donn Welton. New York: Cornell Univ. Press, 1981.

The work discusses Husserl's criticism of Cartesianism and his integration of history and the living world in his later writings.

2551. Landgrebe, Ludwig. DER WEG DER PHANOMENOLOGIE: DAS PROBLEM EINER URSPRUNGLICHEN ERFAHRUNG. Gutersloh: Gutersloher Verlagshaus Mohn, 1978.

2552. Landmann, Michael. PHILOSOPHISCHE ANTHROPOLOGIE: MENSCHLICHE SELBSTDEUTUNG IN GESCHICHTE UND GEGENWART. Berlin and New York: De Gruyter, 1976.

2553. Lang, Dieter. WERTUNG UND ERKENNTNIS: UNTERSUCHUNGEN ZU AXEL HAGERSTROM'S MORALTHEORIE. Amsterdam: Rodopi, 1981.

2554. LaPointe, Francois H. EDMUND HUSSERL AND HIS CRITICS: AN INTERNA-TIONAL BIBLIOGRAPHY, 1894-1979. Bibliographies of Famous Philosophers, Vol. 4. Bowling Green, OH: Philosophy Documentation Center, 1980.

This volume contains a complete bibliography of Husserl's writings and publications, including a listing of the HUSSERLIANA, his works and publications by year, translations, and anthologies. The extensive bibliography of secondary sources includes books and reviews devoted to Husserl and dissertations and theses. The primary and secondary entries total over 3,800.

2555. Lauth, Reinhard. THEORIE DES PHILOSOPHISCHEN ARGUMENTS. Berlin and New York: De Gruyter, 1979.

2556. Lehmann, Gerhard. KANTS TUGENDEN: NEUE BEITRAGE ZUR GESCHICHTE UND INTERPRETATION DER PHILOSOPHIE KANTS. Berlin and New York: De Gruyter, 1980.

This work includes "Die Schriften von Gerhard Lehmann" on pages 277-284.

2557. Leibniz, Gottfried Wilhelm. DISCOURSE ON THE NATURAL THEOLOGY OF THE CHINESE. Tr. of LETTRE SUR LA PHILOSOPHIE CHINOIS A NICOLAS DE REMOND. Tr. by Henry Rosemont, Jr. and Daniel J. Cook. Honolulu: Univ. Of Hawaii Press, 1977.

2558. Lenk, Hans. HANDLUNGSTHEORIEN INTERDIZIPLINAR. 4 Vols. Munich: Fink, 1977.

2559. Lindauer, Martin and Alfred Schope. WIE ERKENNT DER MENSCH DIE WELT?: GRUNDLAGEN DES ERKENNENS, FUHLENS UND HANDELNS: GEISTES-UND NATURWISSENSCHAFTLER IM DIALOG: SYMPOSIUM DER UNIVERSITAT WURZBURG. Stuttgart: E. Klett, 1984.

2560. Lipps, Hans. WERKE. Vol. 1, UNTERSUCHUNGEN ZUR PHANOMENOLO-GIE DER ERKENNTNIS. Vol. 2, UNTERSUCHUNGEN ZU EINER HERMENEU-TISCHEN LOGIK. Vol. 3, DIE MENSCHLICHE NATUR. Vol. 4, DIE VERBIND-LICHKEIT DER SPRACHE. Vol. 5, DIE WIRKLICHKEIT DES MENSCHEN. Frankfurt am Main: Klostermann, 1976-1977.

2561. Lorenz, Kuno. KONSTRUKTIONEN VERSUS POSITIONEN: BEITRAGE ZUR DISKUSSION UM DIE KONSTRUKTIVE WISSENSCHAFTSTHEORIE. PAUL LORENZEN ZUM 60 GEBURTSTAG. 2 Vols. Berlin and New York: De Gruyter, 1978.

The second volume contains a bibliography of the works of Paul Lorenzen on pages 394-400.

2562. Lorenzen, Paul. CONSTRUCTIVE PHILOSOPHY. Tr. by Richard Pavlovic. Amherst: Univ. of Massachusetts Press, 1987.

2563. Lorenzen, Paul. NORMATIVE LOGIC AND ETHICS. 2d annotated ed. Mannheim: Bibliographisches Institut, 1984.

2564. Low, Reinhard. OIKEIOSIS: FESTSCHRIFT FUR ROBERT SPAEMANN. Weinheim: Acta Humaniora, VCH, 1987.

The contributions are in German, Latin and French.

2565. Low, Reinhard. PHILOSOPHIE DES LEBENDIGEN: DER BEGRIFF DES ORGANISCHEN BEI KANT, SEIN GRUND UND SEINE AKTUALITAT. Frankfurt am Main: Suhrkamp, 1980.

This volume contains a bibliography on pages 323-349.

2566. Lowith, Karl. MEIN LEBEN IN DEUTSCHLAND VOR UND NACH 1933: EIN BERICHT. Stuttgart: J.B. Metzler, 1986.

2567. Lubbe, Hermann. UNSERE STILLE KULTURREVOLUTION. Zurich: Interfrom, 1976.

2568. Lubbe, Hermann. WOZU PHILOSOPHIE?: STELLUNGNAHMEN EINES ARBEITKREISES. Berlin and New York: De Gruyter, 1978.

These are papers presented at the Arbeitkreise Rolle und Funktion der Philosophie. There is a bibliography on pages 356-388.

2569. Luhrs, George, et al. KRITISCHER RATIONALISMUS UND SOZIALDEMOKRATIE. Berlin and Bonn-Bad Godesberg: Dietz, 1975-.

This work includes bibliographical references and bio-bibliographical notes about the authors.

2570. Maluschke, Gunther. PHILOSOPHISCHE GRUNDLAGEN DES DEMOKRATISCHEN VERFASSUNGSSTAATES. Reihe Praktische Philosophie, Vol. 16. Freiburg: K. Alber, 1982.

This is the author's Habilitationsschrift, Universitat Tubingen.

2571. Mannheim, Karl. STRUCTURES OF THINKING. Ed. by David Kettler, et al. Tr. of STRUKTUREN DES DENKENS. Frankfurt am Main: Suhrkamp, 1980. Tr. by Jeremy J. Shapiro and Sherry Weber Nicholson. London and Boston: Routledge and Kegan Paul, 1982.

This work includes two hitherto unpublished manuscripts: "A Sociological Theory of

Culture and Its Knowability (conjunctive and communicative thinking)" (1924?) and "The Distinctive Character of Cultural-Sociological Knowledge" (1922).

2572. Marcuse, Herbert. THE AESTHETIC DIMENSION: TOWARD A CRITIQUE OF MARXIST AESTHETICS. Tr. and revision of DIE PERMANENZ DER KUNST. Munich and Vienna: Hanser, 1977. Boston: Beacon Press, 1977.

This work has been translated into Italian by Federico Caobbio-Codelli, LA DIMEN-SIONE ESTETICA. Milan: A. Monadori, 1978 and into Chinese, SHEN MEI CHIH WEI: MA-ERH-KU-SAI MEI HSUEH LUN CHU CHI. Pei-ching: San lien shu tien, 1989.

2573. Marquard, Odo. FAREWELL TO MATTERS OF PRINCIPLE: PHILOSOPHI-CAL STUDIES. Tr. of ABSCHIED VOM PRINZIPIELLEN: PHILOSOPHISCHE STUDIEN. Stuttgart: Reclam, 1981. New York: Oxford Univ. Press, 1989.

2574. Marquard, Odo, et al. SCHICKSAL, GRENZEN DER MACHBARKEIT: SYMPOS-IUM. Munich: Deutscher Taschenbuch Verlag, 1977.

This meeting was sponsored by the Carl Friedrich von Siemens Stiftung.

2575. Marx, Werner. INTRODUCTION TO ARISTOTLE'S THEORY OF BEING AS BEING. Tr. of EINFUHRUNG IN ARISTOTELES' THEORIE VOM SEIENDEN. Freiburg: Rombach, 1972. Tr. by Robert S. Schine. The Hague and Boston: Nijhoff, 1977.

2576. May, Gerhard. SCHOPFUNG AUS DEM NICHTS: DIE ENTSTEHUNG DER LEHRE VON DER CREATIO EX NIHILO. Berlin and New York: De Gruyter, 1978.

2577. Meggle, Georg. ANALYTISCHE HANDLUNGSTHEORIE. Vol. 1, HANDLUN-GSBESCHREIBUNGEN. Vol. 2, HANDLUNGSERKLARUNGEN. Frankfurt am Main: Suhrkamp, 1985c1977.

Vol. 2 was edited by Ansgar Beckermann.

2578. Meinong, Alexius. GESAMTAUSGABE. Bd. 1, ABHANDLUNGEN ZUR PSY-CHOLOGIE. Bd. 2, ABHANDLUNGEN ZUR ERKENNTNISTHEORIE UND GEGEN-STANDSTHEORIE. Bd. 3, ABHANDLUNGEN ZUR WERTTHEORIE. Bd. 4, UBER ANNAHMEN. Bd. 5, UBER PHILOSOPHISCHE WISSENSHAFT UND IHRE PROPA-DEUTIK. UBER DIE STELLUNG DER GEGENSTANDSTHEORIE IM SYSTEM DER WISSENSCHAFTEN. UBER DIE ERFAHRUNGSGRUNDLAGEN UNSERES WIS-SENS. ZUM ERWEISE DES ALLGEMEINEN KAUSALGESETZES. Bd. 6, UBER MOGLICHKEIT UND WAHRSCHEINLICHKEIT. Bd. 7, SELBSTDARSTELLUNG. VERMISCHTE SCHRIFTEN. Ed. by Rudolf Haller and Rudolf Kindinger. Graz: Akademische Druck-und Verlagsanstalt, 1968-1978.

2579. Meinong, Alexius. ON ASSUMPTIONS. Ed. by James E. Heanue. Tr. of UBER ANNAHMEN. Leipzig: J.A. Barth, 1910. Berkeley: Univ. of California Press, 1983.

2580. Merker, Nicolao. DIE AUFKLARUNG IN DEUTSCHLAND. Tr. of L'ILLUMI-NISMO TEDESCO. Bari: Laterza, 1968. Munich: Beck, 1982.

This volume contains an annotated survey of the Enlightenment in Germany. It focuses on rationalism, aesthetics, philosophy of religion, and historiography. It also features discussions of the works of Lessing, Wolff, Herder, Mendelssohn, and Kant.

2581. Merleau-Ponty, Maurice. DIE STRUKTUR DES VERHALTENS. Tr. of STRUC-TURE DU COMPORTEMENT. Paris: Univerisitaires de France, 1942. Tr. by Bernard Waldenfels. Berlin and New York: De Gruyter, 1976.

2582. Meyer, Rudolf W., et al. STUDIEN ZUM ZEITPROBLEM IN DER PHILOSOPHIE DES 20. JAHRHUNDERTS. Freiburg: K. Alber, 1982.

The volume consists chiefly of papers of the Zeit-Symposium organized by the Deutsche Gesellschaft fur Phanomenologische Forschung and held Mar. 31-Apr.3, 1982 in the Husserl Archives at Louvain.

2583. Meyer-Abich, Klaus. FRIEDEN MIT DER NATUR. Freiberg: Herder, 1979.

2584. Mitias, Michael H. MORAL FOUNDATION OF THE STATE IN HEGEL'S PHILOSOPHY OF RIGHT: ANATOMY OF AN ARGUMENT. Elementa. Amsterdam: Rodopi, 1984.

2585. Mittelstrass, Jurgen. ENZYKLOPADIE PHILOSOPHIE UND WISSENSCHAFT-STHEORIE. Mannheim: Bibliographisches Institut, 1980-.

2586. Mittelstrass, Jurgen and Manfred Riedel. VERNUNFTIGES DENKEN: STUDIEN ZUR PRAKTISCHEN PHILOSOPHIE UND WISSENSCHAFTSTHEORIE. Berlin and New York: De Gruyter, 1978.

2587. Mollenstedt, Ulrich. KRITIK DER PSYCHOANALYTISCHEN WISSENSCHAFTS-THEORIE. Bern: Peter Lang, 1976.

2588. Mueller-Vollmer, Kurt. THE HERMENEUTICS READER: TEXTS OF THE GERMAN TRADITION FROM THE ENLIGHTENMENT TO THE PRESENT. New York: Continuum, 1985.

This volume contains an introduction and notes written by the editor, as well as a bibliography on pages 347-361.

2589. Neumann, Walter. NEGATIVE TOTALITAT: ERFAHRUNGEN AN HEGEL, MARX, UND FREUD. Frankfurt am Main: Materials Verlag, 1983.

2590. Neurath, Otto. GESAMMELTE PHILOSOPHISCHE UND METHODOLO-GISCHE SCHRIFTEN. 2 Vols. Ed. by Rudolf Haller and Heiner Rutle. Vienna: Holder-Pichler-Tempsky, 1981.

2591. Neurath, Otto. PHILOSOPHICAL PAPERS, 1913-1946. Ed. by Robert Sonne Cohen and Marie Neurath. Vienna Circle Collection, Vol. 16. Dordrecht and Boston: Reidel, 1983.

This book contains a bibliography of Otto Neurath's works in English on pages 247-264.

2592. Neurath, Otto. WISSENSCHAFTLICHE WELTAUFFASSUNG, SOZIALISMUS UND LOGISCHER EMPIRISMUS. Ed. by Rainer Hegselmann. Frankfurt am Main: Suhrkamp, 1979.

2593. Neususs, Arnhelm. MARXISMUS: EIN GRUNDRISS DER GROSSEN METHODE. Munich: Fink, 1981.

This volume is based on a series of radio programs with the title MARXISTISCHE THEORIE, WAS IST EIGENTLICH? and broadcast by Sender Freies Berlin 1978-1979.

2594. Niehues-Probsting, Heinrich. DER KYNISMUS DES DIOGENES UND DER BEGRIFF DES ZYNISMUS. Munich: Fink, 1979.

2595. Nietzsche, Friedrich W. KRITISCHE GESAMTAUSGABE. Ed. by Giorgio Colli and

Mazzino Montinari. Berlin: De Gruyter, 1967-.

2596. Noack, Hermann. DIE PHILOSOPHIE WESTEUROPAS IM ZWANGZIGSTEN JAHRHUNDERT. 2d ed. Basel and Stuttgart: Schwabe, 1976.

2597. Oehler, Klaus. DER UNBEWEGTE BEWEGER DES ARISTOTELES. Frankfurt am Main: V. Klostermann, 1984.

2598. Oehler, Klaus. ZEICHEN UND REALITAT: AKTEN DES 3. SEMIOTISCHEN KOLLOQUIUMS DER DEUTSCHEN GESELLSCHAFT FUR SEMIOTIK E. V., HAMBURG 1981. 3 Vols. Tubingen: Stauffenburg, 1984.

These volumes contain contributions in English, French, and German.

2599. Oelmuller, Willi. KOLLOQUIUM KUNST UND PHILOSOPHIE. Vol. 1, AESTHE- TISCHE ERFAHRUNG. Vol. 2, ASTHETISCHER SCHEIN. Vol. 3, DAS KUN- STWERK. Paderborn: Schoningh, 1981-.

These three works comprise volumes 4-6 of the Kolloquien zur Gegenwartsphilosophie.

2600. Oelmuller, Willi. KOLLOQUIUM RELIGION UND PHILOSOPHIE. Vol. 1, WIEDERKEHR VON RELIGION?: PERSPEKTIVEN, ARGUMENTE, FRAGEN. Vol. 2, WAHRHEITSANSPRUCHE DER RELIGIONEN HEUTE. Vol. 3, LEIDEN. Pader- born: Schoningh, 1984-1986.

These three works comprise Volumes 7-9 of the Kolloquien zur Gegenwartsphilosophie.

2601. Oelmuller, Willi. MATERIALIEN ZUR NORMENDISKUSSION. Vol. 1, TRANS- ZENDENTALPHILOSOPHISCHE NORMENBEGRUNDUNGEN. Vol. 2, NORMEN- BEGRUNDUNG - NORMENDURCHSETZUNG. Vol. 3, NORMEN UND GES- CHICHTE. Paderborn: Schoningh, 1978-.

These three works comprise Volumes 1-3 of the Kolloquien zur Gegenwartsphilosophie.

2602. Oestreich, Gerhard. NEOSTOICISM AND THE MODERN STATE. Ed. by Birgitta Oestreich and Helmut Georg Konigsberger. Tr. of GEIST UND GESTALT FRUHMOD- ERNEN STAATES. Berlin: Duncker and Humblot, 1969. Tr. by David McClintock. New York and Cambridge: Cambridge Univ. Press, 1982.

This work focuses on the neo-Stoic political philosophy of Justus Lipsius, the Dutch humanist, and its influence on scholarship, poetry, and art up to the Enlightenment.

2603. Opitz, Peter Joachim and Gregor Sebba. THE PHILOSOPHY OF ORDER: ESSAYS ON HISTORY, CONSCIOUSNESS AND POLITICS. Stuttgart: Klett-Cotta, 1981.

This festschrift for Eric Voegelin on his eightieth birthday, January 3, 1981, is printed in English, French and German. There is a bibliography on pages 466-477.

2604. Ottmann, Horst Henning. INDIVIDUUM UND GEMEINSCHAFT BEI HEGEL. Berlin and New York: De Gruyter, 1977.

2605. Otto, Rudolf. AUFSATZE ZUR ETHIK. Ed. by Jack Stewart Boozer. Munich: Beck, 1981.

This work includes five posthumous essays showing the relations of ethics to the sacred and to the complex forces and structures of political economy and society.

2606. Patzig, Gunther, et al. LOGIK, ETHIK, THEORIE DER GEISTESWISSENSCHAF- TEN. Hamburg: Meiner, 1977.

This is the eleventh Deutsche Kongress fur Philosophie held in Gottingen, October 5-9, 1975.

2607. Patzig, Gunther, et al. SYMPOSIUM ZUM GEDENKEN AN NICLOLAI HART-MANN: DIREKTOR DES PHILOSOPHISCHEN SEMINARS DER UNIVERSITAT GOTTINGEN, 1946-1950. Gottingen: Vandenhoek & Ruprecht, 1982.

2608. Plessner, Helmuth. GESAMMELTE SCHRIFTEN. Vol. 1, FRUHE PHILOSO-PHISCHE SCHRIFTEN. Vol. 3, ANTHROPOLOGIE DER SINNE. Vol. 4, DIE STU-FEN DES ORGANISCHEN UND DER MENSCH: EINLEITUNG IN DIE PHILOSO-PHISCHE ANTHROPOLOGIE. Vol. 5, MACHT UND MENSCHLICHE NATUR. Vol. 6, DIE VERSPATETE NATION. Vol. 7, AUSDRUCK UND MENSCHLICHE NATUR. Vol. 8, CONDITIO HUMANA. Vol. 9, SCHRIFTEN ZUR PHILOSOPHIE. Vol. 10, SCHRIFTEN ZUR SOZIOLOGIE UND SOZIALPHILOSOPHIE. Ed. by Gunter Dux, et al. Frankfurt am Main: Suhrkamp; Boston: Insel, 1980-.

2609. Poggeler, Otto. HEIDEGGER UND DIE HERMENEUTISCHE PHILOSOPHIE. Freiburg: K. Alber, 1983.

2610. Poser, Hans. PHILOSOPHIE UND MYTHOS: EIN KOLLOQUIUM. Berlin and New York: De Gruyter, 1979.

2611. Poser, Hans. PHILOSOPHISCHE PROBLEME DER HANDLUNGSTHEORIE. Freiburg: K. Alber, 1982.

2612. Poser, Hans. WANDEL DES VERNUNFTBEGRIFFS. Freiburg: K. Alber, 1981.

This book contains revisions of papers presented at the Wissenschaftliche Tagung of the Engerer Kreis der Allgemeinen Gesellschaft fur Philosophie, held in 1988. It includes papers by Hans Michael Baumgartner, Herbert Schnadelbach, Wolfgang Rod, Odo Marquard, Walther Ch. Zimmerli, Rudolf Haller, Christian Thiel, and Lorenz Kruger.

2613. Radnitzky, Gerard and William Warren Bartley. EVOLUTIONARY EPISTEMOLO-GY, THEORY OF RATIONALITY, AND THE SOCIOLOGY OF KNOWLEDGE. Peru, IL: Open Court, 1987.

This volume is a collection of essays by the leading proponents of evolutionary epistemology, which has been called the most significant development in epistemology since the 18th century.

2614. Reiner, Hans. DUTY AND INCLINATION: THE FUNDAMENTALS OF MORAL-ITY DISCUSSED AND REDEFINED WITH SPECIAL REGARD TO KANT AND SCHILLER. The Hague and Lancast: Nijhoff, 1983.

2615. Reinhart, Kosselleck von, et al. OBJECKTIVITAT UND PARTEILICHKEIT. Munich: Deutscher Taschenbuch Verlag, 1977.

2616. Riedel, Manfred. BETWEEN TRADITION AND REVOLUTION: THE HEGELIAN TRANSFORMATION OF POLITICAL PHILOSOPHY. Tr. of ZWISCHEN TRADI-TION UND REVOLUTION: STUDIEN ZU HEGELS RECHTSPHILOSOPHIE. Stuttgart: Klett-Cotta, 1982. Tr. by Walter Wright. Cambridge and New York: Cambridge Univ. Press, 1984.

ZWISCHEN TRADITION UND REVOLUTION: STUDIEN ZU HEGELS RECHT-SPHILOSOPHIE is a revised edition of STUDIEN ZU HEGELS RECHTSPHILOSO-PHIE which was published in Frankfurt am Main by Suhrkamp in 1969.

2617. Rintelen, Fritz-Joachim von. PHILOSOPHIE DES LEBENDIGEN GEISTES IN

DER KRISE DER GEGENWART: SELBSTDARST. Gottingen, Zurich, Frankfurt am Main: Musterschmidt, 1977.

This volume contains a bibliography of the author's works on pages 77-78.

2618. Ropohl, Gunter. EINE SYSTEMTHEORIE DER TECHNIK: ZUR GRUNDLE-GUNG D. ALLG. TECHNOLOGIE. Munich and Vienna: Hanser, 1979.

2619. Rudolph, Enno. SKEPSIS BEI KANT: EIN BEITRAG ZUR INTERPRETATION DER KRITIK DER REINEN VERNUNFT. Munich: W. Fink, 1978.

2620. Rudolph, Enno and Eckhart Stove. GESCHICHTSBEWUSSTSEIN UND RATIONA-LITAT: ZUM PROBLEM DER GESCHICHTLICHKEIT IN DER THEORIEBILDUNG. Stuttgart: Klett-Cotta, 1982.

2621. Rusen, Jorn. FUR EINE ENEURETE HISTORIK: STUDIEN ZUR THEORIE D. GESCHICHTSWISS. Stuttgart-Bad Canstatt: Frommann Holzboog, 1976.

The volume contains a bibliography on pages 240-251.

2622. Salamun, Kurt. SOZIALPHILOSOPHIE ALS AUFKLARUNG: FESTSCHRIF-TEN FUR ERNST TOPITSCH. Tubingen: Mohr, 1979.

There is a bibliogaphy of Ernst Topitsch's works on pages 494-504. One contribution to the book is in English.

2623. Sandkuhler, Hans-Jorg. EUROPAISCHE ENZYKLOPADIE ZU PHILOSOPHIE UND WISSENSCHAFTEN. 4 Vols. Hamburg: Meiner, 1990.

From a primarily continental European perspective, this encyclopedia covers all major fields in philosophy in some 600 articles by over 380 authorities from 22 countries. All of the articles contain bibliographies of works cited and other pertinent works.

2624. Sass, Hans-Martin. LUDWIG FEUERBACH IN SELBSTZEUGNISSEN BILDDO-KUMENTEN. Reinbeck bei Hamburg: Rowohlt, 1978.

2625. Sass, Hans-Martin. MARTIN HEIDEGGER: BIBLIOGRAPHY AND GLOSSARY. Bibliographies of Famous Philosophers. Bowling Green, OH: Philosophy Documentation Center, 1982.

This volume contains over 6,350 entries in sections covering works by Heidegger, lists of translations, works on Heidegger, Heidegger conferences, a comprehensive Heidegger glossary, and five indices.

2626. Sass, Hans-Martin and Robert U. Massey. HEALTH CARE SYSTEMS: MORAL CONFLICTS IN EUROPEAN AND AMERICAN PUBLIC POLICY. Dordrecht and Boston: Kluwer Academic Publishers, 1988.

This volume is based on the twenty-first Trans-disciplinary Symposium on Philosophy and Medicine, held July 23-26, 1985 at the Werner-Reimers Stiftung in Bad Hamburg von der Hohe, Federal Republic of Germany, sponsored by the Werner-Reimers Stiftung and the School of Medicine of the University of Connecticut Health Center in Farmington.

2627. Sauerland, Karol. EINFUHRUNG IN DIE ASTHETIK ADORNOS. Berlin and New York: De Gruyter, 1979.

2628. Schaeffler, Richard. RELIGIONSPHILOSOPHIE. Freiburg: K. Alber, 1983.

2629. Scheer, Brigitte and Gunter Wohlfart. DIMENSIONEN DER SPRACHE IN DER PHILOSOPHIE DES DEUTSCHEN IDEALISMUS. Worzburg: Konigshausen and Neumann, 1982.

This collection includes articles by Josef Simon, Gunter Wohlfart, Brigitte Scheer, Dietrich Gutterer, Dimitrios Markis, Werner Heinrich Schmitt, Rudiger E. Bohle, and Fritz Zimbrich.

2630. Scheler, Max. PROBLEMS OF A SOCIOLOGY OF KNOWLEDGE. Ed. by Kenneth Strikkers. Tr. by Manfred S. Frings. London and Boston: Routledge and Kegan Paul, 1980.

This is the translation of an essay which originally appeared as the introduction to the anthology VERSUCHE ZU EINER SOZIOLOGIE DES WISSENS. Munich: Duncker and Humlot, 1924.

2631. Schelling, Friedrich Wilhelm Joseph von. THE UNCONDITIONAL IN HUMAN KNOWLEDGE: FOUR EARLY ESSAYS, 1794-1796. Tr. by Fritz Marti. Lewisburg: Bucknell Univ. Press; London: Associated Univ. Presses, 1980.

The essays are: 1. On the Possibility of a Form of All Philosophy. 2. Of the Principle of Philosophy, or On the Unconditional in Human Knowledge. 3. Philosophical Letters on Dogmatism and Criticism. 4. New Deduction of Natural Right.

2632. Schelling, Friedrich Wilhelm Joseph von. WERKE. Vol. 1, ELEGIE (1790). DE MALORUM ORIGINE (1782). UBER MYTHEN (1793). FORM DER PHILOSOPHIE (1794). ERKLARUNG (1795). Vol. 2, VOM ICH ALS PRINCIP DER PHILOSOPHIE (1795). DE MARCIONE (1795). Vol. 3, PHILOSOPHISCHE BRIEFE. UBER DOGMA- TISMUS UND KRITICISMUS (1795). NEUE DEDUCTION DES NATURRECHTS (1795/97). ANTIKRITIK (1796). Vol. 4, ALLEGEMEINE UBERSICHT (1797- 1798). OFFENBARUNG UND VOLSUNTERRICHT (1798). SCHLOSSER-REZENSION (1798). Ed. by Wilhelm G. Jacobs, et al. Stuttgart-Bad Cannstatt: Frommann-Holzboog, 1976-.

2633. Schirmacher, Wolfgang. ZEIT DER ERNTE: STUDIEN ZUM STAND DER SCHOPENHAUER-FORSCHUNG: FESTSCHRIFT FUR ARTHUR HUBSCHER ZUM 85. GEBURTSTAG IM NAMEN DES VORSTANDES DER SCHOPENHAUER- GESELLSCHAFT. Stuttgart-Ban Canstatt: Frommann-Holzboog, 1982.

2634. Schleiermacher, Friedrich Daniel Ernst. HERMENEUTIK UND KRITIK: MIT EINEM ANHANG SPRACHPHILOSOPHISCHER TEXTE SCHLEIERMACHERS. Ed. by Manfred Frank. Frankfurt: Suhrkamp, 1977.

2635. Schleiermacher, Friedrich Daniel Ernst. ON THE GLAUBENSLEHRE: TWO LETTERS TO DR. LUCKE. Tr. of SENDSCHREIBEN UBER SEINE GLAUBENS- LEHRE AN LUCKS. Tr. by James Duke and Francis Fiorenza. Chico, CA: Scholars Press, 1981.

2636. Schmidt, Alfred. HISTORY AND STRUCTURE: AN ESSAY ON HEGELIAN- MARXIST AND STRUCTURALIST THEORIES OF HISTORY. Tr. of GESCHICHTE UND STRUKTUR: FRAGEN EINER MARXISTISCHEN HISTORIK. Munich: Hanser, 1971. Tr. by Jeffrey Herf. Cambridge: MIT Press, 1981.

2637. Schmidt, Gerhart and Gerd Wolandt. DIE AKTUALITAT DER TRANSZEN- DENTAL PHILOSOPHIE: HANS WAGNER ZUM 60. GEBURTSTAG. Bonn: Bouvi- er, 1977.

This volume contains contributions by J. Barion, W. Flach, E. Winterhager, K. Hartmann, W. Rod, J. Vuillemin, E. Hufnagel, J. Derbolev, and the editors.

2638. Schmucker, Josef. DIE ONTOTHEOLOGIE DES VORKRITISCHEN KANT. Ed. by Gerhard Funke and Joachim Kopper. Berlin and New York: De Gruyter, 1980.

2639. Schnadelbach, Herbert. PHILOSOPHY IN GERMANY, 1831-1933. Tr. of PHILOSOPHIE IN DEUTSCHLAND, 1831-1933 Frankfurt am Main: Suhrkamp, 1983. Tr. by Eric Matthews. Cambridge and New York: Cambridge Univ. Press, 1984.

2640. Schneider, Hansjorg A. W. HYPOTHESE, EXPERIMENT, THEORIE: ZUM SELBSTVERSTANDNIS DER NATURWISSENSCHAFT. Berlin and New York: De Gruyter, 1978.

2641. Schneiders, Werner. AUFKLARUNG UND VORURTEILSKRITIK: STUDIEN ZUR GESCHICHTE DER VORURTEILSTHEORIE. Stuttgart Bad Cannstatt: Frommann Holzboog, 1983.

The text is in German with summaries in French and English.

2642. Scholem, Gershom Gerhard. WALTER BENJAMIN: THE STORY OF A FRIENDSHIP. Tr. of WALTER BENJAMIN: DIE GESCHICHTE E. FREUNDSCHAFT. Frankfurt: Suhrkampf, 1975. Tr. from the German by Harry Zohn. Philadelphia: Jewish Publication Society of America, 1981.

2643. Schussler, Ingeborg. ARISTOTELES. PHILOSOPHIE UND WISSENSCHAFT: DAS PROBLEM DER VERSELBSTANDIGUNG DER WISSENSCHAFTEN. Frankfurt am Main: Klostermann, 1982.

2644. Schutz, Alfred. LIFE FORMS AND MEANING STRUCTURE. Tr. of LEBENSFORMEN UND SINNSTRUKTUR. Tr. by Helmut R. Wagner. London and Boston: Routledge and Kegan Paul, 1982.

Helmut R. Wagner wrote both the introduction and the annotations for this volume.

2645. Schutz, Alfred. THEORIE DER LEBENSFORMEN: FRUHE MANUSKRIPTE AUS DER BERGSON-PERIOD. Ed. by Ilja Srubar. Frankfurt am Main: Suhrkamp, 1981.

2646. Schwemmer, Oswald. THEORIE DER RATIONALEN ERKLARUNG: ZU DEN METHODOLOGISCHEN GRUNDLAGEN DER KULTURWISSENSCHAFTEN. Munich: Beck, 1976.

2647. Seidel, George J. ACTIVITY AND GROUND: FICHTE, SCHELLING, AND HEGEL. Hildesheim: G. Olms, 1976.

2648. Seubold, Gunter. HEIDEGGERS ANALYSES DER NEUZEITLICHEN TECHNIK. Freiberg: K. Alber, 1986.

2649. Sheehan, Thomas. KARL RAHNER, THE PHILOSOPHICAL FOUNDATIONS. Series in Continental Thought, Vol. 9. Athens: Ohio Univ. Press, 1987.

2650. Simon, Josef. FREIHEIT: THEORETISCHE UND PRAKTISCHE ASPEKTE DES PROBLEMS. Freiburg and Munich: Alber, 1977.

This anthology, celebrating the five-hundredth anniversary of the founding of Eberhard Karls University, Tubingen, includes contributions by B. Baron v. Freytag Loringhoff, L. Oeing-Hanoff, H. Krings, H. Fahrenbach, A. Schwann, J. Schwartlander, H. Kramer, A. Stern, W. Schulz, K. Hartmann, B. Liebrucks and the editor.

2651. Simon, Josef. WAHRHEIT ALS FREIHEIT: EIN VERSUCH ZUR ENTWICK
LUNG DER WAHRHEITSFRAGE IN DER NEUERER PHILOSOPHIE. Berlin and
New York: De Gruyter, 1978.

2652. Simons, Eberhard. DAS EXPRESSIVE DENKEN ERNST BLOCHS: KATEGOR-
IEN UND LOGIK KUNSTLERISCHER PRODUKTION UND IMAGINATION.
Freiburg: K. Alber, 1983.

This work was originally presented as the author's thesis at the University of Munich in
1978 under the title: FREIHEIT UND METHODE.

2653. Spaemann, Robert. CRITICA DE LAS UTOPIAS POLITICAS. Spanish tr. of
ZUR KRITIK DER POLITISCHEN UTOPIE. Stuttgart: Klett, 1977. Pamplona:
Ediciones Universidad de Navarra, 1980.

2654. Spaemann, Robert and Reinhard Low. DIE FRAGE WOZU? GESCHICHTE UND
WIEDERENTDECKUNG DES TELEOLOGISCHEN DENKENS. Munich: Piper, 1981.

2655. Stallmach, Josef. SUCHE NACH DEM EINEN: GESAMMELTE ABHAND-
LUNGEN ZUR PROBLEMGESCHICHTE DER METAPHYSIK. Ed. by Norbert Fischer. Bonn: Bouvier Verlag H. Grundmann, 1982.

2656. Stegmuller, Wolfgang. COLLECTED PAPERS ON EPISTEMOLOGY, PHILOSO-
PHY OF SCIENCE AND HISTORY OF PHILOSOPHY. 2 Vols. Translated from the
German. Dordrecht and Boston: Reidel, 1977.

A bibliography of the works of Stegmuller is included in Volume 2, pages 278-283.

2657. Stegmuller, Wolfgang. CREER SABER, CONOCER Y OTROS ENSAYOS. Tr. of
GLAUBEN, WISSEN UND ERKENNEN: DAS UNIVERSALIENPROBLEM EINST
UND JETZT. Darmstadt: Wissenschaftliche Buchgesellschaft, 1967. Tr. by Ernesto
Garzon Valdes. Buenos Aires: Alfa, 1978.

2658. Stegmuller, Wolfgang. KRIPKES DEUTUNG DER SPATPHILOSOPHIE WITT-
GENSTEINS: KOMMENTARVERSUCH UBER EINEN VERSUCHTEN KOMMEN-
TAR. Stuttgart: A. Kroner, 1986.

2659. Stegmuller, Wolfgang. NEUE WEGE DER WISSENSCHAFTSPHILOSOPHIE.
Berlin, Heidelberg and New York: Springer, 1980.

2660. Stegmuller, Wolfgang. PROBLEME UND RESULTATE DER WISSENSCHAFTS-
THEORIE UND ANALYTISCHEN PHILOSOPHIE. Bd. 1, WISSENSCHAFTLICHE
ERKLARUNG UND BEGRUNDUNG. Bd. 2, THEORIE UND ERFAHRUNG. Bd. 3,
STRUKTURTYPEN DER LOGIK. Bd. 4, STATISTISCHANALYSE (2 Vols.). Berlin
and New York: Springer-Verlag, 1969-.

There is a bibliography in Volume 1 on pages 1080-1099.

2661. Stegmuller, Wolfgang. RATIONALE REKONSTRUCKTION VON WISSEN-
SCHAFT UND IHREM WANDEL: MIT E. AUTOBIOGRAPHI. EINL. Stuttgart:
Reclam, 1979.

The volume contains a bibliography of Stegmuller's works on pages 205-206.

2662. Stegmuller, Wolfgang. THE STRUCTURALIST VIEW OF THEORIES: A POSSI-
BLE ANALOGUE OF THE BOURBAKI PROGRAMME IN PHYSICAL SCIENCE.
Berlin and New York: Springer-Verlag, 1979.

2663. Stegmuller, Wolfgang. DAS UNIVERSALIEN-PROBLEM. Darmstadt: Wissenschaftliche Buchgesellschaft, 1978.

2664. Stegmuller, Wolfgang, et al. EPISTEMOLOGY, METHODOLOGY, AND PHILOSOPHY OF SCIENCE: ESSAYS IN HONOR OF CARL G. HEMPEL ON THE OCCASION OF HIS 80th BIRTHDAY, JANUARY 8, 1985. Dordrecht and Boston: Reidel, 1985.

This is a reprint in German and English from ERKENNTNIS, Vol. 22, Nos. 1, 2, and 3.

2665. Stegmuller, Wolfgang, et al. PHILOSOPHY OF ECONOMICS: PROCEEDINGS, MUNICH, JULY, 1981. Berlin and New York: Springer, 1982.

2666. Sternberger, Dolf. SCHRIFTEN. Frankfurt am Main: Insel-Verlag, 1977-.

2667. Sticker, Bernhard. ERFAHRUNG UND ERKENNTNIS: VORTRAGE UBER AUFSATZE ZUR GESCHICHTE DER NATURWISSENSCHAFTLICHEN DENK WEISEN 1943-1973. Hildesheim: Gerstenberg, 1976.

This volume is printed chiefly in German but has one essay in English. There is also a bibliography of Sticker's works on pages 305-310.

2668. Strasser, Stephan. JENSEITS VON SEIN UND ZEIT: EIN EINFUHRUNG IN EMMANUEL LEVINAS' PHILOSOPHIE. The Hague: Nijhoff, 1978.

2669. Stroker, Elisabeth. INVESTIGATIONS IN PHILOSOPHY OF SPACE. Tr. of PHILOSOPHISCHE UNTERSUCHUNGEN ZUM RAUM. Frankfurt am Main: Klostermann, 1965. Tr. by Algis Mickunas. Series in Continental Thought, Vol. 11. Athens: Ohio Univ. Press, 1986.

2670. Stroker, Elisabeth. WISSENSCHAFTSGESCHICHTE ALS HERAUSFORDERUNG: MARGINALIEN ZUR JUNGSTEN WISSENSCHAFTSTHEORETISCHEN KONTROVERSE. Frankfurt am Main: Klostermann, 1976.

This volume was originally published in TENDENZEN DER WISSENSCHAFTS-THEORIE, HEFT 6/7, 1974, under the title, GESCHICHTE ALS HERAUSFORDERUNG.

2671. Stroker, Elisabeth, et al. WISSENSCHAFTSTHEORIE DER NATURWISS-ENSCHAFTEN: GRUNDZUGE IHRER SACHPROBLEMATIK UND MODELLE FUR DEN UNTERRICHT. Teil 1, WISSENNSCHAFTSTHEORIE DER NATURWISS-ENSCHAFTEN IN DEN GRUNDZUGEN IHRER SACHPROBLEMATIK. Teil 2, WISSENSCHAFTSTHEORIE DER NATURWISSENSCHAFTEN IM UNTERRICHT. Freiburg: K. Alber, 1981.

2672. Stuhlmann-Laeisz, Rainer. KANTS LOGIK: EINE INTERPRETATION AUF DER GRUNDLAGE VON VORLESUNGEN, VEROFFENTLICHTEN WERKEN UND NACHLASS. Berlin and New York: De Gruyter, 1976.

2673. Tar, Zoltan. THE FRANKFURT SCHOOL: THE CRITICAL THEORIES OF MAX HORKHEIMER AND THEODOR W. ADORNO. New York: Wiley, 1977.

There is a bibliography on pages 209-233.

2674. Teichner, Wilhelm. REKONSTRUKTION ODER REPRODUKTION DES GRUNDES: DIE BEGRUNDUNG DER PHILOSOPHIE ALS WISSENSCHAFT DURCH KANT UND REINHOLD. Bonn: Bouvier Verlag Grundmann, 1976.

2675. Theunissen, Michael. KRITISCHE THEORIE DER GESELLSCHAFT: ZWEI STUDIEN. Berlin and New York: De Gruyter, 1981.

2676. Theunissen, Michael. THE OTHER: STUDIES IN THE SOCIAL ONTOLOGY OF HUSSERL, HEIDEGGER, SARTRE AND BUBER. Tr. of DER ANDERE: STUDIEN ZUR SOZIALONTOLOGIE DER GEGENWART. 2d. enl. ed. Berlin and New York: De Gruyter, 1977. Tr. by Christopher MaCann. Cambridge: MIT Press, 1984.

2677. Theunissen, Michael. SEIN UND SCHEIN: DIE KRITISCHE FUNKTION D. HEGELISCHEN LOGIK. Frankfurt am Main: Suhrkamp, 1978.

2678. Theunissen, Michael. SELBSTVERWIRKLICHUNG UND ALLGEMEINHEIT: ZUR KRITIK DES GEGENWARTIGEN BEWUSSTSEINS. Berlin and New York: De Gruyter, 1981.

2679. Thiel, Udo. LOCKES THEORIE DER PERSONALEN IDENTITAT. Bonn: Bouvier Verlag Grundmann, 1983.

2680. Topitsch, Ernst. ERKENNTNIS UND ILLUSION: GRUNDSTRUKTUREN UNSERER WELTAUFFASSUNG. Hamburg: Hoffmann und Campe, 1979.

2681. Tugendhat, Ernst. SELF-CONSCIOUSNESS AND SELF-DETERMINATION. Tr. of SELBSTBEWUSSTSEIN UND SELBSTBESTIMMUNG: SPRACHANALYTISCHE INTERPRETATIONEN. Frankfurt am Main: Suhrkamp, 1979. Tr. by Paul Stein. Cambridge: MIT Press, 1986.

2682. Tugendhat, Ernst. TRADITIONAL AND ANALYTICAL PHILOSOPHY: LEC-TURES IN THE PHILOSOPHY OF LANGUAGE. Tr. of VORLESUNGEN ZUR EINFUHRUNG IN DIE SPRACHANALYTISCHE PHILOSOPHIE. Frankfurt am Main: Suhrkamp, 1976. Tr. by P. A. Gorner. Cambridge and New York: Cambridge Univ. Press, 1982.

2683. Ueberweg, Friedrich. GRUNDRISS DER GESCHICHTE DER PHILOSOPHIE. Rev ed. Basel: Schwabe, 1983-.

The following volumes have been published: under DIE PHILOSOPHIE ANTIKE, Bd. 3: ALTERE AKADEMIE ARISTOTELES-PERIPATOS, edited by Helmut Flashar, 1983; under DIE PHILOSOPHIE DES 17 JAHRHUNDERTS, Bd. 3: ENGLAND, edited by Jean-Pierre Schobinger, 1988.

2684. Uehlein, Friedrich A. KOSMOS UND SUBJEKTIVITAT: LORD SHAFTES-BURY'S PHILOSOPHICAL REGIMEN. Freiburg and Munich: Alber, 1976.

2685. Waismann, Friedrich. PHILOSOPHICAL PAPERS. Ed. by Brian McGuinness. Vienna Circle Collection, Vol. 8. Dordrecht and Boston: Reidel, 1977.

This work contains an introduction by Anthony Quinton and a bibliography of works by Friedrich Waismann on pages 186-188.

2686. Weimer, Wolfgang. SCHOPENHAUER. Darmstadt: Wissenschaftliche Buchge-sellschaft, 1982.

2687. Weischedel, Wilhelm. DIE FRAGE NACH GOTT IM SKEPTISCHEN DENKEN. Ed. by Wolfgang Muller-Lauter. Berlin and New York: De Gruyter, 1976.

2688. Widmann, Joachim. JOHANN GOTTLIEB FICHTE: EINFUHRUNG IN SEINE PHILOSOPHIE. Berlin and New York: De Gruyter, 1982.

2689. Wiedmann, Franz. RELIGION UND PHILOSOPHIE. VERSUCH ZUR WIEDERGE-WINNUNG EINER DIMENSION. Wurzburg: Konigshausen and Neumann, 1985.

2690. Wiehl, Reiner. ANTIKE PHILOSOPHIE IN IHRER BEDEUTUNG FUR DIE GEGENWART: KOLLOQUIUM ZU EHREN DES 80 GEBURTSTAGES VON HANS-GEORGE GADAMER. Heidelberg: C. Winter, 1981.

2691. Wiehl, Reiner. DIE VERNUNFT IN DER MENSCHLICHEN UNVERNUNFT: DAS PROBLEM DER RATIONALITAT IN SPINOZAS AFFEKTENLEHRE. Hamburg: Joachim Jungius-Gesellschaft der wissenschaften; Gottingen: in Kommission beim Verlag Vandenhoeck and Ruprecht, 1983.

2692. Wieland, George. ETHICA-SCIENTIA PRACTICA: DIE ANFANGE DER PHIL-OSOPHISCHEN ETHIK IM 13. JAHRHUNDERT. Munster Westfalen: Aschendorff, 1981.

2693. Wohlfart, Gunter. DER AUGENBLICK: ZEIT UND ASTHETISCHE BEI KANT, HEGEL, NIETZSCHE UND HEIDEGGER MIT EINEM EXKURS ZU PROUST. Freiburg: Alber, 1982.

2694. Wohlfart, Gunter. DENKEN DER SPRACHE: SPRACHE UND KUNST BEI VICO, HAMANN, HUMBOLDT UND HEGEL. Freiburg: K. Alber, 1984.

The introduction and chapters consist of revisions of lectures and contributions, 1980-1982, two of which were previously published in other sources, and one of which has been revised into German from the original Italian.

2695. Wohlfart, Gunter. DER PUNKT: ASTHETISCHE MEDITATIONEN. Freiburg: K. Alber, 1986.

2696. Wohlfart, Gunter. DER SPEKULATATIVE SATZ: BEMERKUNGEN ZUM BE-GRIFF DER SPEKULATION BEI HEGEL. Berlin and New York: de Gruyter, 1981c1980.

2697. Wolters, Gereon. BASIS UND DEDUKTION: STUDIEN ZUR ENTSTEHUNG UND BEDEUTUNG DER THEORIE DER AXIOMATISCHEN METHODE BEI J. H. LAMBERT (1728-1777). Berlin and New York: De Gruyter, 1980.

2698. Wuchterl, Kurt. METHODEN DER GEGENWARTSPHILOSOPHIE. Stuttgart: Paul Haupt, 1977.

2699. Zilsel, Edgar. DIE SOZIALEN URSPRUNG DER NEUZEITLICHEN WISS-ENSCHAFT. Ed. by Wolfgang Krohn. Essays translated from English by Wolfgang Krohn. Frankfurt am Main: Suhrkamp, 1976.

There is a bibliography on pages 251-274 and also a bio-bibliographical note by Jorn Behrman.

LATIN
AMERICA

Latin America

2700. Fornet-Betancourt, Raul. PROBLEMAS ACTUALES DE LA FILOSOFIA EN HISPANO AMERICA. Buenos Aires: Ediciones FEPAI, 1985.

2701. Gonzalez Lopez, Jesus and Fritz-Joachim von Rintelen. CRISES DE VALORES, REFLEXION INTERDISCIPLINAR DESDE AMERICA LATINA: UN HOMENAJE FILOSOFICO A FRITZ-JOACHIM VON RINTELEN. Spanish tr. of Fritz-Joachim Von Rintelen. PHILOSOPHIE DES LEBENDIGEN GEISTES IN DER KRISES DER GEGENWART. Gottingen: Musterschmidt, 1977. Quito: Ediciones de la Universidad Catolica, 1982.

2702. Gracia, Jorge Jesus Emiliano, ed. DIRECTORY OF LATIN AMERICAN PHILOSO-PHERS-REPERTARIO DE FILOSOFOS LATINOAMERICANOS. Buffalo, Buenos Aires and Mexico: CISP (Council on International Studies and Programs, State Univ. of New York), 1988.

This work is published in association with the Society on Iberian and Latin American Thought, Asociacion Argentina de Investigaciones Eticos, Colezio de Estudios Latinoamer-icanos-Uam.

2703. Gracia, Jorge Jesus Emiliano, ed. LATIN AMERICAN PHILOSOPHY IN THE TWENTIETH CENTURY: MAN, VALUES, AND THE SEARCH FOR PHILOSOPHI-CAL IDENTITY. Translations by William Cooper, et al. Frontiers of Philosophy. Buffalo, NY: Prometheus Books, 1986.

2704. Martin, Dolores Moyano, ed. HANDBOOK OF LATIN AMERICAN STUDIES. Gainesville, FL: Univ. of Florida Press, 1935-.

Every two years this annual series devotes a volume to the humanities which includes a selective bibliographic guide with annotations in Spanish to articles and books in philoso-phy published in Latin America. This biennial bibliography of Latin American philosophi-cal writings is by Juan Carlos Torchia Estrada and covers Central America, the Caribbean, and South America. Since 1976 the humanities volumes are Nos. 38 (1976); 40 (1978); 42 (1980); 44 (1982); 46 (1984); 48 (1986); and 50 (1990).

2705. Masmela, Carlos. TEORIA KANTIANA DEL MOVIMIENTO: UNA INVESTIGA-CION SOBRE LOS PRINCIPIOS METAFISICOS DE LA FORONOMIA. Tr. by Carlos Masmela. Antioquia: Universidad de Antiguia, 1982.

2706. Sambarino, Mario. IDENTIDAD, TRADICION, AUTENTICIDAD: TRES PROB-
LEMAS DE AMERICA LATINA. Caracas: Centro de Estudios Latinoamericanos
Romulo Gallegos, 1980.

2707. Sergio, Sarti. PANORAMA DELLA FILOSOFIA ISPANOAMERICANA CON-
TEMPORANEA. Milan: Cisalpino-Goliardica, 1976.

ARGENTINA

2708. Agassi, Joseph and Robert Sonne Cohen, eds. SCIENTIFIC PHILOSOPHY TODAY:
ESSAYS IN HONOR OF MARIO BUNGE. Dordrecht and Boston: Reidel, 1982.

This volume includes a list of Mario Bunge's publications on pages 489-500.

2709. Aguero, Able, et al. EL MOVIMIENTO POSITIVISTA ARGENTINO. Ed. by
Hugo Edgardo Biagini. Buenos Aires: Editorial de Belgrano, 1985.

2710. Alberini, Coriolano. EPISTOLARIO: CORIOLANO ALBERINI. Mendoza:
Universidad Nacional de Cuto, Facultad de Filosof y Letras, Instituto
de Filosofia, 1981-.

2711. Ardao, Arturo, et al, eds. FRANCISCO ROMERO, MAESTRO DE LA FILOSOFIA
LATINOAMERICANA. Caracas: Sociedad Interamericana de Filosofia, Secretaria, 1983.

The text is in English, French and Spanish.

2712. Atiennza, Manuel. LA FILOSOFIA DEL DERECHO ARGENTINA ACTUAL.
Buenos Aires: Ediciones Depalma, 1984.

The prologue to the volume was written by Francisco Miro Quesada. There is also a
bibliography on pages 335-363.

2713. Biagini, Hugo Edgardo. FILOSOFIA AMERICANA E IDENTITDAD: EL CON-
FLICTIVO CASO ARGENTINIO. Buenos Aires: Editorial Universitaria de Buenos
Aires, 1989.

2714. Biagini, Hugo Edgardo. PANORAMA FILOSOFICO ARGENTINO. Buenos
Aires: Editorial Universitaria de Buenos Aires, 1985.

Arturo Andres Roig wrote the prologue to this volume.

2715. Biagini, Hugo Edgardo, et al. LA REVISTA DE FILOSOFIA (1915-1929): ESTUDIO
E INDICES ANALITICOS. Buenos Aires: Academia Nacional de Ciencias de Buenos
Aires, Centro Estudios Filosofico, 1984.

2716. Bunge, Mario Augusto. CAUSALITY AND MODERN SCIENCE. 3d. rev. ed. New
York: Dover, 1979.

2717. Bunge, Mario Augusto. MATERIALISMO Y CIENCIA. Barcelona: Ariel, 1981.

2718. Bunge, Mario Augusto. THE MIND-BODY PROBLEM: A PSYCHOLOGICAL
APPROACH. Oxford and New York: Pergamon Press, 1980.

2719. Bunge, Mario Augusto. SCIENCE, TECHNICAL EXPERTISE, AND THE QUES-
TION OF VALUE AND CHOICE IN MODERN SOCIETY. Berkeley: Berkeley California Extension Media Center, 1977.

This is a sound recording in 2 cassettes.

2720. Bunge, Mario Augusto. SCIENTIFIC MATERIALISM. Dordrecht and Boston: Reidel, 1981.

2721. Bunge, Mario Augusto. TREATISE ON BASIC PHILOSOPHY. Dordrecht and Boston: Reidel, 1974-.

The following volumes have been published: 1, SEMANTICS I: SENSE AND REFERENCE (1974); 2, SEMANTICS II: INTERPRETATION AND TRUTH (1974); 3, ONTOLOGY I: THE FURNITURE OF THE WORLD (1977); 4, ONTOLOGY II: A WORLD OF SYSTEMS (1979); 5, EPISTEMOLOGY AND METHODOLOGY I: EXPLORING THE WORLD (1983); 6, EPISTEMOLOGY AND METHODOLOGY II: UNDERSTANDING THE WORLD (1983); 7, EPISTEMOLOGY AND METHODOLOGY III: PHILOSOPHY OF SCIENCE AND TECHNOLOGY: PART I. FORMAL AND PHYSICAL SCIENCES and PART II. LIFE SCIENCE, SOCIAL SCIENCE AND TECHNOLOGY (1985); 8, ETHICS: THE GOOD AND THE RIGHT (1989).

2722. Bunge, Mario Augusto, et al. SEMANTIQUE DANS LES SCIENCES: COLLOQUE DE L'ACADEMIE INTERNATIONAL DE PHILOSOPHIE DES SCIENCES. Paris: Beauschene, 1978.

The text is in French, English or German.

2723. Bunge, Mario Augusto and Eli de Gortari. METHODOLOGIA: UNA DISCUSSION. Mexico: Universidad Autonoma de Nuevo Leon, Facultad de Filosofia y Letras, 1976.

2724. Cardenas, Rodolfo Marcelo. EL HOMBRE, ALIENADO O CULPABLE? Buenos Aires: Plus Ultra, 1976.

2725. Carpio, Adolfo P. EL SENTIDO DE LA HISTORIA DE LA FILOSOFIA: ENSAYO ONTOLOGICO SOBRE LA "ANARQUIA" DE LOS SISTEMAS Y LA VERDAD FILOSOFICA. Buenos Aires: Editorial Universitaria de Buenos Aires, 1977.

2726. Castillo Arraez, Alberto. COMENTARIOS A LAS IDEAS ETICAS DE ALEJANDRO KORN. Caracas: Ediciones MRI, 1982.

2727. Caturelli, Alberto. LA METAFISICA CRISTIANA EN EL PENSAMIENTO OCCIDENTAL. Buenos Aires: Ediciones de Cruzamante, 1983.

There is a bibliography of the author's works on pages 154-155.

2728. Caturelli, Alberto. METAFISICA TRAJO. Buenos Aires: Editorial Huemul, 1980.

2729. Caturelli, Alberto. REFLEXIONS PARA UNA FILOSOFIA CRISTIANA DE LA EDUCACION. Cordoba: Direccion General de Publicaciones Universidad Nacional de Cordoba, 1982.

2730. Ciapuscio, Hector. EL PENSAMIENTO FILOSOFICO-POLITICO DE ALBERDI. Buenos Aires: Ediciones Culturales Argentinas: Secretaria de Cultura, Ministerio de Educacion y Justicia, 1985.

2731. Cuyo (Mendoza, Argentina). CUYO: ANUARIO DE FILOSOFIA ARGENTINA Y AMERICANA. Mendoza, Argentina: Universidad Nacional de Cuyo, Facultad de Filosofia y Letras, Instituto de Filosofia Argentina y Americana, 1984-.

2732. Dussel, Enrique D. ETHICS AND THE THEOLOGY OF LIBERATION. Tr. of TEOLOGIA DE LA LIBERACION Y ETICA [i.e. HISTORIA]: CAMINOS DE LIB-

ERACION LATINOAMERICANA. 3d. ed. Buenos Aires: Latinoamericos Libros, 1975. Tr. by Bernard F. McWilliams. Maryknoll, NY: Orbis Books, 1978.

The contents of this book were originally delivered as lectures in a course organized by the Justice and Peace Center, Buenos Aires, 1972.

2733. Dussel, Enrique D. PHILOSOPHY OF LIBERATION. Tr. of FILOSOFIA DE LA LIBERACION. Mexico: Editorial Edicol, 1975. Tr. from the Spanish by Aquilina Martinez and Christine Morkovsky. Maryknoll, NY: Orbis Books, 1985.

2734. Farre, Luis and Celina Ana Lertora Mendoza. LA FILOSOFIA EN LA ARGENTINA. Buenos Aries: Editorial Docencia: Proyectto CINAE, Centro de Investigacion y Accion Educativa, 1981.

2735. Fornet-Betancourt, Raul and Celina Ana Lertora Mendoza, eds. ETHIK IN DEUTSCHLAND UND LATEINAMERIKA HEUTE: AKTE DER ERSTEN GERMANO-IBEROAMERIKANISCHEN ETHIK-TAGE. Frankfurt am Main and New York: Peter Lang, 1987.

The text is written in Spanish and German. The meeting was held Sept. 11-13, 1985 in Buenos Aires and was sponsored by the Fundacion para el Estudio del Pensamiento Argentino e Iberamericano and the Lehrstuhl fur Praktische Philosophie und Geschichte der Philosophie at the Catholische Universitat Eichstatt.

2736. Frondizi, Risieri. ENSAYOS FILOSOFICOS. Mexico: Fondo de Cultura Economica, 1986.

Jorge J. E. Gracia wrote the prologue and contributed an essay to this work.

2737. Frondizi, Risieri. INTRODUCCION A LOS PROBLEMAS FUNDAMENTALES DEL HOMBRE. 1st ed. Madrid: Fondo de Cultura Economica, 1977.

2738. Grand Ruiz, Beatriz Hilda. EL TIEMPO EN JEAN PAUL SARTRE. APENDICE: EL TIEMPO EN CARLOS ASTRADA. Buenos Aires: Ediciones Clepsidra, 1982.

2739. Guariglia, Osvaldo Norberto. IDOLOGIA, VERDAD Y LEGITIMACION. Buenos Aires: Editoria Sudamericana, 1986.

2740. Guerrero, Cesar H. LAS IDEAS FILOSOFICAS EN SAN JUAN. San Juan, Argentina: Ediciones Agon, 1982.

2741. Klimovsky, Gregorio. NOTAS PRELIMINARES SOBRE CONVENCION Y MODALIDAD. Buenos Aires: Instituto Torcuato Di Tella, Centro Investigaciones Sociales, 1976.

2742. Kusch, Rodolfo. ESBOZO DE UNZ ANTROPOLOGIA FILOSOFICA AMERICANA. Buenos Aires: Ediciones Castaneda, 1978.

2743. Lertora Mendoza, Celina Ana. BIBLIOGRAFIA FILOSOFICA ARGENTINA (1900-1975). Ed. by Matilde Isabel Garcia Losada. Buenos Aires: Fundacion para Educacion, la Ciencia y la Cultura, 1983.

2744. Lertora Mendoza, Celina Ana. LA ENSENANZA DE LA FILOSOFIA EN TIEMPOS DE LA COLONIA: ANALISIS DE CURSOS MANUSCRITOS. Buenos Aires: Fundacion para la Educacion, la Ciencia y la Cultura, 1980c1979.

The text is in Latin and Spanish.

2745. Lores Arnaiz, Maria del Rosario. HACIA UN EPISTEMOLOGIA DE LAS CIENCIAS HUMANAS. Buenos Aires: Editorial de Belgrano, 1986.

2746. Maliandi, Ricardo. CULTURA Y CONFLICTO: INVESTIGACIONES ETICAS Y ANTROPOLOGICAS. Buenos Aires: Editorial Biblos, 1984.

2747. Nino, Carlos Santiago. ETICA Y DERECHOS HUMANOS: UN ENSAYO DE FUNDAMENTACION. 2d, enl. and rev ed. Buenos Aires: Editoria Astrea, 1989.

2748. Noussan-Lettry, Luis. CUESTIONES DE HERMENEUTICA HISTORICO-FILOSO-FICA. Mendoza, Argentina: Universidad Nacional de Cuyo, Facultad de Filosofia y Letras, Instituto de Filosofia, 1980-.

2749. Olaso, Ezequiel de. ESCEPTICISMO E ILLUSTRACION: LA CRISIS PIRRONICA E HUME Y ROUSSEAU. Cuadernos de Historica de las ideas. Valencia, Venezuela: Universidad De Carabobo, 1981.

2750. Orayen, Raul, ed. ENSAYOS ACTUALES SOBRE ADAM SMITH Y DAVID HUME. Buenos Aires: Editorial del Instituto, 1978.

2751. Ortiz, Hector. LA FILOSOFIA HOY EN ALEMANIA Y AMERICA LATINA: JORNADAS REALIZADAS EN CORDOBA ENTRE EL 21 Y EL 24 DE SEPTIEMBRE DE 1983. Ed. by Konrad Cramer, et al. Cordoba: Circulo de Amigos del Instituto Goethe, 1984.

This meeting was sponsored by the Instituto Goethe de Cordoba and the Sociedad Argentina de Filosofia under the direction of Professor Hector V. Ortiz.

2752. Pro, Diego F. ENTRE LA ONTOLOGIA Y LA ANTROPOLOGIA FILOSOFICA. Mendoza: Facultad de Filosofia y Letras, Universidad Nacional de Cuyo, Instituto de Filosofia, 1981.

2753. Quiles, Ismael. AUTORRETRATO FILOSOFICO. Buenos Aires: Editiones Universidad del Salvador, 1981.

2754. Quiles, Ismael. FILOSOFIA Y VIDA. Buenos Aires: Ediciones Depalma, 1983.

2755. Ravera, Rosa Maria. ESTETICA Y SEMIOTICA. Rosario, Santa Fe, Argentina: Editorial Fundacion Ross, 1988.

2756. Schuster, Felix Gustavo. EXPLICACION Y PREDICCION: LA VALIDEZ DEL CONOCIMIENTO EN CIENCIAS SOCIALES. Buenos Aires: Consejo Latinoamericano de Ciencias Sociales, 1982.

BOLIVIA

2757. Albarracin Millan, Juan. EL PENSAMIENTO FILOSOFICO DE TAMAYO Y EL IRRACIONALISMO ALEMAN. La Paz, Bolivia: Akapana, 1981.

This is the text of a lecture delivered at the Goethe Institut, La Paz, and published in EL DIARIO of La Paz in June/July, 1979.

2758. Francovich, Guillermo. ALCIDES ARGUEDAS Y OTROS ENSAYOS SOBRE LA HISTORIA. La Paz: Libreria Editoria Juventud, 1979.

2759. Francovich, Guillermo. EL MUNDO, EL HOMBRE Y LOS VALORES. La Paz: Libreria Editorial Juventud, 1981.

These lectures were given in Ducre and published in LA RAZON, La Paz, in 1945.

2760. Francovich, Guillermo. EL ODIO AL PENSAMIENTO: LOS NUEVOS FILOSOFOS FRANCESES. Buenos Aires: Ediciones Depalma, 1982.

2761. Francovich, Guillermo. ENSAYOS PASCALLANOS. Sucre, Bolivia: Division de Extension Universitaria, 1979.

2762. Francovich, Guillermo. LOS CAMINOS DEL EXCESO. Sucre, Bolivia: Division Extension Universitaria, 1977.

This work contains essays previously published in the REVISTA FILOSOFIA Y LETRAS, Universidad Autonoma, Mexico and in PRESENCE LITERARIA, La Paz.

2763. Francovich, Guillermo. PACHAMAMA, DIALOGO SOBRE EL PROVENIT DE LA CULTURE EN BOLIVIA; HUMANISMO LATINOAMERICANO. 3d ed. La Paz: Libreria Editorial Juventud, 1980.

BRAZIL

2764. Amaral, Marcio Tavares d'. ARTE E SOCIEDADE, UMA VISAO HISTORICO-FILOSOFICA. Rio de Janeiro: Edicoes Antares em convenio com o Instituto Nacional do Livro, Fundocao Nacional Pro-Memoria, 1984.

2765. Beaini, Thais Curi. AESCUTA DO SILENCIO: UM ESTUDO SOBRE A LINGUA-GEM NO PENSAMENTO DE HEIDEGGER. Sao Paulo: Cortez Editora: Autores Associados, 1981.

2766. Beaini, Thais Curi. HEIDEGGER: ARTE COMO CULTIVO DO INAPARENTE. Sao Paulo: Nova Stella: Editora da Universidade de Sao Paulo, 1986.

This work was originally presented as the author's doctoral thesis at the Universidade de Sao Paulo in 1986 under the title, A ARTE COMO FRUTO DAS CONCEPCOES EPOCAIS DO SER.

2767. Brito, Rosa Mendon ca de. FILOSOFIA, EDUCACAO, SOCIEDADE E DIREITO NA OBRA DE ARTHUR ORLANDO DA SILVA, 1858-1916. Recife: Fundacao Joaquim Nabuco: Editora Massamgana, 1980.

2768. Correia, Alexandre. ENSAIOS POLITICOS E FILOSOFICOS. Sao Paulo: Editora Convivio: Editora da Universidade de Sao Paulo, 1984.

2769. Crippa, Adolpho. AS IDEIAS FILOSOFICAS NO BRASIL. 3 Vols. Sao Paulo: Editora Convivio, 1978.

2770. Dascal, Marcelo. DIALOGUE: AN INTERDISCIPLINARY APPROACH. Amsterdam and Philadelphia: J. Benjamins, 1985.

This volume consists of papers presented at the 1st International Encounter on the Philosophy of Language held at Campinas, Brazil in August, 1981.

2771. Dascal, Marcelo. FUNDAMENTOS METODOLOGICOS DA LINGUISTICA. Sao Paulo: Global Editora, 1978-.

2772. Dascal, Marcelo. LEIBNIZ, LANGUAGE, SIGNS, AND THOUGHT: A COLLEC-TION OF ESSAYS. Amsterdam and Philadelphia: J. Benjamins, 1987.

This work contains writings of Leibniz previously untranslated into English.

2773. Dascal, Marcelo. PRAGMATICS AND THE PHILOSOPHY OF MIND. Amsterdam and Philadelphia: J. Benjamins, 1983-.

2774. Dascal, Marcelo. SEMIOLOGIE DE LEIBNIZ. Paris: Aubier-Montaigne, 1978.

This volume contains a bibliography on pages 233-251.

2775. Fernandes, Sergio L. de. FOUNDATION OF OBJECTIVE KNOWLEDGE: THE RELATIONS OF POPPER'S THEORY OF KNOWLEDGE TO THAT OF KANT'S. Boston Studies in the Philosophy of Science, Vol. 86. Dordrecht and Boston: Reidel, 1985.

2776. Fonseca, Eduardo Giannetti da. BELIEFS IN ACTION: ECONOMIC PHILOSOPHY AND SOCIAL CHANGE. Cambridge and New York: Cambridge Univ. Press, 1991.

2777. Franciatto, Claudir, ed. A FACANHA DA LIBERDADE: UMA DISCUSSAO SOBRE A VITALIZA CAO NO MUNDO, DOS PENSAMENTOS LIBERAL E LIBERTARIO COM A PARTICIPACAO DE ANTONIO PAIM... Sao Paulo: O Estado de Sao Paulo, 1985?

2778. Francovich, Guillermo. FILOSOFOS BRASILEIROS. Tr. of FILOSOFOS BRASILENOS. Buenos Aires: Editorial Losada, 1943. Tr. by Nisia Nobrega. Rio de Janeiro: Presenca Ediciones, 1979.

2779. Guerreiro, Mario A. L. PROBLEMAS DE FILOSOFIA DA LINGUAGEM. Niteroi-RJ: Universidade Federal Fluminense/EDUFF, PROED--Programa de Estimulo a Editora cao'as IES, 1985.

2780. Guimaraes, Aquiles Cortes. FARIAS BRITO E AS ORIGENS DO EXISTENCIALISMO NO BRASIL. 2d. rev. and enl ed. Biblioteca de Pensamiento Brasileiro. Sao Paulo: Editora Convivio, 1984.

2781. Ladusans, Stanislavs, ed. RUMOS DA FILOSOFIA ATUAL NO BRASIL, EM AUTO-RETRATOS. Sao Paulo: Edicoes Loyola, 1976-.

2782. Machado, Geraldo Pinheiro. 1,000 TITULOS DE AUTORES BRASILEIROS DE FILOSOFIA. Sao Paulo: Pontificia Universidade Catolica de Sao Paulo, Unidade Central de Documenta cao e informa cao Cientifica Professor Casemiro dos Reis Filho, 1983-.

The following volumes have been published to date: Vol. 1, LIVROS E CAPITULOS DE LIVROS. Vol. 2, ARTIGOS DE PERIODICOS. Vol. 3, EVENTOS. Vol. 4, RESENHAS. These volumes contain 1,000 titles by Brazilian philosophers.

2783. Machado, Geraldo Pinheiro. A FILOSOFIA NO BRAZIL. 3d ed. Sao Paulo: Cortez e Moraes, 1976.

2784. Nunes, J. Paulo. TEILHARD DE CHARDIN, O SANTO TOMAS DOS ECULO XX; PARALELISMO FILOSOFICO-TEOLOGICO, CONVERGENCIAS E DIVER GENCIAS. Sao Paulo: Edicoes Loyola, 1977.

2785. Oliveira, Beneval de. A FENOMENOLOGIA NO BRASIL. Rio de Janeiro: Pallas Editora e Distribuidora, 1983.

2786. Olmedo Llorente, Francisco. A FILOSOFIA CRITICA DE MIGUEL REALE. Sao Paulo: Editora Convivio, 1985.

2787. Padilha, Tarcisio Meirelles. UMA FILOSOFIA DA ESPERANCA. Rio de Janeiro: Pallas, 1984 or 1985.

2788. Paim, Antonio Ferreira. BIBLIOGRAFIA FILOSOFICA BRASILEIRA, 1808/1930. Ed. by Vivaldo da Costa Lima. Salvador, Bahia: Centro de Documenta cao do Pensamento Brasileiro, 1983.

2789. Paim, Antonio Ferreira. BIBLIOGRAFIA FILOSOFICA BRASILEIRA: PERIODO CONTEMPORANEO (1931/1977). Ed. by Regina Helena Garcia Dorea. Sao Paulo: Edicoes GRD, 1979.

2790. Paim, Antonio Ferreira. CORRENTE ECLETICA NA BAHIA. Ed. by Anna Maria Moog Rodrigues. Rio de Janeiro: Pontificia Universidade Catolica; Rio de Janeiro: Conselho Federal de Cultura: Editora Documentario, 1979.

The introduction and notes were written by Antonio Paim.

2791. Paim, Antonio Ferreira. A FILOSOFIA DA ESCOLA DO RECIFE. 2d. ed. Sao Paulo: Editora Convivio, 1981.

2792. Paim, Antonio Ferreira, ed. A FILOSOFIA POLITICA POSITIVISTA. Rio de Janeiro: Pontificia Universidade Catolica/Rio, 1979.

2793. Paim, Antonio Ferreira. HISTORIA DES IDEIAS FILOSOFICAS NO BRASIL. 3d., rev. and augm ed. Sao Paulo: Editora Convivio. em convenio com o Instituto Nacional do Livro. Fundacao Nacional Pro-Memoria, 1984.

2794. Paim, Antonio Ferreira. INDICE DA REVISTA BRASILEIRA DE FILOSOFIA (1951-1980). Salvador-Bahia: Centro de Documenta cao de Pensamento Brasileiro, 1983.

2795. Paim, Antonio Ferreira. O ESTUDO DO PENSAMENTO FILOSOFICO BRASILEIRO. 2d., rev and enl ed. Sao Paulo: Editora Convivio, 1986.

2796. Paim, Antonio Ferreira, et al. EVOLUCAO HISTORICA DO LIBERALISMO. Belo Horizonte: Editora Itatiaia, 1987.

2797. Pepe, Albano. RACIALISMO APLICADO: UMA CATEGORIA BACHELARDIANA. Porto Alegre-RS-Brasil: Movimento: Centro de Estudos Sociais, Politicos e Educacionais, Faculdades Integradas de Santa Cruz do Sul, 1985.

2798. Reale, Miguel. EXPERIENCIA E CULTURA PARA A FUNDACAO DE UMA TEORIA GERAL DA EXPERIENCIA. Sao Paulo: Editora da Universidade de Sao Paulo, 1977.

2799. Reale, Miguel. FILOSOFIA EM SAO PAULO. 2d. rev ed. Sao Paulo: Editorial Grijalbo, 1976.

2800. Reale, Miguel. A FILOSOFIA NA OBRA DE MACHADO DE ASSIS & "ANTOLOGIA FILOSOFICA DE MACHADO DE ASSIS". Sao Paulo: Livraria Pioneira Editora, 1982.

2801. Reale, Miguel. VERDAD E CONJETURA. Rio de Janeiro: Editora Nova Fronteira, 1983.

2802. Rouanet, Sergio Paulo. AS RAZOES DO ILUMINISMO. Sao Paulo: Companhia das Letras, 1987.

2803. Rouanet, Sergio Paulo. EDIPO E O ANJO: ITINERARIOS FREUDIANOS EM

WALTER BENJAMIN. Rio de Janeiro: Edicoes Tempo Brasileiro, 1981.

2804. Rouanet, Sergio Paulo. A RAZAO CATIVA: AS ILUSOES DA CONSCIENCIA DE PLATAO A FREUD. Sao Paulo: Editora Brasiliense, 1987.

2805. Rouanet, Sergio Paulo. TEORIA CRITICA E PSICANALISE. Rio de Janeiro: Tempo Brazileiro; Forteleza: Edicoes Universidade Federal do Ceara, 1983.

2806. Sanson, Vitorino Felix. A METAFISICA FARIAS BRITO. Caxias do Sul, Brazil: Editora da Universidade de Caxias do Sul, 1984.

2807. Santiago, Silviano. GLOSSARIO DE DERRIDA. Rio de Janeiro: Livraria F. Alves Editora, 1976.

2808. Severino, Antonio Joachim. PESSOA E EXISTENCIA: INICIA CAO AO PERSON-ALISMO DE EMMANUEL MOUNIER. Sao Paulo: Editora Autores Associados: Cortez Editora, 1983.

This work was originally presented as the author's thesis at Pontificcia Universidade Catolica de Sao Paulo, 1971.

2809. Sociedade Brasileira de Filosofos Catolicos. FILOSOFIA E DESENVOLVIMENTO. 2 Vols. Rio de Janeiro: Sociedade Brasileira de Folosofos Catolicos, 1977.

These are the Proceedings of the Third Semana Internacional de Filosofia, held in Salvador-Bahia on July 17-23, 1976. This work contains material written in English, German, French, Italian, Portuguese, or Spanish.

2810. Sociedade Brasileira de Filosofos Catolicos. FILOSOFIA E REALIDADE BRASI-LEIRA. 2 Vols. Rio de Janeiro: Sociedade Brasileira de Filosofos Catolicos, 1976.

These are the Proceedings of the Second Semana Internacional de Filosofia, held in Petropolis, Rio de Janeiro, July 14-20, 1974. This work contains material in Portuguese, English, French, German, Italian, or Spanish.

2811. Souza Filho, Danilo Marcondes de, ed. SIGNIFICADO, VERDADE E A CAO: ENSAIOS DE FILOSOFIA ANALITICA DA LINGUAGEM. Niteroi: EDUFF, 1986.

The collection includes contributions by Guido Antonio de Almeida, Vera Cristina de Andrade Bueno, Paulo Alcoforado, Raul Ferreira Landim Filho, Mario Guerreiro and the editor.

2812. Universidade Gama Filho, Departamento de Filosofia. FILOSOFIA LUSO-BRASI-LEIRA. Rio de Janeiro: O Departamento, 1983.

This work contains essays by Ricardo Velez Rodriguez, Eduardo Abranches de Soveral, Antonio Braz Teixeira, Beatriz Nizza da Silva. Geraldo Pinheiro Machado and Nelson Saldanha.

2813. Van Acker, Leonardo. O TOMISMO E O PENSAMENTO CONTEMPORANEO. Sao Paulo: Editora Convivio: Editora da Universidade de Sao Paulo, 1983.

2814. Vaz, Henrique C. de Lima. ESCRITOS DE FILOSOFIA: PROBLEMAS DE FONT-EIRA. Sao Paulo: Edicoes Loyola, 1986-.

2815. Wolff, Francis. LOGIQUE DE L'ELEMENT: CLINIMEN. Paris: Presses Universitaires de France, 1981.

CHILE

2816. Arruda, Ayda, et al, eds. MATHEMATICAL LOGIC: PROCEEDINGS OF THE FIRST BRAZILIAN CONFERENCE ON MATHEMATICAL LOGIC. New York: M. Dekker, 1978.

These proceedings were sponsored by the Center of Logic, Epistemology, and the History of Science, and by the Institute of Mathematics, Statistics, and Computing Science of the State University of Campinas.

2817. Astorquiza Pizarro, Fernando, ed. BIO-BIBLIOGRAFIA DE LA FILOSOFIA EN CHILE DESDE 1980 HASTA 1984. Santiago, Chile: Universidad, Facultad de Filosofia, Humanidades y Educacion: Instituto Profesional de Santiago, Escuela de Bibliotecologia y Documentacion 1985. Santiago, Chile: Barcelona, Empresa Industrial Grafica, 1985.

2818. Astorquiza Pizarro, Fernando, ed. BIO-BIBLIOGRAFIA DE LA FILOSOFIA EN CHILE DESDE EL SIGLO XVI HASTA 1980. Universidad de Chile, Facultad de Filosofia, Humanidades y Educacion y el Instituto Profesional de Santiago, Departemento de Bibliotecologia. Nueva Biblioteca Mexicana, Vol. 84. Santiago, Chile: Barcelona, Empresa Industrial Grafica, 1982.

2819. Biblioteca del Congreso Nacional (Chile). BIBLIOGRAFIA CHILENA DE FILOSO-FIA: DESDE FINES DEL SIGLO XVI HASTA EL PRESENTE. Santiago: La Biblioteca, 1979c1978.

2820. Celis M., Luis, ed. LA PRESENCIA DE LA FILOSOFIA EN LA UNIVERSIDAD CATOLICA (1888-1973). Ed. by Jaime Caiceo E. Santiago: Pontificia Universidad Catolica de Chile, 1982.

2821. Centro de Documenta cao do Pensamento Brasileiro. SILVESTRE PINHEIRO FERREIRA, 1769-1846: BIBLIOGRAFIA E ESTUDOS CRITICOS. Salvador-Bahia: O Centro, 1983.

2822. Chuaqui, Rolando Basim. AXIOMATIC SET THEORY: IMPREDICATIVE THEO-RIES OF CLASSES. Amsterdam and New York: North-Holland, 1981.

2823. Chuaqui, Rolando Basim. INTERNAL AND FORCING MODELS FOR THE IMPREDICATIVE THEORY OF CLASSES. Warsaw: P. W. N., 1980.

2824. Chuaqui, Rolando Basim, et al. MATHEMATICAL LOGIC IN LATIN AMERICA. Amsterdam and New York: North-Holland, 1980.

These are the Proceedings of the Fourth Latin-American Symposium on Mathematical Logic held in Santiago, December, 1978.

2825. Chuaqui, Rolando Basim, et al. NON-CLASSICAL LOGICS, MODEL THEORY AND COMPUTABILITY. Amsterdam and New York: North-Holland, 1977.

These are the Proceedings of the third Latin-American Symposium on Mathematical Logic, Campinas, Brazil, July 11-17, 1976.

2826. Costa Leiva, Miguel Da. EL PENSAMIENTO FILOSOFICO DE ENRIQUE MOLINA GARMENDIA. 2 Vols. Madrid: Universidad Complutense de Madrid, 1978.

2827. Costa Leiva, Miguel Da. LOS FILOSOFOS PRESOCRATICOS. DESDE LOS ORIGENES HASTA LOS ATOMISTAS. 2 Vols. Concepcion: Universidad de Concepcion, Instituto de Filosofia, 1977.

2828. Edwards, Annibal. PARMENIDES: TRAS LA PISTA DE KARL REINHARDT Y WALTER F. OTTO. Santiago: Ediciones Universidad Catolica de Chile, 1986.

2829. Escobar, Roberto. LA FILOSOFIA EN CHILE. Santiago: Universidad Tecnica del Estado, 1976.

2830. Escobar, Roberto. NIETZSCHE E IL TRAGICO: POLITICA DELL'ESPERIANZA E VOLONTA DI POTENZA. Milan: Il Formichiere, 1980.

2831. Escobar, Roberto. NIETZSCHE E LA FILOSOFIA POLITICA DEL XIX SECOLO. Milan: Il Formichiere, 1978.

2832. Espindola, Walter Hanisch. JUAN IGNACO MOLINA, SABIO DE SU TIEMPO. 2d. rev ed. Santiago: Editorial "Nihi Mihi", 1976.

2833. Estrella, Jorge. ARGUMENTOS FILOSOFICOS. Santiago: Editorial Andres Bello, 1983.

2834. Estrella, Jorge. CIENCIA Y FILOSOFIA. Santiago: Editorial Universitaria, 1982.

2835. Estrella, Jorge. LA FLOR EN LA PIEDRA. Santiago: Editorial Universitaria, 1981.

2836. Garcia De La Huerta, Marcos. LA TECNICA Y EL ESTADO MODERNO HEIDEGGER Y PROBLEMA DE LA HISTORIA. Santiago: Universidad de Chile, Dept. de Estudios Humanisticos, 1980.

2837. Giannini Iniguez, Humberto. DESDE LAS PALABRAS. Santiago: Ediciones Nueva Universidad, 1981.

2838. Giannini Iniguez, Humberto. TIEMPO Y ESPACIO EN ARISTOTELES Y KANT. Santiago: Editorial Andres Bello, 1982.

2839. Guzman Brito, Alejandro. LA FIJACION DEL DERECHO. Valparaiso: Ediciones Universitarias de Valparaiso, 1977.

2840. Ibanez Santa Maria, Gonzalo. PERSONA Y DERECHO EN EL PENSAMIENTO DE BERDIAEFF, MOUNIER Y MARITAIN. Santiago: Ediciones Universidad Catolica de Chile, 1984.

This work was originally presented as the author's doctoral thesis at the Universidad de Derecho Economia y Ciencias Sociales de Paris (Paris II) under the title, BERDIAEFF, MOUNIER, MARITAIN, FILOSOFIA DEL DERECHO EN EL MOVIMIENTO DEL PERSONALISMO CRISTIANO EN FRANCIA.

2841. Mielas Jimenez, Jorge. LA VIOLENCIA Y SUS MASCARAS. DOS ENSAYOS DE FILOSOFIA. Santiago: Aconcagua, 1978.

2842. Munizaga Aguirre, Roberto. PRINCIPIOS DE EDUCACION. 4th ed. Santiago: Editorial Universitaria, 1978.

2843. Rivano, Juan. THE IDEAS OF MARSHALL MCLUHAN. Tr. of EL PENSAMIENTO DE MARSHALL MCLUHAN. Santiago: s.n., 1972. Tr. by Ivan Jaksic. Amherst: Council on International Studies, State Univ. of New York at Buffalo, 1979.

2844. Rivano, Juan. JOACHIM ISRAEL ON THE EPISTEMOLOGY OF THE SOCIAL SCIENCES: A REVIEW ESSAY. Amherst: Council on International Studies, State Univ. of New York at Buffalo, 1981.

2845. Sanchez Correa, Elena. TRES ENSAYOS SOBRE FILOSOFIA DE LA EDUCA-CION. Santiago: Universidad Catolica de Chile, 1977.

2846. Schultz, Margarita and Jorge Estrella. LA ANTROPOLOGIA DE FELIX SCHWARTZMANN. Santiago: Editorial Universitaria, 1978.

2847. Squella, Agustin. ESTRUCTURA Y CONOCIMIENTO CIENTIFICO. Buenos Aires: Editorial Paidos, 1977.

2848. Torretti, Roberto. PHILOSOPHY OF GEOMETRY FROM RIEMANN TO POIN-CARE. Dordrecht and Boston: Reidel, 1978.

There is a bibliography on pages 420-439.

2849. Torretti, Roberto. RELATIVITY AND GEOMETRY. Oxford and New York: Pergamon, 1983.

There is a bibliography on pages 351-379.

2850. Vial Larrain, Juan De Dios. LA FILOSOFIA DE ARISTOTELES COMO TEOLO-GIA DEL ACTO. Santiago: Editorial Universitaria, 1980.

2851. Vidal Munoz, Santiago. ANDRES BELLO, AMERICANISTA Y FILOSOFO. Madrid: Oriens, 1982.

2852. Wagner De Reyna, Alberto. ANALOGIA Y EVORACION. Madrid: Gredos, 1976.

2853. Zapata, Rene. LUTTES PHILOSOPHIQUES EN U. S. S. R., 1922-1931. Paris: Presses Universitaires de France, 1983.

COLOMBIA

2854. Arroyave de la Calle, Julio Cesar. LA FILOSOFIA EN AMERICA: FENOMENOL-OGIA DEL CONOCIMIENTO, FILOSOFIA DEL SER Y LOS VALORES, TEORIA DE LA CIENCIA. Medellin: Editorial Etcetera, 1979.

2855. Hoyos Vasquez, Guillermo. INTERNATIONALITAT ALS VERANTWORTUNG: GESCHICHTSTELEOLOGIE UND TELEOLOGIE DER INTENTIONALITAT BEI HUSSERL. The Hague: Nijhoff, 1976.

2856. Hoyos Vasquez, Guillermo, et al. EL SUJETO COMO OBJETO DE LAS CIENCIAS SOCIALES. Bogota: Centro De Investigacion y Educacion Popular, [1982 or 1983].

This is a collection of papers presented at the Third Seminar of the Grupo de Tabajo Epistemologia y Politica of the Conpejo Sociales, July 1-3, 1981. The Seminar was held in cooperation with the Sociedad Columbiana de Epistemologia.

2857. Hoyos Vasquez, Guillermo, et al. EPISTEMOLOGIA POLITICA: CRITICA A POSITIVISMO DE LA CIENCIAS SOCIALES EN AMERICA LATINA DESDE LA RACIONALIDAD DIALECTICA. Bogota: Fundacion Friedrich Naumann; Columbia Centro De Investigacion Y Educacion Popular, 1980.

2858. Marquinez Argote, German, ed. SOBRE FILOSOFIA ESPANOLA Y LATINOA-MERICANA. Bogota: Universidad Santo Tomas, Facultad de Filosofia, Centro de Inves-tigaciones, 1987.

2859. Marquinez Argote, German, et al. LA FILOSOFIA EN COLOMBIA: HISTORIA DE LAS IDEAS. Bogota: Editorial el Buho, 1988.

This work contains contributions by Roberto J. Salazar Ramos, Joaquin Zabalza Iriarte, Leonardo Tovar Gonzalez, Eudoro Rodriguez Albarracin, Daniel Herrera Restrepo, and German Marquinez Argote.

2860. Ordenes. Jorge. EL SER MORAL EN LAS OBRAS DE FERNANDO GONZALEZ. Medellin: Associacion Medica de Antioquia, 1983.

This work was presented originally as the author's thesis at George Washington University in 1979.

2861. Pinzon Garzon, Rafael. LA FILOSOFIA EN COLOMBIA. Bogota: Universidad Santo Tomas, Centro de Investigaciones de la Facultad de Filosofia, 1987-.

2862. Sierra Mejia, Ruben, ed. ENSAYOS FILOSOFICOS. Bogota: Instituto Colombiano de Cultura Subdireccion de Communicaciones Culturales Division de Publicaciones, 1978.

2863. Sierra Mejia, Ruben. LA FILOSOFIA EN COLOMBIA: SIGLIO XX. Bogota: Procultura, Presidencia de la Republica, 1985.

2864. Sierra Mejia, Ruben. LOGICA Y FILOSOFIA DEL LENGUAJE EN BERTRAND RUSSELL. Bogota: Faculted de Filosofia y Letras, Universidad de los Andes, 1979.

2865. Tellez, Freddy. DE LA PRAXIS. Bogota: Universidad Nacional de Colombia, 1985.

2866. Universidad Santo Tomas. Facultad de Filosofia. Centro de Investigaciones. LA FILOSOFIA EN COLOMBIA: BIBLIOGRAFIA DEL SIGLIO XX. Bogota: Universidad Santo Tomas, Centro de Investigaciones de la Facultad de Filosofia, 1985.

COSTA RICA

2867. Camacho, Luis, ed. CAUSALIDAD Y DETERMINACION. San Jose: Editorial de la Universidad de Costa Rica, 1979.

2868. Gutierrez, Claudio. NUEVE ENSAYOS EPISTEMOLOGICOS. San Jose: Editorial Costa Rica, 1982.

CUBA

2869. D'Angelo, Edward, ed. CUBAN AND NORTH AMERICAN MARXISM. Amsterdam: B. R. Gruner, 1984.

This book consists of papers presented at the Cuban-North American Marxist Philosophers Conference held in May, 1982, in Havana.

2870. Gracia, Jorge Jesus Emiliano, ed. EL HOMBRE Y SU CONDUCTA: ENSAYOS FILOSOFICOS EN HONOR DE RISIERI FRONDIZI. (MAN AND HIS CONDUCT: PHILOSOPHICAL ESSAYS IN HONOR OF RISIERI FRONDIZI). Rio Piedras: Editorial Universitaria, 1980.

This work contains essays by Latin American and North American philosophers.

2871. Gracia, Jorge Jesus Emiliano. INTRODUCTION TO THE PROBLEM OF INDIVIDUATION IN THE EARLY MIDDLE AGES. Washington, DC: Catholic Univ. of

America Press; Munich: Philosophia Verlag, 1984.

2872. Gracia, Jorge Jesus Emiliano, et al. PHILOSOPHICAL ANALYSIS IN LATIN AMERICA. Dordrecht and Boston: Reidel, 1984.

2873. Instituto de Filosofia (Academia de Ciencias de Cuba). Departamento de Materialismo Dialectico. PROBLEMAS FILOSOFICOS METODOLOGICOS DEL CONOCIMIENTO CIENTIFICO. Havana: Editorial de Ciencias Sociales, 1985.

These are the proceedings of a seminar entitled Problemas Filosoficos Metodologi os del Conocimiento Cientifico, sponsored by the Instituto de Filosofia de la Academia de Ciencias de Cuba, Departamento de Materialismo Dialectico which was held at the Institute in 1984.

2874. Mariategui, Jose Carlos. OBRAS. Ed. by Francisco Baeza. Havana: Casa de la Americas, 1982-.

2875. Marti, Oscar Raphael. THE REACTION AGAINST POSITIVISM IN LATIN AMERICA: A STUDY IN THE PHILOSOPHIES OF CARLOS VAZ FERREIRA AND JOSE INGENIEROS. New York: City Univ. of New York, 1978.

This is the author's thesis. A microfilm of the transcript is available from University Microfilms, Ann Arbor, MI.

2876. Rodriguez Ugidos, Zaira. FILOSOFIA, CIENCIA Y VALOR: CRITICA DEL ALTHUSSERIANISMO Y DE ALGUNAS VARIANTES NEOALTHUSSERIANAS EN LATINOAMERICA. Havana: Editorial de Ciencias Sociales, 1985.

2877. Sosa, Ernest, ed. ESSAYS ON THE PHILOSOPHY OF RODERICK M. CHISHOLM. Amsterdam: Rodopi, 1979.

2878. Sosa, Ernest, ed. THE PHILOSOPHY OF NICHOLAS RESCHER: DISCUSSION AND REPLIES. Dordrecht and Boston: Reidel, 1979.

2879. Ternovoi, Oleg Sergeevich. LA FILOSOFIA EN KUBY 1790-1878. Tr. of FILOSO-FIIA A KUBY, 1790-1878 Minsk: Izd-vo BGU, 1972. Havana: Editorial de la Ciencias Sociales, 1981.

This volume contains an extensive bibliography on pages 327-341. The original Russian work contains a table of contents and a summary in Spanish.

ECUADOR

2880. Malo Fonzalez, Hernan. EL HABITO EN LA FILOSOFIA DE FELIX RAVAISSON. Quito: Centro de Publicaciones de la Pontificia Universidad Catolica de Ecuador, 1976.

This work includes a translation of DE L'HABITUDE by Ravaisson.

2881. Roig, Arturo Andres. EL HUMANISMO ECUATORIANO DE LA SEGUNDA MITAD DEL SIGLO XVIII. 2 Vols. Quito: Banco Central del Ecuador: Corporacion Editora Nacional, 1984.

There is an extensive bibliography on pages 259-282.

2882. Roig, Arturo Andres. ESQUEMAS PARA UNA HISTORIA DE LA FILOSOFIA ECUATORIANA. 2d. corr & aug ed. Quito: Ediciones de la Universidad Catolica, 1982.

MEXICO

2883. Basave Fernandez Del Valle, Augustin. FILOSOFIA DE HOMBRE: FUNDAMEN-
TOS DE ANTROPOSAFIA METAFISICA. Mexico: Espasa-Calpe Mexicana, 1978.

2884. Basave Fernandez Del Valle, Augustin. LA COSMOVISION DE FRANZ KAFKA.
Mexico: Jus, 1978.

2885. Basave Fernandez Del Valle, Augustin. TRATADO DE METAFISICA: TEORIA
DE LA "HABENCIA". Mexico: Editorial Limusa, 1982.

2886. Basave Fernandez Del Valle, Augustin. TRES FILOSOFOS ALEMANES DE
NUESTRO TIEMPO. Mexico: Universidad Autonoma de Nuevo Leon, 1977.

2887. Beller, Walter, et al. EL POSITIVISMO MEXICANO. Mexico, D.F.: Universidad
Autonoma Metropolitana Xochimilco, 1985.

2888. Beuchot, Mauricio. LA FILOSOFIA DEL LENGUAJE EN LA EDAD MEDIA.
Mexico: Universidad Nacional Autonoma de Mexico, Instituto de Investigaciones Filosoficas, 1981.

2889. Cardiel Reyes, Raul. RETORNO A CASO. Mexico: Universidad Nacional Autonoma
de Mexico, Facultad de Filosofia y Letras, 1986.

2890. Cerutti Guldberg, Horacio. DE VARIA UTOPICA. Bogota: Publicaciones Universidad Central: Instituto Colombiano de Estudios Latinoamericano y del Caribe, 1989.

2891. Cerutti Guldberg, Horacio. FILOSOFIA DE LA LIBERACION LATINOAMERICA-
NA. Mexico: Fondo de Cultura Economica, 1983.

There is a bibliography on pages 311-324.

2892. Cerutti Guldberg, Horacio. HACIA UNA METODOLOGIA DE LA HISTORIA
DE LAS IDEAS (FILOSOFICAS) EN AMERICANA LATINA. Guadalajara, Jalisco,
Mexico: Universidad de Guadalajara, 1986.

2893. De Ipola, Emilio. DISCUSION SOBRE IDEOLOGIA. Caracas: Ediciones
Faces/UCV, 1981.

This work contains contributions by Emilio de Ipola, Jeanette Abouhamad and
Rigoherto Lanz.

2894. Escobar Valenzuela, Gustavo Alberto. LA ILUSTRACION EN LA FILOSOFIA
LATINOAMERICANO. Mexico, D.F.: Editorial Trillas, 1980.

2895. Facultad de Filosofia y Letras, Universidad Nacional Autonoma de Mexico. ESTU-
DIOS DE HISTORIA DE LA FILOSOFIA EN MEXICO. 4th ed. Mexico, D. F.: Universidad Nacional Autonoma de Mexico, 1985.

This book includes contributions by Miguel Leon-Portilla, Edmundo O'Gorman, Jose
M. Gallegos Racafull, Rafael Moreno, Luis Villoro, Abelardo Villegas, Leopoldo Zea,
Fernando Salmeron, and Ramon Xirau.

2896. Gaos, Jose. ANTOLOGIA DEL PENSAMIENTO DE LENGUA ESPANOLA EN
LA EDAD CONTEMPORANEA. Introduccion y textos del Dr. Jose Gaos. Culiaca,
Sinaloa, Mexico: Universidad Autonoma de Sinaloa, 1982.

2897. Gaos, Jose. EN TORNO A LA FILOSOFIA MEXICANA. Mexico, DF: Alianza

Editorial Mexicana, 1980.

2898. Gaos, Jose. FILOSOFIA "AMERICANA". Mexico: Universidad Nacional Autonoma de Mexico, Coordinacion de Humanidades Centro de Estudios Latinoamericanos Facultad de Filosofia y Letras: Union de Universidades de America Latina, 1979.

2899. Gaos, Jose. FILOSOFIA DE LA FILOSOFIA E HISTORIA DE LA FILOSOFIA. Ed. by Fernando Salmeron. 2d ed. Ciudad Universitaria, Mexico: Universidad Nacional Autonom de Mexico, Coordinacion de Humanidades, 1987.

2900. Gaos, Jose. INTRODUCCION A EL SER Y EL TIEMPO DE MARTIN HEIDEGGER. 2d aug. and rev ed. Mexico: Fondo de Cultural Economica, 1977.

2901. Gaos, Jose. OBRAS COMPLETAS. Mexico: Nacional Autonoma de Mexico, Coordinacion de Humanidades, 1982.

2902. Garcia Maynez, Eduardo. ALGUNOS ASPECTOS DE LA DOCTRINIA KELSENIANA: EXPOSION Y CRITICA CONFERENCIAS DEL AUTOR EN EL COLEGIO NACIONAL. Mexico: Editorial Porrua, 1978.

2903. Garcia Maynez, Eduardo. DIALOGOS JURIDICOS. Mexico: Editorial Porrua, 1978.

2904. Garcia Maynez, Eduardo. FILOSOFIA DEL RECHO. 4th rev ed. Mexico: Editorial Porrua, 1983.

2905. Gonzalez, Juliana. EL MALESTAR EN MORAL: FREUD Y LA CRISIS DE LA ETICA. Mexico: J. Mortiz, 1986.

2906. Gonzalez, Juliana. LA METAFISICA DIALECTICA DE EDUARDO NICOL. Mexico: Universidad Nacional Autonoma de Mexico, 1981.

2907. Gonzalez, Juliana. PRESENCIA DE RAMON XIRAU. Mexico, D.F.: UNAM, Coordinacion de Difusion Cultural, 1986.

There is a list of works by the author on pages 219-221.

2908. Gonzalez, Juliana and Lizbeth Sagols, eds. EL SER Y LA EXPRESION: HOMENAJE A EDUARDO NICOL. Mexico, D.F.: Facultad de Folosofia y Letras, Universidad Nacional Autonoma de Mexico, 1990.

2909. Gortari, Eli de. REFLEXIONES HISTORICAS Y FILOSOFICAS SOBRE MEXICO. Mexico, D.F.: Editorial Grijalbo, 1982.

2910. Guillen, Fedro. JESUS SILVA HERZOG, ISIDRO FABELA, JOSE VASCONCELOS. Mexico: Universidad Nacional Autonoma Mexico, 1980.

2911. Hernandez Luna, Juan. SAMUEL RAMOS: ETAPAS DE SU FORMACION ESPIRITUAL. Moralia, MI: Universidad Michoacana de San Nicolas de Hidalgo, 1982.

2912. Krauze de Kolteniuk, Rosa. LA FILOSOFIA DE ANTONIO CASO. Mexico, D. F.: Universidad Nacional Autonoma de Mexico, Seminario de Filosofia en Mexico, Colegio de Filosofia, 1985.

2913. Lipp, Solomon. LEOPOLDO ZEA: FROM MEXICANIDAD TO A PHILOSOPHY OF HISTORY. Waterloo, Ontario: Wilfrid Laurier Press, 1980.

2914. Lizcano, Franciso. LEOPOLDO ZEA: UNA FILOSOFIA DE LA HISTORIA. Madrid: ICI, 1986.

2915. Lopez-Diaz, Pedro. UNA FILOSOFIA PARA LA LIBERTAD: LA FILOSOFIA DE LEOPOLDO ZEA. Mexico, D.F.: Costa-Amic Editores, S.A., 1989.

2916. Medin, Tzvi. LEOPOLDO ZEA: IDEOLOGIA, HISTORIA Y FILOSOFIA DE AMERICA LATINA. Mexico: Universidad Nacional Autonoma de Mexico, Coordinacion de Humanidades, 1983.

2917. Nicol, Eduardo. CRITICA DE LA RAZON SIMBOLICA: LA REVOLUCION EN LA FILOSOFIA. Mexico: Fondo de Cultura Economica, 1982.

2918. Nicol, Eduardo. HISTORICISMO Y EXISTENCIALISMO. 3d ed. Mexico, D.F.: Fondo Cultura Economica, 1981.

2919. Nicol, Eduardo. LA IDEA DEL HOMBRE. Mexico: Fondo de Cultura Economica, 1977.

2920. Nicol, Eduardo. LA PRIMERA TEORIA DE LA PRAXIS. Mexico: Universidad Nacional Autonoma de Mexico, 1976.

2921. Nicol, Eduardo. LA REFORMA DE LA FILOSOFIA. Mexico: Fondo de Cultura Economica, 1980.

2922. Olmedo, Raul. EL ANTIMETODO: INTRODUCCION A LA FILOSOFIA MARX-ISTA. Mexico: Editorial J. Mortiz, 1980.

2923. Rabossi, Eduardo A. ANALISIS FILOSOFICO, LENGUAJE Y METAFISICA: ENSAYOS SOBRE LA FILOSOFIA ANALITICA Y EL ANALISIS FILOSOFICO "CLASICO". Caracas: Monte Avila Editore, 1977.

2924. Rabossi, Eduardo A. LA JUSTIFICACION MORAL DEL CASTIGO: EL TEMA DEL CASTIGO LAS TEORIAS TRADICO. Buenos Aires: Editorial Astrea, 1976.

2925. Ramos, Samuel. OBRAS COMPLETAS. 2d ed. Mexico: Universidad Nacional Autonoma de Mexico, 1985-.

2926. Redmond, Walter Bernard and Mauricio Beuchot. LA LOGICA MEXICANA EN EL SIGLO DE ORO. Mexico: Instituto de Investigaciones Filosoficas, Universidad Nacional Autonoma de Mexico, 1985.

2927. Ribeiro, Darcy. LA CULTURA LATINOAMERICANA. Mexico: Universidad Nacional Autonoma de Mexico, Coordinacion de Humanidades, Facultad de Filosofia y Letras; Union de Universidades de America Latina, 1978.

2928. Roig, Arturo Andres. FILOSOFIA, UNIVERSIDAD Y FILOSOFOS EN AMERICA LATINA. Mexico: Universidad Nacional Autonoma de Mexico, Coordinacion de Human-idades, Centro Coordinador y Difusor de Estudios Latinoamericanos, 1981.

2929. Rossi, Alejandro. LENGUAJE Y SIGNIFICADO. 3d ed. Mexico: Siglio Veintiuno Editores, 1978.

2930. Rossi, Alejandro, et al. JOSE ORTEGA Y GASSET. Mexico: Fondo de Cultura Economica, 1984.

2931. Salmeron, Fernando. LA FILOSOFIA Y LAS ACTITUDES MORALES. 3d ed. Mexico: Siglio Veintiuno Editores, 1986.

2932. Salmeron, Fernando. LAS MOCEDADES DE ORTEGA Y GASSET. 3d ed. Mexico: Universidad Nacional Autonoma de Mexico Facultad de Filosofia y Letras, 1983.

2933. Sanchez Vazquez, Adolfo. ENSAYOS MARXISTAS SOBRE HISTORIA Y POLITI-CA. Mexico, D.F.: Ediciones Oceano, 1985.

2934. Sanchez Vazquez, Adolfo. SOBRE FILOSOFIA Y MARXISMO. Ed. by Gabriel Vargas Lozano. Puebla, Mexico: Escuela de Filosofia y Letras, Ediciones de la Universidad Autonoma de Puebla, 1983.

2935. Serrano Caldera, Alejandro. INTRODUCCION AL PENSAMIENTO DIALECTICO. Mexico: Fondo de Cultura Economica, 1976.

2936. Suarez, Francisco. SUAREZ ON INDIVIDUATION: METAPHYSICAL DISPUTA-TION V, INDIVIDUAL UNITY AND ITS PRINCIPLE. Tr. of DE UNITATE INDI-VIDUALE EUISQUE PRINCIPIO. Translation from Latin with introduction, notes, glossary and bibliography by Jorge J. E. Gracia. Milwaukee: Marquette Univ. Press, 1982.

2937. Tamayo y Salmoran, Rolando. EL DERECHO Y LA CIENCIA DEL DERECHO: INTRODUCCION A LA CIENCIA JURIDICA. Mexico: Universidad Nacional Autonoma de Mexico, Instituto de Investigaciones Juridicas, 1984.

2938. Tamayo y Salmoran, Rolando, ed. FILOSOFIA JURIDICA. Mexico: Universidad Nacional Autonoma de Mexico, Instituto de Investigaciones Juridicas, 1979.

This book contains writings by Edgar Bodenheimer, Luis Recasens Siches, and Michel Villey.

2939. Trejo, Wonfilio. ENSAYOS EPISTOMOLOGICOS. Mexico: Universidad Nacional Autonoma de Mexico, 1976.

2940. Trejo, Wonfilio. FENOMENALISMO Y REALISMO. Mexico: Universidad Nacional Autonoma de Mexico, 1977.

2941. Vargas Lozano, Gabriel. MARX Y SU CRITICA DE LA FILOSOFIA. Mexico, D.F.: Universidad Autonoma Metropolitana, Unidad Iztapalapa, Division de Ciencias Sociales y Humanidades, Departamento de Filosofia, Area de Filosofia de las Ciencias Sociales, 1984.

2942. Vera y Cuspinera, Margarita. EL PENSIAMIENTO FILOSOFICO DE VASCONCE-LOS. Mexico: Extemporaneos, 1979.

2943. Vera y Cuspinera, Margarita. HOMENAJE DE LA FACULTAD DE FILOSOFIA Y LETRAS. Mexico: Universidad Nacional Autonoma de Mexico, 1981.

2944. Villanueva, Enrique. ARGUMENTO DEL LENGUAJE PRIVADO: INTRODUC-CION, SELECCION, DE TEXTOS Y BIBLIOGRAFIA. Mexico: UNAM Instituto de Investigaciones Filosoficas, 1979.

2945. Villanueva, Enrique. LENGUAJE Y PROVACIDAD. Mexico: Universidad Nacional Autonoma de Mexico, Insituto de Investigaciones Filosoficas, 1984.

2946. Villegas, Abelardo, ed. LA FILOSOFIA. Mexico: Direccion General Difusion Cultural Universidad Nacional Autonoma de Mexico, 1979.

2947. Villegas, Abelardo. LA FILOSOFIA DE LO MEXICANO. 2d ed. Mexico: Universidad Nacional Autonoma de Mexico, 1979.

2948. Villegas, Abelardo and Gustavo Escobar, eds. FILOSOFIA ESPANOLA E HISPA-NOAMERICANA CONTEMPORANEAS: ANTOLOGIA. Mexico: Extemporaneos, 1983.

2949. Villegas, Abelardo and Ramon Xirau. LA FILOSOFIA. Mexico: Direccion General de Difusion Cultural, Universidad Nacional Autonoma de Mexico, 1979.

2950. Villoro, Luis. CREER, SABER, CONOCER. Mexico, DF: Siglio Veintiuno Editores, 1982.

This volume contains a bibliography on pages 266-305.

2951. Villoro, Luis. LOS GRANDES MOMENTOS DEL INDIGEISMO EN MEXICO. 2d ed. Mexico: Edicione de la Casa Chata, 1979.

2952. Weinstein, Michael A. THE POLARITY OF MEXICAN THOUGHT: INSTRU-MENTALISM AND FINALISM. Univ. Park: Pennsylvania State Univ. Press, 1976.

2953. Xirau, Ramon. ENTRE IDOLOS Y DIOSES: TRES ENSAYOS SOBRE HEGEL. Mexico: Editorial de El Colegio Nacional, 1980.

2954. Yamuni Tabush, Vera. JOSE GAOS: EL HOMBRE Y SU PENSAMIENTO. Mexico: Universidad Nacional Autonoma de Mexico, 1980.

The text is in Spanish and French.

2955. Zamora, Francisco. IDEALISMO Y MATERIALISMO DIALECTICO: UNO POLEMICA CON EL DOCTOR ANTONIO CASO. Mexico: Editorial Nuestro Tiempo, 1978.

2956. Zea, Leopoldo, ed. AMERICA LATINA EN SUS IDEAS. Paris: Unesco; Mexico: Siglo Veintiuno Editores, 1986.

2957. Zea, Leopoldo. DIALECTICA DE LA CONCIENCIA AMERICANA. Mexico: Alianza Editorial Mexicana, 1976.

2958. Zea, Leopoldo. FILOSOFIA DE LA HISTORIA AMERICANA. Mexico: Fondo de Cultura Economica, 1978.

2959. Zea, Leopoldo. LATINOAMERICA TERCER MUNDO. Mexico: Extemporaneos, 1977.

2960. Zea, Leopoldo. LATINOAMERICA, UN NUEVO HUMANISMO. Tunja, Boyaca, Colombia: Editoria Bolivariana Internacional, 1982.

PARAGUAY

2961. Benitez, Justo Pastor. INFLUENCIAS DEL POSITIVISMO EN LA VULTURA NACIONAL: PARA UNA HISTORIA DE LAS IDEAS. Asuncion, Paraguay: NAPA, 1983.

2962. Duarte Prado, Bacon. CUESTIONES DE ESTETICA. Asuncion, Paraguay: Editora Litocolor, 1983.

2963. Abugattas, Juan, et al. EL FACTOR IDOLOGICOS EN LA CIENCIA Y LA TECHNOLGIA. Lima: Asociacion Cultural Peruano Alemana: Mosi Azul Editores, 1984.

This is a collection of papers from a meeting held in October and November, 1982, in Lima, sponsored by the Asociacion Cultural Peruano-Alemana and the Instituto Goethe de Lima.

2964. Arico, Jose. MARX Y AMERICA LATINA. 2d ed. Mexico City: Alianza Editorial Mexicana, 1982.

2965. Falcon, Jorge. MARIATEGUI, MARX-MARXISMO: EL PRODUCTOR Y SU PRODUCTOR. Lima, Peru: Empresa Editora Amauta, 1983.

2966. Himelblau, Jack. ALEJANDRO O. DEUSTUA: PHILOSOPHY IN DEFENSE OF MAN. Gainesville: Univ. Presses of Florida, 1979.

This work gives a knowledgeable account of the trajectory of the Peruvian aesthetician's thought as well as a detailed description of its substance.

2967. Kossok, Manfred, ed. MARIATEGUI Y LAS CIENCIAS SOCIALES. Lima: Biblioteca Amauta, 1982.

This work includes contributions by Manfred Kossok, Antonio Melis, Anatoly Shulgovsky, Raimundo Prado Redondez, and Kinichiro Harada.

2968. Miro Quesada Cantuarias, Francisco. FILOSOFIA DE LAS MATEMATICAS. Logica, Vol. 1. Lima, Peru: Ignacio Prado Pastor, 1980-.

2969. Miro Quesada Cantuarias, Francisco. IMPACTO DE LA METAFISICA EN LA IDEOLOGIA LATINOAMERICANA. Mexico: Union de Universidades de America Latina, 1978.

2970. Miro Quesada Cantuarias, Francisco. LA FILOSOFIA DE LO AMERICANO, TREINTA ANOS DESPUES. Mexico, D. F.: Universidad Nacional Autonoma de Mexico, Coordinacion de Humanidades, Centro de Estudios Latinoamericanos, Facultad de Filosofia y Letras, Union de Universidades de America Latina, 1979.

2971. Miro Quesada Cantuarias, Francisco. PROYECTO Y REALIZACION DEL FILOSO-FAR LATINOAMERICANO. Mexico: Fondo de Cultura Economica, 1981.

2972. Quijano, Aibal. REENCUENTRO Y DEBATE: UNA INTRODUCCION A MARIA-TEGUI. Lima: Mosca Azul Editores, 1981.

2973. Salazar Bondy, Augusto. EXISTE UNA FILOSOFIA DE NUESTRA AMERICA? 8th ed. Mexico: Siglio Veintiuno Editores, 1982.

2974. Salazar Bondy, Augusto. SENTIDO Y PROBLEMA DEL PENSAMENTO FILOSO-FICO HISPANOAMERICANO. Mexico: Union de Universidades de America Latina, 1978.

URUGUAY

2975. Assuncao, Fernando O., et al. JOSE ORTEGA Y GASSET, 1883-1955: SEIS CONFERENCIAS EN SU CENTENARIO: HOMENAJE. Montevideo: Casa del Autor Nacional, 1984.

VENEZUELA

2976. Ardao, Arturo. ANDRES BELLO, FILOSOFO. Caracas: Academia Nacional de la Historia, 1986.

2977. Ardao, Arturo. ESPACIO E INTELIGENCIA. Caracas: Editorial Equinoccio, 1983.

2978. Ardao, Arturo. ESTUDIOS LATINOAMERICANOS: HISTORIA DE LAS IDEAS. Caracas: Monte Avila Editores, 1978.

2979. Ardao, Arturo, ed. LA FILOSOFIA ACTUAL EN AMERICANA LATINA. Mexico: Editorial Grijalbo, 1976.

These are papers presented at the First Coloquio Nacional de Filosofia held at Moretia, Mexico, in 1975.

2980. Barragan, Julia. IIIPOTESIS METODOLOGICAS. Caracas: Editorial Juridica Venezolana, 1983.

2981. Beuchot, Mauricio. EL PROBLEMA DE LOS UNIVERSALES. Mexico: Universidad Nacional Autonoma de Mexico, Colegio de Filosofia Facultad de Filosofia y Letras, 1981.

There is a prologue by Carlos Ulises Moulina and a bibliography on pages 503-518.

2982. Cappelletti, Angel J. ENSAYOS SOBRE LOS ATOMISTAS GRIEGOS. Caracas: Sociedad Venezolana de Ciencias Humanas, 1979.

2983. Cappelletti, Angel J. LA IDEA DE LA LIBERTAD EN EL RENACIMIENTO. Barcelona: Editoria Laia, 1986.

2984. Cappelletti, Angel J. LA IDEOLOGIA ANARQUISTA. Caracas: Alfadil Ediciones; Barcelona: Editoria Laia, 1985.

2985. Cappelletti, Angel J. LAO-TSE Y CHUANG-TSE. Caracas: Ediciones de la Direccion General de Cultura de la Gobernacion del Distrito Federal y del Centro Simon Bolivar, 1976.

2986. Cappelletti, Angel J. PREHISTORIA DEL ANARQUISMO. Madrid: Queimada, 1983.

2987. Garcia Bacca, Juan David. TRANSFINITUD E INMORTALIDAD: ENSAYO. Caracas: s.n., 1984.

2988. Imaz, Eugenio. FILOSOFIA DE LA HISTORIA: EMMANUEL KANT. Tr. by Eugenio Imaz. Mexico: Fondo de Cultura Economica, 1978.

2989. Imaz, Eugenio. PENSAMIENTO DE DILTHEY. Mexico: Fondo de Cultura Economica, 1979,1978.

2990. Lluberes, Pedro. CIENCIA Y ESCEPTICISMO: APROXIMACION A DESCARTES. Caracas: Equinoccio, 1976.

2991. Mayz Vallenilla, Ernesto. CLASE MAGISTRAL DEL RECTOR. Sartenejas: Universidad Simon Bolivar, 1978.

2992. Mayz Vallenilla, Ernesto. EL PROBLEMA DE AMERICA. Mexico, D.F.: Universidad Nacional Autonoma de Mexico, Coordinacion de Humanidades, Centro de Estudios Latinoamericanos, Facultad de Filosofia y Letras, Union de Universidades de America

Latina, 1979.

2993. Mayz Vallenilla, Ernesto. FENOMENOLOGIA DEL CONOCIMIENTO: El PROB-
LEMA D LA CONSTITUCION DEL OBJETO EN LA FILOSOFIA DE HUSSERL.
Caracas: Equinoccio, 1976.

2994. Mayz Vallenilla, Ernesto. RATIO TECHNICA. Caracas: Monte Avila Editores,
1983.

2995. Moulines, Carles Ulises. EXPLORACIONES METACIENTIFICAS: ESTRUCTURA,
DESARROLO Y CONTENIDO DE LA CIENCIA. Madrid: Alianza, 1982.

2996. Moulines, Carles Ulises, et al. LA POLEMICA DEL MATERIALISMO. Madrid:
Tecnos, 1982.

2997. Nuno Montes, Juan Antonio. COMPROMISO Y DESVIACIONES: ENSAYOS
DE FILOSOFIA Y LITERATURA. Caracas: Ediciones de la Biblioteca Universidad
Central de Venezuela, 1982.

2998. Nuno Montes, Juan Antonio. DOBLE VERDAD Y LA NARIZ DE CLEOPATRA.
Caracas: Academia Nacional de la Historia, 1988.

2999. Nuno Montes, Juan Antonio. LA FILOSOFIA DE BORGES. Mexico: Fondo de
Cultura Economica, 1986.

3000. Nuno Montes, Juan Antonio. SENTIDO DE LA FILOSOFIA CONTEMPORANEA.
2d ed. Caracas: Universidad Central de Venezuela, 1980.

There is a bibliography on pages 273-301.

3001. Ramis, Pompeyo. VEINTE FILOSOFOS VENEZOLANOS: (1946-1976). Merida,
Venzuela: Universidad de Los Andes, Consejo de Publicaciones, 1978.

3002. Schmill, Ulises and Roberto Jose Vernengo. PUREZA METODICA Y RACIONALI-
DAD EN LA TEORIA DEL DERECHO: TRES ENSAYOS SOBRE KELSEN. Mexico:
Universidad Nacional Autonoma de Mexico, 1984.

3003. Tosco, Carlos, ed. LA FILOSOFIA EN AMERICA: TRABAJOS PRESENTADOS
EN EL IX CONGRESO INTERAMERICANO DE FILOSOFIA. Vol. 1, LA REALIDAD
LATINOAMERICANA COMO PROBLEMA PARA EL PENSAR FILOSOFICO. Vol. 2,
LAS TENDENCIAS ACTUALES DE LA FILOSOFIA EN EL CONTINENTE AMERI-
CANO. Caracas: Sociedad Venezolana de Filosofia, 1979.

The text is printed in Spanish, English, French, or Portuguese.

3004. Vernengo, Roberto Jose. CURSO DE TEORIA GENERAL DEL DERECHO. 2d
ed. Buenos Aires: Cooperadora de Derecho Y Ciencias Sociales, 1976.

NORTH
AMERICA

NORTH AMERICA

CANADA/ANGLOPHONE

3005. Amore, Roy C., ed. DEVELOPMENTS IN BUDDHIST THOUGHT: CANADI-
AN CONTRIBUTIONS TO BUDDHIST STUDIES. Waterloo, Ontario: Wilfried
Lauriers Univ. Press, 1979.

This is a collection of nine essays mainly on Buddhism in its cultural contexts, particularly India and China, by such scholars as Klaus Klostermaier, H.V. Guenther, Bimal K.
Matilal and others. It was published for the Canadian Corporation for Studies in Religion.

3006. Anderson, C. Anthony and Joseph Owens, ed. PROPOSITIONAL ATTITUDES:
THE ROLE OF CONTENT IN LOGIC, LANGUAGE, AND MIND. Stanford, CA:
Center for the Study of Language and Information, 1990.

Most of these papers were presented at a conference held at the University of Minneso-
ta, Twin Cities Campus, during October 14--16, 1988. Contributors to this volume include
Kit Fine, Hans Kamp, Ernest LePore and Barry Loewer, Tyler Burge, Robert Stalnaker,
Joseph Owens, John Wallace , H. E. Mason, Keith S. Donnellan, Nathan Salmon, Stephen
Schiffer, John R. Searle, and Keith Gunderson.

3007. Aquinas, St Thomas. QUODLIBETAL QUESTIONS 1 AND 2. Tr. of QUAES-
TIONES QUODLIBETALES 1-2. Tr. with an introduction and notes by Sandra S.
Edwards. Mediaeval Sources in Translation, Vol. 27. Toronto: Pontifical Institute of
Mediaeval Studies, 1983.

3008. Armour, Leslie and Edward T. Bartlett. THE CONCEPTUALIZATION OF THE
INNER LIFE: A PHILOSOPHICAL EXPLORATION. Atlantic Highlands, NJ: Humanities Press, 1980.

3009. Armour, Leslie and Elizabeth Trott. THE FACES OF REASON: AN ESSAY ON
PHILOSOPHY AND CULTURE IN ENGLISH CANADA 1850-1950. Waterloo, Ont:
Wilfrid Laurier Univ. Press, 1981.

3010. Black, Deborah L. LOGIC AND ARISTOTLE'S RHETORIC AND POETICS IN
MEDIEVAL ARABIC PHILOSOPHY. Leiden and New York: E. J. Brill, 1990.

3011. Blair, J. Anthony and Ralph Henry Johnson, eds. INFORMAL LOGIC: THE FIRST INTERNATIONAL SYMPOSIUM. Inverness, CA: Edgepress, 1980.

3012. Block, Irving, ed. PERSPECTIVES ON THE PHILOSOPHY OF WITTGENSTEIN. Cambridge: MIT Press; Oxford: B. Blackwell, 1981.

This work consists mainly of edited papers from the Wittgenstein Colloquium held in London, Ontario, Canada, 1976.

3013. Bond, Edward James. REASON AND VALUE. Cambridge Studies in Philosophy. Cambridge and New York: Cambridge Univ. Press, 1983.

3014. Bracken, Harry M. MIND AND LANGUAGE: ESSAYS ON DESCARTES AND CHOMSKY. Dordrecht and Cinnaminson, NJ: Foris Publications, 1984.

3015. Brand, Myles and Douglas Walton, ed. ACTION THEORY: PROCEEDINGS OF THE WINNIPEG CONFERENCE ON HUMAN ACTION HELD AT WINNIPEG, MANITOBA, CANADA, 9-11 MAY, 1975. Dordrecht and Boston: Reidel, 1976.

3016. Braybrooke, David. MEETING NEEDS. Princeton: Princeton Univ. Press, 1987.

This volume contains a bibliography on pages 307-327.

3017. Bronaugh, Richard, ed. PHILOSOPHICAL LAW: AUTHORITY, EQUALITY, ADJUDICATION, PRIVACY. Westport, CT: Greenwood Press, 1978.

3018. Buczynska-Garewicz, Hanna, et al. STUDIES IN PEIRCE'S SEMIOTIC. Ed. by David Savan. Toronto: Victoria Univ., 1982.

3019. Burbridge, John. ON HEGEL'S LOGIC: FRAGMENTS OF A COMMENTARY. Atlantic Highlands, NJ: Humanities Press, 1982.

The author reworks some of the arguments in SCIENCE OF LOGIC by suggesting that the movement of thought is an intellectual activity purified of contingent and relative associations.

3020. Butts, Robert E. KANT AND THE DOUBLE GOVERNMENT METHODOLO-GY: SUPERSENSIBILITY AND METHOD IN KANT'S PHILOSOPHY OF SCIENCE. Dordrecht and Boston: Reidel, 1984.

3021. Campbell, Richmond. SELF-LOVE AND SELF-RESPECT: A PHILOSOPHICAL STUDY OF EGOISM. Ottawa: Published for the Canadian Association for Publishing in Philosophy by the Department of Philosophy of Carleton University, 1979.

3022. Campbell, Richmond and Lanning Sowden, eds. PARADOXES OF RATIONALITY AND COOPERATION: PRISONER'S DILEMMA AND NEWCOMBE'S PROBLEM. Vancouver, BC: Univ. of British Columbia Press, 1985.

3023. CANADIAN JOURNAL OF PHILOSOPHY. SUPPLEMENTARY VOLUMES. Vol. 1, Pt. 1, NEW ESSAYS IN THE HISTORY OF PHILOSOPHY (1975), ed by Terence Penelhum and Roger A. Shiner; Pt. 2, NEW ESSAYS IN THE PHILOSOPHY OF MIND (1975), ed. by John King-Farlow and Roger A. Shiner. Vol. 2, NEW ESSAYS ON PLATO AND THE PRE-SOCRATICS (1976), ed. by Roger A. Shiner and John King-Farlow. Vol. 3, NEW ESSAYS ON CONTRACT THEORY (1977), ed. by Kai Nielsen and Roger A. Shiner. Vol. 4, NEW ESSAYS ON RATIONALISM AND EMPIRICISM (1978), ed. by Charles E. Jarrett, John King-Farlow, and F.J. Pelletier. Vol. 5, NEW ESSAYS ON JOHN STUART MILL AND UTILITARIANISM (1979), ed. by Wesley E. Cooper, Kai Nielsen, and Steven C. Patten. Vol. 6, NEW ESSAYS IN PHILOSOPHY OF

LANGUAGE (1980), ed. by F. J. Pelletier and Calvin G. Normore. Vol. 7, MARX AND MORALITY (1981), ed. by Kai Nielsen and Steven C. Patten. Vol. 8, NEW ESSAYS IN ETHICS AND PUBLIC POLICY (1982), ed. by Kai Nielsen and Steven C. Patten. Vol. 9, NEW ESSAYS ON PLATO (1983), ed. by F. J. Pelletier and John King-Farlow. Vol. 10, NEW ESSAYS ON ARISTOTLE (1984), ed. by F. J. Pelletier and John King-Farlow. Vol. 11, NEW ESSAYS IN PHILOSOPHY OF MIND, SERIES II (1985), ed. by David Copp and J.J. MacIntosh. Vol. 12, NUCLEAR WEAPONS, DETERRENCE, AND DISARMAMENT (1986), ed. by David Copp. Vol. 13, SCIENCE, MORALITY AND FEMINIST THEORY (1987), ed. by Marsha Hanen and Kai Nielsen. Vol. 14, PHILOSO- PHY AND BIOLOGY (1988), ed. by Mohan Matthen and Bernard Linsky, and Vol. 15, ANALYZING MARXISM: NEW ESSAYS IN ANALYTICAL MARXISM (1989), ed. by Robert Ware and Kai Nielsen. Guelph, Ontario: Canadian Association for Publishing in Philosophy, 1975-.

3024. Canfield, John V., ed. THE PHILOSOPHY OF WITTGENSTEIN. 15 Vols. New York: Garland, 1986.

This collection reproduces over 250 major articles about Wittgenstein's philosophy, ranging from his early philosophy of language as picture, to logic and ontology in his later philosophy, and to his growing influence outside of analytic philosophy. Vol. 1, THE EARLY PHILOSOPHY: LANGUAGE AS PICTURE. Vol. 2, LOGIC AND ONTOLO- GY. Vol. 3, MY WORLD AND ITS VALUE. Vol. 4, THE LATER PHILOSOPHY: VIEWS AND REVIEWS. Vol. 5, METHOD AND ESSENCE. Vol. 6, MEANING. Vol. 7, CRITERIA. Vol. 8, KNOWING, NAMING AND CERTAINTY, AND IDEALISM. Vol. 9, THE PRIVATE LANGUAGE ARGUMENT. Vol. 10, LOGICAL NECESSITY AND RULES. Vol. 11, PHILOSOPHY OF MATHEMATICS. Vol. 12, PERSONS. Vol. 13, PSYCHOLOGY AND CONCEPTUAL RELATIVITY. Vol. 14, AESTHETICS, ETHICS, AND RELIGION. Vol. 15, ELECTIVE AFFINITIES.

3025. Carr, David. INTERPRETING HUSSERL: CRITICAL AND COMPARATIVE STUDIES. Dordrecht and Boston: Nijhoff, 1987.

3026. Carr, David. TIME, NARRATIVE, AND HISTORY. Bloomington: Indiana Univ. Press, 1986.

3027. Cell, Howard R. and James I. MacAdam. ROUSSEAU'S RESPONSE TO HOBBES. New York: P. Lang, 1988.

3028. Chapman, Tobias H. TIME: A PHILOSOPHICAL ANALYSIS. Dordrecht and Boston: Reidel, 1982.

3029. Conway, Anne. THE PRINCIPLES OF THE MOST ANCIENT AND MODERN PHILOSOPHY. Ed. by Peter J. Loptson. The International Archives of the History of Ideas, Vol. 101. The Hague and Boston: Nijhoff, 1982.

This Latin and English text of Conway's one surviving work, her metaphysical treatise, THE PRINCIPLES OF THE MOST ANCIENT AND MODERN PHILOSOPHY, in- cludes an introduction to her life and thought and a commentary on her system by Peter Loptson. There are discussions of her links to Henry More and a 17th Century Christian Cabalist tradition typified by Francois Mercure van Helmont and of her significance as a philosopher of essence.

3030. Coward, Harold G. and Terence Coward, eds. THE CALGARY CONFERENCE ON MYSTICISM, 1976. Waterloo, Ont: Corporation Canadienne des Sciences Religieuses and Wilfrid Laurier Univ. Press, 1977.

3031. Cunningham, Frank. DEMOCRATIC THEORY AND SOCIALISM. Cambridge and New York: Cambridge Univ. Press, 1987.

There is an extensive bibliography on pages 293-360.

3032. Daniels, Charles R., et al. TOWARD AN ONTOLOGY OF NUMBER, MIND AND SIGN. Aberdeen: Aberdeen Univ. Press, 1986.

3033. Davis, Steven, ed. PRAGMATICS: A READER. Oxford: Oxford Univ. Press, 1991.

3034. Demopoulos, William and Zenon W. Pylyshyn. MEANING AND COGNITIVE STRUCTURE: ISSUES IN THE COMPUTATIONAL THEORY OF MIND. Norwood, NJ: Ablex pub. Corp., 1986.

This volume consists of papers presented at a 3 day meeting at the University of Western Ontario Centre for Cognitive Science, Oct. 1981.

3035. Despland, Michel. THE EDUCATION OF DESIRE: PLATO AND THE PHILOSO-PHY OF RELIGION. Toronto: Univ. of Toronto Press, 1985.

3036. Dorter, Kenneth. PLATO'S PHAEDO: AN INTERPRETATION. Toronto: Univ. of Toronto Press, 1982.

3037. Dray, William H. ON HISTORY AND PHILOSOPHERS OF HISTORY. Leiden and New York: E.J. Brill, 1989.

3038. Dray, William H. PERSPECTIVES ON HISTORY. Boston: Routledge & Kegan Paul, 1980.

3039. Englebretsen, George. LOGICAL NEGATION. Assen: Van Gorcum, 1981.

3040. Englebretsen, George. THREE LOGICIANS: ARISTOTLE, LEIBNIZ, AND SOMMERS AND THE SYLLOGISTIC. Assen: Van Gorcum, 1981.

3041. Faghfoury, Mostafa, ed. ANALYTICAL PHILOSOPHY OF RELIGION IN CANADA. Ottawa: Univ. of Ottawa Press, 1982.

3042. Fischer, Norman, et al, eds. CONTINUITY AND CHANGE IN MARXISM. New Jersey: Humanities Press, 1982.

3043. Fox, Michael Allen. THE CASE FOR ANIMAL EXPERIMENTATION. Berkeley: Univ. of California Press, 1986.

3044. Fox, Michael Allen. SCHOPENHAUER: HIS PHILOSOPHICAL ACHIEVEMENT. Brighton: Harvester Press; Totowa, NJ: Barnes and Noble, 1980.

3045. Hacking, Ian, ed. SCIENTIFIC REVOLUTIONS. Oxford and New York: Oxford Univ. Press, 1981.

3046. Hacking, Ian. THE TAMING OF CHANCE. Cambridge and New York: Cambridge Univ. Press, 1990.

3047. Hare, William F. IN DEFENSE OF OPEN-MINDEDNESS. Montreal: McGill-Queen's Univ. Press, 1985.

3048. Harper, William Leonard and Clifford Alan Hooker, eds. FOUNDATIONS OF PROBABILITY THEORY, STATISTICAL INFERENCE, AND STATISTICAL THEORIES OF SCIENCE. Vol. 1, FOUNDATIONS AND PHILOSOPHY OF EPIS-TEMIC APPLICATION OF PROBABILITY THEORY; Vol. 2, FOUNDATIONS AND PHILOSOPHY OF STATISTICAL INFERENCE; Vol. 3, FOUNDATIONS AND

PHILOSOPHY OF STATISTICAL THEORIES IN THE PHYSICAL SCIENCES. Dordrecht and Boston: Reidel, 1976.

This volume consists of the Proceedings of an International Research Colloquium held at the University of Western Ontario, London, Canada, May 10-13, 1973.

3049. Harris, Henry Silton. HEGEL'S DEVELOPMENT: NIGHT THOUGHTS (JENA 1801- 1806). New York: Oxford Univ. Press; Oxford: Clarendon Press, 1983.

This work is a sequel to the author's HEGEL'S DEVELOPMENT: TOWARD THE SUNLIGHT. Clarendon Press, 1972.

3050. Hellman, John. EMMANUEL MOUNIER AND THE CATHOLIC LEFT, 1930-1950. Toronto and Buffalo: Univ. of Toronto Press, 1981.

3051. Hendley, Brian Patrick. DEWEY, RUSSELL, WHITEHEAD: PHILOSOPHERS AS EDUCATORS. Carbondale: Southern Illinois Univ. Press, 1986.

3052. Hutter, Horst. POLITICS AS FRIENDSHIP: THE ORIGINS OF CLASSICAL NOTIONS OF POLITICS IN THE THEORY AND PRACTICE OF FRIENDSHIP. Waterloo, Ont: Wilfrid Laurier Univ. Press, 1978.

3053. Joos, Ernest. LUKACS' LAST AUTOCRITICISM: THE ONTOLOGY. Atlantic Highlands, NJ: Humanities Press, 1983.

This work includes a translation of DIE ONTOLOGISCHEN GRUNDLAGEN DES MENSCHLICHEN DENKENS UND HANDELNS, a lecture delivered in Vienna in 1969.

3054. Kain, Philip J. MARX'S METHOD, EPISTEMOLOGY, AND HUMANISM: A STUDY OF THE DEVELOPMENT OF HIS THOUGHT. Dordrecht and Boston: Reidel, 1986.

3055. Kain, Philip J. SCHILLER, HEGEL, AND MARX: STATE, SOCIETY AND THE AESTHETIC IDEAL OF ANCIENT GREECE. Kingston, Ont: McGill-Queen's Univ. Press, 1982.

3056. King-Farlow, John, ed. THE CHALLENGE OF RELIGION TODAY: ESSAYS ON THE PHILOSOPHY OF RELIGION. New York: Science History Publication, 1976.

3057. King-Farlow, John, ed. SELF-KNOWLEDGE AND SOCIAL RELATIONS: GROUNDWORK OF UNIVERSAL COMMUNITY. New York: Science History Publication, 1978.

3058. Kluge, Eike-Henner W. THE METAPHYSICS OF GOTTLOB FREGE: AN ESSAY IN ONTOLOGICAL RECONSTRUCTION. The Hague and Boston: Nijhoff, 1980.

3059. Kontos, Alkis, ed. POWERS, POSSESSIONS, AND FREEDOM: ESSAYS IN HONOUR OF C. B. MACPHERSON. Toronto and Buffalo: Univ. of Toronto Press, 1979.

This volume contains essays by C. Taylor, J. Shklar, E. J. Hobsbawm, S. Lukes, and others.

3060. Kuehn, Manfred. SCOTTISH COMMON SENSE IN GERMANY, 1768-1800: A CONTRIBUTION TO THE HISTORY OF CRITICAL PHILOSOPHY. Kingston, Ont.: Mc-Gill Queen's Univ. Press, 1987.

3061. Lennon, Thomas, et al. PROBLEMS OF CARTESIANISM. Kingston, Ont: McGill-Queen's Press, 1982.

3062. Lipton, David Robert. ERNST CASSIRER: THE DILEMMA OF A LIBERAL INTELLECTUAL IN GERMANY, 1914-1933. Toronto and Buffalo: Univ. of Toronto Press, 1978.

3063. Lonergan, Bernard Joseph Francis. THE COLLECTED WORKS OF BERNARD LONERGAN. Vol. 3, INSIGHT: A STUDY OF HUMAN UNDERSTANDING. 5th ed. rev. and aug. (1992). Vol. 4, COLLECTION. 2d. ed., rev. and aug. (1988). Vol. 5, UNDERSTANDING AND BEING: THE HALIFAX LECTURES ON INSIGHT. 2d. ed. rev. and aug. (1990). Ed. by Frederick E. Crowe and Robert M. Doran. Toronto: Univ. of Toronto Press for Lonergan Research Institute of Regis College, 1988-.

In addition to the volumes listed above, the COLLECTED WORKS will consist of the following: Vol. 1, GRACE AND FREEDOM. Vol. 2, VERBUM: WORD AND IDEA IN AQUINAS. Vol. 6, PHILOSOPHICAL AND THEOLOGICAL PAPERS. Vol. 7, THE ONTOLOGICAL AND PSYCHOLOGICAL CONSTITUTION OF CHRIST. Vol.8, THE INCARNATE WORD. Vol. 9, THE TRIUNE GOD. Vol. 10, TOPICS IN EDUCATION. Vol. 11, A SECOND COLLECTION. Vol. 12, METHOD IN THEOLOGY. Vol. 13, MORE PHILOSOPHICAL AND THEOLOGICAL PAPERS. Vol. 15. ESSAY IN CIRCULATION ANALYSIS. Vol. 16, EARLY LATIN THEOLOGY. Vol. 17, SHORTER PAPERS. Vol. 18, LECTURES FROM THE ROMAN YEARS. Vol. 19, EARLY WORKS ON THEOLOGICAL METHOD I. Vol. 20, EARLY WORKS ON THEOLOGICAL METHOD II. Vol. 21, ARCHIVAL MATERIAL. Vol. 22, GENERAL INDEX.

3064. Lukes, Timothy J. THE FLIGHT INTO INWARDNESS: AN EXPOSITION AND CRITIQUE OF HERBERT MARCUSE'S THEORY OF LIBERATIVE AESTHETICS. Selinsgrove: Susquehanna Univ. Press; London and Toronto: Associated Univ. Presses, 1985.

There is a bibliography on pages 167-174.

3065. MacAdam, James I., et al, eds. TRENT ROUSSEAU PAPERS: PROCEEDINGS OF THE ROUSSEAU BICENTENNIAL CONGRESS, TRENT UNIVERSITY, JUNE, 1978=ETUDES ROUSSEAU-TRENT. Ottawa: Univ. of Ottawa Press, 1980.

This volume contains English translations of NARCISSE by Jean-Jacques Rousseau and LA DISPUTE by Pierre Marivaux. The text is in English and French.

3066. Macpherson, Crawford Brough. BURKE. Toronto: Oxford Univ. Press, 1980.

3067. MacPherson, Crawford Brough. THE LIFE AND TIMES OF LIBERAL DEMOCRACY. Oxford and New York: Oxford Univ. Press, 1977.

3068. Macpherson, Crawford Brough, ed. PROPERTY, MAINSTREAM AND CRITICAL POSITIONS. Oxford: Blackwell, 1978.

3069. Macpherson, Crawford Brough, et al. MARX AND MARXISM RECONSIDERED. Canadian Journal of Political and Social Theory. V. 3, no. 1, Winter, 1979. Downsview, Ont: Univ. of Toronto Press, 1979.

This number of the journal is devoted, in part, to papers and commentaries from a conference held in San Francisco in March, 1978, under the sponsorship of the Conference for the Study of Political Thought.

3070. Madison, Gary Brent. THE PHENOMENOLOGY OF MERLEAU-PONTY: A SEARCH FOR THE LIMITS OF CONSCIOUSNESS. Tr. of LA PHENOMENOL-

OGIE DE MERLEAU-PONTY: UNE RECHERCHE DES LIMITES DE LA CON-
SCIENCE. Preface by Paul Ricoeur. Paris: Klincksieck, 1973. Series in Continental
Thought, Vol. 3. Athens: Ohio Univ. Press, 1981.

3071. Madison, Gary Brent. UNDERSTANDING, A PHENOMENOLOGICAL-PRAG-
MATIC ANALYSIS. Westport, CT: Greenwood Press, 1982.

3072. Marcil-Lacoste, Louise. CLAUDE BUFFIER AND THOMAS REID: TWO
COMMON-SENSE PHILOSOPHERS. Kingston, Ont.: McGill-Queen's Univ. Press,
1982.

This is a comparative study of the writings of Buffier and Reid.

3073. Martin, Julian. FRANCIS BACON, THE STATE AND THE REFORM OF
NATURAL PHILOSOPHY. Cambridge and New York: Cambridge Univ. Press, 1991.

3074. Matthen, Mohan and Bernard Linsky, eds. PHILOSOPHY AND BIOLOGY. Calgary:
Univ. of Calgary Press, 1988.

These are papers from a conference held in Edmonton, May 8-10, 1987.

3075. McCormick, Peter J. HEIDEGGER AND THE LANGUAGE OF THE WORLD:
AN ARGUMENTATIVE READING OF THE LATER HEIDEGGER'S MEDITA-
TIONS ON LANGUAGE. Ottawa: Univ. of Ottawa Press, 1976.

3076. McMurty, John M. THE STRUCTURE OF MARX'S WORLD VIEW. Princeton,
NJ: Princeton Univ. Press, 1978.

3077. McRae, Robert F. LEIBNIZ: PERCEPTION, APPERCEPTION, AND THOUGHT.
Toronto and Buffalo: Univ. of Toronto Press, 1976.

3078. Michalos, Alex. FOUNDATIONS OF DECISION-MAKING. Ottawa: Published for
the Canadian Association for Publishing in Philosophy by the Department of Philosophy of
Carleton University, 1978.

3079. Mill, John Stuart. COLLECTED WORKS. Ed. by John Mercel Robson and Jack Stil-
linger. Toronto: Univ. of Toronto Press, 1963-.

Vol. 1, AUTOBIOGRAPHY AND LITERARY ESSAYS. Vol. 2-3, PRINCIPLES OF
POLITICAL ECONOMY. Vol. 4-5, ESSAYS ON ECONOMY AND SOCIETY, 1824-
1879. Vol. 7-8., A SYSTEM OF LOGIC: RATIOCINATIVE AND INDUCTIVE. Vol. 9,
AN EXAMINATION OF SIR WILLIAM HAMILTON'S PHILOSOPHY OF THE
PRINCIPAL PHILOSOPHICAL QUESTIONS DISCUSSED IN HIS WRITINGS. Vol.
10, ESSAYS ON ETHICS, RELIGION AND SOCIETY. Vol. 11, ESSAYS ON PHILOS-
OPHY AND THE CLASSICS. Vol. 12-13, THE EARLIER LETTERS, 1812-1848. Vol.
14-17, THE LATER LETTERS, 1848-1873. Vol. 18-19, ESSAYS ON POLITICS AND
SOCIETY. Vol. 20, ESSAYS ON FRENCH HISTORY AND HISTORIANS. Vol. 21,
ESSAYS ON EQUALITY, LAW, AND EDUCATION. Vol. 26-27, JOURNALS AND
DEBATING SPEECHES. Vol. 28-29, PUBLIC AND PARLIAMENTARY SPEECHES.

3080. Neufeldt, Ronald Wesley, ed. KARMA AND REBIRTH: POST-CLASSICAL
DEVELOPMENTS. Albany: State Univ. of New York Press, 1985.

3081. Nielsen, Kai. AFTER THE DEMISE OF TRADITION: RORTY, CRITICAL
THEORY, AND THE FATE OF PHILOSOPHY. Boulder: Westview Press, 1991.

3082. Nielsen, Kai. EQUALITY AND LIBERTY: A DEFENSE OF RADICAL EGALI-
TARIANISM. Totawa, NJ: Rowman and Allanheld, 1984.

3083. Nielsen, Kai. GOD, SKEPTICISM AND MODERNITY. Ottawa: Univ. of Ottawa Press, 1989.

3084. Nielsen, Kai. PHILOSOPHY AND ATHEISM: THE DEFENSE OF ATHEISM. Buffalo: Prometheus Books, 1985.

3085. Nielsen, Kai. WHY BE MORAL? Buffalo: Prometheus Books, 1989.

3086. Nisbet, Euan George. LEAVING EDEN: TO PROTECT AND MANAGE THE EARTH. Cambridge and New York: Cambridge Univ. Press, 1991.

3087. Norton, David Fate. DAVID HUME, COMMON-SENSE MORALIST, SCEPTICAL METAPHYSICIAN. Princeton: Princeton Univ. Press, 1982.

3088. Norton, David Fate, et al. MCGILL HUME STUDIES. Studies in Hume and Scottish Philosophy, Vol. 1. San Diego: Austin Hill Press, 1979.

This volume contains contributions by J. Moore, G. Davie, L.W. Beck, and others.

3089. Owens, Joseph. AQUINAS ON BEING AND THING. Niagra University Publications in Honor of Jacques and Raissa Maritain. Niagra, NY: Niagra Univ. Press, 1981.

3090. Owens, Joseph. ARISTOTLE, THE COLLECTED PAPERS OF JOSEPH OWENS. Ed. by John R. Catan. Albany: State Univ. of New York Press, 1981.

This work contains a complete bibliography of the writings of Joseph Owens.

3091. Owens, Joseph. THE DOCTRINE OF BEING IN THE ARISTOTELIAN META-PHYSICS: A STUDY IN THE GREEK BACKGROUND OF MEDIAEVAL THOUGHT. 3d. rev ed. Toronto: Pontifical Institute of Medieval Studies, 1978.

3092. Owens, Joseph. HUMAN DESTINY: SOME PROBLEMS FOR CATHOLIC PHI-LOSOPHY. Washington, DC: Catholic Univ. of America Press, 1985.

3093. Owens, Joseph. PHILOSOPHICAL TRADITION OF ST. MICHAEL'S COL-LEGE. Toronto: Univ. of St. Michael's College Archives, 1979.

3094. Owens, Joseph. ST. THOMAS AQUINAS ON THE EXISTENCE OF GOD: COLLECTED PAPERS OF JOSEPH OWENS. Ed. by John R. Catan. Albany: State Univ. of New York Press, 1980.

3095. Owens, Joseph. TOWARDS A CHRISTIAN PHILOSOPHY. Studies in Philosophy and the History of Philosophy, Vol. 21. Washington, D.C.: Catholic Univ. of America Press, 1990.

3096. Penelhum, Terence. GOD AND SKEPTICISM: A STUDY IN SKEPTICISM AND FIDEISM. Philosophical Studies Series in Philosophy, Vol. 28. Dordrecht and Boston: Reidel, 1983.

3097. Plantinga, Theodore. HISTORICAL UNDERSTANDING IN THE THOUGHT OF WILHELM DILTHEY. Toronto and Buffalo: Univ. of Toronto Press, 1980.

3098. Prado, Carlos Gonzales. MAKING BELIEVE: PHILOSOPHICAL REFLECTIONS ON FICTION. Westport, CT: Greenwood Press, 1984.

3099. Rist, John M. HUMAN VALUE: A STUDY IN ANCIENT PHILOSOPHICAL ETHICS. Leiden: E. J. Brill, 1982.

3100. Rist, John M. THE STOICS. Berkeley: Univ. of California Press, 1978.

3101. Robson, John Mercel, ed. ORIGIN AND EVOLUTION OF THE UNIVERSE: EVIDENCE FOR DESIGN. Kingston: McGill-Queen's Univ. Press, 1987.

The papers in this volume originated in a symposium at McGill University, May 30-June 1, 1985, sponsored by the Royal Society of Canada with the cooperation of the Canadian Institute of Advanced Research.

3102. Robson, John Mercel and Michael Laine, eds. JAMES AND JOHN STUART MILL: PAPERS OF THE CENTENARY CONFERENCE. Toronto, Buffalo, and London: Univ. of Toronto Press, 1976.

3103. Rosenberg, Aubrey. NICOLAS GUEUDEVILLE AND HIS WORK. The International Archives of the History of Ideas, Vol. 99. The Hague and Boston: Nijhoff, 1982.

The subject of this study, a former Benedictine monk, attacked absolutism as exemplified by the French political system and the Catholic religion.

3104. Ruse, Michael. DARWINISM DEFENDED: A GUIDE TO THE EVOLUTION CONTROVERSIES. Menlo Park, CA: Benjamin Cummings Pub. Co.; Reading, MA: Addison-Wesley, Advanced Book Program/World Science Division, 1982.

3105. Ruse, Michael. IS SCIENCE SEXIST?: AND OTHER PROBLEMS IN THE BIOMEDICAL SCIENCES. Dordrecht and Boston: Reidel, 1981.

3106. Ruse, Michael. LA HOMOSEXUALIDAD. Tr. of HOMOSEXUALITY: A PHILOSOPHICAL INQUIRY. Oxford and New York: Blackwell, 1988. Tr. by Carlos Laguna. Madrid: Catedra, 1989.

3107. Ruse, Michael. SOCIOBIOLOGY: SENSE OR NONSENSE? 2d rev ed. Dordrecht and Boston: Reidel, 1984.

3108. Ruse, Michael. TAKING DARWIN SERIOUSLY: A NATURALISTIC APPROACH TO PHILOSOPHY. New York: Blackwell, 1986.

3109. Ruse, Michael, ed. WHAT THE PHILOSOPHY OF BIOLOGY IS: ESSAYS DEDICATED TO DAVID HULL. Dordrecht and Boston: Reidel, 1989.

This work includes a bibliography of publications by David L. Hull.

3110. Shanker, Stuart G., ed. LUDWIG WITTGENSTEIN: CRITICAL ASSESSMENTS. Vol. 1, FROM THE NOTEBOOKS TO PHILOSOPHICAL GRAMMAR. Vol. 2, FROM PHILOSOPHICAL INVESTIGATIONS TO ON CERTAINTY. Vol. 3, FROM THE TRACTATUS TO REMARKS ON THE FOUNDATIONS OF MATHEMATICS. Vol. 4, FROM THEOLOGY TO SOCIOLOGY , WITTGENSTEINS' IMPACT ON CONTEMPORARY THOUGHT. Vol. 5, A WITTGENSTEIN BIBLIOGRAPHY. London and Dover, NH: Croom Helm, 1986.

Volume 5, which was issued separately, was edited by V. A. and S. G. Shanker.

3111. Shanker, Stuart G., ed. PHILOSOPHY IN BRITAIN TODAY. London: Croom Helm; Albany: State Univ. of New York Press, 1986.

This collection contains essays by Gordon Baker, Renford Bambrough, Antony Flew, Ernest Gellner, R. M. Hare, Rom Harre, Stephan Korner, Czeslaw Lejewski, Karl R. Popper, Crispin Wright and the editor. Each contributor was asked to give either a brief intellectual autobiography and resume of their approach to philosophy, or else a statement on what they regard as a major problem in philosophy and how it should be solved.

3112. Shanker, Stuart G. WITTGENSTEIN AND THE TURNING-POINT IN THE PHILOSOPHY OF MATHEMATICS. Albany: State Univ. of New York Press, 1987.

The volume contains a bibliography on pages 342-353.

3113. Shea, William R. and John King-Farlow, eds. CONTEMPORARY ISSUES IN POLITICAL PHILOSOPHY. New York: Science History Publications, 1976.

3114. Shea, William R. and John King-Farlow, eds. VALUES AND THE QUALITY OF LIFE. New York: Science History Publication, 1976.

3115. Sparshott, Francis Edward. THE THEORY OF THE ARTS. Princeton: Princeton Univ. Press, 1982.

There is an extensive bibliography on pages 685-711.

3116. Sprung, Mervyn, ed. THE QUESTION OF BEING: EAST-WEST PERSPECTIVES. University Park: Pennsylvania State Univ. Press, 1978.

The volume consists of papers read at a symposium at Brock University, St. Catherines, Ontario.

3117. Sumner, Leonard Wayne, et al, eds. PRAGMATISM AND PURPOSE: ESSAYS PRESENTED TO THOMAS A. GOUDGE. Toronto, Buffalo and London: Univ. of Toronto Press, 1981.

This work contains twenty essays on pragmatism in honor of Goudge. There is a bibliography of the published works of Thomas A. Goudge on pages 329-336.

3118. Taylor, Barry M. MODES OF OCCURRENCE: VERBS, ADVERBS, AND EVENTS. Aristotelian Society Series, Vol. 2. Oxford and New York: Blackwell, 1985.

3119. Taylor, Charles. PHILOSOPHICAL PAPERS. Vol. 1, HUMAN AGENCY AND LANGUAGE; Vol. 2, PHILOSOPHY AND THE HUMAN SCIENCES. Cambridge and New York: Cambridge Univ. Press, 1985-.

3120. Taylor, Charles. SOURCES OF THE SELF: THE MAKING OF MODERN IDENTITY. Cambridge: Cambridge Univ. Pres; Cambridge: Harvard Univ. Press, 1989.

The author criticizes what he claims to be the reductionism and oversimplification of currently fashionable political and social philosophies in both the Anglo-American and continental European philosophical traditions.

3121. Tennessen, Herman. PROBLEMS OF KNOWLEDGE: ESSAYS AT UNRIDDLING SOME PERPLEXING NEXUS OF KNOWLEDGE NOTIONS. Assen: Van Gorcum, 1980.

3122. Van Fraassen, Bastiaan C. THE SCIENTIFIC IMAGE. Oxford: Clarendon Press; New York: Oxford Univ. Press, 1980.

The author develops three mutually reinforcing theories as a constructive alternative to scientific realism.

3123. Weisheipl, James A. NATURE AND MOTION IN THE MIDDLE AGES. Ed. by William E. Carroll. Washington, DC: Catholic Univ. of America Press, 1985.

This volume reprints essays originally published from 1954 to 1981.

3124. Wernham, James C. S. JAMES'S WILL-TO BELIEVE DOCTRINE: A HERETICAL VIEW. Kingston: McGill-Quenn's Univ. Press, 1987.

CANADA/FRANCOPHONE

3125. Aristotle. LES ATTRIBUTIONS (CATEGORIES): LE TEXTE ARISTORELICIEN ET LES PROLEGOMENES D'AMMONIOS D'HERMEIAS. Tr. by (with notes and introduction) Yvan Pelletier. Montreal: Bellarmin; Paris: Societe d'Edition Les Belles Lettres, 1983c1982.

3126. Baum, Hermann, et al. DE LA PHILOSOPHIE COMME PASSION DE LA LIBERTE: HOMMAGE A ALEXIS KLIMOV. Quebec: Editions du Beffroi, 1984.

3127. Croteau, Jacques. L'HOMME, SUJET OU OBJET?: PROLEGOMENES PHILOSO-PHIQUES A UNE PSYCHOLOGIE SCIENTIFICO-HUMANISTE. Montreal: Bellarmin; Tournai: Declee et Cie, 1981.

This work presents a Neo-Thomist and existentialist critique of Cartesian-Kantian rationalism and empirical psychology on behalf of human freedom of the will.

3128. Danek, Jaromir, ed. VERITE ET ETHOS: RECEUIL COMMEMORATIF D'EDIE A ALPHONSE MARIE PARENT. Quebec: Presses de l'Universite Laval, 1982.

3129. Duchesneau, Francois. ACTES DU CONGRES D'OTTAWA SUR KANT DANS LES TRADITIONS ANGLO-AMERICAINE ET CONTINENTALE=PROCEEDINGS OF THE OTTAWA CONGRESS ON KANT IN THE ANGLO-AMERICAN AND CONTINENTAL TRADITIONS: TENU DU 10 AU 14 OCTOBRE, 1974. Ed. by Francois Duchesneau, et al. Ottawa: Editions de l'Universite d'Ottawa, 1976.

3130. Duchesneau, Francois. LA PHYSIOLOGIE DES LUMIERES: EMPIRISME, MODELES ET THEORIES. Archives internationales d'histoirie des idees, Vol. 95. The Hague: Nijhoff, 1982.

3131. Fortin, Ernest L. DISSIDENCE ET PHILOSOPHIE AU MOYEN AGE: DANTE ET SES ANTECEDENTS. Montreal: Bellarmin; Paris: J. Vrin, 1981.

3132. Gauthier, Yvon. FONDEMENTS DES MATHEMATIQUES: INTRODUCTIONS A UNE PHILOSOPHIE CONSTRUCTIVISTE. Montreal: Presses de l'Universite de Montreal, 1976.

3133. Gauthier, Yvon. METHODES ET CONCEPTS DE LA LOGIC FORMELLA. 2d. ed. rev. and enl. Montreal: Presses de l'Universite de Montreal, 1981.

This book is based on notes for a course taught at the University of Toronto and the University of Montreal from 1972 to 1974.

3134. Gauthier, Yvon. THEORETIQUES, POUR UNE PHILOSOPHIE CONSTRUC-TIVISTE DES SCIENCES. Longuevil, Quebec, Canada: Preambule, 1982.

3135. Geraets, Theodore F., ed. HEGEL: L'ESPRIT ABSOLU=THE ABSOLUTE SPIRIT. Ottawa: Editions de l'Universite d'Ottawa, 1984.

This international colloquium on the meaning of Hegel's Absolute Spirit was held November 6, 1981 at the University of Ottawa, Canada.

3136. Geraets, Theodore F., ed. RATIONALITY TODAY/LA RATIONALITE AUJOUR-D'HUI. Ottawa: Univ. of Ottawa Press, 1979.

3137. Klimov, Alexis. DE L'ABIME: PETIT TRAITE A L'USAGE DES CHERCHEURS D'ABSOLU. Quebec: Editions du Beffroi, 1985.

3138. Klimov, Alexis. TERRORISME ET BEAUTE. Quebec: Editions du Beffroi, 1986.

3139. Klimov, Alexis. VEILLEURS DE NUIT: ESQUISSE POUR UN ESSAI. Turnbull, Quebec: Editions du Beffroi, 1984.

These papers were presented to the General Assembly of the Presence de Gabriel Marcel at the Palais du Luxembourg in Paris on October 8, 1983.

3140. LaFrance, Yvon. LA THEORIE PLATONICIENNE DE LA DOXA. Montreal: Bellarmin; Paris: Les Belles Lettres, 1981.

3141. LaFrance, Yvon. METHODE ET EXEGESE EN HISTOIRE DE LA PHILOSOPHIE. Montreal: Editions Bellarmin, 1983.

3142. Lamonde, Yvan, et al. PHILOSOPHIE ET SON ENSEIGNEMENT AU QUEBEC (1665-1920): COLLECTION PHILOSOPHIE. Cahiers du Quebec, Vol. 58. Quebec: Hurtubise HMH, 1980.

3143. Levesque, Claude. L'ETRANGETE DU TEXTE: ESSAIS SUR NIETZSCHE, FREUD, BLANCHOT ET DERRIDA. Montreal: V. L. B., 1976.

3144. Montpetit, Raymond. COMMENT PARLER DE LA LITTERATURE. Montreal: Hurtubise HMH, 1976.

3145. Murin, Charles. NIETZSCHE-PROBLEME: GENEALOGIE D'UNE PENSEE. Montreal: Presses de l'Universite de Montreal; Paris: Vrin, 1979.

3146. Roy, Jean. HOBBES AND FREUD. Tr. of HOBBES ET FREUD. Halifax: Dalhousie Univ. Press for the Canadian Association for Publishing in Philosophy, 1976. Tr. by Thomas G. Osler. Toronto: Published by Canadian Philosophical Monographs for the Canadian Association of Publishing in Philosophy, 1984.

3147. Vanderveken, Daniel. MEANING AND SPEECH ACTS. Vol. 1, PRINCIPLES OF LANGUAGE USE; Vol. 2, FORMAL SEMANTICS OF SUCCESS AND SATISFACTION. Cambridge and NEw York: Cambridge Univ. Press, 1990.

UNITED STATES

3148. Abelson, Raziel. PERSONS: A STUDY IN PHILOSOPHICAL PSYCHOLOGY. London: Macmillan; New York: St. Martin's Press, 1977.

3149. Abelson, Raziel and Marie Louis Friquenon. ETHICS FOR MODERN LIFE. 2d ed. New York: St. Martin's Press, 1982.

3150. Ackermann, Robert John. THE PHILOSOPHY OF KARL POPPER. Amherst: Univ. of Massachusetts Press, 1976.

3151. Adler, Mortimer Jerome. HOW TO THINK ABOUT GOD: A GUIDE FOR THE 20TH- CENTURY PAGAN. New York: Macmillan, 1980.

3152. Adler, Mortimer Jerome. THE PAIDEIA PROPOSAL: AN EDUCATIONAL

MANIFESTO. New York: Macmillan; London: Collier Macmillan, 1982-.

This is the first volume of the author's trilogy; the second volume is PAIDEIA PROB-
LEMS AND POSSIBILITIES, and the third volume is THE PAIDEIA PROGRAM: AN
EDUCATIONAL SYLLABUS.

3153. Adler, Mortimer Jerome. PHILOSOPHER AT LARGE: AN INTELLECTUAL
AUTOBIOGRAPHY. New York: Macmillan, 1977.

This volume contains a bibliography of Adler's writings through 1976.

3154. Adler, Mortimer Jerome. SOME QUESTIONS ABOUT LANGUAGE. La Salle,
IL: Open Court, 1976.

3155. Adler, Mortimer Jerome. TEN PHILOSOPHICAL MISTAKES. New York: Macmillan; London: Collier Macmillan, 1985.

3156. Allen, Reginald E. PLATO'S PARMENIDES: TRANSLATION AND ANALYSIS.
Minneapolis: Univ. of Minnesota Press; Oxford: Blackwell, 1983.

The author argues that Plato's dialogue sheds light on Aristotle's account of substance,
form, and universality.

3157. Allison, David B., ed. THE NEW NIETZSCHE: CONTEMPORARY STYLES OF
INTERPRETATION. New York: Dell Pub. Co., 1977.

This collection includes contributions by Derrida, Heidegger, Deleuze, Klossowski,
Blanchot, and others.

3158. Allison, Henry E. KANT'S TRANSCENDENTAL IDEALISM: AN INTERPRE-
TATION AND DEFENSE. New Haven: Yale Univ. Press, 1984.

3159. Almeder, Robert F. THE PHILOSOPHY OF CHARLES S. PEIRCE: A CRITI-
CAL INTRODUCTION. Totowa, NJ: Rowman and Littlefield, 1980.

3160. American Catholic Philosophical Association. PROCEEDINGS. Washington, D. C.:
Office of the National Secretary of the Association, Catholic Univ. of America, 1935-.

Each volume in the series is the proceedings of a conference devoted to a particular
philosophical topics. Since 1976, Vol. 50, FREEDOM (1976) edited by George F. McLean;
Vol. 51, ETHICAL WISDOM EAST &-OR WEST (1977) edited by George F. McLean;
Vol. 52, IMMATERIALITY (1978) edited by George F. McLean; Vol. 53, THE HUMAN
PERSON (1979) edited by George F. McLean; Vol. 54, PHILOSOPHICAL KNOWL-
EDGE (1980) edited by John B. Brough; Vol. 55, INFINITY (1981) edited by Leo Swee-
ney; Vol. 56, THE ROLE & RESPONSIBILITY OF THE MORAL PHILOSOPHER
(1982) edited by John T. Noonan; Vol. 57, THE ACPA IN TODAY'S INTELLECTUAL
WORLD (1984) edited by Marc F. Griesbach; Vol. 58, PRACTICAL REASONING
(1985) edited by Daniel O. Dahlstrom; Vol. 59, REALISM (1985); Vol. 60, EXISTEN-
TIAL PERSONALISM (1987) editied by Daniel O. Dahlstrom; Vol. 61, METAPHYSICS
OF SUBSTANCES (1987) edited by Daniel O. Dahlstrom; Vol. 62, HERMENEUTICS &
THE TRADITION (1988) edited by Daniel O. Dahlstrom; Vol. 63, ETHICS OF HAVING
CHILDREN (1989) edited by Lawrence P. Schrenk.

3161. Ameriks, Karl. KANT'S THEORY OF MIND: AN ANALYSIS OF THE PARALOG-
ISMS OF PURE REASON. Oxford: Clarendon Press; New York: Oxford Univ. Press,
1982.

3162. Anastaplo, George. THE ARTIST AS THINKER: FROM SHAKESPEARE TO

JOYCE. Chicago: Swallow Press, 1983.

3163. Anderson, Thomas C. FOUNDATION AND STRUCTURE OF SARTREAN ETH-ICS. Lawrence: Regent Press of Kansas, 1979.

3164. Angeles, Peter Adam. A DICTIONARY OF PHILOSOPHY. London and San Francisco: Harper & Row; New York: Barnes & Noble Books, 1981.

3165. Anglemayer, Mary, et al, comps. A SEARCH FOR ENVIRONMENTAL ETHICS: AN INITIAL BIBLIOGRAPHY. Washington, DC: Smithsonian Institution Press, 1980.

This bibliography was compiled under the auspices of the Rachel Carson Council and contains an introduction by S. Dillon Ripley.

3166. Anton, John Peter. CRITICAL HUMANISM AS A PHILOSOPHY OF CULTURE, THE CASE OF E.P. PAPANOUTSOS: A TALK. Ed. by Theofanis George Stavrou. St. Paul, MN: North Central Publishing Company, 1981.

This volume contains a list of the major works of Evangelos P. Papanoutsos in English and Greek on pages 42-45.

3167. Anton, John Peter, ed. SCIENCE AND THE SCIENCES IN PLATO. New York: Eidos; Delmar, NY: Caravan, 1980.

3168. Anton, John Peter, et al, ed. ESSAYS IN ANCIENT GREEK PHILOSOPHY. Albany: State Univ. of New York Press, 1971-.

This series of volumes consist of papers originally presented at the annual meetings of the Society for Ancient Greek Philosophy, 1953-.

3169. Arato, Andrew and Andrew Breines. THE YOUNG LUKACS AND THE ORIGINS OF WESTERN MARXISM. New York: Seabury Press, 1979.

3170. Arendt, Hannah. LECTURES ON KANT'S POLITICAL PHILOSOPHY. Ed. by Ronald Beiner. Chicago: Univ. of Chicago Press; Brighton: Harvester, 1982.

The volume includes an interpretive essay by Ronald Beiner.

3171. Aschenbrenner, Karl. ANALYSIS OF APPRAISIVE CHARACTERIZATION. Dordrecht and Boston: Reidel, 1983.

3172. Ashcraft, Richard and John Greville Agard Pocock. JOHN LOCKE. Los Angeles: Univ. of California Press, 1980.

3173. Attfield, Robin. THE ETHICS OF ENVIRONMENTAL CONCERN. New York: Columbia Univ. Press; Oxford: Basil Blackwell, 1983.

3174. Audi, Robert. BELIEF, JUSTIFICATION, AND KNOWLEDGE. Belmont, CA: Wadsworth Press, 1988.

3175. Aune, Bruce. KANT'S THEORY OF MORALS. Princeton: Princeton Univ. Press, 1979.

3176. Aune, Bruce. REASON AND ACTION. Dordrecht and Boston: Reidel, 1977.

3177. Austin, Scott. PARMENIDES: BEING, BOUNDS, AND LOGIC. New Haven and London: Yale Univ. Press, 1986.

3178. Auxter, Thomas P. KANT'S MORAL TELEOLOGY. Macon, GA: Mercer Univ. Press, 1982.

The author traces Kant's precritical ethics and its dilemmas to Aristotle's teleology.

3179. Averroes. AVERROES' MIDDLE COMMENTARIES ON ARISTOTLE'S CATE-GORIES AND DE INTERPRETATIONE. Tr. by Charles E. Butterworth. Princeton: Princeton Univ. Press, 1983.

3180. Bach, Kent and Robert M. Harnish. LINGUISTIC COMMUNICATION AND SPEECH ACTS. Cambridge: MIT Press, 1979.

3181. Bahm, Archie J. COMPARATIVE PHILOSOPHY: WESTERN, INDIAN AND CHINESE PHILOSOPHIES COMPARED. Albuquerque, NM: Universal Publications, 1977.

3182. Bahm, Archie J., ed. DIRECTORY OF AMERICAN PHILOSOPHERS, 1990-91. 15th ed. Bowling Green, OH: Philosophy Documentation Center, Bowling Green State Univ., 1990.

This comprehensive directory covers the United States and Canada. It includes the addresses and telephone numbers of philosophy departments, department chairpersons, philosophy faculty, centers and institutes, societies, journals, and publishers.

3183. Ballard, Edward Goodwin. MAN AND TECHNOLOGY: TOWARD THE MEAS-UREMENT OF A CULTURE. Pittsburgh: Duquesne Univ. Press, 1978.

3184. Ballard, Edward Goodwin. PRINCIPLES OF INTERPRETATION. Series in Continental Thought, Vol. 5. Athens: Ohio Univ. Press, 1983.

3185. Banner, William Augustus. MORAL NORMS AND MORAL ORDER: THE PHI-LOSOPHY OF HUMAN AFFAIRS. Gainesville: Univ. Presses of Florida, 1981.

Banner presents an argument for not separating questions of justice from those of legality. In this book, written in general agreement with Aristotle's inclusive view of human affairs, the reader is given a philosophical alternative to two influential views in the modern world: legal positivism and utilitarianism.

3186. Barnes, Hazel Estella. SARTRE AND FLAUBERT. Chicago and London: Univ. of Chicago Press, 1981.

3187. Barrett, William. DEATH OF THE SOUL: FROM DESCARTES TO THE COM-PUTER. Garden City, NY: Anchor Press, 1986.

3188. Barrett, William. THE ILLUSION OF TECHNIQUE: A SEARCH FOR MEANING IN A TECHNOLOGICAL CIVILIZATION. Garden City, NY: Anchor Press, 1978.

3189. Bartley, William Warren. THE RETREAT TO COMMITMENT. 2d. rev. and enl ed. La Salle, IL: Open Court, 1984.

3190. Bartley, William Warren. WITTGENSTEIN. 2d., rev. and enl. ed. La Salle, IL: Open Court, 1985.

3191. Bauman, Zygmunt. HERMENEUTICS AND SOCIAL SCIENCE. London: Hutchinson; New York: Columbia Univ. Press, 1978.

3192. Bayles, Michael D., ed. ETHICS AND POPULATION. Cambridge, MA: Schenkman, 1976.

3193. Bayles, Michael D. MORALITY AND POPULATION POLICY. University: Univ. of Alabama Press, 1980.

3194. Baynes, Kenneth, et al, eds. AFTER PHILOSOPHY: END OR TRANSFORMA-TION? Cambridge: MIT Press, 1986.

3195. Bealer, George. QUALITY AND CONCEPT. Clarendon Library of Logic and Philosophy. Oxford: Clarendon Press; New York: Oxford Univ. Press, 1982.

3196. Beardsley, Monroe C. THE AESTHETIC POINT OF VIEW: SELECTED ESSAYS. Ed. by Michael Wreen and Donald Callen. Ithaca: Cornell Univ. Press, 1982.

3197. Beauchamp, Tom L. and Alexander Rosenberg. HUME AND THE PROBLEM OF CAUSATION. New York: Oxford Univ. Press, 1981.

3198. Beck, Lewis White, et al, eds. KANT'S LATIN WRITINGS: TRANSLATIONS, COMMENTARIES AND NOTES. New York: Peter Lang, 1986.

3199. Becker, Lawrence C. PROPERTY RIGHTS: PHILOSOPHIC FOUNDATIONS. Boston and London: Routledge & Kegan Paul, 1977.

3200. Becker, Lawrence C. and Charlotte B. Becker, eds. THE ENCYCLOPEDIA OF ETHICS. New York: Garland, 1992.

This encyclopedia contains more than 400 signed articles by over 250 internationally recognized authorities. It emphasizes the application of ethics in all areas of modern life. There is an extensive index of names and subjects.

3201. Bedau, Hugo Adam, ed. THE DEATH PENALTY IN AMERICA. 3d ed. New York: Oxford Univ. Press, 1982.

3202. Bell, David E., et al, eds. CONFLICTING OBJECTIVES IN DECISIONS. New York and London: Wiley, 1977.

This book contains an edited version of a workshop held at the International Institute for Applied Systems Analysis, Laxenburg, Austria on October 20-24 1975.

3203. Benacerraf, Paul and Hilary Putnam, eds. PHILOSOPHY OF MATHEMATICS: SELECTED READINGS. 2d ed. Cambridge and New York: Cambridge Univ. Press, 1983.

The second edition is an extensive revision of the first.

3204. Bencivenga, Ermanno, et al. LOGIC BIVALENCE AND DENOTATION. Atasca-dero, CA: Ridgeview Pub., 1986.

3205. Bennett, Jonathan Francis. LINGUISTIC BEHAVIOR. London and New York: Cambridge Univ. Press, 1976.

3206. Bennett, Jonathan Francis. A STUDY OF SPINOZA'S ETHICS. Cambridge: Cambridge Univ. Press, 1984.

3207. Benton, Robert J. KANT'S SECOND CRITIQUE AND THE PROBLEM OF TRANSCENDENTAL ARGUMENTS. The Hague: Nijhoff, 1977.

3208. Berger, Fred R. HAPPINESS, JUSTICE AND FREEDOM: THE MORAL AND POLITICAL PHILOSOPHY OF JOHN STUART MILL. Berkeley: Univ. of California Press, 1984.

3209. Berndtson, Arthur. POWER, FORM, AND MIND. Lewisburg: Bucknell Univ. Press, 1981.

3210. Bernstein, Richard J. BEYOND OBJECTIVISM AND RELATIVISM: SCIENCE, HERMENEUTICS AND PRAXIS. Philadelphia: Univ. of Pennsylvania Press; Oxford: Blackwell, 1983.

3211. Bernstein, Richard J., ed. HABERMAS AND MODERNITY. Cambridge: MIT Press, 1985.

All of the essays in this volume were published in PRAXIS INTERNATIONAL.

3212. Bernstein, Richard J. PHILOSOPHICAL PROFILES: ESSAYS IN A PRAGMATIC MODE. Philadelphia: Univ. of Pennsylvania Press, 1985.

3213. Bernstein, Richard J. THE RESTRUCTURING OF SOCIAL AND POLITICAL THEORY. New York: Harcourt Brace Jovanovich; Oxford: B. Blackwell, 1976.

3214. Bien, Joseph, ed. PHENOMENOLOGY AND THE SOCIAL SCIENCES: A DIALOGUE. The Hague and Boston: Nijhoff, 1978.

3215. Black, Max. THE PREVALENCE OF HUMBUG AND OTHER ESSAYS. Ithaca: Cornell Univ. Press, 1982.

3216. Blackwell, Richard J., comp. BIBLIOGRAPHY OF THE PHILOSOPHY OF SCIENCE, 1945-1981. Westport, CT: Greenwood Press, 1983.

3217. Block, Ned J., ed. IMAGERY. Montgomery, VT: Bradford Books, 1980.

3218. Blum, Lawrence. FRIENDSHIP, ALTRUISM AND MORALITY. London and Boston: Routledge and Kegan Paul, 1980.

Blum argues that moral philosophers have concentrated on rationality in morality and have neglected the role of feelings, such as compassion, concern and sympathy, as motivating forces.

3219. Bogan, James and James E. McGuire, eds. HOW THINGS ARE: STUDIES IN PREDICATION AND THE HISTORY OF PHILOSOPHY AND SCIENCE. Dordrecht and Boston: Reidel, 1985.

This volume includes papers from a conference sponsored by Pitzer College in 1981.

3220. Bok, Sissela. LYING: MORAL CHOICE IN PUBLIC AND PRIVATE. Hassocks: Harvester Press; New York: Pantheon, 1978.

3221. BonJour, Nelson. THE STRUCTURE OF EMPIRICAL KNOWLEDGE. Cambridge: Harvard Univ. Press, 1985.

3222. Bourgeois, Patrick L. and Sandra B. Rosenthal. PRAGMATISM AND PHENOME-NOLOGY: A PHILOSOPHIC ENCOUNTER. Amsterdam: B. R. Gruner, 1980.

This work seeks to discover points of convergence between pragmatism and phenomenology while taking full account of the differences between these two philosophical positions. The author attempts to develop each position further by drawing on insights in the other.

3223. Bourgeois, Patrick L. and Sandra B. Rosenthal. THEMATIC STUDIES IN PHE-NOMENOLOGY AND PRAGMATICISM. Amsterdam: B. R. Gruner, 1983.

3224. Bouwsma, Oets Koek. WITTGENSTEIN: CONVERSATIONS, 1949-1951. Ed. by Jimmy Lee Craft and Ronald E. Hustwit. Indianapolis: Hackett, 1986.

3225. Boyle, Joseph M., et al. FREE CHOICE: A SELF-REFERENTIAL ARGUMENT. Notre Dame, IN: Univ. of Notre Dame Press, 1976.

3226. Brandt, Richard B. A THEORY OF THE GOOD AND THE RIGHT. Oxford: Clarendon Press; New York: Oxford Univ. Press, 1979.

The author develops a concept of a moral code and attempts a definition of "morally right" which incorporates the notion of a moral code supported by rational persons.

3227. Breazele, J. Daniel, ed. PHILOSOPHY AND TRUTH: SELECTIONS FROM NIETZSCHE'S NOTEBOOKS OF THE EARLY 1870'S. Tr. (with introduction) by J. Daniel Breazele. Atlantic Highlands, NJ: Humanities Press, 1979.

3228. Brenkert, George G. MARXIST ETHICS OF FREEDOM. London and Boston: Routledge and Kegan Paul, 1983.

This work offers an analysis of the system of ethics allegedly underlying Marx's entire body of thought.

3229. Brezik, Victor B., ed. ONE HUNDRED YEARS OF THOMISM: AETERNI PATRIS AND AFTERWARDS: A SYMPOSIUM. Houston: Center for Thomistic Studies, Univ. of St. Thomas, 1981.

The text of the AETERNI PATRIS is included on pages 173-197.

3230. Bricke, John. HUME'S PHILOSOPHY OF MIND. Princeton, NJ: Princeton Univ. Press; Edinburgh: Univ. Press, 1980.

3231. Brittain, Gordon G. KANT'S THEORY OF SCIENCE. Princeton, NJ: Princeton Univ. Press, 1978.

3232. Bronowski, Jacob. THE VISIONARY EYE: ESSAYS IN THE ARTS, LITERA-TURE, AND SCIENCE. Ed. by Piero Ariotti and Rita Bronowski. Cambridge: MIT Press, 1978.

3233. Brown, Robert F. THE LATER PHILOSOPHY OF SCHELLING: THE INFLU-ENCE OF BOEHME ON THE WORKS OF 1809-1815. Lewisburg, PA: Bucknell Univ. Press, 1977.

3234. Brown, Robert F. SCHELLING'S TREATISE ON "THE DEITIES OF SAMOTH-RACE". Tr (with interpretation) by Robert F. Brown. AAR Studies in Religion. Missoula: Scholar's Press, 1977.

3235. Brubacher, John S. ON THE PHILOSOPHY OF HIGHER EDUCATION. San Francisco: Jossey-Bass, 1977.

3236. Bruzina, Ronald and Bruce W. Wilshire, eds. CROSS CURRENTS IN PHENOME-NOLOGY. The Hague and Boston: Nijhoff, 1978.

3237. Bruzina, Ronald and Bruce W. Wilshire, eds. PHENOMENOLOGY, DIALOGUES AND BRIDGES. Albany: State Univ. of New York Press, 1982.

3238. Bugliarello, George and Dean B. Doner, eds. THE HISTORY AND PHILOSOPHY OF TECHNOLOGY. Urbana: Univ. of Illinois Press, 1979.

This work is based on a Symposium on the History and Philosophy of Technology, Chicago, 1973, sponsored by the College of Engineering and the College of Liberal Arts and Sciences of the University of Illinois at Chicago Circle.

3239. Burke, John P., et al. MARXISM AND THE GOOD SOCIETY. Cambridge and New York: Cambridge Univ. Press, 1981.

This volume contains ten essays by five philosophers, three political scientists, a sociologist of science and the editor of MONTHLY REVIEW.

3240. Buroker, Jill Vance. SPACE AND INCONGRUENCE: THE ORIGIN OF KANT'S IDEALISM. Dordrecht and Boston: Reidel, 1981.

3241. Burrell, David B. AQUINAS: GOD AND ACTION. Notre Dame, IN: Univ. Press, 1979.

3242. Butchvarov, Panayot. BEING QUA BEING: A THEORY OF IDENTITY, EXISTENCE, AND PREDICATION. Bloomington: Indiana Univ. Press, 1979.

3243. Butts, Robert E. and Jaakko Hintikka, eds. BASIC PROBLEMS IN METHODOLOGY AND LINGUISTICS. Dordrecht and Boston: Reidel, 1977.

3244. Cahn, Steven M., ed. NEW STUDIES IN THE PHILOSOPHY OF JOHN DEWEY. Hanover, NH: Univ. Press of New England, 1977.

3245. Cahn, Steven M. and David Shatz, eds. CONTEMPORARY PHILOSOPHY OF RELIGION. New York and Oxford: Oxford Univ. Press, 1982.

This anthology contains essays by Peter Thomas Geach, Nicholas Wolterstorff, Terence Penelhum, Kai Nielsen, Alvin Plantinga, Ninian Smart, and other contemporary Anglo-American philosophers.

3246. Campbell, Keith. BODY AND MIND. 2d ed. Notre Dame: Univ. of Notre Dame Press, 1984.

3247. Caplan, Arthur L. THE SOCIOBIOLOGY DEBATE: READINGS ON ETHICAL AND SCIENTIFIC ISSUES. New York: Harper and Row, 1978.

There is a bibliography on pages 489-503.

3248. Caputo, John D. THE MYSTICAL ELEMENT IN HEIDEGGER'S THOUGHT. Athens: Ohio Univ. Press, 1978.

3249. Cargile, James. PARADOXES: A STUDY IN FORM AND PREDICATION. Cambridge and New York: Cambridge Univ. Press, 1979.

3250. Carnap, Rudolf. DEAR CARNAP, DEAR VAN: THE QUINE-CARNAP CORRESPONDENCE AND OTHER MATERIAL. Ed. by Richard Creath. Berkeley: Univ. of California, 1990.

3251. Carter, Richard Burnett. DESCARTES' MEDICAL PHILOSOPHY: THE ORGANIC SOLUTION TO THE MIND-BODY PROBLEM. Baltimore: Johns Hopkins Univ. Press, 1983.

3252. Cassirer, Ernst. KANT'S LIFE AND THOUGHT. Tr. of KANTS LEBEN UND LEHRE. 2d. ed. Berlin: Cassirer, 1921. Tr. by James Haden. New Haven: Yale Univ. Press, 1981.

3253. Cassirer, Ernst. SYMBOL, MYTH, AND CULTURE: ESSAYS AND LECTURES OF ERNST CASSIRER 1935-1945. Ed. by Donald Phillip Verene. New Haven: Yale Univ. Press, 1979.

3254. Castaneda, Hector-Neri. AGENT, LANGUAGE, AND THE STRUCTURE OF THE WORLD: ESSAYS PRESENTED TO HECTOR-NERI CASTANEDA WITH HIS REPLIES. Ed. by James E. Tomberlin. Indianapolis: Hackett, 1983.

3255. Castaneda, Hector-Neri. ON PHILOSOPHICAL METHOD. Nous Publications, No. 1. Detroit: Castaneda, 1980.

3256. Castaneda, Hector-Neri. THINKING, LANGUAGE AND EXPERIENCE. Minneapolis: Univ. of Minnesota Press, 1989.

3257. Catalano, Joseph S. COMMENTARY ON JEAN-PAUL SARTRE'S "CRITIQUE OF DIALECTICAL REASON." Vol. 1, THEORY OF PRACTICAL ENSEMBLES. Chicago: Univ. of Chicago Press, 1986.

3258. Catalano, Joseph S. A COMMENTARY ON JEAN-PAUL SARTRE'S BEING AND NOTHINGNESS. Chicago: Univ. of Chicago Press, 1980.

3259. Cauman, Leigh S., et al, eds. HOW MANY QUESTIONS?: ESSAYS IN HONOR OF SIDNEY MORGENBESSER. Indianapolis: Hackett, 1983.

3260. Cavell, Stanley. THE CLAIM OF REASON: WITTGENSTEIN, SKEPTICISM, MORALITY, AND TRAGEDY. Oxford: Clarendon Press; New York: Oxford Univ. Press, 1979.

3261. Cavell, Stanley. IN QUEST OF THE ORDINARY: LINES OF SKEPTICISM AND ROMANTICISM. Chicago: Univ. of Chicago Press, 1988.

This work argues for the philosophical basis of romanticism, particularly in works of classical American writers such as Emerson, Thoreau, and Poe.

3262. Cavell, Stanley. PURSUITS OF HAPPINESS: THE HOLLYWOOD COMEDY OF REMARRIAGE. Harvard Film Studies. Cambridge: Harvard Univ. Press, 1981.

3263. Cavell, Stanley. THE SENSES OF WALDEN. Expanded ed. San Francisco: North Point Press, 1981.

3264. Cavell, Stanley. THIS NEW YET UNAPPROACHABLE AMERICA: LECTURES AFTER EMERSON AFTER WITTGENSTEIN. Albuquerque: Living Batch Press, 1989.

These essays examine Wittgenstein as a critic of culture who balanced a philosophy of the ordinary against the world's decline and traces this philosophy back to Emerson.

3265. Cavell, Stanley. THE WORLD VIEWED: REFLECTIONS ON THE ONTOLOGY OF FILM. Enl ed. Cambridge: Harvard Univ. Press, 1979.

3266. Caws, Peter. SARTRE. The Arguments of the Philosophers. London and Boston: Routledge and Kegan Paul, 1979.

3267. Caws, Peter, ed. TWO CENTURIES OF PHILOSOPHY IN AMERICA. Totowa, NJ: Rowman and Littlefield, 1980.

This book consists mainly of papers presented at the Bicentennial Symposium of Philosophy held in New York City, Oct. 7-10, 1976.

3268. Chappell, Vere Claiborne and Willis Doney, eds. TWENTY-FIVE YEARS OF DESCARTES SCHOLARSHIP, 1960-1984: A BIBLIOGRAPHY. New York: Garland, 1987.

This work includes nearly 2,500 books, chapters, articles, discussions, and reviews about Descartes's life work and influence as a philosopher, mathematician, scientist, and writer. Publications in English, French, German, Italian, Spanish, Portuguese, Swedish, and Dutch are covered. More than 200 editions and tranlations of Descartes's works are listed. There is a comprehensive subject index.

3269. Cherniss, Harold Frederik. SELECTED PAPERS. Ed. by Leonard Taran. Leiden: E. J. Brill, 1977.

A bibliography of the author's works appears on pages 524-530.

3270. Chisholm, Roderick M. BRENTANO AND MEINONG STUDIES. New York: Humanities Press; Amsterdam: Rodopi, 1982.

3271. Chisholm, Roderick M. THE FIRST PERSON: AN ESSAY ON REFERENCE AND INTENTIONALITY. Minneapolis: Univ. of Minnesota Press; Brighton: Harvester, 1981.

3272. Chisholm, Roderick M. THE FOUNDATIONS OF KNOWING. Minneapolis: Univ. of Minnesota Press; Brighton: Harvester Press, 1982.

3273. Chisholm, Roderick M. PERSON AND OBJECT: A METAPHYSICAL STUDY. London: G. Allen and Unwin, 1976.

3274. Chomsky, Noam. KNOWLEDGE OF LANGUAGE: ITS NATURE, ORIGIN, AND USE. New York: Praeger, 1986.

3275. Chomsky, Noam. LANGUAGE AND RESPONSIBILITY: BASED ON CONVER-SATIONS WITH MITSOU RONAT. Tr. of DIALOGUES AVEC MITSOU RONAT. Paris: Flammarion, 1977. Tr. from the French by John Viertel. New York: Pantheon Books; Sussex: Harvester, 1979.

3276. Chomsky, Noam. RULES AND REPRESENTATIONS. New York: Columbia Univ. Press; Oxford: Blackwell, 1980.

This is number 11 of the Woodbridge lectures delivered at Columbia University.

3277. Chomsky, Noam, et al. CHOMSKY O SKINNER: LA GENESIS DEL LENGUAJE. Ed. by Ramon Bayles. Barcelona: Fontanella, 1977.

3278. Churchland, Patricia Smith. NEUROPHILOSOPHY: TOWARD A UNIFIED SCIENCE OF THE MIND-BRAIN. Cambridge: MIT Press, 1986.

This work contains a bibliography on pages 491-523.

3279. Claus, David B. TOWARD THE SOUL: AN INQUIRY INTO THE MEANING OF [PSYCHE] BEFORE PLATO. New Haven: Yale Univ. Press, 1981.

3280. Clendenning, John. THE LIFE AND THOUGHT OF JOSIAH ROYCE. Madison: Univ. of Wisconsin Press, 1985.

3281. Cobb, John B. and Franklin I. Gamwell, eds. EXISTENCE AND ACTUALITY: CONVERSATIONS WITH CHARLES HARTSHORNE. Chicago: Univ. of Chicago Press, 1984.

This is a selection of papers presented at a conference held at the Divinity School, University of Chicago, in the fall of 1981.

3282. Cohen, Marshall, ed. RONALD DWORKIN AND CONTEMPORARY JURIS-PRUDENCE. Philosophy and Society series. Totawa, NJ: Rowman and Allanheld, 1984c1983.

This is a collection of philosophical essays on Dworkin's thought by H. L. A. Hart, A. D. Woozley, David Lyons and others.

3283. Cohen, Marshall, et al. EQUALITY AND PREFERENTIAL TREATMENT. Princeton: Princeton Univ. Press, 1977.

With one exception, the essays in this book originally appeared in the journal PHILOSOPHY AND PUBLIC AFFAIRS.

3284. Cohen, Richard A., ed. FACE TO FACE WITH LEVINAS. Albany: State Univ. of New York Press, 1986.

3285. Cohen, Robert Sonne, et al, eds. ESSAYS IN MEMORY OF IMRE LAKATOS. Dordrecht and Boston: Reidel, 1976.

3286. Cohen, Robert Sonne and Larry Laudan, eds. PHYSICS, PHILOSOPHY AND PSYCHOANALYSIS: ESSAYS IN HONOR OF ADOLF GRUNBAUM. Dordrecht and Boston: Reidel, 1983.

3287. Cohen, Robert Sonne and Marx W. Wartofsky. EPISTEMOLOGY, METHODOLO-GY, AND THE SOCIAL SCIENCES. Dordrecht and Boston: Reidel, 1983.

3288. Cohen, Robert Sonne and Marx W. Wartofsky. HEGEL AND THE SCIENCES. Dordrecht and Boston: Reidel, 1984.

3289. Cohen, Robert Sonne and Marx W. Wartofsky, eds. LANGUAGE, LOGIC AND METHOD. Dordrecht and Boston: Reidel, 1982.

3290. Cohen, Robert Sonne and Marx W. Wartofsky. METHODOLOGY, METAPHYSICS AND THE HISTORY OF SCIENCE: IN MEMORY OF BENJAMIN NELSON. Boston Studies in the Philosophy of Science, Vol. 84. Dordrecht and Boston: Reidel, 1984.

3291. Cohen, Ted and Paul Guyer, eds. ESSAYS IN KANT'S AESTHETICS. Chicago: Univ. of Chicago Press, 1982.

3292. Coleman, Earle Jerome, ed. VARIETIES OF AESTHETIC EXPERIENCE. Lanham, MD: Univ. Press of America, 1983.

3293. Colish, Marcia. THE MIRROR OF LANGUAGE: A STUDY IN THE MEDIE-VAL THEORY OF KNOWLEDGE. Rev ed. Lincoln: Univ. of Nebraska Press, 1983.

3294. Coomaraswamy, Ananda Kentish. COOMARASWAMY: SELECTED PAPERS. Vol. 1; SELECTED PAPERS--TRADITIONAL ART AND SYMBOLISM. Vol. 2; SELECTED PAPERS--METAPHYSICS. Vol. 3; HIS LIFE AND WORK. Ed. by Roger Lipsey. Princeton: Princeton Univ. Press, 1977.

3295. Cooney, Timothy J. TELLING RIGHT FROM WRONG: LANGUAGE, ANGER, AND MORALITY. New York: Random House, 1984.

3296. Cooper, David E. AUTHENTICITY AND LEARNING: NIETZSCHE'S EDUCA-

TIONAL PHILOSOPHY. International Library of the Philosophy of Education. London and Boston: Routledge & Kegan Paul, 1983.

Nietzsche's educational theory is presented in detail, elucidating the philosopher's belief that the purpose of education is to produce individuals who are responsible for their lives.

3297. Cooper, Robin. QUANTIFICATION AND SYNTACTIC THEORY. Dordrecht and Boston: Reidel, 1983.

3298. Cornman, James W. SKEPTICISM, JUSTIFICATION, AND EXPLANATION. Dordrecht and Boston: Reidel, 1980.

This volume includes a bibliographic essay by Walter N. Gregory.

3299. Cox, Ronald R. SCHUTZ'S THEORY OF RELEVANCE: A PHENOMENOLOGI-CAL CRITIQUE. The Hague and Boston: Nijhoff, 1978.

3300. Craft, Jimmy Lee and Ronald E. Hustwit, eds. TOWARD A NEW SENSIBILITY. Lincoln: Univ. of Nebraska Press, 1982.

3301. Craft, Jimmy Lee and Ronald E. Hustwit, eds. WITHOUT PROOF OR EVIDENCE: ESSAYS OF O. K. BOUWSMA. Lincoln: Univ. of Nebraska Press, 1984.

3302. Crocker, David A. PRAXIS AND DEMOCRATIC SOCIALISM: THE CRITICAL SOCIAL THEORY OF MARKOVIC AND STOJANOVIC. Atlantic Highlands, NJ: Humanities Press; Brighton, Sussex: Harvester Press, 1983.

This volume evaluates, analyzes and strengthens the author's concept of praxis and the normative basis for Markovic's and Stojanovic's conception of individual and social excellence, critique of bureaucratic socialism and advanced capitalism, and vision of a humane and democratic socialism.

3303. Crosson, Frederick James, ed. THE AUTONOMY OF RELIGIOUS BELIEF: A CRITICAL INQUIRY. Notre Dame, IN: Univ. of Notre Dame Press, 1981.

3304. Cua, Antonio S. DIMENSIONS OF MORAL CREATIVITY: PARADIGMS, PRIN-CIPLES, AND IDEALS. Univ. Park: Pennsylvania State Univ. Press, 1978.

3305. Culler, Jonathan D. ON DECONSTRUCTION: THEORY AND CRITICISM OF STRUCTURALISM. Ithaca: Cornell Univ. Press, 1982.

This book contains a bibliography on pages 281-302.

3306. Culver, Charles M. and Bernard Gert. PHILOSOPHY IN MEDICINE: CONCEPTU-AL AND ETHICAL ISSUES IN MEDICINE AND PSYCHIATRY. New York: Oxford Univ. Press, 1982.

3307. Cumming, Robert Denoon. PHENOMENOLOGY AND DECONSTRUCTION. Vol. 1, THE DREAM IS OVER. Chicago: Univ. of Chicago Press, 1991.

3308. Cunningham, Suzanne. LANGUAGE AND THE PHENOMENOLOGICAL REDUC-TIONS OF EDMUND HUSSERL. The Hague: Nijhoff, 1976.

3309. Curley, Edwin M. DESCARTES AGAINST THE SKEPTICS. Cambridge: Harvard Univ. Press; Oxford: B. Blackwell, 1978.

3310. Curtler, Hugh Mercer. A THEORY OF ART, TRAGEDY AND CULTURE: THE PHILOSOPHY OF ELISEO VIVAS. New York: Haven Publications, 1981.

3311. Curtler, Hugh Mercer, ed. WHAT IS ART? New York: Haven Publications, 1983.

3312. D'Amico, Robert. MARX AND PHILOSOPHY OF CULTURE. Gainesville: Univ. Presses of Florida, 1981.

This work presents a reevaluation of Marx's general theory of human action. The book contains one of the first discussions in English of the French philosophers Baudrillard, Goux, Deleuze, and Guatari.

3313. D'Angelo, Edward, et al. CONTEMPORARY EAST EUROPEAN MARXISM. Amsterdam: B. R. Gruner, 1980-.

The essays in Vol. 1 were published previously in REVOLUTIONARY WORLD and in EAST-WEST DIALOGUES.

3314. Dahm, Helmut, et al, eds. PHILOSOPHICAL SOVIETOLOGY: THE PURSUIT OF SCIENCE. Dordrecht and Boston: Reidel, 1988.

3315. Danto, Arthur Coleman. NARRATION AND KNOWLEDGE: INCLUDING THE INTEGRAL TEXT OF ANALYTICAL PHILOSOPHY OF HISTORY. This is a revised edition of the author's ANALYTICAL PHILOSOPHY OF HISTORY, 1968. New York: Columbia Univ. Press, 1985.

3316. Danto, Arthur Coleman. THE PHILOSOPHICAL DISENFRANCHISEMENT OF ART. New York: Columbia Univ. Press, 1986.

3317. Danto, Arthur Coleman. THE TRANSFIGURATION OF THE COMMONPLACE: A PHILOSOPHY OF ART. Cambridge: Harvard Univ. Press, 1981.

3318. Dauben, Joseph Warren. GEORG CANTOR: HIS MATHEMATICS AND PHILOS-OPHY OF THE INFINITE. Cambridge: Harvard Univ. Press, 1979.

3319. Dauenhauer, Bernard P. SILENCE: THE PHENOMENON AND ITS ONTOLOGI-CAL SIGNIFICANCE. Bloomington: Indiana Univ. Press, 1980.

3320. Davidson, Donald. ESSAYS ON ACTION AND EVENTS. Oxford: Clarendon Press, 1980.

This is a companion volume to INQUIRIES INTO TRUTH AND INTERPRETA-TION.

3321. Davidson, Donald. INQUIRIES INTO TRUTH AND INTERPRETATION. Oxford: Clarendon Press: New York: Oxford Univ. Press, 1984.

This is a companion volume to ESSAYS ON ACTION AND EVENTS.

3322. Davis, Martin. MEANING, QUANTIFICATION, NECESSITY: THEMES IN PHILOSOPHICAL LOGIC. London and Boston: Routledge and Kegan Paul, 1981.

3323. DeGeorge, Richard T. THE PHILOSOPHER'S GUIDE: TO SOURCES, RESEARCH TOOLS, PROFESSIONAL LIFE AND RELATED FIELDS. Lawrence: Regents Press of Kansas, 1980.

3324. DeGeorge, Richard T., ed. SEMIOTIC THEMES. Lawrence, KS: Univ. of Kansas Humanistic Publications, No. 53, 1981.

This volume includes essays on Saussure and Peirce, literary and cultural semiotics, and biosemiotics.

3325. DeGrood, David H. CONSCIOUSNESS AND SOCIAL LIFE. Amsterdam: B. R. Gruner, 1976.

3326. Den Uyl, Douglas J. POWER, STATE, AND FREEDOM: AN INTERPRETATION OF SPINOZA'S POLITICAL PHILOSOPHY. Assen: Van Gorcum, 1983.

3327. Den Uyl, Douglas J. and Douglas B. Rasmussen, eds. THE PHILOSOPHIC THOUGHT OF AYN RAND. Urbana: Univ. of Illinois Press, 1984.

3328. Dennett, Daniel Clement. BRAINSTORMS: PHILOSOPHICAL ESSAYS ON MIND AND PSYCHOLOGY. 1st ed. Montgomery, VT: Bradford Books, 1978.

3329. Dennett, Daniel Clement. CONSCIOUSNESS EXPLAINED. Boston: Little Brown; London: Allen Lane; Penguin Press, 1991.

Dennett develops a new, counterinituitive model of consciousness based on new facts and theories from neuroscience, psychology, and artificial intelligence.

3330. Dennett, Daniel Clement. ELBOW ROOM: THE VARIETES OF FREE WILL WORTH HAVING. Cambridge: MIT Press; Oxford: Clarendon Press; New York: Oxford Univ. Press, 1984.

This volume is based on the author's John Locke lectures at Oxford in 1983.

3331. Deutsch, Eliot. ON TRUTH: AN ONTOLOGICAL THEORY. Honolulu: Univ. of Hawaii, 1979.

3332. Deutsch, Eliot. PERSONHOOD, CREATIVITY, AND FREEDOM. Honolulu: Univ. of Hawaii, 1982.

3333. Devine, Elizabeth, et al, eds. THINKERS OF THE TWENTIETH CENTURY: A BIOGRAPHICAL, BIBLIOGRAPHICAL AND CRITICAL DICTIONARY. Detroit: Gale, 1983.

Philosophers comprise about a fourth of this selection of 400 scholars, scientists, and other writers. Each individual is covered in terms of a brief life sketch, a list of books published, a list of critical studies, and an interpretive essay. The biobibliographies tend to be more complete than those in comparable reference works. There is no subject index. Although some individuals such as Gandhi are treated, the focus of the work is western, not world-wide.

3334. Dewey, John. THE COMPLETE WORKS OF JOHN DEWEY. Ed. by Jo Ann Boydston. Carbondale, IL: Southern Illinois Univ. Press, 1967-.

The complete 5 volumes of THE EARLY WORKS OF JOHN DEWEY, 1882-1898 and the complete 15 volumes of THE MIDDLE WORKS OF JOHN DEWEY, 1899-1924 have been published. So far 17 volumes of THE LATER WORKS OF JOHN DEWEY, 1925-1953 have appeared.

3335. Dewey, Robert E. PHILOSOPHY OF JOHN DEWEY: A CRITICAL EXPOSITION OF HIS METHOD, METAPHYSICS AND THEORY OF KNOWLEDGE. The Hague: Nijhoff, 1977.

3336. Dicker, Georges. PERCEPTUAL KNOWLEDGE: AN ANALYTICAL AND HISTORICAL STUDY. Dordrecht and Boston: Reidel, 1980.

3337. Dickie, George T. THE ART CIRCLE: A THEORY OF ART. New York: Haven Publications, 1984.

3338. Dickie, George T. EVALUATING ART. Philadelphia: Temple Univ. Press, 1988.

3339. Donagan, Alan. THE THEORY OF MORALITY. Chicago: Univ. of, Chicago Press, 1979.

3340. Donagan, Alan, et al, eds. HUMAN NATURE AND NATURAL KNOWLEDGE: ESSAYS PRESENTED TO MARJORIE GRENE ON THE OCCASION OF HER SEVENTY-FIFTH BIRTHDAY. Dordrecht and Boston: Reidel, 1986.

This volume contains a list of the publications of Marjorie Grene on pages 371-374.

3341. Dreyfus, Hubert L. WHAT COMPUTERS CAN'T DO: THE LIMITS OF ARTIFICIAL INTELLIGENCE. Rev ed. New York: Harper & Row, 1979.

3342. Dreyfus, Hubert L. and Stuart E. Dreyfus. MIND OVER MACHINE: THE POWER OF HUMAN INTUITION AND EXPERTISE IN THE ERA OF THE COMPUTER. New York: Free Press; Oxford: B. Blackwell, 1986.

3343. Durfee, Harold A., ed. ANALYTIC PHILOSOPHY AND PHENOMENOLOGY. The Hague: Nijhoff, 1976.

3344. Dutton, Denis, ed. THE FORGER'S ART: FORGERY AND THE PHILOSOPHY OF ART. Berkeley: Univ. of California Press, 1983.

3345. Dutton, Denis and Michael Krausz, eds. THE CONCEPT OF CREATIVITY IN SCIENCE AND ART. The Hague and Boston: Nijhoff, 1981.

3346. Dworkin, Ronald M. LAW'S EMPIRE. Cambridge: Belknap Press, 1986.

3347. Dworkin, Ronald M. A MATTER OF PRINCIPLE. Cambridge: Harvard Univ. Press, 1985.

3348. Dworkin, Ronald M. TAKING RIGHTS SERIOUSLY. London: Duckworth; Cambridge: Harvard Univ. Press, 1977.

3349. Dworkin, Gerald. THE THEORY AND PRACTICE OF AUTONOMY. Cambridge and New York: Cambridge Univ. Press, 1988.

3350. Eames, Samuel Morris. PRAGMATIC NATURALISM: AN INTRODUCTION. Carbondale: Southern Illinois Univ. Press, 1977.

3351. Earle, William. PUBLIC SORROWS AND PRIVATE PLEASURES. Studies in Phenomenology and Existential Philosophy. Bloomington: Univ. of Indiana Press, 1976.

3352. Earman, John, et al. FOUNDATIONS OF SPACE-TIME THEORIES. Minneapolis Studies in the Philosophy of Science, Vol. 8. Minneapolis: Univ. of Minnesota Press, 1977.

This anthology contains recent essays on the general subject of its title by Adolf Grunbaum, Wesley C. Salmon, Laurence Sklar, Clark Glymour and other philosophers of science.

3353. Ecker, David W. and Stanley S. Madeja. PIONEERS IN PERCEPTION: A STUDY OF AESTHETIC PERCEPTION: CONVERSATIONS WITH ARNHEIM, GIBSON, GOODMAN, SCHAEFER-SIMMERN, AND SHERMAN. St. Louis: CEMREL, 1979.

3354. Edel, Abraham. ARISTOTLE AND HIS PHILOSOPHY. Chapel Hill: Univ. of North Carolina Press; London: Croom Helm, 1982.

3355. Edel, Abraham. SCIENCE, IDEOLOGY AND VALUE. Vol. 1, ANALYZING CONCEPTS IN SOCIAL SCIENCE. Vol. 2, EXPLORING FACT AND VALUE. Vol. 3, INTERPRETING EDUCATION. New Brunswick, NJ: Transaction Books, 1979-1985.

3356. Edie, James M. SPEAKING AND MEANING: THE PHENOMENOLOGY OF LANGUAGE. Bloomington: Indiana Univ. Press, 1976.

This work has an extensive bibliography on pages 245-271.

3357. Edwards, James C. ETHICS WITHOUT PHILOSOPHY: WITTGENSTEIN AND THE MORAL LIFE. Tampa: Univ. Presses of Florida, 1982.

The author provides arguments for the relationship between Wittgenstein's famous philosophical doctrines and his ethical and religious concerns.

3358. Edwards, Paul. HEIDEGGER ON DEATH: A CRITICAL EVALUATION. Monist Monograph, Vol. 1. La Salle: The Hegeler Institute, 1980.

3359. Eisele, Carolyn. STUDIES IN THE SCIENTIFIC AND MATHEMATICAL PHILOSOPHY OF CHARLES S. PEIRCE: ESSAYS. Ed. by Richard Milton Martin. The Hague and New York: Mouton, 1979.

3360. Elgin, Catherine Zincke. WITH REFERENCE TO REFERENCE. Indianapolis: Hackett, 1983.

Nelson Goodman wrote the foreward for this volume.

3361. Elliston, Frederick A., ed. HEIDEGGER'S EXISTENTIAL ANALYTIC. 's-Gravenhage and New York: Mouton, 1978.

3362. Elliston, Frederick A. and Peter J. McCormick, eds. HUSSERL: EXPOSITIONS AND APPRAISALS. Notre Dame, IN: Univ. of Notre Dame Press, 1977.

3363. Elrod, John W. KIERKEGAARD AND CHRISTENDOM. Princeton: Princeton Univ. Press, 1981.

3364. Elvee, Richard Q., ed. MIND IN NATURE. San Francisco: Harper & Row, 1982.

This volume includes six essays contributed by John A. Wheeler, Sir Karl Popper, Richard Rorty, Ragnar Granit, Eugene Wigner, and Wolfhart Pannenburg to the Nobel Conference XVII at Gustavus Adolphus College, St. Peter MN.

3365. Emmett, Kathleen and Peter Machamer. PERCEPTION: AN ANNOTATED BIBLIOGRAPHY. New York: Garland, 1976.

3366. Ermarth, Michael. WILHELM DILTHEY: THE CRITIQUE OF HISTORICAL REASON. Chicago: Univ. of Chicago Press, 1978.

3367. Evans, C. Stephen. KIERKEGAARD'S "FRAGMENTS" AND "POSTSCRIPT": THE RELIGIOUS PHILOSOPHY OF JOHANNES CLIMACUS. Atlantic Highlands: Humanities, 1983.

3368. Farber, Marvin. THE SEARCH FOR AN ALTERNATIVE: PHILOSOPHICAL PERSPECTIVES ON SUBJECTIVISM AND MARXISM. Philadelphia: Univ. of Pennsylvania Press, 1984.

3369. Fay, Thomas A. HEIDEGGER: THE CRITIQUE OF LOGIC. The Hague: Nijhoff, 1977.

3370. Feenberg, Andrew L. LUKACS, MARX, AND THE SOURCES OF CRITICAL THEORY. Totowa, NJ: Rowman & Littlefield, 1981.

3371. Feibleman, James Kern. ADAPTIVE KNOWING: EPISTEMOLOGY FROM A REALISTIC STANDPOINT. The Hague: Nijhoff, 1976.

3372. Feibleman, James Kern. ASSUMPTIONS OF GRAND LOGICS. The Hague and Boston: Nijhoff, 1979.

3373. Feibleman, James Kern. JUSTICE, LAW AND CULTURE. Dordrecht and Boston: Nijhoff, 1985.

3374. Feibleman, James Kern. TECHNOLOGY AND REALITY. The Hague and Boston: Nijhoff, 1982.

3375. Feinberg, Joel. THE IDEA OF THE OBSCENE. Lawrence: Univ. of Kansas Press, 1979.

3376. Feinberg, Joel. THE MORAL LIMITS OF CRIMINAL LAW. Vol. 1, HARM TO OTHERS. Vol. 2, OFFENSE TO OTHERS. Vol. 3, HARM TO SELF. Vol. 4, HARM-LESS WRONGDOING. Oxford and New York: Oxford Univ. Press, 1984-1988.

3377. Feinstein, Howard M. BECOMING WILLIAM JAMES. Ithaca: Cornell Univ. Press, 1984.

3378. Fell, Joseph P. HEIDEGGER AND SARTRE: AN ESSAY ON BEING AND PLACE. New York: Columbia Univ. Press, 1979.

3379. Ferre, Frederick, et al, eds. THE CHALLENGE OF RELIGION: CONTEMPORARY READINGS IN PHILOSOPHY OF RELIGION. New York: Seabury Press, 1982.

3380. Fetzer, James H., ed. PRINCIPLES OF PHILOSOPHICAL REASONING. Totowa, NJ: Rowman and Allanheld, 1984.

This collection of twelve original essays by distinguished contemporary philosophers investigates the existence and character of distinctively philosophical patterns of reasoning and principles of inquiry. The authors include Jaakko Hintikka and George Schlesinger.

3381. Field, Hartry H. SCIENCE WITHOUT NUMBERS: A DEFENCE OF NOMINAL-ISM. Oxford: B. Blackwell;,Princeton: Princeton Univ. Press, 1980.

3382. Findlay, John Niemeyer. KANT AND THE TRANSCENDENTAL OBJECT: A HERMENEUTIC STUDY. Oxford: Clarendon Press; New York: Oxford Univ. Press;, 1981.

3383. Fisch, Max Harold. PEIRCE, SEMIOTIC, AND PRAGMATISM. Ed. by Kenneth Lane Ketner and Charles J. W. Kloesel. Bloomington, IN: Univ. of Indiana Press, 1986.

3384. Fisher, John, ed. ESSAYS ON AESTHETICS: PERSPECTIVES ON THE WORK OF MONROE C. BEARDSLEY. Philadelphia: Temple Univ. Press, 1983.

3385. Fitting, Melvin Chris. PROOF METHODS FOR MODAL AND INTUITIONISTIC LOGICS. Dordrecht and Boston: Reidel, 1983.

3386. Flower, Elizabeth and Murray G. Murphey. A HISTORY OF PHILOSOPHY IN AMERICA. 2 Vols. New York: Capricorn Books, 1977.

3387. Flynn, Thamas. SARTRE AND MARXIST EXISTENTIALISM: THE TEST CASE

OF COLLECTIVE RESPONSIBILITY. Chicago: Univ. of Chicago Press, 1984.

The volume contains a bibliography on pages 245-255.

3388. Fodor, Jerry A. MODULARITY OF MIND: AN ESSAY ON FACULTY PSY-CHOLOGY. Cambridge: MIT Press, 1983.

3389. Fodor, Jerry A. REPRESENTATIONS: PHILOSOPHICAL ESSAYS ON THE FOUNDATIONS OF COGNITIVE SCIENCE. Montgomery, VT: Bradford Books, 1980.

3390. Fogelin, Robert J. HUME'S SKEPTICISM IN THE TREATISE OF HUMAN NATURE. London: Routledge & Kegan Paul, 1985.

3391. Fogelin, Robert J. WITTGENSTEIN. 2d ed. The Arguments of the Philosophers. London and New York: Routledge & Kegan Paul, 1976.

3392. Folse, Henry J. THE PHILOSOPHY OF NIELS BOHR: THE FRAMEWORK OF COMPLEMENTARITY. Amsterdam and New York: North-Holland, 1985.

3393. Forbes, Graeme. THE METAPHYSICS OF MODALITY. Oxford and New York: Oxford Univ. Press, 1985.

3394. Fox, Marvin. INTERPRETING MAIMONIDES: STUDIES IN METHODOLOGY, METAPHYSICS, AND MORAL PHILOSOPHY. Philadelphia: Jewish Publication Society, 1989.

3395. Frankena, William K., ed. THE PHILOSOPHY AND FUTURE OF GRADUATE EDUCATION. Ann Arbor: Univ. of Michigan Press, 1980.

3396. Freeman, Eugene, ed. THE RELEVANCE OF CHARLES PEIRCE. LaSalle, IL: Hegler Institute, 1983.

This work contains contributions from over 20 American and Western European philosophers. There is an extensive bibliography on pages 373-405.

3397. French, Peter A., et al, eds. MIDWEST STUDIES IN PHILOSOPHY. Vol. 1, STUDIES IN THE HISTORY OF PHILOSOPHY (1976); Vol. 2, STUDIES IN THE PHILOSOPHY OF LANGUAGE (1977); Vol. 3, STUDIES IN ETHICAL THEORY (1978); Vol. 4, STUDIES IN METAPHYSICS (1979); Vol. 5, STUDIES IN EPISTE-MOLOGY (1980); Vol. 6, THE FOUNDATIONS OF ANALYTIC PHILOSOPHY (1981); Vol. 7, SOCIAL AND POLITICAL PHILOSOPHY (1982); Vol. 8, CONTEM-PORARY PERSPECTIVES ON THE HISTORY OF PHILOSOPHY (1983); Vol. 9, CAUSATION AND CAUSAL THEORIES (1984); Vol. 10, STUDIES IN THE PHILOS-OPHY OF MIND (1986); Vol. 11, STUDIES IN ESSENTIALISM (1987); Vol. 12, REALISM AND ANTI-REALISM (1988); Vol. 13, ETHICAL THEORY (1988); Vol. 14, CONTEMPORARY PERSPECTIVES IN THE PHILOSOPHY OF LANGUAGE II (1989); Vol. 15, THE PHILOSOPHY OF THE HUMAN SCIENCES 1990); Vol. 16, PHILOSOPHY AND THE ARTS (1991). Minneapolis: Univ. of Minnesota Press, 1976-.

Beginning with volume 13, ETHICAL THEORY, this series now is published by the Univ. of Notre Dame Press, Notre Dame, Indiana.

3398. Frey, Raymond Gillespie. INTERESTS AND RIGHTS: THE CASE AGAINST ANIMALS. Clarendon Library of Logic and Philosophy. Oxford: Clarendon Press; New York: Oxford Univ. Press, 1980.

This volume contains a bibliography on pages 241-254.

3399. Frey, Raymond Gillespie. RIGHTS, KILLING, AND SUFFERING: MORAL VEGETARIANISM AND APPLIED ETHICS. Oxford: B. Blackwell, 1983.

3400. Friedman, George. THE POLITICAL PHILOSOPHY OF THE FRANKFURT SCHOOL. Ithaca: Cornell Univ. Press, 1981.

3401. Friedman, Maurice S. MARTIN BUBER'S LIFE AND WORK. Vol.1, THE EARLY YEARS, 1878-1923. Vol.2, THE MIDDLE YEARS, 1923-1945. Vol.3, THE LATER YEARS, 1945-1965. New York: Dutton, 1981-1983.

3402. Fumerton, Richard A. METAPHYSICAL AND EPISTEMOLOGICAL PROBLEMS OF PERCEPTION. Lincoln: Univ. of Nebraska Press, 1985.

3403. Gardner, Howard. THE QUEST FOR MIND: PIAGET, LEVI-STRAUSS, AND THE STRUCTURALIST MOVEMENT. 2d ed. Chicago: Univ. of Chicago Press, 1981.

3404. Gardner, Martin. ORDER AND SURPRISE. Buffalo: Prometheus Books, 1983.

This is a sequel to SCIENCE: GOOD, BAD AND BOGUS.

3405. Gardner, Martin. SCIENCE: GOOD, BAD AND BOGUS. Buffalo: Prometheus Books, 1981.

3406. Gardner, Martin. THE WHYS OF A PHILOSOPHICAL SCRIVENER. New York: W. Morrow, 1983.

3407. Garfinkel, Alan. FORMS OF EXPLANATION: RETHINKING THE QUESTIONS IN SOCIAL THEORY. New Haven and London: Yale Univ. Press, 1981.

3408. Geuss, Raymond. THE IDEA OF A CRITICAL THEORY: HABERMAS AND THE FRANKFURT SCHOOL. Cambridge and New York: Cambridge Univ. Press, 1981.

3409. Gewirth, Alan. HUMAN RIGHTS: ESSAYS ON JUSTIFICATION AND APPLICA-TION. Chicago: Univ. of Chicago Press, 1982.

3410. Gewirth, Alan. REASON AND MORALITY. Chicago: Univ. of Chicago Press, 1982.

3411. Gibson, Roger F. THE PHILOSOPHY OF W. V. QUINE: AN EXPOSITORY ESSAY. Tampa: Univ. Presses of Florida, 1982.

This book includes a foreward by W. V. Quine.

3412. Gilmour, John C. PICTURING THE WORLD. Albany: State Univ. of New York Press, 1986.

3413. Glymour, Clark N. THEORY AND EVIDENCE. Princeton: Princeton Univ. Press, 1980.

3414. Goddman, Lenn Evan. MONOTHEISM; A PHILOSOPHIC INQUIRY INTO THE FOUNDATIONS OF THEOLOGY AND ETHICS. Totowa, NJ: Allanheld, Osmun, 1981.

This is an American Philosophical Association David Baumgardt Memorial Lecture.

3415. Goldthwait, John T. VALUE, LANGUAGE AND LIFE. Buffalo: Prometheus Books, 1985.

3416. Goodman, Nelson. FACT, FICTION AND FORECAST. 4th ed. Cambridge: Harvard Univ. Press, 1983.

3417. Goodman, Nelson. LANGUAGES OF ART: AN APPROACH TO A THEORY OF SYMBOLS. 2d. ed. Indianapolis: Hackett, 1976.

This work has been translated into Spanish as LOS LENGUAJES DEL ARTE: APROXIMACION A LA TEORIA DE LOS SIMBOLOS. Barcelona: Editorial Seix Barral, 1976.

3418. Goodman, Nelson. OF MIND AND OTHER MATTERS. Cambridge: Harvard Univ. Press, 1984.

In this collection Goodman brings up to date the discussion of many topics in his earlier books.

3419. Goodman, Nelson. RECONCEPTIONS IN PHILOSOPHY AND OTHER ARTS AND SCIENCES. Indianapolis: Hackett; London: Routledge and Kegan Paul, 1988.

3420. Goodman, Nelson. THE STRUCTURE OF APPEARANCE. 3d ed. Dordrecht and Boston: Reidel, 1977.

3421. Goodman, Nelson. WAYS OF WORLDMAKING. Indianapolis: Hackett; Hassocks: Harvester Press, 1978.

3422. Gorowitz, Samuel. DOCTORS' DILEMMAS. New York: Macmillan; London: Collier Macmillan, 1982.

3423. Gottinger, Hans-Werner and Werner Leinfellner, eds. DECISION THEORY AND SOCIAL ETHICS: ISSUES IN SOCIAL CHOICE. Dordrecht and Boston: Reidel, 1978.

3424. Gouinlock, James. EXCELLENCE IN PUBLIC DISCOURSE: JOHN STUART MILL, JOHN DEWEY, AND SOCIAL INTELLIGENCE. New York: Teachers College Press, Columbia Univ., 1986.

This is the John Dewey Lecture delivered at Columbia University Teachers College.

3425. Gould, Carol C., ed. BEYOND DOMINATION: NEW PERSPECTIVES ON WOMEN AND PHILOSOPHY. Totowa, NJ: Rowman and Allenheld, 1984c1983.

3426. Gould, Carol C. MARX'S SOCIAL ONTOLOGY: INDIVIDUALITY AND CONTINUITY IN MARX'S THEORY OF SOCIAL REALITY. Cambridge: MIT Press, 1978.

3427. Gould, Carol C. and Marx W. Wartofsky, eds. WOMEN AND PHILOSOPHY: A THEORY OF LIBERATION. New York: Putnam, 1976.

3428. Gram, Moltke S. DIRECT REALISM: A STUDY OF PERCEPTION. The Hague and Boston: Nijhoff, 1983.

3429. Greene, Maxine. LANDSCAPES OF LEARNING. New York: Teachers College Press, 1978.

3430. Grene, Marjorie. PHILOSOPHY IN AND OUT OF EUROPE. Berkeley: Univ. of California Press, 1976.

3431. Grene, Marjorie and Everett Mendelsohn, eds. TOPICS IN THE PHILOSOPHY OF BIOLOGY. Dordrecht and Boston: Reidel, 1976.

3432. Griffiths, Paul J. ON BEING MINDLESS: BUDDHIST MEDITATION AND THE MIND-BODY PROBLEM. La Salle, IL: Open Court, 1986.

3433. Griswold, Charles L. SELF-KNOWLEDGE IN PLATO'S PHAEDRUS. New Haven: Yale Univ. Press, 1986.

3434. Grood, David H. de. DIALECTICS AND REVOLUTION. Amsterdam: B. R. Gruner, 1978-.

3435. Grunbaum, Adolf. FOUNDATIONS OF PSYCHOANALYSIS. Berkeley: Univ. of California Press, 1985.

3436. Gunderson, Keith. MENTALITY AND MACHINES. 2d ed. Minneapolis: Univ. of Minnesota Press, 1985.

3437. Gurwitsch, Aron. HUMAN ENCOUNTERS IN THE SOCIAL WORLD. Ed. by Alexander Metraux. Tr. of MITMENSCHLICHEN BEGEGNUNGEN IN DER MILI-EUWELT. Ed. by Alexander Metraux. Berlin and New York: de Gruyter, 1977. Tr. by Fred Kersten. Phanomenologische-psychologische Forschungen, Vol. 16. Pittsburgh: Duquesne Univ. Press, 1979.

This work is Gurwitsch's HABILITATIONSSCHRIFT, Gottingen, finished in 1931 but not published.

3438. Gurwitsch, Aron. MARGINAL CONSCIOUSNESS. Ed. by Lester Embree. Series in Continental Thought, Vol. 7. Athens: Ohio Univ. Press, 1985.

This volume contains a bibliography on pages 107-123.

3439. Gustafson, Donald F. and L. Tapscott Bangs, eds. BODY, MIND, AND METHOD: ESSAYS IN HONOR OF VIRGIL C. ALDRICH. Dordrecht and Boston: Reidel, 1979.

3440. Guyer, Paul. KANT AND THE CLAIMS OF TASTE. Cambridge: Harvard Univ. Press, 1979.

3441. Hahn, Lewis Edwin, ed. THE PHILOSOPHY OF CHARLES HARTSHORNE. LaSalle, IL: Open Court, 1991.

In addition to Hartshorne's intellectual autobiography and a complete bibliography of his writings up to the date of publication, this volume contains 29 descriptive and critical essays on Hartshorne's philosophy by other philosophers and Hartshorne's detailed replies to his critics.

3442. Hamrick, William S., ed. PHENOMENOLOGY IN PRACTICE AND IN THEORY: ESSAYS FOR HERBERT SPIEGELBERG. The Hague and Boston: Nijhoff, 1984.

3443. Harari, Josue V., ed. TEXTUAL STRATEGIES: PERSPECTIVES IN POST-STRUCTURALIST CRITICISM. Ithaca: Cornell Univ. Press, 1979.

3444. Harbert, David L. EXISTENCE, KNOWING AND PHILOSOPHICAL SYSTEMS. Washington, DC: University Press of America, 1982.

3445. Harding, Sandra and Merrill Bristow Hintikka, eds. DISCOVERING REALITY: FEMINIST PERSPECTIVES ON EPISTEMOLOGY, METAPHYSICS, METHODOLO-GY, AND PHILOSOPHY OF SCIENCE. Dordrecht and Boston: Reidel, c1983.

3446. Harman, Gilbert. CHANGE IN VIEW: PRINCIPLES OF REASONING. Cambridge: MIT Press, 1986.

3447. Harman, Gilbert, ed. ON NOAM CHOMSKY: CRITICAL ESSAYS. 2d ed. Amherst: Univ. of Massachusetts Press, 1982.

3448. Harris, Ransom Baine. NEOPLATONISM AND INDIAN THOUGHT. Norfolk: International Society for Neoplatonic Studies, 1982.

3449. Hartmann, Geoffrey A. SAVING THE TEXT: LITERATURE, DERRIDA, PHILOSOPHY. Baltimore: Johns Hopkins Univ. Press, 1981.

3450. Hartshorne, Charles. AQUINAS TO WHITEHEAD: SEVEN CENTURIES OF METAPHYSICS OF RELIGION. Milwaukee: Marquette Univ. Publications, 1976.

3451. Hartshorne, Charles. THE DARKNESS AND THE LIGHT: A PHILOSOPHER REFLECTS UPON HIS FORTUNATE CAREER AND THOSE WHO MADE IT POSSIBLE. Albany: State Univ. Press of New York, 1990.

3452. Hartshorne, Charles. INSIGHTS AND OVERSIGHTS OF GREAT THINKERS: AN EVALUATION OF WESTERN PHILOSOPHY. Albany: State Univ. of New York Press, 1983.

3453. Hartshorne, Charles. LA CREATIVIDAD EN LA FILOSOFIA ESTADOUNIDENSE. Tr. of CREATIVITY IN AMERICAN PHILOSOPHY. Albany: State University of New York Press, 1984. Tr. by Mariluz Caso. Mexico: EDAMEX, 1987.

3454. Hartshorne, Charles. OMNIPOTENCE AND OTHER THEOLOGICAL MISTAKES. Albany: State Univ. of New York, 1984.

3455. Hartshorne, Charles. WISDOM AS MODERATION: A PHILOSOPHY OF THE MIDDLE WAY. Albany: State Univ. of New York, 1987.

3456. Hartshorne, Charles and Creighton Peden. WHITEHEAD'S VIEW OF REALITY. New York: Pilgrim Press, 1981.

3457. Harvey, Charles W. HUSSERL'S PHENOMENOLOGY AND THE FOUNDATIONS OF NATURAL SCIENCE. Series in Continental Thought, Vol. 15. Athens: Ohio Univ. Press, 1989.

3458. Healey, Richard, ed. REDUCTION, TIME AND REALITY: STUDIES IN THE PHILOSOPHY OF THE NATURAL SCIENCES. New York and London: Cambridge Univ. Press, 1981.

These essays examine questions concerning various kinds of scientific entities, and the truth of various kinds of scientific statement: theoretical explanation, statistical theories, intentional psychology, modal reality, essences and the laws of nature.

3459. Hegel, George Wilhelm Friedrich. HEGEL: THE LETTERS. Tr. by Clark Butler and Christine Seiler. Bloomington: Indiana Univ. Press, 1984.

For the first time available in English, the letters reveal the crucial role of historical and existential concerns in the shaping of Hegel's grand philosophical system.

3460. Held, Virginia. RIGHTS AND GOODS: JUSTIFYING SOCIAL ACTION. New York: Free Press; London: Collier Macmillan, 1984.

3461. Heller, Erich. IN THE AGE OF PROSE: LITERARY AND PHILOSOPHICAL ESSAYS. Cambridge and New York: Cambridge Univ. Press, 1984.

3462. Hempel, Carl Gustav, et al. THE PHILOSOPHY OF NELSON GOODMAN. Hamburg: Reidel, 1978.

3463. Hetzler, Florence M. and Austin H. Kutscher. PHILOSOPHICAL ASPECTS OF THANATOLOGY. New York: MSS Information Corp., 1978.

3464. Hickman, Larry A. MODERN THEORIES OF HIGHER LEVEL PREDICATES: SECOND INTENTIONS IN THE NEUZEIT. Munich: Philosophia, 1980.

3465. Hochberg, Herbert I. THOUGHT, FACT, AND REFERENCE: THE ORIGINS AND ONTOLOGY OF LOGICAL ATOMISM. Minneapolis: Univ. of Minnesota Press, 1978.

3466. Hodson, John D. THE ETHICS OF LEGAL COERCION. Dordrecht and Boston: Reidel, 1983.

3467. Hofstadter, Douglas R. GODEL, ESCHER, BACH: AN ETERNAL GOLDEN BRAID. New York: Basic Books; Sussex: Harvester, 1979.

3468. Hofstadter, Douglas R. and Daniel Clement Dennett, eds. MIND'S I: FANTASIES AND REFLECTIONS ON SELF AND SOUL. New York: Basic Books; Sussex, Harvester, 1981.

This collection includes selected writings of philosophers and others with comments by the authors.

3469. Hohler, Thomas P. IMAGINATION AND REFLECTION: INTERSUBJECTIVITY: FICHTE'S GRUNDLAGE OF 1794. The Hague and Boston: Nijhoff, 1982.

3470. Hollinger, Robert, ed. HERMENEUTICS AND PRAXIS. Notre Dame, IN: Univ. of Notre Dame Press, 1985.

3471. Hook, Sidney. MARXISM AND BEYOND. Totowa, NJ: Rowman and Littlefield, 1983.

3472. Hook, Sidney. OUT OF STEP: AN UNQUIET LIFE IN THE 20TH CENTURY. New York: Harper and Row, 1987.

3473. Hook, Sidney. PHILOSOPHY AND PUBLIC POLICY. Carbondale: Southern Illinois Univ. Press, 1980.

3474. Hull, David L. THE METAPHYSICS OF EVOLUTION. Albany: State Univ. of New York Press, 1989.

3475. Ihde, Don. CONSEQUENCES OF PHENOMENOLOGY. Albany: State Univ. of New York, 1986.

3476. Ihde, Don. TECHNOLOGY AND THE LIFEWORLD: FROM GARDEN TO EARTH. Bloomington: Indiana Univ. Press, 1990.

3477. Ihde, Don and Richard M. Zaner, eds. INTERDISCIPLINARY PHENOMENOLOGY. The Hague: Nijhoff, 1977.

3478. Inada, Kenneth K., ed. EAST-WEST DIALOGUES IN AESTHETICS. Buffalo: Council on International Studies, State Univ. of New York, 1978.

3479. Inada, Kenneth K. GUIDE TO BUDDHIST PHILOSOPHY. Boston: G. K. Hall, 1985.

The basic objective "...has been to provide an authoritative guide to the literature, both texts in translation and commentary and analysis, for teachers and advanced undergraduate and beginning graduate students who are not specialized scholars with access to primary texts in their original languages." Although some of the books and articles go back to the early 1900's, the bulk of the entries fall in the period 1950-1980.

3480. Jackson, Carl T. THE ORIENTAL RELIGIONS AND AMERICAN THOUGHT: NINETEENTH CENTURY EXPLORATIONS. Westport CT: Greenwood Press, 1981.

3481. Jacobson, Nolan Pling. BUDDHISM AND THE CONTEMPORARY WORLD. Carbondale and Edwardsville: Southern Illinois Univ. Press, 1983.

3482. Jacoby, Russell. DIALECTIC OF DEFEAT: CONTOURS OF WESTERN MARXISM. New York and Cambridge: Cambridge Univ. Press, 1981.

This is a critique of the "conformist" Marxism of the Russian and Chinese revolutions in favor of Lukacs, the Dutch and Frankfurt Schools.

3483. Jaggar, Alison. FEMINIST POLITICS AND HUMAN NATURE. Totowa, NJ: Rowman and Allanheld, 1983.

3484. James, William. WILLIAM JAMES: SELECTED UNPUBLISHED LETTERS, 1885- 1910. Ed. by Frederick J. Down Scott. Columbus: Ohio Univ. Press, 1986.

There is an extensive bibliography on pages 561-594.

3485. James, William. THE WORKS OF WILLIAM JAMES. PRAGMATISM (1975). THE MEANING OF TRUTH (1975). ESSAYS IN RADICAL EMPIRICISM (1976) (The first three volumes are introduced by H. S. Thayer). A PLURALISTIC UNIVERSE (1977) (Introduced by Richard J. Bernstein). ESSAYS IN PHILOSOPHY (1978) (Introduced by John J. McDermott). THE WILL TO BELIEVE (1979) (Introduced by Edward H. Madden). SOME PROBLEMS OF PHILOSOPHY (1979) (Introduced by Peter H. Hare). THE PRINCIPLES OF PSYCHOLOGY. 3 Vols. 1981-1983 (Introduced by Rand B. Evans and Gerald E. Myers). ESSAYS IN RELIGION AND MORALITY (1982) (Introduced by John J. McDermott). TALKS TO TEACHERS ON PSYCHOLOGY AND TO STUDENTS ON SOME OF LIFE'S IDEALS (1983) (Introduced by Gerald E. Myers). ESSAYS IN PSYCHOLOGY (1983) (Introduced by William R. Woodward). PSYCHOLOGY, BRIEFER COURSE (1984) (Introduced by Michael M. Sokal). VARIETIES OF RELIGIOUS EXPERIENCE (1985) (Introduced by John E. Smith). ESSAYS IN PSYCHICAL RESEARCH (1986) (Introduced by Robert A. McDermott). ESSAYS, COMMENTS AND REVIEWS (1987) (Introduced by Ignas K. Skrupskelis). MANUSCRIPT ESSAYS AND NOTES (1988). MANUSCRIPT LECTURES (1988). Ed. by Frederick H. Burkhardt and Fredson Bowers. Cambridge: Harvard Univ. Press, 1975-.

3486. Jensen, Kenneth Martin. BEYOND MARX AND MACH: ALEKSANDR BOGDANOV'S PHILOSOPHY OF LIVING EXPERIENCE. Dordrecht and Boston: Reidel, 1978.

3487. Johnson, Mark, ed. PHILOSOPHICAL PERSPECTIVES ON METAPHOR. Minneapolis: Univ. of Minnesota Press, 1981.

This is an anthology of essays by Monroe C. Beardsley, Timothy Binkley, Max Black, Ted Cohen, Donald Davidson, Nelson Goodman, Paul Henle, Mark Johnson, George Lakoff, Ina Loewenberg, I. A. Richards, Paul Ricoeur, and John R. Searle.

3488. Johnstone, Henry W. CATEGORIES: A COLLOQUIUM. University Park: Pennsylvania State Univ., Dept. of Philosophy, 1978.

This volume contains The 1978 Dotterer lecture by Wilfrid Sellars: THE ROLE OF THE IMAGINATION IN KANT'S THEORY OF EXPERIENCE.

3489. Johnstone, Henry W. VALIDITY AND RHETORIC IN PHILOSOPHICAL ARGUMENT: AN OUTLOOK IN TRANSITION. Univ. Park, Pennsylvania: Dialogue Press of Man and World, 1978.

3490. Jones, Edwin. READING THE BOOK OF NATURE: A PHENOMENOLOGICAL STUDY OF CREATIVE EXPRESSION IN SCIENCE AND PAINTING. Series in Continental Thought, Vol. 14. Athens: Ohio Univ. Press, 1989.

3491. Jones, William Frank. NATURE AND NATURAL SCIENCE: THE PHILOSOPHY OF F. J. E. WOODBRIDGE. Buffalo: Prometheus Book, 1983.

3492. Kainz, Howard P. ETHICA DIALECTICA: A STUDY OF ETHICAL OPPOSITIONS. The Hague: Nijhoff, 1979.

3493. Kaminsky, Jack. ESSAYS IN LINGUISTIC ONTOLOGY. Carbondale: Southern Illinois Univ. Press, 1982.

3494. Kashap, S. Paul. SPINOZA AND MORAL FREEDOM. Albany: State Univ. of New York Press, 1987.

3495. Kateb, George. HANNAH ARENDT: POLITICS, CONSCIENCE, EVIL. Philosophy and Society Series. Totowa, NJ: Rowman and Allanheld, 1984c1983.

3496. Katz, Jerrold J. COGITATIONS: A STUDY OF THE "COGITO" IN RELATION TO THE PHILOSOPHY OF LOGIC AND LANGUAGE, AND A STUDY OF THEM IN RELATION TO THE "COGITO". New York: Oxford Univ. Press, 1986.

3497. Katz, Jerrold J. PROPOSITIONAL STRUCTURE AND ILLOCUTIONARY FORCE: A STUDY OF THE CONTRIBUTION OF SENTENCE MEANING TO SPEECH ACTS. Hassocks, Eng: Harvester Press; New York: Crowell, 1977.

3498. Kaufmann, Walter A. EXISTENTIALISM, RELIGION, AND DEATH: THIRTEEN ESSAYS. New York: New American Library, 1976.

3499. Kaufmann, Walter A. FROM SHAKESPEARE TO EXISTENTIALISM: AN ORIGINAL STUDY: ESSAYS ON SHAKESPEARE AND GOETHE: HEGEL AND KIERKEGAARD: NIETZSCHE, RILKE, AND FREUD: JASPERS, HEIDEGGER, AND TOYNBEE. Princeton, NJ: Princeton Univ. Press, 1980.

3500. Kaufmann, Walter Arnold. DISCOVERING THE MIND. Vol. 1, GOETHE, KANT, AND HEGEL. Vol. 2, NIETZSCHE, HEIDEGGER, AND BUBER. Vol. 3, FREUD VERSUS ADLER AND JUNG. New York: McGraw-Hill, 1980.

3501. Kellner, Douglas. HERBERT MARCUSE AND THE CRISIS OF MARXISM. Los Angeles: Univ. of California, 1985.

3502. Kelly, Michael. MODERN FRENCH MARXISM. Baltimore: Johns Hopkins Univ. Press, 1982.

3503. Kelly, Michael. PIONEER OF THE CATHOLIC REVIVAL: THE IDEAS AND INFLUENCE OF EMMANUEL MOUNIER. London: Sheed and Ward, 1979.

3504. Kennedy, C. and Jack C. Marier, eds. THOMISTIC PAPERS II. Notre Dame, IN: Univ. of Notre Dame Press, 1985.

3505. Kersey, Ethel M. WOMEN PHLOSOPHERS: A BIO-CRITICAL SOURCEBOOK. Westport, CT: Greenwood Press, 1989.

3506. Kestenbaum, Victor. THE PHENOMENOLOGICAL SENSE OF JOHN DEWEY: HABIT AND MEANING. Atlantic Highlands, NJ: Humanities Press, 1977.

3507. Ketner, Kenneth Lane. A COMPREHENSIVE BIBLIOGRAPHY OF THE PUB-LISHED WORKS OF CHARLES SANDERS PEIRCE WITH A BIBLIOGRAPHY OF SECONDARY STUDIES. 2d. rev ed. Bibliographies of Famous Philosophers. Bowling Green, OH: Philosophy Documentation Center, Bowling Green Univ., 1986.

This work contains a bibliography of Peirce's published works and a bibliography of secondary studies compiled by C.J.W. Kloesel and Joseph M. Ransdell.

3508. Ketner, Kenneth Lane, et al. PROCEEDINGS OF THE C. S. PEIRCE BICENTEN-NIAL INTERNATIONAL CONGRESS, 1976, Amsterdam, Netherlands. Lubbock: Texas Tech Univ. Press, 1981.

3509. Kim, Sang-Ki. THE PROBLEM OF THE CONTINGENCY OF THE WORLD IN HUSSERL'S PHENOMENOLOGY. Amsterdam: Gruner, 1976.

3510. Kirk, Robert. TRANSLATION DETERMINED. New York: Oxford Univ. Press; Oxford: Clarendon Press, 1986.

3511. Kivy, Peter. THE SEVENTH SENSE: A STUDY OF FRANCIS HUTCHINSON'S AESTHETHICS AND IT'S INFLUENCE IN 18TH CENTURY BRITAIN. New York: Franklin, 1976.

3512. Klemke, Elmer D. STUDIES IN THE PHILOSOPHY OF KIERKEGAARD. The Hague: Nijhoff, 1976.

3513. Klemm, David Eugene. HERMENEUTICAL INQUIRY. Vol. 1, THE INTER-PRETATION OF TEXTS. Vol. 2, THE INTERPRETATION OF EXISTENCE. Atlanta, GA: Scholars Press, 1986.

3514. Klemm, David Eugene. HERMENEUTICAL THEORY OF PAUL RICOEUR: A CONSTRUCTIVE ANALYSIS. Lewisburg, PA: Bucknell Univ. Press; London: Associated Univ. Presses, 1983.

3515. Klenk, Virginia H. WITTGENSTEIN'S PHILOSOPHY OF MATHEMATICS. The Hague: Nijhoff, 1976.

3516. Kockelmans, Joseph J. HEIDEGGER AND SCIENCE. Washington, DC: Center for Advanced Research in Phenomenology: Univ. Press of America, 1985.

This volume developed from a series of lectures on philosophy and natural science at Duquesne University in April, 1979 and a seminar on the philosophy of science at Pennsylvania State University. There is a bibliography on pages 283-298.

3517. Kockelmans, Joseph J. HEIDEGGER ON ART AND ART WORKS. Dordrecht and Boston: Nijhoff, 1985.

3518. Kockelmans, Joseph J. ON THE TRUTH OF BEING: REFLECTIONS ON HEI-DEGGER'S LATER PHILOSOPHY. Bloomington: Indiana Univ. Press, 1984.

The author focuses on the important question of the relationship of truth and Being by providing a systematic treatment of the central themes and topics of Heidegger's later writings.

3519. Kockelmans, Joseph J. PHENOMENOLOGICAL PSYCHOLOGY: THE DUTCH SCHOOL. Dordrecht and Boston: Nijhoff, 1987.

3520. Krausz, Michael and Jack W. Meiland, eds. RELATIVISM, COGNITIVE AND MORAL. Notre Dame, IN: Notre Dame Press, 1982.

This work includes contributions by Nelson Goodman, Maurice Mandelbaum, Donald Davidson, Chris Swoyer, Gerald Doppelt, Philippa Foot, Bernard Williams, Gilbert Harman, David Lyons, and Geoffrey Harrison.

3521. Kretzmann, Norman, eds. INFINITY AND CONTINUITY AND MEDIEVAL THOUGHT. Ithaca: Cornell Univ. Press, 1982.

3522. Kretzmann, Norman and Eleonore Stump, eds. LOGIC AND THE PHILOSOPHY OF LANGUAGE. Cambridge and New York: Cambridge Univ. Press, 1988.

3523. Kripke, Saul A. LA LOGIQUE DES NOMS PROPRES. Tr. of NAMING AND NECESSITY. Cambridge: Cambridge Univ. Press, 1980. Tr. by Pierre Jacob and Francois Recanati. Paris: Editions de minuit, 1982.

3524. Kripke, Saul A. WITTGENSTEIN UBER REGELN UND PRIVATSPRACHE: EINE ELEMENTARE DARSTELLUNG. Tr. of WITTGENSTEIN ON RULES AND PRIVATE LANGUAGE: AN ELEMENTARY EXPOSITION. Oxford: Blackwell, 1982. Frankfurt: Suhrkamp, 1987.

3525. Kristeller, Paul Oskar. HANDSCHRIFTEN-FORSCHUNG UND GEISTES-GESCHICHTE DER ITALIENISCHEN RENAISSANCE. Mainz: Academie der Wissenschaften und der Literatur; Wiesbaden: Steiner, 1982.

3526. Kristeller, Paul Oskar. A LIFE OF LEARNING. Charles Homer Haskins Lecture. New York: American Council of Learned Societies, 1990.

3527. Kristeller, Paul Oskar. RENAISSANCE THOUGHT AND THE ARTS: COLLECTED ESSAYS. Expanded edition with a new afterword. Princeton: Princeton Univ. Press, 1990.

3528. Kuhn, Thomas S. THE ESSENTIAL TENSION: SELECTED STUDIES IN SCIENTIFIC TRADITION AND CHANGE. Chicago: Univ. of Chicago Press, 1977.

3529. Kuhns, Richard Francis. PSYCHOANALYTIC THEORY OF ART: A PHILOSOPHY OF ART ON DEVELOPMENTAL PRINCIPLES. New York: Columbia Univ. Press, 1983.

3530. Kuhns, Richard Francis. TRAGEDY: CONTRADICTION AND REPRESSION. Chicago: Univ. of Chicago Press, 1991.

3531. Kuklick, Bruce. CHURCHMEN AND PHILOSOPHERS: FROM JONATHAN EDWARDS TO JOHN DEWEY. New Haven: Yale Univ. Press, 1985.

3532. Kuklick, Bruce. THE RISE OF AMERICAN PHILOSOPHY: CAMBRIDGE MASSACHUSETTS, 1860-1930. New Haven: Yale Univ. Press, 1977.

3533. Kurtz, Paul. PHILOSOPHICAL ESSAYS IN PRAGMATIC NATURALISM. Buffalo: Prometheus Books, 1990.

3534. Kurtz, Paul, ed. SIDNEY HOOK: PHILOSOPHER OF DEMOCRACY AND HUMANISM. Buffalo: Prometheus Books, 1983.

This volume contains a complete bibliography of the writings of Sidney Hook up to 1983 compiled by Jo Ann Boydston and Kathleen Poulos on pages 311-347. A review of Sidney Hook's works appears on pages 348-355.

3535. Lang, Berel, ed. THE DEATH OF ART. New York: Haven, 1984.

This collection of essays devoted to the theme of the end of art includes a lead essay by Arthur Danto and pieces by Richard Kuhns, Joyce Brodsky, Norman Miller, Anita Silvers and others.

3536. Langer, Susanne K. MIND: AN ESSAY ON HUMAN FEELING. Abridged ed. Baltimore and London: Johns Hopkins Univ. Press, 1988.

3537. Langley, Patrick W., et al. SEARCH FOR REGULARITY: FOUR ASPECTS OF SCIENTIFIC DISCOVERY. Pittsburgh: Carnegie-Mellon Univ. for Robotics Institute, 1984.

3538. Lanigan, Richard L. SPEECH ACT PHENOMENOLOGY. The Hague and Boston: Nijhoff, 1977.

3539. Laudan, Larry. PROGRESS AND ITS PROBLEMS: TOWARD A THEORY OF SCIENTIFIC GROWTH. Berkeley: Univ. of California Press; London: Routledge and Kegan Paul, 1977.

3540. Lauer, Quentin. HEGEL'S CONCEPT OF GOD. Albany: State Univ. of New York Press, 1982.

3541. Lauer, Quentin. HEGEL'S IDEA OF PHILOSOPHY WITH A NEW TRANSLA-TION OF HEGEL'S INTRODUCTION TO THE HISTORY OF PHILOSOPHY. 2d ed. New York: Fordham Univ. Press, 1983.

3542. Lauer, Quentin. THE NATURE OF PHILOSOPHICAL INQUIRY. Milwaukee: Marquette Univ. Press, 1989.

3543. Lauer, Quentin. A READING OF HEGEL'S PHENOMENOLOGY OF SPIRIT. New York: Fordham Univ. Press, 1976.

3544. Lazerowitz, Morris. THE LANGUAGE OF PHILOSOPHY: FREUD AND WITT-GENSTEIN. Dordrecht and Boston: Reidel, 1977.

3545. Lazerowitz, Morris and Alice Ambrose. ESSAYS IN THE UNKNOWN WITTGEN-STEIN. Buffalo, NY: Prometheus Books, 1984.

3546. Lazerowitz, Morris and Alice Ambrose. NECESSITY AND LANGUAGE. New York: St. Martin's Press; London: Croom Helm, 1985.

3547. Lazerowitz, Morris and Alice Ambrose. PHILOSOPHICAL THEORIES. The Hague: Mouton, 1976.

3548. LeBlanc, Hugues. EXISTENCE, TRUTH AND PROVABILITY. Albany: State Univ. of New York, 1982.

This collection of 35 essays contains some of the most influential contributions to logic and the philosophy of logic during the past 20 years. The volume has been thoroughly revised and the material placed in context by new texts discussing its history and scope.

3549. Lehrer, Keith. METAMIND. Oxford: Clarendon Press; New York: Oxford Univ. Press, 1989.

3550. Lehrer, Keith and Ernest Sosa, eds. THE OPENED CURTAIN: A U. S.-SOVIET PHILOSOPHY SUMMIT. Boulder, CO: Westview Press, 1991.

This work consists of papers presented at meetings of Soviet and American philosophers held in Moscow and Providence in 1988. It includes contributions by William P. Alston, Hector-Neri Castaneda, Alvin I. Goldman, Jaakko Hintikka, Jaegwon Kim, Keith Lehrer, Sydney Shoemaker, N.S. Avtonomova, D. P. Gorsky, M. S. Burgin, D. I. Dubrovsky, A. A. Ivin, A. L. Nikiforov, V. V. Petrov, V. S. Shvyrev, V. S. Stepin, A. L. Subbotin, and V. P. Zinchenko.

3551. Lehrer, Keith and Carl Wagner. RATIONAL CONSENSUS IN SCIENCE AND SOCIETY: A PHILOSOPHICAL AND MATHEMATICAL STUDY. Dordrecht and Boston: Reidel, 1981.

3552. Levi, Albert William. NATURE AND ART. New Orleans: The Graduate School of Tulane Univ., 1980.

3553. Levi, Isaac. DECISIONS AND REVISION: PHILOSOPHICAL ESSAYS ON KNOWLEDGE AND VALUE. Cambridge and New York: Cambridge Univ. Press, 1984.

3554. Levinson, Henry Samuel. THE RELIGIOUS INVESTIGATIONS OF WILLIAM JAMES. Chaple Hill: Univ. of North Carolina Press, 1981.

3555. Lewis, David Kellog. PHILOSOPHICAL PAPERS. 2 Vols. New York: Oxford Univ. Press, 1983-1986.

This volume consists of reprints of fifteen papers unchanged from their original form, but new postscripts have been added to eight of them.

3556. Ligota, C. R. and Robert Strassfeld, eds. BIBLIOGRAPHY OF WORKS IN THE PHILOSOPHY OF HISTORY, 1973-1977. Middletown, Conn: Wesleyan Univ. Press, 1979.

This series is issued annually as the fourth number of the periodical "HISTORY AND THEORY" and two other four-year cumulations have been published in book form covering 1978-1982 (compiled by Zdenek V. David and Robert Strassfeld), and 1983-1987 (compiled by Zdenek V. David).

3557. Lineback, Richard H. THE PHILOSOPHER'S INDEX THESAURUS. 2d ed. Bowling Green, OH: Philosophy Documentation Center, 1990.

3558. Lingis, Alphonso. EXCESSES: EROS AND CULTURE. Albany: State Univ. of New York Press, 1983.

3559. Lingis, Alphonso. LIBIDO: THE FRENCH EXISTENTIAL THEORIES. Bloomington, IN: Indiana Univ. Press, 1985.

3560. Lingis, Alphonso. PHENOMENOLOGICAL EXPLANATIONS. Dordrecht and Boston: Reidel, 1986.

3561. Linsky, Leonard. NAMES AND DESCRIPTIONS. Chicago: Univ. of Chicago Press, 1977.

3562. Linsky, Leonard. OBLIQUE CONTEXTS. Chicago: Univ. of Chicago Press, 1983.

3563. Loscerbo, John. BEING AND TECHNOLOGY: A STUDY IN THE PHILOSOPHY OF MARTIN HEIDEGGER. The Hague and Boston: Nijhoff, 1981.

3564. Love, Frederick R. NIETZSCHE'S SAINT PETER: GENESIS AND CULTIVA-
TION OF AN ILLUSION. Berlin and New York: De Gruyter, 1981.

3565. Lovekin, David and Donald Phillip Verene, eds. ESSAYS IN HUMANITY AND
TECHNOLOGY. Dixon,IL: Sauk Valley College, 1977.

3566. Lovin, Robin W. and Frank E. Reynolds, eds. COSMOGONY AND ETHICAL
ORDER: NEW STUDIES IN COMPARATIVE ETHICS. Chicago: Univ. of Chicago
Press, 1985.

This volume consists mainly of papers presented in a series of conferences held at the
Divinity School, University of Chicago, in March, 1981, April, 1982, and October, 1982.

3567. Lowe, Victor. ALFRED NORTH WHITEHEAD: THE MAN AND HIS WORK.
Vol. 1, 1871-1910. Vol. 2, 1910-1947. Baltimore: Johns Hopkins Press, 1985.

3568. Lucey, Kenneth and Tibor R. Machan, eds. RECENT WORK IN PHILOSOPHY.
Totowa, NJ: Rowman and Allanheld, 1983.

The essays in this volume are by prominent philosophers specializing in the areas of
philosophy about which they write. Although some bibliographic citations are as late as
1980, the majority of them fall in the period from the 1950's to 1976.

3569. Luckmann, Thomas, ed. PHENOMENOLOGY AND SOCIOLOGY: SELECTED
READINGS. Harmondsworth, Eng. and New York: Penguin Books, 1978.

3570. Lukashevich, Steven. THUS SPAKE MASTER CHUANG: A STRUCTURAL
EXEGESIS OF TAOIST PHILOSOPHY. New York: Peter Lang, 1987.

3571. Lyons, David. ETHICS AND THE RULE OF LAW. Cambridge: Cambridge Univ.
Press, 1984.

3572. MacIntyre, Alasdair C. AFTER VIRTUE: A STUDY IN MORAL THEORY.
Notre Dame, IN: Univ. of Notre Dame Press; London: Duckworth, 1981.

3573. MacIntyre, Alasdair C. THREE RIVAL VERSIONS OF MORAL ENQUIRY:
ENCYCLOPAEDIA, GENEALOGY, AND TRADITION: BEING GIFFORD LEC-
TURES DELIVERED IN THE UNIVERSITY OF EDINBURGH IN 1988. Notre Dame:
Univ. of Notre Dame Press; London: Duckworth, 1990.

These Gifford Lectures compare and contrast the additions to moral inquiry represent
ed by the nineteenth century ninth edition of the ENCYCLOPEDIA BRITANNICA: the
genealogical mode of inquiry in terms of Nietzsche and some contemporary French philosophers, and the Augustinian Thomistic tradition.

3574. Magel, Charles R. A BIBLIOGRAPHY ON ANIMAL RIGHTS AND RELATED
MATTERS. Lanham, MD: Univ. Press of America, 1981.

3575. Magnus, Bernd. NIETZSCHE'S EXISTENTIAL IMPERATIVE. Bloomington:
Indiana Univ. Press, 1978.

3576. Mahoney, Edward P., ed. PHILOSOPHY AND HUMANISM: RENAISSANCE
ESSAYS IN HONOR OF PAUL OSKAR KRISTELLER. Leiden: E.J. Brill; New York:
Columbia Univ. Press, 1976.

This work contains a bibliography of the publications of Kristeller for the years 1929-
1974 on pages 546-589.

3577. Mahowald, Mary Briody. PHILOSOPHY OF WOMAN: AN ANTHOLOGY OF CLASSIC AND CURRENT CONCEPTS. 2d ed. Indianapolis: Hackett, 1983.

3578. Malcolm, Norman. LUDWIG WITTGENSTEIN: A MEMOIR. 2d ed. Oxford and New York: Oxford Univ. Press, 1984.

This volume contains a biographical sketch of Wittgenstein by G. H. von Wright and Wittgenstein's letters to Malcolm.

3579. Malcolm, Norman. NOTHING IS HIDDEN: WITTGENSTEIN'S CRITICISM OF HIS EARLY THOUGHT. Oxford and New York: Blackwell, 1986.

The author discusses some 15 theses of Wittgenstein's TRACTATUS in relation to the development of his position in the later PHILOSOPHICAL INVESTIGATIONS. The author also critically discusses what he believes to be some basic misunderstandings of Wittgenstein by John Searle and Saul Kripke, along with a comparison of Wittgenstein and Descartes on certainty.

3580. Manheimer, Ronald J. KIERKEGAARD AS EDUCATOR. Berkeley: Univ. of California Press, 1977.

3581. Manicas, Peter T. A HISTORY AND PHILOSOPHY OF THE SOCIAL SCIENCES. Oxford and New York: B. Blackwell, 1987.

3582. Manuel, Frank E. and Fritzie P. Manuel. UTOPIAN THOUGHT IN THE WESTERN WORLD. Cambridge: Belknap Press; Oxford: Blackwell, 1979.

3583. Margolis, Joseph Zalman. CULTURE AND CULTURAL ENTITIES: TOWARD A NEW UNITY OF SCIENCE. Synthese library, Vol. 170. Dordrecht and Boston: Reidel, 1984.

3584. Margolis, Joseph Zalman. PERSONS AND MINDS: THE PROSPECTS OF NON-REDUCTIVE MATERIALISM. Dordrecht and Boston: Reidel, 1978.

3585. Martin, Michael. ATHEISM: A PHILOSOSPHICAL JUSTIFICATION. Philadelphia: Temple Univ. Press, 1990.

3586. Martin, Rex. HISTORICAL EXPLANATION: REENACTMENT AND PRACTICAL INFERENCE. Ithaca: Cornell Univ. Press, 1977.

3587. Martin, Richard Milton. PRAGMATICS, TRUTH, AND LANGUAGE. Boston Studies in the Philosophy of Science, Vol. 38. Dordrecht and Boston: Reidel, 1979.

3588. Martin, Richard Milton. PRIMORDIALITY, SCIENCE, AND VALUE. Albany: State Univ. of New York Press, 1980.

3589. Matson, Wallace I. SENTIENCE. Berkeley: Univ. of California Press, 1976.

3590. Matthews, Gareth B. PHILOSOPHY AND THE YOUNG CHILD. Cambridge: Harvard Univ. Press, 1980.

3591. May, Thomas. PHILOSOPHY BOOKS, 1982-1986. Bowling Green, OH: Philosophy Documentation Center, Bowling Green State Univ., 1990.

This bibliography contains citations and abstracts of the 650 English language books published during 1982-1986 that are claimed to have "...received the most attention from the philosophic community during 1987-1989." It is organized into sixteen major areas of philosophy which, in turn, are divided into a number of subdivisions.

3592. Mazzeo, Joseph Anthony. VARIETIES OF INTERPRETATION. Notre Dame, IN: Univ. of Notre Dame Press, 1978.

3593. McAlister, Linda L. THE DEVELOPMENT OF FRANZ BRENTANO'S ETHICS. Elementa. Amsterdam: Rodopi, 1980.

The author traces the actual development of Brentano's ethics from the earlier to the later period, adding background information about his methodology, psychology and epistemology.

3594. McAlister, Linda L., ed. THE PHILOSOPHY OF BRENTANO. London: Duckworth, 1976.

The volume includes a bibliography of the writings of Brentano on pages 240-247.

3595. McCarthy, Thomas A. THE CRITICAL THEORY OF JURGEN HABERMAS. London: Hutchinson; Cambridge: MIT Press, 1978.

This volume contains a list of works by Habermas on pages 442-445.

3596. McCarthy, Vincent A. THE PHENOMENOLOGY OF MOODS IN KIERKEGAARD. The Hague and Boston: Nijhoff, 1978.

3597. McClellan, James E. PHILOSOPHY OF EDUCATION. Englewood Cliffs, NJ: Prentice-Hall, 1976.

3598. McCormick, Peter J. and Frederick A. Elliston, eds. HUSSERL: SHORTER WORKS. Notre Dame, IN: Univ. of Notre Dame Press; Brighton, Sussex: Harvester Press, 1982.

This book contains twenty one essays with introductions to Husserl's articles on phenomenology. logic and psychologism, science and phenomenology, space and time, and the social and personal world. It also includes comprehensive bibliographies and a glossary.

3599. McDermott, John Joseph. STREAMS OF EXPERIENCE: REFLECTIONS ON THE HISTORY AND PHILOSOPHY OF AMERICAN CULTURE. Amherst: Univ. of Massachusetts Press, 1986.

3600. McDonough, Richard M. THE ARGUMENT OF THE TRACTATUS: ITS RELEVANCE TO CONTEMPORARY THEORIES OF LOGIC, LANGUAGE, MIND, AND PHILOSOPHICAL TRUTH. Albany: State Univ. of New York Press, 1985.

3601. McKenna, William R. HUSSERL'S "INTRODUCTIONS TO PHENOMENOLOGY": INTERPRETATION AND CRITIQUE. The Hague and Boston: Nijhoff, 1982.

3602. McKenna, William R., et al, eds. A PRIORI AND WORLD: EUROPEAN CONTRIBUTIONS TO HUSSERLIAN PHENOMENOLOGY. The Hague and Boston: Nijhoff, 1981.

This collection includes essays on the theme of the title by J. N. Mohanty, E. Fink, G. Funke, T. Pentzopolow-Valalas, L. Landgrebe, J. Wahl, and R. Toulemont.

3603. McKeon, Richard. FREEDOM AND HISTORY AND OTHER ESSAYS: AN INTRODUCTION TO THE THOUGHT OF RICHARD MCKEON. Ed. by Zahava Karl McKeon. Chicago: Univ. of Chicago Press, 1990.

3604. McKirahan, Richard D. PLATO AND SOCRATES: A COMPREHENSIVE BIBLIOGRAPHY, 1958-1973. New York: Garland, 1978.

3605. McLaughlin, Robert J., ed. WHAT? WHERE? WHEN? WHY?: ESSAYS ON INDUCTION, SPACE AND TIME, EXPLANATION: INSPIRED BY THE WORK OF WESLEY C. SALMON AND CELEBRATING HIS FIRST VISIT TO AUSTRALIA, SEPTEMBER- DECEMBER,1978. Dordrecht and Boston: Reidel, 1982.

3606. Mensch, James R. THE QUESTION OF BEING IN HUSSERL'S LOGICAL INVESTIGATIONS. The Hague and Boston: Nijhoff, 1981.

3607. Meynell, Hugo Anthony. THE INTELLIGIBLE UNIVERSE: A COSMOLOGI-CAL ARGUMENT. Totowa, NJ: Rowman and Littlefield; London: Macmillan, 1982.

3608. Meynell, Hugo Anthony. THE NATURE OF AESTHETIC VALUE. Albany: State Univ. of New York Press; London: Macmillan, 1986.

3609. Mijuskovic, Ben Lazare. CONTINGENT IMMATERIALISM: MEANING, FREE-DOM, TIME, AND MIND. Amsterdam; B.R. Gruner, 1984.

3610. Mijuskovic, Ben Lazare. LONELINESS. 2d. ed. Millwood, NY: Associated Faculty Press, 1985.

This is a revised edition of LONELINESS IN PHILOSOPHY, PSYCHOLOGY, AND LITERATURE. Assen: Van Gorcum, 1979.

3611. Miller, David Leslie, ed. THE INDIVIDUAL AND THE SOCIAL SELF: UNPUB-LISHED WORK OF GEORGE HERBERT MEAD. Chicago: Univ. of Chicago Press, 1982.

3612. Miller, David Leslie. PHILOSOPHY AND IDEOLOGY IN HUME'S POLITICAL THOUGHT. Oxford: Clarendon Press; New York: Oxford Univ. Press, 1981.

3613. Miller, Harlan B. and William H. Williams, eds. ETHICS AND ANIMALS. Clifton, NJ: Humana Press, 1983.

3614. Miller, James Edwin. HISTORY AND HUMAN EXISTENCE: FROM MARX TO MERLEAU-PONTY. Berkeley and London: Univ. of California Press, 1979.

3615. Miller, Jim. ROUSSEAU: DREAMER OF DEMOCRACY. New Haven: Yale Univ. Press, 1984.

3616. Miller, Joan M., comp. FRENCH STRUCTURALISM: A MULTIDISCIPLINARY BIBLIOGRAPHY. New York: Garland, 1981.

This volume includes a checklist of sources for Louis Althusser, Roland Barthes, Jacques Derrida, Michel Foucault, Lucien Goldmann, Jacques Lacan and an update on works by Claude Levi-Strauss.

3617. Miller, Mitchell H. THE PHILOSOPHER IN PLATO'S STATESMAN. The Hague and Boston: Nijhoff, 1980.

3618. Miller, Richard W. ANALYZING MARX: MORALITY, POWER AND HISTO-RY. Princeton, NJ: Princeton Univ. Press, 1984.

3619. Mohanty, Jitendranath N. EDMUND HUSSERL'S THEORY OF MEANING. The Hague: Nijhoff, 1976.

3620. Mohanty, Jitendranath N. HUSSERL AND FREGE. Studies in Phenomenology and Existential Philosophy. Bloomington: Indiana Univ. Press, 1982.

This is the first extensive study in any language of the important philosophical relationship between Edmund Husserl and Gottlob Frege.

3621. Mohanty, Jitendranath N., ed. READINGS ON EDMUND HUSSERL'S LOGICAL INVESTIGATIONS. The Hague: Nijhoff, 1977.

3622. Moline, Jon. PLATO'S THEORY OF UNDERSTANDING. Madison: Univ. of Wisconsin Press, 1981.

3623. Monetta, Giuseppina Chiara. ON IDENTITY: A STUDY IN GENETIC PHENOM-ENOLOGY. The Hague: Nijhoff, 1976.

3624. Morewedge, Parviz, ed. PHILOSOPHIES OF EXISTENCE: ANCIENT AND MEDIEVAL. Bronx, NY: Fordham Univ. Press, 1982.

These thirteen studies by various scholars discuss the treatment of ontological problems in ancient and medieval times not only in the West but also in Islamic, Indic and Manichaean philosophies.

3625. Morgenbesser, Sidney, ed. DEWEY AND HIS CRITICS. New York: The Journal of Philosophy, 1977.

This book contains writings by John Dewey and his interpreters and critics which appeared in the American Journal of Philosophy from 1904 until Dewey's death in 1952.

3626. Moser, Paul. EMPIRICAL JUSTIFICATION. Dordrecht and Boston: Reidel, 1985.

3627. Moser, Paul. KNOWLEDGE AND EVIDENCE. Cambridge and New York: Cambridge Univ. Press, 1989.

3628. Mossner, Ernest Campbell. THE LIFE OF DAVID HUME. 2d ed. Oxford: Clarendon Press, 1980.

The author has updated the bibliography, corrected errors of fact, and added a textual supplement which includes recent Hume scholarship.

3629. Mulvaney, Robert J. and Philip M. Zeltner, eds. PRAGMATISM: ITS SOURCES AND PROSPECTS. Columbia: Univ. of South Carolina Press, 1981.

These are papers from a symposium at the University of South Carolina in 1975 by H. S. Thayer, W. V. O. Quine, E. Gellner, John J. McDermott, and J. Gouinlock on the origins of pragmatism, its place in empiricism, and theory of values of various pragmatists.

3630. Munevar, Gonzalo. RADICAL KNOWLEDGE: A PHILOSOPHICAL INQUIRY INTO THE NATURE AND LIMITS OF SCIENCE. Indianapolis, IN: Hackett, 1981.

3631. Mungello, David E. LEIBNIZ AND CONFUCIANISM, THE SEARCH FOR ACCORD. Honolulu: Univ. Press of Hawaii, 1977.

3632. Murphy, Richard Timothy. HUME AND HUSSERL: TOWARDS RADICAL SUBJECTIVISM. The Hague and Boston: Nijhoff, 1980.

3633. Murray, Michael, ed. HEIDEGGER AND MODERN PHILOSOPHY: CRITICAL ESSAYS. New Haven: Yale Univ. Press, 1978.

This collection includes a complete bibliography of Heidegger's writings translated into English before 1978.

3634. Myers, Gerald Eugene. WILLIAM JAMES: HIS LIFE AND THOUGHT. New Haven and London: Yale Univ. Press, 1986.

This is a comprehensive, analytical and critical study of all aspects of William James's philosophy. The volume contains a chronology of key writings and an extensive bibliography on pages 483-614.

3635. Nagel, Thomas. MORTAL QUESTIONS. Cambridge and New York: Cambridge Univ. Press, 1979.

This collection of essays ranges over a wide variety of subjects, such as death, moral luck, sexual perversion, war, equality, panpsychism, consciousness, and the subjective and the objective.

3636. Nagel, Thomas. THE VIEW FROM NOWHERE. New York: Oxford Univ. Press, 1986.

3637. Natoli, Charles M. NIETZSCHE AND PASCAL ON CHRISTIANITY. New York: Peter Lang, 1985.

3638. Navia, Luis E. PYTHAGORAS: AN ANNOTATED BIBLIOGRAPHY. New York: Garland, 1990.

This annotated bibliography lists almost 1,200 works on Pythagoras and Pythagoreanism, including books, journal articles, doctoral dissertations, plays, poems, and musical compositions. All the important works in most modern languages and Latin since the 16th century are covered. There are author and proper name indexes.

3639. Navia, Luis E. and Ellen L. Katz. SOCRATES: AN ANNOTATED BIBLIOGRAPHY. New York: Garland, 1988.

3640. Navickas, Joseph L. CONSCIOUSNESS AND REALITY: HEGEL'S PHILOSOPHY OF SUBJECTIVITY. The Hague: Nijhoff, 1976.

3641. Needleman, Jacob. CONSCIOUSNESS AND TRADITION. New York: Crossroads, 1982.

3642. Nehamas, Alexander. NIETZSCHE: LIFE AS LITERATURE. Cambridge: Harvard Univ. Press, 1985.

There is an extensive bibliography on pages 239-255.

3643. Nelson, Raymond John. THE LOGIC OF MIND. Dordrecht and Boston: Reidel, 1982.

3644. Nielsen, Harry A. WHERE THE PASSION IS: A READING OF KIERKEGAARD'S PHILOSOPHICAL FRAGMENTS. Tallahassee: Univ. Presses of Florida, 1983.

The author sets out to keep the two spheres (Christianity and human thought) separate by making Kierkegaard's distinctions more accessible.

3645. Noone, John B. ROUSSEAU'S SOCIAL CONTRACT: A CONCEPTUAL ANALYSIS. Athens: Univ. of Georgia Press, 1980.

3646. Norton, Bryan G. LINGUISTIC FRAMEWORKS AND ONTOLOGY: A REEXAMI-NATION OF CARNAP'S METAPHILOSOPHY. The Hague: Mouton, 1977.

3647. Notturno, Mark Amadeus. OBJECTIVITY, RATIONALITY, AND THE THIRD REALM: JUSTIFICATION AND THE GROUNDS OF PSYCHOLOGISM: A STUDY OF FREGE AND POPPER. Dordrecht and Boston: Nijhoff, 1985.

3648. Nozick, Robert. THE EXAMINED LIFE: PHILOSOPHICAL MEDITATIONS. New York: Simon and Schuster, 1989.

3649. Nozick, Robert. PHILOSOPHICAL EXPLANATIONS. Cambridge: Belknap Press of Harvard Univ. Press, 1981.

3650. Nussbaum, Martha Craven. THE FRAGILITY OF GOODNESS: LUCK AND ETHICS IN GREEK TRAGEDY AND PHILOSOPHY. Cambridge and New York: Cambridge Univ. Press, 1986.

3651. Nussbaum, Martha Craven. LOVE'S KNOWLEDGE: ESSAYS ON PHILOSO-PHY AND LITERATURE. New York: Oxford Univ. Press, 1990.

3652. O'Connell, Robert J. ART AND THE CHRISTIAN INTELLIGENCE IN ST. AUGUSTINE. Cambridge: Harvard Univ. Press; Oxford: Blackwell, 1978.

3653. O'Connell, Robert J. WILLIAM JAMES ON THE COURAGE TO BELIEVE. New York: Fordham Univ. Press, 1984.

3654. O'Connor, David. THE METAPHYSICS OF G. E. MOORE. Dordrecht and Boston: Reidel, 1982.

3655. O'Meara, Dominic J., ed. NEOPLATONISM AND CHRISTIAN THOUGHT. Norfolk, VA: International Society for Neoplatonic Studies, 1981.

3656. Oliver, Harold H. RELATEDNESS: ESSAYS IN METAPHYSICS AND THEOLO-GY. Macon, GA: Mercer, 1984.

3657. Oliver, Harold H. A RELATIONAL METAPHYSIC. Studies in Philosophy and Religion, Vol. 4. The Hague and Boston: Nijhoff, 1981.

3658. Olson, Alan M. TRANSCENDENCE AND HERMENEUTICS: AN INTERPRE-TATION OF THE PHILOSOPHY OF KARL JASPERS. The Hague and Boston: Nijhoff, 1978.

3659. Ong, Walter J. FIGHTING FOR LIFE: CONTEST, SEXUALITY AND CON-SCIOUSNESS. Ithaca: Cornell Univ. Press, 1981.

3660. Orenstein, Alex. WILLARD VAN ORMAN QUINE. Twayne's World Leader Series, Vol. 65. Boston: Twayne Pub, 1977.

3661. Organ, Troy Wilson. THIRD EYE PHILOSOPHY: ESSAYS IN EAST-WEST THOUGHT. Athens: Ohio Univ. Press, 1987.

3662. Outlaw, Lucius. PHILOSOPHY, ETHNICITY, AND RACE. Hamden, CT: Quinnipiac College, 1989.

3663. Paikeday, Thomas M. THE NATIVE SPEAKER IS DEAD: AN INFORMAL DISCUSSION OF A LINGUISTIC MYTH WITH NOAM CHOMSKY AND OTHER LINGUISTS, PHILOSOPHERS, PSYCHOLOGISTS, AND LEXICOGRAPHERS. Toronto and New York: Paikeday Pub., 1985.

3664. Pappas, George Sotiros and Marshall Swain, eds. ESSAYS ON KNOWLEDGE AND JUSTIFICATION. Ithaca: Cornell Univ. Press, 1978.

3665. Parsons, Charles. MATHEMATICS IN PHILOSOPHY: SELECTED ESSAYS. Ithaca: Cornell Univ. Press, 1983.

3666. Parsons, Howard L. SELF, GLOBAL ISSUES, AND ETHICS. Amsterdam: B. R. Gruner, 1980.

3667. Parsons, Howard L. and John Somerville, eds. MARXISM, REVOLUTION, AND PEACE. Amsterdam: B. R. Gruner, 1977.

The contents of this volume are from the Proceedings of the Society for the Philosophical Study of Dialectical Materialism.

3668. Paul, Jeffrey, ed. READING NOZICK: ESSAYS ON ANARCHY, STATE, AND UTOPIA. Totowa, NJ: Rowman & Littlefield; London: B. Blackwell, 1981.

3669. Peirce, Charles Sanders. CHARLES SANDERS PEIRCE (microform): COMPLETE PUBLISHED WORKS INCLUDING SELECTED SECONDARY MATERIALS. Ed. by Kenneth Lane Ketner. Greenwich, CT: Johnson Associates, 1977.

3670. Peirce, Charles Sanders. CHARLES SANDERS PEIRCE: CONTRIBUTIONS TO THE NATION. PART ONE, 1869-1893; PART TWO, 1894-1900; PART THREE, 1901-1908; PART FOUR, INDEX. Ed. by Kenneth Lane Ketner and James Edward Cook. Lubbock: Texas Tech Univ. Press, 1975-1987.

The first three parts comprise all of Peirce's contributions to the NATION. Part Four is an index to all of those contributions.

3671. Peirce, Charles Sanders. WRITINGS OF CHARLES S. PEIRCE: A CHRONOLOGICAL EDITION. Vol. 1, 1857-1866. Vol. 2, 1867-1871. Vol. 3, 1872-1878. Vol. 4, 1879-1884. Vol. 5, 1884-1886. Ed. by Max Harold Fisch. Bloomington: Indiana Univ. Press, 1982-.

This new definitive edition of Peirce's writings, arranged in chronological order, contains hitherto unpublished material and is projected to run to eighteen volumes.

3672. Pennock, James Roland. DEMOCRATIC POLITICAL THEORY. Princeton: Princeton Univ. Press, 1979.

This volume contains an extensive bibliography on pages 527-557.

3673. Pennock, James Roland and John William Chapman, eds. NOMOS. New York: New York Univ. Press, 1958-.

Vol. 17, HUMAN NATURE IN POLITICS (1977); Vol. 18, DUE PROCESS (1977); Vol. 19, ANARCHISM (1978); Vol. 20, ??; Vol. 21., COMPROMISE IN ETHICS, LAW, AND POLITICS (1979); Vol. 22, PROPERTY (1980); Vol.23, HUMAN RIGHTS (1981), Vol. 24, ETHICS, ECONOMICS, AND THE LAW (1982); Vol. 25, LIBERAL DEMOCRACY (1983); Vol. 26, MARXISM (1983); Vol. 27, CRIMINAL JUSTICE (1985); Vol. 28, JUSTIFICATION (1986).

3674. Perkins, Robert L., ed. KIERKEGAARD'S FEAR AND TREMBLING: CRITICAL APPRAISALS. University: Univ. of Alabama Press, 1981.

3675. Perreiah, Alan R. PAUL OF VENICE: A BIBLIOGRAPHIC GUIDE. Bibliographies of Famous Philosophers. Bowling Green, OH: Philosophy Documentation Center, Bowling Green Univ., 1986.

3676. Perry, Thomas A., ed. EVIDENCE AND ARGUMENTATION IN LINGUISTICS. Berlin and New York: De Gruyter, 1980.

3677. Perry, Thomas D. PROFESSIONAL PHILOSOPHY: WHAT IT IS AND WHY IT MATTERS. Dordrecht and Boston: Reidel, 1986.

3678. Pharies, David A. CHARLES S. PEIRCE AND THE LINGUISTIC SIGN. Amsterdam and Philadelphia: J. Benjamins, 1985.

3679. Pojman, Louis P. THE LOGIC OF SUBJECTIVITY: KIERKEGAARD'S PHILOSOPHY OF RELIGION. University: Univ. of Alabama Press, 1984.

3680. Pols, Edward. THE ACTS OF OUR BEING: A REFLECTION ON AGENCY AND RESPONSIBILITY. Amherst: Univ. of Massachusetts Press, 1982.

3681. Popkin, Richard Henry. THE HIGH ROAD TO PYRRHONISM. Ed. by Richard A. Watson and James E. Force. Studies in Hume and Scottish Philosophy, Vol. 2. San Diego: Austin Hill Press, 1980.

3682. Popkin, Richard Henry. HISTORY OF SCEPTICISM FROM ERASMUS TO SPINOZA. Rev. and expanded ed. Berkeley: Univ. of California Press, 1979.

This is a revised edition of a work published in New York by Humanities Press under the title: THE HISTORY OF SKEPTICISM FROM ERASMUS TO DESCARTES (1964).

3683. Prier, Raymond Adolph. ARCHAIC LOGIC: SYMBOL AND STUCTURE IN HERACLITUS, PARMENIDES AND EMPEDOCLES. The Hague: Mouton, 1976.

3684. Prior, William J. UNITY AND DEVELOPMENT IN PLATO'S METAPHYSICS. La Salle, IL: Open Court, 1985.

3685. Prosch, Harry. MICHAEL POLANYI: A CRITICAL EXPOSITION. Ithaca: State Univ. of New York Press, 1986.

This volume includes a complete bibliography of Polanyi's humanistic publications, as well as all of his earlier works.

3686. Putnam, Hilary. HOW NOT TO SOLVE ETHICAL PROBLEMS. The Lindley Lectures. Lawrence: Univ. of Kansas Press, 1983.

3687. Putnam, Hilary. THE MANY FACES OF REALISM. THE PAUL CARUS LECTURES. 16TH SERIES. La Salle, IL: Open Court, 1987.

3688. Putnam, Hilary. MEANING AND THE MORAL SCIENCES. London and Boston: Routledge and Kegan Paul, 1978.

This volume includes the author's six John Locke lectures given at Oxford University in 1976.

3689. Putnam, Hilary. PHILOSOPHICAL PAPERS. Vol. 1, MATHEMATICS, MATTER AND METHOD. Vol. 2, MIND, LANGUAGE, AND REALITY. Vol. 3, REALISM AND REASON. 2d ed. London and New York: Cambridge Univ. Press, 1979-.

3690. Putnam, Hilary. REASON, TRUTH AND HISTORY. Cambridge and New York: Cambridge Univ. Press, 1981.

3691. Putnam, Hilary and Paul Benacerraf, eds. PHILOSOPHY OF MATHEMATICS: SELECTED READINGS. 2d ed. Cambridge and New York: Cambridge Univ. Press, 1983.

There is an extensive bibliography on pages 571-600.

3692. Quine, Willard Van Orman. PURSUIT OF TRUTH. Cambridge: Harvard Univ. Press, 1990.

3693. Quine, Willard Van Orman. SAGGI FILOSOFICI 1970-1981. (SELECTIONS). Ed. by Michele Leonelli. Rome: Armando, 1982.

There is a bibliography on pages 225-238.

3694. Quine, Willard Van Orman. THEORIES AND THINGS. Cambridge: Harvard Univ. Press, 1981.

3695. Quine, Willard Van Orman. THE TIME OF MY LIFE. Cambridge: MIT Press, 1985.

3696. Quine, Willard Van Orman. THE WAYS OF PARADOX, AND OTHER ESSAYS. Rev. and enl ed. Cambridge: Harvard Univ. Press, 1976.

3697. Rader, Melvin Miller. MARX'S INTERPRETATION OF HISTORY. Oxford and New York: Oxford Univ. Press, 1979.

3698. Rader, Melvin Miller. THE RIGHT TO HOPE: CRISIS AND COMMUNITY. Seattle and London: Univ. of Washington Press, 1982.

This is a collection of essays written between 1946 and 1980.

3699. Radner, Daisie. MALEBRANCHE: A STUDY OF A CARTESIAN SYSTEM. Assen: Van Gorcum, 1978.

3700. Rajchman, John. MICHEL FOUCAULT: THE FREEDOM OF PHILOSOPHY. New York: Columbia Univ. Press, 1985.

3701. Rajchman, John and Cornel West, eds. POST-ANALYTIC PHILOSOPHY. New York: Columbia Univ. Press, 1985.

Contributors to this volume include Richard Rorty, Hilary Putnam, Thomas Nagel, Donald Davidson, Thomas D. Kuhns, and others writing on science, literary culture, and moral theory.

3702. Randall, Jr., John Herman. PHILOSOPHY AFTER DARWIN: CHAPTERS FOR THE CAREER OF PHILOSOPHY VOLUME III, AND OTHER ESSAYS. Ed. by Beth J. Singer. New York: Columbia Univ. Press, 1977.

This work is a sequel to the first two volumes of Randall's projected history of modern Western philosophy. Illness prevented him from completing this third volume. The "Other Essays" critically discuss the ontology of Paul Tillich, religious experience, and Ernst Cassirer and John Dewey on the history of philosophy.

3703. Rawls, John, et al. LIBERTY, EQUALITY AND THE LAW. Salt Lake City: Univ. Of Utah Press, 1987.

3704. Reagan, Charles E., ed. STUDIES IN THE PHILOSOPHY OF PAUL RICOEUR. Athens: Ohio Univ. Press, 1979.

This volume includes a bibliography of Paul Ricoeur compiled by Franz D. Vansina on pages 180-194.

3705. Regan, Donald. UTILITARIANISM AND CO-OPERATION. Oxford: Clarendon Press; New York: Oxford Univ. Press, 1980.

3706. Regan, Tom. ALL THAT DWELL THEREIN: ANIMAL RIGHTS AND ENVI-RONMENTAL ETHICS. Berkeley: Univ. of California Press, 1981.

This volume consists of papers and lectures written and delivered over the past six years or so on the general topic of human obligations to non-humans.

3707. Regan, Tom. BLOOMSBURY'S PROPHET: G. E. MOORE AND THE DEVEL-OPMENT OF HIS MORAL PHILOSOPHY. Philadelphia: Temple Univ. Press, 1986.

3708. Regan, Tom. THE CASE FOR ANIMAL RIGHTS. Berkeley: Univ. of California Press; London: Routledge and Kegan Paul, 1983.

3709. Regan, Tom, ed. MATTERS OF LIFE AND DEATH: NEW INTRODUCTORY ESSAYS IN MORAL PHILOSOPHY. 2d ed. New York: Random House, 1986.

This is a collection of original essays by various philosophers on such practical ethical questions as abortion, euthanasia, capital punishment, suicide, and war.

3710. Regan, Tom and Peter Singer, eds. ANIMAL RIGHTS AND HUMAN OBLIGA-TIONS. Englewood Cliffs, NJ: Prentice-Hall, 1976.

3711. Rescher, Nicholas. ETHICAL IDEALISM: AN INQUIRY INTO THE NATURE AND FUNCTION OF IDEALS. Berkeley: Univ. of California Press, 1987.

3712. Rescher, Nicholas. INDUCTION: AN ESSAY ON THE JUSTIFICATION OF INDUCTIVE REASONING. Oxford: B. Blackwell; Pittsburgh: Univ. of Pittsburgh Press, 1980.

3713. Rescher, Nicholas. LEIBNIZ'S METAPHYSICS OF NATURE: A GROUP OF ESSAYS. Western Ontario Series, Vol. 18. Dordrecht and Boston: Reidel, 1981.

3714. Rescher, Nicholas. MID-JOURNEY: AN UNFINISHED AUTOBIOGRAPHY. Washington, DC: Univ. Press of America, 1983.

3715. Rescher, Nicholas. THE RIDDLE OF EXISTENCE: AN ESSAY IN IDEALISTIC METAPHYSICS. Lanham, MD: Univ. Press of America, 1984.

3716. Rescher, Nicholas. SCEPTICISM: A CRITICAL REAPPRAISAL. Totowa, NJ: Rowman and Littlefield; Oxford: B. Blackwell, 1980.

3717. Rescher, Nicholas. SCIENTIFIC PROGRESS: A PHILOSOPHICAL ESSAY ON THE ECONOMICS OF RESEARCH IN A NATURAL SCIENCE. Oxford: B. Blackwell; Pittsburgh: Univ. of Pittsburgh Press, 1978.

3718. Rescher, Nicholas. THE STRIFE OF SYSTEMS: AN ESSAY ON THE GROUNDS AND IMPLICATIONS OF PHILOSOPHICAL DIVERSITY. Pittsburgh: Univ. of Pittsburgh Press, 1985.

3719. Rescher, Nicholas. UNPOPULAR ESSAYS ON TECHNOLOGICAL PROGRESS. Pittsburgh: Univ. of Pittsburgh Press, 1980.

3720. Richter, Melvin. POLITICAL THEORY AND POLITICAL EDUCATION. Princeton, NJ and Guildford, Surrey: Princeton Univ. Press, 1980.

3721. Rieber, Robert W., ed. DIALOGUES ON THE PSYCHOLOGY OF LANGUAGE AND THOUGHT: CONVERSATIONS WITH NOAM CHOMSKY, CHARLES OSGOOD, JEAN PIAGET, ULRIC NEISSER, AND MARCEL KINSBOURNE. New York: Plenum Press, 1983.

3722. Riley, Patrick. THE GENERAL WILL BEFORE ROUSSEAU: THE TRANSFORMATION OF THE DIVINE INTO THE CIVIC. Studies in Moral, Political and Legal Philosophy. Princeton: Princeton Univ. Press, 1986.

3723. Riley, Patrick. KANT'S POLITICAL PHILOSOPHY. Totowa, NJ: Rowman and Littlefield, 1983.

3724. Riley, Patrick. WILL AND POLITICAL LEGITIMACY: A CRITICAL EXPOSITION OF SOCIAL CONTRACT THEORY IN HOBBES, LOCKE AND ROUSSEAU AND HEGEL. Cambridge: Harvard Univ. Press, 1982.

3725. Robb, Kevin, ed. LANGUAGE AND THOUGHT IN EARLY GREEK PHILOSOPHY. La Salle, IL: Hegeler Institute, 1983.

This work includes essays by the editor and Eric Havelock, G. S. Kirk, Jonathan Barnes, Charles H. Kahn, J. P Hershbell, Julius M. Moravcsik, Arthur W. H. Adkins, Joseph Margolis, Dallas Willard, Wallace I. Matson, Robert S. Brumbaugh and Joanne Bell.

3726. Robinson, Daniel N. PHILOSOPHY OF PSYCHOLOGY. New York: Columbia Univ. Press, 1985.

3727. Rockmore, Tom, et al. MARXISM AND ALTERNATIVES: TOWARDS THE CONCEPTUAL INTERACTION AMONG SOVIET PHILOSOPHY, NEO-THOMISM, PRAGMATISM, AND PHENOMENOLOGY. Sovietica, Vol. 45. Dordrecht and Boston: Reidel, 1981.

3728. Roemer, John E., ed. ANALYTICAL MARXISM. Cambridge and New York: Cambridge Univ. Press; Paris: Editions de la Maison des sciences de l'homme, 1986.

3729. Romanell, Patrick. JOHN LOCKE AND MEDICINE: A NEW KEY TO LOCKE. Buffalo: Prometheus Book, 1984.

3730. Romanos, George David. QUINE AND ANALYTIC PHILOSOPHY: THE LANGUAGE OF LANGUAGE. Cambridge: MIT Press, 1983.

3731. Rorty, Amelie Oksenberg, ed. ESSAYS ON ARISTOTLE'S ETHICS. Berkeley: Univ. of California Press, 1980.

3732. Rorty, Amelie Oksenberg, ed. ESSAYS ON DESCARTES' MEDITATIONS. Berkeley: Univ. of California Press, 1986.

3733. Rorty, Amelie Oksenberg, ed. EXPLAINING EMOTIONS. Berkeley: Univ. of California Press, 1980.

3734. Rorty, Amelie Oksenberg, ed. THE IDENTITIES OF PERSON. Berkeley: Univ. of California Press, 1976.

3735. Rorty, Richard. CONSEQUENCES OF PRAGMATISM: ESSAYS 1972-1980. Minneapolis: Univ. of Minnesota Press, 1982.

3736. Rorty, Richard. CONTINGENCY, IRONY, AND SOLIDARITY. Cambridge and New York: Cambridge Univ. Press, 1989.

The author argues that such thinkers as Nietzsche, Freud, and Wittgenstein have enabled societies to see themselves as historical contingencies rather than as historical expressions of human nature. Rorty attempts to show how literature can advance Liberalism's social and political goals by providing a genuine sense of human solidarity.

3737. Rorty, Richard. L'HOMME SPECULAIRE. Tr. of PHILOSOPHY AND THE MIRROR OF NATURE. Princeton: Princeton Univ. Press, 1979. Tr. from the English by Thierry Marchaisse. Paris: Seuil, 1990.

The German translation by Michael Gebauer was published in 1981 as DER SPIEGEL DER NATUR: EINE KRITIK DER PHILOSOPHIE in Frankfurt am Main by Suhrkamp.

3738. Rorty, Richard. PHILOSOPHICAL PAPERS. Vol. 1, OBJECTIVITY, RELATIVISM, AND TRUTH. Vol. 2, ESSAYS ON HEIDEGGER AND OTHERS. Cambridge and New York: Cambridge Univ. Press, 1991.

3739. Rorty, Richard, et al. PHILOSOPHY IN HISTORY: ESSAYS IN THE HISTORIOGRAPHY OF PHILOSOPHY. Cambridge and New York: Cambridge Univ. Press, 1984.

Part I emphasizes theoretical and methodological issues, while the essays in Part II discuss a number of case histories drawn from the history of philosophy from ancient times to the present. The above volume is the first in the projected series of volumes under the title IDEAS IN CONTEXT.

3740. Rosen, Stanley. THE ANCIENTS AND THE MODERNS: RETHINKING MODERNITY. New Haven: Yale Univ. Press, 1989.

3741. Rosen, Stanley. HERMENEUTICS AS POLITICS. New York: Oxford Univ. Press, 1988.

3742. Rosen, Stanley. THE LIMITS OF ANALYSIS. New York: Basic Books, 1980.

3743. Rosen, Stanley. THE QUARREL BETWEEN PHILOSOPHY AND POETRY: STUDIES IN ANCIENT THOUGHT. New York: Routledge, 1988.

3744. Rosenberg, Jay F. ONE WORLD AND OUR KNOWLEDGE OF IT: THE PROBLEMATIC OF REALISM IN POST-KANTIAN PERSPECTIVE. Dordrecht and Boston: Reidel, 1980.

3745. Rosenberg, Jay F. THINKING CLEARLY ABOUT DEATH. Englewood Cliffs, NJ: Prentice-Hall, 1983.

3746. Rosenberg, Jay F. THE THINKING SELF. Philadelphia: Temple Univ. Press, 1986.

3747. Rosenkrantz, Roger D. FOUNDATIONS AND APPLICATIONS OF INDUCTIVE PROBABILITY. Atascadero, CA: Ridgeview Publishing, 1981.

3748. Rosenkrantz, Roger D. INFERENCE, METHOD AND DECISION: TOWARDS A BAYESIAN PHILOSOPHY OF SCIENCE. Dordrecht and Boston: Reidel, 1977.

3749. Ross, Stephen David. A THEORY OF ART: INEXHAUSTIBILITY BY CONTRACT. Albany: State Univ. of New York Press, 1982.

3750. Roth, Norman. MAIMONIDES: ESSAYS AND TEXTS. 850TH ANNIVERSARY. Madison, WI: Hispanic Seminary of Medieval Studies, Ltd, 1985.

This volume includes a basic bibliography of Maimonides on pages 155- 164.

3751. Rothbard, Murray Newton. ETHICS OF LIBERTY. Atlantic Highlands, NJ: Humanities Press, 1982.

3752. Rowell, Lewis Eugene. THINKING ABOUT MUSIC: AN INTRODUCTION TO THE PHILOSOPHY OF MUSIC. Amherst: Univ. of Massachusetts Press, 1983.

3753. Rubinstein, David. MARX AND WITTGENSTEIN: SOCIAL PRAXIS AND SOCIAL EXPLANATION. London and Boston: Routledge & Kegan Paul, 1981.

3754. Rudavsky, Tamar, ed. DIVINE OMNISCIENCE AND OMNIPOTENCE IN MEDIEVAL PHILOSOPHY: ISLAMIC, JEWISH, AND CHRISTIAN PERSPECTIVES. Dordrecht and Boston: Reidel, 1985.

3755. Saatkamp, Herman J. GEORGE SANTAYANA: BIBLIOGRAPHICAL CHECK-LIST, 1880-1980. Bibliographies of Famous Philosophers. Bowling Green, OH: Philosophy Documentation Center, 1982.

3756. Sacksteder, William. HOBBES STUDIES (1879-1979): A BIBLIOGRAPHY. Bibliographies of Famous Philosophers. Bowling Green, OH: Philosophy Documentation Center, 1982.

3757. Sallis, John C., ed. DECONSTRUCTION AND PHILOSOPHY: THE TEXTS OF JACQUES DERRIDA. Chicago and London: Univ. of Chicago Press, 1987.

This volume consists of papers from the international conference Deconstruction and Philosophy: The Texts of Jacques Derrida held at Loyola University of Chicago on March 22-28, 1985. It also includes "Geschlecht II; Heidegger`s Hand," a previously untranslated essay by Derrida.

3758. Sallis, John C. THE GATHERING OF REASON. Series in Continental Thought, Vol. 2. Athens: Ohio Univ. Press, 1980.

3759. Sallis, John C., ed. HUSSERL AND CONTEMPORARY THOUGHT. Atlantic Highlands, NJ: Humanities Press, 1983.

This is a reprint from RESEARCH IN PHENOMENOLOGY, 1982, Vol. 12.

3760. Sallis, John C., ed. PHILOSOPHY AND ARCHAIC EXPERIENCE: ESSAYS IN HONOR OF EDWARD G. BALLARD. Pittsburgh: Duquesne Univ. Press, 1982.

3761. Sallis, John C., et al, eds. THE COLLEGIUM PHAENOMENOLOGICUM: THE FIRST TEN YEARS. Dordrecht and Boston: Kluwer Academic Publishers, 1988.

3762. Salmon, Wesley C., ed. HANS REICHENBACH: LOGICAL EMPIRICIST. Dordrecht and Boston: Reidel, 1979.

3763. Samuelson, Norbert M. AN INTRODUCTION TO MODERN JEWISH PHILOSO-PHY. Albany: State Univ. of New York Press, 1981.

3764. Santas, Gerasimos Xenophon. SOCRATES, PHILOSOPHY IN PLATOS'S EARLY DIALOGUES. The Arguments of the Philosophers. London and Boston: Routledge & Kegan Paul, 1979.

3765. Santayana, George. THE WORKS OF GEORGE SANTAYANA. Vol. 1, PERSONS AND PLACES: FRAGMENTS OF AN AUTOBIOGRAPHY. Vol. 2, THE SENSE OF BEAUTY: BEING THE OUTLINES OF AESTHETIC THEORY. Vol. 3, INTERPRETA-

TIONS OF POETRY AND RELIGION. Ed. by William G. Holzberger and Herman J. Saatkamp. Cambridge: MIT Press, 1986-.

3766. Sayre, Kenneth M. CYBERNETICS AND THE PHILOSOPHY OF MIND. London: Routledge and Kegan Paul; Atlantic Highlands, NJ: Humanities Press, 1976.

3767. Schacht, Richard. CLASSICAL MODERN PHILOSOPHERS: DESCARTES TO KANT. London and Boston: Routledge and Kegan Paul, 1984.

The thought of the seven philosophers Descartes, Leibniz, Spinoza, Locke, Berkeley, Hume and Kant is held to constitute the core and to define the themes of classical modern philosophy.

3768. Schacht, Richard. NIETZSCHE. The Arguments of the Philosophers. London and Boston: Routledge and Kegan Paul, 1983.

Concentrating on Nietzsche's writings in the last ten years of his life, the author explores his philosophizing on truth and knowledge, human nature, values, moralities and art.

3769. Scheffler, Israel. BEYOND THE LETTER: A PHILOSOPHICAL INQUIRY INTO AMBIGUITY, VAGUENESS AND METAPHOR IN LANGUAGE. London and Boston: Routledge and Kegan Paul, 1979.

3770. Scheffler, Israel. OF HUMAN POTENTIAL: AN ESSAY IN THE PHILOSOPHY OF EDUCATION. Boston: Routledge and Kegan Paul, 1985.

3771. Scheffler, Samuel. THE REJECTION OF CONSEQUENTIALISM: PHILOSOPH-ICAL INVESTIGATION OF THE CONSIDERATIONS UNDERLYING RIVAL MORAL CONCEPTIONS. Oxford: Clarendon Press; New York: Oxford Univ. Press, 1982.

This volume was originally presented as the author's thesis at Princeton University in 1977.

3772. Schilpp, Paul Arthur, ed. THE PHILOSOPHY OF BRAND BLANSHARD. Library of Living Philosophers, Vol. XV. La Salle, IL: Open Court, 1980.

Thirty philosophers critically discuss various aspects of Blanshard's philosophy. The work also includes Blanshard's philosophical autobiography, his detailed reply to his critics, and a bibliography of his writings to 1980.

3773. Schilpp, Paul Arthur, ed. THE PHILOSOPHY OF KARL JASPERS. New aug. cd. Library of Living Philosophers, Vol. IX. Chicago: Open Court, 1981.

This is a reissue with addenda of the 1957 edition. It includes a 90 page philosophical autobiography and a 121 page reply to contributors by Jaspers. It also includes Jaspers's previously suppressed comments on Martin Heidegger. The bibliography of Jaspers's writings does not go beyond 1957.

3774. Schilpp, Paul Arthur and Lewis Edwin Hahn, eds. THE PHILOSOPHY OF W. V. QUINE. The Library of Living Philosophers, Vol. XVIII. LaSalle, IL: Open Court, 1986.

In addition to Quine's intellectural autobiography and a complete bibliography of his writings up to the date of publication, this volume contains critical articles on Quine's philosophy by other philosophers and Quine's replies to each of them.

3775. Schlesinger, George. RELIGION AND SCIENTIFIC METHOD. Dordrecht: Reidel, 1977.

3776. Schneewind, Julius B. SIDGWICK'S ETHICS AND VICTORIAN MORAL PHI-LOSOPHY. Oxford and New York: Oxford Univ. Press, 1977.

3777. Schrag, Calvin O. COMMUNICATIVE PRAXIS AND THE SPACE OF SUB-JECTIVITY. Bloomington: Indiana Univ. Press, 1986.

3778. Schrag, Calvin O. RADICAL REFLECTION AND THE ORIGIN OF THE HUMAN SCIENCES. West Lafayette: Purdue Univ. Press, 1987.

3779. Schutz, Alfred. THEORY OF SOCIAL ACTION: THE CORRESPONDENCE OF ALFRED SCHUTZ AND TALCOTT PARSONS. Ed. by Richard Grathoff. Blooming-ton, IN: Indiana Univ. Press, 1978.

3780. Schwartz, Stephen P., ed. NAMING, NECESSITY, AND NATURAL KINDS. Ithaca: Cornell Univ. Press, 1977.

3781. Searle, John R. INTENTIONALITY: AN ESSAY IN THE PHILOSOPHY OF MIND. Cambridge and New York: Cambridge Univ. Press, 1983.

3782. Searle, John R. MEANING: PROTOCOL OF THE FORTY-FOURTH COLLO-QUY, 3 OCTOBER 1982. Ed. by Julian Boyd. Berkeley: Center for Hermeneutical Studies in Hellenistic and Modern Culture, 1981.

3783. Searle, John R. MINDS, BRAINS, AND SCIENCE: THE 1984 REITH LEC-TURES. Cambridge: Harvard Univ. Press; London: British Broadcasting Corporation, 1984.

3784. Searle, John R., et al, eds. SPEECH ACT THEORY AND PRAGMATICS. Dordrecht and Boston: Reidel, 1980.

3785. Searle, John R. and Daniel Vanderveken. FOUNDATIONS OF ILLOCUTION-ARY LOGIC. Cambridge and New York: Cambridge Univ. Press, 1985.

3786. Seigel, Jerrold. MARX'S FATE: THE SHAPE OF A LIFE. Princeton: Princeton Univ. Press, 1978.

3787. Seigfried, Charlene Haddock. CHAOS AND CONTEXT: A STUDY IN WILLIAM JAMES. Athens: Ohio Univ. Press, 1978.

3788. Seigfried, Charlene Haddock. WILLIAM JAMES'S RADICAL RECONSTRUC-TION OF PHILOSOPHY. Albany: State Univ. of New York Press, 1990.

3789. Sellars, Wilfrid. NATURALISM AND ONTOLOGY. Reseda, CA: Ridgeview, 1979.

This volume is a revised and expanded version of the John Dewey lectures given at the University of Chicago in May, 1974.

3790. Sellars, Wilfrid. PURE PRAGMATICS AND POSSIBLES: THE EARLY ESSAYS OF WILFRID SELLARS. Ed. by Jeffrey Sicha. Reseda, CA: Ridgeview Press, 1980.

3791. Sellars, Wilfrid, et al, contributors. FOUNDATIONS FOR A METAPHYSICS OF PURE PROCESS. The Carus Lectures. Ed. by Eugene Freeman. LaSalle, IL: Hegel-er Institute, 1981.

3792. Seung, Thomas K. STRUCTURALISM AND HERMENEUTICS. New York: Columbia Univ. Press, 1982.

3793. Shahan, Robert W. and John Ivan Biro, eds. SPINOZA: NEW PERSPECTIVES.

Norman: Univ. of Oklahoma, 1978.

3794. Shahan, Robert W. and Chris Swoyer, eds. ESSAYS ON THE PHILOSOPHY OF W. V. QUINE. Norman: Univ. of Oklahoma; Sussex: Harvester Press, 1979.

This book consists of eleven essays on various aspects of Quine's philosophical work by such philosophers as Gilbert Harman, J. N. Mohanty, Michael E. Levin, Mark Pastin, and others, as well as a contribution by Quine.

3795. Shalvey, Thomas J. CLAUDE LEVI-STRAUSS: SOCIAL PSYCHOTHERAPY AND THE COLLECTIVE UNCONSCIOUS. Amherst: Univ. of Massachusetts Press, 1979.

3796. Shapere, Dudley. REASON AND THE SEARCH FOR KNOWLEDGE: INVESTIGATIONS IN THE PHILOSOPHY OF SCIENCE. Boston Studies in the Philosophy of Science, Vol. 78. Dordrecht and Boston: Reidel, 1983.

3797. Shapiro, Marianne and Michael Shapiro. STRUCTURE AND CONTENT: ESSAYS IN APPLIED SEMIOTICS. Toronto: Victoria Univ., 1979.

3798. Shapiro, Michael. THE SENSE OF GRAMMAR: LANGUAGE AS SEMIOTIC. Bloomington: Indiana Univ. Press, 1983.

3799. Shaw, William H. MARX'S THEORY OF HISTORY. London: Hutchinson, 1978.

3800. Shelp, Earl E., ed. THE CLINICAL ENCOUNTER: THE MORAL FABRIC OF THE PATIENT-PHYSICIAN RELATIONSHIP. Dordrecht and Boston: Reidel, 1983.

3801. Shoemaker, Sidney. IDENTITY, CAUSE, AND MIND: PHILOSOPHICAL ESSAYS. Cambridge and New York: Cambridge Univ. Press, 1984.

3802. Shoemaker, Sidney and Richard Swinburne. PERSONAL IDENTITY. New York: Blackwell, 1984.

3803. Sia, Santiago. GOD IN PROCESS THOUGHT: A STUDY IN CHARLES HARTSHORNE'S CONCEPT OF GOD. Dordrecht and Boston: Nijhoff, 1985.

This volume includes a postscript by Charles Hartshorne.

3804. Silverman, Hugh J., ed. CONTINENTAL PHILOSOPHY. New York: Routledge, 1988-.

The following volumes have appeared: Vol. 1, PHILOSOPHY AND NON PHILOSOPHY SINCE MERLEAU-PONTY (1988). Vol. 2, DERRIDA AND DECONSTRUCTION (1989). Vol. 3, POSTMODERNISM: PHILOSOPHY AND THE ARTS (1990).

3805. Silverman, Hugh J., et al. CONTINENTAL PHILOSOPHY IN AMERICA. Pittsburgh: Duquesne Univ. Press, 1983.

All of the essays in this volume are published here for the first time and represent what are judged to be the best works presented at the annual meetings of the Husserl, Heidegger, and Merleau-Ponty Circles.

3806. Silverman, Hugh J. and Frederick A. Elliston, eds. JEAN-PAUL SARTRE: CONTEMPORARY APPROACHES TO HIS PHILOSOPHY. Pittsburgh: Duquesne Univ. Press, 1980.

3807. Silverman, Hugh J. and Donn Welton, eds. POSTMODERNISM AND CONTINENTAL PHILOSOPHY. Albany: State Univ. of New York Press, 1988.

3808. Simon, Herbert Alexander. MODELS OF DISCOVERY AND OTHER TOPICS IN THE METHODS OF SCIENCE. Studies in the Philosophy of Science, Vol. 44. Dordrecht and Boston: Reidel, 1977.

3809. Singer, Irving. THE NATURE OF LOVE, 1: PLATO TO LUTHER; 2: COURTLY AND ROMANTIC; 3. THE MODERN WORLD. 2d ed. Chicago and London: Univ. of Chicago Press, 1984-1987.

This work ranges over the development of ideas about love in philosophy and literature to discover the sources of our contemporary thinking about love.

3810. Singer, Peter. THE EXPANDING CIRCLE: ETHICS AND SOCIOBIOLOGY. New York: Farrar, Strauss and Giroux, 1981.

3811. Skrupskelis, Ignas K. WILLIAM JAMES: A REFERENCE GUIDE. Boston: G. K. Hall, 1977.

3812. Sluga, Hans D. GOTTLOB FREGE. The Arguments of the Philosophers. London and Boston: Routledge and Kegan Paul, 1980.

3813. Smith, David Woodruff and Ronald McIntyre. HUSSERL AND INTENTIONALITY: A STUDY OF MIND, MEANING AND LANGUAGE. Dordrecht and Boston: Reidel, 1982.

3814. Smith, John Edwin. PURPOSE AND THOUGHT: THE MEANING OF PRAGMATISM. New Haven: Yale Univ. Press, 1978.

3815. Smith, John Edwin. THE SPIRIT OF AMERICAN PHILOSOPHY. Rev ed. Albany: State Univ. of New York Press, 1983.

3816. Smith, Joseph H., ed. KIERKEGAARD'S TRUTH: THE DISCLOSURE OF THE SELF. New Haven: Yale Univ. Press, 1981.

3817. Smith, Joseph H., ed. THOUGHT, CONSCIOUSNESS AND REALITY. Psychiatry and the Humanitites, Vol. 2. New Haven: Yale Univ. Press, 1977.

3818. Smith, Joseph H. and William Kerrigan, eds. INTERPRETING LACAN. Psychiatry and the Humanities, Vol. 6. New Haven and London: Yale Univ. Press, 1983.

3819. Sober, Elliot. THE NATURE OF SELECTION: EVOLUTIONARY THEORY IN PHILOSOPHICAL FOCUS. Cambridge: MIT Press, 1984.

3820. Soble, Alan. PORNOGRAPHY: MARXISM, FEMINISM, AND THE FUTURE OF SEXUALITY. New Haven: Yale Univ. Press, 1986.

3821. Sokolowski, Robert. MORAL ACTION: A PHENOMENOLOGICAL STUDY. Bloomington: Indiana Univ. Press, 1985.

3822. Sokolowski, Robert. PRESENCE AND ABSENCE: A PHILOSOPHICAL INVESTIGATION OF LANGUAGE AND BEING. Bloomington: Indiana Univ. Press, 1978.

3823. Solomon, Robert C. IN THE SPIRIT OF HEGEL: A STUDY OF G.W.F. HEGEL'S `PHENOMENOLOGY OF SPIRIT'. New York and Oxford: Oxford Univ. Press, 1983.

3824. Solomon, Robert C., ed. NIETZSCHE: A COLLECTION OF CRITICAL ESSAYS. Garden City, NY: Doubleday Anchor, 1980.

3825. Soltis, Jonas F., ed. PHILOSOPHY AND EDUCATION: EIGHTIETH YEAR-BOOK OF THE NATIONAL SOCIETY FOR THE STUDY OF EDUCATION, Part I. Chicago: Univ. of Chicago Press, 1981.

3826. Spiegelberg, Herbert. THE CONTEXT OF THE PHENOMENOLOGICAL MOVEMENT. The Hague and Boston: Nijhoff, 1981.

3827. Spiegelberg, Herbert. THE PHENOMENOLOGICAL MOVEMENT: A HISTOR-ICAL INTRODUCTION. 3d. rev. and enl ed. Dordrecht, The Hague and Boston: Nijhoff, 1982.

This third edition has new sections on Roman Ingarden and Hedwig Conrad-Martius, as well as a new chapter on Emmanuel Levinas. All chapters have been enlarged.

3828. Spiegelberg, Herbert and Eberhard Ave-Lallemant, eds. PFANDERSTUDIEN. The Hague and Boston: Nijhoff, 1982.

3829. Stack, George Joseph. SARTRE'S PHILOSOPHY OF SOCIAL EXISTENCE. St. Louis: W. H. Green, 1977.

3830. Stambaugh, Joan. THE REAL IS NOT THE RATIONAL. Albany: State Univ. of New York Press, 1986.

3831. Staten, Henry. WITTGENSTEIN AND DERRIDA. Lincoln: Univ. of Nebraska Press, 1984.

3832. Steinkraus, Warren E., ed. REPRESENTATIVE ESSAYS OF BORDEN PARKER BOWNE. Utica, NY: Meridian, 1981.

There is an introductory essay by Herbert W. Schneider and a bibliography on pages 198-215.

3833. Steinkraus, Warren E. and Kenneth Schmitz, eds. ART AND LOGIC IN HEGEL'S PHILOSOPHY. Atlantic Highlands, NJ: Humanities Press; Sussex: Harvester Press, 1980.

3834. Stepelevich, Lawrence S. and David Lamb, eds. HEGEL'S PHILOSOPHY OF ACTION. Atlantic Highlands, NJ: Humanities Press, 1983.

These papers were delivered at the Joint meeting of the Hegel Society of America and the Hegel Society of Great Britain held at Merton College, Oxford, Sept, 1-4, 1981, to mark the 150th anniversary of Hegel's death.

3835. Sterba, James P. THE DEMANDS OF JUSTICE. Notre Dame: Univ. of Notre Dame Press, 1980.

3836. Stern, Raphael, et al, eds. CREATION AND INTERPRETATION. New York: Haven Publications, 1985.

3837. Stich, Stephen P. FROM FOLK PSYCHOLOGY TO COGNITIVE SCIENCE: THE CASE AGAINST BELIEF. Cambridge, MA: MIT Press, 1983.

3838. Stroud, Barry. THE SIGNIFICANCE OF PHILOSOPHICAL SKEPTICISM. Oxford: Clarendon Press; New York: Oxford Univ. Press, 1984.

3839. Suckiel, Ellen Kappy. THE PRAGMATIC PHILOSOPHY OF WILLIAM JAMES. Notre Dame: Univ. of Notre Dame Press, 1982.

3840. Sukale, Michael. COMPARATIVE STUDIES IN PHENOMENOLOGY. The Hague: Nijhoff, 1976.

3841. Suppe, Frederick, ed. THE STRUCTURE OF SCIENTIFIC THEORIES. 2d ed. Urbana: Univ. of Illinois Press, 1977.

The volume contains a critical introduction and an afterword by Fredrick Suppe and a bibliography on pages 731-772.

3842. Suppes, Patrick. PROBABILISTIC METAPHYSICS. Oxford and New York: B. Blackwell, 1984.

3843. Taylor, Edward. WILLIAM JAMES ON EXCEPTIONAL MENTAL STATES: THE 1896 LOWELL LECTURES. New York: Scribner, 1983.

A reconstruction of William James's lectures on topics ranging from hypnosis and hysteria to witchcraft and genius. These lectures come between THE PRINCIPLES OF PSYCHOLOGY and THE VARIETIES OF RELIGIOUS EXPERIENCE.

3844. Teloh, Henry. THE DEVELOPMENT OF PLATO'S METAPHYSICS. University Park and London: Pennsylvania State Univ. Press, 1981.

3845. Teloh, Henry. SOCRATIC EDUCATION IN PLATO'S EARLY DIALOGUES. Notre Dame: Univ. of Notre Dame Press, 1986.

3846. Thalberg, Irving. PERCEPTION, EMOTION AND ACTION: A COMPONENT APPROACH. Oxford: Blackwell; New Haven: Yale Univ. Press, 1977.

3847. Thomas, Paul. KARL MARX AND THE ANARCHISTS. London and Boston: Routledge and Kegan Paul, 1980.

3848. Thro, Linus J., ed. HISTORY OF PHILOSOPHY IN THE MAKING: A SYMPOSIUM OF ESSAYS TO HONOR JAMES D. COLLINS ON HIS 65TH BIRTHDAY BY HIS COLLEAGUES AND FRIENDS. Washington, DC: Univ. Press of America, 1982.

This work consists of: Part I, 10 Essays on "Source Thinkers Under Historical Questioning" (Plato, Boethius, St. Thomas, Duns Scotus, Suarez, Hobbes, Wolff, Kierkegaard, C. S. Peirce.); and Part II, 7 essays on problems in contemporary philosophy.

3849. Tice, Terrence N. and Thomas P. Slavens, eds. RESEARCH GUIDE TO PHILOSOPHY. Sources of Information in the Humanities, Vol. 3. Chicago: American Library Association, 1983.

The work consists of brief descriptive and evaluative essays followed by short selective bibliographies divided into two main parts: (1) A history of Western philosophy from ancient Greece to the date of publication; and (2) Areas or fields of philosophy such as aesthetics, epistemology, ethics, philosophy of language, and so on. The volume concludes with an annotated bibliography of reference works. The selective bibliographies list only works in English published since World War II.

3850. Toews, John Edward. HEGELIANISM: THE PATH TOWARD DIALECTICAL HUMANISM, 1805-1841. Cambridge and New York: Cambridge Univ. Press, 1980.

3851. Tomberlin, James E. and Peter Van Inwagen, eds. ALVIN PLANTINGA. Dordrecht and Boston: Reidel, 1985.

3852. Tragesser, Robert S. HUSSERL AND REALISM IN LOGIC AND MATHEMATICS. Cambridge and New York: Cambridge Univ. Press, 1984.

3853. Turbayne, Colin Murray, ed. BERKELEY: CRITICAL AND INTERPRETIVE ESSAYS. Minneapolis: Univ.of Minnesota, 1982.

These are some of the papers delivered at the Berkeley Commemorative Conference held at Newport, Rhode Island, September 27-30, 1979. This volume contains a bibliography of George Berkeley, 1963-1979, on pages 313-329.

3854. Unger, Peter K. PHILOSOPHICAL RELATIVITY. Minneapolis: Univ. of Minnesota Press; Oxford: B. Blackwell, 1984.

The author hypothesizes that for many problems there are no right or best solutions; consequently a belief that there are indefinite objective answers should be examined.

3855. Van Inwagen, Peter. AN ESSAY ON FREE WILL. Oxford: Clarendon Press, 1983.

3856. Van Inwagen, Peter, ed. TIME AND CAUSE: ESSAYS PRESENTED TO RICHARD TAYLOR. Dordrecht and Boston: Reidel, 1980.

This work contains a bibliography of the philosophical writings of Richard Taylor on pages 301-306.

3857. Vendler, Zeno. THE MATTER OF MINDS. Oxford: Clarendon Press; New York: Oxford Univ. Press, 1984.

3858. Verbeke, Gerard. THE PRESENCE OF STOICISM IN MEDIEVAL THOUGHT. Washington, DC: Catholic Univ. Press of America, 1983.

3859. Verdu, Alfonso. EARLY BUDDHIST PHILOSOPHY IN LIGHT OF THE FOUR NOBLE TRUTHS. Washington: Univ. Press of America, 1979.

3860. Verdu, Alfonso. THE PHILOSOPHY OF BUDDHISM: A "TOTALISTIC" SYNTHESIS. The Hague and Boston: Nijhoff, 1980.

3861. Verene, Donald Phillip. HEGEL'S SOCIAL AND POLITICAL PHILOSOPHY: THE PHILOSOPHY OF OBJECTIVE SPIRIT. Atlantic Highlands, NJ: Humanities Press; Sussex: Harvester Press, 1980.

This is a collection of papers from the biennial conference of the Hegel Society of America, held at Villanova Univ., Villanova, PA, November 11-13, 1976.

3862. Verene, Donald Phillip. VICO'S SCIENCE OF IMAGINATION. New York: Cornell Univ. Press, 1981.

3863. Vlastos, Gregory. SOCRATES, IRONIST AND MORAL PHILOSOPHER. Ithaca, NY: Cornell Univ. Press, 1991.

3864. Wainwright, William J. PHILOSOPHY OF RELIGION: AN ANNOTATED BIBLIOGRAPHY OF TWENTIETH-CENTURY WRITINGS IN ENGLISH. New York: Garland, 1978.

3865. Waithe, Mary Ellen, ed. A HISTORY OF WOMEN PHILOSOPHERS. Vol. 1, ANCIENT WOMEN PHILOSOPHERS, 600 B.C.-500 A.D. Vol. 2, MEDIEVAL, RENAISSANCE, AND ENLIGHTENMENT WOMEN PHILOSOPHERS, A.D. 500-1600. Dordrecht and Boston: Nijhoff, 1987-.

3866. Walton, Kendall L. MIMESIS AS MAKE BELIEVE: ON THE FOUNDATIONS OF THE REPRESENTATIONAL ARTS. Cambridge: Harvard Univ. Press, 1990.

3867. Wang, Hao. BEYOND ANALYTIC PHILOSOPHY: DOING JUSTICE TO WHAT WE KNOW. Cambridge: MIT Press, 1986.

The author criticizes the tradition of modern analytical philosophy as represented by the work of Russell, Carnap, and Quine and offers his own original view of what philosophy could and should be.

3868. Wang, Hao. POPULAR LECTURES ON MATHEMATICAL LOGIC. New York: Van Nostrand Reinhold, 1981.

3869. Wang, Hao. REFLECTIONS ON KURT GODEL. Cambridge: MIT Press, 1987.

3870. Warren, Mary Anne. GENDERCIDE: THE IMPLICATIONS OF SEX SELEC-TION. Totowa, NJ: Rowman and Allanheld, 1985.

3871. Wartofsky, Marx W. FEUERBACH. London, Cambridge [Eng] and New York: Cambridge Univ. Press, 1977.

3872. Wartofsky, Marx W. MODELS: REPRESENTATION AND THE SCIENTIFIC UNDERSTANDING. Dordrecht and Boston: Reidel, 1979.

3873. Wasserstrom, Richard A. PHILOSOPHY AND SOCIAL ISSUES: FIVE STUD-IES. Notre Dame: Univ. of Notre Dame Press, 1980.

3874. Webb, Rodman B. THE PRESENCE OF THE PAST: JOHN DEWEY AND ALFRED SCHUTZ ON THE GENESIS AND ORGANIZATION OF EXPERIENCE. Gainesville: Univ. of Florida Presses, 1976.

3875. Weinberg, Julius Rudolph. OCKHAM, DESCARTES, AND HUME: SELF-KNOWLEDGE, SUBSTANCE, AND CAUSALITY. Madison: Univ. of Wisconsin Press, 1977.

This volumes includes a bibliography of the writings of Julius R. Weinberg, pages 173-176.

3876. Weiss, Paul. FIRST CONSIDERATIONS: AN EXAMINATION OF PHILO-SOPHICAL EVIDENCE. Carbondale: Southern Illinois Univ. Press, 1977.

3877. Weiss, Paul. PHILOSOPHY IN PROCESS. Albany: State Univ. of New York Press, 1966-.

Volumes 1-8 were published by the Southern Illinois Univ. Press, Carbondale. Volume 7, Part 2, and volumes 8, 9, 10, and 11 have been published by the State Univ. of New York Press. These are Weiss's working journals or intellectual diaries.

3878. Weiss, Paul. TOWARD A PERFECTED STATE. Albany: State Univ. of New York Press, 1986.

3879. Weissman, David. INTUITION AND IDEALITY. Albany: States Univ. of New York Press, 1987.

3880. Welby, Lady Victoria. SIGNIFICS AND LANGUAGE: THE ARTICULATE FORM OF OUR EXPRESSIVE AND INTERPRETIVE RESOURCES. Ed. by H. Walter Schmitz. Amsterdam and Philadelphia: J. Benjamins, 1985.

This work contains Lady Welby's "Meaning and Metaphor," "Sense, Meaning and Inter-pretation" and her last book "Significs and Language: The Articulate Form of Our Expres-sive and Interpretive Resources." Also included are two previously unpublished articles

"Primal Sense" and "The Social Value of Expression," the unpublished letters of Lady Welby and F. C. S. Schiller, and Schiller's previously unpublished "Mother Sense."

3881. Wellbank, Joseph H. JOHN RAWL'S THEORY OF JUSTICE: A BIBLIOGRA-PHY. Bowling Green, KY: Philosophy Documentation Center, Bowling Green State Univ., 1976.

3882. Wellbank, Joseph H., et al. JOHN RAWLS AND HIS CRITICS: AN ANNOTAT-ED BIBLIOGRAPHY. New York and London: Garland, 1982.

3883. Wellman, Carl. THEORY OF RIGHTS: PERSONS UNDER LAWS, INSTITU-TIONS, AND MORALS. Totowa, NJ: Rowman and Allanheld, 1985.

3884. Wellman, Carl. WELFARE RIGHTS. Philosophy and Society Series. Totowa, NJ: Rowman and Littlefield, 1982.

3885. Welton, Donn. THE ORIGINS OF MEANING: A CRITICAL STUDY OF THE THRESHOLDS OF HUSSERLIAN PHENOMENOLOGY. The Hague and Boston: Nijhoff, 1983.

3886. Welton, Donn and Hugh J. Silverman, eds. CRITICAL AND DIALECTICAL PHENOMENOLOGY. Albany: State Univ. of New York, 1987.

3887. Werkmeister, William Henry, ed. FACETS OF PLATO'S PHILOSOPHY. Assen: Van Gorcum, 1976.

3888. Wessell, Leonard P. G.E. LESSING'S THEOLOGY: A REINTERPRETATION: A STUDY IN THE PROBLEMATIC NATURE OF THE ENLIGHTENMENT. The Hague, Paris and New York: Mouton, 1977.

3889. Westbrook, Robert B. JOHN DEWEY AND AMERICAN DEMOCRACY. Ithaca: Cornell Univ. Press, 1991.

3890. Westphal, Merold. GOD, GUILT, AND DEATH: AN EXISTENTIAL PHENOME-NOLOGY OF RELIGION. Bloomington: Indiana Univ. Press, 1984.

3891. Westphal, Merold. HISTORY AND TRUTH IN HEGEL'S PHENOMENOLOGY. Atlantic Highlands, NJ: Humanities Press, 1978.

3892. Westphal, Merold, ed. METHOD AND SPECULATION IN HEGEL'S PHENOME-NOLOGY. Atlantic Highlands, NJ: Humanities Press, 1981.

This book consists of essays presented at the 1978 meeting of the Hegel Society of America. The papers on the theme of THE PHENOMENOLOGY OF THE SPIRIT fall into three groups: Hegel's phenomenological method and the place of his book shaped by that method in the larger Hegelian works; analyses of specific portions of the text; and the comparison of Hegel to Kierkegaard and Marx.

3893. White, David A. HEIDEGGER AND THE LANGUAGE OF POETRY. Lincoln: Univ. of Nebraska Press, 1978.

3894. White, David A. LOGIC AND ONTOLOGY IN HEIDEGGER. Columbus: Ohio State Univ. Press, 1985.

3895. White, Morton Gabriel. THE PHILOSOPHY OF THE AMERICAN REVOLU-TION. New York: Oxford Univ. Press, 1978.

3896. White, Morton Gabriel. WHAT IS AND WHAT OUGHT TO BE DONE: AN ESSAY ON ETHICS AND AN ESSAY ON ETHICS AND EPISTEMOLOGY. New York: Oxford Univ. Press, 1981.

3897. White, Morton Gabriel and Lucia White. JOURNEYS TO THE JAPANESE, 1952-1979. Vancouver: Univ. of British Columbia Press, 1985.

3898. Whitehead, Alfred North. PROCESS AND REALITY: AN ESSAY IN COSMOLOGY. New York: Free Press, 1978.

This is a corrected edition by David Ray Griffin and Donald W. Sherburn.

3899. Whittemore, Robert C. REACH OF PHILOSOPHY: ESSAYS IN HONOR OF JAMES KERN FEIBLEMAN. Dordrecht: Nijhoff; New Orleans: Tulane Univ. Press, 1977.

This volume contains essays by R. L. Barber, S. C. Feldman, A. J. Reck, R. C. Whittemore, and others.

3900. Wilbur, James B., ed. SPINOZA'S METAPHYSICS: ESSAYS IN CRITICAL APPRECIATION. Assen: Van Gorcum, 1976.

3901. Willard, Dallas. LOGIC AND THE OBJECTIVITY OF KNOWLEDGE: A STUDY IN HUSSERL'S EARLY PHILOSOPHY. Series in Continental Thought, Vol. 6. Athens: Ohio Univ. Press, 1984.

3902. Wilshire, Bruce W. ROLE PLAYING AND IDENTITY: THE LIMITS OF THEATRE AS METAPHOR. Bloomington: Univ. of Indiana Press, 1982.

The author makes use of a phenomenological methodology to establish theatre as the art of imitation that reveals imitation.

3903. Wilson, Daniel J. ARTHUR O. LOVEJOY AND THE QUEST FOR INTELLIGIBILITY. Chapel Hill: Univ. of North Carolina Press, 1980.

3904. Wilson, Daniel J. ARTHUR O. LOVEJOY: AN ANNOTATED BIBLIOGRAPHY. New York and London: Garland, 1982.

3905. Wilson, Daniel J. SCIENCE, COMMUNITY, AND THE TRANSFORMATION OF AMERICAN PHILOSOPHY, 1860-1930. Chicago: Univ. of Chicago Press, 1990.

3906. Wohlgelernter, Maurice, ed. HISTORY, RELIGION, AND SPIRITUAL DEMOCRACY: ESSAYS IN HONOR OF JOSEPH L. BLAU. New York: Columbia Univ. Press, 1980.

This volume includes "Joseph L. Blau: A Bibliography," by Sam Dekay on pages 341-364.

3907. Wolff, Kurt H., ed. ALFRED SCHUTZ: APPRAISALS AND DEVELOPMENTS. Hingham, MA: Kluwer, 1984.

3908. Wolfson, Harry Austryn. REPERCUSSIONS OF THE KALEM IN JEWISH PHILOSOPHY. Cambridge: Harvard Univ. Press, 1979.

3909. Wolz, Henry G. PLATO AND HEIDEGGER: IN SEARCH OF SELFHOOD. Lewisburg, PA: Bucknell Univ. Press; London: Associated Univ. Press, 1981.

3910. Wood, Allen W. KARL MARX. The Arguments of the Philosophers. London and Boston: Routledge & Kegan Paul, 1981.

3911. Woodbridge, Barry A. ALFRED NORTH WHITEHEAD: A PRIMARY-SECONDARY BIBLIOGRAPHY. Bibliographies of Famous Philosophers. Bowling Green, OH: Philosophy Documentation Center, 1977.

3912. Woozley, Anthony Douglas. LAW AND OBEDIENCE: THE ARGUMENTS OF PLATO'S CRITO. Chapel Hill: Univ. of North Carolina Press, c1979.

3913. Wright, John P. THE SCEPTICAL REALISM OF DAVID HUME. Minneapolis: Univ. of Minnesota Press, 1983.

Hume's philosophy is presented in its historical context, and the author argues that Hume's thought is both skeptical and realist.

3914. Wright, Larry. TELEOLOGICAL EXPLANATIONS: AN ETIOLOGICAL ANALYSIS OF GOALS AND FUNCTIONS. Berkeley: Univ. of California Press, 1976.

3915. Wyschograd, Edith. SPIRIT IN ASHES: HEGEL, HEIDEGGER, AND MAN-MADE MASS DEATH. New Haven: Yale Univ. Press, 1985.

3916. Zaner, Richard M. THE CONTEXT OF SELF: A PHENOMENOLOGICAL INQUIRY USING MEDICINE AS A CLUE. Series in Continental Thought, Vol. 1. Athens: Ohio Univ. Press, 1981.

3917. Ziff, Paul. ANTIAESTHETICS: AN APPRECIATION OF THE COW WITH THE SUBTILE NOSE. Dordrecht and Boston: Reidel, 1984.

3918. Zimmerman, Michael E. ECLIPSE OF THE SELF: THE DEVELOPMENT OF HEIDEGGER'S CONCEPT OF AUTHENTICITY. Rev. ed. Athens: Ohio Univ. Press, 1986.

3919. Zimmerman, Michael E., ed. THE THOUGHT OF MARTIN HEIDEGGER. Tulane Studies in Philosophy, Vol. 32. New Orleans: Tulane Univ. Press, 1984.

Author Index

The numbers after the names of each author refer to the numbers of the bibliographic entries, not to pages. Works with more than two authors or editors are listed only after the name of the first author or editor. In those few instances where there is no individual author or editor named, the entries are listed by title or corporate author such as an association, symposium, series, and so on.

Aagaard-Mogensen, Lars 2281, 2282, 2283, 2284, 2285, 2286, 2287
Aarnio, Aulis 779, 1103, 1104, 1105, 1106, 1107, 1108, 1109, 1183
Abe, Masao 382
Abel, Gunter 2351
Abellan, Jose Luis 2242
Abelson, Raziel 3148, 3149
Abensor, Miguel 1058
Abraham, William James 1442
Abugattas, Juan 2963
Acham, Karl 2352
Ackermann, Robert John 3150
Ackrill, John Lloyd 1443
Adachi, Kazuhiro 383
Adelmann, Frederick J. 528, 810
Adler, Mortimer Jerome 3151, 3152, 3153, 3154, 3155
Adloff, Jean Gabriel 1199
Adorno, Theodor Wiesengrund 2353, 2354, 2355
Afanasev, Viktor Grigorevich 811
Agassi, Joseph 128, 129, 130, 131, 148, 2708
Agazzi, Evandro 1868, 1869, 1870, 1871, 1872, 1873, 1874, 1875, 1876 ,1877
Agrawal, Murari Mohan 77, 78
Aguero, Able 2709
Airaksinen, Timo 1110, 1111, 1112, 1113, 1114, 1128, 1178
Ajdukiewicz, Kazimierz 711
Alanen, Lilli 1115
Al-Attas, Muhammed Naguib 98
Albarracin Millan, Juan 2757
Alberini, Coriolano 2710
Albert, Hans 2356, 2357, 2358, 2359, 2360, 2361, 2362, 2363, 2364, 2365
Albertoni, Ettore A. 1878
Alekseev, Igor Serafimovich 812
Alekseev, Peter Vasilevich 813
Alexander, Peter 1444
Alexy, Robert 1146
Al-Ghazzali 57

Alici, Luigi 1879
Allen, Douglas 780
Allen, Reginald E. 3156
Allinson, Robert E. 529
Allison, David B. 3157
Allison, Henry E. 3158
Almasi, Miklos 689
Almeder, Robert F. 3159
Alther, Eduard 2366
Althusser, Louis 1200, 1201, 1202, 1203
Amadi, Elechi 79
Amado Levy-Valensi, Eliane 132, 133
Amaral, Marcio Tavares d' 2764
Ambrose, Alice 1056, 3545, 3546, 3547
American Catholic Philosophical Association 3160
Ameriks, Karl 3161
Ames, Roger T. 530, 557
Amore, Roy C. 3005
Amsterdamski, Stefan 712, 1204
Anacker, Stefan 198
Anand, Kewal Krishna 199
Anastaplo, George 3162
Anawati, Georges C. 58, 59
Anderberg, Thomas 2288
Anderson, C. Anthony 3006
Anderson, Janet 918
Anderson, Thomas C. 3163
Andersson, Gunnar 2367, 2368
Andropov, Iurii Vladmirovich 814, 815
Angehern, Emil 2369
Angeles, Peter Adam 3164
Anglemayer, Mary 3165
Anismov, Sergei Fedorovich 816
Ankersmit, Franklin R. 2098
Annas, Julia 1445, 1446, 1447
Anscombe, Gertrude Elizabeth Margaret 1050, 1051, 1054, 1448
Anton, John Peter 3166, 3167, 3168
Anufriev, Evgenii Aleksandrovich 817
Anyanwu, K. Chukwulozie 48
Apel, Karl-Otto 1116, 2370, 2371, 2372, 2373

Subject Index

The numbers after each subject heading refer to the numbers of the bibliographic entries, not to pages. Anyone desiring to make the most efficient use of this index is advised to search first for the most specific topics of interest. Since each bibliographic category has a different emphasis, when searching Epistemology and political philosophy or other conjunctions of areas of philosophy, scan both areas or fields for related listings, e.g., consult Epistemology and Political philosophy and also Political philosophy and Epistemology, etc. Nearly all of the bibliographic entries are listed after more than one subject heading for the purposes of greater accuracy, specificity, and reliability in finding every relevant book and monograph. Titles of works are printed entirely in capital letters.

2277
Bowne, Borden Parker 3832
Boyle, Robert 1444, 1792
Bradley, Francis Herbert 1683
Brailas-Armenis, Petros 1853
Braithwaite, R. B. (Festschrift) 1699
Brandt, Richard (Festschrift) 948
Brazilian philosophy 2769, 2778, 2780,
    2781, 2783, 2785, 2790, 2791, 2792,
    2809, 2810, (Bibliography) 2782, 2788,
    2789, 2795, (Index) 2794
Brazilian philosophy, History of 2788,
    2789, 2793, 2799, 2802, 2812
Brentano, Franz 1042, 1047, 2429, 3270,
    3593, (Bibliography) 3594
Breton, Stanislas 1639
British philosophy, Contemporary 169,
    1662, 2167, 3111
British philosophy, History of 1749
British philosophy, History of contempo-
    rary 1756, 1820
British philosophy, History of modern
    1892
Brito, Raymundo de Farias 2780,
Brodda, Benny 2316
Bruno, Giordano 1936
Buber, Martin 152, 154, 2676, 3500,
    (Bibliography) 159, (Biography) 3401
Buddha 444, 447, (Biography) 284, 443
Buddhism 18, 29, 198, 445, 3005, 3860,
    (Asanga) 379, (Bibliography) 3479,
    (Chinul) 509, (Dogen) 416, 465, (Hume)
    151, (Joshu) 386, (Kukai) 465, (Nagarju-
    na) 282, (Shin) 491, (Shinran) 490,
    (Wittgenstein) 269
Buddhism and aesthetics, 441, Asian civili-
    zation, 287, 3005, Christianity, 467,
    epistemology, 269, 281, 309, 310, 342,
    425, 3432, eschatology, 446, ethics, 29,
    269, 281, Indian philosophy, 309, logic,
    274, 310, 425, meaning, 311, meditation,
    288, metaphysics, 231, 253, 260, 267,
    281, 381, 425, 542, 576, 3830, mind and
    body, 465, mind-body problem, 507,
    3432, perception, 309, phenomenology,
    465, 1742, philosophy of man, 295,
    psychology, 198, 270, 1742, 3432, reve-
    lation, 259, science, 279, secularism,
    235, self, 151, 253, 414, 467, social
    philosophy, 325, 3481
Buddhism, Ch'an 566, 2303
Buddhism, Chinese 259, 360, 542, 566,
    3005
Buddhism, Hinayana 295
Buddhism, History of 281, 448
Buddhism, History of Korean 523
Buddhism, Hua-yen 509, 542
Buddhism, Indian 231, 235, 248, 250,

259, 262, 269, 270, 274, 282, 283, 287,
    296, 297, 311, 318, 326, 327, 360, 379,
    381, 3005, 3859
Buddhism, Japanese 382, 386, 387, 388,
    389, 390, 391, 392, 393, 394, 395, 416,
    423, 425, 445, 446, 448, 454, 457, 465,
    467, 481, 489, 490, 491, (Dictionary of
    original writings) 413
Buddhism, Korean 509
Buddhism, Mahayana 230, 281, 292, 347,
    379, 467
Buddhism, Primitive 485
Buddhism, Sacred books 439, 440
Buddhism, Theravada 253, 279, 281, 288
Buddhism, Tibetan 259, 287, 318, 360,
    379, 554, 576, 596
Buddhism, Zen 281, 382, 386, 414, 416,
    448, 457, 509, 566, (Dogen) 388, 389,
    390, 391, 392, 393, 394, 395, 423, 489,
    (Kido) 387
Buddhist scriptures (Bibliography) 254
Buddhist Sutras 432
Buffier, Claude 3072
Bulgarian philosophy (Bibliography) 599
Bunge, Mario Augusto (Festschrift) 2708
Burckhardt, Jacob 469
Bureaucracy 958, 960
Burke, Edmund 1604, 3066
Burleigh, Walter (see Burley, Walter) 2119
Burley, Walter 2119
Burmese philosophy, Contemporary 197
Burnet, John 1524
Butler, Joseph 1738
Byzantine philosophy 1866

Cajetan, Cardinal 2262
Cambridge Platonism 3029
Canadian philosophy, Contemporary
    (Directory) 3182
Canadian philosophy, History of 3093
Canadian philosophy, History of An-
    glophone 3009
Canadian philosophy, History of Franco-
    phone 3142
Candrakirti 225
Cantor, Georg 3318
Capitalism 555, 556, 953, 1004, 1245,
    1246, 1785
Cardan, Girolamo 1985
Carnap, Rudolf 1039, 1921, 2064, 3646,
    3867, (Correspondence) 3250
Carpaccio, Vittore 1427
Carroll, Lewis 2038
CARTE POSTALE (Derrida) 1377
Cartesianism 1100, 1115, 1205, 1308,
    1968, 1987, 2550, 2990, 3061, 3329,
    3699, (Bibliography) 3268
Carvaka *See Lokayata*

654, 658, 659, 660, 661, 662, 665, 668, 677, 678, 679, 682, 688, 730, 747, 805, 810, 811, 813, 824, 834, 835, 837, 845, 848, 853, 855, 857, 858, 859, 865, 870, 877, 880, 881, 882, 883, 884, 885, 886, 887, 890, 893, 894, 906, 907, 908, 912, 914, 942, 1203, 1301, 1314, 1327, 1418, 1700, 1767, 2060, 2148, 2307, 2403, 2593, 2636, 2876, 2922, 2955, 3042, 3370, 3667, (Bibliography) 26

Materialism, Historical 633, 644, 646, 647, 648, 649, 655, 676, 703, 745, 747, 881, 884, 894, 900, 906, 2491, 2933, 3228, 3618

Mathematics, Philosophy of 184, 1012, 1045, 1046, 1050, 1053, 1135, 1250, 1431, 1466, 1527, 1633, 1870, 1876, 1877, 1964, 1992, 2023, 2434, 2447, 2460, 2461, 2462, 2463, 2533, 2535, 2562, 2816, 2848, 2849, 2968, 3046, 3132, 3203, 3285, 3318, 3381, 3397, 3467, 3515, 3546, 3665, 3689, 3691, 3794, 3852, (Frege) 1125, 1529, 2204, (Godel) 602, (Kant) 2449, (Peirce) 3359, (Ramsey) 2323, (Wittgenstein) 1055, 1838, 3024, 3112

Matter 1100, 3689

MATTOSHO (Shinran) 490

Maupassant, Guy de 1302, 1304

Mauss, Marcel 1496

Maya 223, 330, 372

McLuhan, Marshall 2843

McTaggert, John Ellis 1569

Mead, George Herbert 2529, 3611

Meaning See also Language, Philosophy of; Logic; Semantics; Semiotics 158, 311, 353, 383, 404, 433, 546, 551, 779, 810, 913, 975, 1055, 1056, 1077, 1133, 1160, 1218, 1264, 1281, 1305, 1344, 1347, 1364, 1399, 1402, 1405, 1426, 1436, 1465, 1467, 1509, 1528, 1541, 1568, 1591, 1598, 1631, 1690, 1759, 1802, 1872, 2193, 2203, 2224, 2261, 2308, 2644, 2721, 2929, 3006, 3024, 3034, 3147, 3322, 3356, 3506, 3510, 3562, 3600, 3619, 3620, 3651, 3688, 3692, 3774, 3782, 3789, 3790, 3794, 3813, 3880, 3885

Mechanism 1295, 2198, 2465, 3643

Medicine, Philosophy of 82, 148, 679, 963, 991, 1003, 1224, 2211, 2317, 2318, 2319, 2626, 3105, 3251, 3306, 3422, 3431, 3800, 3916, (Locke) 3729, (Schelling) 2338

Medieval European philosophy, History of early 1685

Medieval philosophy 99, 161, 162, 762, 1117, 1568, 1897, 1901, 2164, 2871, 2888, 3007, 3090, 3091, 3094, 3624, 3754, 3858, 3908

Medieval philosophy, History of 1655, 1849, 1900, 2119, 2131, 2183, 2389, 2692, 3131, 3293, 3521

Medieval philosophy, History of early 1493, 1684

MEDITATIONS (Descartes) 3732

Mehta, Jarava Lal 313

Meinong, Alexius 1043, 3270, (Collected works) 2578

Memory 1289, 1997

Mencius 512, 553

Merleau-Ponty, Maurice 1266, 1267, 1325, 1896, 2272, 2582, 3070, 3307, 3430, 3614, 3805, (Bibliography) 1336

Metaphor 1405, 1509, 1944, 2198, 2406, 2496, 3418, 3487, 3769, 3902

METAPHYSICS (Aristotle) 100, 1473, 2041, 2418, 2575, 2597, 3091

Metaphysics See also Ontology 1006, 1008, 2179, 2728, 2885, 3270, 3294, 3397, 3439, 3568, 3623, 3876, (Anaxagoras) 2326, (Anderson) 927, (Anscombe) 1448, (Aquinas) 2131, 2262, (Asanga) 381, (Averroes) 100, (Avicenna) 60, (Berkeley) 3853, (Bhattacharyya, K. C.) 355, (Blanshard) 3772, (Boyle) 1444, (Brentano) 3270, (Brito) 2806, (Cajetan) 2262, (Condillac) 1248, (Conway) 3029, (Davidson) 945, (Derrida) 3831, (Descartes) 1308, 1379, 1501, 2387, 3300, 3732, (Dewey) 3874, (Encyclopedia) 2426, (Fichte) 2484, 2647, (Frege) 1125, (Freud) 2196, (Gurwitsch) 1069, (Hamelin) 1437, (Hartshorne) 3281, 3441, (Hegel) 720, 722, 755, 1657, 1823, 1918, 2196, 2444, 2484, 2647, 2677, 3540, 3541, 3543, 3640, 3891, (Heidegger) 1383, 2097, 2454, 2499, 2502, (Hobbes) 142, (Hume) 3087, (Husserl) 1069, 1250, 2551, 3509, (James) 3634, (Kant) 720, 1019, 1380, 1819, 2565, 2631, 2638, 2705, 3020, 3158, 3161, 3240, 3382, (Kierkegaard) 1097, (Lavelle) 3139, (Leibniz) 3713, (Lenin) 408, (Levinas) 2668, (Locke) 1444, (Maimonides) 3394, (Marcel) 1949, 3139, (Marx) 720, 1696, (McTaggert) 1569, (Meinong) 1043, 2578, 3270, (Merleau-Ponty) 1069, 1266, 1267, (Moore) 1716, 3654, (Nicol) 2906, (Nietzsche) 1251, 2502, 3157, (Parmenides) 2454, 2828, (Peirce) 3508, (Plato) 1100, 1318, 1439, 1986, 2454, 2484, 3036, 3684, 3844, (Quine) 3774, (Rosmini) 1948, (Royce) 3280, (Ryle) 1764, (Sabzavari) 125, (Sartre) 722, (Schelling) 1438, 2497, 2647, (Schopen-

theology, 1097, 1513, 2157, 2576, 2638, 2727, 3450, 3656, things, 460, time, 1233, 1601, 1698, 1719, 1786, 2366, 2668, 2693, 3713, 3856, totality, 1359, truth, 206, 755, 1009, 1069, 1660, 1794, 2801, 3738, 3891, universals, 321, 921, 1601, 2663, 2981, unknowable, 459, value, 211, 1383, Vedanta, 77, 200, 217, 267, 301, 312, 340, 372, 376, voluntarism, 3044, yoga, 333

Metaphysics, Destruction of 1383

Metaphysics, History of 1898, 2131, 2179, 2426, 2484

Metaphysics, Nature of 1652, 2343

Methodology *See also Causality; Dialectic; Epistemology; Explanation; Logic; Science, Philosophy of; Social science, Philosophy of* 1700, 2260, (Descartes) 1501, 1881, (Dewey) 3335, (Dignaga) 415, (Galileo) 1136, (Kant) 3020, (Lenin) 408, (Maimonides) 3394, (Marx) 2424, 3054, (Peirce) 505, 2238, (Quine) 3774, (Wittgenstein) 473, 475, 3024

Methodology and action, 1167, 1763, aesthetics, 1183, 2475, 3419, 3902, analytic philosophy, 478, 2660, 3742, axiology, 1128, 3553, biology, 669, Buddhism, 269, computers, 1236, contemporary philosophy, 498, 2698, culture, 2646, 3081, definition, 840, dialectic, 428, 435, 436, 449, 461, 468, 478, 500, 502, 505, 1157, 2935, dialectical materialism, 408, 502, 659, 682, 835, 865, 914, 2307, 2922, discovery, 1032, 1990, 3808, epistemology, 664, 850, 1157, 1621, 2300, 2507, 2660, 2664, 2721, 3121, 3287, 3335, 3445, ethics, 818, 1183, 1612, 3455, 3573, 3593, evidence, 2300, existentialism, 1418, 3257, explanation, 1179, 3122, 3407, feminism, 3445, hermeneutics, 384, 2475, history, 420, 3037, history of philosophy, 2171, 2892, 3141, 3739, history of science, 1136, 3290, intuition, 3742, language, 153, 156, 473, 475, 1136, 1763, 2771, 3289, 3689, law, 2, 779, 1103, 1106, 1109, 1165, 1183, 1676, 2190, 2191, 2297, 2300, 3002, linguistics, 156, 2771, logic, 384, 408, 415, 420, 428, 435, 436, 449, 461, 468, 473, 478, 500, 502, 505, 611, 659, 664, 669, 682, 739, 757, 775, 778, 809, 840, 850, 914, 1032, 1136, 1179, 1507, 1614, 1621, 1678, 1881, 1984, 1990, 2238, 2507, 2590, 2592, 2644, 2659, 2660, 2664, 2980, 2995, 3133, 3134, 3289, 3385, 3593, 3779, 3808, Marxism, 408, 502, 659, 682, 747, 818, 823, 835, 865, 888, 914, 1418, 2307,

2593, 2922, mathematics, 3689, metaphysics, 408, 502, 659, 3290, 3335, 3439, 3445, 3456, 3689, 3876, mindbody problem, 546, 3439, ontology, 412, phenomenology, 2467, 3437, 3892, 3902, philosophical systems, 3718, physics, 2435, political philosophy, 1711, praxis, 916, 1418, proof, 2300, 3385, science, 659, 664, 669, 739, 756, 772, 778, 888, 914, 934, 955, 1032, 1057, 1136, 1179, 1339, 1501, 1507, 1614, 1621, 1678, 1718, 1875, 1881, 1984, 1990, 2024, 2027, 2294, 2305, 2335, 2435, 2507, 2515, 2590, 2640, 2659, 2660, 2664, 2670, 2671, 2723, 2873, 2995, 3020, 3122, 3134, 3289, 3445, 3537, 3553, 3775, 3808, semantics, 3255, semiotics, 449, 505, 1306, social philosophy, 747, 809, 1128, 2622, 3407, 3437, social science, 611, 682, 746, 775, 809, 916, 931, 1057, 1086, 1306, 2515, 2622, 2644, 3287, 3407, 3437, 3779, statistics, 746, 2660, structuralism, 157, 3255, systems theory, 823, 865, 1128

Mexican philosophy 2897, 2909, 2913, 2914, 2915, 2947, 2951, 2952

Mexican philosophy, History of 2887, 2895, 2926

Meyer, Rudolf W. (Festschrift) 2511

Mill, James 3102

Mill, John Stuart 999, 1586, 1729, 1892, 2147, 3023, 3102, 3208, (Collected Works) 3079

Mimamsa 266, 267, 278, 358

Mimesis 2127, 3866

Mind 923, 1601, 3032, 3070, 3438, 3643

Mind, Philosophy of *See also Consciousness; Epistemology; Metaphysics; Psychology, Philosophy of; Self* 14, 132, 231, 249, 402, 460, 465, 560, 571, 920, 1100, 1115, 1189, 1208, 1240, 1279, 1645, 1664, 1679, 1732, 1764, 1894, 1928, 1929, 2135, 2176, 2198, 2207, 2330, 2378, 2388, 2571, 2773, 3006, 3014, 3023, 3034, 3161, 3187, 3230, 3328, 3364, 3388, 3397, 3432, 3439, 3468, 3500, 3536, 3549, 3555, 3568, 3609, 3635, 3643, 3733, 3746, 3766, 3781, 3783, 3817, 3843, (Anscombe) 1448, (Dictionary) 1590, (Hegel) 3640, (Husserl) 3813, (Spinoza) 1928, (Wittgenstein) 378, 1465

Mind, Philosophy of, and causality, 923, 1625, 3801, epistemology, 1115, identity, 1578, 1678, 2679, 3329, 3734, 3801, 3802, law, 1829, perception, 1669, 1731, 3857

Mind-body problem 507, 546, 923, 1034,

3544, 3548, 3561, 3692, 3780, 3790, 3880, (Mill) 2147, (Wittgenstein) 1465
Semiotics 449, 717, 751, 752, 753, 872, 908, 1073, 1074, 1207, 1209, 1264, 1270, 1302, 1303, 1304, 1306, 1398, 1944, 1945, 1946, 1947, 2165, 2346, 2372, 2488, 2509, 2598, 2755, 2888, 3324, 3784, 3797, (Bibliography) 832, 2450, (Dictionary) 2265, (Greimas) 1078, 1305, (Leibniz) 2425, 2446, 2772, 2774, (Lotman) 895, (Peirce) 505, 3018, 3383, 3678, 3798, (Saussure) 1234
Semiotics, and literature, 1305, poetics 1305, 2264
Sensation 1669, 3536, 3589
Sentential calculus 742, 777
Serres, Michel (Festschrift) 1433
Set theory 744
Sex 1111, 1288, 3105, 3558, 3559, 3635, 3659, 3870
Shaftesbury, Third Earl of 2684
SHARH AL-MAN ZUMAH FI AL-HIKMAH (Sabzavari) 125
SHEN-CHIEN (Hsun Yueh) 534
Sherman, Hoyt Leon 3353
Shih, Tao 543
Shinran 491 (Correspondence) 490
SHINTAI (Yasuo Yuasa) 507
SHOBOGENZO (Dogen) 388, 390, 391, 392, 394, 395, 457
Sidgwick, Henry 3776
Significs 3880
Signs 610, 752, 753, 1218, 1940, 2005, 2172, 2637, 2772, 3032, 3417, 3508, 3678
Sikhism and secularism 235
Silence 3319
Silva, Arthur Orlando da 2767
Similarity 180
Simplicity 3609
Sin 731, 1037
Siromani, Raghunatha 340
Skepticism 180, 259, 721, 723, 947, 976, 1073, 1369, 1447, 1468, 1470, 1589, 1771, 1795, 2073, 2217, 2543, 2619, 2687, 2749, 2990, 3047, 3083, 3096, 3124, 3261, 3298, 3309, 3390, 3585, 3653, 3664, 3681, 3716, 3837, 3838, 3913 (Encyclopedia) 31
Skepticism, History of 3682
Skinner, Burrhus Frederic 3277
Skjervheim, Hans (Festschrift) 2218
Sleep 2201
Smith, Adam 2750
Snellman, Johan Wilhelm 1156, 1189
Social change 741
Social contract 1703, 2043, 3023, 3645, 3724

Social philosophy *See also Ethics; Law, Philosophy of; Political philosophy; Social philosophy; Social science, Philosophy of; political and social movements* 1596, 3397, 3568, 3882, 3899, (Adorno) 1637, 1757, (Anderson) 926, 927, (Arendt) 1068, 3495, (Benjamin) 2390, (Bolivar) 2890, (Buber) 2676, (Burke) 3066, (Dewey) 3424, 3889, (Dilthey) 1883, (Domat) 2088, (Foucault) 1781, (Freud) 3146, (Gramsci) 2007, (Habermas) 701, 1808, 3211, 3408, 3595, (Hegel) 1346, 1736, 2604, 3055, 3850, 3861, (Heidegger) 2676, (Hess) 135, (Hobbes) 1954, 3027, 3146, (Hook) 3534, (Hume) 1616, (Husserl) 2676, (James) 3634, (Krause) 2251, (Levinas) 1060, (Lukacs) 692, (Mandeville) 2057, 2071, (Marcuse) 3501, (Marx) 1499, 2138, 3055, 3069, (Mead) 2529, (Mill) 999, 1586, 3424, (Nozick) 3668, (Pascal) 2088, (Plato) 2197, 3912, (Rawls) 2508, 3881, (Rousseau) 3027, 3645, (Royce) 3280, (Sartre) 1516, 2676, 3257, 3829, (Schiller) 3055, (Schutz) 3299, (Vico) 1954, (Weber) 1702, (Wittgenstein) 1534
Social philosophy, and action, 354, 1185, 1623, 2493, aesthetics, 657, 692, 790, 792, 1201, 1213, 1245, 1370, 1946, 2034, 2311, 2390, 2482, 2764, 3262, 3337, 3736, alienation, 689, 758, 1664, anarchism, 1804, 3668, 3673, animal rights, 989, 1703, 3708, 3710, anthropology, 2, 1277, 2746, axiology, 1128, 2719, Buddhism, 325, 3481, bureaucracy, 960, business ethics, 925, capitalism, 1004, 1246, 1785, Chinese philosophy, 567, Christianity, 2088, communication, 2491, 2493, 3424, community, 3698, comparative philosophy, 837, conflict, 1606, Confucianism, 567, cooperation, 1804, criminal law, 998, culture, 697, 800, 803, 1979, 2390, 3262, 3736, decision theory, 956, 3423, democracy, 917, 944, 1658, 1677, 2359, 3067, 3889, 3906, dharma, 203, dialectic, 2148, ecology, 472, 943, 970, 2227, 2231, 2234, 3086, 3710, economic, 2776, economics, 1016, 1246, 1785, 2231, 2295, 2665, 3199, education, 1217, 1555, 2233, epistemology, 239, 645, 808, 955, 1014, 1290, 1781, 2373, 2571, 2630, 3635, equality, 11, 1553, 1555, 2043, 3082, 3283, 3703, ethics, 35, 72, 163, 183, 203, 472, 567, 748, 795, 803, 939, 943, 963, 970, 988, 990, 991, 1003, 1110, 1182, 1287, 1288, 1321, 1596, 1605, 1606, 1607, 1616, 1643, 1664,

About the Editors

JOHN R. BURR is Professor of Philosophy at the University of Wisconsin–Oshkosh. He has authored numerous articles on philosophy and is the editor of the *Handbook of World Philosophy: Contemporary Developments Since 1945* (Greenwood Press, 1980).

CHARLOTTE A. BURR is the Reference Librarian at Ripon College. Before becoming a librarian, she was a member of the Music Department faculty at the University of Wisconsin–Superior.